FrontPage® 2002:
The Complete Reference

Martin S. Matthews
Erik B. Poulsen

Osborne/**McGraw-Hill**

New York   Chicago   San Francisco
Lisbon   London   Madrid   Mexico City
Milan   New Delhi   San Juan
Seoul   Singapore   Sydney   Toronto

Osborne/**McGraw-Hill**
2600 Tenth Street
Berkeley, California 94710
U.S.A.

To arrange bulk purchase discounts for sales promotions, premiums, or fund-raisers, please contact Osborne/**McGraw-Hill** at the above address. For information on translations or book distributors outside the U.S.A., please see the International Contact Information page immediately following the index of this book.

FrontPage® 2002: The Complete Reference

1234567890 CUS CUS 01987654321

Book p/n 0-07-213223-X and CD p/n 0-07-213224-8
parts of
ISBN 0-07-213222-1

Publisher
   Brandon A. Nordin

Vice President & Associate Publisher
   Scott Rogers

Acquisitions Editor
   Ann Sellers

Project Editor
   Patty Mon

Acquisitions Coordinator
   Tim Madrid

Technical Editor
   John Cronan

Copy Editors
   Sally Engelfried
   Mike McGee

Proofreader
   Stefany Otis

Indexer
   Valerie Robbins

Computer Designer
   Dick Schwartz
   Kelly Stanton-Scott

Illustrators
   Michael Mueller
   Lyssa Sieben-Wald

Series Design
   Peter F. Hancik

This book was composed with Corel VENTURA™ Publisher.

About the Authors

Martin S. Matthews is the best-selling author of over 50 books, including *Windows 2000: A Beginner's Guide, FrontPage 2000: The Complete Reference, Windows 98 Answers! Certified Tech Support,* and *Office 2000 Answers! Certified Tech Support.* Martin, who has more than 30 years of computer experience, also does consulting and training on a wide variety of computer topics with a number of firms nationwide.

Erik B. Poulsen is the Senior Web Developer for Arcadia Web Service. Erik has more than 14 years of computer experience and works with major corporations to develop ASP and database-driven web applications. He has also collaborated with Marty on a number of book projects, including *FrontPage 2000: The Complete Reference.*

For John Cronan,
who for many years
and over many books
has maintained a careful, critical
eye on their technical accuracy
while being a very good friend.

Martin Matthews

For Gregers Bjørn Poulsen,
who went for help and returned with a camera.
It's a pleasure to be able to continue the
conversation we started 25 years ago, Gregers.
Thanks for staying around.

Erik Poulsen

Contents at a Glance

Contents

Part I

Getting Started

Part III

Working Behind the Scenes

Part IV

Extending Your Web Site

Part V

Appendixes

Acknowledgments

Mark Hammock wrote Chapter 14 and significantly revised chapters 20 and 23, and did so with much expertise, on time, and he was very easy to work with. Thanks Mark!

John Cronan, technical editor and friend, corrected many errors, added many tips and notes, and otherwise significantly improved the book while always being there for us. Thanks, John!

Greg Sherman, database programmer and musician extraordinaire, has provided much guidance over the years. Greg's understanding of the hidden nature of data and how to reveal its secrets constantly expands my horizons. His music accompanied much of the writing of this book and has enriched my life beyond words. Thanks, Greg!

Cynthia Daniel, a pioneer web developer, provided much appreciated feedback and advice, and her son, **John Shields**, provided really incredible meals. Thanks, Cynthia and John!

Ann Sellers, acquisitions editor, made working with her easy and a joy. Thanks, Ann!

Tim Madrid, editorial assistant, kept the book moving through the editorial process, handling all the little things that often get overlooked. Thanks, Tim!

George Henny, **Jeff Wallace**, and **Terry Keller** of WhidbeyNet, Marty's Internet service provider, have been helpful in setting up the several web sites he needed and in answering his questions. Thanks, George, Jeff, and Terry!

Carole Boggs Matthews, Marty's life partner, sharer of their parenting adventure, and an author in her own right, provided him with the necessary support without which no project like this could ever get done. In addition, Carole had the daunting task of contacting a myriad of software publishers, determining what should be included on the companion CD, and then making that happen. Thanks, my love!

Introduction

As the interest in the Internet and its World Wide Web has skyrocketed, so has the desire of organizations and individuals to have a presence there, to put up their own web sites and be a part of the Internet phenomenon. At the same time, organizations are using the same technology to install intranets at a geometric rate, and therefore they have the need to create their own web sites to use internally. The problem has been that the tools to create both Internet and intranet web sites have been very crude and anything but easy to use. FrontPage has changed all of that. FrontPage provides a very easy-to-use, full-featured set of tools for the full-featured creation, delivery, and maintenance of web sites. And FrontPage does this in a WYSIWYG (What You See Is What You Get) environment where you can see what you are doing as you are doing it.

Unfortunately, FrontPage comes with a slim manual that gives only the briefest of instructions. *FrontPage 2002: The Complete Reference* fills this void by giving you a clear, concise, hands-on guide to this extremely powerful product.

About This Book

FrontPage 2002: The Complete Reference leads you through the planning, creation, testing, deployment, and maintenance of both intranet and Internet web sites with FrontPage. It does this using substantial real-world examples and clear, step-by-step instructions. All of the major features of FrontPage are explained and demonstrated in such a way that you can follow along and see for yourself how each is used, including database connectivity, the addition of multimedia, the creation of an e-commerce site, and the incorporation of Active Server Pages (ASP), ASP.NET, Java Server Pages, JavaScript, and Visual Basic Script. In addition, this book takes you beyond basic FrontPage web site creation and introduces you to HTML, DHTML, and XML and how to use them with FrontPage, as well as how to set up an intranet site, with and without SharePoint, how to manage Internet and intranet security, and how to publish and promote your web site. *FrontPage 2002: The Complete Reference* provides the one complete reference on how to make the most of FrontPage. If you are going to purchase FrontPage, or if you already use it, you need this book!

How This Book Is Organized

FrontPage 2002: The Complete Reference is written the way most people learn. It starts by reviewing the basic concepts and then uses a learn-by-doing method to demonstrate the major features of the product. Throughout, the book uses detailed examples and clear explanations to give you the insight needed to make the fullest use of FrontPage.

Part I, "Getting Started," introduces you to web sites and FrontPage; it includes Chapters 1 through 4.

- Chapter 1, "Designing Quality Web Applications," explores the world of the Internet and intranets and looks at what makes good web pages.

- Chapter 2, "Exploring FrontPage," takes you on a tour of the major FrontPage features, giving you a taste of the power inherent in this product.

- Chapter 3, "Using Wizards and Themes," shows you how to create webs and web pages with these powerful tools.

- Chapter 4, "Using Templates," demonstrates not only the use of templates in creating both webs and web pages, but also how to create templates themselves.

Part II, "Creating Web Sites," demonstrates each of the major features of FrontPage by leading you through examples of their implementation; it includes Chapters 5 through 11.

- Chapter 5, "Creating and Formatting a Web Page from Scratch," sets aside the wizards and templates and looks at the steps necessary to create a full-featured web on your own.

- Chapter 6, "Adding and Managing Hyperlinks and Hotspots," explores how to add interactivity and interconnectedness to your web.

- Chapter 7, "Using Tables and Frames," describes two completely different methods of segmenting a page and shows how you can make the best use of these tools.

- Chapter 8, "Working with Forms," explains ways to let the web user communicate back to you, the web creator.

- Chapter 9, "Using Web Components," describes how to automate some of the web creation process and extend a web's interactive features.

- Chapter 10, "Advanced Formatting Techniques," covers customizing themes, creating and using style sheets, positioning and wrapping text, and choosing web-safe colors.

- Chapter 11, "Importing and Integrating Office and Other Files," shows you how to use existing (or *legacy*) files in your intranet and Internet webs.

Part III, "Working Behind the Scenes," delves into the inner workings of a web site by exploring the languages behind and ways of activating a web; it includes Chapters 12 through 20.

- Chapter 12, "Working with HTML," provides an extensive introduction to the HTML language and how to use it with FrontPage.

- Chapter 13, "Using Dynamic HTML," demonstrates how you can easily add motion and animation to your web site.

- Chaapter 14, "Extensible Markup Language (XML)," provides a thorough and usable introduction to this very powerful addition to the programming used in web sites.

- Chapter 15, "Web Scripting Languages," describes and shows you how to use JavaScript and Visual Basic Script with your FrontPage webs.

- Chapter 16, "Active Server Pages," explores how to create and use JavaScript and VBScript to control and run tasks on the web server to greatly expand the capability of a web.

- Chapter 17, "Introducing ASP.NET," looks at Microsoft's newest web creation tool, ASP.NET, which uses complied programming languages in place of scripts to enhance the functionality of Active Server Pages.

- Chapter 18, "JavaServer Pages," demonstrates how to build the same functionality that you can achieve with Microsoft's ASP on Windows-based servers into webs hosted on UNIX and Linux servers using Sun Microsystem's Java and Java Server Pages.

- Chapter 19, "Working with Databases," introduces you to interactive databases and shows you how to incorporate them in your own FrontPage webs to dynamically change the webs' contents.

- Chapter 20, "Activating Your Webs," describes how Java and ActiveX can be used to activate web sites and then shows you how to incorporate them in your own webs.

Part IV, "Extending Your Web Site," covers ways of extending and enhancing what you can do with FrontPage; it includes Chapters 21 through 25.

- Chapter 21, "Adding Multimedia to Your Webs," shows you how to add regular and streaming audio files, both prerecorded and live, to your web site.
- Chapter 22, "Security on the Web," looks at what the Internet and intranet security issues are and explains what you can do to minimize the risks.
- Chapter 23, "Doing E-Commerce," explores the issues behind doing business on the Web and then explains how to build a web store.
- Chapter 24, "Setting Up an Intranet Web Site," leads you through the steps to create an intranet in your organization and how to set up a SharePoint team collaboration web within an intranet.
- Chapter 25, "Publishing and Promoting Webs on the Internet," looks at how to locate an Internet service provider, how to transfer your completed webs to their servers, and how to promote your webs once they're online.

Part V, "Appendixes," concludes *FrontPage 2002: The Complete Reference*.

- Appendix A, "FrontPage 2002 Installation," provides a detailed set of instructions on how to install the FrontPage related components in Microsoft Office XP or stand-alone FrontPage 2002 packages.
- Appendix B, "FrontPage's Shortcut Keystrokes," lists the shortcut keystrokes that can be used to perform many of the functions in FrontPage.
- Appendix C, "Constructing Web Templates," shows you a thorough example of how to create a web template.
- Appendix D, "Using the Companion CD," describes the many pieces of third-party software that are contained on the CD that is packaged with this book, as well as the files that are used or created in this book.

Conventions Used in This Book

FrontPage 2002: The Complete Reference uses several conventions designed to make the book easier for you to follow. Among these are

- **Bold type** is used for text that you are to type from the keyboard.
- *Italic type* is used for a word or phrase that is being defined or otherwise deserves special emphasis.
- The Courier typeface is used for the HTML and other code that is either produced by FrontPage or entered by the user.
- SMALL CAPITAL LETTERS are used for keys on the keyboard such as ENTER and SHIFT.
- When you are expected to enter a command, you are told to press the key(s). If you are to enter text or numbers, you are told to type them.

The Complete Reference

FrontPage 2002

Part I

Getting Started

In this book, you will learn how you can be part of the Internet or intranet revolution. You will learn how to use FrontPage to create and maintain a presence on the Web for your business, your organization, or for yourself. This book will take you through all the steps necessary to create your own web application—from initial design to placing your content on a web server where it can be accessed by anyone on the Web.

In the first of the four chapters of Part I, you will be introduced to the Internet and intranet, see what makes a quality web site, and how such a web site is designed. In Chapter 2, you will explore FrontPage 2002, looking at its components, and seeing how they are used to create a web site. In Chapters 3 and 4, you will learn how to use FrontPage's wizards, themes, and templates to build a web site.

Chapter 1

Designing Quality Web Applications

Communication, whether it be within a small group, throughout a large organization, or among many organizations, can almost always be improved—made faster, easier to receive, and easier to respond to. The *web application*, a multimedia form of communication including text, graphics, audio, video, and scripts transmitted by computers, is the latest improvement. While computers sit on the sending and receiving ends of web communication, it is what links the computers that gives web applications one of their most important features. The link means that senders and receivers can operate independently—senders can put the web content up according to their schedule, and receivers can get it anytime thereafter. The link used for the transmission of web content is one of two forms of networking, either the public *Internet,* which uses public and private networks, including phone lines; or a private *intranet,* which uses a *local area network* (*LAN*), generally within an organization.

The Internet is at the foundation of a global communications revolution that has changed the way people communicate, work, and conduct business. It has made it easier and cheaper to exchange information, ideas, and products around the globe. For instance, accessing a web site halfway around the world is as easy as accessing one across the street.

The Internet

The Internet is a network infrastructure of computers, communications lines, and switches (really other computers) that use a set of computer hardware and software standards, or *protocols,* that allow computers to exchange data with other computers. The computers can be in the same room, or they can be located around the world from each other. They can use the same operating system software, such as Windows 2000, or each can use a different computer operating system, such as the Macintosh operating system, Linux, or UNIX. The standards that make up the Internet have become a modern *lingua franca*—a language enabling any computer connected to the Internet to exchange information with any other computer also connected to the Internet, regardless of the operating systems the computers use.

The birth of the Internet can be traced back to the late 1960s when the use of computers by the Department of Defense Advanced Research Projects Agency (ARPA) and other government agencies had expanded so much that a way for the computer systems to share data was needed. ARPANET, the predecessor to what we now know as the Internet, was created to meet this need.

Another milestone in the history of the Internet came in the mid-1980s, when the National Science Foundation (NSF) added its five supercomputing centers (NSFNET) to the Internet. This gave educational centers, the military, and other NSF grantees access to the power of these supercomputers and, more importantly, created the backbone of today's information superhighway. This backbone is made up of all the high-capacity (or wide-bandwidth) phone lines and data links needed to effectively transfer all the information now on the Internet. Until this wide-bandwidth infrastructure existed, the potential of ARPANET, NSFNET, and now the Internet couldn't be realized. As a result, by the end of the 1980s, almost all the pieces were in place for a global telecommunications revolution.

The World Wide Web

By 1990, the Internet had grown to be a highway linking computers across the United States and around the world, but it was still a character-based system. That is, what appeared on computer screens connected to the Internet was simply text. There were no graphics or hyperlinks. A *graphical user interface* (*GUI*) to the Internet needed to be developed. Tim Berners-Lee, a scientist working at the European Laboratory for Particle Physics (CERN) in Geneva, Switzerland, proposed a set of protocols for the transfer of graphical information over the Internet in 1989. Berners-Lee's proposals were adopted by other groups, and thus the World Wide Web was born.

The Internet is a *wide area network* (*WAN*), as compared with a local area network (LAN), among computers in proximity. For computers to share information over a WAN, there must be a physical connection (the communications infrastructure created by ARPA and the NSF, and now maintained by private industry) and a common software standard that the computers use to transfer data. The physical connection depends on whether you use a modem to dial up to the Internet, or whether your computer is part of a LAN with an Internet connection. The physical layer includes the modem or network interface card in your computer. You also need a phone or dedicated network line that connects you to the Internet backbone. In either case, your computer, connected to the Internet either with a dial-up or network connection, is capable of sharing information with any other computer connected to the Internet anywhere in the world.

> **Note** *The term "modem," as used here, includes DSL and ISDN "adapters." Such devices provide the means to use ordinary phone lines to connect to the Internet.*

LANs and an Intranet

As important as the Internet has become to society, local area networks have become even more important to the exchange of information and communication within organizations. LANs started out as a way to share programs and data files among several people in an organization. This was then augmented by electronic mail (e-mail) for sending and receiving messages over the LAN. Then intranets were added to LANs to provide a miniature version of the World Wide Web within an organization—a place for people to post and read text and graphics documents whenever they choose.

A good example of how an intranet can be put to use is a project report. Instead of e-mailing a weekly update to a long list of potentially uninterested people (and filling up everybody's inbox in the process), you could post a web page on the intranet that would give not only the current status, but also other, more static information, such as the people working on the project, its goals, and its funding. In this way, those people who are truly interested can get the information.

With Active Server Pages (ASP, which are included with Microsoft's Internet Information Services) and Microsoft Office, even more intranet interactivity is possible.

Users can send commands to a web site, which with ASP become a web application, and receive customized responses. Any Microsoft Office document can be included in a web page. Databases can be queried, and custom web pages can automatically be generated to display query results. Integrating Office and other files with your FrontPage web sites is covered in Chapter 11, Active Server Pages is covered in Chapters 16 and 17, and working with databases is covered in Chapter 19.

Note *Internet Information Services (IIS) is included with Microsoft's Windows NT Server, as well as Windows 2000 Professional (a limited version), Server, and Advanced Server. IIS and FrontPage provide all the software tools you need to set up a full-scale intranet or World Wide Web site. FrontPage, along with the Microsoft Personal Web Server (PWS), which is available in Windows 98, can even host limited web sites by themselves.*

Except for possibly the content, there is no difference between a web site on the World Wide Web and a web site on an intranet. They are created the same way and can have the same features and components. The discussion and instructions throughout this book are aimed equally at both the World Wide Web and an intranet, and there are examples included of each. So, in learning to create a web application, you can apply that knowledge to either form of dissemination.

Tip *Think of the Internet and a LAN as equivalent means of information transmission—one public, the other private. And think of the World Wide Web and an intranet as equivalent means of posting and reading information being transmitted over the Internet or a LAN, respectively. The World Wide Web and an intranet are just advanced electronic bulletin boards, while a web page is an electronic document posted on that bulletin board.*

Note *In a unique blending of two concepts, intranets can be extended to outside users, creating an* extranet. *For example, a corporation may provide other businesses, such as vendors or customers, access to a select subset of corporate data as well as a way to exchange the information.*

Internet Protocols

The Internet and the Web are built upon several protocols, which can also be used in LANS and intranets:

- **Transmission Control Protocol/Internet Protocol (TCP/IP)** controls how information is packaged before being transferred between computers connected through the Internet or a LAN.

- **Hypertext Transfer Protocol (HTTP)** is the language the computers use to exchange information on the Web or an intranet.

- **Hypertext Markup Language (HTML)** is the programming language used to create the documents that are distributed on the Web or an intranet and displayed on your monitor. Chapter 12 discusses HTML in depth.
- **Extensible Markup Language (XML)** is the second generation programming language used to create and display Internet and intranet documents. XML is discussed in Chapter 14.

TCP/IP

To transfer information over the Internet or within a LAN, several requirements must be met. These include a way to assign each computer or site on the network a unique address (just like having a unique postal address), as well as a means of "packaging" the information for transmission. These functions are handled by the Transmission Control Protocol and the Internet Protocol.

Internet Protocol

The foundation of the system is the Internet Protocol (IP). The IP converts data into packets and provides an address for each site on the Internet. *Packets* are like the pages of a book. An entire book contains too much information to be printed on one page, so it is divided into multiple pages. This makes the information in the book much more manageable. The Internet Protocol does the same thing with the information in a file slated to be transmitted over the Internet or a LAN. It divides the information into packets that can be handled more easily by the network.

The other primary function of the IP is to provide addresses for the computers connected to the Internet. Each computer needs its own *IP address*—a group of four decimal numbers that provides a unique address for the computer. Examples of IP addresses are 198.68.191.10 and 204.250.144.70. These IP addresses are actually decimal representations of single 32-bit binary numbers. While a computer may be comfortable with 11000110 01000100 10111111 00001010 or 11001100 11111010 10010000 01000110 as an address, most people find decimal numbers easier to work with. This system of numbering allows for about 4.3 billion (2^{32}) possible combinations. If you are setting up a web server, you will need to get an IP address. You may also need a domain name. A *domain name* is a unique name that identifies a computer or network, much like the name of a city in a postal address, and is matched to a unique IP address. Examples of domain names are "microsoft.com" and "whidbey.net." The .COM extension identifies the domain as commercial, while .NET identifies an Internet service provider or ISP. Other domain extensions include .ORG for nonprofit organizations and .GOV for government agencies. These are assigned by Internet registrars, a list of which can be found at the Internet Network Information Center (InterNIC, **http://www.internic.net**). Your Internet service provider (ISP) can help you get an IP address and domain name. You can also have a new web site located in an existing domain. If you will be using an existing web server, the network administrator or webmaster will be able to tell you what the domain name and IP addresses are.

Tip *If you can't find the name you want with a .COM, .ORG, or .NET extension, in the very near future (possibly by the time you read this) you will be able to register a name with the .AERO, .BIZ, .COOP, .INFO, .MUSEUM, .NAME, and .PRO extensions. Right now you can register a name with a .CC extension (http://www.ccnames.cc), a .NF extension (http://www.names.nf), or a .TO extension (http://www.register.to). These are, in fact, foreign registrations, but they are still legitimate domain names that you can use. .CC is for the Cocos (Keeling) Islands, .NF is for Norfolk Island, and .TO is for Trinidad and Tobago. Domainit.com (http://www.domainit.com) provides a registration site for a number of extensions including .COM, .ORG, .NET, .CC, .TO, .AC, and .SH, and provides a means for searching all these extensions.*

Transmission Control Protocol

While the Internet Protocol provides the basics for sharing information over the Internet, it leaves some things to be desired. The two most important objectives are ensuring that all the packets reach their destination and that they arrive in the proper order. This is where the Transmission Control Protocol (TCP) steps in. To understand how it works, assume you want to send a book to someone, and you have to mail it one page (or packet) at a time. Also assume that there are no page numbers in the book.

How will recipients know that they have received all the pages, and how will they know the proper order of the pages? TCP solves these problems by creating an "envelope" for each packet generated by the IP. Each envelope has a serialized number that identifies the packet inside it. As each packet is sent, the TCP assigns it a number that increases by 1 for each packet. When the packets are received, the numbers are checked for continuity and sequence. If any numbers are missing, the receiving computer requests that the missing packet be re-sent. If the packets are out of sequence, the receiving computer puts them back in order. TCP also makes sure the information arrives in the same condition it was sent (in other words, that the data was not corrupted in transit).

TCP/IP provides the basic tools for transferring information over the Internet. The next layer up the ladder is the Hypertext Transfer Protocol, the traffic director for the Web.

Note *To set up an intranet on a LAN, you must add the TCP/IP protocols to the existing networking protocols—possibly either IPX/SPX (Integrated Packet Exchange/ Sequenced Packet Exchange) or NetBEUI (NetBIOS Extended User Interface)— on both the server and all clients. Chapter 24 tells you how to do this.*

Hypertext Transfer Protocol

The Hypertext Transfer Protocol (HTTP) is the heart of the World Wide Web and is also used with an intranet. HTTP composes the messages and handles the information that is sent between computers on the Internet using TCP/IP. To understand how HTTP works, you first need to understand the nature of client/server relationships.

Client/Server Relationships

The basic function of the Internet or a LAN is to provide a means for transferring information between computers. To do this, one computer (the *server*) will contain information and another (the *client*) will request it. The server will process a client's request and transfer the information. The server may be required to process the request before it can be filled. For example, if the request is for information contained in a database, such as a request submitted to a web search engine, the server would first have to extract the information from the database before it could be sent to the client.

The passing of information between a client and a server has six basic steps:

1. A connection is made between the client and the server. This is handled by TCP/IP.

2. The client creates a request to the server in the form of an HTTP message.

3. The request is sent to the server using TCP/IP.

4. The server processes the request and creates a response to the client, again in the form of an HTTP message.

5. The response is sent to the client using TCP/IP.

6. The connection between the client and the server is terminated by TCP/IP.

TCP/IP creates the connection between the client and the server, and HTTP composes the request for information and the response from the server. This is how HTTP is used to transfer information over a TCP/IP connection.

To access information on the Web or an intranet, you need an application that can send requests to a server as well as process and display the server's response. This is the function of web browsers. The two most common web browsers are Microsoft's Internet Explorer and Netscape's Navigator/Communicator.

Note *Recent releases of both Microsoft's browser, Internet Explorer, and Netscape's browser, Navigator, have grown into integrated suites of applications. Microsoft has kept the name Internet Explorer for their browser suite while Netscape renamed theirs Communicator. Netscape Navigator is available both as a stand-alone browser and as part of Communicator. The term Netscape Navigator, or just Netscape is used to refer both to the stand-alone Navigator and the browser component of Communicator.*

Hypertext Markup Language

The parts of the Web or an intranet covered so far, TCP/IP and HTTP, control how information is transferred over the network. Hypertext Markup Language (HTML) is the component that controls how the information is displayed. The information sent from a web server is an HTML document. Here's what a simple HTML document looks like:

```
<HTML>
<HEAD>
<TITLE>A Simple HTML Document</TITLE>
</HEAD>
<BODY>
<H1>A Simple HTML Document</H1>
<P><B>This text is bold</B> and <I>this text is italic</I>.</P>
</BODY>
</HTML>
```

Figure 1-1 shows how a web browser displays this HTML document. Web browsers interpret the HTML document and display the results on your monitor. HTML files are simple ASCII text files that contain formatting tags controlling how information (text and graphics) is displayed and how other file types are executed (audio and video files, for example).

HTML tags are usually used in pairs. An HTML document must begin with the <HTML> opening tag and end with the </HTML> closing tag. The <HEAD></HEAD> tags enclose information about the beginning of a web page, such as the title, which is defined by the <TITLE></TITLE> tags and displayed in the title bar of the web browser. The body of the web page is enclosed by the <BODY></BODY> tags. The <H1></H1>

Figure 1-1. *A browser displaying the Simple HTML document*

tags define the enclosed text as a level-1 heading. The <B></B> and <I></I> tags, respectively, define text as bold or italic, as you saw in the preceding listing. Each paragraph is usually enclosed in the <P></P> tags.

Note	*HTML tags are not case-sensitive. They can be upper- or lowercase, or mixed case, such as <Body>.*

In the early days of the Web, these tags were typed in using a simple text editor to create web pages. This was time-consuming and not much fun. Today, you can use FrontPage, a true WYSIWYG (What You See Is What You Get) HTML editor, to create your web pages. Gone are the days when you had to learn all the HTML tags and proper syntax. With FrontPage, you design a page, and the proper HTML is created automatically. It's never been easier to create your own web site.

What Is a Web Page?

A web application consists of one or more web pages that are interconnected. Since the focus of this book is how to create web applications that are collections of web pages, here's a more detailed definition of what a web page is. A good way to think of it is that a *web page* is a text file containing Hypertext Markup Language (HTML) formatting tags, and links to graphics files and other web pages. The text file is stored on a *web server* and can be accessed by other computers connected to the server, via the Internet or a LAN. The file can be accessed by the use of *web browsers*—programs that download the file to your computer, interpret the HTML tags and links, and display the results on your monitor. Another definition is that a web page is an interactive form of communication that uses a computer network.

There are two properties of web pages that make them unique: they are interactive and they can use multimedia. The term *multimedia* is used to describe text, audio, animation, and video files that are combined to present information—for example, in an interactive encyclopedia or a game. When those same types of files are distributed over the Internet or a LAN, you can use the term *hypermedia* to describe them. With the World Wide Web, it is now possible to have true multimedia over the Internet. However, unless your clients have a high-speed service, such as the Integrated Services Digital Network's (ISDN) 128-Kbps service or Digital Subscriber Line (DSL) from 56 Kbps to over 1 Mbps, downloading the large hypermedia files can take too long to routinely use them. On most LANs, which are considerably faster, this is much more feasible, but there are still limitations and a potential need to keep the LAN open for high-volume data traffic.

Web pages are interactive to allow the reader or user to send information or commands back to the web site that hosts the web application. For example, Figure 1-2 shows the home page of the AltaVista web search engine. The AltaVista home page gives you access to an application that searches the AltaVista database of web sites. You can use

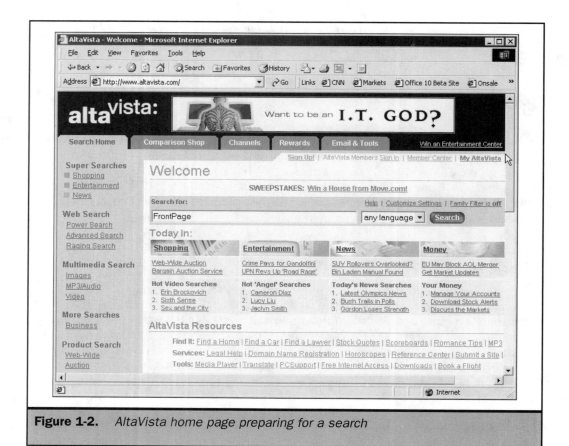

Figure 1-2.   *AltaVista home page preparing for a search*

this and other search engines to locate sites on the Web. From this web page you can select which part of the Internet to search, how the results of the search will be displayed, and the keywords that the search will be based on. When you click the Search button, the information you've entered is sent to the AltaVista web server. The database is then searched, and the results are used to create a new web page, which is displayed by your web browser. Figure 1-3 shows the results of a search using the keyword "FrontPage."

Each web page has an address called the *uniform resource locator* (*URL*), which is displayed in the Address combo box (a combination of a text box and a drop-down list) at the top of the screen (below the toolbar). A URL is the path on the Internet to a specific web page (for instance, the URL for the AltaVista home page is **http://www.altavista.com**) and is used the same way you use a path name to locate files on your computer. In this case, the URL tells you that the web page is located on a web server with the domain

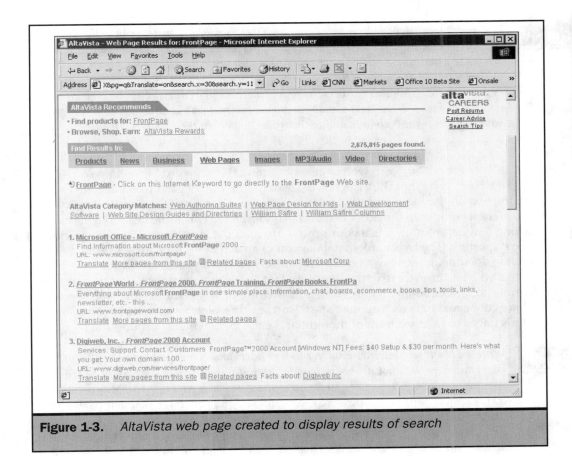

Figure 1-3.   *AltaVista web page created to display results of search*

name *altavista.com* connected to the World Wide Web ("www"). While a *domain* is one or more networked computers, the *domain name* provides a single address to access the network from the Internet. The network's domain server, meanwhile, routes the request to the correct place within the network. The actual filename of the *home page* (the top-level page of the web, which usually serves as a table of contents for the web) is usually either Default.htm or Index.htm (or Default.asp or Index.asp when using Active Server Pages, see Chapter 16); it is implied by being unstated. The default web page filename is set on a web server. This is the page that will be displayed if no web page filename is specified. On a LAN, the URL is similar; it uses the server name in a format like http://*servername*/ *folder*/*homepage filename*. The server name is the functional equivalent of the domain name in this case. The home page filename can also be left off if it is the default filename.

Note   *Web pages located on web servers using the UNIX operating system generally have an .HTML extension, while web pages located on Windows NT web servers generally have an .HTM extension. Active Server web pages have an .ASP extension. Also, not all URLs include the "www." This is determined by how the URL is programmed into the network routers. Routers perform the task of matching IP (Internet Protocol) addresses to domain names. It's a good idea to have your Internet service provider (ISP) program your domain name both with and without the "www" in their routers. IP addresses and domain names were covered in the "TCP/IP" section earlier in this chapter.*

AltaVista found 2,675,815 web pages containing the keyword "FrontPage." The web page created by the AltaVista server displays the title of each web page, an excerpt from the text on the page, and the URL for the page. The title of the page is displayed in a different color than the other text and is underlined. This indicates it is a *hyperlink.* Clicking a hyperlink will cause your browser to load the location (web page) specified in the hyperlink. The hyperlink may take you to an actual location, or *bookmark,* within the same document, the way a bookmark works in a word processor file, or it may link you to a web site anywhere in the world. In fact, if a web page doesn't have an obvious identifier to its location, you may not even be aware of what country the web server you are connected to is in. You may start "surfing" the Web by clicking hyperlinks on various pages to follow a train of thought and end up "traveling" around the world.

Tip   *With the Microsoft Internet Explorer (3.0 or later) and Netscape Navigator (3.0 or later) browsers, it is not necessary to enter **http://** in the Address box. With Microsoft's Internet Explorer 3.0 or later you can also access a search engine by typing **go**, followed by the keywords in the Address box—for example, **go FrontPage** (without the "http://" prefix). In IE 5.0 and later you need only type **FrontPage** and click Go on the right of the Address box. In Netscape 6.0 or later, you can type FrontPage and click Search to access a search engine and see sites that relate to the word "FrontPage."*

Note   *Hyperlinks do not have to be underlined, although they should be displayed in a color different from the body text. With Netscape Navigator (and Communicator) 4.03 and later, you can use the Preferences option in the Edit menu; with Microsoft Internet Explorer, you can use the Internet Options option in the View menu (IE 4.0) or Tools menu Internet Options Advanced tab (IE 5.0) to control whether hyperlinks will be underlined, as well as what color they should be displayed in (Internet Options | General tab | Colors buttons).*

When you submit keywords or other information to a web site, such as AltaVista, you are actually running an application on the web server. Web servers can also download applications—for example, a Java applet or an ActiveX control—to your computer. *Java* is a programming language that extends the flexibility and functions of the Web. *Applets* are small programs that are downloaded to your computer and then executed. *ActiveX controls* are similar in use and function to Java applets, but are written in programming languages such as Visual Basic. Java applets and ActiveX controls are used to add games, chat, menus, and other interactive components to web pages. You do not have to know how to program in Java or Visual Basic to use a Java applet or ActiveX control—a growing library of applets and controls is already available on the Web. A good place to start looking for Java applets is the Java home page, **http://www.java.sun.com**, or the Gamelan home page, **http://www.gamelan.com**. For ActiveX controls, Microsoft's web site, **http://www.microsoft.com**, is the place to start. Java and ActiveX are described in Chapters 18 and 20; Visual Basic Scripting Edition (VBScript) and JavaScript are described in Chapter 15.

> **Tip** *You can turn support for Java applets on or off in Internet Explorer by opening the Internet Options dialog box from the View menu (IE 4.0) or Tools menu (IE 5.0), selecting the Advanced tab, and clicking the Java JIT Compiler Enabled check box. In Netscape Navigator 4.5, you can turn support for Java applets and JavaScript on or off by opening the Network Preferences dialog box from the Options menu, selecting the Languages tab, and then clicking the Enable Java and Enable JavaScript check boxes. In Netscape Communicator and Navigator 4.0 or later, Java and JavaScript support are turned on or off by opening the Preferences dialog box from the Edit menu, selecting Advanced in the Category list box, and then clicking the Enable Java and Enable JavaScript check boxes.*

As you can see, the World Wide Web is a flexible and powerful means of communication. Next, look at how you can design and create a web application to use this powerful medium.

Designing Quality Web Applications

To many, web application design is limited to what is often called the look and feel of the web pages—things like where do you put the navigation bar or buttons, what kind of graphics should you use, and how should they be arranged on the web page. Good web design, though, also means having a clear understanding of the goals of the web application and a good feeling for the information's organization in the web application.

A lot of decisions about the design of the page are based on general design practices seen in the print media. The Web is its own medium with its own peculiarities. How it is different is partially based on the nature of the Internet and the World Wide Web. The differences are also caused by the medium with which you view the Web: the computer and its monitor. Understanding these differences is important because some things that work in print just do not translate well to the Web. But the Web can also do things that print cannot do. On the Web, you can read about a performer and see them, hear the performer live, even interact with that performer in real time. Try that in a magazine!

Designing for a web application is also a process. You just don't decide that you are going to design a web application and start laying out a web page, expecting to end up with a useable product without going back and filling in the details numerous times. Good design, in addition to knowing your media and tools, has four major components:

- Gathering requirements
- Organizing information
- Structuring the web application
- Developing a navigation scheme

This chapter outlines a process that will take you from an initial concept to a completed web application that you, your customer, and most important, the end user of the web application, can all be happy with.

So where do you start? The best place is at the beginning. Ask yourself: Just why are you creating a web application?

Gathering Requirements

Start by posing these questions to yourself:

- What is the purpose of this web application?
- What is it supposed to do?
- What are the goals of the web application?
- Is it to amuse, amaze, educate, or sell a product?
- Is it to show off your web development skills, record a family event, or cybercast a live event?

It could be one or several of these, but the basic reason is to communicate, and you need to be clear on what it is you are communicating.

Most often, you are creating the web application for up to three groups of people. The first, although often considered last, is the end user. This is the person who will not only use the web application, but is your audience. The second group is the person or party that wants the web application built—your customer, the party that you, the web designer, are working for. And last, and usually least, you are doing it for yourself, to create something that will be a good example of what you can do. What do all three of these groups want? What do all three need? The answers to these questions will provide the requirements for the web application. The answers, unfortunately, can also produce three *different* sets of requirements, which are often conflicting.

The web developer needs to integrate these requirements and satisfy as many of them as possible before communicating effectively with the customer so both have the same understanding of what the web application is supposed to do and where it is going. Everything that comes after this needs to be bounced back against these requirements. If it supports the requirements, it is the right thing to do. If it doesn't, it shouldn't be done unless you want to go back and revise the requirements.

The requirements stage will determine what the content and functionality will be. Once this is understood, you can start gathering and organizing the contents of your web application.

Organizing Information

Once you have defined the requirements, you then have the job of collecting and organizing the contents. This means locating the images and articles that will make up the site, and then sorting them into logical groups of information. This stage, and the previous one of figuring out why you are doing the web application in the first place, are not glamorous and often are not nearly as fun as making impressive graphics, but your customer and audience will certainly appreciate it when they try to use your web application. It is here that you set the stage for the structure of your web application. Every web application presents a different problem, but there are some general approaches. Keep the end user in mind when organizing information. Does it make sense? Will it enable the user to develop a mental map of the web application? And most important, can the user easily find and use what they're looking for?

The following are some common ways of organizing information. They are meant to get you thinking about different ways of organizing your material, but they are not the only ways to do so. One of the following may not work for your project. If it doesn't, see if you can come up with another scheme. Again, keep the end user in mind.

There are two general classes of schemes. The first are those that rely on an obvious order such as the alphabetical order of the phone book's white pages—a place where the organization of its contents are clear. The second class are those schemes that are arranged in an order that is not so obvious—such as the phone book's yellow pages, which uses topics that may or may not be well understood.

Obvious Order

Schemes with an obvious order are the easy ones to use. Once you decide to use one of them, organizing the material becomes a no-brainer. They do have their limitations, however, since they require that the user knows what they are looking for. Three obvious orders are alphabetical, chronological, and geographical.

Alphabetical   The white pages of the phone book are a good example of alphabetical organization. The names are arranged in the order of the letters of the alphabet. It is easy to find a person if you know their name.

The drawback is that a person can be difficult to find if you don't know how to spell the name, or if you are not sure of the name, or if all you know about the person is that he or she is a web developer. Alphabetical organization can be used for arranging any list of things, from departments of a company to a list of recipes.

Chronological   Events, or anything that is associated with a date, lend themselves to a chronological organization. A list of concert dates is often arranged chronologically. Press releases, being that they are dated, can be organized similarly. Chronological organization is useful, as long as there is a clear date or time attached to what you are organizing. Figure 1-4 shows the schedule of the Seattle Mariners baseball team, arranged in chronological order.

You also need to ask yourself: Does your user want to look for a game by date? A list like this puts the priority on *when* rather than *whom*. People may find the date more important when they are looking for a specific game, but some may prefer to search by the name of the opposing team or a specific pitcher rather than by date. In this case, an alphabetical listing of opponents or pitchers would be more appropriate.

Geographical   Some things are tied to a geographic location. For instance, a business may want to organize the information on its different sites according to the location of each office. Weather is also tied to this system of arrangement. When you look at

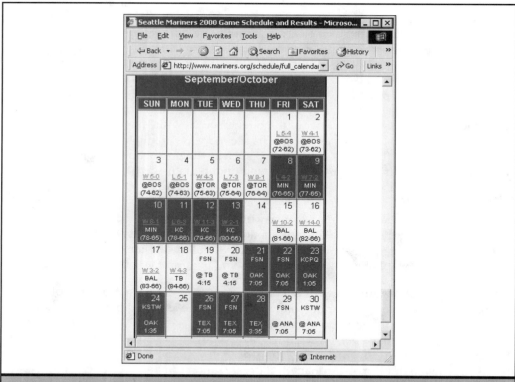

Figure 1-4.   *A baseball team schedule arranged in chronological order*

a weather report, you typically want to check a specific location. The sizes of the areas may range widely—for instance, a city like Duluth as opposed to the whole continent of Asia—nevertheless both are geographical locations. A similar system is shown in Figure 1-5, which shows a map used to select airfares by clicking a part of the world. This map is created in Chapter 6.

Not-So-Obvious Order

These schemes are more difficult to set up and more open to interpretation, but people often don't know exactly what they are looking for when they begin searching. Because of that, these schemes are often very useful. Four less obvious orders are topical, task, priority, and metaphor.

Topical   Many, if not most, sites provide a topical index to their contents because people tend to know the topic they are looking for rather than a specific item, and because the list

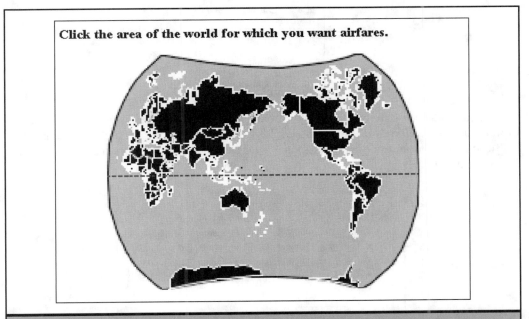

Figure 1-5.   *Geographically selecting airfares*

of specific items is often too large to search. For example, the Amazon.com music page lists music by type, like this:

If you are looking for a classical composer, you would click Classical, then use an alphabetical search to find the composer. If you are just looking for a classical album without a clear preference as to composer, you can click Classical, then select from this second list of topics:

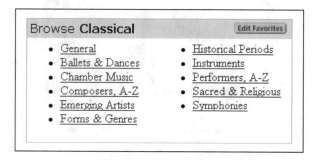

But are the topics clear? Is there a definite understanding of what constitutes "General" or "Forms & Genres"? Isn't Symphonies a form of classical music and therefore included in "Forms & Genres" (it is)? And who is included in "Emerging Artists"? There isn't always a clear definition, but it is still useful to categorize them this way even though you may run into some gray areas. It is important to organize topics in a sensible way that makes things easy to find. It is frequently better to organize topics in order of interest rather than alphabetical order, because it allows people to quickly find what they are looking for. Try to keep the gray areas to a minimum. Keep it simple!

Task   Task schemes are organized around things that you do. The menus in a web browser are set up that way with selections for *File*, *Edit*, and *View*. Task-oriented schemes are useful if the web application is dealing with processes, tasks, or actions that you want the user to do. Task lists always start with or include a verb, like *Track, Use, See,* or *Read* in the following task list on Amazon.com.

Where's My Stuff?
- Track your recent orders.
- Use Your Account to view or change your orders.

Shipping & Returns
- See our Shipping Rates & Policies.
- Read our Returns Policy.

Need Help?
- Forgot your password? Click here.
- Redeem or buy a gift certificate.
- Visit the Help Desk.

Priority   Sometimes things need to be arranged around their importance or priority. If you are organizing the departments of a corporation alphabetically, you would put *Accounting* in front of the *Office of the President*. But if you are organizing by importance, or priority, the *Office of the President* will be first.

Unfortunately, this type of organizational scheme can be fraught with political implications, for what constitutes an obvious order of importance to those inside an organization may be completely different to those outside it.

Metaphor   *Metaphor* is the use of one object's meaning transferred to another to make a new idea easier to understand. One of the great metaphors on the computer desktop is Apple's use of the trashcan as a metaphor for deleting files. Figure 1-6 shows a site organized around metaphors.

Metaphorical organization must be used carefully because not all metaphors have the clear connection of the Macintosh trashcan. The associations people make may be unexpected, or there may be no association at all. For example, what is the *Lounge* in Figure 1-6? It also may not be clear what the *Mailroom* and the *Reception* areas are.

Mixing Organizational Schemes

One of the greatest causes of confusion to the user is the mixing of organizing schemes. The organizing scheme is what helps the user create a mental map of the web application. When you mix schemes, it becomes very difficult to develop a mental map of the web application, and this causes confusion. It is the old apples-and-oranges comparison. While apples and oranges share the status of fruit, they are also dissimilar enough to be seen as completely different. So it is with organizing schemes. The mind tries to make patterns out of what it sees, and when things the mind expects to be the same are actually far apart, there is a mental grinding of gears in trying to reconcile them.

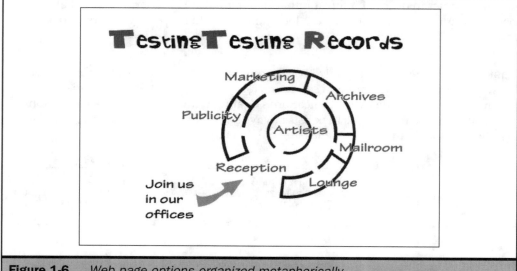

Figure 1-6. *Web page options organized metaphorically*

Put yourself in the mind of the user. How will they perceive and use the information? Figuring this out often requires a pair of fresh eyes—something you may not be equipped with if you're too close to your material. It requires looking at organizing material with fresh eyes. That is always hard to do with something you are very close to. Therefore it's often worthwhile to get users to look at what you have done. If they don't understand your organizing scheme, don't assume it's their fault. At least you know there's a problem, and you can correct it.

With the material now organized, you can begin laying out the structure of the web application.

Structuring the Web Application

How you have organized your material will determine how you structure your web application. Three major ways to structure a web application are hierarchical, hypertext, and database. These methods can be used alone or in different combinations, as the material requires.

Hierarchical Structure

Hierarchical structure is the traditional top-down approach. It is creating high-level categories and then arranging material underneath in logical subcategories. You can divide music into:

- Types (Rock, Classical, etc.)
- Musical periods (Baroque, Classical, etc.)

- Composers of the period (Bach, Mozart, etc.)
- Forms of music the composer wrote (symphonies, sonatas, etc.)
- Specific pieces the composer wrote (*Symphony No. 41, Eine Kleine Nachtmusik,* etc.)

Each of these is a level in a hierarchical structure, like this:

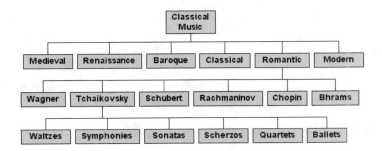

This is a very common classification scheme that most people are familiar with. It helps users create a mental map of the structure of the site that in turn helps them move around it without getting confused or lost.

In designing a hierarchical structure, you want to keep a balance between the width and depth of the hierarchy. The extremes are the *narrow and deep hierarchy* and the *broad and shallow hierarchy.*

Narrow and Deep Hierarchy   A narrow and deep hierarchy is organized so that there are just a few classifications at the top. As a result, the user is forced to move down through many levels to get the information desired. This constitutes extra work for the user, making it difficult to keep track of where he or she is in the web application. In this example, it takes seven clicks to get from *Page A* to *Page B.*

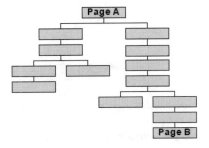

A good rule of thumb for depth is to structure the web application so that users access the information they want in three levels. Once they hit four or five levels without getting what they want, confusion and frustration set in.

Broad and Shallow Hierarchy   The opposite problem occurs when classifications at the top level greatly outnumber the levels underneath. This can present the user with too many choices to keep track of, as illustrated here:

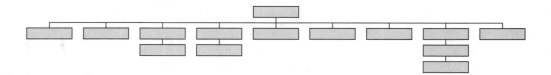

The human short-term memory is limited to around seven items. When they get to the eighth or ninth, users start forgetting earlier ones. As the items become more complex, the ability to remember them decreases. You can list up to nine items, if they are simple, or keep it down to five, if the material is more complex.

   It is useful to draw a diagram of your site hierarchy showing the pages and their relationships to one another. You can refer to this diagram, or storyboard, when you create your web pages.

Hypertext Structure

Hypertext is text or images that are linked to other text, images, or audio or video pieces without a specific structure. These links can be located throughout the page and provide a way to move quickly to related data. This is a very nonlinear approach to structure, and looks like this:

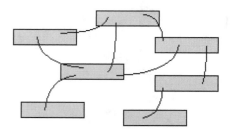

Using hypertext can be very confusing and should be employed carefully. It works best as a secondary, or supporting, structure. Because of its nonlinearity, the user can get lost quickly and will find it difficult to make a mental map of the web application. Using hypertext works best if the link is to data that is at a dead end. The user would then move back to the main hierarchical structure and not have other choices that would move him or her further away.

Database Structure

A database can be used for structuring a site by building pages of information out of a database as the information is requested. This works well for large sites with related information. Using a database can also give a lot of flexibility in presenting only the information requested. Chapter 19 describes using databases with FrontPage.

Once you have a structure for your web application, you will next develop the tools the user needs to navigate through this structure.

Developing a Navigation Scheme

The navigation scheme of your web application is highly dependent on the structure you have developed, and directly affects how the user will move around your site and access the material you present.

There are a lot of ways to provide navigation. If you have been on the Web for a while, you have seen many of them and probably gotten lost using some. There is a natural tendency for web developers to come up with new ways to dazzle their audience. But it is often best to keep navigation simple, or your audience may end up more confused than dazzled.

The next several sections discuss the major issues that need to be considered in setting up navigation schemes, including browser navigation, maintaining the hierarchy and structure of your design, providing flexibility in navigation, and the use of navigation bars, frames, and menus. This will be followed by an example of a navigation scheme.

Browser Navigation

Because your web application will run inside a web browser, it has navigation tools before you even start building it. Most modern web browsers provide the following variety of tools independent of your web application:

- Forward and backward arrows, which let the user move forward and backward through web pages

- *Bookmark* or *Favorites* lists, which allow the user to save the URL of a page and return directly there without going through the front door of the web application

- Page URLs, which allow the user to go directly to any page desired

- Status bar display of a link's URL, which gives users a sense of where they are going if you have carefully labeled your folders and files

However, one of the most useful navigation features that the browser provides is one that web developers try to subvert most often—the use of blue underlined type to indicate an unvisited text link, and purple underlined type to indicate a visited link. It is a navigation scheme common to all browsers and one that every beginning web user learns very early. It makes it easy to scan a page and see where the links are and to know whether you have used a particular link. No other navigation scheme provides that much information or is as universally understood. To use any other scheme is to force your user to stop and learn your scheme before being able to proceed.

Maintaining the Design Hierarchy and Structure

Your navigation scheme will be the primary way for the user to get a sense of the structure of your web application. The user is not using the navigation scheme to just find places to go, but also to see where they are and how they are related to the rest of the web application.

When using a hierarchical structure, it is useful for the navigation scheme to reflect that. But many such schemes do not differentiate between pages that are at different levels of the hierarchy. They treat them as if they are equal, as the following hypothetical navigation bar would imply:

| Music Home Page | Alternative | Blues | Classical | Folk | Jazz | Rock |

One of the most recognized ways of showing hierarchy and structure is the outline form. The top levels of the hierarchy are flush left and each level down is indented to the right an equal amount, as shown here:

```
I.  Classical Music
      A. Modern
      B. Romantic
            1. Bhrams
            2. Chopin
            3. Rachmaninov
            4. Shubert
            5. Tchaikovsky
                  a) Ballets
                  b) Quartets
                  c) Scherzos
                  d) Sonatas
                  e) Symphonies
                  f) Waltzes
            6. Wagner
      C. Classical
      D. Baroque
      E. Renaissance
      F. Medieval
```

This outline structure visually shows where each section is and how it relates to the hierarchy. Your navigation scheme should provide this kind of information. One way is to show the user where they are as they progress down a structure, which Amazon does like this:

 Music > Styles > Classical > Forms & Genres

Providing Flexibility in Navigation

Providing flexibility in navigation is a balancing act. The web developer is acting as *Director of Traffic* when designing the navigation scheme. How do you get the users to their destination quickly without getting them lost? Look at the extremes in order to see the middle.

The least flexibility is provided by links that only go down or up the hierarchy tree one level at a time with no lateral links, as you can see here:

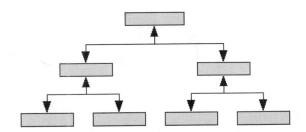

This forces the user to travel back up, one page at a time, and then back down the tree, one page at a time, to go from one part of the web application to another. This may keep users from getting lost, but they are not going to be able to get around the web application quickly.

The most flexibility, the other extreme, is when everything is linked to everything else, like this:

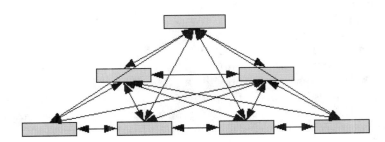

The user has maximum flexibility to move around the web application and, as you can see, a maximum opportunity for confusion. This presents the user with too much information. The trick is to balance the amount of information to maximize flexibility without confusing the user.

As you move down the hierarchy tree, it is recommended that you provide links back up the tree to the home page so that the user can quickly return there. It is also useful to provide lateral links to pages on the same level since these pages should all be related information if the hierarchy tree is set up correctly. Lateral links to pages one level above may be useful, but be careful you don't offer so many choices that the user becomes confused. Here is a reasonable set of links:

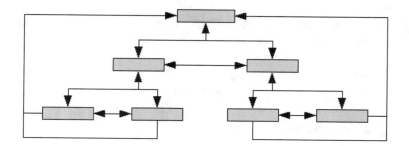

Consistent Labeling

The labels used for navigation links need to reflect the material they represent. This isn't the place to get fancy. Users need to be able to scan your navigation links and have a clear understanding of where they are going.

If you have organized your material well, your labels should fall into place. If the material is arranged by task, the labels should identify those tasks. If it is arranged by topic, the labels should identify the topics.

The wording for the labels should be consistent. The words should use the same verb tense, punctuation, capitalization, and so on. Put yourself in the place of a user new to your material: will your labels be clear to them? To make sure, keep your labels concise, but avoid abbreviations and acronyms because the confusion they cause is always greater then the space they save.

Once you have labels that are consistent and clear, be sure to use the same ones throughout the web site. A useful technique is to repeat the navigation link in the heading of each page. This should show the links used to arrive at that page using the exact same labels users selected to get there. If the labels are different, users will think they have clicked the wrong link and gone to the wrong page. As important, if users are not where they want to be, they are reminded of the choices they made and can go back and change those choices.

Navigation Bars

When you have come up with a navigation scheme and identified all the labels for the links, you need to determine where to put the links. The simplest answer is to gather all the navigation links on a *navigation bar*, which is a set of buttons or text links that allow you to jump to another place in your web application. Navigation bars can be on the top, the bottom, the left side, or the right side of a web page. The major concern is that the location is consistent. Every page must use the same scheme for navigation. The home page defines where it is and what it looks like. All the other pages of the web application should follow that lead.

There are certain limitations with navigation bars on top of the page. The horizontal layout makes it difficult to show hierarchy, and the width of the page limits the entries in the navigation bar unless you go to a smaller font. The top navigation bar can be in the way of the object of the page, which is its content. Here are horizontal navigation bars used by MSN.com, Amazon.com, and CNN.com:

Navigation bars on the bottom of the page should only be there if there is also one on the top. Bottom navigation bars have the same limitations as far as content, and become yet another element to maintain. There may be a bit of confusion here, too. When you look at the navigation bar, are you at the top or the bottom of the page? When the navigation bar is in one place, it acts like an anchor to the page. It becomes a consistent visual point of reference as to where you are on that page. When it is in two places, it doesn't provide that reference.

The left side of the page has become a standard place to put navigation bars. It is not so limiting on the length of the labels and gives more room to show hierarchy without getting in the way of the content. The vertical navigation bar should be placed high so that when the users are at the top of the page, they will also see the top of the navigation bar. Here are vertical navigation bars from MSN.com, Amazon.com, and CNN.com (many sites use both horizontal and vertical navigation bars):

○ **Autos**
○ **Business**
○ **Careers**
○ **City Guides**
○ **Computing & Web**
○ **Entertainment**
○ **Games**
○ **Health**
○ **Home & Loans**
○ Learning & Research
○ **Love & Relationships**
○ **News**
○ **Radio & Video**
○ **Sports**
○ Sydney 2000
○ **Travel**
○ **Women**
	BROWSE
	[Add Favorites]
	• Books
	• Music
	• DVD
	• Video
	• Electronics
	• Toys
	• Health & Beauty
	• Software
	• Computer &
	  Video Games
	• Kitchen
	• Tools &
	  Hardware
	• Lawn & Patio
	• New Cars
	• Auctions
	• sothebys.
	  amazon.com
	• zShops
	• Gift Ideas
	• Free e-Cards
		MAINPAGE
		WORLD
		U.S.
		WEATHER
		BUSINESS
		SPORTS
		TECHNOLOGY
		SPACE
		HEALTH
		ENTERTAINMENT
		POLITICS
		LAW
		TRAVEL
		FOOD
		ARTS & STYLE
		BOOKS
		NATURE
		IN-DEPTH
		ANALYSIS
		LOCAL

Putting the navigation bar on the right side is not a common approach, but is useful in certain limited conditions. Often in a large web application, the home page becomes more of an index of links to the rest of the web application. In such cases it makes sense to use a right navigation bar to link to important pages within the web application, as long as it's set up so a user with a small display will not have to scroll horizontally.

Text vs. Icons   They say a picture is worth a thousand words, but it took words to say that. Try saying it in a picture. Try saying it in a very little picture. Icons have a very limited use unless it is for a very common function, such as returning to the home page. Whenever you see an icon, there is usually a text link along with it. So what is the purpose of the icon? Typically it is no more than eye candy, as shown here:

At most, an icon can supplement a text link. It can provide some additional visual information that supports the text link, but the text link is still the primary link that users will focus on. Icons also take additional time to create, maintain, and download, so use them carefully. Seldom can they stand on their own.

Text Links vs. Navigation Buttons   In a navigation bar you can use either text links (text with a link associated with it) or navigation buttons (small graphics with a text label and an associated link). Navigation buttons allow the web developer to use a variety of fonts and backgrounds for the link. This is usually done for aesthetic reasons to better integrate the text of the links into the design of the other graphics used on the page. The following example shows navigation buttons and text links.

However, whenever you use something other than the default text links, you slow users down because they have to decipher what are links and what are not. The default text link has the advantage of already being familiar to many users. Using alternatives also forfeits the ability to tell if you have used that link or not. With the default text link, the color changes when it has been used. It is also easier to modify a text link in a navigation bar than it is to change or create a new graphic every time you want to edit or insert a new link.

Drop-Down List Boxes

Drop-down list boxes can put a number of selections or links in a small space. The drop-down list (or pull-down menu) only takes up one line until it is selected, and then it opens and displays its contents for selection. The user, though, cannot see what is in the drop-down list until it is selected. If there are several drop-down list boxes, users will not be able to remember what is in each one and will end up clicking back and forth to find what they want. The following example shows how a drop-down list box will show its information when selected.

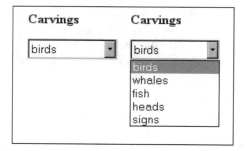

It is better to have everything the user needs clearly visible. Navigation is not a treasure hunt. Make it easy.

Image Maps

Image maps (graphics with "hotspots" that are essentially links the user can click) can be especially useful if your information is organized around geographical locations. It is often not clear that an image can be used to select links. Any navigation system should be usable without instructions on how to use it. To force users to wave their cursor over an image to see if there are any links is to put them on another treasure hunt, which they don't often have the patience for. Even when it is clear that there are hotspots on the image for selection, care must be taken to make it obvious where those hotspots are. Figure 1-7 shows the image map first seen in Figure 1-5 with boxes defining the hotspots. Image maps and hotspots are discussed further in Chapters 2 and 6.

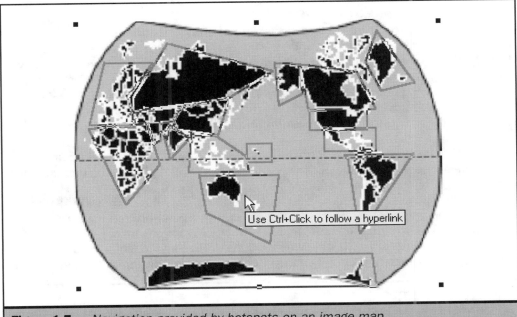

Figure 1-7.   *Navigation provided by hotspots on an image map*

Additional Navigation Aids

Sometimes a site map, an index, and/or a table of contents are used to supplement the primary navigation scheme. Generally speaking, these are admissions of defeat. They are mostly used as an alternative to good organization and a well-designed navigation scheme. They have possibilities as a supplement to the primary navigation scheme, but usually the time spent on these aids would be better spent on improving the organization and primary navigation.

Subsites

After all the emphasis on consistency of navigation devices throughout your web application, there is a situation for which it makes sense to change the navigation: in large sites, particularly large corporate intranets. As you move down the tree to lower levels, you come to sections where the content is very different and therefore needs to be organized differently. Sites representing various organizations in a large corporation are a good example of this. These become subsites, and there is often a lot of latitude in how they are presented as long as they are consistent within themselves and still provide navigation links back up to the primary site.

An Example Navigation Scheme

What does a navigation scheme that meets the preceding requirements look like? The following is an example of one acceptable scheme. Users have found it easy to use this scheme, but that doesn't mean there aren't other ways to get them to where they need to go. If you find a better way that's even easier to use, then use that scheme. Just remember to keep your focus on the needs of the user when designing it.

The following navigation scheme is for classical music. It will start at the top level and break down into individual types of music by composer. Figure 1-8, example a, shows the top level.

The home page is at the top. Since this is the page you are on, there is no link. It is frustrating to users to have the page they are on have a link to itself. The unlinked text is bold to distinguish it from the linked text. The links are all text links in the default colors, and they are all indented evenly like an outline. This shows they are all on the same level and one level below the home page in the web application hierarchy. Users will thus know where they are and what the structure is for one level.

This example is built with a table within a table to align and indent the links. The link labels are for the different standard genres of classical music. The genres are date-related

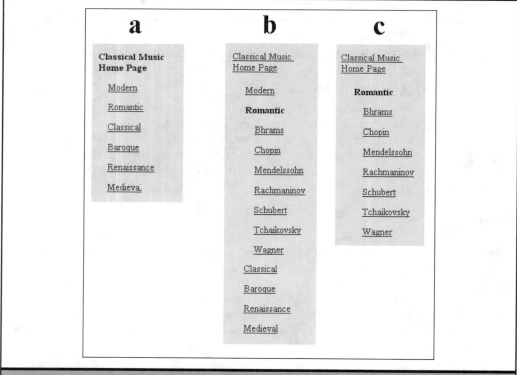

Figure 1-8.   *Sample navigation scheme, first and second levels*

and are chronologically ordered, with the most recent on top. The dates could have been included in labels. This is also a good illustration of how not to do labels. The label *Classical* appears in both levels. Since this is common usage, it is used here, but it always causes confusion.

Next, go down one level by selecting the link *Romantic*. Figure 1-8, example b, shows what this would look like.

Another level opens up that has composers from the Romantic period. It is indented to the right, indicating another level down in the web application hierarchy. Since the page you are on is *Romantic*, it is bold and not linked. You can see where you are. You can also see the pages one level below, as well as those at the same level and the page one level up. This allows you to move down, laterally, and up.

Figure 1-8, example c, shows another way this might be displayed.

Here the lateral moves have been eliminated but you can still move up and down from this point. Whether you want to collapse the structure like this depends on the material and the number of links shown.

Go down one more level by selecting Tchaikovsky. Figure 1-9, example a, shows what the navigation bar might now look like.

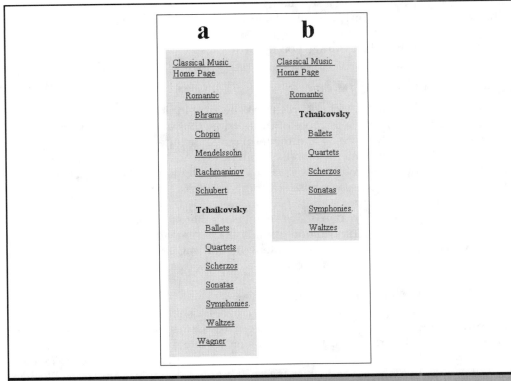

Figure 1-9. *Sample navigation scheme, third level*

Now Tchaikovsky is unlinked and bold since that is where the user is. The pages one level below are shown, along with those on the same level. But the pages on the level above have been collapsed. To add all the pages at that level would start overloading the navigation bar. From here you can go down, laterally, or up to either level above.

If it starts to get confusing you might want to collapse the lateral links as in Figure 1-9, example b.

Using this scheme will tell you where you are and what is around you in the web application. You can collapse the levels, depending on the material and number of links, so that the resulting navigation bar provides the most flexibility in moving up, down, and laterally without becoming too confusing.

With the navigation bar designed for the site you are building, look at how to handle the graphics.

Working with Graphics

The work you have done on organizing, structuring, and developing the navigation of your web application results in a site that is easy to use. All the graphics in the world are not going to make a poorly organized site any easier to use. Graphics can, however, make your site attractive and fun to use. This section will provide some highlights on graphics for the Web and encourage you to learn more.

What Are Graphics For?

What are graphics anyway? Most people think the term indicates pictures, icons, and illustrations. And, for the purpose of this section, that is what it will mean (in FrontPage they are all "pictures"). But the term really includes much more. Graphics include not only picture elements but also typography. And typography isn't just about the shapes of letters and typefaces, but also about white spaces: the spaces between letters, lines, and paragraphs. The term "graphics" refers to how all the visual elements on a page are put together.

What are graphics for? In a broad sense, they are there to support the content. They are there to make the information visually interesting and understandable. As such, they play a supporting role. The content, the message, this is what's primary. If the graphics help that message jump off the page, and be easily understood, they are good graphics. If they become dominant, if they are done for their own sake, if they get in the way of the message, they are bad graphics.

Do you really need graphics? Graphics—and here we shift back to their definition as picture elements—are useful but not always necessary. Using pictures and illustrations is often a case of less is more. A lone red rose lying on a white sheet becomes a much more powerful image than the same rose lying on a pile of multicolored rags. There are many beautiful pages with only text and white spaces. It is how the graphics are arranged and how they serve the content that are important.

What Kinds of Graphics Are There?

There are several different formats for digital images. Many are unique to the graphics program they are created in, and many formats are created to be universal formats that can be read by many programs. Another consideration in digital formats is file size, because of the time they take to download on the Web. Some digital formats have been created that can compress their file size yet still retain their universal file types.

The Web uses two of these compression formats: GIF and JPEG. There are new file types being developed, but these two are the most widely supported and used today.

GIF

The *Graphic Interchange Format (GIF)* was originally developed by CompuServe and is a *lossless* compression scheme. Lossless compression compresses and decompresses a file, returning it exactly as it started without losing any pieces.

GIF files contain only 256 colors or less. This is compatible with many computers, which have 8-bit, or 256-color, displays. The user can define the 256 colors.

The way a GIF file is compressed gives us some clues as to how it is best used. The GIF compression is based on horizontal pixel transitions. It creates a number that defines the color and the horizontal span of the color. If you have a solid color or solid horizontal lines, there is a much higher compression than if you had a lot of changes in color horizontally. For example, if you took the graphic shown next with horizontal lines and compressed it as a GIF, the GIF file size would be very small. If you rotate the graphic and compress it as a GIF this way, the file size increases to six times the size of the previous compression.

One of the best ways to keep file size down when using GIF compression is to create illustrations that use large areas of solid colors. When you have continuous tone images, like a photograph where the colors change every pixel, the file size will be much larger.

 Create your web graphics at 72 pixels per inch since the GIF compression scheme converts your graphic to 72 pixels per inch.

There are two types of GIF compressions: GIF87a and GIF89a. GIF89a builds on the older GIF87a by adding interlacing, transparency, and animation.

Interlacing   When an image is *interlaced,* it is loaded and displayed at full size, but not all the information is immediately used. The image appears "out of focus" and gets sharper in a series of passes. It takes four passes to display an interlaced GIF in its final form. Interlaced GIFs are only used for larger graphics that will take a while to download. They can be annoying. *Noninterlaced* GIFs are displayed one stripe at a time, and each stripe is displayed at the final resolution. FrontPage has an option that allows you to make a GIF file interlaced.

Transparency   *Transparent backgrounds* are created when one color in the GIF is replaced by the color of the background it is displayed on. This is a very useful feature for placing text closely around an irregular-shaped image rather than around a rectangular box that includes the original background. The fish on the left, shown next, is the full graphic where you can see the rectangular shape with its original background, while the fish on the right has a background that has been made transparent.

Animation   *Animated GIFs* are a series of static GIF images that are displayed in succession to create the illusion of movement. These static GIFs, along with the timing information, are saved as a single animated GIF image file. An example of this is the Microsoft Internet Explorer logo button. Animated GIFs are supported by Netscape Navigator 2.0 and later, and by Internet Explorer 3.0 and later. To create animated GIFs, you need a program such as the GIF Construction Set for Windows (available at **http://www.mindworkshop.com/alchemy/gifcon.html**).

Care must be taken to keep an animated GIF'S file size down since there is no compression between GIF frames. If you create an animated GIF file with ten 4K files, you will have a 40K file.

Animated GIFs should be used with caution. Any motion, particularly repetitive motion, is very distracting. It draws the eye every time it moves.

JPEG

The *Joint Photographic Experts Group (JPEG)* format is a *lossy* format. Image data is lost whenever the file is compressed. Compression can be as much as 100:1. The amount of compression is variable depending on the graphic program.

Low compression will change the picture little, while high compression will cause noticeable change. Run some tests to see how much you can compress and still get an image you like.

Create your graphics at 72 pixels per inch. Unlike GIF compression, JPEG compression will retain the resolution of the original graphic. The screen resolution on a Macintosh computer is 72 pixels per inch. Windows monitors have a slightly higher resolution but use 72 pixels per inch. If you exceed 72 pixels per inch, you will create detail that will not be seen, and you will have a large file because of the extra detail.

JPEG is a 24-bit format, which gives it over 16.7 million colors. However, if the viewer's computer only has an 8-bit display, it will only display 256 colors. JPEG compression works best on continuous tone images like photographs.

Where Do Graphics Come From?

Graphics for your web application can be purchased as clip art, created in graphics programs, scanned from existing images, or taken with a digital camera.

Clip Art

Clip art are images that are already created and usable as they are. Clip art used to mean little line drawings, but that has changed. Now the term includes all manner of images including large collections of photographs on CDs.

A good place to get clip art is on the Web. Go to Yahoo and search for *clip art*. You will find sites with collections of clip art that are both free or for sale over the Web. Always be aware of copyright infringement when using clip art. When people give away free clip art, it may not be theirs to give away.

 Make sure you have the right to display an image before using it in your web application.

There are many collections of clip art CDs available at computer stores. There are also many stock photo houses currently putting their photo collections on CDs or the Web. The reputable photo CDs are not inexpensive, but you do get the legal right to use high-quality images.

The big disadvantage of clip art is that you aren't the only one using these images. They show up all over the place. You've probably seen print ads from different companies that used the same image. Clip art also often has a sameness about it that screams *clip art*. Originality does count, after all.

Graphics Programs

When you decide you want to be original and create your own graphics, you can use any one of a number of different graphics programs. The problem is that using them isn't simple. There are paint programs, draw programs, and combinations of the two. (There are also programs such as Imaging for Windows—from Kodak—that comes with Windows 98, Windows 2000, and Windows ME and is primarily a viewing program for many different formats with only limited drawing capabilities.)

Paint Programs   Paint programs are the mainstay of web graphics. A paint program is a pixel-based, or bitmap, program. Whether you bring in a photograph, put in some type, or create some shapes, the program only recognizes the pixels it has created. It doesn't know what the pixels represent. It only knows that they are pixels and what the hue and values are. This is also called *raster graphics*. But a paint program has a lot of flexibility in color control for creating web graphics. It is the best program for dealing with photographic images.

Adobe Photoshop is the most popular paint program used for web graphics. Fractal Paint offers a lot of artistic flexibility in making interesting graphics and is a good supplement to Photoshop. Corel PHOTO-PAINT is also widely used. In addition, there are some good shareware programs if Photoshop is too expensive for you. Paint Shop Pro is very popular. Microsoft PhotoDraw is another option for a paint program.

Draw Programs   Draw programs use vector graphics. They are not pixel-based. The shapes are defined mathematically and are always editable. For example, text always remains editable (it doesn't become mere pixels when you leave the text function), and you can change the font, colors, or any other characteristic at any time. When you zoom in on a graphic created by a paint program, you see the individual pixels. There are no pixels in a draw program. You can zoom in all you want and still have sharp edges and clean colors.

However, paint programs like Adobe Photoshop are better for final preparation of web graphics since GIFs and JPEGs are pixel-based. It often works well to use the draw program for elements, such as text, that it does well and then export the file to the paint program. You can see the difference between paint and draw programs (or between raster and vector graphics) here, where the draw program with vector graphics is on the left and the paint program with bitmap or raster graphics is on the right:

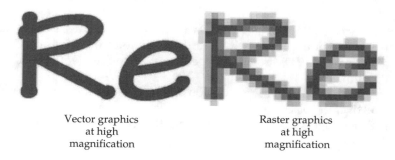

Vector graphics
at high
magnification

Raster graphics
at high
magnification

CorelDRAW and Adobe Illustrator are two very popular draw programs, and provide much better control of text and precise line drawings than do paint programs.

Scanners

A scanner can be a powerful tool to use with a paint program. You can convert any image on a flat surface into a digital image. These images are scanned into bit-mapped graphic files or directly into a paint program where they can be manipulated and integrated into your web graphics. Scanners often come with a low-end paint program not really suitable for serious web graphics.

While high-end flatbed scanners go for up to $1,000, you can get a very good scanner in the $100 to $200 range.

Scanners can be used for more than copying images. They also come with optical character recognition (OCR) programs. These programs scan text documents, turn them into bitmap images, compare the shapes of the text to the shapes of letters in its memory, and create a text file that can be edited in a word processing program.

Digital Cameras

One of the new ways to get images is with a digital camera. Although they are more expensive than a film-based camera, they allow you to eliminate all the film and developing costs. A reasonable camera for web application use can be purchased in the $300 to $500 range. For $1,000 you get a camera with more pixels that can make high-quality photographic prints with a good ink-jet printer.

The images can be downloaded into your computer and manipulated with a paint program. Actually, digital cameras come with their own paint programs, but unfortunately they are fairly simple and are no substitute for a higher-end paint program when it comes to doing web graphics.

Monitor Color Settings

On a PC, the number of colors a monitor displays can be 16, 256, 64,000 (16-bit High Color), or 16 million (24-bit True Color) or more. Keep in mind, though, you have no control over how many colors will be displayed when your work goes onto the Web; some monitors still display only 16 colors.

You can expect the number of colors available to continue increasing; you may even have 32-bit True Color on your own system. Regardless, you can count on your work being displayed at minimum on a 16-color system.

The decision you have as a web page designer is whether to limit yourself to the lowest common denominator (16-color, 640×480 resolution) or to work at a higher standard. If you are designing a simple page with minimal graphics, limiting your design to 16 colors may make sense. It ensures compatibility with virtually all the systems your work will be displayed on. (If someone is using a monochrome monitor to view your work, the point is moot, of course.)

However, if you limit yourself to 16 colors, you will not be able to effectively use scanned photographs or graphics with subtle shadings. In that case it would be better to use at least 256 colors. You cannot limit yourself to the lowest common denominator in every case. You simply have to accept that your work will not look its best on lower-end systems. (The people with these systems hopefully will upgrade them as they discover that other people's systems look a lot better!)

Another point to remember about color is that every monitor will display colors a little differently. There are many factors at play here, ranging from the age of the monitor to the amount and type of light in the room. If you've worked with programs like Adobe Photoshop and have output to color printers, you know how difficult it can be to get the printed output to exactly match the colors you see on the monitor. If it's important that a particular color appear exactly the correct shade on a web page—when it's part of a logo, for example—you're simply out of luck. You can calibrate your own monitor and ensure the color is correct on a calibrated system, but once you turn it loose on the Web, you have no control over how it will appear.

If you design your web pages to be displayed on a 256-color, 640×480-resolution monitor and then remember it will look different at other video resolutions, you can count on most people seeing your work the way you intended. See "Monitor Display" later in this chapter for more information on how a monitor's resolution affects the way a web page appears to the user.

Some Tips for Professional Looking Graphics

Creating web graphics can fill up a whole book—actually, many books, judging from bookstore shelves. But the following three tips cover a lot of mistakes that beginners make.

Browser-Safe Palette

GIFs use up to 256 colors. But which 256 colors? Well, it can be any 256 colors. And this is not good. You painstakingly create a graphic with a nice solid color, and when you look at it on your monitor, it isn't solid anymore. What happened? If your monitor is set to display 256 colors, it is displaying a defined set of 256 colors. And they may not be the same colors you used in your graphic.

When the computer runs across a color outside of its 256-color palette, it approximates that color by combining two of its colors. This is called *dithering*. When you look closely, you can see that the dithered color has clumps of different-colored pixels while the non-dithered example does not—as in the dithered example here on the left:

Dithered color   Solid color

Fortunately, browsers use a common palette of colors, although it has been reduced to 216. If you use these 216 colors when creating your graphics, they will display as solid, non-dithered, colors. FrontPage's standard palette (labeled "More Colors") displays 134 of these colors and if you stick to these you are safe. You can find out more about these colors at two excellent web sites on web graphics: Lynda Weinman's site at **http://www.lynda.com/hex.html** and David Siegal's *Creating Killer Web Sites* at **http://www.killersites.com/1-design**.

Lynda's site has two graphics that give the Red, Green, Blue (RGB) values for all 216 browser-safe colors. You can use these RGB values in FrontPage for defining the background colors, or in your graphics program to make sure your colors will not dither. Both Lynda's and David's site have a graphic with these colors that you can load into Adobe Photoshop and turn into a palette which will allow you to select the colors directly.

Anti-aliasing

Why do some web graphics have little jagged edges and others do not? It is because the smooth-edged web graphics use *anti-aliasing*. GIFS are created at 72 pixels per inch. When you put a solid color, irregular-shaped image on top of a solid-color background, the edge is visibly jagged. Anti-aliasing creates a buffer zone of transition colors between the shape and the background. This tricks the eye into seeing the edge as smooth. Make sure your paint program has anti-aliasing turned on when you create text and shapes. Here's a comparison of aliased (on the right) and anti-aliased characters (on the left):

Anti-aliased character   Aliased character

Halos

A possible problem with anti-aliasing is that halos appear around an image when the image has been anti-aliased, compressed as a GIF, and had the background made transparent. That process causes the white line or halo to appear around this fish head:

The buffer pixels between the image and background that anti-aliasing introduces are color keyed to the background color of the graphic and not the web page background. The solution is to not use the transparent function of GIF89a, but to create the graphic with the graphic background using the same browser-safe color as the web page background. Then the rectangular edges of the graphic blend in with the web page background. Of course, if you change the page background, you must change the graphic background.

This won't work with textured or tiled backgrounds since there is no way to control the registration of the background image with the graphic.

It is not recommended to use images as a background since the background then starts to fight with the foreground for attention, and it is the foreground that has your content.

Next, put all you have previously learned together and make a set of web pages or a web application.

Laying Out Web Pages

Successfully laying out a web page, like many things in life, is making the most of a less than perfect situation. There are a number of limitations inherent in the Web environment that you must live within and you have a fixed set of tools and techniques that are available to you. How you use those tools and techniques to work around the limitations will determine your success.

Layout Limitations

Layout limitations include those in the language used to create a web page (HTML), the limitations of both a browser and the user's monitor, and the fact that everything on your page must be downloaded to users at the speed of their modem or LAN connection. All of these factors require serious consideration when laying out a page.

HTML Limitations

Your web application is created using the Hypertext Markup Language (HTML). As you read earlier in this chapter, HTML is a formatting language that consists of ASCII text and, since ASCII text contains extremely limited formatting information, a system of formatting tags is used to contain the formatting information.

There are tags that begin and end a web page, define the sections of the web page, tags that call for images, execute programs, and affect how the text is displayed. There are lots of tags and more of them are on their way. In fact, there are far more tags than you probably want to deal with, and with a program like FrontPage, thankfully, you really don't have to deal with tags at all. Just in case you do, however, Chapter 12 goes into some depth on HTML.

FrontPage is a WYSIWYG (What You See Is What You Get) HTML editor. It allows you to create the page layout much as you would if using a word processor—a pretty stupid word processor, unfortunately. This is not a shortcoming of FrontPage, but a result of HTML's limitations. Like everything on the Web, though, this is changing.

Although you don't need to know HTML to produce excellent web applications with FrontPage, there will come a time when you have to look at the HTML to troubleshoot something and it is a great help to know what you are looking at. Chapter 12 will give you a good start on this, and the HTMLLIB (an HTML library) on the CD that accompanies this book provides all the detail you need.

Note *As a historical aside, in the early 1980s, personal computer word processing programs were ASCII text editors with formatting tags that were interpreted when the document was printed, much like a web browser does today when it displays a web page.*

Browser Display

When you want to view a web page on your browser, you are requesting an HTML document with its ASCII text and HTML tags. The browser analyzes the HTML tags to determine what formatting to use. When it comes to a tag that indicates an image, it sends another request to the server for that image. Each time it comes to an image, it sends another request. It goes through the entire document getting images and other secondary files, and then displays the page.

The HTML document leaves all the actual decisions of how the text is to be displayed up to the browser software. This wouldn't be a problem if there were just one browser. But there are different browser manufacturers, and each manufacturer has different versions of their browser. Each manufacturer displays the standards slightly differently, each version of a browser adheres to different standards, and each manufacturer has created their own nonstandard standards. This is why browsers display web pages differently.

If you keep to the industry-standard tags, everything works pretty well even though the display will look slightly different from one manufacturer's browser to the other. When you move into the more advanced browser capabilities, like cascading style sheets or Java scripts, you may run into headaches, because what works on one browser may not work on a competitor's. And they won't work at all on older browsers.

Note *Scripting languages like JavaScript and VBScript give the web developer a lot of capabilities, but there are so many problems if you use them on the client (browser) side that it is recommended you keep them on the server side.*

There is no one good source that documents all the differences among browsers. The only way to deal with these is to keep your design and layout simple and look at your page in recent versions of Netscape Navigator and Microsoft Internet Explorer. If you are working in an intranet environment where everyone has the same browser, you are blessed.

Monitor Display

Monitor resolution affects the width of the page displayed. It is measured by the width of the screen in pixels by the height of the screen in pixels. The three most common displays are 640×480 pixels, 800×600 pixels, and 1024×768 pixels.

When you lay out your page, you need to consider that it will be viewed in all three formats and that it should look good, or at least acceptable in all three. It certainly isn't going to look the same, however. Figures 1-10 through 1-12 show how a web page designed for 800×600 will look in the three formats.

The best way to tell how your design will appear is to test it on your monitor at each of the three different sizes.

Tip   *You can set the dimensions of your web browsers using the FrontPage Preview In Browser command (located in the File menu). If you are using Windows 9x, ME, or 2000 you can often change your resolution without rebooting by right-clicking the desktop, choosing Properties, selecting Settings, and changing the Screen Area.*

Note   *If you design your pages to display full screen on an 800×600 display, as many pages are, users viewing a 640×480 display will have to scroll both horizontally and vertically to see the full page. It can be disorienting to scroll in both directions.*

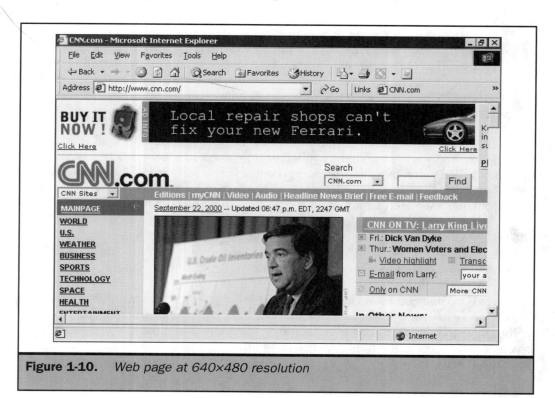

Figure 1-10.   *Web page at 640×480 resolution*

Figure 1-11.   *Web page at 800×600 resolution*

Data Transfer

Making people wait too long for your web page to download is a sure way to get your viewers to go elsewhere. And elsewhere is only a few clicks of the mouse away. The two major factors in long downloads are the user's connection speed, usually a modem being the slowest, and the total file size of your HTML and any other files, such as images, that your web page uses. Some users are still on 28.8-Kbps modems, but these are becoming rarer. 33.6 Kbps is still very common. Try to keep your download times under 30 seconds for a 28.8-Kbps modem user.

> **Tip**   *FrontPage tells you in the lower-right corner of the Page view window the average download time of a page with a 28.8 or other speed modem.*

You can't control the user's modem speed, but you can control the size of the files that make up your web page. Keep unnecessary graphics off your page. When you do have graphics, make their file size small. You can keep the user's attention longer if there is text to read while images lower down in the page are loading. You also can make the page shorter so that there is not as much on it. Users are not nearly as impressed with pages that have lots of fancy graphics and a long download time as they are with quick-loading pages.

Page Elements

There are some page elements to consider adding to every web application, such as banner identification, a simple page background, short line length, and contact information. On the other hand, some page elements such as horizontal lines and bullets may be overused and so better left off the site in the end.

Banner Identification

Using a banner at the top of every page is the best way to identify the web application from page to page. Using the same banner on all the pages provides an effective visual anchor. If the banner always stays the same, and the page underneath it changes, it is clear to the users that they are in the same web application.

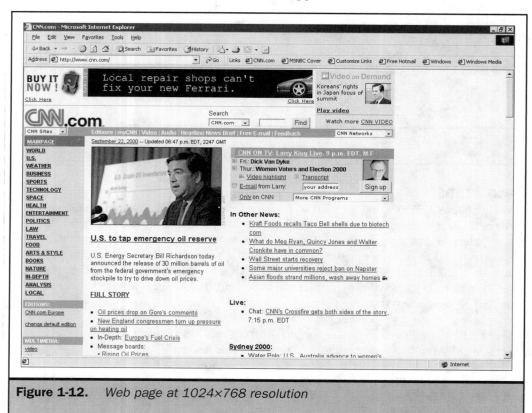

Figure 1-12.   *Web page at 1024×768 resolution*

It also helps to visually differentiate the banner on the home page from the following pages. Making the banners on the following pages smaller than the home page helps establish the position of the home page in the hierarchy of the web application.

Page Background

The default background for web pages is either white or, in older browsers, gray. This color can be changed to other solid colors, or an image can be tiled in the background. Always be careful about placing anything other than a solid color under text. If there is a textured background, the text can be hard to read, which will only get in the way of your message. If you use a dark color, you will have to use a lighter-colored text to make it readable. This is called *inverted text* and is more difficult to read. Using colored text on a colored background may be useful, as is inverted text, for setting off a piece of text, but for larger areas of text it is better to maximize contrast for readability. Black letters on a white background are the easiest to read. Ever read a book that was anything other than black letters on a white page?

Line Length

In the early days of web design, most web developers let their text run the width of the page. Some still do. This makes reading very difficult; when the eye gets to the end of the line it is reading, it must traverse back to the beginning of the line below. If it's a long line, the eye gets confused about which is the next line, and the text becomes tiring to read. This concept is even more important for screen text than print text. It is ideal to have no more than 10-12 words on a line or no more than 60 to 80 characters. Putting your text in a table whose cells are 400 to 420 pixels wide will accomplish this.

Contact Information

One of the beauties of the Web is its interactivity. The user can speak back. Provide a way for this to happen with at least an e-mail address. Let the user of the site communicate directly with the owner of the site. This is normally done at the bottom of the home page with a copyright notice and the name, address, e-mail address, and sometimes the phone number of the owner of the web application.

Horizontal Rules

Horizontal rules are seen everywhere on the Web and are sometimes misused to separate elements of a page. Horizontal rules can separate too much. They don't cause the eye to pause; they cause it to come to a halt. It is often better to use well-organized white space for vertical separation. On the other hand, when you want the eye to make a clear break, such as between a banner and a navigation bar, or between a navigation bar and the body text, then a horizontal rule may make sense. When there is a need to provide a stronger break between two sections, you can use what's called a *printer's mark*. This is a small graphic such as a 10×10-pixel square or diamond, as shown here:

If you want to use a horizontal line, try something other than the 2-pixel-high, full-width horizontal rule. It is easy in FrontPage to make the horizontal rule thinner and shorter. Try a 1-pixel thick rule at 50% of your page width.

Page Layout

Page layout is about placing all these elements along with the text, images, and navigation bars on the page, then controlling where everything goes. This can sometimes be a sporting proposition using HTML, but there are some tools—most importantly, tables—that let you put things down and have them stay there whether the display is 640 or 1024 pixels wide.

Tables vs. Frames

There are two basic approaches for controlling space on the web page: tables and frames. Frames, which are like pages within a page and allow separate scrolling of different areas of a web page, can lead to navigation and printing difficulties because each frame is a separate page. Frames also present problems for page layout. They take up valuable real estate on the page and do not begin to offer the much finer control that tables offer. Tables do not offer the same degree of control that you get from a page layout program such as PageMaker or Microsoft Publisher, but tables are the best tool currently available for complex layout of a web page.

FrontPage makes using tables much easier than doing it directly in HTML since the table structure is easy to see and manipulate in FrontPage's Page view. Trying to use tables extensively in a text editor is almost impossible, but in FrontPage they can be constructed quickly and modified easily. This doesn't mean that they don't do weird things sometimes, so keep checking the page in a browser to see just how it is going to look. Tables and frames are discussed in depth in Chapter 7.

Invisible Tables

When you use tables, you normally want to turn off all borders since they often get in the way of the information they surround. Borders are a visual element meant to provide separation for the text they enclose, but unfortunately they often fight for the eye's attention. It is better to use vertical and horizontal white space to separate and accentuate a table's contents.

Nested Tables

A table within a table is called a *nested table*. After establishing the table and cell structure for the overall page, it may be necessary to control page elements within individual cells. The indented links in the navigation bar are accomplished with nested tables. The following example, which is used to indent options in a navigation bar, has the table borders turned on so you can see where the tables are and how a nested table is used within a cell of an outer table. Nested tables are a very powerful tool for controlling the layout of a web page.

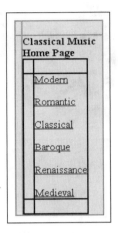

Absolute and Relative Cell Size

Tables can be very elastic and change size based on the screen resolution and the screen area given to the browser. In order to control where elements are placed on the page, you need to control cell width, which can be unconstrained, relative, or absolute.

Unconstrained Width   If the width of the cell is not otherwise defined, the text and images that are in it will define its width. When you create a table with undefined sizes for both the table and the cells, put in text and images, and move the width of the browser in and out, you will see how the cells change their size to match the browser width. It is impossible to control how a page looks with this scheme. The top of Figure 1-13 shows how this looks in a 640×480-pixel display, while the bottom shows how it changes in a 1024×768-pixel display.

Relative Size   Tables and cells can be defined as a percentage of the browser width. This becomes an improvement over the undefined size, but it is still not enough to accurately control the page layout. When using relative size, the look of the page changes significantly between a 640×480 display, shown at the top of Figure 1-14, and a 1024×768 display, shown in the bottom of that figure.

Figure 1-13. *A table with unconstrained cell width in both 640×480 and 1024×768 resolutions*

Absolute Size   Defining table and cell size by pixels is the only way to control the placement of the elements in your page. If you apply pixel values to a table's widths and move the browser width in and out, the page stays the same, independent of whether your display is 640×480, as shown in the top of Figure 1-15, or 1024×768, as shown in the bottom. The page and its elements are stable.

Table Weirdness

Even when using absolute-size tables, weird things can happen. When you stuff a big image in a smaller cell, the table will try to adjust the best it can. If you are using empty cells to control vertical space, they may not display, which means you will need to specify the height and width of the image cell. Always look at the page in a browser at several resolutions to see how the table is going to display.

FrontPage makes it easier to work with tables, but when you start nesting tables, you need to be careful they don't start interacting with each other. Pay attention to the widths of the tables being nested and keep checking it in the browser.

Using Color in Page Layout

Separate colors are often used to separate areas of a page. For example, a separate color can be placed behind a navigation bar to separate it from the rest of the page, or a separate color can be placed behind a particular article to call attention to it.

Therefore the sage manages affairs without doing anything, and conveys his instructions without the use of speech.

Therefore the sage manages affairs without doing anything, and conveys his instructions without the use of speech.

Therefore the sage manages affairs without doing anything, and conveys his instructions without the use of speech.

Therefore the sage manages affairs without doing anything, and conveys his instructions without the use of speech.

Figure 1-14. *A table with relative cell width in both 640×480 and 1024×768 resolutions*

Therefore the sage manages affairs without doing anything, and conveys his instructions without the use of speech.

Therefore the sage manages affairs without doing anything, and conveys his instructions without the use of speech.

Therefore the sage manages affairs without doing anything, and conveys his instructions without the use of speech.

Therefore the sage manages affairs without doing anything, and conveys his instructions without the use of speech.

Figure 1-15. *A table with absolute cell width in both 640×480 and 1024×768 resolutions*

There are three ways to add colors to a specific area of a page:

- Create a background image for the page with the desired area separately colored.
- Use frames and make the desired area a separate frame with its own color.
- Create a table with the desired area occupying one or more cells containing a unique color.

Background Image Layout

The background image layout was developed before table cells could be colored, but it still has its uses. With it you can color any area of a page including circles and other non-rectangular shapes and you can use more than one color. The greatest drawback to a background image is that an image that is balanced at 640×480 becomes unbalanced at 800×600 and very unbalanced at 1024×768 because of all the extra white space that is added at the higher resolutions. For example, if a background image is created with a colored stripe on the left that highlights a navigation bar and has a balancing white stripe on the right that fills a browser in a 640×480 display, it will become unbalanced when white space is automatically added on the right at 800×600 and 1024×768.

The scroll bar in a browser takes up screen width, so make a background image or table no more than 600 pixels wide to fit within a 640-pixel-wide window.

Frame-Colored Layout

You can create separate frames only in designated areas of a page including the top, the left and right sides, and the bottom. If you want any of those areas colored, you can use a frame to do it. Each frame is considered a separate page to which you can assign a separate background color. Also, within each frame you can use a background image or a table with separate cell colors. The frame itself is the biggest drawback to this approach at coloring a part of the layout, suffering from the navigation, printing, and usage of page space problems mentioned earlier in the chapter.

Cell-Colored Layout

The cell-colored layout uses the coloring of individual cells within a table to highlight specific areas of a web page. Because of table offset within a page, the color cannot go to the edge or to the top of the screen. You are also limited to one color within a cell, but since there is not an image to download and possibly tile, a cell-colored layout will be a little quicker to load. Since you don't have to place your content over a background, you can center the layout, allowing white space to be added on all sides at higher screen resolutions. Figure 1-16 is an example of the cell-colored layout with the table borders turned on so you can see the added white space on either side at 1024×768.

The cell-colored layout in Figure 1-16 has a fixed width and is centered in the browser. It is set up to fill the browser in a 640×480 display. In an 800×600 or 1024×768 display, there will be equal amounts of white space on the sides.

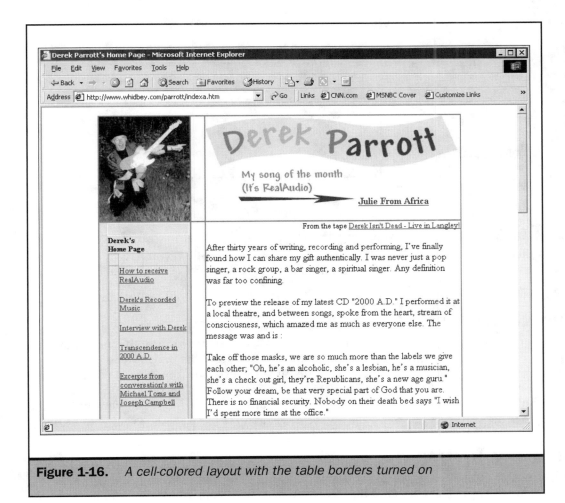

Figure 1-16. *A cell-colored layout with the table borders turned on*

The basic table structure is a three-cell table. The left cell holds the navigation bar, and the right cell holds the content of the page. The middle cell acts as a spacer between the right and left cells. The width of this cell is adjusted so that the content has enough white space between itself and navigation bar background. The left cell uses nested tables to lay out the content.

There is a built-in offset in a browser between the left edge of the browser and the left edge of the table, so the left side of the image is not the same as the left side of the table. To make it worse, the offset is different between Microsoft and Netscape browsers. All you can do is look at it in both browsers and adjust as best you can.

To control what you want colored, you can set the background color of a single cell, a group of cells, such as a column, or you can set the color of individual nested cells. This is the most precise of all the methods, as shown next:

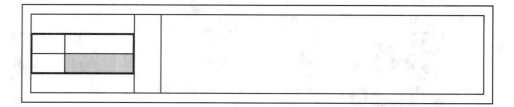

Testing, Testing, Testing

When you finish laying out the pages of your web application, you have to test them to see if they actually work the way you want them to. This process is in two parts: functional testing and usability testing.

Functional Testing

Functional testing determines whether the web application works at the functional level. Do all the links work? Do all the forms work? Do all the images load? FrontPage offers a lot of checks to make sure everything will work well, but there is no substitute for clicking all the links and using all the functionality you have designed into the web application in a real-world situation. Surprises always appear. Use the web application under the same conditions the user will experience to see what really is going to happen.

Usability Testing

The most enlightening testing is usability testing. This is where you test the human element, how a human, other than you, interacts with your web page. And those pesky humans always seem to do things you didn't expect.

Large corporations hire focus groups to do this testing. All you need to do is invite some friends over and, without telling them anything, watch them use your web application. No coaching! Look at what they click. Notice how they move through your web application. Watch when they pause. Are they confused? Are they getting the message? Again, no coaching!

They are giving you a lot of valuable information just by how they use your web application. And if they do something wrong, it is probably because your design is unclear and needs more work. Listen to them carefully. Afterwards, ask them for their comments. They may have some solutions for you.

Keep Them Coming Back

No matter what the subject of your web site or application, you should expect competition. So how do you keep people coming back to your web application? If it is a hobby, such as an application for a favorite pastime, encouraging return visits may not matter to you. However, if you want it to be profitable, you have basically three paths: advertising, subscriptions, or selling merchandise. In each case you need to build and maintain a high volume of users.

Good design for your web pages is only half the battle. You must also make them interesting—there has to be a reason for people to visit them. Keep the following guidelines in mind when creating your web pages: they have to be rich in content, they must stay fresh, and they must make the user feel part of a community.

Rich Content

First and foremost, your web application has to be rich in content, not hype. For example, if it was created for marketing your line of kayaks, include the history of the sport, stories (with photos) of trips your users have taken, information for people new to the sport, hyperlinks to related sites (not necessarily your competitors'), and anything else you can think of that might be interesting to kayakers. Don't just put up an online catalog and expect people to come back.

Stay Fresh

Keep your web application fresh. Update as often as you can. People are not going to come back to see the same old stuff. In the kayaking example, consider updating the trips featured every month. In winter (in the Northern Hemisphere), feature trips in New Zealand. Compare your web application to a magazine—no one would subscribe to a magazine that was the same every month; it would be boring. Your web application is no different.

Community

Design and content only go so far in getting people to come back. The final element for a successful web application is a sense of community. The Web is not a one-way environment. It allows the user to respond back to the owners of the web application and also to other users.

There are three tools that can help you achieve this: guest books, message boards, and chat.

- **Guest books** are the simplest way for the user to interact with the owner of the web application and other users. The user enters their comments in a form, and these comments are added on top of a page with the other users' comments.

- **Message boards** are simply the familiar electronic bulletin boards that have been a mainstay of electronic communication. By creating a place for your users to post their ideas and engage in conversation with other users, you give them an additional reason to come back to your site often. With FrontPage's Discussion Web (see Chapter 3), you can easily create your own message boards.

- **Chat** is a more immediate form of message board. The conversation takes place in real time, with each user's comments appearing on the other users' screens shortly after they are typed in. Due to the inevitable delays, this can be similar to having a conversation at a party, with several conversational threads going at once. You must be careful with chat rooms to stay focused on supporting your application or it can get out of control. You need to monitor what is going on. FrontPage's Discussion Web can also be used for this purpose.

The proper balance of design, content, and community is the foundation of a successful web application.

Do It!

Putting together a useful web application can be a lot of work. There's a lot to know, but the best way to learn it is to just do it. Build your web application, and see what works and what doesn't work. Change it and remember what to do for the next time. Not all web applications need to be high-powered business applications. You could just be putting up pictures of your daughter's wedding, or your child's first birthday, or pictures of your vacation.

You can communicate throughout the world using the Web. This book will show you how to do it using FrontPage.

The
Complete
Reference

FrontPage
2002

Chapter 2

Exploring FrontPage

59

Microsoft FrontPage is an authoring and publishing system for creating and delivering formatted content over the Internet or over a local area network (LAN). FrontPage provides the means to design, organize, and deliver an online application, called a *web*, which may be one or more pages on the Internet's World Wide Web (the *Web*) or on a LAN's intranet. To both create and deliver web content requires two or, for the best results, three major modules:

- **FrontPage** itself, which allows you to create, format, and lay out text; add pictures created in or outside of FrontPage; establish hyperlinks; and organize your webs and their links by using several views of the pages in a web in a drag-and-drop environment.

- **A web server** such as Microsoft's **Internet Information Services (IIS)**, which is included in Windows XP or 2000 Server, Windows NT 4.0 Server, and in a limited edition in Windows XP or 2000 Professional, or the Microsoft Personal Web Server (PWS), which came with Windows 98 (First or Second Edition) or FrontPage 98. A web server allows you to directly deliver your webs to someone seeking them, as well as provide file-management support for your webs.

- **FrontPage Server Extensions**, which are available for most popular web servers, add the functionality needed to implement the interactive parts of a FrontPage web.

Creating a Web

The FrontPage process of creating a web is unique. The following steps provide an overview:

1. Plan the web—what the goals are; what text, pictures, forms, and hyperlinks it will contain; how it will flow; how the user will get around; and roughly what the pages will look like.

2. In FrontPage, create the structure of the new web by using a wizard and/or template, or simply by starting with a blank page. If desired, you can also import existing webs into yours.

3. Open FrontPage's Tasks view, and create the items you want to include on the list of tasks to be completed before your web is ready to publish. If you used a wizard to create your structure, you will automatically have items in the Tasks list you can edit.

4. Open FrontPage's Folders view and double-click the first page you want to work on to open it in Page view.

5. In FrontPage's Page view, enter, format, and position the text you want to use. Insert the pictures, sound, video, hyperlinks, frames, tables, and forms.

6. As each page is completed, save it and mark the task as complete. From Folders view, select the next page you want to work on, and open it in Page view.

7. Periodically open a web browser such as Microsoft Internet Explorer or Netscape Navigator from Page view using the Preview In Browser toolbar button, and look at the web you are creating (better yet, use both browsers to see what your web will look like). This allows you to test the full functionality of your web with your local web server. You will be able to see and interact with the web as the user will. You can then revise the web by changing or updating the content, adjusting the page layouts, and reordering the pages and sections using one or more of the FrontPage views.

8. In FrontPage's Reports view, look for errors and potential problems with the web in the reports that are available on files, links, tasks, and themes.

9. In FrontPage's Hyperlinks view, verify the hyperlinks that you have placed in your web.

10. When you are satisfied with your web, publish it on the server from which you want to make it available.

11. Using your browser, download, view, and manipulate the web as the user would. Note the load times and the impression you are getting of the web. Ask others to view and use your web and to give you their impressions and suggestions.

12. Revise and maintain the web as necessary, either by directly editing the copy on the server, or by editing your local copy and then replacing the server copy.

Tip   *If someone other than yourself has permission to edit a web you are about to work on, you should import the current version from the server and then edit it, rather than trusting the copy on your local machine. This avoids the "Twilight Zone Effect," where a web is edited by more than one person at one time.*

Creating a web with FrontPage gives you important advantages over using other authoring systems. You can:

- Graphically visualize and organize a complex web with a number of pages, images, and other elements by using Folders view

- Create and edit a complex web page in a WYSIWYG environment by using Page view without having to use or know HTML, the language of the Web

- Easily manage the tasks that are required to build a web, who has responsibility for them, and their completion by using Tasks view

- Quickly create an entire web, a page, or an element on a page by using wizards or templates

- Easily add interactive functions such as forms, text searches, and discussion forums without the use of programming by using Web Components (formerly WebBots)

- Directly view and use a web on your hard disk by using a local web server

FrontPage is a true client/server application that provides all of the pieces necessary to create and deliver formatted text and graphical information over both a LAN and the Internet. FrontPage is the client side, while a combination of a web server (IIS or PWS) and the FrontPage Server Extensions constitutes the server side.

FrontPage Views

FrontPage offers six different views you can use when creating or managing a web:

- **Page view** allows you to create and edit a web page by adding and laying out formatted text, pictures, sounds, video, frames, tables, forms, hyperlinks, and other interactive elements. Page view provides a WYSIWYG (what you see is what you get) editing environment where you can edit new webs and existing webs, including those created elsewhere on the Web. In Page view you can use page wizards, templates, and themes, apply Web Components for interactive functions, create forms and tables, add image maps with clickable hotspots, and convert popular image formats into GIF and JPEG formats used on the Web.

- **Folders view** allows you to look at and manage an entire web from its files and folders level.

- **Reports view** allows you to look for errors or potential problems, added or changed files, review and publishing status, and usage of a web site using any one of 26 reports on such subjects as unlinked files, slow pages, recently changed files, publishing status, and daily page hits.

- **Navigation view** allows you to check and change the way a user would get from one page to another and then back to the "Home" page.

- **Hyperlinks view** allows you to check and organize the hyperlinks in a web in a drag-and-drop environment.

- **Tasks view**, which displays the Tasks list, allows you to track the tasks required to produce a web, identifying who is responsible for them, their priority, and status.

In the next several sections of this chapter you will further explore the FrontPage views. While it is not mandatory, it will be beneficial if you are looking at these on your own computer. To do that, start FrontPage by opening the Windows Start menu, choosing Programs, and selecting Microsoft FrontPage.

Page View

When you first start FrontPage, Page view is normally the view that you will see. If you have chosen to use a template or a wizard to create a web, or you have imported a web, FrontPage may open in Folders view. In that case, double-click the page you want to work on to open it in Page view. You can also click the Page view icon in the Views bar or choose Page in the View menu. In any case, when you are in Page view, you'll see a window that looks very much like most word processors—in particular, Microsoft Word—as you can see in Figure 2-1. This is where you can enter and edit text. It is also where you can add pictures, frames, tables, forms, sound, video, hyperlinks (including hotspots on pictures), and active Web Components to your page, as you'll read about in a moment.

As you read in Chapter 1, a web page is a lot of HTML (Hypertext Markup Language) and a little bit of text. If you use a normal word processor or text editor (without any optional HTML features added) to create a web page, you must learn and use HTML. With the FrontPage Page view, you don't need to know HTML. You simply enter the text you want, format it using normal word processing formatting tools, and add pictures, tables, forms, and other elements. When you are done, FrontPage will generate the HTML for you. It is no harder than creating and formatting any other document, and what you see on the screen is very close to what you would see in a web browser. Not only does Page view convert the text and formatting that you enter to HTML, but you can also import RTF, ASCII, and Microsoft Office files into Page view, and they will have the HTML added to them.

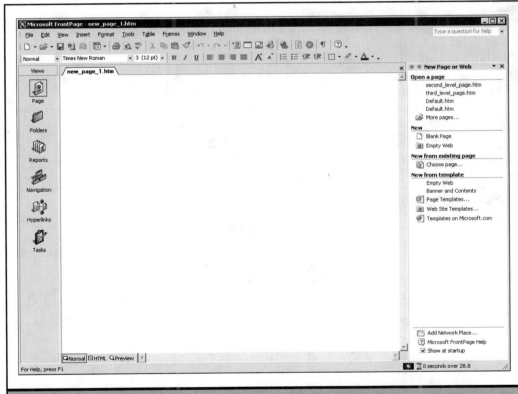

Figure 2-1. *FrontPage Page view, where all editing is done*

If you want to see the HTML behind a web page, select the HTML tab at the bottom of Page view. If you are comfortable with directly editing HTML, you can do so in this HTML window of Page view. If you're not familiar with editing HTML, directly changing the HTML could create a problem.

Formatting Text

The formatting that is available from Page view is quite extensive, but it is limited to the type of formatting that is available with HTML. For example, HTML predefines a number of formatting styles whose names and definitions are unique to the Web. Some formatting tags are dependent on the web browser being used to display your web page. For example, both Internet Explorer and Netscape Navigator accept a Font tag that allows you to change the font (for example, <FONT FACE="Arial">*text to be formatted*</FONT>), but other browsers may not. The paragraph styles supported in FrontPage are described in Table 2-1 and shown in Figure 2-2. They are applied from the Style drop-down list on the left of the Formatting toolbar.

 *To have text displayed in a specified font, the browser must support the Font tag, and the specified font must be installed on the user's computer. More information about using fonts on the Web, as well as a selection of fonts that can be downloaded, can be found on Microsoft's web site, **http://www.microsoft.com/truetype/**.*

Note *The Formatted paragraph style is the only tag that allows you to use multiple spaces in text. HTML throws out all but one space when it encounters multiple spaces, except when the Formatted style is used. This can be used for forms, to get labels to right-align and text boxes to left-align. You can also use tables to align labels and form fields (see Chapters 7 and 8).*

Paragraph Style	How It Looks
Normal	Displayed with the proportional font, normally Times New Roman.
Formatted	Displayed with the fixed-width font, normally Courier.
Address	Displayed with the proportional font in an italic style. Often used to display information on how to contact the owner of the web.
Heading 1-6	Displayed with the proportional font in a bold style in six sizes.

Table 2-1. *Paragraph Styles*

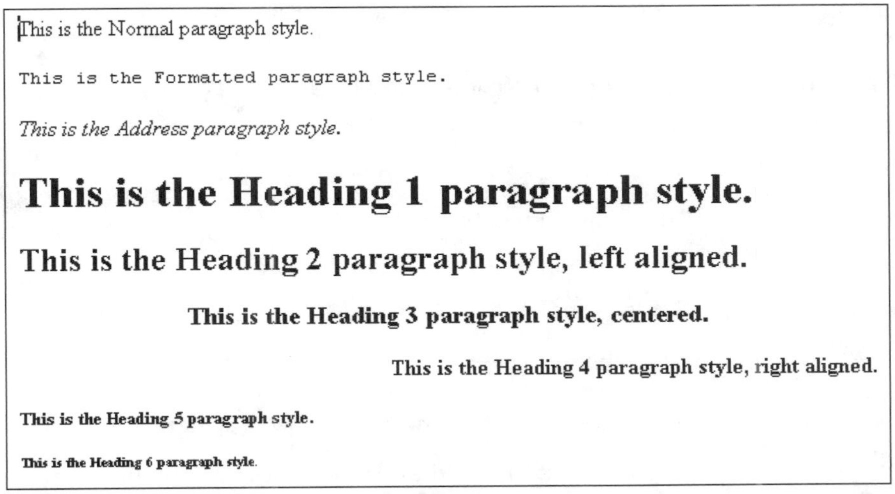

This is the Normal paragraph style.

This is the Formatted paragraph style.

This is the Address paragraph style.

This is the Heading 1 paragraph style.

This is the Heading 2 paragraph style, left aligned.

This is the Heading 3 paragraph style, centered.

This is the Heading 4 paragraph style, right aligned.

This is the Heading 5 paragraph style.

This is the Heading 6 paragraph style.

Figure 2-2.   *Examples of the paragraph styles*

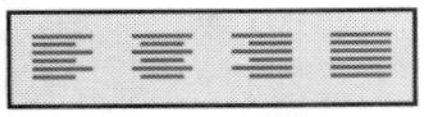

Any of the paragraph styles can use left, center, right, or justify (both the left and right) paragraph alignment applied either from the Paragraph dialog box (accessed by opening the Format menu and choosing Paragraph) or with the alignment buttons in the toolbar.

Standard font (or character) styles that are available are regular, bold, italic, and bold italic. These are applied using the Formatting toolbar buttons for that purpose. In addition, there are 18 font effects described in Table 2-2 (some samples are shown in Figure 2-3). The font effects are applied in the Font dialog box, which is opened with the Font option on the Format menu.

Font Effect	What It Does
Underline	Makes text underlined.
Strikethrough	Puts a line through text.
Overline	Puts a line above the text.
Blink	Makes text blink (defined only in Netscape Navigator).
Superscript	Raises text above the baseline.
Subscript	Lowers text below the baseline.

Table 2-2.   *Font Effects*

Font Effect	What It Does
Small Caps	Makes normally lowercase letters small capitals.
All Caps	Makes all letters capitals.
Capitalize	Makes the leading character of all words a capital.
Hidden	The affected text will not be displayed.
Strong	Usually makes text bold.
Emphasis	Usually makes text italic.
Sample	Formats text in the Sample style, normally in a fixed-width font.
Definition	Formats text in the Definition style, normally italic.
Citation	Formats text in the Citation style, normally italic.
Variable	Formats text in the Variable style, normally italic.
Keyboard	Formats text in the Keyboard style, normally the fixed-width font with a bold style.

Table 2-2. *Font Effects* (continued)

Strong, Emphasis, Sample, Definition, Citation, Variable, Keyboard, and Code effects are *logical* styles. The appearance of the text with these tags is determined by the browser. Older browsers allowed you to change the defaults for these tags, but this feature seems to have disappeared. Bold, Italic, Underline, Strikethrough, Overline, Blink, Superscript, Subscript, Small Caps, All Caps, Capitalize, and Hidden are *physical* styles that are not changeable by the browser.

Note *Beginning with FrontPage 2000, FrontPage generates the <B> tag for bold and the <I> tag for italic. If you want the <STRONG> and <EM> tags, you must select Strong and Emphasis from the Font dialog box.*

Characters in any style can be one of seven preset sizes from 8 points to 36 points (as shown in Figure 2-4), one of 16 preset colors or a custom color, and designated as either superscript or subscript. Character size and color can be changed with the respective toolbar drop-down list or button, shown here, or through the Font dialog box.

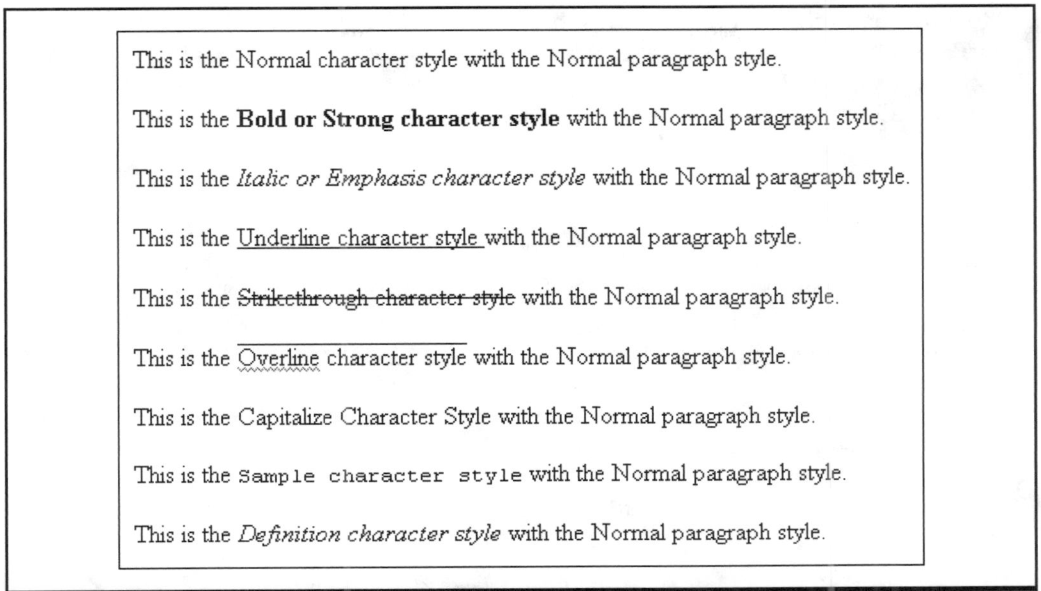

This is the Normal character style with the Normal paragraph style.

This is the **Bold or Strong character style** with the Normal paragraph style.

This is the *Italic or Emphasis character style* with the Normal paragraph style.

This is the <u>Underline character style</u> with the Normal paragraph style.

This is the ~~Strikethrough character style~~ with the Normal paragraph style.

This is the Overline character style with the Normal paragraph style.

This is the Capitalize Character Style with the Normal paragraph style.

This is the Sample character style with the Normal paragraph style.

This is the *Definition character style* with the Normal paragraph style.

Figure 2-3. *Examples of some of the available font effects*

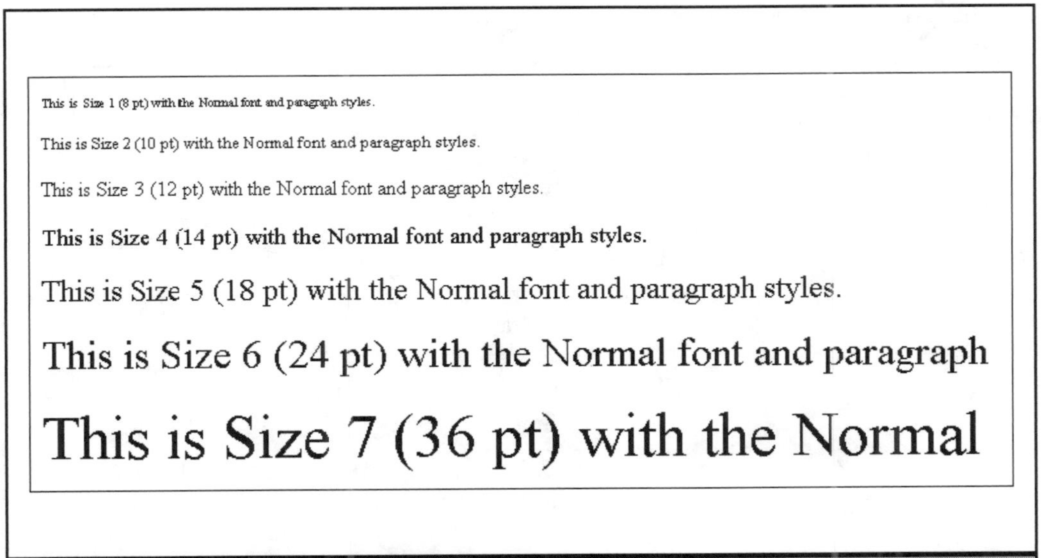

This is Size 1 (8 pt) with the Normal font and paragraph styles.

This is Size 2 (10 pt) with the Normal font and paragraph styles.

This is Size 3 (12 pt) with the Normal font and paragraph styles.

This is Size 4 (14 pt) with the Normal font and paragraph styles.

This is Size 5 (18 pt) with the Normal font and paragraph styles.

This is Size 6 (24 pt) with the Normal font and paragraph

This is Size 7 (36 pt) with the Normal

Figure 2-4. *The seven preset font sizes*

In addition to the paragraph styles that you have already seen, HTML and FrontPage allow you to define several types of lists. Table 2-3 describes the available list styles, which are shown in Figure 2-5. Note that at this time there is no difference between bulleted, directory, and menu lists. It is possible this will change in the future.

Tip   *You can end any list by pressing CTRL+ENTER.*

Not all web browsers treat the formatting in a web the same; they may even ignore some formatting. Blink, in particular, is a style that is ignored by all but Netscape Navigator. Also, several styles may produce exactly the same effect in many browsers. For example, in most instances, the Emphasis, Citation, Definition, and Italic styles often produce the same effect. If you are creating a web for a broad public audience, it is worthwhile to test it in recent versions of the two primary web browsers: Netscape Navigator and Microsoft Internet Explorer.

Tip   *Use only the physical styles that exclude Blink to be assured of the greatest consistency.*

The Font dialog box or the Font Color button on the toolbar allow you to set the color of selected text. You can also set the color of text for an entire page through the Background tab on the Page Properties dialog box, which is opened from the File menu (you may have to extend it) and shown in Figure 2-6. Colored text is useful on colored backgrounds to create an unusual look on a page.

List Style	How It Looks
Numbered List	Series of paragraphs with a hanging indent and a number on the left
Bulleted List	Series of paragraphs with a hanging indent and a bullet on the left
Directory List	Series of short (normally less than 20 characters) paragraphs
Menu List	Series of paragraphs, one line or less in length, in a vertically compact format
Definition and Definition Term	Pairs of paragraphs as terms, which are left-aligned, and definitions, which are indented similarly to dictionary definitions

Table 2-3.   *List Styles*

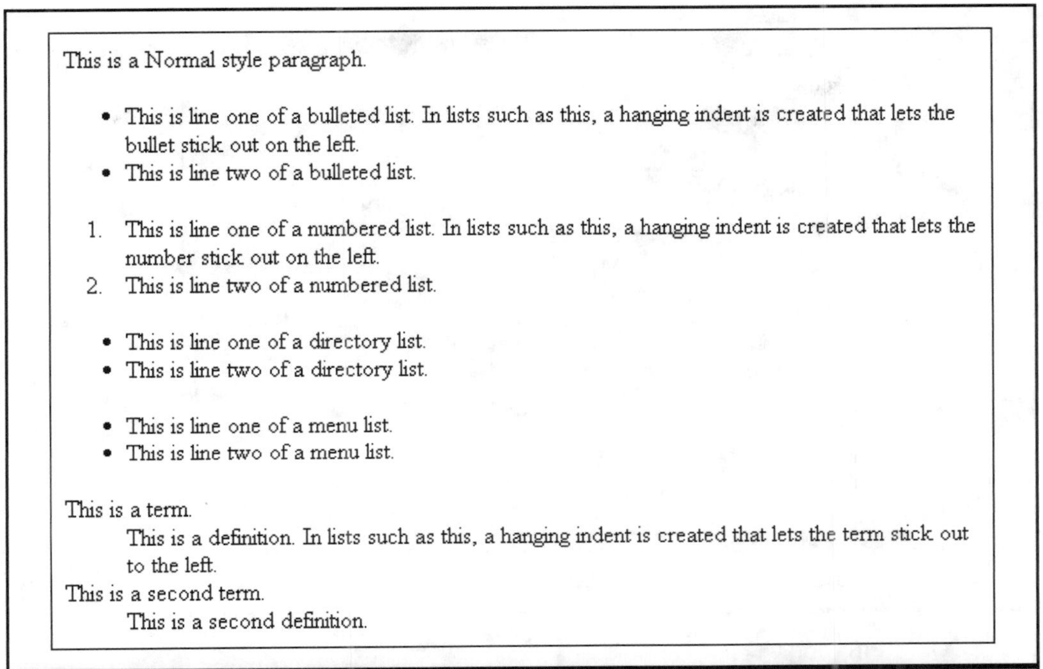

This is a Normal style paragraph.

- This is line one of a bulleted list. In lists such as this, a hanging indent is created that lets the bullet stick out on the left.
- This is line two of a bulleted list.

1. This is line one of a numbered list. In lists such as this, a hanging indent is created that lets the number stick out on the left.
2. This is line two of a numbered list.

- This is line one of a directory list.
- This is line two of a directory list.

- This is line one of a menu list.
- This is line two of a menu list.

This is a term.
   This is a definition. In lists such as this, a hanging indent is created that lets the term stick out to the left.
This is a second term.
   This is a second definition.

Figure 2-5.   *Examples of list styles*

Tip   *You can open the Page Properties dialog box by right-clicking the page and selecting Page Properties from the context menu.*

Inserting Pictures

FrontPage allows you to add pictures to a web page in three ways:

■ You can add a background picture, which you can specify in the Page Properties dialog box (Figure 2-6), that fills a page. By placing a picture in the background, you can enter text on top of it.

Note   *A background picture will be tiled if it doesn't fill the screen. Even if it fills the screen at 640×480, it may be tiled at higher resolutions.*

■ You can add a group of pictures in a photo gallery by opening the Insert menu and choosing Picture | New Photo Gallery. This opens the Photo Gallery Properties dialog box where you can select the pictures to be in the gallery, as well as choose the gallery's layout. Figure 2-7 shows a group of pictures in the horizontal layout.

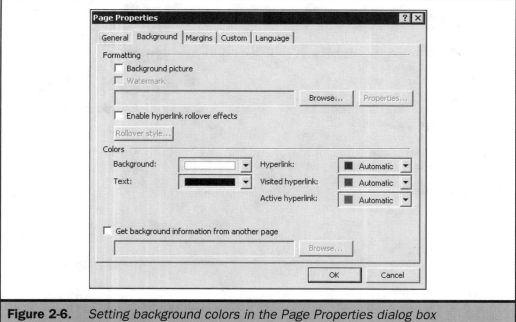

Figure 2-6. *Setting background colors in the Page Properties dialog box*

■ You can add a stand-alone picture from the Picture dialog box opened from the Insert menu (Insert | Picture) and then specify if the picture is from a clip art library, a file, or a scanner or camera. You can also use the Insert Picture From File button on the toolbar. You can size the picture either before you insert it (using a graphics program) or after using FrontPage. Once it is inserted and selected, the Picture toolbar appears either as a floating toolbar in the FrontPage window or as an additional toolbar at the top of the window (as seen in Figure 2-8). You also can right-click the picture and select Picture Properties to open the Picture Properties dialog box. Here you can enter: the alignment; the amount of space to place above and to the left of a picture; the thickness of a border, if any; and, on the General tab, the alternative text to display if the picture is not displayed. You can also identify a hyperlink to follow if the user clicks on the picture.

You can left-, center-, or right-align a picture by selecting it and clicking the Align Left, Center, or Align Right buttons in the toolbar normally used to align text.

Pictures that are included in web pages must be GIF, JPEG, or PNG format. This has presented a problem in the past, because many clip-art and graphics programs use other formats. FrontPage has solved this problem by allowing you to import other file

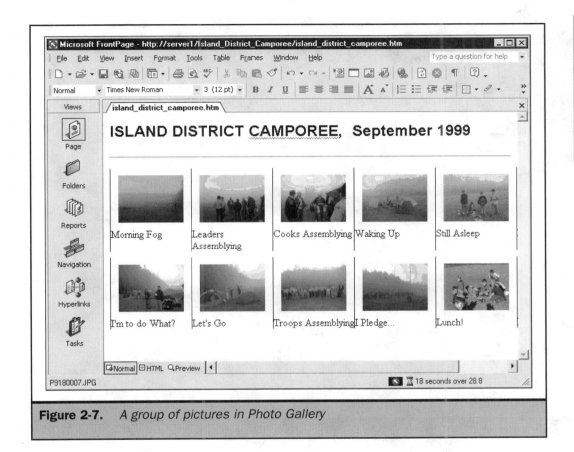

Figure 2-7. *A group of pictures in Photo Gallery*

formats that FrontPage will convert to GIF, JPEG, or PNG. The file formats that
FrontPage can accept are

GIF (.GIF)
JPEG (.JPG, .JPEG, .JFF, .JTF)
PNG (.PNG)
Kodak PhotoCD (.PCD)
PCX (.PCX)
Encapsulated PostScript (.EPS)
SUN Raster (.RAS)
Targa (.TGA)
TIFF (.TIF)
Windows Metafile (.WMF)
Windows or OS/2 bitmap (.BMP)

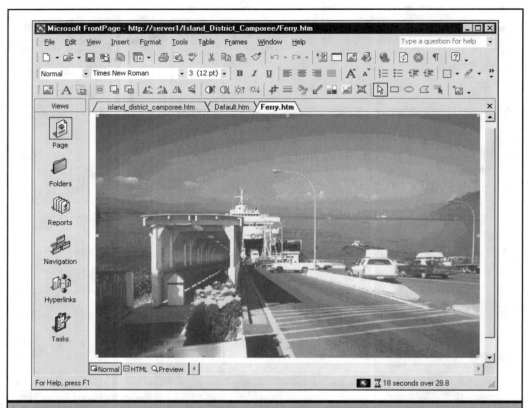

Figure 2-8.   *The Picture toolbar appears when a picture is selected and allows you to edit it*

Note   *FrontPage converts pictures with up to 256 colors to GIF files and pictures with more than 256 colors to JPEG files.*

Remember, pictures take a long time to download and therefore become frustrating for the user who has to wait for them. Even though a picture may look really neat, if users have to wait several minutes for it to download, they probably are not going to appreciate it or stick around to look at it.

Tip   *You can tell how long a page will take to download using a 28.8-Kbps modem (or whatever speed you choose through right-clicking on it) by the number of seconds on the right of the status bar, like this:*

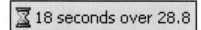

Adding Forms

So far you have seen how to display text and pictures on a web page—in other words, how to deliver information to the user. In Page view you can also add a form in which the user of your web can send you information. You can create a form either field-by-field, or all at once by using the Form Page Wizard. You'll see how the Form Page Wizard works in a later section of this chapter ("Working with Templates and Wizards"). For now, let's look at the field-by-field approach. You can use the Form option on the Insert menu to create a Form toolbar with the forms options on it by "dragging off" the menu, as shown in Figure 2-9. The Form toolbar buttons are described in Table 2-4.

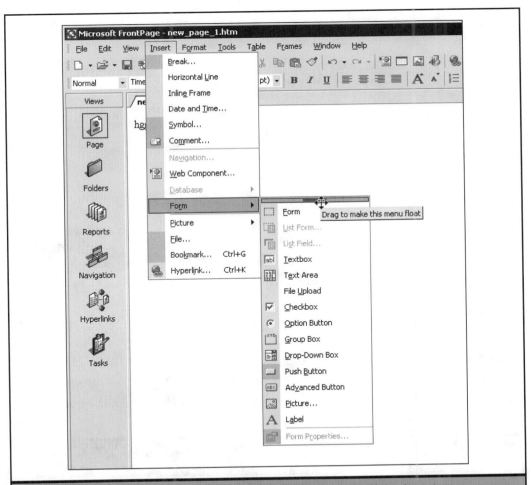

Figure 2-9. *You can create a Form toolbar by dragging it off the Insert menu*

Button	Description	Example(s) in Figure 2-10
	Form	Dashed outline of form
	List Form	Adds a list form, see the discussion of lists in this chapter (not shown in Figure 2-10)
	List Field	Adds a list field, see the discussion of lists in this chapter (not shown in Figure 2-10)
	One-line text box	Address
	Scrolling text area	Comments
	File Upload	Allows a user to browse for a file before submitting it (not shown in Figure 2-10)
	Check box	Using our products?
	Radio or Option button	Age
	Group box	Adds a border and label with which to group a set of controls within a form (not shown in Figure 2-10)
	Drop-down menu	Which products?
	Push button	Submit and Reset
	Advanced button	A sizable, editable push button (not shown in Figure 2-10)
	Picture	Adds a picture (not shown in Figure 2-10)

Table 2-4. *Form Field Creation Buttons*

Button	Description	Example(s) in Figure 2-10
A	Label separate from field	E-mail address
	Form Properties	Opens the Form Properties dialog box (not shown in Figure 2-10)

Table 2-4.   *Form Field Creation Buttons* (continued)

To use the Form toolbar, simply place the cursor or insertion point where you want the field, and then click the type of field you want. The form field will appear on the page. After adding a new field you can right-click it and choose Form-Field Properties. A dialog box will open and ask you to name the field and specify other aspects of it, such as the width of the box on the form and the number of characters that can be entered. Figure 2-10 shows one way a form can be built. In Chapter 8, you'll go through the detailed steps of designing and building a form.

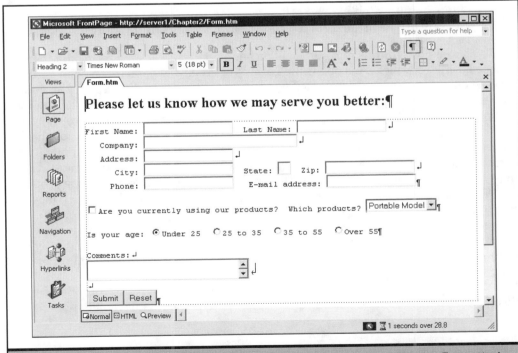

Figure 2-10.   *A form created with all fields in the same block using the Formatted paragraph style*

If you put form fields in the same form block (area created by the Form button and enclosed by a dashed line) and use SHIFT+ENTER to create a new line, you can stack the fields closer together, and they will all have the same form properties.

If you format form fields with the Formatted paragraph style, you can align the labels and text boxes using multiple spaces as shown in Figure 2-10. However, it's not always possible to get all the form elements to line up exactly using Formatted text. This is because a space in a form text box is not the same width as a character space. As you will see in the section "Working with Templates and Wizards" later in this chapter, you can also use tables to align form elements, often with better results.

When you create a form field by field, you need to provide a means of gathering the data that is entered on it. With FrontPage, you can handle the form data in a number of ways:

- You can save the information to a file as HTML, as formatted text, as a text database that can be imported into most database programs, or directly into an Access (.MDB) database.

- You can also have the results sent as an e-mail or posted to a discussion group, or register the sender to access a password-protected area of a web.

- You can also have the form results sent to a custom script for processing.

To choose how your form results will be handled, right-click the form, and then choose Form Properties. This opens the Form Properties dialog box, shown in Figure 2-11, where you can select or create a file to save the form information, specify an e-mail address to send it to, or select a custom script to process the information. Clicking the Options button opens the Saving Results dialog box, where you can set the options for each method of processing the form data. You may or may not want to include the field names in the output or in the additional information. You must repeat these steps for each field that is in a separate form block (the area enclosed within the outermost dashed line) with the options under the Saved Fields tab of the Saving Results dialog box.

When you create a form, you may have certain fields that must be filled in (such as first and last name) or fields that have to contain a certain type of information (such as numeric for a phone number). To force the user to enter the proper type of information where required, you can create validation rules for each form field. You do this by right-clicking the form field you want validated, then selecting Form Field Properties from the context menu and clicking Validate to open a validation dialog box. The Text Box Validation dialog box is shown in Figure 2-12. (Different types of form fields will display different validation dialog boxes, while some do not display validation dialog boxes at all.)

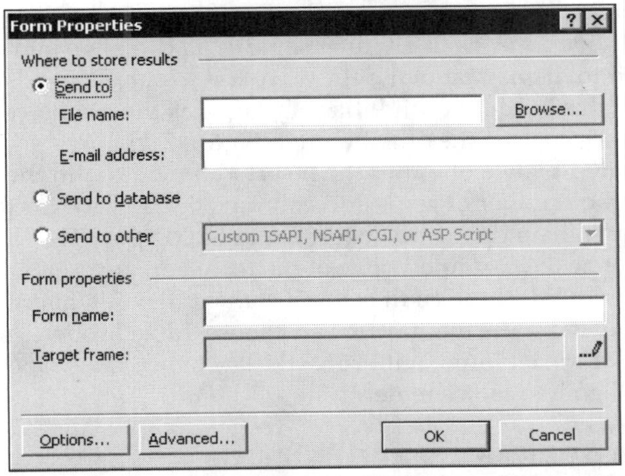

Figure 2-11.   *Determining what to do with the contents of a form*

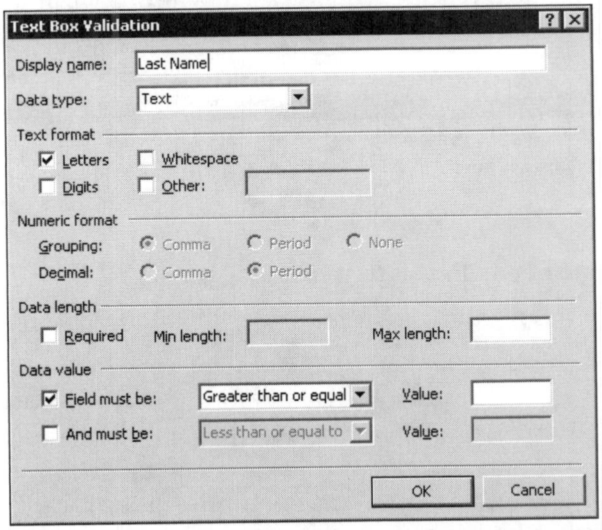

Figure 2-12.   *Validate a field to force the information you need*

Using Tables

In webs, tables provide a means of dividing some or all of a page into rows and columns. Tables can be used to display tabular data as well as to simply position information on a page, perhaps with a border around it. FrontPage has the extensive ability to create and work with tables such as the one shown in Figure 2-13.

Tables are created by use of either the Insert Table button in the toolbar (which allows you to set the number of rows and columns in the table) or the Insert option on the Table menu, which opens the Insert Table dialog box. This dialog box allows you to specify the size, layout, and width of the table you are creating. Once a table is created, you can modify it through the table's context menu, which appears when you right-click the table. From the menu, you can choose Table Properties to change the overall properties of the table, or Cell Properties to change the properties of a single cell. Chapter 7 will go into tables in depth.

Working with Templates and Wizards

Templates and wizards allow you to automatically create a new page or a new web with many features on it. Templates differ from wizards only in the amount of interaction between you and the computer during the creation process. *Templates* create a ready-made page or web without interacting with you. *Wizards* use one or more dialog boxes to ask you a series of questions during creation. Based on your answers to these questions, a customized page is created. Whether you use a template or a wizard, you can customize the resultant web pages. The New From Template section of the New Page Or Web task

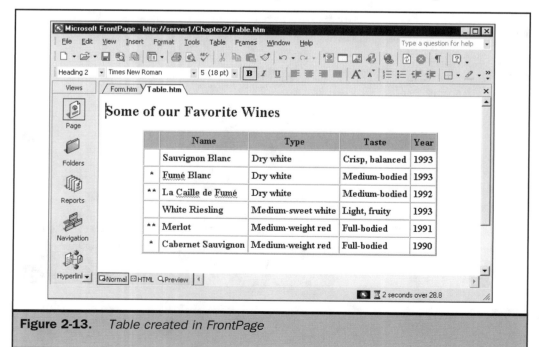

Figure 2-13.   *Table created in FrontPage*

pane (opened by choosing New | Page Or Web from the File menu) provides access to both page and web templates including several wizards (both included in FrontPage and on the Microsoft web site) to help you create many specialized pages. Selecting Page Templates from the New Page Or Web task pane opens the Page Templates dialog box shown in Figure 2-14.

Note *Figure 2-14 shows two wizards, Document Library View Page Wizard and List View Page Wizard that you may not see when you open the Page Templates dialog box. To display these wizards, you must install SharePoint and be in an open web. SharePoint and the Team Web Site that uses SharePoint are discussed briefly at the end of this chapter, again in Chapter 4, and at some length in Chapter 24.*

Note *Both CTRL+N and the New Page button itself on the toolbar give you a new page using the Normal Page template—they do not open the New Page Or Web task pane, which provides access to templates and wizards. The down arrow on the right of the New Page button gives you a choice of Page or Web, which in turn directly opens the Page Templates and Web Site Templates dialog boxes, bypassing the New Page Or Web task pane.*

For example, to use a wizard to create a custom form similar to the one created earlier, you would select the Form Page Wizard. This opens a series of dialog boxes that ask you questions about what you want on the form you want to build. One such dialog box is shown in Figure 2-15. When you are done, a form is automatically created, which you can see in Figure 2-16.

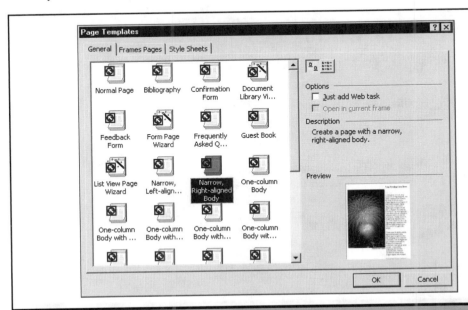

Figure 2-14. *Page templates and wizards used to create new pages*

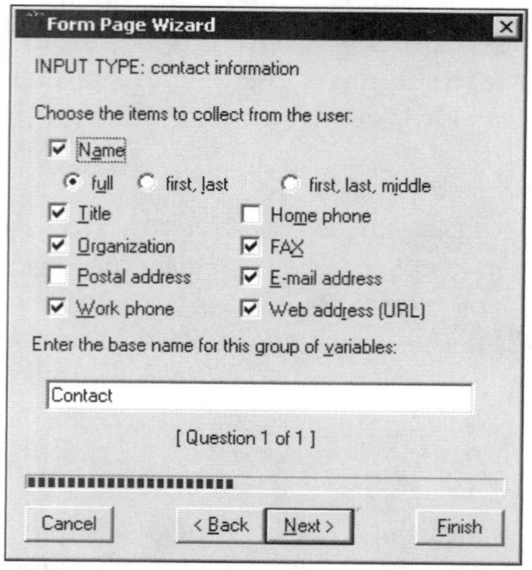

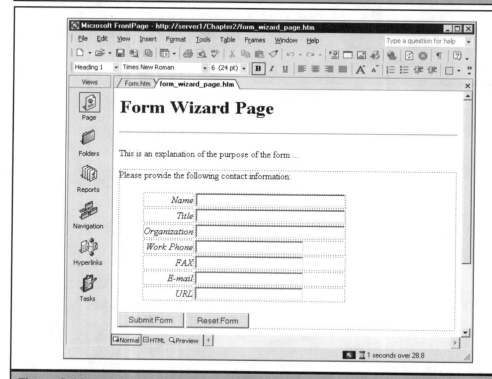

Figure 2-15.   *One of the Form Page Wizard's dialog boxes used to create a form*

Figure 2-16.   *A form created with the Form Page Wizard*

The form in Figure 2-16 was created by use of a table. The Form Wizard can also generate Formatted text for aligning labels and form fields.

Web templates and wizards, like their page counterparts, create multipage webs for you that you can customize as you see fit. Web templates and wizards are discussed later in this chapter under "Folders View." Page templates and wizards provide an excellent way to get a quick start on a large variety of web pages, as described in Table 2-5.

Tip   *Templates and wizards quickly get you over the "where do I start" hurdle and give you a "first cut" that you can customize.*

Template	What Is Created on a New Page
Normal Page	Blank page
Bibliography	List of references to other pages or works
Confirmation Form	Acknowledgment of the receipt of input from the user
Document Library View Page Wizard	Page for viewing a document library created with SharePoint and the Team Web Site
Feedback Form	Form for a user to give you comments
Form Page Wizard	Custom form you have designed using this wizard
Frequently Asked Questions	List of questions and their answers
Guest Book	Form for users of your web to leave their identification and comments
List View Page Wizard	Page for viewing a list created with SharePoint and the Team Web Site
Narrow, Left-aligned Body	Body text formatted in a narrow, left-aligned column on the left
Narrow, Right-aligned Body	Body text formatted in a narrow, right-aligned column on the right
One-column Body	Single-column body text centered on the page
One-column Body with Contents and Sidebar	Body text in a single column with the contents on the left and a sidebar on the right

Table 2-5.   *Page Templates and Wizards*

Template	What Is Created on a New Page
One-column Body with Contents on Left	Contents in a narrow column on the left with body text on the right
One-column Body with Contents on Right	Contents in a narrow column on the right with body text on the left
One-column Body with Staggered Sidebar	Body text in one column on the right with two columns of staggered sidebars on the left
One-column Body with Two Sidebars	Body text in a center column with a two-column staggered sidebar on the left and a one-column sidebar on the right
One-column Body with Two-column Sidebar	Body text in a single column on the left with a two-column sidebar on the right
Photo Gallery	Thumbnail pictures and captions
Search Page	Search engine for finding keywords within the pages of a web
Table of Contents	List, in outline format, of hyperlinks to the other pages in your web
Three-column Body	Body text in three columns
Two-column Body	Body text in two columns
Two-column Body with Contents and Sidebar	Body text in two columns with a sidebar-like contents column on the left and a sidebar on the right
Two-column Body with Contents on Left	Body text in two right-aligned columns with contents in a left-aligned column
Two-column Staggered Body	Body text in two staggered columns
Two-column Staggered Body with Contents and Sidebar	Body text in two staggered columns in the center with a contents column on the left and a sidebar on the right
User Registration	Form for registering to use a secure web
Wide Body with headings	Body text in a single wide body with subheadings

Table 2-5. *Page Templates and Wizards* (continued)

Frames

Frames are a way to organize a web page by combining several pages onto one, each in a tile or *frame*. You use the Frames Pages tab of the Templates dialog box to create the several pages necessary for a given layout, called a *frame set*. In the Frames Pages tab, you can choose one of several frame templates, each of which is a frame set (described in Table 2-6). After creating the layout you want, you are shown the layout and asked how you want to determine the page contents, as shown in Figure 2-17. Frames are discussed in depth in Chapter 7.

Note   *Frames are another area of HTML programming that is not supported by all browsers, though Netscape Navigator has supported them since version 2.0, and Internet Explorer has supported them since version 3.0. As you will learn in Chapter 7, you can create alternate pages meant to be loaded by browsers that do not support frames when a frame page is encountered. (A frame page defines and identifies the set of pages, each containing the contents of one frame, which go together to create the single frame page in a browser.)*

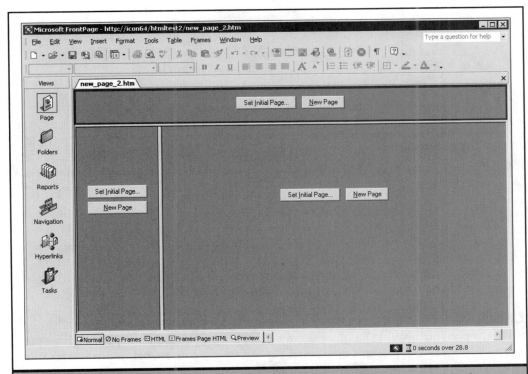

Figure 2-17.   *A frame page layout allows you to create the content in each frame*

Template	What Is Created on a New Frame Page
Banner and Contents	Creates three frames: a banner across the top, a contents frame on the left, and a main frame.
Contents	Creates two frames: a contents frame on the left and a main frame.
Footer	Creates a main frame with a narrow footer frame across the bottom.
Footnotes	Creates a main frame with a footnote frame across the bottom.
Header	Creates a main frame with a narrow header frame across the top.
Header, Footer, and Contents	Creates four frames: a header frame across the top, a contents frame on the left side, a main frame, and a footer frame across the bottom.
Horizontal Split	Creates two frames, split horizontally.
Nested Hierarchy	Creates a full-height contents frame on the left, a header frame, and a main frame.
Top-Down Hierarchy	Creates three frames, split horizontally.
Vertical Split	Creates two frames, split vertically.

Table 2-6.   *Frame Templates*

All of the frame pages discussed so far require that you create a frame set that divides the "page" a user sees into a set of frames that cover the entire page. There is also an *inline frame* that allows you to have a single floating frame anywhere on a regular page. This does not require a frame set, but is a single frame that has all the properties of a normal individual frame. Examples of an inline frame are a form or a complex list of items that the user would scroll to fully see.

Using Web Components

Web components provide automation in a web, giving you the ability to do more than just provide text and pictures on a page. For example, components return information to you that have been entered on a form, or enable users to participate in a discussion group. Most of FrontPage's components, though, just make creating and maintaining a web easier. In other web-authoring packages, this same capability requires various levels of programming. In FrontPage, you simply have to set up and enable a component.

The Discussion Component is automatically enabled when you create a new web using the Discussion Web Wizard. The Save Results Component is automatically enabled when you use the Form Page Wizard, or as you saw earlier, you can also add it from the Form toolbar. All other components are enabled through the Insert Web Component dialog box (shown in Figure 2-18) opened by choosing Web Component from the Insert menu. The components that you can place on a page are described in Table 2-7.

Adding Hyperlinks and Mapping Hotspots

In Page view you can add hyperlinks (or *links*), which allow the user of a web to quickly jump from one page to another, or to a particular element on the same page or another page (called a *bookmark*), or to a different web or web site. You can make either text or a picture be the element the user clicks to make the link, and you can map certain areas of a picture to be designated as different links (called *hotspots*). You create a link by first selecting the object that you want the user to click and then clicking the Insert Hyperlink button in the toolbar, or by choosing Hyperlink from either the context menu (opened by right-clicking the item) or the Insert menu. In either case, the Insert Hyperlink dialog box will open as shown in Figure 2-19.

Within the Insert Hyperlink dialog box, you can select a bookmark that has been previously placed on any open page or just an open page without a bookmark, any page in the current web with or without a bookmark, any URL or address on the World Wide Web, a new page yet to be defined in the current web, or an e-mail address. When you have created a hyperlink, the object on which the user is to click changes to a different color and may become underlined.

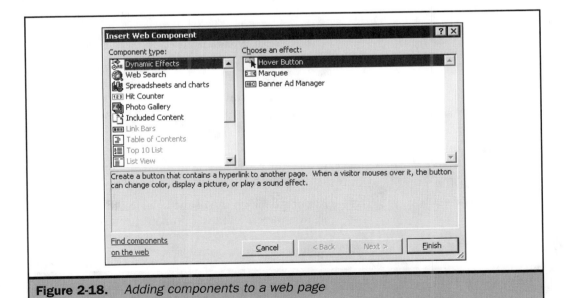

Figure 2-18. *Adding components to a web page*

Component	Capability Added to a Web Page
Dynamic Effects Hover Button	Creates a button that can change color, display a picture, or play a sound when the mouse pointer hovers over it.
Dynamic Effects Marquee	Inserts a marquee on a web page in which text is scrolled or slid across the marquee.
Dynamic Effects Banner Ad Manager	Inserts a banner in a web page within which a series of pictures will be rotated.
Web Search – Current Web	Adds a search form to allow the user to search the current web.
Spreadsheets and Charts	Adds an interactive spreadsheet, chart, or pivot table to a web page in which the web viewer can change the data and see the results.
Hit Counter	Allows you to choose from several counters, which record the number of times a page has been downloaded.
Photo Gallery	Provides for the automatic display of a series of photos on a page with a horizontal, vertical, montage, or slide show layout.
Included Content	Allows you to include one web page's content, picture, banner, or creation information (such as author and date last changed) on another page. For example, a page header can be put on one page and included on every other page.
Link Bars	Adds a link bar with hyperlinks to other pages specified by the user, or to the next or previous page, or based on the structure of the current web.
Table of Contents	Creates a table of contents that lists all of the pages in a web either hierarchically or based on chosen categories.
Top 10 List	Reports back on the usage of a site: the top 10 visited pages, referring domains, referring URLs, search strings, visiting users, operating systems (OSs), and browsers.

Table 2-7.   *Components Inserted from the Insert Web Component Dialog Box*

Component	Capability Added to a Web Page
List View	Provides access to lists in a SharePoint Team Web Site.
Document Library View	Provides access to document libraries in a SharePoint Team Web Site.
BCentral Web Components MSN Components MSNBC Components	Adds content from Microsoft web sites, such as stock quotes and weather forecasts, and lets you exchange banner ad time.
Additional Components	Adds a Visual InterDev type of navigation bar.
Advanced Controls	Adds HTML content, a Java applet, a plug-in, an ActiveX control, or design-time control to a web page.
Advanced Controls: Confirmation Field	Echoes the information entered on a form by users, so you can show them what they entered.

Table 2-7.   *Components Inserted from the Insert Web Component Dialog Box* (continued)

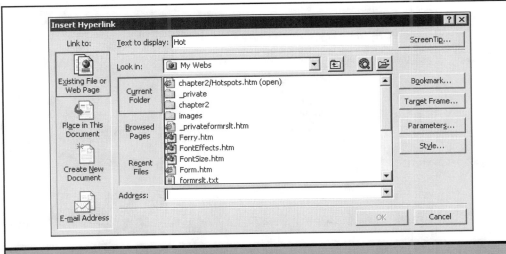

Figure 2-19.   *Insert Hyperlink dialog box*

A picture can have its entire area defined as a link, or you can identify specific areas in a picture as separate links, while any unidentified areas are assigned a default link. For example, you could provide a map that allows the user to quickly get to information about a particular area of the world by simply clicking that area, as you can see in Figure 2-20.

 The left end of the status bar informs you of the link under the mouse pointer.

You place hotspots on a picture by using the hotspot drawing tools (shown next) located on the right side of the Pictures toolbar. The Pictures toolbar will be displayed when you select the picture, if it isn't already displayed. (If you don't see the Pictures toolbar, it may be partially hidden by another toolbar. Look carefully and you'll see a part of the Pictures toolbar sticking out on the left or right which you can drag to its own row or on to the page.)

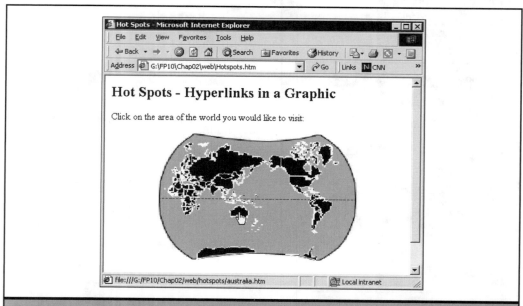

Figure 2-20. *Selecting a hyperlink that is a hotspot in a picture*

First select the picture, then select the rectangle, circle, or polygon tool. Use it to draw a border around the area of the picture you want to be the hotspot. When you complete a closed area, you'll be asked to enter the URL (bookmark, web site, or page reference) where the browser should transfer when that area is clicked. When you are done identifying all the hotspots, your picture will look something like this (although users won't see the lines in a browser):

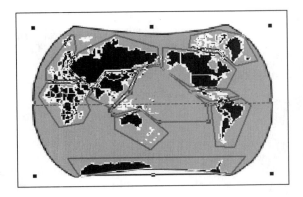

 Another useful tool on the Pictures toolbar is the Set Transparent Color tool. This tool lets you click any color in the picture and make it transparent, allowing the page background to show through.

 Transparent backgrounds only work with GIF89a files. If you try using a transparent background with a JPEG, you'll get a dialog box that says the JPEG will be converted to a GIF.

Using Drawing, AutoShapes, and WordArt

Besides adding clip art and pictures, FrontPage gives you the capability of adding your own drawings, AutoShapes, and WordArt. The drawing that can be done is with the Drawing toolbar, which is opened from the View menu by selecting Toolbars | Drawing and is shown here:

The Drawing toolbar provides a number of tools, described in Table 2-8, that allow you to create and enhance simple line drawings. Two of the tools on the Drawing toolbar, AutoShapes and WordArt, are themselves clusters of tools and can be separately opened from the Insert | Picture menu.

Tool	Name	Purpose
Draw ▾	Draw menu	Manipulate a drawing including group, ungroup, order, and align objects; snap, nudge, and rotate an object; and edit points on a line or curve.
	Select object	Select elements in a drawing such as lines, curves, and text.
AutoShapes ▾	AutoShapes	Insert predefined shapes. See following section.
	Line	Draw lines, initially straight, but through editing make curved.
	Arrow	Draw lines with an arrowhead at the end. Again the lines are initially straight, but through editing can be made to curve.
	Rectangle	Draw rectangles that can be edited.
	Oval	Draw ovals that can be edited.
	Text Box	Insert a text box.
	WordArt	Give text an artistic flair. See upcoming section.
	ClipArt	Insert clip art.
	Picture	Insert a picture from a file.
	Fill	Fill a closed object with a color, texture, pattern, or picture.
	Line Color	Change the color or pattern of a line.

Table 2-8. *Drawing Toolbar*

Tool	Name	Purpose
A ▾	Font Color	Change the color of text.
≡	Line Style	Change the type and width of lines.
⋯	Dash Style	Make a line dashed in various ways.
⇄	Arrow Style	Change the arrow type and its affixed end.
▣	Shadow	Add a shadow in various ways to an object.
▣	3-D	Add various 3-D effects to an object.

Table 2-8.   *Drawing Toolbar* (continued)

AutoShapes   AutoShapes are a set of ready-made shapes that includes basic shapes, block arrows, and flowchart elements (as shown next), as well as lines, stars, banners, and callouts.

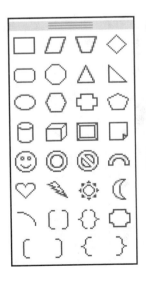 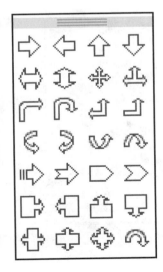 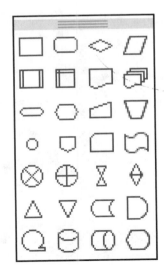

Once you have selected the shape, you can place it anywhere on the page by moving the mouse pointer to that area and clicking. In this manner, you can lay down a "normal-sized" object, or size it by dragging the mouse. To resize the object once it's on the page, simply select it and drag one of the selection handles in or out. You can also fill an enclosed shape with color and/or change its outline color by using the Fill and Line Color tools.

WordArt   WordArt takes selected text that you have entered and applies one of 30 effects that you select from the WordArt Gallery shown in Figure 2-21. After you have selected the effect, the Edit WordArt Text dialog box opens allowing you to make any changes to the text you want. When you click OK, the text with the applied effect will appear on your current work page. When the text is selected, a WordArt toolbar appears allowing you to: edit the text; select a different effect from the gallery; change the color, size, layout, and rotation of the text; make all the characters the same size; make them vertical, change their alignment, and alter their spacing.

Other FrontPage Views

While Page view is the place where you construct the individual pages that make up a web, FrontPage offers you five other views that let you look at the web in other ways. You can look at the complete web and see all of its pages, files, and links, or you can look at a segment of the web and see the components of that segment. As you saw earlier in this chapter, the other views are Folders view, Reports view, Navigation view, Hyperlinks view, and Tasks view.

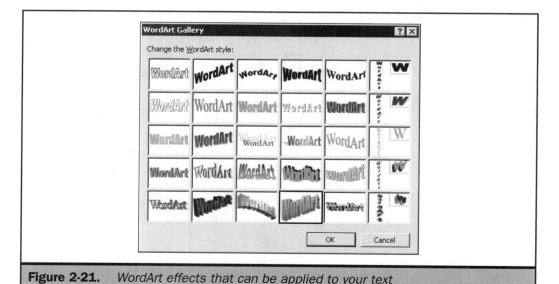

Figure 2-21.   *WordArt effects that can be applied to your text*

Folders View

Folders view is similar in a number of ways to the Windows Explorer. In Folders view, for example, the left pane (or Folder List) displays a hierarchical structure of folders, while the right pane (or Contents pane) displays a list of the files supporting the web, as shown in Figure 2-22.

By clicking the plus and minus icons in the left pane, you can expand or collapse the view of the hierarchy. If you right-click an object in either pane, its context menu will open, which, among other options, allows you to open the object's Properties dialog box. A final way that Folders view is like the Windows Explorer is that in Folders view, you can sort the list of files by clicking the column name immediately above the list.

In either Page or Folders view, you can use wizards and templates to automatically create entire webs, including a full set of pages, links, and other elements. As in Page view, wizards and templates differ only in the amount of interaction between you and the computer during the creation process. Web templates create a ready-made web without interacting with you. Web wizards, on the other hand, use one or more dialog boxes to ask you a series of questions during creation. Based on your answers to these

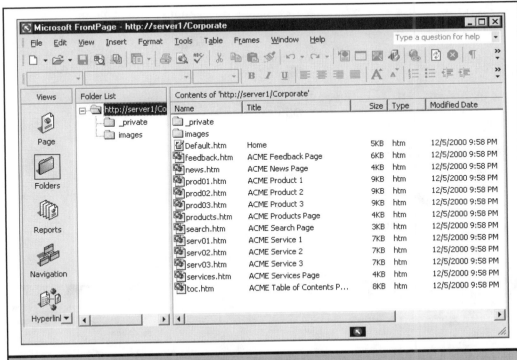

Figure 2-22. *A web displayed in Folders view*

questions, a customized web is created. You can customize the resultant web pages and elements with Page view. You can also create an empty web by clicking the Empty Web icon in the New Web Or Page task pane, or import an existing web by choosing Web Site Templates and then double-clicking the Import Web Wizard icon.

The web templates and wizards that are currently available in FrontPage are shown in Table 2-9. You can use these templates and wizards to create either new webs or additions to existing webs. Also, wizards and templates automatically create the tasks in Tasks view that support the created pages. As you'll see in Chapter 4 and Appendix C, you can build your own templates to create a standard look—for example, across all departments in a corporate intranet.

Template or Wizard	Characteristics of Web Created
Templates	
One Page Web	Has a single blank page.
Customer Support Web	Tells customers how to contact you and provides a form where they can leave information so you can contact them. Includes an FTP download area, a frequently asked questions (FAQ) area, and a form for leaving suggestions and contact information.
Empty Web	Has no pages, so you can import pages from another web.
Personal Web	Has a single page with personal and professional information and ways to be contacted.
Project Web	Provides a way to communicate the status of a project including its schedule, who is working on it, and its accomplishments.
SharePoint Team Web Site	Has pages for collaboration among team members. To be used with SharePoint (see discussion later in this chapter).

Table 2-9. *Web Templates and Wizards*

GETTING STARTED

Template or Wizard	Characteristics of Web Created
Wizards	
Corporate Presence	Provides information about a company, including what it does, what its products and services are, how to contact it, and a means to leave feedback for it.
Database Interface	Sets up a connection with a database whose records can then be viewed and modified.
Discussion Web	Is an electronic bulletin board where users can leave messages and others can reply to those messages.
Import Web	Provides assistance in collecting all of the components of a web and bringing them into FrontPage.

Table 2-9.   *Web Templates and Wizards* (continued)

Reports View

Reports view provides a series of reports that tell you about your web (as you can see in Figure 2-23). To see the detail of any report, click its name. You can then return to the Site Summary by opening the Reports menu on the Reporting toolbar and choosing Site Summary (see Tip that follows). There is a great amount of valuable information in the reports that FrontPage provides. The best way to get familiar with it is to open each of the reports and study the contents.

Some of the reports do not open and only provide information at the summary level.

You can open a Reporting toolbar from the View menu Toolbars option (once open, it will automatically appear whenever you open the Reports view). The Reporting toolbar lets you select what is displayed in the Reports view. You can also edit and verify hyperlinks, and using the down arrow in the lower-right corner, you can add or remove (customize) the other toolbar contents.

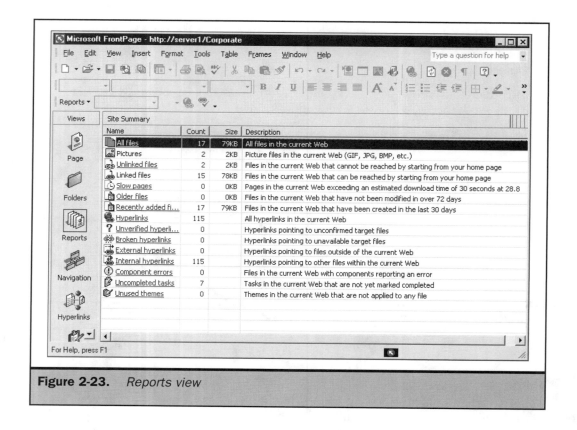

Figure 2-23. *Reports view*

Navigation View

Navigation view, shown in Figure 2-24, gives you a graphical overview of how the web is organized. A list of the files supporting the web is displayed in the left pane, and a graphical representation of the hyperlinks used to go from page to page is shown in the right pane. By clicking the plus and minus signs in the right pane, you can expand or collapse the hierarchy of links. You can also drag a page from one position to another and change its link by doing so.

Hyperlinks View

Hyperlinks view allows you to look at the links among the pages in a web, as well as the links to external sites. Web pages and their links create a hierarchical structure that is shown in the Folder List, which is the left pane of the Hyperlinks view, as shown in Figure 2-25. You create this structure either by adding pages one at a time and then linking them, or by using one of the web wizards or templates to automatically create the desired pages and their links.

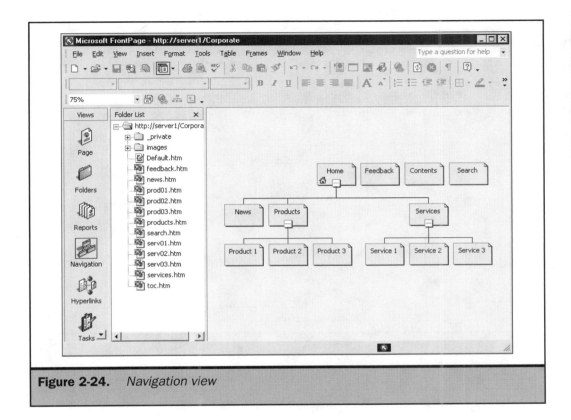

Figure 2-24.   *Navigation view*

Tasks View

Tasks view (Figure 2-26) lists the tasks that must be accomplished to complete the web application you are building. The items on the Tasks list are placed there either by a web wizard or by you. You can add tasks in any view by opening the File menu and choosing New | Task, or clicking the arrow to the right of the New button and choosing Task. You can also add tasks by opening the Edit menu and choosing Tasks | Add Task in any view.

When you add a new task, the New Task dialog box will appear in which you can give the task a name, assign it to an individual, give it a priority, and type in a description. Once you have a complete Tasks list, use it to go to the various sections of a web that still require work by right-clicking a task and selecting Start Task. This will open Page view and display the page that needs work. When you have completed the task, you can return to Tasks view, right-click the task, and select Mark Complete from the context menu, which will mark the task as completed and leave it in the list, or select Delete Task from the context menu to delete the task from the list. By right-clicking an uncompleted task and selecting Edit Task from the context menu, you can modify who the task is assigned to, its priority, its description, and the task name. For a completed task, you can only edit the description.

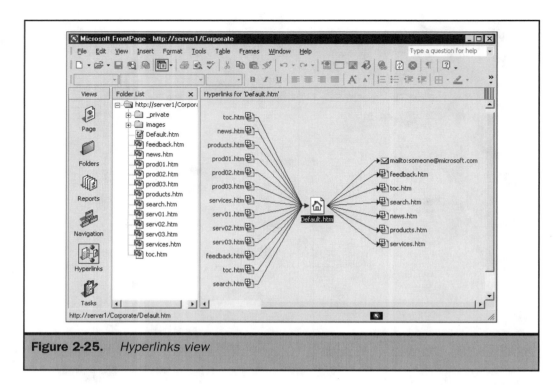

Figure 2-25. Hyperlinks view

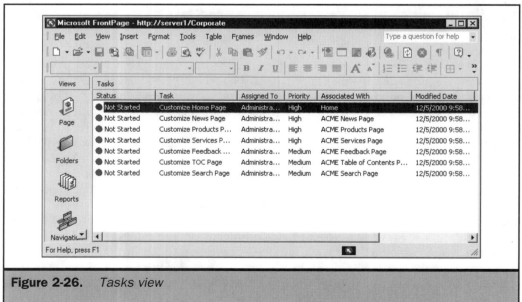

Figure 2-26. Tasks view

You can sort the tasks in Tasks view on any column by clicking the column name at the top of the list.

Accessing Other Functions in FrontPage

As you are working on your web, you can open Page view in several ways. The following are just a few methods:

- Use either the Page option in the View menu or the Page button in the Views bar
- Double-click the page filename (or icon) you want to edit in one of several views of FrontPage

 When you are done creating a web, you can test a hyperlink by right-clicking the link in Hyperlinks view and selecting Verify Hyperlink. Also, if you have edited a web and removed or changed some of the pages, use the Recalculate Hyperlinks option in the Tools menu to update all of the internal links so there is no reference to a nonexistent page. Finally, when everything is the way you want it, you can publish your web on a server (provided you weren't already working on the server) by using the Publish Web option in the File menu or by using the Publish Web button on the toolbar.

Distributing FrontPage Webs

So far, this chapter has dealt with the creation of FrontPage webs—that, after all, is the purpose of FrontPage. A web page, though, is worthless if it isn't distributed to those who wish to see it. The distribution side of FrontPage has three components: servers, FrontPage Server Extensions, and SharePoint.

Web Servers

You can use any web server to publish FrontPage webs. As was said at the beginning of this chapter, this book assumes you are using one of the Microsoft web servers: Internet Information Services (IIS) in Windows XP or 2000 Server, NT Server, or Windows XP or 2000 Professional, or personal web server (PWS) in FrontPage 98 or Windows 98. The web server can be on your computer, another computer on your LAN, or a computer on the Internet. If your web server is on your computer or a local computer on your LAN, it gives you added flexibility to test your webs. IIS or PWS on your computer simply sit in the background as a task and take very little management. IIS is often on a dedicated server and is all the web server you need to run a full World Wide Web site.

Appendix A details the installation and setup of IIS and PWS. From here on, this book will assume that either IIS or PWS is running and available to you.

 Though Windows Me does not ship with PWS, you can use the PWS from a Windows 98 CD.

FrontPage Server Extensions

If you want to use all of the components of FrontPage, especially the interactive components, you need to have the FrontPage Server Extensions installed on both the server you use to build your webs and the server your Internet service provider (ISP) or Web Presence Provider (WPP) is using. If your Web Presence Provider is not using the FrontPage Server Extensions, you should suggest that they do so (see Chapter 24 for information on using the server extensions on a web server). The server extensions are available from Microsoft (**http://www.microsoft.com/workshop/languages/fp/**) for virtually every popular Windows NT- and UNIX-based server. If your WPP doesn't want to run the server extensions, then you might consider changing providers. There are now a great many WPPs that offer FrontPage Server Extensions, both locally and across the country. Remember that, with the Web, it is not necessary to be physically close to your provider to have a successful working relationship. Features and quality of service are more important.

> **Note**   *Though the terms Internet service provider (ISP) and Web Presence Provider (WPP) are sometimes used interchangeably, there is a difference. An ISP provides access to the Internet, usually through a dial-up (modem) connection. A WPP hosts web sites. That is, a WPP stores the web files on a server that is accessible over the Internet. Often your ISP and your WPP will be the same company. In this book, the terms presence provider and web host refer to a WPP.*

Among the components and advance features in FrontPage that require FrontPage Server Extensions are:

- Forms
- Hotspot image maps
- Web Components that are active while a web is being used in a browser, such as:
  - Confirmation Field Component
  - Discussion Component
  - Registration Component
  - Save Results Component
  - Search Component

The focus of this book is on creating webs that use the Microsoft Internet Information Services and the FrontPage Server Extensions on both your local machine and the web server your webs will be hosted on. In the following chapters, you will use all of the elements of FrontPage and many of their features to build your own webs.

SharePoint

SharePoint is a special way of distributing workgroup or team webs to facilitate the collaboration and management of a project within a web site. SharePoint provides three tools that are only available there: lists, surveys, and document libraries. With these tools, the following functions are set up and available to the entire team:

- Tasks can be documented and tracked
- Events can be scheduled and followed up
- Announcements can be made and archived
- Contacts can be identified and maintained
- Favorite references, styles, procedures, web sites, and other preferences can be cataloged
- Opinions can be sought and documented
- Libraries of documents, drawings, pictures, sounds, video images, scripts, and code can be indexed and maintained

SharePoint Lists

SharePoint lists are used to share information among a team. Examples of lists are contacts, team members, events, dates, milestones, and products. Based on team members' permissions, they can add, delete, modify, and view the lists. You can create and manage lists in FrontPage using the List View Web Component previously described under Using Web Components.

SharePoint Document Libraries

SharePoint document libraries are used to share documents among a team. Examples of items in a library include correspondence, reports, procedures, plans, and policies. Based on team members' permissions, they can add, delete, modify, and view the libraries. You can create and manage document libraries in FrontPage using the Document Library View FrontPage component described earlier under Using Web Components.

SharePoint Surveys

SharePoint surveys are used to collect information from team members. Surveys can be used to collect current project status, determine availability for a meeting, and gather opinions on a subject. In addition, you can add a survey to a web using the SharePoint Create web function.

SharePoint Administration

You, as an administrator, can set up and maintain SharePoint using FrontPage 2002 and Internet Explorer. Your SharePoint web can have just the features you want to use, and the team members can have the set of permissions to use these features that is appropriate both for the team and for the individual. SharePoint depends on an SQL database to store the lists, libraries, and surveys that make up each web. (A runtime version of SQL comes with SharePoint.) As administrator, you can set up the database in a manner appropriate to the web site.

SharePoint is not installed in the default install of Office XP. You must separately install it by opening the Sharept folder on the Office XP CD in Windows Explorer, double-clicking Setupse, and following the instructions.

SharePoint is administered through the Server Administration pages that are opened through Start | Programs | Administrative Tools | Microsoft SharePoint Administrator. This provides the page shown in Figure 2-27, which contains the primary controls that allow you to change the configuration settings as well as back up, upgrade, and uninstall SharePoint.

A SharePoint web can be created using the Team Web Site template that you read about previously under Folders view. Chapter 4 describes SharePoint further and Chapter 24 describes how to use SharePoint in detail, showing how it can manage projects.

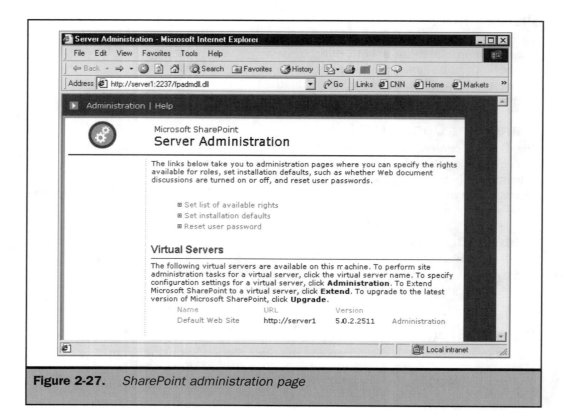

Figure 2-27.   *SharePoint administration page*

FrontPage 2002

Chapter 3

Using Wizards and Themes

s you saw in Chapter 2, the easiest way to create a web with FrontPage is by using a wizard or a template. You'll remember that *wizards* ask you questions about the web you want to create and then build a web based on your answers. *Templates* create a particular kind of web without input from you. In this chapter, you'll see how to use wizards to create webs, and the results that they produce. (Templates are covered in Chapter 4.) The purpose of this is twofold: to acquaint you with the wizards and to demonstrate many of FrontPage's features, which have been included in the wizard-produced webs.

Most of the wizards are web wizards, which create the folder structure and pages that make a complete web. A few are page wizards that create only a single page.

Web Wizards

Begin looking at the FrontPage wizards by loading FrontPage as you did in Chapter 2. (For the remainder of this book, it is assumed you have either Internet Information Services (IIS) or Personal Web Server (PWS), both with the FrontPage Server Extensions, running on your computer or another computer on your network, as explained in Appendix A.)

After FrontPage has loaded, you can start a new web in three ways:

- You can simply begin creating the first web page and then add additional pages to it as necessary.

- You can open the New toolbar button by clicking the down arrow on its right and choosing Web, as shown left.

- You can open the File menu, choose New, and then select Page or Web to open the New Page Or Web task pane. Click Web Site Templates.

In the last two alternatives, the Web Site Templates dialog box will be displayed, as shown in Figure 3-1. In this dialog box, icons for the following web wizards are displayed:

- **Corporate Presence Wizard** creates a complete web site to promote your company or business. With it you can:

  - Create web pages that tell customers what's new with your company (for example, by using press releases)

  - Inform customers about your products and services

  - Create a table of contents to help visitors navigate your web site

  - Provide a feedback form so your customers can give you their opinions

  - Provide a search form that visitors to your web site can use to quickly find specific information on your site

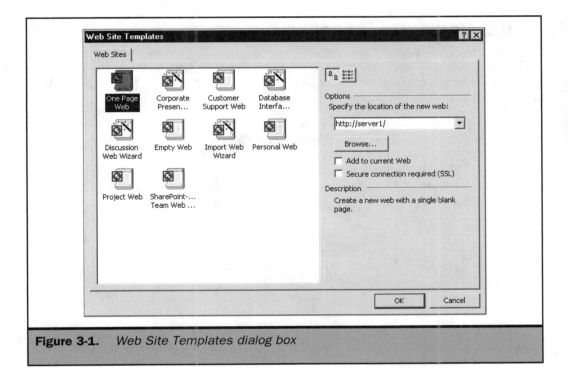

Figure 3-1.   *Web Site Templates dialog box*

- **Database Interface Wizard** builds a web site with which you can connect to and manage a database, including viewing, adding, changing, and deleting database records.

- **Discussion Web Wizard** creates web pages that allow the web user to submit comments to a discussion. It also provides a table of contents, a search form, a page to follow threaded replies, and a confirmation page so users know their comments have been received. *Threaded replies* link multiple comments on the same subject. This allows the reader to go directly from one comment to the next on a given subject.

- **Import Web Wizard** lets you quickly convert existing web pages and content into a FrontPage web by collecting web pages from your local drive, or from an intranet or the Internet, and organize them into a FrontPage web. This is an important feature if you need to convert a number of existing webs into FrontPage, to update them, or to incorporate any of FrontPage's active elements, Web Components, or other dynamic FrontPage elements in them.

Using the Corporate Presence Wizard

The Corporate Presence web is one of the more sophisticated webs that FrontPage creates. By using a wizard, you get to do a lot of customizing as you build. In this section, you will create a Corporate Presence web ("Corporate web," for short). Do that now with these instructions (FrontPage should be loaded and Page view open on your screen):

1. Open the File menu, choose New | Page or Web, and then click Web Site Templates. Click the Corporate Presence Wizard in the Web Site Templates dialog box Web Sites tab, and enter the URL or address for the new web (**Corporate** will work well for the name) in the Specify The Location Of The New Web drop-down list. For example, on a computer named "Server1," this is the URL:

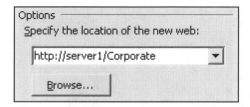

   - If you will be normally working directly on your web server, the URL is the domain name plus the name of the web, for example: **http://Excitingtravel.com/Corporate**.

   - If you are working on your local computer and intend to later publish your web on a web server, this would be the name of your computer (as it was in the case of "Server1" just a paragraph ago). (You may also use "localhost" for the computer you are working on. Localhost is a default network name for your computer—see the discussion on installing a web server in Appendix A.)

   - If you are creating a disk-based web, you would enter the path to the folder on your hard drive that will contain the web. For example: **C:\Webs\Corporate**.

2. If you do not have a server name entered, select or enter the URL for the server or computer where your web will reside. The Secure Connection Required (SSL) check box should be unchecked. (See Chapter 22 for a discussion of Secure Sockets Layer or SSL.)

3. Click OK to close the Web Site Templates dialog box. If your server requires it, you will be prompted to enter your user name and password in the Name And Password Required dialog box. This is to verify that you are authorized to create webs on your server. Enter your name and password and click OK.

4. The first Corporate Presence Web Wizard dialog box will be displayed, explaining that you will be asked a series of questions. Click Next, opening the second wizard dialog box (shown in Figure 3-2), which displays the list of pages that can be included in the web.

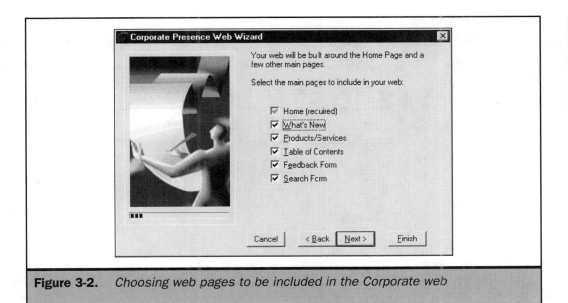

Figure 3-2. *Choosing web pages to be included in the Corporate web*

5. Select all of the options (to include all the possible pages) and click Next. This brings up a list of topics that can be included on the home page.

6. Choose all the check boxes and default options in this and the following wizard dialog boxes, and supply requested information about your company or organization. (One of the choices is whether you want to use the Under Construction icon on your pages. See the following Tip on this choice, although in the illustrations here it was included.) So that you don't have to come up with pictures at this time, do not select a company logo or a product image. After you select web options and supply information about your site, you will reach the dialog box that gives you the option of choosing the web theme you want to use in your web. Click Choose Web Theme in this dialog box (you will explore Themes in detail later in this chapter).

Tip *Using the Under Construction icon is generally not a good idea. If at all possible, finish the web before putting it on the server for public consumption. (The icon is shown on the screen shots later in this chapter so you can see what it looks like.)*

7. In the Choose Theme dialog box (see Figure 3-3) that appears, select the All Pages option (if it isn't already selected) and look at a number of the options.

8. Choose the one you want (Modular is used in the figures in this chapter). Make sure all four check boxes are selected in the Choose Theme dialog box so you can experience all the theme features. If you have a limited list of themes and

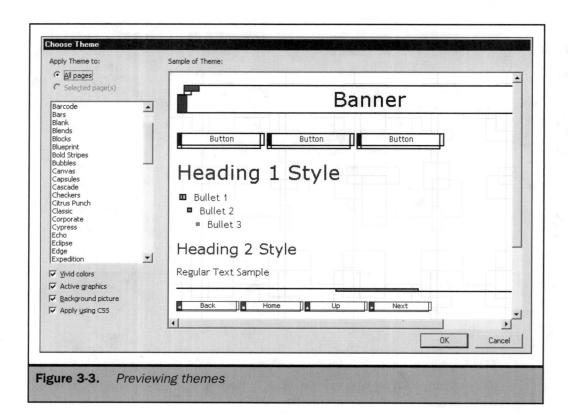

Figure 3-3. *Previewing themes*

can't find Modular, additional themes can be installed from the Office or FrontPage CD by choosing Install Additional Themes from the top of the list of themes in the Choose Theme dialog box. If you don't see Install Additional Themes, they have all been installed.

Note *"CSS," in the check box in the lower left of the Choose Theme dialog box stands for "cascading style sheets," which are used to apply consistent styles in a web site. CSS is discussed further in Chapters 10 and 12.*

9. Click OK and then click Next. In the final dialog box of the Corporate Presence Web Wizard, make sure the Show Tasks View After Web Is Uploaded check box is checked and then click Finish. The web will be created and displayed in Tasks view. The Tasks view shows what you need to do to finish the web that was generated by the Corporate Presence Web Wizard, as you can see in Figure 3-4.

10. Click the Navigation view icon in the Views bar on the left side of the FrontPage window to show the Corporate web in Navigation view, as in Figure 3-5. This shows all of the main web pages and their relationship to each other.

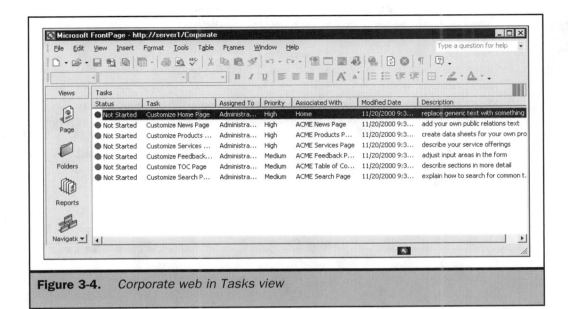

Figure 3-4.   *Corporate web in Tasks view*

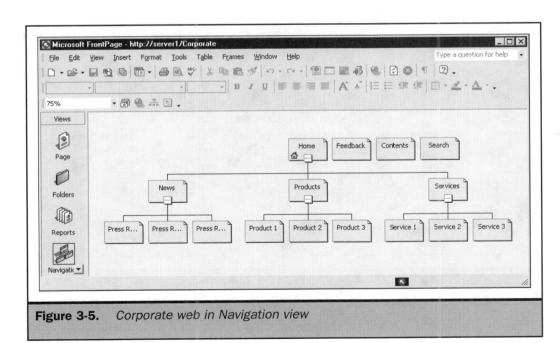

Figure 3-5.   *Corporate web in Navigation view*

11. Select Hyperlinks view by clicking the Hyperlinks view icon in the Views bar. As you can see in Figure 3-6, the Corporate Presence Web Wizard has not only created all the pages you selected in the wizard, but it has also created the basic hyperlinks between the pages, represented by the arrows in the right pane of the FrontPage window.

12. Right-click the Home Page file, which is either Default.htm or Index.htm, in either pane of Hyperlinks view, and choose Properties from the context menu that opens. The Properties dialog box for the Home page, similar to the one shown in Figure 3-7, will open. Here you can see the filename, title, and URL that have been generated for the Home page. In the Summary tab you can see when and by whom the page was created and modified. You can also add comments.

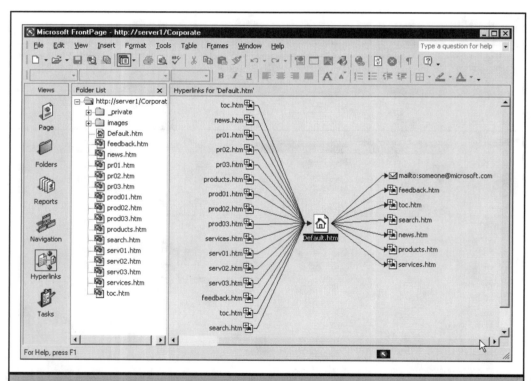

Figure 3-6.   *Links between web objects are shown in Hyperlinks view*

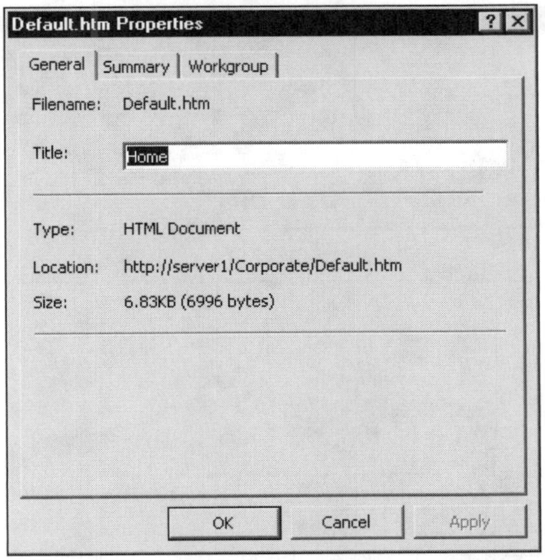

Default.htm Properties   ? X

General | Summary | Workgroup |

Filename: Default.htm

Title: Home

Type: HTML Document

Location: http://server1/Corporate/Default.htm

Size: 6.83KB (6996 bytes)

OK   Cancel   Apply

Figure 3-7.   *Examining Properties for the Home page*

Note *Since we are using IIS as our web server, FrontPage has named the Home page Default.htm. It would also do this with PWS. With other servers FrontPage would name the Home page Index.htm. The name of the home page for a web is important since this will determine whether your web server will display the home page when accessed without the home page filename (http://webname/) or whether the full URL will be required (http://webname/pagename.htm). Different web servers have different default settings for the home page name. Check with your web server administrator for the default home page name on your web server.*

13. Click OK. The Properties dialog box closes. Click the Tasks view icon in the Views bar to return to the Tasks list (shown previously in Figure 3-4).

14. Right-click the first task (Customize Home Page), and choose Start Task from the context menu. Page view will open with the Home page displayed, as shown in Figure 3-8. On the Home page you can see some of the features incorporated in this web (scroll through the page to make sure you see

Figure 3-8. *Corporate web Home page in Page view*

everything). Here are some of the features to note (see Figure 3-8 for the first four features):

Tip

If the folder list is still open, click the Toggle Pane icon in the toolbar (sixth icon from the left, which toggles between no pane on the left, a folder list pane, or a navigation pane) to close it and gain more screen area to display the page.

- Hyperlink buttons ("Home," "Feedback," "Contents," and "Search") at the top of the page, called a "link bar," allow visitors to jump to other pages in your web site.

- The page title, "Home," called a "page banner," and the page background are graphics. You can create such graphics in Microsoft PhotoDraw, CorelDRAW, Adobe PhotoShop, Fractal Design Painter, or other graphics packages and then place them in FrontPage.

- The link bar down the left side, similar to the one at the top, is a series of graphics, one for each of the hyperlinks, and is included in a *shared border* that is used at the top, left, and bottom of each regular web page. In Figure 3-8, there are three link bars: one at the top ("Home," "Feedback," "Contents," and "Search"); one under the Home banner (you must edit it for the buttons to be visible); and one on the left ("News," "Products," and "Services"). There is also a link bar in the bottom-shared border that you cannot see in Figure 3-8. You will explore shared borders toward the end of this chapter.

- The line beneath the first Comment is a graphic.

- The phone numbers, postal address, and e-mail addresses near the bottom of the page are entered and maintained through the Substitution Web Component. (Web Components are discussed in Chapter 9.)

15. Select Open from the File menu or click Open on the toolbar to display the Open File dialog box.

16. Double-click News.htm. When the News.htm file is loaded in Page view, you can see the common elements that are included on each page created with the Corporate Presence Web Wizard. Notice that the "Home" page banner below the top link bar has been replaced by one that says "News." Each page in the Corporate web will have its own page banner to identify it.

If you do not see file extensions (the ".htm" in "News.htm"), you can turn them on by opening the Windows Explorer and its Tools menu, choosing Folder Options, selecting the View tab, and clearing the Hide File Extensions For Known File Types check box.

On any of the pages, you can enter and format text, insert graphics, and add forms, tables, and other elements, as you saw in Chapter 2. In later chapters, you will do all of these tasks. The purpose here is simply to see that the Corporate Presence Web Wizard does, in fact, create a complete web. It also creates all of the structure (shown in Figures 3-5 and 3-6) behind a web in FrontPage.

The web pages generated by the Corporate Presence Web Wizard include text and graphics, as well as content stored in shared borders. The shared borders—on the top, bottom, and left of the page—will be explored later in this chapter, after you have examined the rest of the page contents.

Looking at the News Page

The News page of your Corporate web serves as a central location to list press releases, information on media coverage, changes to your web site, and to provide hyperlinks to the individual pages that describe the items in more detail.

Each element on the page has its own properties which you can view and change by right-clicking the object and selecting Properties from the context menu. In the following steps, you will look at the Properties dialog boxes for the different types of objects on the News page.

1. Scroll down the News page and right-click the small "NEW" image on the left of your company name ("Acme Industries, Inc." if you didn't change the wizard default). In the context menu, select Picture Properties to open the Picture Properties dialog box in Figure 3-9.

   ■ In the Appearance tab of the Picture Properties dialog box, you can set the alignment of the graphic within text on the page, specify horizontal and vertical spacing around the graphic, create a border for it, and specify the size.

   ■ In the General tab, you can select the image to be shown, provide text that will appear in browsers that do not display graphics (this text will also be displayed for a few seconds if you point on the graphic in a browser), and create a hyperlink for the graphic.

   ■ The Video tab is where you select a video file and modify how the video appears, how long it plays, and when it starts.

2. Close the Picture Properties dialog box, and right-click any of the horizontal lines on the page. Select Horizontal Line Properties from the context menu.

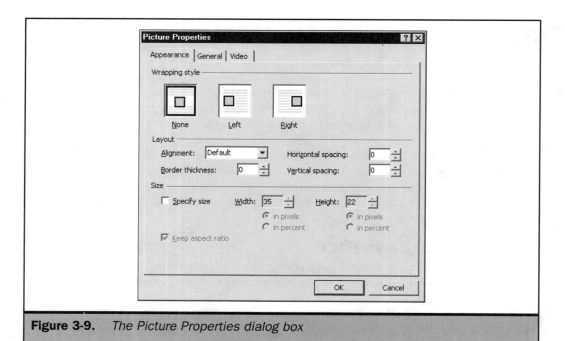

Figure 3-9.   *The Picture Properties dialog box*

GETTING STARTED

Many of the properties for the horizontal line on this page are defined by the web's theme, but you can edit these settings in the dialog box as shown next.

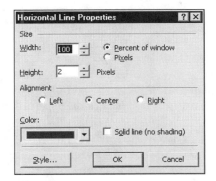

3. Close the Horizontal Line Properties dialog box and right-click the hyperlink Press Release in the line following the "NEW" image. Select Hyperlink Properties to display the Edit Hyperlink dialog box shown in Figure 3-10. You use this dialog box to set hyperlinks on either text or graphics in your web pages that connect to other locations in your web, to other intranet webs, or to the World Wide Web. You can also set hyperlinks to bookmarks on the same page.

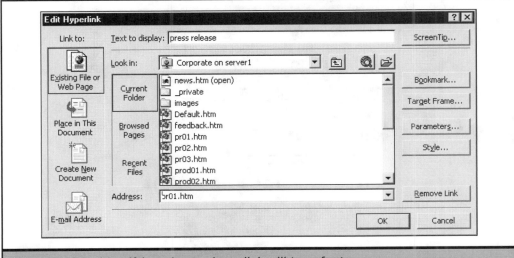

Figure 3-10.   *Identifying where a hyperlink will transfer to*

4. Click Cancel to close the Edit Hyperlink dialog box. Right-click the same Press Release hyperlink again, and select Follow Hyperlink in the context menu (or press and hold CTRL while clicking the hyperlink) to open the Press Release 1 page (pr01.htm) in Page view, as shown in Figure 3-11. The Press Release 1 template includes space for the title of your announcement, the date of the release, and contact information for the press.

Tip *In Page view, you have to press and hold CTRL while clicking the hyperlink, or you can open the context menu and select Follow Hyperlink to open the target of a link. In a web browser or the Preview tab, you simply click the hyperlink.*

Note *The Press Release pages, as well as the Product and Service pages, are all numbered 1 through 3. In the Corporate Presence Web Wizard, the default number of pages to be created for these three types of web pages is three. The next time you create a web with this wizard, you can choose the number of Product and Service pages that best fits your needs.*

5. Close the Press Release 1 page by selecting Close from the File menu.

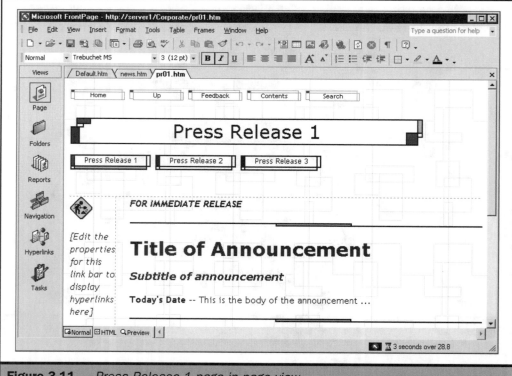

Figure 3-11. *Press Release 1 page in page view*

The Table of Contents Page

The Table of Contents page provides the user with a single location to open any page in a web.

1. Open the Table of Contents page in Page view by double-clicking Toc.htm in the Open File dialog box. (Recall that the Open File dialog box is accessed either by use of the Open toolbar button or by selecting Open in the File menu.) Figure 3-12 shows the page in Page view.

   The pages listed in the Table of Contents are automatically generated, starting from the home page. In Page view this does not look like much, but in a browser this is automatically expanded to include references to each page and to each bookmark on those pages.

2. Open the File menu and select Preview In Browser. (You may have to fully extend the menu.) In the Preview In Browser dialog box that appears (shown next), you can select a web browser to view your page, add a browser you have installed on your computer, and select the size at which the browser will be

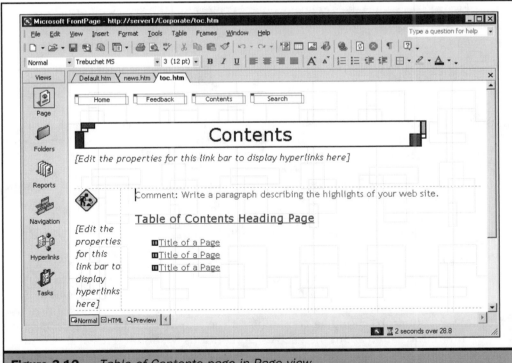

Figure 3-12. *Table of Contents page in Page view*

opened. (If you click the Preview In Browser toolbar button, you do not get a choice of browsers; your default browser automatically opens instead. Of course, if you have only one browser installed, that is what you get in either case.) Depending on your server and network configuration, you may be prompted to log onto the Internet first.

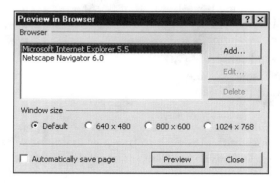

3. Click Preview to open the Table of Contents page in your selected browser. Figure 3-13 shows the Table of Contents page after the Web Component has created the hyperlinks.

4. Close your browser, return to Page view, and close the Table of Contents page.

The Feedback Page

There are many reasons to get feedback from the people who visit your web site. If your site is designed to promote a product or service, you will want to know what visitors think of your products, and as a result you'll give users a simple way of contacting you with questions. The Feedback page in the Corporate web does exactly that, as you will see by following these instructions:

1. Open the Feedback page in Page view by selecting Feedback.htm in the Open File dialog box and clicking Open.

2. When the Feedback page is opened, scroll through it to see all the elements. The lower part of the page should look like Figure 3-14.

The body of the Feedback page is a form. As you saw in Chapter 2, a form is used to gather information on a web page and then transfer the information to a Web Component or another application. This Feedback form includes a scrolling text box to enter the users' comments, a drop-down menu for users to select the subject of their comments, seven one-line text boxes for users to enter information about themselves, and buttons to submit or clear the form.

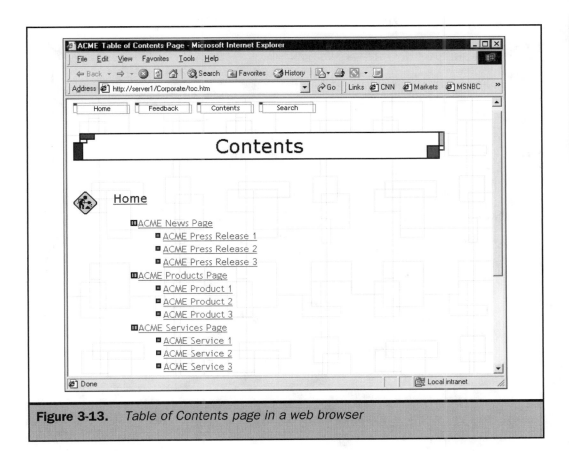

Figure 3-13.   *Table of Contents page in a web browser*

Tip   *To see the contents of a drop-down menu on a form field in Page view, double-click the drop-down menu. Click Cancel when you are done looking at this dialog box.*

3. Right-click anywhere on the form except on one of the form fields, and select Form Properties from the context menu. The file in the File Name box of the Form Properties dialog box shows the file to which the input data will be saved.

4. Click the Options button to open the Saving Results dialog box, shown in Figure 3-15. Here you can set the name and location of the file to which the data is being saved, as well as the format of the file. Additional information (for example, date, time, and username) can be selected in the Saved Fields tab of the dialog box and included in the file.

5. Close the Saving Results dialog box and then the Form Properties dialog box. Then close the Feedback page in Page view.

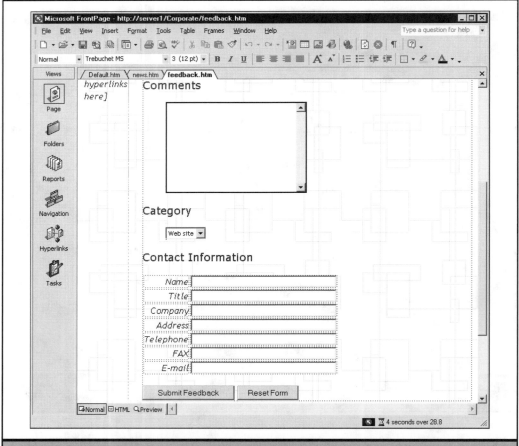

Figure 3-14.   *Lower part of the form on the Feedback page*

The Search Page

In a large web site, a table of contents does not always provide the quickest method for a user to find specific information. The Search page, on the other hand, allows users to search your web using any of the keywords that describe the information they are looking for. The

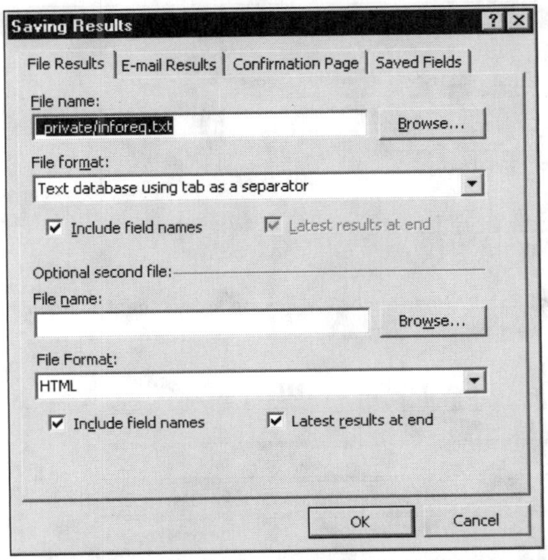

Figure 3-15.   *Setting where, what, and how to save feedback information*

Search page uses the Web Search Component to search the web and generate a results page that contains hyperlinks to web pages matching the search criterion. Figure 3-16 shows the results of a search of the Corporate web for the word "products."

You can hide pages, such as style pages or pages you are using only to include in other pages, from the Web Search Component by placing the pages in the special web folder Webname_private. The Search Form does not search this folder.

1. Open the Corporate web Search page in Page view (Search.htm in the Open File dialog box) and click Preview in the bottom left to see the full Search page shown in Figure 3-17.

2. The body of the Search page is a simple form with a single text box and two buttons. The user enters the word(s) to search for in the text box and then clicks the Start Search button. Click Normal to return to the Normal view.

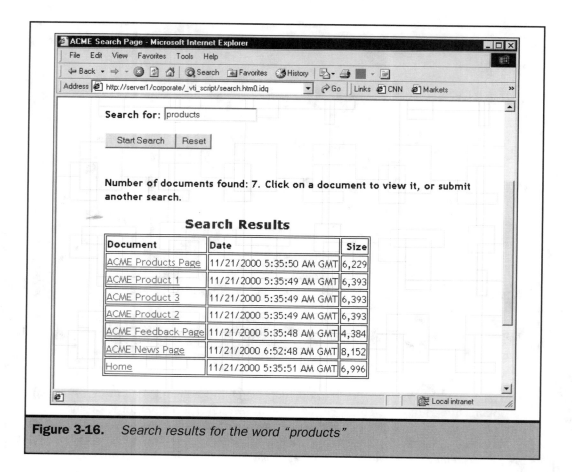

Figure 3-16. *Search results for the word "products"*

3. Right-click the form (the Search For text box), and select Search Form Properties from the context menu. In the Search Form Properties dialog box (shown next), you can set the labels for the text box and the buttons, as well as set the width of the text box. In the Search Results tab of the dialog box, you can set the options for the search results.

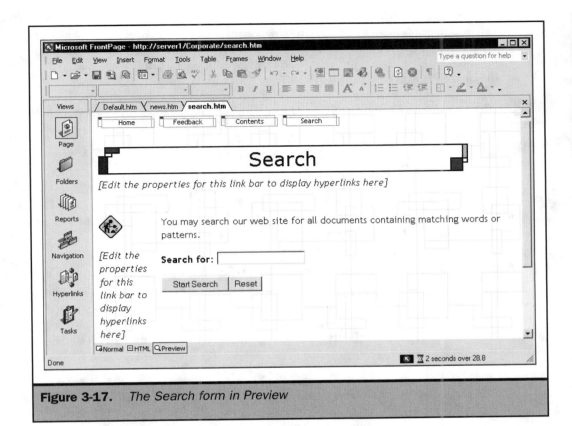

Figure 3-17.   *The Search form in Preview*

4. Click Cancel to close the Search Form Properties dialog box.

5. Click the Preview In Browser toolbar button and examine your web.

6. Use the navigation buttons in the Corporate home page to look at other pages in the web. Go to the Search page and search for the word "press." After you generate a list of pages that match that criterion, go to the Feedback page and enter some constructive criticisms of the site. Notice that when you click the Submit Feedback button in the Feedback form, you will see a confirmation page that tells you that your feedback was received.

Note *On a Windows 2000 computer, if you get the message "Service is not running" when you do a search, it is because the Indexing Service is not started. To do that, right-click My Computer and choose Manage. Open Services And Applications and select Indexing Service. Open the Action menu and choose Start. Click Yes to begin the Indexing Service when the computer is started. Be aware that it may take a few minutes for the Indexing Service to create an index.*

7. When you are finished viewing the Corporate web in your browser, close your browser, and then delete the Corporate web by choosing Delete Web from the File menu, selecting Delete This Web Entirely in the Confirm Delete dialog box that appears, and clicking OK.

Note *If you do not have Delete Web in your File menu, you can add it by opening the Tools menu and choosing Customize. Under the Commands tab of the Customize dialog box, select File in the Categories list. Scroll the Commands list until you see Delete Web, then drag Delete Web to the File menu and drop it just below Close Web.*

The Corporate web shows how easy it is to create a complete web site with the FrontPage wizards. To actually put the web on the World Wide Web, you need only add your content to the pages. In Chapter 11, you'll learn how to import word processor documents and other files into a FrontPage web.

Connecting with the Database Interface Wizard

Connecting a web site to a database allows you to dynamically change the web site's content based on the selections made by the user. This can be a complex subject and is fully described in Chapter 19. To make the process easier, FrontPage includes a Database Interface Wizard that leads you through the process. See how this is done with these steps:

1. Click the down arrow on the right of the New toolbar icon, choose Web, then when the Web Site Templates dialog box opens, select Database Interface Wizard, enter a web server and web name, and click OK. The first Database Interface Wizard dialog box will open, as you can see in Figure 3-18.

2. Click Use A Sample Database Connection, and then click Next. When you are told the database connection is made, click Next again. You are asked to select a table or view to use for the database connection.

3. Click Customers and then Next. You will be shown a list of fields that will be used to display, edit, and add entries to the database. For an existing database, you can only modify the field type on the right, but for new databases, you can add and delete records and modify all fields.

4. Click Next. You are asked to select the database interface pages you would like created. Select all three page types, and click Next. If you want the database protected with a username and password, enter them, or click Don't Protect My Database (the example shown in this chapter is not protected). Click Next.

5. You are told the Database Interface Wizard will create the pages you selected and place the results in a specified folder. Click Finish. Three pages will be created in FrontPage; one of which, the Database Editor, is shown in Figure 3-19.

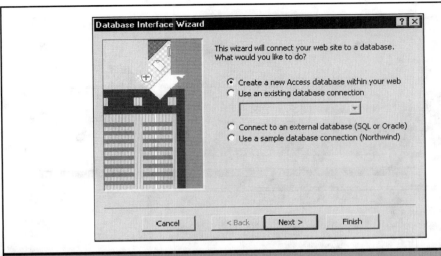

Figure 3-18.   *Choosing the type of database connection you want to use*

6. Open the Results Page (View.asp) and the Submission Page (New.asp). At first, these pages don't look like much, but by scrolling to the right you'll see something is actually there. These are database forms meant to be viewed in a browser—so do that.

7. Reopen the Database Editor page and click Preview In Browser. If you are told you haven't saved your changes (the creation of the web site), click Yes to do so. The Database Editor will then open in a browser.

8. Click the CustomerID hyperlink for a name and it will be displayed in the lower pane, as you can see in Figure 3-20. Here you can edit and delete a record. Click Results Page at the top of the Database Editor page. Here, a set of five or less database records are displayed along with a group of buttons that enable you to move from one set to the next, or jump to the first or last set of records.

9. Click Submission Form at the top of the Results Page. Here you can enter a record into the database by entering the desired contents into each field and clicking OK at the bottom of the form.

10. Return to the Database Editor page and click Add New Record. The same Submission form you just saw will open in the lower pane. Note also that you can check a record to select it and then click Delete Selected Records.

11. Close the browser and then delete the web.

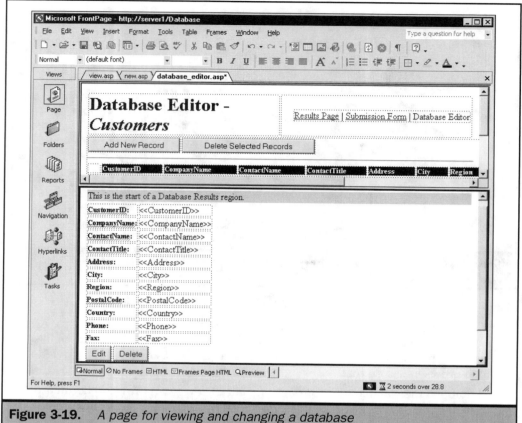

Figure 3-19. *A page for viewing and changing a database*

This gives you a brief introduction of the Database Interface Wizard. Besides using the sample database, you can create a new database in FrontPage with which you can interface, or create an interface to an existing Access database, or an external SQL or Oracle database. In Chapter 19, you'll see how to directly work with a database.

Working with the Discussion Web Wizard

Discussion groups provide a means for people to have online conversations. They provide a simple way for you to link comments about a single subject, or to find comments about a specific subject in the discussion group. You can create a separate discussion web or incorporate a discussion group in another web by using the Discussion Web Wizard:

1. Choose New | Page or Web from the File menu and click Web Site Templates, or click the down arrow next to the New toolbar button and select Web. The Web Site Templates dialog box will open. Click Discussion Web Wizard, enter

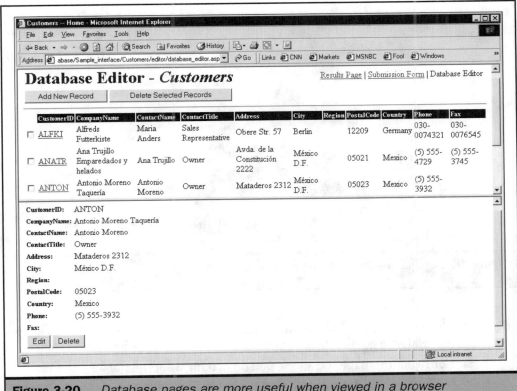

Figure 3-20.   *Database pages are more useful when viewed in a browser*

http://*server*/Discussion, in the Specify The Location Of The New Web box, and click OK. The first Discussion Web Wizard dialog box will explain how the wizard works.

2. Click Next. The second dialog box will ask you the features of a discussion group that you want to include, as you can see in Figure 3-21. Your choices include the following:

- **Submission Form** is the form used to submit comments to the discussion and is required for a discussion group.

- **Table Of Contents** provides a means of organizing and finding previously submitted comments by subject. If you want readers to read and comment about what previous contributors have submitted, then you need to include a table of contents.

- **Search Form** is an alternative way for readers to find previously contributed information. It allows a reader to find a contribution containing words other than those in the subject.

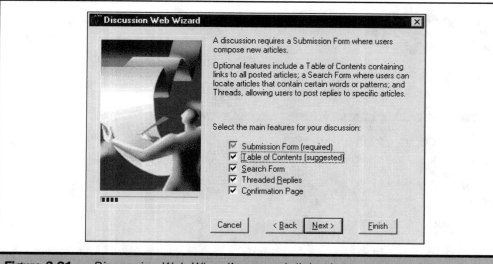

Figure 3-21. *Discussion Web Wizard's second dialog box*

- ■ **Threaded Replies** links multiple comments on the same subject. This allows the reader to go directly from one comment to the next on a given subject.

- ■ **Confirmation Page** shows the person making a submission of what the system has received.

3. Check all of the options if they are not already checked, so you can look at them, and click Next. The third dialog box will open and ask for the title you want to use as well as the folder name for the discussion group messages. Accept **Discussion** for the title, and accept the default folder name (note that discussion folder names must begin with an underscore).

4. Again, click Next. The fourth Discussion Web Wizard dialog box will ask for the fields you want to start with on the submission form such as the default fields named "Subject" and "Comments." You will be able to add more later in Page view.

5. Keep the defaults and click Next. The fifth dialog box will ask if you want to restrict the contributors to the discussion group.

6. Accept No, Anyone Can Post Articles, and click Next. Also accept the defaults in the next five dialog boxes by clicking Next in each of them, noting each time the content being generated for the Discussion Group web. (You may want to choose a web theme, which you can do when the choice is offered to you. I did here to get better illustrations.) Click Finish in the final dialog box.

7. Click Navigation view and double-click the single box in the right pane of Navigation view to open the Discussion Group Home page in Page view. From here you can open any of the pages and make any changes you desire. To try a page, though, you need to look at it in a browser. Since one of the defaults chosen was to use frames, you need to use Netscape Navigator 2.0 or later, or Internet Explorer 3.0 or later, to see the frames.

8. Preview your web in your Internet browser, and your Discussion Group web Home page will appear as shown in Figure 3-22.

9. Click Post A New Article. In the form that appears, enter a subject, your name, and some comments, then click Post Article. (If you get a message saying you are about to send information over the Internet and other people might see it, click Yes.) The confirmation should appear showing the subject you entered.

10. In the Confirmation page, click the Refresh The Main Page hyperlink. Back at the Home page you saw in Figure 3-22, you should again see the subject you entered

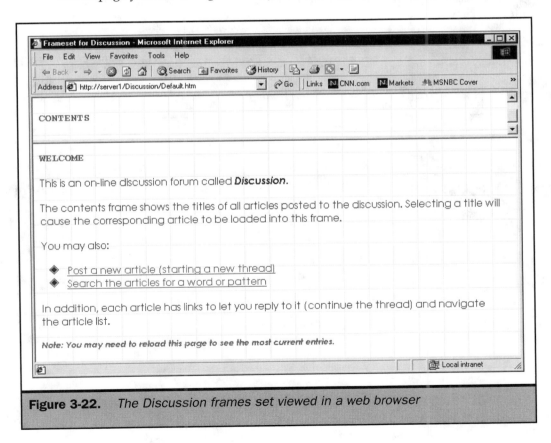

Figure 3-22. *The Discussion frames set viewed in a web browser*

under Contents. You may need to click the Refresh button in your browser to see articles that were just entered. Click your subject and that message will appear in the bottom frame, as shown in Figure 3-23. You will see the name, the date and time you made the submission, and the comments you entered. Depending on the options you selected for your discussion group, you may see other information about the person who submitted the comment as well.

11. The link bar in the bottom frame now has several new entries: Contents, Search, Post (to start a new thread), Reply (to add a comment to an existing thread), Next and Previous (to go forward and backward, respectively, in the current thread), and Up (to go to the next thread).

12. Try these new link bar entries by making several submissions, both independent and in reply to another submission, so you can see how the navigation works. When you are done, close the browser and delete the web.

A discussion group can be a powerful means of communication, and FrontPage offers an easy way to create one.

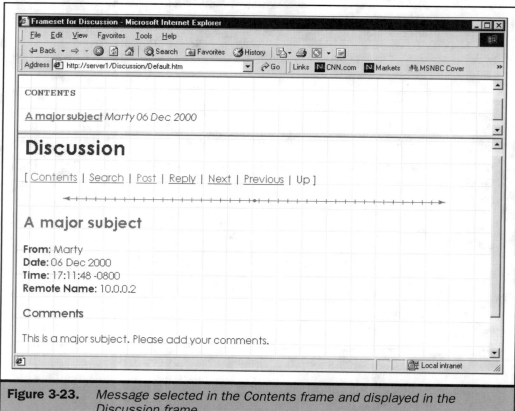

Figure 3-23.   *Message selected in the Contents frame and displayed in the Discussion frame*

Using the Import Web Wizard

If FrontPage 2002 is the first version of FrontPage you've used, you may have a number of existing webs that you will want to convert to FrontPage webs. The process is extremely simple when you use the Import Web Wizard.

1. If it isn't open already, open the New Page Or Web task pane on the right, and as you have done previously, select Web Site Templates, click Import Web Wizard, and enter a location and name for the new web. Click OK and the first wizard dialog box will be displayed.

2. In the Import Web Wizard dialog box, shown in Figure 3-24, select a source for your web—either from your local computer or network, or from the World Wide Web. If you choose a source on your local computer or network, enter the complete path name of the folder where the web is located, or click the Browse button to locate the folder. Select the Include Subfolders check box. If you choose the World Wide Web, enter the complete URL and whether it requires a secure connection. Then click Next.

3. If you select a folder on your computer, then the next dialog box will display a list of the files located in the selected folder. Select the files you want to *exclude* from the new FrontPage web (if any) and click the Exclude button. Click Next and then click Finish.

4. If you select a web site, then the next dialog box will display a set of limits that you can impose on what you import. Select the limits that you want to impose, click Next, and then click Finish.

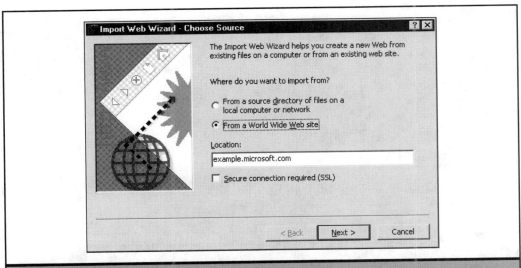

Figure 3-24.   *The Import Web Wizard opening dialog box*

That's all there is to it. Your imported web will be displayed in FrontPage, ready for you to work on it.

Page Wizards

In addition to the wizards that create a full web site, FrontPage comes with several wizards that create a single page. Depending on your installation you may see either one or three page wizards in the Page Templates dialog box, shown in Figure 3-25. If you see only one wizard, it is the Form Page Wizard, which leads you through the creation of a single page form by allowing you to select the information you want the form to collect. This was briefly demonstrated in Chapter 2 and will be covered further in Chapter 8. The other two page wizards will only appear if you are connected to a server with SharePoint installed (see *Teaming Up with the Team Web Site* in Chapter 4) and have an open web in FrontPage. These are the Document Library View Page Wizard, which creates a page to view the Team Web Site's document library, and the List View Page Wizard, which creates a page to view a Team Web Site list. SharePoint and the Team Web Site are described briefly in Chapter 4 and in more detail in Chapter 24.

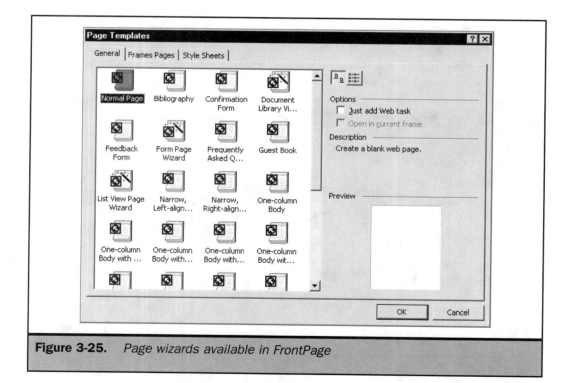

Figure 3-25. *Page wizards available in FrontPage*

Themes

FrontPage 2002 comes with a selection of 67 themes that can be applied to an entire FrontPage web or to individual pages. Themes apply and control many different elements of a web page and can consistently apply these elements to *every* page in a web.

Having coordinated graphic elements, background images, and link bars gives a unifying feel to your web site. Visitors will see familiar color schemes, navigation tools, and graphic images at each page in your site.

Some of the elements that are applied to pages incorporating a theme include:

- Text colors
- Bullet styles and colors
- Font sizes and types
- Link bars and buttons
- Heading styles
- Horizontal lines
- Page background images
- Page banners

Themes are applied to an entire FrontPage web using the Themes dialog box (called "Choose Theme" when using a wizard) you saw in Figure 3-3. You have already seen that when you create a FrontPage web using one of the wizards, you are prompted to apply a theme. You can change or remove this theme at any time.

Each FrontPage theme can be modified by selecting or deselecting one of the top-three check boxes in the lower-left of each theme. Those check boxes allow you to include Vivid Colors, Active Graphics, or a Background Picture. The bottom check box, Apply Using CSS, lets you choose whether to apply the theme using cascading style sheets (CSS), which uses special HTML commands to apply the styles associated with the theme. CSS is discussed further in Chapters 10 and 12.

Assigning Themes to FrontPage Webs

You can assign a theme to your FrontPage web whether or not that web already has a theme applied to it. So, for example, if you generate a FrontPage web using a template or wizard, you can change the theme of that web. Or if you create a web from scratch, you can also assign a theme to it. The process is the same regardless of whether your web already has a theme.

1. Open (or create) a FrontPage web. A web page without formatting or themes tends to leave the pages looking a bit barren, as you can see in Figure 3-26. You can, however, always elect to format pages one at a time. You will learn to do this in Chapter 6.

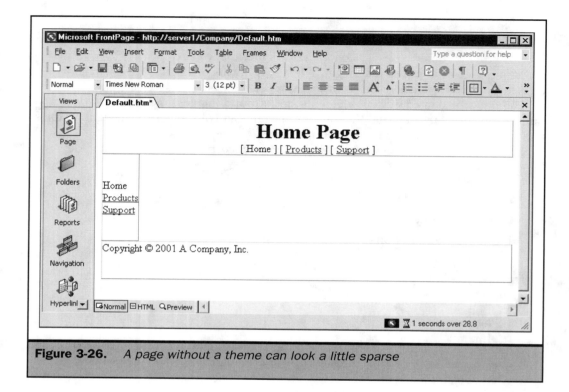

Figure 3-26.   *A page without a theme can look a little sparse*

2. Open the Format menu and choose Theme. The Themes dialog box that you saw in Figure 3-3 will open.

3. Click All Pages to apply the theme to all pages in the web, select a theme, and view the results in the Sample Of Theme area. You can experiment with any theme by selecting different combinations of the theme effects check boxes before you apply the theme. Note some of the objects that are included in a theme:

   ■ A banner at the top of the page

   ■ Navigation buttons at the top of the page

   ■ A horizontal line above the bottom navigation buttons

   ■ A matching set of different-sized bullets for bullet lists

   ■ A color scheme that color coordinates page text, banners, bullets, and horizontal lines

   ■ A unified color scheme for links, followed links, and active links

4. Below the list of Themes are four check boxes which add special effects to a selected theme or apply them using CSS. As soon as you click one of the first three check boxes, the effect of that selection is applied immediately in the Sample Of Theme area. (You do not see any effect from using CSS.)

- Choosing the Vivid Colors option brightens the color scheme and generally transforms your site from subtle to brash.

- Choosing the Background Picture check box replaces the solid color background with a tiled graphic image.

  While you can test the effects of the Vivid Colors and Background Picture check boxes in the Sample Of Theme area, you will not see the full effect of active graphics when you select the Active Graphics check box. This option transforms navigation buttons in your web pages into dynamic hover buttons. To test these hover buttons, you will have to apply your theme and open your web page using a browser that interprets Java applets. In Figure 3-27, the Hover Button effect causes the arrows to be vertical when the mouse moves over the button.

5. After you decide which theme and theme options to apply to your web pages, click OK. If you are applying the theme to an existing web, you are warned that applying the theme will permanently change some existing formatting. If you want to do that, click Yes. Then look at the effect in your web pages by opening them in Page view or in your browser.

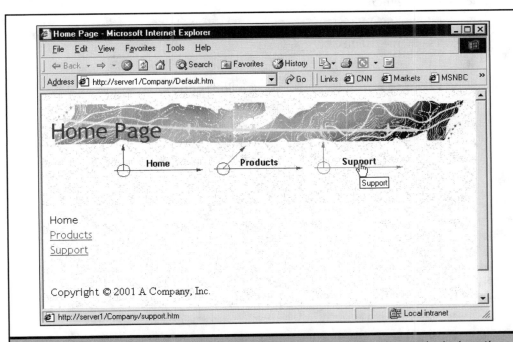

Figure 3-27.   *The Active Graphics option causes the arrow to be vertical when the mouse hovers over it*

Assigning Themes to Web Pages

Themes can be assigned to a single web page as well as to an entire FrontPage web. You assign themes to pages by selecting the page and then choosing Selected Pages in the Themes dialog box. When you do that, you affect only the selected web page.

Overall, the purpose of a theme is to provide a cohesive, unifying look and feel to your entire web site. Therefore, themes are usually applied to entire webs. However, there are a number of reasons why you might want to assign themes to an individual page. You could decide that one or more pages in your web should not look like they are part of the overall web site. These pages might include legal disclaimers, pages that provide information that isn't integral to the overall message of the web, or pages you want to stand out from the rest of the web.

To apply a theme to a single web page, open it in Page view and edit the theme assigned to the page using the following steps:

1. With your web page open in Page view, open the Format menu and choose Theme.
2. The Themes dialog box opens. By default, the Themes dialog box will first display the theme that is applied to the entire FrontPage web.
3. The buttons in the upper-left of the Themes dialog box allow two options. You can:
   - Apply the theme you choose to all pages, or
   - Apply the theme you choose to just the selected pages.
4. From the theme list box, choose to:
   - Use the web's default theme, which is automatically applied to a new page
   - Use one of the 67 themes that come with FrontPage 2002
   - Have no theme, or
   - Modify one of the existing themes and save it as a new theme.
5. Once you have previewed your theme in the Sample Of Theme area of the Themes dialog box, click OK to apply the theme. The selected theme and theme options are applied to the open page.

There are a couple of other ways to see what theme is applied to a page, as well as remove a theme from a page. You can remove themes in the Page Properties dialog box. With your web page open in Page view, right-click anywhere on the page and choose Page Properties from the context menu. If a theme has been applied to the web page, the Page Properties dialog box has a Custom tab (see Figure 3-28) that lists the applied theme in the User Variables section. You can delete a theme by selecting the theme from the User Variables list and clicking the Remove button.

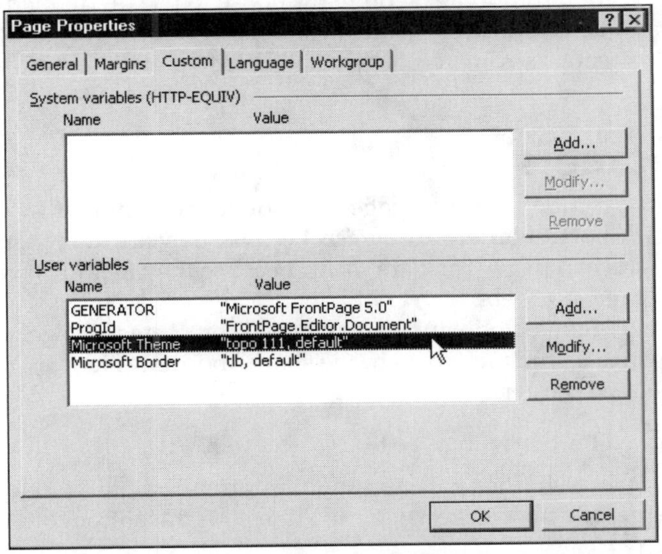

Figure 3-28.   *A page's theme can be removed in the Page Properties Custom tab*

You can also view or remove themes in the HTML view by clicking HTML in the bottom left of the Page view window. The HTML code

```
<meta name="Microsoft Theme" content="topo 111">
```

indicates that the Topo theme has been applied to the page. You can remove a theme by selecting this line of HTML code in the HTML tab and pressing the DEL key.

Along with applying a new theme to an open web page, you can also edit many of the page format elements using page formatting. For example, you can change font color, font size, and paragraph alignment. However, other formatting options cannot be changed after applying a theme, such as the background and the default text and hyperlink colors. If you open the Themes dialog box from a page with an existing theme, there is a Modify button that lets you change the colors, graphics, and styles used in a theme and then save it as a new theme or a replacement for an existing theme.

Themes have many advantages, including the fact that they create attractive, professional, coordinated, and useful web pages very quickly. The downside is that your ability to fine-tune the look and feel of your web site is constrained by themes.

While learning about FrontPage, you may choose to use predefined themes to provide layout and design ideas. As you become proficient with FrontPage, you may use other tools to create coordinated pages that are completely unique to your site.

Shared Borders

Shared borders are sections of a web page set aside for content that will appear on each page of your web. Shared borders are *borders* because they are at the top, bottom, left, or (rarely) right side of a page. They are *shared* because they include content that is shared by every page in a web.

Shared borders often include link bars. All the FrontPage webs generated by wizards or templates include link bars in the shared borders. Here are some examples of other useful shared borders:

- A top shared border with page titles
- A bottom shared border with copyright information, site contact information, and other text or images you want to appear on the bottom of every page in your site
- A left shared border with general information you want to place in every page in your site, such as links

Tip   *Shared borders are rarely placed on the right side of web pages because your users may not see them. Depending on the size and resolution of the users' screen, and the size of their browser window, the right side of your web pages may not be visible to them unless they use the horizontal scroll bar to see it. Since shared borders often include link bars, you will normally want the shared border to be visible as soon as your web page downloads.*

All FrontPage themes assign some combination of shared borders to web pages. These shared borders can be changed. So, for example, even though a theme may apply three shared borders to every page in a FrontPage web, you can change it so only two shared borders appear on a given page.

If you did not create your FrontPage web from a template or wizard, you can still assign shared borders to your web. But FrontPage will not insert link bars in your shared borders unless you use the Navigation view to assign how the pages in your web relate to each other (or generate the web from a template or wizard).

Assigning Shared Borders to a FrontPage Web

Global changes can affect the layout of shared borders in every page. Use the following steps to see how this works:

1. Open or create a FrontPage web and select Shared Borders from the Format menu. (You may have to fully extend the menu.) The Shared Borders dialog box opens, as shown in Figure 3-29.

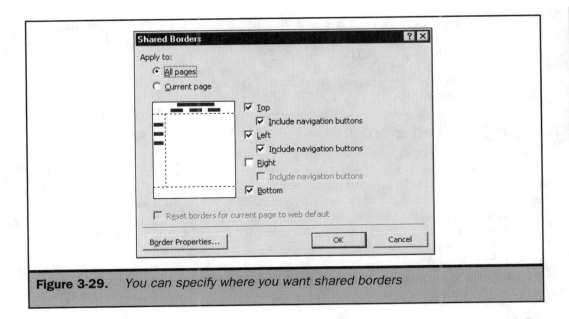

Figure 3-29.   *You can specify where you want shared borders*

2. Use the Top, Left, Right, and Bottom check boxes in the Shared Borders dialog box to select or turn off any of the four borders; use the three Include Navigation Buttons check boxes to add navigation buttons to the borders. If All Pages is selected, the borders you select will be applied to or removed from every page in your web by default, although you can turn them off or change them for specific pages.

Tip   *The shared borders you assign in the Shared Borders dialog box will override any shared borders assigned by a theme.*

3. When you have chosen which shared borders to add or remove, click OK. The shared borders are applied immediately to the pages in your web that do not have specific shared borders.

Assigning Shared Borders to a Web Page

Shared borders can be edited and customized for individual web pages. For example, you can apply a bottom shared border to some but not all pages in your web:

1. Open the page in Page view on which you want to customize the shared borders.

2. Open the Format menu and select Shared Borders (you may have to extend the menu).

3. Choose the Current Page option in the Shared Borders dialog box, and define additional shared borders or remove current shared borders by selecting or clearing the applicable check boxes.

After you create a new shared border for a page, the content of that shared border is available to other pages.

Changing Shared Borders

You can define a maximum of four shared borders for a FrontPage web. You can elect to apply or not apply different borders to different pages, but you can make only limited changes to shared borders on individual pages. If you want to place different content on each web page (and you will), do so independently of shared borders. The purpose of shared borders is to place the same content on multiple pages.

Think of shared borders as being similar to headers and footers in printed documents. They are there to include content that you want to repeat on each page. Therefore, when you change a shared border in one page, for the most part you change that shared border on every page to which the shared border is applied. Both the content and the properties of shared borders can be changed.

Editing the Content of Shared Borders

The content of the shared borders is edited in Page view:

1. Click the content of any shared border to edit it.

2. You can add text to any shared border by simply typing it in. For example, type **Copyright 2001, A Company, Inc.** in the bottom shared border. (You can add a copyright symbol after the word "Copyright" by opening the Insert menu, choosing Symbol, locating and double-clicking the copyright symbol, and clicking Close.)

3. Click outside the shared border when you are done entering or editing its contents.

After you edit a shared border for a particular page, the shared border content will appear on all other pages. In Figure 3-30, a bottom-shared border has been assigned to a page in a web.

Changing the Properties of Shared Borders

Besides the content of a shared border, you can also change the border properties that include either or both the background color and/or a background picture. You can do this by right-clicking any shared border and choosing Border Properties or by choosing

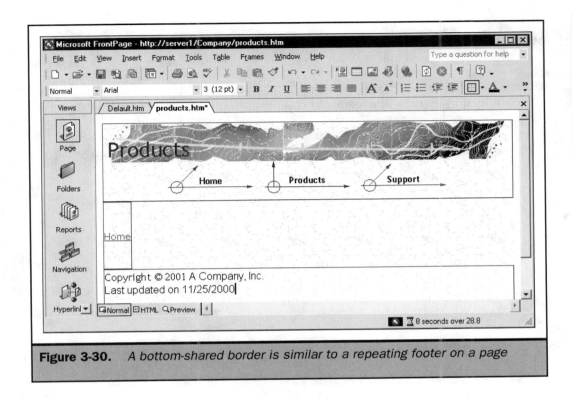

Figure 3-30.   *A bottom-shared border is similar to a repeating footer on a page*

Border Properties in the Shared Borders dialog box you saw in Figure 3-29. This opens the Border Properties dialog box, like this:

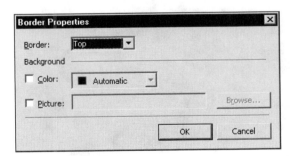

In the Border Properties dialog box, you can choose the border you want to change and the color and/or picture you want contained in that border.

Editing Link Bars

Link bars are generated automatically in FrontPage. They include hyperlinks to other pages within your web site. How does FrontPage know the relationship between pages in your web site? FrontPage uses the page relationships shown in Navigation view to place navigation buttons. The hierarchy you assign when you create a web (shown in Navigation view) determines the options available to you for link bars.

To assign link bars to shared borders, you must choose the Include Navigation Buttons option in the Shared Borders dialog box that was described earlier. If you created your FrontPage web using a wizard or template, or independently chose the Include Navigation Buttons option, link bars are created automatically. The actual page-to-page relationships utilized by the link bars are best viewed and changed in Navigation view. Try defining new relationships by following these steps:

1. Open a FrontPage web, choose Navigation view, and open the Folder List by clicking the Toggle Pane icon on the toolbar.

2. Drag web pages from the Folder List (left pane) into the Navigation view (right pane) as shown in Figure 3-31.

3. You can define the relationship between pages by how you place them in relation to each other.

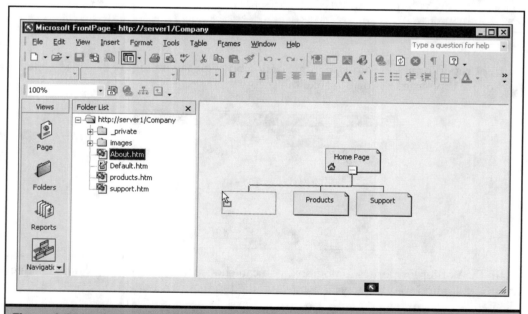

Figure 3-31.   *Define and change link bar relationships in Navigation view*

Note

The view shown in Figure 3-31 is the default portrait view of a web hierarchy (and the one referred to in the following points). Using the Navigation toolbar (which is normally open when you are in Navigation view), you can switch to landscape view.

- A page that is connected to and below another page in Navigation view is referred to as a *child level* page.

- A page that is connected to and above another page is a *parent level* page.

- Pages that are connected by a horizontal line are referred to as *same level* pages. These relationships determine the buttons that can be included in link bars.

Once you have defined page relationships in Navigation view, you can assign link bars in Page view:

1. Open a web page in Page view.

2. Click a shared border in which you will place or edit a link bar.

3. If a link bar already exists, double-click it. If there is no link bar, select Navigation from the Insert menu, choose Link Bars | Bar Based On Navigation Structure, then select a style and orientation. The Link Bar Properties dialog box appears as shown in Figure 3-32.

4. In the Hyperlinks To Add To Page area, choose one of the six options: Parent Level, Same Level, Back And Next (navigates between pages on the Same Level that are next to each other in Navigation view), Child Level, Global Level (Home page and other pages at that top level), or Child Pages Under Home.

Tip

To fully understand where the link bar hyperlinks go, turn off the Home Page and Parent Page check boxes and try out each of the six options (several times) in the Hyperlinks To Add To Page area and look at the diagram on the left (keep turning off the Home Page and Parent Page check boxes to see just the effect of the six options).

5. Regardless of which option you choose, you can include a link to the home page and/or the parent page for the open page by selecting one or both of the Additional Pages check boxes.

6. In the Style tab, you can choose a style for the link bar by scrolling down the list and clicking the one you want. In the Orientation And Appearance area of the dialog box you can define the layout of navigation buttons that will appear on your link bar and whether or not they use vivid colors and active graphics. Horizontal and vertical layouts are previewed in the small preview area on the left side of the Orientation And Appearance area of the dialog box.

7. When you have selected all your link bar options, click OK.

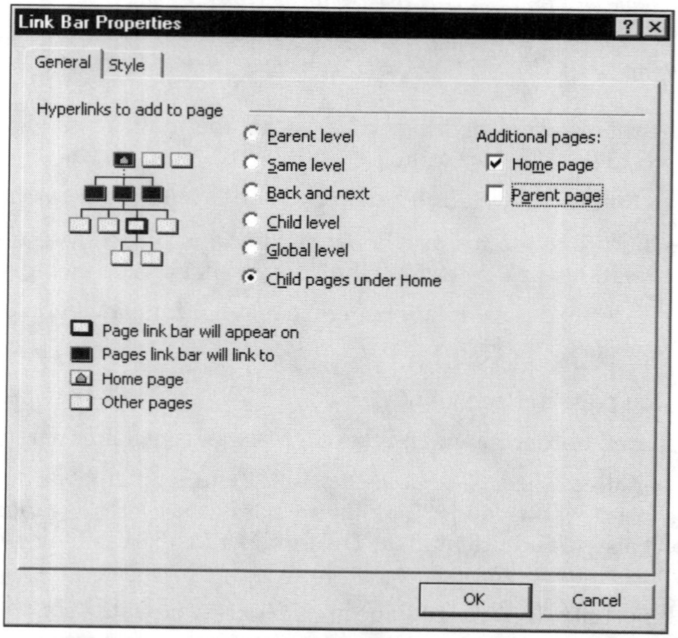

Figure 3-32. The Link Bar Properties dialog box determines the function of navigation buttons

By combining FrontPage web templates and wizards with themes, shared borders, and link bars, you can create professional and sophisticated integrated web applications with ease.

The
Complete
Reference

Chapter 4

Using Templates

As you now know, wizards and templates provide easy ways to create webs with FrontPage. In Chapter 3, you saw how to use wizards to create complete webs and pages by answering questions about the web you want to build. In the first part of this chapter, you'll see how to use templates to build both webs and pages without input from you, and the results that they produce. In the second part of this chapter, you'll learn how to create your own page templates. This will allow you to easily create new webs or add pages to existing webs without having to re-create a design or layout each time.

Web Templates

FrontPage provides templates at both the web level and the page level. Begin looking at the web level by loading FrontPage. When this is complete, if you are not in Folders view, click Folders in the Views bar. Then click the arrow to the right of New on the toolbar, and choose Web. The Web Site Templates dialog box will open and display the templates and wizards you can use. There are six web templates:

- One Page Web
- Customer Support Web
- Empty Web
- Personal Web
- Project Web
- SharePoint Team Web Site

Using the One Page Web Template

The usual starting place for creating a general-purpose web is with the One Page Web template. This template creates a web folder structure for your server with a single page. Do that now with these instructions (the Web Site Templates dialog box should be open on your screen):

1. Click One Page Web in the Web Sites tab of the Web Site Templates dialog box.

2. Enter the server and folder names where you want the new web stored in the Specify The Location Of The New Web drop-down list box. For the lack of any other name, type **Onepage**, and then click OK.

3. If you are not already there, click Folders in the Views bar. As you can see in Figure 4-1, this creates a web with a single page, the home page Default.htm.

4. Double-click Default.htm to open the home page in Page view. You will see a blank page. Just to keep track of it, type **Home Page**.

GETTING STARTED

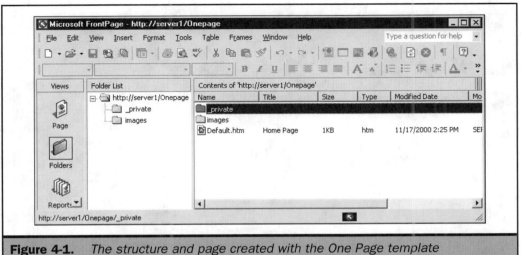

Figure 4-1.   *The structure and page created with the One Page template*

You can easily add pages to a web created with the One Page Web template in Page, Folders, or Navigation view, but in Navigation view you can also easily and graphically specify the relationship of new pages with existing pages. Try the following instructions and see how new pages are integrated into the web that was created in Navigation view.

1. After you generate a new One Page Web, click Navigation in the Views bar, click the Home Page icon in the right pane, and then click New Page on the toolbar. (You can create as many pages as you need by clicking this button.) The first page you generate is called "New Page 1" and is a child page to the Home Page.

2. Create a second page with the New Page button, and continue to click New Page to generate four additional pages for a total of six in addition to the home page.

3. Edit the navigational relationships between pages by dragging the pages in the right (Navigation) pane of the Navigation view such that pages 4 and 5 are under page 2, and page 6 is under page 4, as shown in Figure 4-2.

Right-click an empty area of the right pane of Navigation view, and choose Zoom | Size To Fit to see all the pages in case any are outside the window. If it is open, you can also do this using the Navigation toolbar, as shown in Figure 4-2.

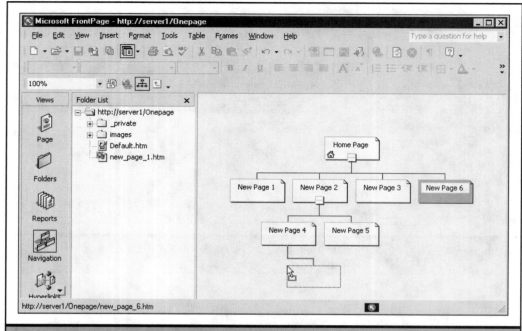

Figure 4-2. *Dragging a page into position in Navigation view*

4. Click the Home Page to select it, open the Format menu, choose Shared Borders (expand the menu if necessary), and make sure All Pages is selected. Next, click Top, Include Navigation Buttons, Bottom, and then click OK.

5. Double-click the Home Page to open it in Page view. Right-click the top comment ("Edit the properties...") for the top-shared border and choose Link Bar Properties. In the Link Bar Properties dialog box, choose Child Level, uncheck Home Page and Parent Page (if checked), and click OK. This puts three buttons at the top of the Home Page to allow you to easily get from the home page to New Pages 1, 2, and 3, as shown next. You can see how easy it is to build a multipage web starting with a One Page Web template.

Note *You replace the comments with your text by clicking the comment and typing your text.*

6. When you are ready, open the File menu, choose Delete Web, then click Delete This Web Entirely, and click OK (if you don't see a Delete Web option on the file menu, you need to drag it there from Tools | Customize | Commands as described in Chapter 3).

As you create your own webs, you'll probably use the One Page Web template often to build the small or custom webs that you'll need.

Applying the Empty Web Template

If you are going to import web content (see Chapter 11 for more on this subject) and want a FrontPage structure in which to place it, then the Empty Web template is the way to start. This template creates a web folder structure for your server, but does not generate any web pages. Do that now with these instructions:

1. Click the down arrow next to New on the toolbar, click Web, click Empty Web in the Web Site Templates dialog box, enter a server and folder name, and click OK.

2. Click Folders in the Views bar and you will see that the folder structure has been created for the web, but with no pages, like this:

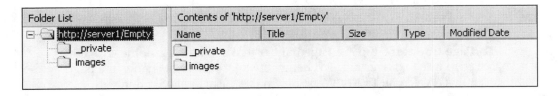

Why go to all this trouble for an empty web? FrontPage needs the folder structure to perform its functions. Since most webs have a number of pages and other elements, such as forms, the folder structure is used for organizing the web and making it easy to use and maintain. You can easily add pages to this web just as you did with the One Page Web.

3. Open the File menu and choose Delete Web, click Delete This Web Entirely, and click OK.

Creating a Personal Web

FrontPage's Personal Web template creates a five-page web to publicize a person or small organization. See what this web is like by building it with the following steps:

1. Open the Web Site Templates dialog box, click Personal Web, enter a server and folder name, and click OK. The new web appears and if you look at Folders view, you will see the six pages (the six .htm files) that you can customize, as shown here:

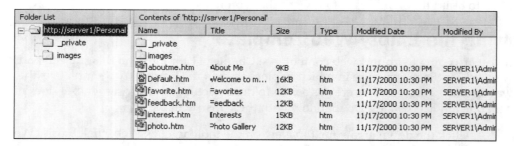

2. Double-click the Welcome Page (the Default.htm file) to open it in Page view. The page that opens has a lot of features incorporated into it, some of which are shown in Figure 4-3. These features are only suggestions and can be removed or customized. They provide a starting set of elements that you can use or delete depending on your needs, and you can add any other features you want. Among the important features are the following:

- **Page title** at the top is a Page Banner that contains a graphic with the page title text overlaid. To change the text, you must change the page title ("Welcome To My Web Site" in this case) in Navigation view by right-clicking the page and choosing Rename. Changing the name in the Page Properties dialog box or editing the text on the page does not permanently change the title.

- **Table framework** is used to separate the various parts of the page. Each of the cells is identified by a dotted line in Normal view, but in Preview view you only see the lines that have been drawn. Tables are discussed in Chapter 7.

- **Link bar** below the table framework and to the left of the title is a series of lines of text that are hyperlinks to other pages in the web. You can edit a link bar by right-clicking the text that is or represents the link bar and then choosing Link Bar Properties. The Link Bar Properties dialog box will open, where you can change the hyperlinks used for navigation and the orientation and appearance of the buttons. You'll work with this dialog box later in the chapter.

Figure 4-3.   *Home Page created with the Personal Web template*

The Link Bar Properties dialog box allows you to determine the link bar buttons from among pages hierarchically above (Parent Level), below (Child Level), or on the same level in the Hyperlinks To Add To Page area of the dialog box. This allows you to direct how the link bar will be built.

- **Plain text** is text that you can replace with your own words by simply editing it as you would in a word processor. For example, Michael Smith might replace "Welcome to my Web site!" with "Welcome to Michael Smith's Web Site!"

- **Hyperlinks** are marked with underlines. They are links to other pages in your web site or other sites on an intranet or the Internet.

- A **Background image** may be included in the page. This is a small graphic file that is *tiled* or repeated across the background of the web page.

- **Text font and colors** have been assigned. These, along with the background image or color, are part of a theme that has been attached to this web.

- A **Search form** is included to search the web. Forms are discussed in Chapter 8.

- A link to a **Photo Gallery** page, where a number of photographs can be automatically displayed with captions, has been provided. See the discussion of the Photo Gallery page template later in this chapter.

- A **Hit Counter**, which counts the number of times a page is opened in a browser, is included on the left of the page under the link bar. A hit counter gives a very rough approximation of the number of visits to a web page and is discussed in Chapter 9.

- **Time stamp** is placed on the page using the Date and Time option of the Insert menu. It will automatically display the date the page was last updated or edited. You can change the time-stamp properties by double-clicking the date to open the Date and Time dialog box, shown here:

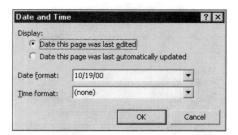

When you are done looking at the Home page, choose Open from the File menu to view other pages that were generated by the Personal Web template. Then close Page view and delete the web you created. The "simple" personal web you can create with the Personal Web template is a good starting point for many webs and offers a number of useful features. Consider using it as you create your own webs.

Using the Project Web Template

The Project Web template creates a multipage web, shown in Figure 4-4, that is used to keep people up-to-date on a project. It lists a project's staff members, schedule, and status, and provides independent page headers and footers, an archive, a search engine, and a discussion bulletin board. (You've seen how some of these features are used in the webs you created with wizards in Chapter 3.) Follow these steps to look at some of the features that are unique to this template:

1. Open the Web Site Templates dialog box, select Project Web, enter a server and folder name for the web, such as "Project," and click OK. A new web will be created and will appear. In Navigation view, it will look like Figure 4-4.

2. Double-click the Home icon in Navigation view to open Page view. The page shown in Figure 4-5 will be displayed.

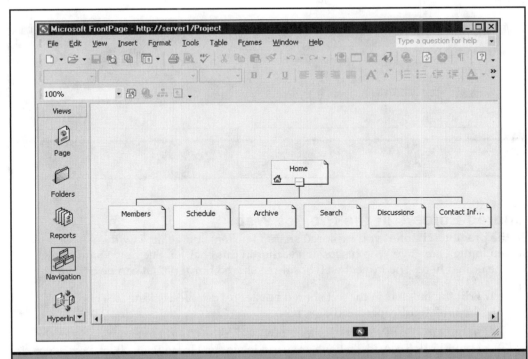

Figure 4-4. *Structure created by the Project Web template*

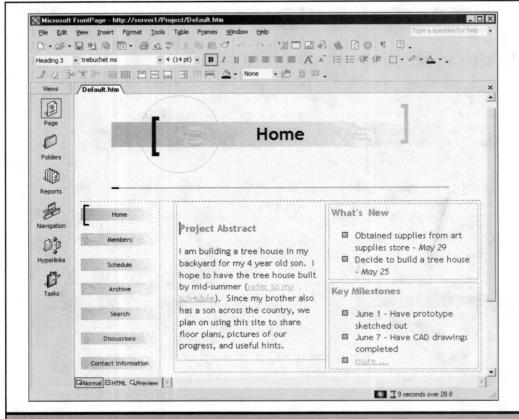

Figure 4-5. *Project Web home page with title and link bars*

Shared Borders in the Project Web

In the previous chapter, you explored shared borders and again saw them added to a web in the One Page Web discussion earlier in this chapter. See how shared borders can be edited here. The Project web has three shared borders that can be edited.

1. Edit the link bar in the left shared border by double-clicking it. This opens the Link Bar Properties dialog box.

2. In the Link Bar Properties dialog box, select the Child Level option from the Hyperlinks To Add To Page area and leave the Home Page check box selected. In the Style tab, leave the style and orientation as they are set (Use Page's Theme and Vertical), and click OK.

3. The names that appear in a link bar are the names of the other pages in the web as determined by the Link Bar Properties dialog box. To change the actual words used in the link bar, you must change the page names in Navigation view by clicking a page twice slowly (not double-clicking) and entering a new name followed by pressing ENTER.

4. Scroll to the bottom of the page. Note the bottom-shared border as shown next. It has the automatic Date and Time component (although it is showing only the date here).

Home | Members | Schedule | Archive | Search | Discussions | Contact Information

Copyright or other proprietary statement goes here.
For problems or questions regarding this web contact [ProjectEmail].
Last updated: 11/18/00.

5. Open and review the Members, Schedule, and Archive pages. On each you'll see the shared borders, as well as other features you saw on the Project Web Home Page.

Note

Since you chose Child Level in the Link Bar Properties dialog box, you only have Home in the link bar of the pages below the Home page. If you change it on the child pages so you have links there, you won't have any links on the Home page (try it and see), but the original default of Child Pages Under Home works for both page types.

Searches and Discussion Groups

The Project web that you created incorporates two other FrontPage-created features—text searches and discussion groups—that add interactivity to the web. You saw how these features worked in the Corporate Presence web you created in Chapter 3. To review how these work in the Project web:

1. Open the Project Web Search page in Page view by choosing Open from the File menu and double-clicking Search.htm. Your screen should look like Figure 4-6. This page includes a one-field form that allows you to search the documents in the current web for a particular text string that you have entered in the form.

Note

Depending on how you left your link bar properties, your link bar may be different than what is shown in Figure 4-6.

2. This search form is another FrontPage Web component. You can edit its characteristics by right-clicking the search area and choosing Search Form Properties.

3. Close the Search page and open the Project Web Discussions page (Discuss.htm), which contains links to two discussion groups (Requirements Discussion and Knowledge Base). The discussion groups are separate. They allow people to enter comments, and others to comment on the original comments, thereby creating threads on a given subject. Most online forums follow this format.

4. To get a better perspective of the Project web, click Preview In Browser on the toolbar and follow the navigation buttons to look at the various pages. When you are finished viewing the Project web, close your browser. Then delete the Project web.

A web that has been created with the Project Web template provides an excellent communications tool, not only for projects, but also for any team, operation, or department.

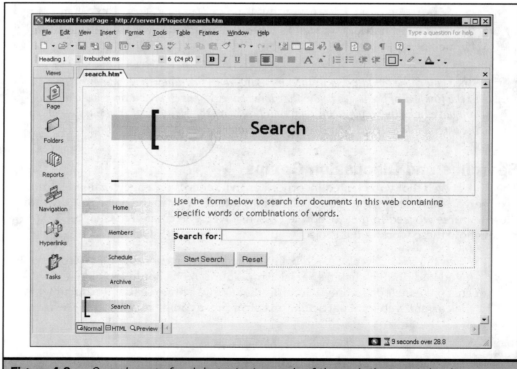

Figure 4-6. *Search page for doing a text search of the web that contains it*

Applying the Customer Support Web Template

The Customer Support Web template, shown in Figure 4-7, makes a lot of information available to users in several ways and allows users to provide information to you in two ways. In doing this, the web uses FrontPage features you have already seen, but with different twists. We'll look at those differences next.

1. Create a Customer Support web using the Customer Support Web template in the Web Site Templates dialog box Web Sites tab. In Navigation view, your result should look like Figure 4-7.

2. Double-click the Customer Support Web page, the home page for this web. This page has a top-, bottom-, and left-shared border, with link bars in all three.

3. Close the home page and then open, look at, and close the What's New and F.A.Q. (frequently asked questions) pages. These pages, well-designed for their purposes, are simply combinations of text and hyperlinks with the included header and footer.

4. Open the Customer Support—Service Request page (Service.htm). If you scroll down the page, you'll see a special form for collecting information about a problem with a product. As with all other features in a wizard- or template-created web, you can customize this, changing the text, size, and content of the fields.

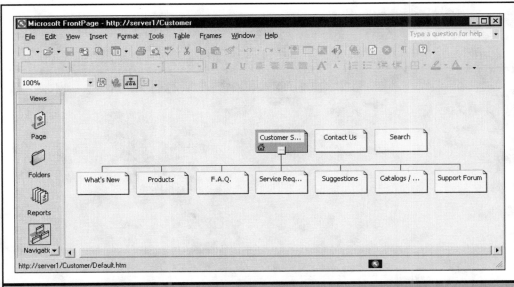

Figure 4-7.   *Customer Support Web template structure*

5. To experience changing one of the fields on the form, right-click the drop-down list box that displays Select Product/Service, and choose Form Field Properties. The field's Properties dialog box will open, as shown in Figure 4-8. Here you can change the name of the field in the top text box and change the choices the field presents to the user by using the Add, Modify, and Remove buttons.

6. Click Product 1 to select it, then click Modify. In the Modify Choice dialog box, delete "Product 1" and replace it with "**Blue Widget**." Click OK.

7. Click Add to open the Add Choice dialog box. Type **Green Widget** in the Choice text box, leave other settings as they are, and click OK. Back in the Drop-Down Box Properties dialog box, click the Product 2 entry to select it, then click Move Down twice to move it below Service 2.

8. Click OK to close the Drop-Down Box Properties dialog box and then close and save the Service Request page; open, look at, and close the Suggestions page (Suggest.htm), which allows customers to use a form to submit suggestions.

9. Open the Suggestions From Customers page (Feedback.htm), which is used to contain the suggestions that customers have entered using the Suggestions page.

10. Close the Suggestions From Customers page and then open, look at, and close the Discussion and Search pages. These contain a discussion group and a search form similar to those you saw in the Project web.

11. Open your Customer Support web in a browser and try its features, submitting a service request and a suggestion. This will show you how these pages work. You should then see a confirmation page.

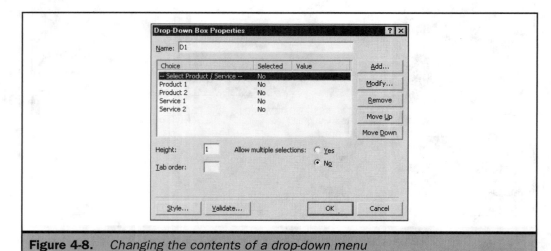

Figure 4-8.   *Changing the contents of a drop-down menu*

12. After you enter and submit input in the Suggestions and Customer Support—Service Request pages, return to FrontPage and select Refresh from the View menu or click the toolbar button. Then use Page view to open and view the Srvclist.htm and Feedback.htm results pages.

13. When you are done, delete the Customer Support web.

Note *As noted in Chapter 3, these webs are deleted when you are done looking at them because they take a fair amount of disk space.*

Teaming Up with the SharePoint Team Web Site

The SharePoint Team Web Site is used to share information within a team of people, such as a project group, a marketing team, a department, or a small company. The Team Web Site provides a way for a team to collect and group information that is useful to all members. As you can see in Figure 4-9, Team Web Site allows team members to add announcements, calendar events, and links on the home page, as well as share documents, participate in a discussion group, and use a common contacts list.

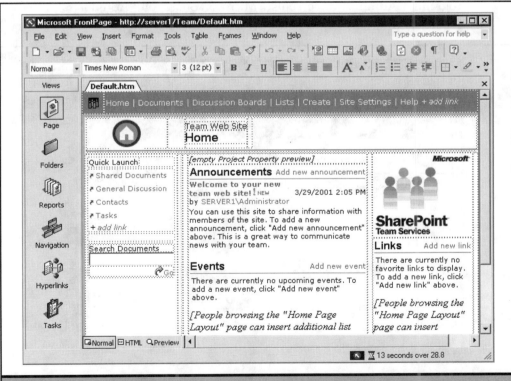

Figure 4-9. *The Team Web Site for collaborating within a web site*

Installing SharePoint

To use the Team Web Site, SharePoint must be installed on your web server. SharePoint is a special-purpose program that facilitates collaboration among team members. SharePoint requires IIS and can only be installed with Windows 2000 or later operating systems (it does not work with Windows 9x and Me). SharePoint is not installed by default, nor are you given an option to install it when you install Office 10. Use these instructions to install Share Point:

1. Place the Office XP or FrontPage 2002 CD in its drive. Windows Explorer will open displaying the contents of the CD. Open the Sharept folder and double-click Setupse.exe. SharePoint Setup will begin. Follow the instruction on the screen.

2. When SharePoint Setup has completed, open the Windows Start menu. If you are using Windows 2000 or XP Professional choose Settings | Control Panel, and double-click Administrative Tools. In the Administrative Tools window, double-click Microsoft SharePoint Administrator to open the administration page in a browser, as you can see in Figure 4-10.

   If you are using Windows 2000 or XP Server, from the Start menu choose Programs | Administrative Tools | Microsoft SharePoint Administrator to open the page shown in Figure 4-10.

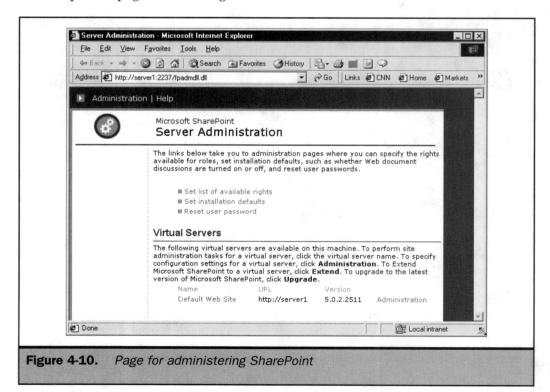

Figure 4-10. *Page for administering SharePoint*

3. Click the Default Web Site. You will see a page for administering the current site, including establishing users and roles, setting up web discussions and subscriptions, managing subwebs, and generally checking on and controlling the site. At the bottom of this page, you can add and delete subwebs, although if you use the Team Web Site template, it will create a subweb you name.

4. Close the Site Administration page and click Administration under Virtual Servers. This gives you an overall administration page where you can uninstall, upgrade, and change the configuration of SharePoint.

5. When you are done exploring SharePoint, close the browser which you were using to look at its administration pages.

Using Team Web Site

Once you have installed SharePoint, you can create a web using the Team Web Site template. Do that next.

1. Open the Web Site Templates dialog box, select the server on which you installed SharePoint, enter a name such as **Team**, and double-click the SharePoint Team Web Site template. This takes a fair amount of time, even on a fast computer. When it is complete, you see a folder view similar to this:

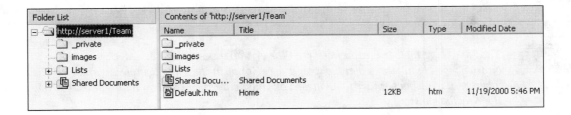

2. Double-click Default.htm and the page you saw in Figure 4-9 will be displayed. Note the many unique features of this web site:

   a) It is built using a table.

   b) The link bars are built using simple page links and not the structure in the Navigation view. You can add link bars to a SharePoint web using the Web Component option on the Insert menu.

   c) Five components of the Home page are meant to be added to by the user: the top link bar and the Quick Launch, Announcements, Events, and Links areas.

3. Click Preview In Browser in the toolbar to open the site in your default browser. Click each of the links in the link bar, each of the links in the Quick Launch area, and each of the forms for adding new announcements, adding

new events, adding new links, and advanced searching. Try each of these features; you'll find all of them fairly sophisticated.

4. Close your browser and delete the Team web.

SharePoint and the Team Collaboration Website are discussed further in Chapter 24 on intranets.

Page Templates

The Web templates create webs with many different page types and features on each page. Sometimes, though, what you want is a single page. For that purpose, FrontPage provides page templates. In this section, you'll see some of the more useful page templates. Begin with these steps:

1. In FrontPage, create a new web using the Empty Web template; name its folder **TestPages**. In Navigation view, add a home page by clicking New Page on the toolbar.

2. Double-click the Home Page icon to open it in Page view.

3. Open the File menu, choose New | Page or Web, and select Page Templates in the task pane. The Page Templates dialog box appears with the General tab selected. Click one of the templates and its thumbnail will be displayed as shown in Figure 4-11.

Note *The New Page toolbar button itself (not the arrow) gives you a new page using the Normal Page template (a blank page); it does not open the Page Templates dialog box where you can choose other templates. You must click the arrow on the right of the New Page toolbar button.*

The templates and wizards listed in the Page Templates dialog box General tab represent a tremendous resource that you can use to build your own webs. Chapter 2 provided a brief description of all the page templates and wizards. Let's look at several of them. As each template is discussed, use it to create a page and look at the results, at least in Page view (and possibly in your browser). You can add a page like the Search Page to a web by opening the web in FrontPage, opening Page view, and then creating a new page with the template or wizard you want to use.

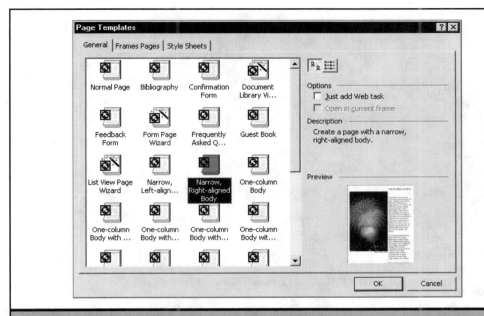

Figure 4-11. *The templates and wizards available to use with a new page*

Feedback Form Template

The Feedback Form template creates a general-purpose form page (as you can see in Figure 4-12) that allows a user to send you comments. The template creates several types of fields, gives them names, and generates files needed to capture the information submitted. Afterward, it's saved in the Feedback.txt file in the _Private subfolder under the web's folder. (If you use the default folder scheme and your web is named TestPages, then the full path for Feedback.txt with Microsoft IIS is C:\Inetpub\Wwwroot\ TestPages_Private\Feedback.txt.)

 Both "folder" and "directory" describe a container of disk files. In this book, we'll use "folder" when talking about the file structure in FrontPage and other Windows applications, and "directory" when referring to the real or "virtual" file structure on many servers such as Windows 2000.

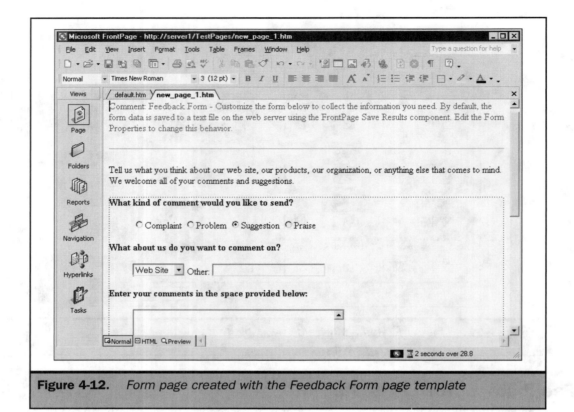

Figure 4-12. *Form page created with the Feedback Form page template*

Confirmation Form Template

A *confirmation page* is used to show someone submitting information to you that his or her submission was received. When you create a submission form—for example, a feedback form or a registration form—FrontPage automatically generates a default confirmation page. You can create a custom confirmation page by using the Confirmation Form template, but you must specify that you want to use your own confirmation page in the Form Properties dialog box of the submission form (from a form's context menu, click Form Properties, click Options, select the Confirmation Page tab, and fill in the URL of the confirmation page). In Hyperlinks view, after saving both the submission form and the confirmation page, you can see the link between them, like this:

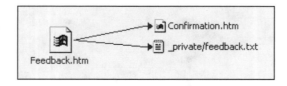

Note *To get the page names shown here, the pages are saved with their template names (Feedback and Confirmation) and then their page title is changed in Navigation view by right-clicking the page and choosing Rename or by using Change Title in the Save As dialog box.*

The Confirmation Form template creates a confirmation page, as shown in Figure 4-13. This page contains fields from the form the user submitted. You can add fields to a confirmation page by opening Insert | Web Component and choosing Advanced Controls | Confirmation Field, as well as change the text and move the existing confirmation fields. The only requirement is that the name of a field on a form must be the same as the name used in the confirmation page. Several submission forms can share the same confirmation page if the forms use identical field names.

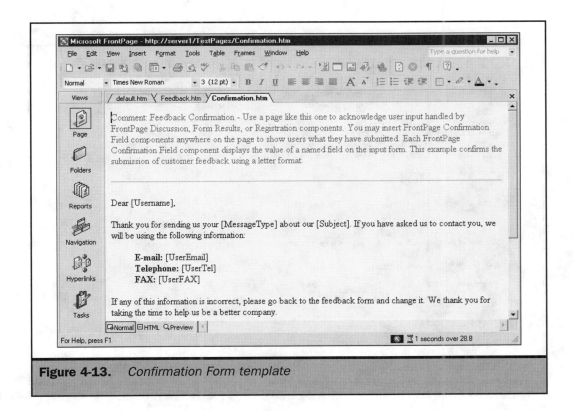

Figure 4-13. *Confirmation Form template*

You must know the field names from the submission form when you are building the confirmation page, because the Insert | Web Component | Advanced Controls | Confirmation Field option or the Confirmation Field Properties dialog box, opened by right-clicking a confirmation field, both require the field name and do not allow you to browse for them.

Search Page Template

The Search Page template provides all the text search features that you saw in the webs earlier in this chapter. It is completely self-contained, including the query language instructions. When you include this page in a web, it will search all of the text in the web without any further effort on your part.

When visitors to your web site use your search page, they will receive a list of pages with content that matches their search criteria, as shown in Figure 4-14. The visitor can click the entries in the list of pages to view the one they want.

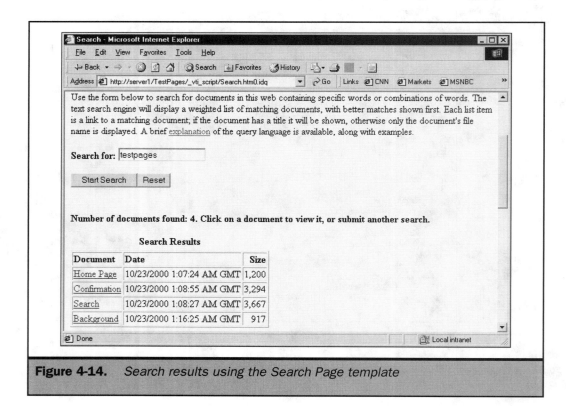

Figure 4-14.   *Search results using the Search Page template*

In Windows 2000 and XP, you must have the Indexing Service turned on (right-click My Computer, choose Manage, open Services and Applications, right-click Indexing Service, and choose Start) for a search to work. Also, after saving the web, you may have to wait several minutes for the indexing to take place.

Table of Contents Template

The page, or more likely a portion thereof, created by the Table of Contents template is probably one of the more useful page templates. When you have finished adding all of the pages to a web, giving them each names and creating links from a home page, add a table of contents page, or incorporate its contents on another page. This will not look like much in Page view, but when you open the page in a browser, you'll have a complete table of contents of all the pages in the web.

Figure 4-15 was taken from a web that contained the pages created with templates discussed in the preceding sections, including the Home page of the web. To do this, a shared border with a page banner (to supply the page title) and a link bar (to supply the links to the other pages) was added to all pages of the web. After creating the Contents page, you need to open the Table of Contents Properties dialog box (on the Contents page,

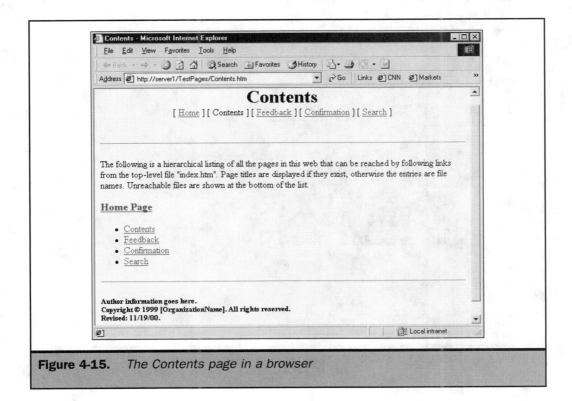

Figure 4-15. *The Contents page in a browser*

right-click the line that says "Table of Contents Heading Page") and specify the filename of the home page, as shown here:

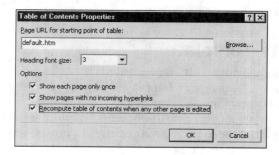

Photo Gallery Template

The Photo Gallery template provides a page on which you can display one or more photographs along with their captions, as shown in Figure 4-16. You add photos,

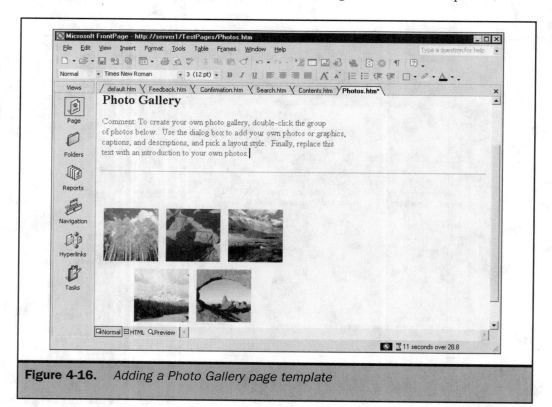

Figure 4-16. *Adding a Photo Gallery page template*

captions, and descriptions to this page by right-clicking the photo-thumbnail area and choosing Photo Gallery Properties. Here, you click Add | Pictures From Files or Pictures From Scanner or Cameras. You then select the files you want to display and enter their captions and descriptions.

The Narrow, Right-Aligned Body Page Template

The templates you have examined so far used components like search boxes, tables of contents, input forms, and a photo gallery. These templates generated valuable features by using the components. There are other page templates that do not use components or any usable text. They provide layout features you can use to design your web pages. Narrow, Right-aligned Body is one such template.

You can preview the layout provided by a template in the Preview area of the Page Templates dialog box. Figure 4-11, earlier in this chapter, shows the Narrow, Right-aligned Body template.

The page generated by the Narrow, Right-aligned Body template is a three-column, two-row table. The lower-left table cell has a large, impressive graphic. The upper-middle cell has a heading, and the lower-middle cell is full of nonsense (or Greeked) text, both of which you will replace with your own content. You will explore tables in detail in Chapter 7, but for now you can still use this template to design pages.

When visitors see your web page, they will not see the dotted lines that define the cells in Page view. Figure 4-17 shows how this page looks in the Preview tab, where table cell boundaries are not visible.

Before going on to create your own templates, delete the TestPages web you have been using.

Creating Your Own FrontPage Templates

As you have been working with templates, you have probably had some ideas for templates that you wished were available. If you are setting up an intranet, this is especially true, because it makes excellent sense to have a template for the entire organization to use to get a consistent web across the company. In any situation where several similar webs are needed, you can use a template to create them. If you are creating a large web with a number of pages that look alike, you can create a page template that will speed up the process.

In the next couple of sections you'll look at the types of templates you can create and their common characteristics, and then see how to build the different types. Building templates does not require programming, as does creating your own wizards, but templates do require getting the right files in the right place. We'll spend some time clarifying the file management and then lead you through a few complete examples so you can see how templates are built.

Figure 4-17.   *Viewing a page generated by the Narrow, Right-aligned Body template*

Types of Templates

Templates are model or prototype webs or web pages, identical in every detail to an actual web or web page. The only thing that distinguishes them is that they are in a special folder. You can view a template in a browser and use it like any other web or web page. In fact, a template is just a web or web page that has been set aside to serve as a model for other webs or web pages.

Because they are stored in different folders, think of web templates and page templates as two distinct types of templates, although there are many similarities. *Page* templates generally create a single page that becomes part of a separately created web, although a page template can include additional linked pages. A *web* template creates a full FrontPage web with one or more interconnected pages. This means that it includes all of the folder structure that is a part of FrontPage. In both cases, though, you create the web or the page in the same way that you would create any other web or page. When the web or page is the way you want it, you then place it in a special folder set up for templates with the extension TEM. For example, Test.tem is a folder containing the files for a template named "Test." The files within the template folder are just the normal HTM extension

HTML web files plus an INF template information file and a DIB file, which is a thumbnail of the template that appears in the Page Templates dialog box Preview section.

FrontPage Folder Structure

The TEM template folders that come with FrontPage 2002 are stored in different folders depending on whether they are pages, webs, frames, or styles. If you used the default installation, these folders have the path

C:\Program Files\Microsoft Office\Templates\1033\

Figure 4-18 shows the contents of the Pages and Webs folders within that path.
If you are using either Windows 2000 with IIS or Windows 98/Windows Me with PWS along with the default installation, you have a folder with the path

C:\Inetpub\Wwwroot

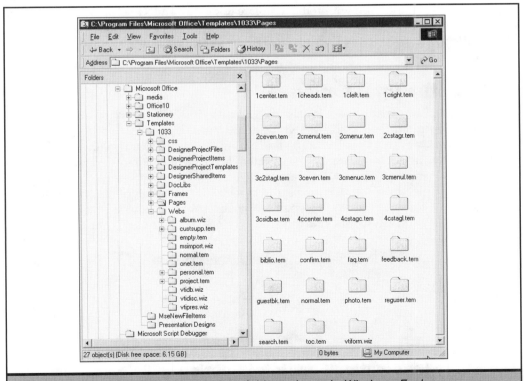

Figure 4-18. *Page and web template folders shown in Windows Explorer*

This folder is the root directory for the webs that you want to let people access with either IIS or PWS on your computer. The folder can store all of the FrontPage webs that you create. It is *not* used to store templates, but comes into play when you create them, as you'll see later in this chapter.

Use the Windows Explorer to open your C:\Program Files\Microsoft Office\ Templates\1033\Pages folder now, and then open the 1center.tem template folder. Within the folder, you will see three files, like this:

Name △	Size	Type
1CENTER.DIB	15 KB	DIB File
1CENTER.HTM	3 KB	HTML Document
1CENTER.INF	1 KB	Setup Information

One of these files is an HTM web file that, if you double-click it, will open your default browser and display the web page produced by the template. In any other folder, this file would be considered just another web page; there is nothing to distinguish it except for the folder it is in. The other files within the template folder are an INF setup information file and a DIB image file, which is a thumbnail of your page template automatically generated by FrontPage and used in the Preview area of the Page Templates dialog box. Look at the INF file next.

The INF (Setup Information) File

The INF (Setup Information) file is used to hold descriptive information about the template. It is similar to a Windows INI file and is read by FrontPage's Page view when it is working with templates. The INF file must have the same name as the TEM folder it is in; so, for example, the Test.tem folder will contain the Test.inf file.

If it isn't open already, open the Pages and 1center.tem folders, then double-click the 1center.inf file. If the INF file type is not associated with an application that can read it on your computer, select Notepad as that application. Notepad will open and display the file's short contents, like this:

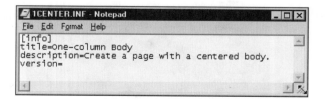

```
[info]
title=One-column Body
description=Create a page with a centered body.
version=
```

The Setup Information File [info] Section

The INF information file will always have an [info] section with at least two items in it—the title of the template and its description—as you just saw. These items are used in the Page Templates or Web Templates dialog box to provide the name of the template and its description (as you saw earlier in Figure 4-11).

If the INF file is not included, FrontPage uses the base name of the template folder ("Test" if the template folder is Test.tem) as the title and leaves the description blank.

Under most circumstances, the INF file will automatically be created for you, as you will see in later sections of this chapter. When it isn't created automatically, you must create it using the INF file format that you saw earlier. There must be a section named "[info]," and it must contain the title and description lines spelled correctly and with the equal signs. Whatever is on the right of the equal sign is data that will appear in the Description area or below the icon representing its title of the Page Templates or Web Templates dialog box. Each of the fields in the [info] section can be up to 255 characters long, including the attribute name ("title" and "description") and the equal sign. As a practical matter, though, to be completely visible within the Page Templates or Web Templates dialog box, the title should be fewer than 30 characters, and the description should be fewer than 100 characters.

> **Tip**   *If you do have to create an INF file, the easiest way is to copy an existing file and change the name, title, and description.*

For page templates, which are displayed in Page view, only the [info] section of the INF file is used. For web templates, with one or more pages within them, the INF file can have additional sections, including [FileList], [MetaInfo], and [TaskList], that are used when the template is loaded into a server.

The Information File [FileList] Section

The [FileList] section, which is shown in Figure 4-19, tells FrontPage how you want the files in the template stored in a web. If a [FileList] section is not included, FrontPage loads all of the files in the TEM folder, but does nothing with any subfolders. The filenames in the TEM folder are converted to all lowercase and become URLs in the web. Also, any JPG or GIF files in the TEM folder are placed in the Images subfolder of the web. The [FileList] section should be included if you have any of the following situations:

- You have subfolders to the TEM folder containing files you want in the web.

- You want to specify the URL and/or the case it uses.

- You want to indicate the specific files in the TEM folder to be placed in the web (files in the TEM folder and not in [FileList] are ignored).

- You want the files to go to folders in the web other than the root folder for the HTM files and the images subfolder for the JPG and GIF files. Another available subfolder is _private used for files that you do not want to be found in a web search.

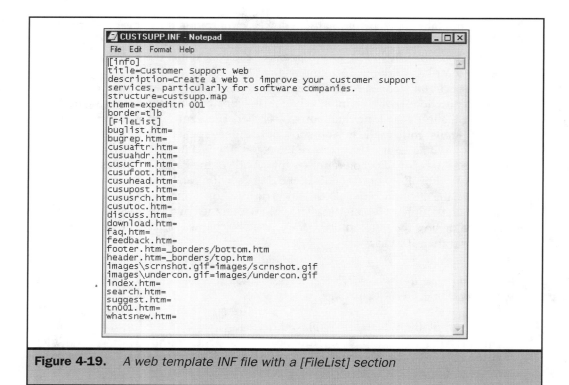

Figure 4-19. *A web template INF file with a [FileList] section*

When you use the [FileList], you must list all of the files you want transferred. If you do not want to change the filename or the path, list just the filename with an equal sign after it. If you want to specify the path, you need to switch from the MS-DOS/Windows use of the *backslash* between subfolders on the *left* of the file list to the URL use of a *slash* between subfolders on the *right* side, as shown about three-quarters of the way down the list in Figure 4-19.

The Information File [MetaInfo] Section

The [MetaInfo] section can be used to store configuration variables used in the Substitution component (discussed in Chapter 9). In this way, the [MetaInfo] section supplies the custom configuration variables that would otherwise have to be manually loaded into the Parameters tab of the FrontPage Web Settings dialog box for each web (opened by selecting Web Settings from FrontPage Tools menu). For example, you might provide the following company information for all users of a template:

```
[MetaInfo]
CompanyName=Exciting Travel, Inc.
CompanyAddress=1 Main St., Some Town, ST 01000
```

The Information File [TaskList] Section

The [TaskList] section is used to provide a list of tasks to be placed in the FrontPage Tasks view for a web template. The tasks in the list have the following format:

TaskNumber=TaskName | Priority | CreatedBy | URL | Cookie | Comment

The elements in the task list are separated by a vertical bar and are described in Table 4-1. Figure 4-20 shows a Tasks view Task Details dialog box in which you can see how the elements are used.

Tip   *Adding tasks to a web template adds significantly to its value and can reduce the amount of support that is needed to help organizations use your template.*

Element	Description	Comments
TaskNumber	A unique number or a key	For example, "t01," "t02," "t03," and so on
TaskName	A short task description	A three- or four-word phrase used as the task name
Priority	An integer describing relative importance	1 = High, 2 = Medium, 3 = Low
CreatedBy	Name of template	Used in the Created By field of the dialog box
URL	The URL for the task	The page or image that the task refers to
Cookie	The location on the page where work is required	Only bookmarks are supported, in the form #bookmark
Comment	Description of task	A longer description of what needs to be done (cannot contain new-line characters)

Table 4-1.   *Description of [TaskList] Elements*

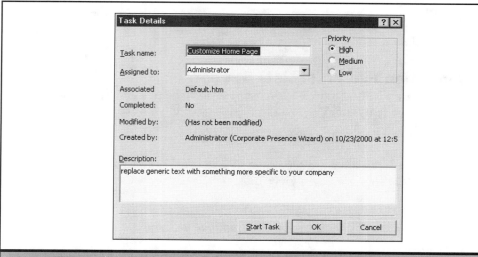

Figure 4-20. *The elements of a task in the Task Details dialog box*

Home Page Renaming

As a default, FrontPage names the home page in its webs Index.htm if you don't specify a server type. If you are using either IIS or PWS, the name is automatically changed to Default.htm. On an NCSA server (a common UNIX-based server), Index.htm is used for the home page and can be left off the URL for a web. For example, the URL **http://www.fairmountain.com/wine** opens the Index.htm page in the Wine web on the Fairmountain NCSA server. Depending on the server to which the web is eventually uploaded, the name for a home page can differ. On a CERN server (another UNIX server), it normally is Welcome.htm. When FrontPage creates a web from a web template, it will automatically rename any file named "Index.htm" to the name appropriate for the specified server. FrontPage, though, *does not change any links to the home page.* To use the automatic renaming feature, you can make all links to the home page be a special ./ (period-slash) link that will force the server to locate the correct home page. If you do not want to use the automatic renaming feature, put the following line in the [info] section of the INF information file:

NoIndexRenaming=1

Creating Page Templates

FrontPage makes it easy to create customized page templates. These templates can then be reused, just like the page templates that come with FrontPage. FrontPage even generates a thumbnail graphic illustrating your page that you can see in Page view's Page Templates dialog box.

Building a single-page template is simplicity itself. Just create a normal web page with the material you want on it, and then save it as a template. That's all there is to it! Try it for yourself:

1. Load the CD that comes with this book in your drive. From FrontPage, choose Open from the File menu, locate the Hometem.htm file in the \Book\Chap04 folder on the CD, and double-click it. The page opens in Page view.

2. From the File menu, click Save As. In the Save As Type drop-down list, select FrontPage Template. Click Save. The Save As Template dialog box will open.

3. Change the title to **Home Page Template**, accept the name **hometem**, type **Create a custom home page.** (including the period) in the Description box, as shown next, and click OK.

Note   *Do not check the Save Template In Current Web check box. It is grayed out in the next illustration, but if you have a web open when you open Hometem, the check box will be available. If you check the box, the template won't be globally available, that is it won't be in the Pages folder, it will be in a Sharedtemplates folder in the current web.*

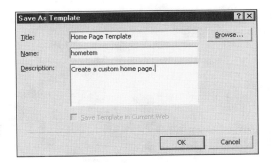

4. Open Windows Explorer, and locate the new template. With the default folder structure in Windows 98 or Me, it will be in

C:\Windows\Application Data\Microsoft\FrontPage\Pages\hometem.tem.

In Windows 2000 or XP or Professional, it will be in

C:\Documents and Settings*username*\Application Data\Microsoft\ FrontPage\Pages\hometem.tem.

Tip   *If you do not see the template name appear in the \Pages subfolder, press F5 to refresh Windows Explorer.*

5. Open the Hometem.tem folder. You should see the three files that were automatically created when you saved the page as a template. These are the HTM web file, the INF information file, and the DIB image file (which is used for a thumbnail picture of the template in the Page Templates dialog box. Double-click the INF (Setup Information) file. It should open and reflect your entries in Step 3 earlier, as shown next.

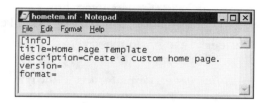

6. Close Notepad, close Hometem.htm in FrontPage, and in FrontPage in Page view open the File menu, choose New | Page or Web, click Page Templates, and select Home Page Template. Figure 4-21 shows what your template should look like in the Page Templates dialog box with the description and a thumbnail image.

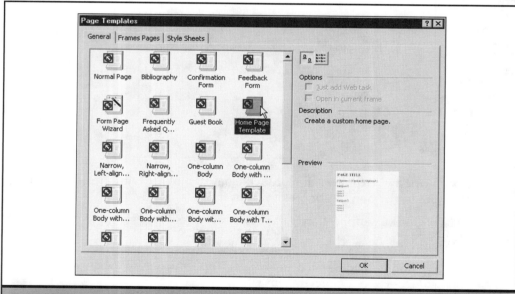

Figure 4-21. *List of templates include the newly created template with a thumbnail preview*

Note   *If you have a web open and have installed SharePoint when you open the Page Templates dialog box, you will have two page wizards (Document Library View Page Wizard and List View Page Wizard) that are not shown in Figure 4-21.*

7. Double-click Home Page Template, and a new page based on your template will open ready for you to customize. When you are finished, save the page with a unique name, and close the web.

Although this example was very simple, you can see that with your template you should be able to substantially reduce the time it takes to create additional pages, and that all the pages you create using templates will be very consistent. In Chapter 5, you will learn about the various elements you can use to customize your web pages and templates. In Appendix C, you can read about creating a web template, which is not as easy as creating page templates.

The Complete Reference

Part II

Creating Web Sites

Part I gave you an overview of webs and how they are built in FrontPage. In Part II, you will actually build a web using many of the tools that FrontPage provides. In Chapter 5, you will build a foundation web that will be built upon in later chapters. In Chapter 6, you will add hyperlinks and hotspots to your foundation web. In Chapter 7, you will add tables and frames, while in Chapter 8 forms and reports will come in to play. Chapter 9 uses Web Components and Chapter 10 looks at advanced formatting techniques. Finally, Chapter 11 discusses how Office and other files can be brought in and utilized within FrontPage.

Chapter 5

Creating and Formatting a Web Page from Scratch

In Chapters 3 and 4, you saw how to build a web and its pages by using a wizard or a template. You learned that using a wizard or template is the easiest way to create a web that incorporates many FrontPage features. Occasionally, you may want to build a web from scratch. In this chapter, we'll do that (and consequently increase your knowledge of the parts of a web).

Note *This chapter uses a number of files that are on the CD included with this book. All files are in the folder \Book\Chap05 on the CD.*

Planning a Web

Chapter 1 talked about the process of designing a web application or web site, and Chapter 2 listed the steps necessary to build a web. In both chapters, planning was the first and probably most important step in making a good web—and the one most often shortchanged. Planning seeks to answer four questions:

- What are the goals of the web?
- What will its content be?
- How will it be organized?
- What do you want it to look like?

Suppose you work for a travel agency named Exciting Travel and have been given the task of creating an intranet web to communicate with the company's agents. Go through each of the four questions with that in mind. (With only small changes, you could alternatively look at this as an Internet web to communicate with your potential clients.)

Whatever your need for a web site is, you should begin by defining your goals.

What Are Your Goals?

Setting the goals of a web is very important—if the goals are well thought out, you will probably end up with an effective web. Keep it simple. Having one or two obtainable goals for your web is better than having a number of goals that cannot all be met. Too many goals will scatter the focus of the web, making it much more difficult to accomplish any one of them.

For Exciting Travel, there is one primary goal for their intranet web: to give their agents a competitive advantage by providing access to a consolidated list of the latest travel offerings. (An Internet web goal might be to get the user to call Exciting Travel and inquire about a possible trip.) There is a secondary and supporting goal: to keep the web frequently updated so the agents will look at it often.

What Is the Content?

To accomplish Exciting Travel's goals, you'll need to include information about current travel specials over a broad range of travel options. The information needs to be complete enough to capture the agents' interest but concise enough for them to read quickly. Therefore, the content needs to include not only a brief description of current packages, but also general information the agents might need, such as the current exchange rates, climates, and latest travel conditions.

How Is It Organized?

How well a web is organized determines how easily users can get the information they seek. The desired information should be within two or three clicks of your home page, and the path should be clear—users shouldn't have to guess how to get what they want. The home page mainly provides links to other pages. The pages below the home page contain the desired information and are a single click or link away from the home page. In a web site with a limited amount of content, this is a relatively simple process, but a web site with a great deal of content requires more planning. The user will have to "drill down" into the web's structure, going from the general to the specific to reach the desired information. How you organize your content will determine the path the user follows. This path should be clear and logical, and should allow the user to jump back to the starting points without having to retrace every step. The home page's links to detailed information give relatively quick answers to those agents who are willing to take a couple of minutes, but following the links may not appeal to those who are in a hurry. For quick answers, you need to have some low-priced specials briefly but prominently listed on the home page.

Your web needs to be based on a simple and obvious tree structure, similar to the one shown in Figure 5-1, so that users always know where they are and how they got there. The lines connecting the pages show how the pages should be hyperlinked. In this example, no page is more than three clicks from the home page, and most of the content is within two clicks. The third-level pages within each second-level area are linked, but the user has to move back up the tree to reach the third-level pages in the other second-level area. While a cross-link between two third-level branches may seem like a quick way to get users from one place to another under certain circumstances, it is also a quick way to confuse users about where they are. It is often better to force users back up the tree and down another branch. If you never have more than two levels from your home page, it is not a big chore to backtrack. Besides, the previously visited pages are already on the user's disk in their browser's cache, so they can quickly backtrack.

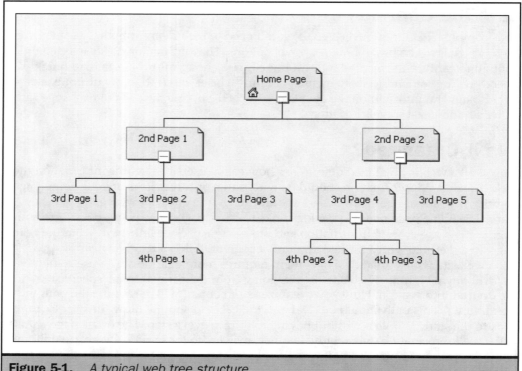

Figure 5-1. *A typical web tree structure*

Note *Web browsers store the web pages and pictures they download in temporary files, called a cache, on the user's local machine. This speeds up subsequent loading of the pages by reading from the hard disk rather than downloading the file over the Internet. The browsers check to see if the file on the web server is newer than the files in cache. If the pages are the same, the cached page is used. If the version on the web server is newer, it is downloaded. In Netscape 4.0 through 6.0, the users control the cache (called "History" by Netscape) in the Preferences dialog box, opened by choosing Preferences from the Edit menu. The cache or History can be cleared anytime, and a time limit for saving cached files can be set. In Internet Explorer, the cache ("Temporary Internet Files," "History" in IE is a set of links to pages you have viewed, not the pages themselves) is controlled from the General tab of the Internet Options dialog box, opened by choosing Internet Options from the View menu (IE 4.0) or the Tools menu (IE 5.0 and on).*

This tree structure can be expanded to hold hundreds or even thousands of pages, all within two or at most three clicks of the home page. The important thing is to remember that, no matter how small your web is at the beginning, a well-organized tree structure will allow you to expand your web to any size in the future.

 Each page in your web, regardless of the level, should have a direct link back to the home page. This allows users to quickly return to the starting point in one click.

What Will It Look Like?

With all the concepts just discussed, what will this web look like? This includes the graphic design as well as the structure of each page. It's best to begin with the structure and then add the graphic elements. This gives you the functionality first, and no web site, no matter how good-looking it is, will be successful if it isn't well structured and easy to use.

The best approach is to begin by sketching the primary types of pages that you will be using. Figure 5-2 shows one way that the information in this web could be laid out to satisfy the desired points brought out in the plan. To keep to the desired three levels, there will be three types of pages:

- A home page with a list of interesting specials and links to all second-level pages with the different types of travel

- A second-level page that contains the main content for a particular type of travel and links to the details for a particular travel type

- A third-level page with the details for a particular type of travel

All three types of pages will have the same footer, which will have a copyright notice, the date last updated, a postal address, and information on how to contact the webmaster (the person responsible for maintaining the web). Each second-level page and the third-level pages below it, of which there will be many, will share the same heading, which will be a link bar, providing links to other pages. The home page will have a unique header and larger, separate sections with links in each.

The web will begin on the home page with major travel options such as cruises, land tours, hotels, and air travel. These will lead to a list of specific offerings for a travel option, such as a list of Alaskan cruises, on the second-level pages. Each entry will lead to the details of a specific offering, such as the specifics of a particular cruise, on the third-level pages. The "Current Specials" on the home page will link directly to the third-level details of those offerings.

The trick is to maintain a balance that doesn't overwhelm users with dozens of links on a page, or make them click until their finger drops to reach the information they want.

This gives you a general view of what your web will look like, which is enough for the planning process. As you actually create the pages, you will fine-tune that look by placing pictures and positioning text. The final home page to be built in this book is shown in Figure 5-3, but it is the product of several chapters, so you'll have to be patient to see this image on your screen.

CREATING
WEB SITES

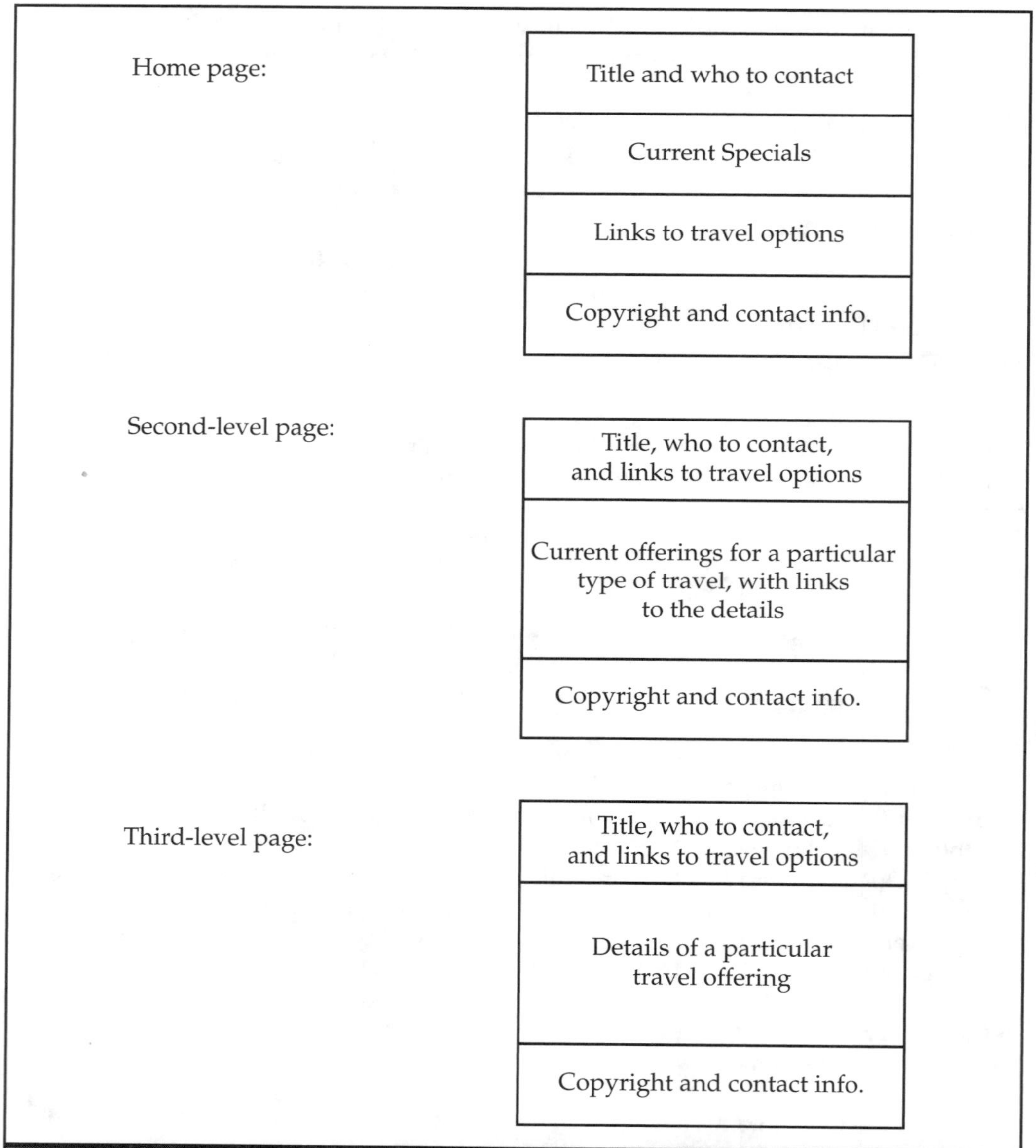

Home page:

| Title and who to contact |
| Current Specials |
| Links to travel options |
| Copyright and contact info. |

Second-level page:

| Title, who to contact, and links to travel options |
| Current offerings for a particular type of travel, with links to the details |
| Copyright and contact info. |

Third-level page:

| Title, who to contact, and links to travel options |
| Details of a particular travel offering |
| Copyright and contact info. |

Figure 5-2. *A way to lay out the Exciting Travel web*

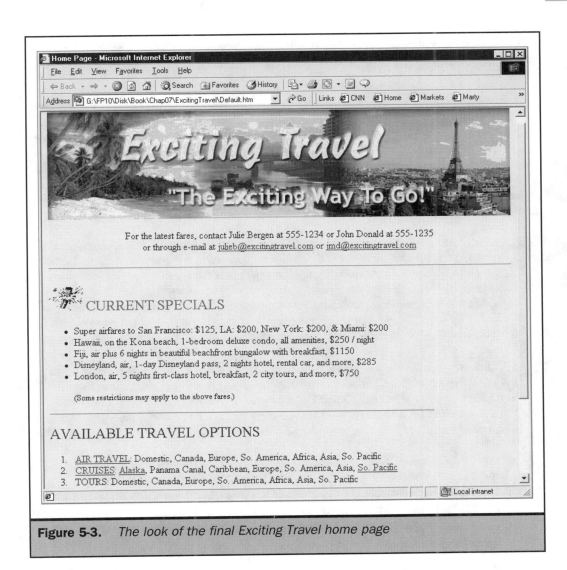

Figure 5-3. *The look of the final Exciting Travel home page*

Starting a Web

The Exciting Travel web will be created in this and the following several chapters. This chapter will look at working with text and pictures and the next four chapters will deal with hyperlinks and hotspots, tables and frames, forms and reports, and Web Components respectively. The reason for this approach is to focus on one topic at a time. As a result, you'll see areas, especially in this chapter, that may be better handled with, for example, a table or a Web component. That discussion will be put off until the appropriate chapter, so each topic can be fully developed without interfering with others.

Developing all but the simplest webs is a long and tedious chore. Look at this proposed travel web—there will be a second-level page for each type of travel, of which there are probably six to ten types. There are then probably six to ten offerings for each type. That means at a minimum there will be 36 third-level pages (not counting those that may be referred to directly from the home page), six second-level pages, and a home page—a total of at least 43 pages! You can let out your breath; in this chapter, you'll only do one of each type of page. It is important to consider, though, how the page count explodes as you develop a web and how adding levels makes the web grow geometrically.

Allow enough time to complete the development of a web. Material created electronically, such as text files and pictures, is the easiest to work with, but you may need to use text for which you only have printed copies. One way to speed the process is to scan printed documents that you want incorporated (like travel brochures for the details of a travel offering) and then use optical character recognition (OCR) to convert them to text. Be sure to carefully edit any OCR-generated text (the process is less than perfect), and make sure you have written permission to reproduce other people's copyrighted material.

It is recommended that you build this web site from scratch, but if you wish, you can download it from the CD that accompanies this book. As a third alternative, there is a Chap5txt.doc file on the CD that can be opened in Microsoft Word 95 or later and contains all of the text that is used on this web site. You can cut and paste this text between Word and FrontPage, saving you the typing.

1. Start FrontPage. Click the down arrow on the right of the New icon on the toolbar and choose Web. The Web Site Templates dialog box will open.

2. Select the One Page Web from the Web Site Template dialog box, enter the folder name **ExcitingTravel**, which becomes the web name, with the path you want to use (the path and folder name should look like **http://***servername***/ExcitingTravel**), and click OK.

3. In Navigation view, right-click the Home Page icon to open its context menu. Choose Properties to open the page's Properties dialog box. Observe that the URL for this page includes the page's filename of Default.htm. The filename of the home page should match the default for the server your web will be hosted on (check with the webmaster of your server if you're not sure). Default.htm is the default filename for IIS and PWS. Click OK to close the Default.htm Properties dialog box.

Note *FrontPage will detect the correct default filename for the selected server and name the home page accordingly. If you are developing your web on IIS or PWS but intend to move it to another server later, you should set the default filename to match the final web server. See Appendix A for instructions on how to set the default filename.*

4. Click New Page on the toolbar. A new page will appear under the home page. Slowly click twice (don't double-click) in the title area of the new page, type **Second Level Page**, and press ENTER to revise the page name.

5. Again click New Page on the toolbar, click twice in the title area of the new page, type **Third Level Page**, and press ENTER. You should see three pages, one under the other, as shown in Figure 5-4.

Note *The web server that webs are developed on is often called the staging server. In this book IIS or PWS is assumed to be the staging server. When the web is ready to go "live," it will be copied, or published, to a production server. All work on a web should be done and tested on the staging server before you publish it to the production server.*

CREATING
WEB SITES

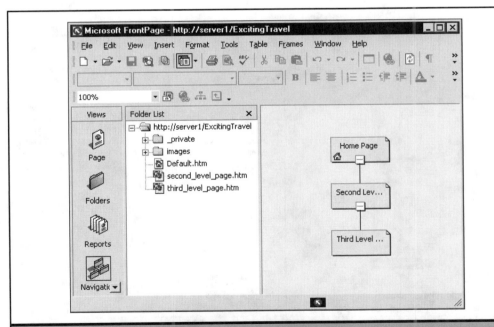

Figure 5-4.   *The initial three pages in Navigation view*

There is a very good structural reason for organizing your web pages in folders. Web servers, like IIS, allow you to create *virtual* directories. These are simply folders that are *aliased* or *mapped* to names that are easier to work with. For example, if you have set up FrontPage and IIS or PWS as recommended in Appendix A, the physical path to the Exciting Travel folder is C:\Inetpub\Wwwroot\ExcitingTravel\, as displayed with the Windows Explorer in Figure 5-5. This can be mapped to the virtual directory /ExcitingTravel. In your web, you can reference any pages in the ExcitingTravel folder using the /ExcitingTravel virtual directory rather than the full path.

When you installed IIS or PWS, certain virtual directories were created by default. The most important is the root directory of the web server. The physical path is, by default, C:\Inetpub\Wwwroot\. This was mapped to the Home virtual directory. This means the URL http://*servername*/ will load the web page whose path is C:\Inetpub\Wwwroot\Default.htm. There can only be one Home virtual directory with IIS or PWS on a client computer running Windows 2000 Professional/Windows

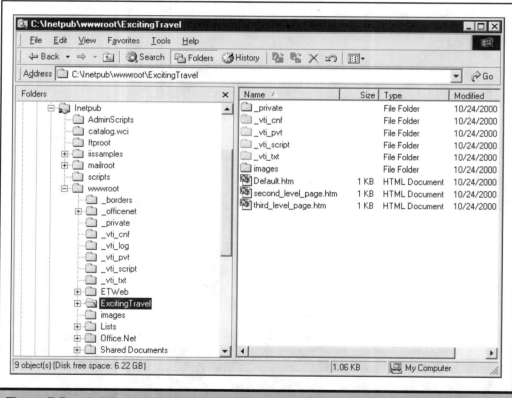

Figure 5-5.   *In Windows Explorer you can see where a new web is placed*

NT Workstation or Windows 98/Me, while web servers like Windows 2000 Server or Windows NT Server running IIS can have multiple home directories, but each one must have a unique IP address.

 The terms folder and directory are interchangeable. FrontPage and Windows 2000 and 98/Me use "folder," while Windows NT, IIS, and PWS uses "directory."

Using virtual directories also allows you to set different levels of permissions for web pages. If you have some web pages that you want to be available to the public, but others to which you want to limit access, you can place the restricted pages in a separate folder and control access to the folder. In a FrontPage web, the _private folder serves this purpose. Chapter 22 covers security on the web in more detail.

The next step in creating your web is to add text and pictures to your pages. In Chapter 6, you will add the hyperlinks that will give the web a structure.

Note *By creating the three pages in FrontPage Navigation view you automatically established a relationship among the pages, as shown by their relative position and the lines between them. This relationship will be used in creating the automatic links in a link bar. Since you will be working with hyperlinks and hotspots in Chapter 6, you won't do anything more with links in this chapter.*

Adding and Formatting Text

The text will be entered in sections corresponding to the home page sections shown in Figure 5-2—for example, the title, the footer (copyright and contact information), and the current specials. Where applicable, this information will be entered and formatted on the home page and then copied to other pages. Begin by entering the footer using FrontPage's Shared Borders feature.

Tip *All of the text that you are asked to enter in this chapter is on the CD that accompanies this book in the \Book\Chap05\ folder and Chap5txt.doc file. You can open that file in Microsoft Word and then cut and paste the text between Word and FrontPage.*

Entering the Footer

The footer goes at the bottom of all the pages and contains the copyright notice and information on how to contact the webmaster. To create the footer:

1. In Navigation view, open the Format menu and choose Shared Borders. In the Shared Borders dialog box, select the Bottom check box, make sure All Pages is selected, and clear all the other check boxes, as shown in Figure 5-6. Click OK.

2. Double-click the Home Page icon in the Navigation pane to open the home page in Page view.

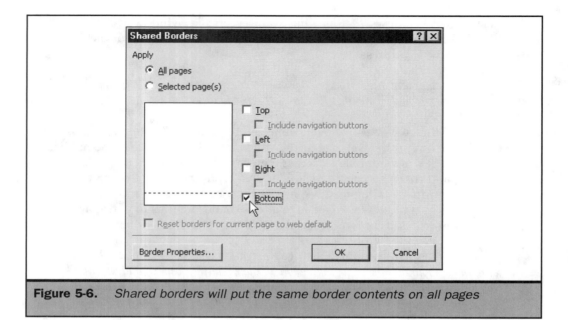

Figure 5-6.   *Shared borders will put the same border contents on all pages*

3. Select the line on the home page that states "Comment: Shared Bottom Border," type the word **Copyright**, and press the SPACEBAR.

4. With the cursor where you left it after Step 3, open the Insert menu and choose Symbol. In the Symbol dialog box, scroll down the set of characters and select the copyright symbol, as shown next, click Insert, and then click Close.

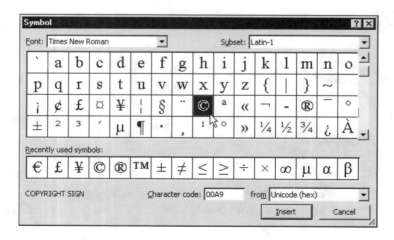

5. Press the SPACEBAR once again to insert a space after the copyright symbol, and then type the following information, just as it is shown here. Press SHIFT+ENTER (new line) at the end of each of the first two lines. Insert the bullet from the Symbol dialog box.

1996-2001 Exciting Travel, Inc. All rights reserved.
1234 W 13th, Ourtown, ST 99999 • (999) 555-1234
Please send comments and suggestions to webmaster@excitingtravel.com

(Remember, if you don't want to type this text, it is in the Chap5txt.doc file in the \Book\Chap05 folder on the CD that comes with this book. When you bring text over from Word it is sometimes advisable to use Paste Special from the Edit menu and choose Treat as HTML. This effectively removes all formatting and gives you just the text, which you can format in FrontPage. Here, a normal paste should work. The text on the CD is bold, so you can either make it all bold or only those parts you choose.)

Note | Using SHIFT+ENTER instead of ENTER reduces the amount of space between lines and helps group related material.

6. To see the new line and paragraph marks in Page view, click Show All on the right of the toolbar.

7. If you look at the paragraph style in the Style drop-down list box on the left of the Formatting toolbar, it should be Normal. This is a little large for the footer, so click the down arrow in the Style drop-down list, and select Heading 5. This reduces the size, but it is still easy to read, as you can see in Figure 5-7.

8. Click Save on the toolbar or press CTRL+S to save your home page with its new footer.

9. Open Folders view and double-click Second Level Page. You'll see that it has the same footer as the home page. Again, open Folders view and double-click Third Level Page. It also has the same footer.

You might need to refresh the Second Level Page and Third Level Page to see the shared border footer. With the page opened in Page view, click Refresh on the right of the toolbar. You now have the footer entered and correctly formatted on each page using shared borders. Next, work on the home page title.

Creating the Home Page Title

The home page title is the introduction to a web. It needs to be inviting and to reflect the company. In this web, it also needs to communicate how certain people can be reached. That is a big order and one that you'll revisit again in this chapter and in later chapters.

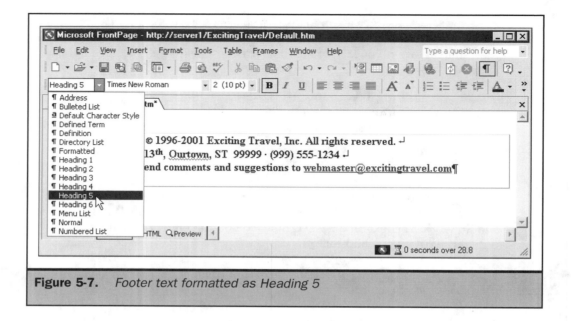

Figure 5-7. Footer text formatted as Heading 5

To start out, create a text-only title with the following instructions. Later in the chapter, you'll replace the text with a graphic.

1. Click the Default.htm tab and click above the footer to return to the top of the home page in preparation for creating the title.

2. Type or copy the following text, pressing SHIFT+ENTER at the end of the first and fourth lines below, and pressing ENTER at the end of the second and sixth lines (the fourth and sixth lines are just continuations of the third and fifth lines). Look at Figure 5-8 to see what the final title will look like (you'll do the formatting in a moment).

   EXCITING TRAVEL

   "The Exciting Way To Go!"

   For the latest fares, contact Julie Bergen at 555-1234

   or John Donald at 555-1235

   or through e-mail at julieb@excitingtravel.com

   or jmd@excitingtravel.com

3. Click anywhere in each of the two paragraphs you just typed, and then, for each paragraph, click Center on the Formatting toolbar.

4. Drag across the first two lines to select them, open the Style drop-down list, select Heading 1, and then click Italic on the Formatting toolbar.

5. Drag across just the first line, open the Font Size drop-down list on the Formatting toolbar, and select 7 (36 pt) to increase the font size to the 36-point maximum.

6. Click Save on the toolbar to protect your work. Your final product should look like Figure 5-8. (The figures and illustrations in this book may look different than your screen because of differences in resolution.)

Listing the Current Specials

The current specials are promotional fares for a particular week. Listing them gives agents immediate access to the latest and lowest fares.

Tip   *It is very important to keep the list of specials updated. First, it provides a reason for people to come back and look at the page. Second, it prevents information in the list from getting out of date.*

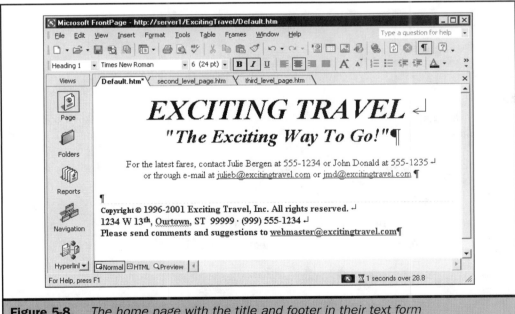

Figure 5-8.   *The home page with the title and footer in their text form*

To create the list of current specials:

1. With the insertion point on the blank line immediately following the two e-mail addresses in the title, press ENTER once to leave another blank line, and make sure that the paragraph style is Normal and the text is left-aligned.

2. Type or copy the following text as it is shown. Press ENTER at the end of every other line shown below. The intervening lines are continued on the next line (see Figure 5-9).

   CURRENT SPECIALS

   **Super airfares to San Francisco: $125,
   LA: $200, New York: $200, & Miami: $200**

   **Hawaii, on the Kona beach, 1-bedroom deluxe condo,
   all amenities, $250 / night**

   **Fiji, air plus 6 nights in beautiful beachfront bungalow
   with breakfast, $1150**

   **Disneyland, air, 1 day Disneyland pass, 2 nights hotel,
   rental car, and more, $285**

   **London, air, 5 nights first-class hotel, breakfast, 2 city tours,
   and more, $750**

   (Some restrictions may apply to the above fares.)

> **Note** *A single paragraph cannot have more than one paragraph style, nor can a single paragraph contain more than one bulleted or numbered line. For that reason, all of the lines in both the Current Specials and Travel Options sections have ENTER placed at the end of each line, even though it takes more space.*

3. Click line 1, and from the Style drop-down menu box, choose Heading 2.

4. Drag across lines 2 through 6, and click Bullets on the Formatting toolbar.

5. Drag over the last line, select 2 (10 pt) from the Font Size drop-down list, and then click Increase Indent on the Formatting toolbar.

6. Click Save. Your Current Specials section should look like Figure 5-9.

Adding the Travel Options

The Travel Options section provides a list (really an index) of the travel options that are available from this agency. In Chapter 6, you'll come back and make these links to the second-level pages.

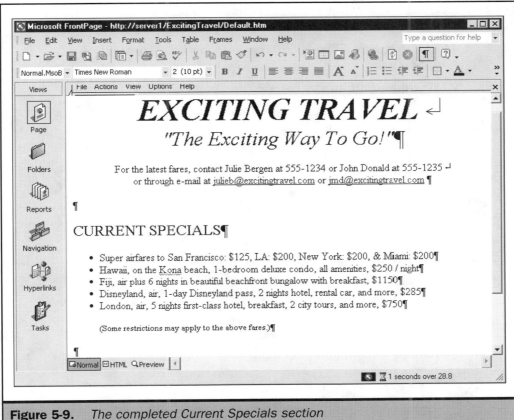

Figure 5-9.   *The completed Current Specials section*

To create the Travel Options section:

1. With the insertion point on the line immediately below the last line typed above, type or copy the following text. Press ENTER at the first line and then at the end of every other line (the intervening lines are continued on the next line). You can copy the list of options on line 3 and use it on lines 6 and on.

   AVAILABLE TRAVEL OPTIONS

   AIR TRAVEL: Domestic, Canada, Europe, So. America, Africa, Asia, So. Pacific

   CRUISES: Alaska, Panama Canal, Caribbean, Europe, So. America, Asia, So. Pacific

   TOURS: Domestic, Canada, Europe, So. America, Africa, Asia, So. Pacific

CREATING WEB SITES

HOTELS: Domestic, Canada, Europe, So. America, Africa, Asia, So. Pacific

AUTO: Domestic, Canada, Europe, So. America, Africa, Asia, So. Pacific

RAIL: Domestic, Canada, Europe, So. America, Africa, Asia, So. Pacific

2. Click line 1 and choose the Heading 2 style.

3. Select lines 2 through 7, and click Numbering on the Formatting toolbar.

4. Delete all but one blank line between the last line of the travel options and the beginning of the footer.

5. Save the home page, the bottom of which should look like Figure 5-10.

This completes the text that you will need on the home page.

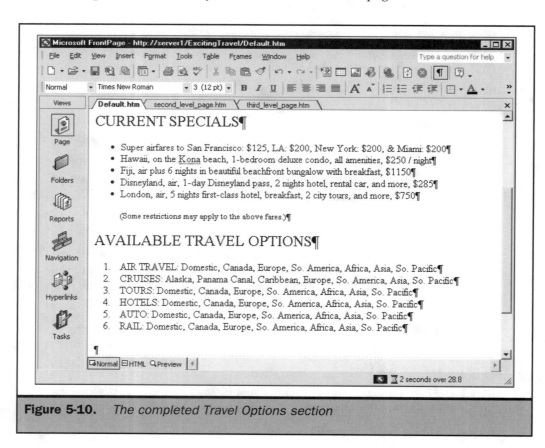

Figure 5-10. *The completed Travel Options section*

Building the Title for Pages 2 and 3

On all but the home page, you want to have a brief title or heading with the ways to contact the specialists and the links to other pages. This keeps the contacts in front of the agents and gives them the primary way to navigate or get around the web. Use the next set of instructions to enter the text related to these items on page 2 and copy them to page 3. Later in this chapter, you'll do some graphics work on this, and in Chapter 6 you'll establish the actual links to implement the navigation.

1. On the home page, drag over the first four lines of text that represent the title of the web, and click Copy on the toolbar.

2. Click the second_level_page.htm tab. After the page opens, click the top left corner to place the insertion point above the footer, and click Paste on the toolbar. The title appears on page 2.

3. If you have an extra blank line above the just-pasted title, press CTRL+HOME to move the insertion point to the very top of the page, and then press DEL to delete the leading paragraph mark.

4. Select the words "Exciting Travel," and choose Heading 2 as the paragraph style. The size doesn't change, because you applied the special character size to these words. The size of the second line ("The Exciting Way To Go!") changes because it is part of the same paragraph, and you did not apply a special character size to it.

5. Open the Format menu, choose Font, and select Normal for the font size. This will change the first line to the actual Heading 2 size, as you can see next. Click OK to close the Font dialog box and resize your text.

Note *"Normal" font size is not a particular size, but rather allows the default size of a given paragraph style to take precedence.*

> *EXCITING TRAVEL* ↵
> *"The Exciting Way To Go!"*¶

6. Select the second line and press DEL twice to delete the line as well as the paragraph mark. This also changes the phone numbers and e-mail addresses to Heading 2.

7. Select the words "For the latest fares, c" (include the comma, the space following it, and the letter "c" from the word "contact") and type an uppercase **C**, without the comma.

8. After the first phone number, type a space and **(julieb)**, without a comma. After the second phone number, add another space and type **(jmd)** to add the e-mail addresses.

9. Delete the new-line symbol and the remainder of the contact information.

10. Select all of the words in the title *except* "**Exciting Travel**," open the Font Size drop-down list, and choose 3 (12 pt) so all of the contact information fits on one line like this (it may wrap to two lines with a different resolution):

EXCITING TRAVEL ↵

Contact Julie Bergen at 555-1234 (julieb) or John Donald at 555-1235 (jmd)¶

Note   *The wavy red lines under the words "julieb," and "jmd" are the spelling checker telling you that these words are not in the spelling dictionary and may be misspelled. You can right-click on these words and get a list of alternative correctly spelled words, as well as commands to ignore the suspected misspelling or add the word to the dictionary.*

11. Click Align Left to left-align the title, and then move the insertion point to the first line after the title.

12. Type or copy the following text, which in Chapter 6 will become a link bar with links to the rest of the web. (Note that there is a space, a vertical bar, and a space between each option.)

   | **Home** | **Air Travel** | **Cruises** | **Tours** | **Hotels** | **Auto** | **Rail** |

13. With the insertion point still in the future link bar, choose Heading 3 for the paragraph style. Press ENTER to add a blank line after the link bar if necessary. Your second-page heading should now look like Figure 5-11. Click Save to save the changes to page 2.

14. Select the two title lines and the link bar, and click Copy on the toolbar.

15. Click the third_level_page.htm tab, click the top left corner of the page to place the insertion point there, and click Paste on the toolbar. The heading appears on page 3. If a small Paste Options appears, click Keep Source Formatting.

16. If you have an extra blank line above the just-pasted title, press CTRL+HOME to move the insertion point to the top of the page. Then, if necessary, press DEL to delete the leading paragraph mark.

17. Click Save to save page 3.

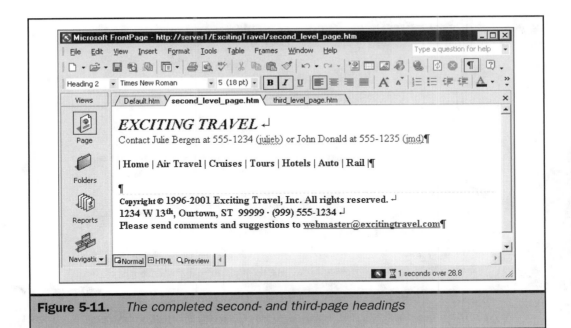

Figure 5-11. *The completed second- and third-page headings*

Entering the Offerings for a Travel Option

The body of information on the second-level pages is a listing of specific offerings for a particular type of travel—for example, a geographically ordered listing of the cruises. That is, of course, a long list. For this example, to keep the typing to a minimum (remember you can use the Chap5txt.doc file on the CD that comes with this book), you'll work on the page for cruises, with only a couple of geographic areas and a couple of cruises in each.

1. Click the Second_level_page.htm tab. When the page opens, place the insertion point at the end of the link bar, and press ENTER twice to leave a blank line.

2. Type **CRUISES**, choose Heading 1, click Center, and press ENTER.

3. Type **ALASKA**, choose Heading 3, click Align Left, and press ENTER.

4. Choose Heading 5 and click Increase Indent on the Formatting toolbar to format and indent the list of cruises.

5. Type or copy the following cruise list, pressing SHIFT+ENTER after the second and fourth lines and ENTER after the last line (the first, third, and fifth lines are continued on the next line; see Figure 5-12):

   Royal Caribbean, Legend of the Seas, 7 nights,
   Vancouver to Skagway & rtn, May-Sept

> Princess Cruises, Regal Princess, 7 nights,
> Vancouver to Skagway & rtn, May-Sept

> Holland American, Nieuw Amsterdam, 7 nights,
> Vancouver to Sitka & rtn, May-Sept

6. Click Decrease Indent, choose Heading 3, type **SOUTH PACIFIC**, and press ENTER.

7. Choose Heading 5, click Increase Indent, and type or copy the following cruise list, pressing SHIFT+ENTER after the second line and ENTER after the last line (the first and third lines are continued on the following lines):

> Princess Cruises, Regal Princess, 12 days,
> Honolulu to Papeete, Oct. 6 only

> Royal Caribbean, Legend of the Seas, 10 days,
> Vancouver to Honolulu, Sept. 15 only

8. Click Decrease Indent, choose Heading 4, and type the following notice:

> Note: Excellent prices are available on these cruises, call for the latest ones.

9. When you are done, your second-level page should look like Figure 5-12.

10. If you have more than one blank line between the last line entered and the beginning of the footer, delete the extra lines, and then save the page.

Importing the Details of a Travel Offering

The third-level page contains the detailed description of one particular travel option. Since this is often better described by the travel provider, it may be helpful to use their material if you have permission to do so (check with your legal department or advisor on the need for this). You can do this by typing in the material, or in some cases it might be faster to scan it in.

Scanning text from brochures and other promotional pieces and then using optical character recognition (OCR) has a much lower success rate than if the text were on plain white paper. For small amounts of text, it is often easier to type it.

In the following exercise, you will use a combination of scanned and typed text to enter the information for the third page. If you have a scanner with OCR capability, you are encouraged to use it with something like a brochure or catalog—anything that is on slick paper with a mixture of text and pictures, and possibly with the text printed on a background image (the material can be about anything; it does not have to be related to travel). You'll then get an understanding of how that works. Of course, if you do not have access to a scanner, you can import the text used here from the Chap5txt.doc file on the CD included with this book.

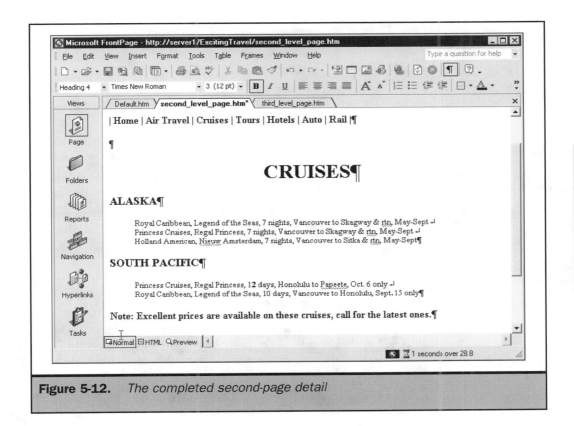

Figure 5-12.   *The completed second-page detail*

The trip used for this detailed description is a cruise from Vancouver, BC Canada, to Skagway, Alaska, offered by Princess Cruises in their 1999 Alaska catalog (used by permission of Princess Cruises, a P&O Company). Several segments of text from this catalog will be scanned into Microsoft Word and then inserted into the Exciting Travel web.

You may use any text to replace that used here. If possible, use a scanner as directed, but if that is unavailable, import the Alaskan.doc files or the applicable portions of Chap5txt.doc on the enclosed CD.

FrontPage can import files from many word processors. Chapter 11 will cover in detail how to import word processor and other files into FrontPage.

To build the body of the third page by use of scanned and typed text, use the following steps:

1. Using your scanner and its software in the normal manner, scan an article of approximately 100 words. Use your OCR program (included with most scanners) to convert the text so that it can be read by Microsoft Word or your word processing program.

2. Similarly, scan and convert to text a table of approximately four columns and ten rows, and then scan and convert to text two articles of 20 to 30 words each.

3. In Microsoft Word or your word processing program, edit the articles and table for scanning errors and make any changes you'd like. Then save the articles.

4. Click the Third_level_page.htm tab. Place the insertion point at the right end of the link bar and press ENTER twice to leave a blank line below the link bar.

5. Type or copy the following text. Use SHIFT+ENTER at the end of the first line and ENTER on the second. Format these lines with Heading 2.

   Princess Cruises' Regal Princess
   7 Days, Vancouver to Skagway and Return

6. Move the insertion point below the heading you just typed, and then from the Insert menu, choose File. In the Select File dialog box, shown next, open the Files Of Type drop-down menu, and choose the type of word processor file you used.

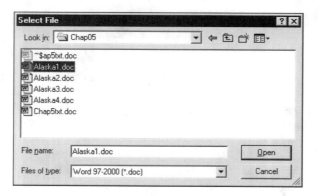

7. Locate the folder, select the name of your 100-word article, and click Open. (Or use the Alaska1.doc file on this book's CD.) You may be told that FrontPage needs to install a converter to display this file. If so, click Yes. The article will appear on your page, as you can see in Figure 5-13.

8. In a similar way, import your table (Alaska2.doc on CD) and then the two short articles (Alaska3.doc and Alaska4.doc).

9. If necessary, add or remove lines so that there is a single blank line before and after your two short articles.

10. On the second line after your short articles, type the following text:

    Material on this page originated from and is used with the permission of Princess Cruises.

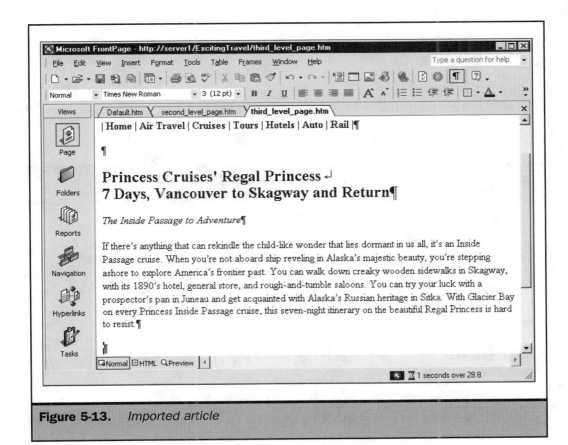

Tip *Getting permission to use other people's work generally depends on whether it is to the advantage of the originator. For example, permission for the material used here from Princess Cruises was easy to get because it publicizes them and one of their cruises.*

11. Select the line you just typed, and click Italic on the Formatting toolbar.

12. Leave one blank line between the line you just typed and the page footer, and then save the page. The bottom of the page should look like Figure 5-14.

Figure 5-13.   *Imported article*

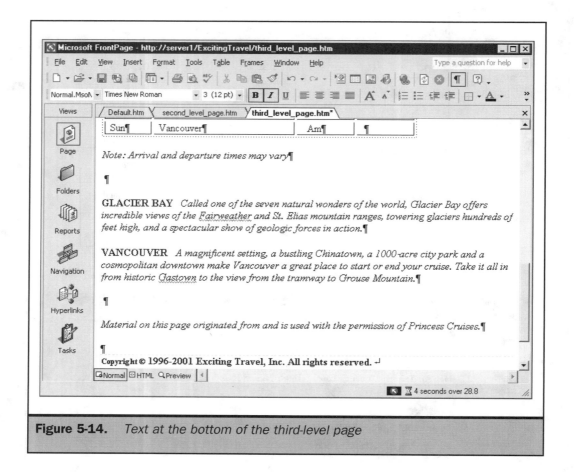

Figure 5-14. *Text at the bottom of the third-level page*

The table in this example was created in Microsoft Word. When it was imported, FrontPage automatically generated an HTML table with the same rows and columns. In Chapter 7, you'll see how to create FrontPage tables.

This completes the entry of all the text you need in this web. Now let's look at sprucing up the text with pictures.

Obtaining and Working with Pictures

There are four sources of pictures for a web:

- Programs like Microsoft PhotoDraw, CorelDRAW, Windows Paint, or Adobe PhotoShop allow you to create your own pictures.

- Clip art from any number of sources including the Internet, FrontPage, PhotoDraw, and CorelDRAW give you ready-made images that you can immediately place into your work.

- Scanners allow you to scan existing photographs and other printed art and put the results into your work.

- Digital cameras, both still and video, allow you to take a shot and immediately place it in a web.

All of these have advantages and disadvantages. Using clip art is fast and easy, but it is often difficult to find exactly what you want. Scanned art gives you a lot of versatility, but you must have access to a scanner, and you must get permission from the art's creator to copy it. Digital is very quick and easy, but you must be in the location where you want the picture taken and some skill helps to create a good image. Also, you may need to get permission to take and publish a picture. Creating your own art in a drawing program has the ultimate versatility, but it takes time and skill. This section will look at several types of pictures.

Pictures can communicate a lot very quickly, and to some people they are far better at communicating than text. Therefore, make pictures an important part of your web, whether it is on the Internet or an intranet. Adding pictures to an intranet page is slightly different from adding them to an Internet page. Intranet pages, for internal consumption, usually emphasize information. Internet pages, for external consumption, usually emphasize selling. Also, LAN connections used by most intranets are much faster at downloading pictures than the modem connections generally used on the Internet. Just keep in mind the objectives of your web and the time pictures take to load.

Creating and Inserting Pictures

In creating pictures for your web pages, you are limited only by your skill, imagination, and time. There are, of course, an infinite number of ways to create your own graphic and a number of different programs to do so. Here you'll look at two title replacements, one drawn and one created with photographs.

> **Tip**
>
> *Before exporting a graphic from a graphics program to a web, it's best to size the graphic as desired. Even though you can resize it in FrontPage, you cannot add more pixels. Enlarging a graphic will make it appear jagged. Also, choose a moderate number of colors or even switch to grayscale to reduce the file size and therefore the download time.*

1. With the CD that comes with this book in your CD drive, open the Windows Explorer and copy the following six files from the \Book\Chap05 folder on the CD to the C:\Inetpub\Wwwroot\ExcitingTravel\Images folder on your hard disk as shown in Figure 5-15: Glacier.gif, Map.gif, Princess.gif, Webtitle.gif, and Webtitle.jpg. (You will also use two other pictures on the CD that you will directly bring in to get a feel for doing it both ways.)

Note   *There are several pictures in this group that are not directly used in the steps in this chapter. They are meant for you to experiment with as you see fit. For example, you might put Glacier.gif near the two small articles, and the Map.gif near the table, all on the Third Level page.*

2. In FrontPage Page view, click the Default.htm tab. Select the words "Exciting Travel" at the top of the page (leaving the new-line symbol), and press DEL.

3. Open the Insert menu, choose Picture | From File. Open the Images folder in the ExcitingTravel web and double-click Webtitle.gif. (If you don't see the Webtitle.gif file you just copied to the ...\ExcitingTravel\Images\ folder, open Look In and navigate to C:\Inetpub\Wwwroot\ExcitingTravel\Images folder.) A title created with drawn art will be placed on your home page as shown here:

4. Select both the new drawn title and the second line, "The Exciting Way To Go!" and press DEL. Open Insert | Picture | From File and double-click Webtitle.jpg. This brings in a title that is made by blending three photographs and overlaying some interesting type, like this:

5. Save the changes to the home page. If you did not have the title file in your Images folder, the Save Embedded Files dialog box will open, allowing you to save the images you are using in this web (the title, in this case) with the web files. Click OK.

Caution   *Always save your images with your web files, so that when you copy the web to a server, they will all be together and FrontPage can do the copying for you.*

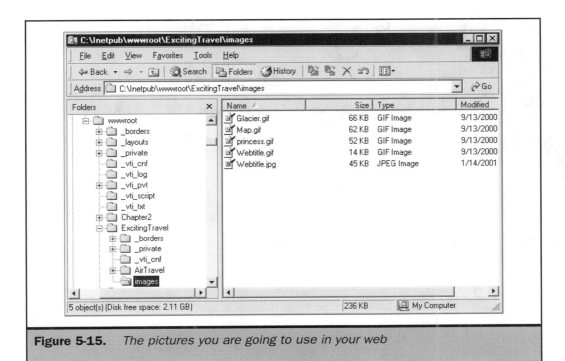

Figure 5-15. *The pictures you are going to use in your web*

Adding Horizontal Lines

Horizontal lines help separate sections of a web page. FrontPage provides an easy way to add such lines through the Insert menu. You can also add your own lines by placing them as pictures. Try both techniques now with these steps:

1. With the Exciting Travel home page displayed in Page view, place the insertion point on the blank line just above "CURRENT SPECIALS."

2. Open the Insert menu and choose Horizontal Line. A horizontal line will appear on your page.

3. Delete the original blank line (the horizontal line creates its own line ending). You now have a line separating the top two sections on your home page, like this:

For the latest fares, contact Julie Bergen at 555-1234 or John Donald at 555-1235 ↵
or through e-mail at julieb@excitingtravel.com or jmd@excitingtravel.com¶

CURRENT SPECIALS¶

4. Move the insertion point down to the left end of the line that reads "AVAILABLE TRAVEL OPTIONS." Press ENTER to create a blank line just above it, move the insertion point to that line, and make it Normal style. Here you'll add a horizontal line graphic that comes with FrontPage.

5. Open the Insert menu, choose Picture | Clip Art. The Insert Clip Art task pane will open. Type **lines** in the Search Text list box, and click Search. A number of different lines appear, like this:

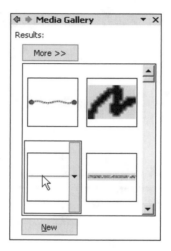

6. Click the line that you want to use (the left one in the second row was used here) and the line will appear on the page, as shown next. You can also choose to open a fly-out menu by clicking the arrow on the right and then clicking Insert.

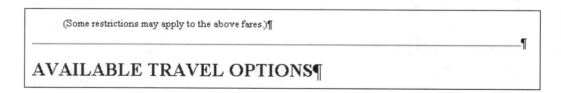

7. Save your home page and click OK to save the embedded file that is the last line you just placed.

Placing Clip Art

Clip art gives you that quick little something to jazz up a page. There are many sources of clip art, especially on the Internet, and some are bundled with FrontPage and Microsoft Office, Corel WordPerfect, and CorelDRAW. To add a firecracker next to the CURRENT

SPECIALS heading by using art from the Office Insert Clip Art collection or art from the CorelDRAW clip-art collection on this book's CD, or any other piece of clip art you have available, do the following:

1. If you want to use your own art or that on this book's CD, open your graphics package and import a firecracker-like piece of clip art (you can use the Firecracker.tif file in this book's CD). Export your firecracker as a .TIF file, sizing it quite small (I used 59×53 pixels) and with 256 colors.

2. In all cases open FrontPage in Page view with the Exciting Travel home page, move the insertion point to the left edge of the CURRENT SPECIALS heading.

3. To use the Office clip art collection, open the Insert menu, choose Picture | Clip Art, type **firecracker**, and click Search. Scroll the set of firecracker pictures, locate the one you want, and double-click it (I've used the right-hand one in the fourth row). It will appear on your page.

Note

If you can't find any firecracker pictures in your search, it could be that you are not connected to the Internet. The clip art search will first look on your computer in both Office and other files, and if the keyword is not found, it will then search the Internet beginning with the Microsoft site.

4. To use your own clip art or the one from this book, open the Insert menu, choose Picture | From File, open the Look In drop-down list and select the path and filename of the file you want to use (\Book\Chap05\Firecracker.tif on the CD that comes with this book). Click Insert when the file is selected.

Note

The Picture dialog box gives you several methods of locating a picture file. To get an image from the Internet, click the Search The Web button on the toolbar; to get an image from a file, open the Look In drop-down list or click one of the buttons on the left. Also, you can type a filename in its box.

5. If necessary, select the graphic, which opens the Pictures toolbar, choose the Set Transparent Color tool, and click the background color to remove it. (If your Pictures toolbar doesn't open when you select a picture, you can open it by opening the View menu and choosing Toolbars | Pictures.) The final result should appear, as shown next:

6. Save the home page. The Save Embedded Files dialog box again appears, allowing you to save the graphic to the current FrontPage web. Click OK to do so, which closes the dialog box.

It's easy to get carried away with adding small clip-art images. They are neat and don't use much memory (the firecracker image on this book's CD is only 2K compared with the Office clip art firecracker, which is 80K), so people think that they add little to the load time. But if you put several of them on a page, such as one for every paragraph, all of a sudden you have a loading problem and the page begins to look cluttered.

Adding Colored Text

FrontPage makes it very easy to color text and, as with clip art, it is easy to get carried away. Also, it is very important that whatever you use does not impair readability. You want the color to have a high contrast with its background. Use the following steps to see how to make text a color other than black:

1. In the Exciting Travel home page, which should be open in Page view on your screen, drag across the words "Current Specials."

2. On the Formatting toolbar, click the down arrow on the right of the Font Color button to open the color palette shown next.

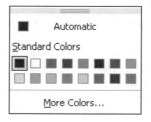

    The color palette can be "torn off" the toolbar to become a floating menu by dragging the bar at the top of the palette. When you move the mouse pointer to this bar, the mouse pointer becomes a four-headed arrow.

3. Click the bright red, the third selection from the right in the second row, to give these words a firecracker color.

4. Select the words "Available Travel Options" and, using the preceding process, make them bright blue, the color next to the red you just used.

5. Once again save your home page.

Adding a Background

The default background used by FrontPage is white, which you have seen in all the figures and illustrations so far in this chapter. You can change this to any color you wish or to a background image by using the Page Properties dialog box. Again, you have to be aware of the load-time impact as your background gets more sophisticated. There are several possibilities for a background.

Creating a Solid-Color Background

Begin by looking at solid-color backgrounds:

> **Tip**   *If you choose black for your text—and there is no reason you need to—then your backgrounds should be very light colors. In any case, you should maintain a very high contrast between the background and text colors so they are easy to read.*

1. With the Exciting Travel home page in Page view, open the File menu, choose Properties, and click the Background tab. The Page Properties dialog box Background tab will appear as shown in Figure 5-16.

2. Click the down arrow for the Colors Background drop-down list. A palette of 16 colors, the default color, possibly a set of custom colors, the colors currently in use in the document, and a More Colors option are displayed, as you saw with font colors.

3. By selecting More Colors, you display the More Colors dialog box, shown in Figure 5-17. You can use any of the predefined 128 colors, or you can use one of the 6 shades of gray. You can also create your own colors with the Custom button, which opens the Color dialog box where you can use either of two numerical schemes, or more simply by clicking a color in the color selector and then adjusting the brightness on the right. One possible color is a very light yellow being selected in Figure 5-17.

4. Select a color of your own, and then click OK. The color appears in the Page Properties dialog box; click OK again. Now the color appears on the web page.

> **Tip**   *Be sure to check how both Netscape Navigator and Microsoft Internet Explorer display any custom color you create. Some colors may end up being dithered and won't look right.*

5. If either your page title or the firecracker now show a different background (the firecracker from the Office clip art collection will), click the graphic to select it and open the Pictures toolbar. Select the Set Transparent Color tool, and click the color you want to be transparent.

6. Save your home page.

> **Tip**   *If you want to make the background the same on several pages in a web, then, after getting the first page the way you want it, open the second page, open its Page Properties dialog box Background tab, click Get Background Information From Another Page, click Browse, and select the first page. Click OK.*

CREATING
WEB SITES

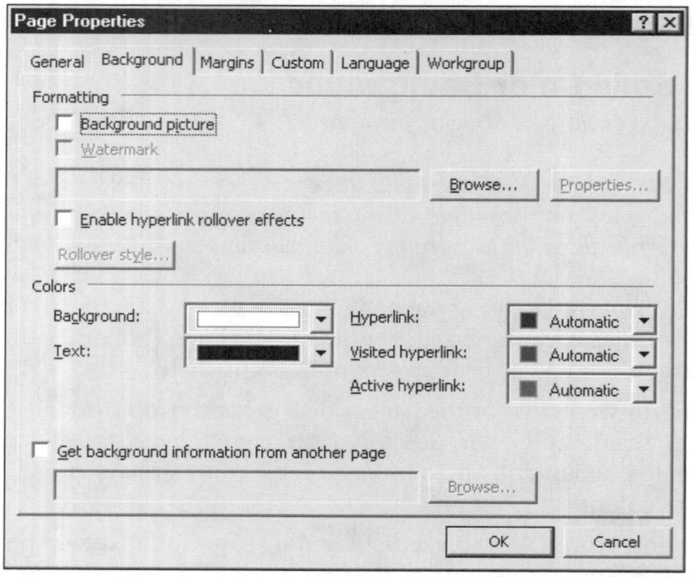

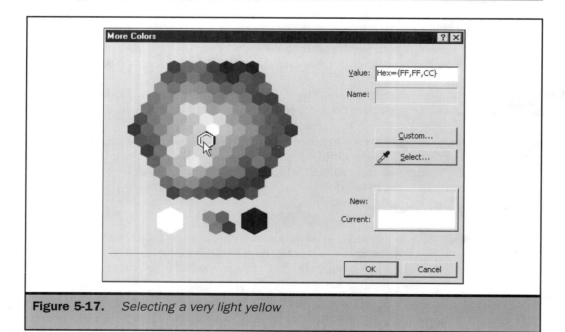

Figure 5-16. *Setting a page's background*

Figure 5-17. *Selecting a very light yellow*

Using a Textured Background

You can also choose one of the many textured backgrounds offered with Office or FrontPage, as well as any of those available on the Internet and elsewhere.

Note *Most textured backgrounds are made by tiling a small graphic. You can make your own with any small image, optimally 96×96 pixels. If the image has a repeatable pattern, it is possible to get it to be reasonably seamless, as FrontPage has done in its samples.*

To add a textured background:

1. Click the Second_level_page.htm tab. Open the Insert menu and choose Picture | Clip Art. If this is the first time you have opened your Office XP clip art collection, you will be asked if you want to catalog your clip art. Click Now. When the cataloging is done, the Insert Clip task pane will appear. Type **texture** in the Search Text box and click Search. Select the one you want and click it (the right one in the second row was used here). A block of the pattern will appear on the page.

2. Save the Second_Level_Page. When the Save Embedded Files dialog box appears, note the name of the texture, and then click OK. Once the page and the texture image are saved, delete the texture image on the page.

3. Right-click a blank area of the page, choose Page Properties, then the Background tab, and click Background Picture. Click Browse and double-click the texture image you just saved (00020662.gif is used here). Finally, click OK to close the Page Properties dialog box. The background appears as shown in Figure 5-18.

4. Save your second-level page.

Using a Single Background Image

You can also use a single background image to cover a page. In most circumstances this is not advised, because the image is quite large (the image used in this example is over 1,000KB or 1MB) and therefore will take a very long time to download. Also, it is hard to get a single text color that shows up well against a multicolored image. Nevertheless, if you know that all your readers have high-speed connections, as they might in an intranet, a single background image can be quite striking. Try it:

1. Select Third_level_page.htm from the Window menu of Page view.

2. Open the Page Properties dialog box, click Background Picture in the Background tab, and browse to locate a large photographic image. (The image I've used is Princess.tif on the CD, scanned from the Princess Cruises catalog and used by permission of Princess Cruises.) Click OK to close the dialog boxes and import the image.

3. If you use the Princess.tif picture you will see that the text is very hard to read against the dark background. To fix that, reopen the Page Properties dialog box Background tab, open the Text color drop-down list, and select White.

4. Click OK to close the Page Properties dialog box. Your background image with white text over it will appear as shown in Figure 5-19.

5. Save your third-level page, clicking OK to save the image with the web.

Using Scanned Images

Using scanned images on web pages is very similar to using other pictures, except for what you can do to the image before bringing it into FrontPage. For example, you can

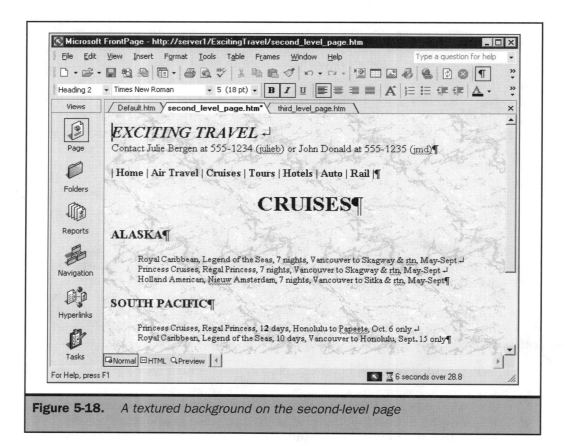

Figure 5-18. *A textured background on the second-level page*

Figure 5-19.   *A single image used as a background
(image used by permission of Princess Cruises)*

scan an image into Adobe PhotoShop, where you can crop it or otherwise edit it. To try that, follow these steps:

1. Using your scanner and its software in the normal manner, scan a picture that you want to bring into your web (I used an image of the *Regal Princess* from the Princess Cruises catalog). This will create a .TIF or other bitmap file (the Princess.tif file previously used).

2. Open Adobe PhotoShop or another program that can edit bitmap files, and crop the image to the size you want. Do any other editing and then resave the file as either a GIF or JPEG file (see discussion in Chapter 1).

3. Click the second-level page tab and place the insertion point to the left of the word "CRUISES." Open the Insert menu, choose Picture | From File, and then

double-click the file you want to import (you can use the Princess.gif file that you copied from the CD). Your result will look something like Figure 5-20, after you left-align the paragraph.

4. Save the second-level page, and click OK in the Save Embedded Files dialog box. Also, close the web by selecting Close Web from the File menu for all open pages and then close FrontPage.

You can use some of the other pictures that you copied off the CD to place other scanned images in this web site.

Text and pictures are the foundation of any web, whether you create the web or it is created with a template or wizard. In Chapter 6, you'll learn about adding hyperlinks, or just "links," to both text and pictures. Then in future chapters, you'll see how to change the look of this web to achieve a professional feel.

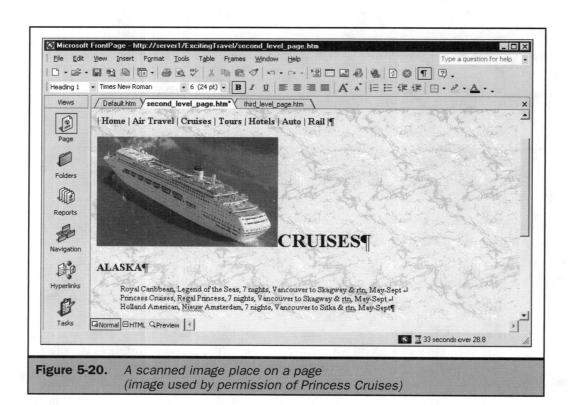

Figure 5-20.   *A scanned image place on a page*
(image used by permission of Princess Cruises)

The Complete Reference

FrontPage 2002

Chapter 6

Adding and Managing Hyperlinks and Hotspots

When you open a web page in a browser, you have access to only the single page in the address given to the browser. There is no way to get to another page without giving the browser its address, unless there is a hyperlink on the first page that provides the address of (and therefore takes you to) the other page.

A *hyperlink* or *link* is an object, either text or graphic, that, when you click it, tells the browser to move to a bookmark on the same page or to open another page. The hyperlink, when clicked, gives the browser an address called a *uniform resource locator (URL)*. The browser then opens the page at that address. The page can be part of the current web, part of another web at the same site, or part of any web at any site anywhere on the Internet, anywhere in the world (unless your intranet limits you to its domain).

A hyperlink is an essential part of a web page. It is the element that allows the page to be interconnected with other pages, producing the "web." Hyperlinks are also why the language behind web pages, HTML, is called *Hyper*text Markup Language. Hyperlinks provide the first and most important level of interactivity in a web page: they give users a choice of where to go when they are done with the current page.

When a hyperlink is viewed in a browser, it is normally a different color than the surrounding text, and it is usually underlined (the person controlling the browser may be able to determine what color a hyperlink is and whether it is underlined). Also, when you move the mouse pointer over a hyperlink, the pointer normally turns into a pointing hand, and either the full or partial URL related to that link is displayed in the status bar at the bottom of the window, as you can see next. (This shows a full path, http:/Server1/ExcitingTravel/Default.htm. A partial URL would be just the page name, Default.htm.)

In this chapter, you will see how to add hyperlinks to text and graphics, how to assign areas of a graphic, or hotspots, to a hyperlink, and how to manage the hyperlinks in a web page.

Adding Hyperlinks to Text and Graphics

Hyperlinks can be assigned to anything you enter on a web page. Any piece of text—be it a word, a phrase, or a paragraph—or any graphic (from a bullet to a large image) can be assigned a link. While there are many similarities, there are also some differences, so let's look separately at assigning hyperlinks to text and to graphics.

Assigning Hyperlinks to Text

Within a web, hyperlinks provide the principal means of getting from one page to another and back again. Begin by assigning hyperlinks for that purpose:

1. If it isn't already loaded, start FrontPage. In FrontPage, open the ExcitingTravel web that you created in Chapter 5, and then open the three pages, one after the other, in Page view.

> *A fast way to open a web you have recently worked on (ExcitingTravel in this case) is to open the File menu and select Recent Webs | http://yourserver/ExcitingTravel.*

2. Display the Home page in Page view, and then scroll the page so you can see the Available Travel Options.

3. Drag across the word "CRUISES" in the second line to select that word. You'll make this word a link to the Second Level page displaying a list of cruises.

4. Click Insert Hyperlink on the toolbar. Alternatively, you can choose Hyperlink from the Insert menu, right-click the word and choose Hyperlink, or press CTRL+K. In any case, the Insert Hyperlink dialog box will open, as you can see in Figure 6-1.

CREATING
WEB SITES

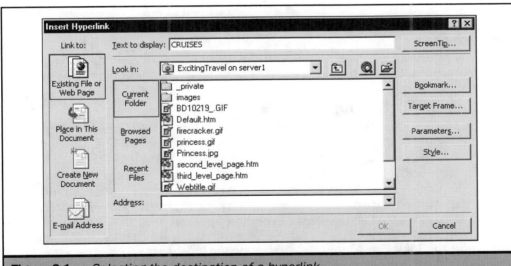

Figure 6-1.   *Selecting the destination of a hyperlink*

5. The Second Level page is the one you want to link to, so double-click the filename (Second_level_page.htm). The Insert Hyperlink dialog box will close. When you return to the Home page, you'll see that the word "CRUISES" has changed. If you move the highlight off it, you'll see that it has changed color, is underlined, and the link destination appears in the bottom status bar when the mouse moves over it, like this:

6. Right-click CRUISES and choose Hyperlink Properties to again open the hyperlink dialog box, now called Edit Hyperlink. You'll see that the address Second_level_page.htm has been assigned to this link. Click Cancel to close the dialog box.

7. Click Save on the toolbar to save the Home page.

8. Press and hold CTRL while clicking (called "CTRL+click") CRUISES to follow the hyperlink and see where it will take you. You should end up on the Second Level page. (If you didn't, you somehow did not select the correct page in Step 5.)

When you simply choose a page as a link, you are taken to the top of that page. This may or may not be what you want. You can control where you go on a page through bookmarks, which are discussed in "Establishing Bookmarks" later in this chapter.

Creating or Activating a Link Bar

Once you are on the second page, you need a way to return to the Home page (ignore for the moment that there is a Back button). To do that you need a link back to the Home page as well as to other pages. This is what a link bar is used for. In Chapter 5, you mocked up a link bar and put it in both the second-level and third-level pages. One way to provide the links back to the Home page and to other pages is simply to activate the words in the existing link bar mockup. An alternative is to let FrontPage build a link bar for you. Let's look at both of these approaches next.

Activating the Link Bar Mockup   Activating the link bar mockup is the same as turning any word into a hyperlink, as you can see with these steps:

1. At the top of the Second Level page, drag across the word "Home" in the link bar, and click Insert Hyperlink on the toolbar. (From now on this will just be called the "Link" button.)

2. Double-click the Home Page (Default.htm) to establish that as the destination of the link.

3. Since you'll copy the link bar to other pages, drag across Cruises in the link bar, click Link, and double-click the Second Level Page. Home and Cruises are the only two link bar elements you can activate at this time, so your link bar should look like this:

Having FrontPage Create a Link Bar   FrontPage uses the relationships established and shown in Navigation view to create a link bar for you. See how with these steps.

1. Click Navigation in the Views bar. The Navigation view of your Exciting Travel web should look like Figure 6-2. If for some reason your Second Level and Third Level pages are not as shown in Figure 6-2, you can drag them from the Folder List to the Navigation pane and they will automatically be connected to the page above where they are being dragged.

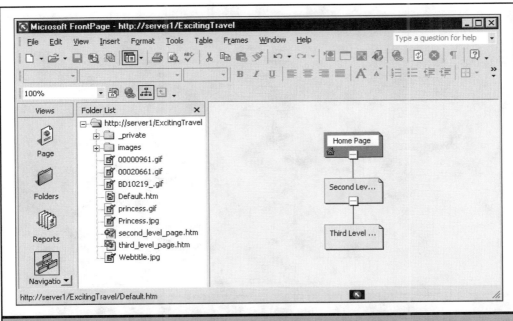

Figure 6-2.   *Navigation view relationships establish the links in a link bar*

2. In the Navigation toolbar, the Included In Link Bars button, the second one from the right, allows you to turn a particular link in the automatic link bars on or off. If you select the Second Level page and click the Included In Link Bars button, both the Second Level and Third Level pages are removed from the Automatic link bars and become gray in color. Try this for yourself with different pages selected. When you are done, make sure that all pages are included in link bars and that your Navigation view looks like Figure 6-2.

3. Double-click the Second Level Page in the navigation pane to open that page in Page view. When the page opens, move the insertion point to the blank line under the manual link bar. If there isn't a blank line there, add one by placing your insertion point at the end of the manual link bar and pressing ENTER.

4. Open the Insert menu and choose Navigation. In the Insert Web Component dialog box, Link Bars should be selected as the Component Type. If not, select it, choose Bar Based On Navigation Structure, and click Next.

5. Choose any style that you like. Here, the first plain style close to the bottom under the buttons, called Bars, is used. Click Next, accept the horizontal orientation, and click Finish. The Link Bar Properties dialog box opens. Select the Child Level option and Home Page check box, as shown in Figure 6-3. Click OK.

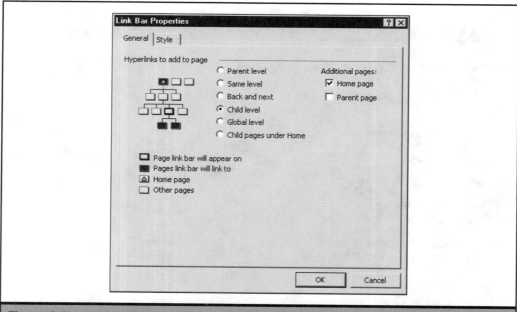

Figure 6-3. *Establishing the links in an automatic link bar*

Note *In the Insert Web Component dialog boxes or in the Style tab of the Link Bar Properties dialog box, you can choose to have the hyperlinks displayed as either graphical buttons or text. For buttons, you apply a theme to the web or choose from one of a number of styles. Alternatively, as in this example, you can choose to have the links displayed as text.*

As you can see next, a link bar is inserted on the page displaying the links you established in Navigation view and selected in the Link Bar Properties dialog box.

In Step 5 of the preceding exercise, you chose to create links to the Home page and Child pages in the link bar. If you were to repeat these steps on the Third Level page link bar, since it doesn't have a child page, the link bar with the same settings as the Second Level page would have only one link, back to the Home page. The Third Level page does have a parent page—the Second Level page—and you'll want to provide a link to that page. You'd do that by changing the link bar properties on the Third Level page to include the Parent Page. Do that with these steps:

1. Click the tab for the Third Level page. On that page, place the insertion point immediately below the mockup of a manual link bar. Add a blank line if required.

2. Open the Insert menu and choose Navigation. In the Insert Web Component dialog box, make sure Link Bars is selected as the Component Type, select Bar Based On Navigation Structure, and click Next.

3. Choose the same plain bar style near the bottom of the list of styles, as was chosen earlier, click Next, accept the horizontal orientation, and click Finish.

4. In the Link Bar Properties dialog box, click Same Level to pick up any future pages that are created at the third level, and click Home Page and Parent Page to create links to those pages. A link bar with Home and Up will appear.

5. Save both your Second Level and Third Level pages.

Note *The normal blue color of a hyperlink is a problem when placed against the blue background in the photo. You can change the color of a hyperlink and a visited hyperlink by right-clicking on the page, choosing Page Properties, selecting the Background tab, and then setting the colors in the lower right.*

Establishing Bookmarks

Since some web pages can be quite long and you may want to direct exactly where on a page a link will take the user, you need to identify a spot on a page where a link will end up. This is done with the use of bookmarks. *Bookmarks* are objects (text or graphics) that have been selected as destinations for a link. Follow these steps to create a bookmark:

You must identify the bookmark before you establish the link, unless you want to go back and edit the link after it is established.

1. Return to the Second Level page and drag across the heading "ALASKA" below the image of a cruise ship.

2. Press CTRL+G or open the Insert menu and choose Bookmark (you may have to extend the menu). The Bookmark dialog box will open, as shown here:

3. Click OK to make the word "ALASKA" a bookmark. You'll see a dashed line appear under "ALASKA."

4. Drag across the heading "SOUTH PACIFIC," press CTRL+G or open the Insert menu, choose Bookmark, and click OK in the Bookmark dialog box. A dashed line will appear under the selected words.

Selecting the bookmarks is only half the procedure; you must also establish the links to the bookmarks. Before going back to the Home page to do that, establish the link to the Third Level page.

Linking to the Third Level Page

The Third Level page is a detailed description of one Alaska cruise listed on the Second Level page. Therefore, set the line that lists the cruise as the link to the page that describes it, using these steps:

1. With the Second Level page displayed, scroll the page so you can see the list of cruises under the Alaska heading.

2. Drag across the line that begins "Princess Cruises, Regal Princess..."

3. Click Link on the toolbar to open the Insert Hyperlink dialog box, and then double-click Third_Level_Page. Your Second Level page with the activated link bars, the two bookmarks, and the link to the third page should look like Figure 6-4.

4. Click Save on the toolbar to save the second page.

5. CTRL+click the Princess Cruises link you established in Step 3 to follow the hyperlink. Your Third Level page should open.

6. Clean up the page and recapture some room by selecting and deleting the manual link bar mockup, leaving the link bar created by FrontPage on the Third Level page, as you can see in Figure 6-5.

CREATING
WEB SITES

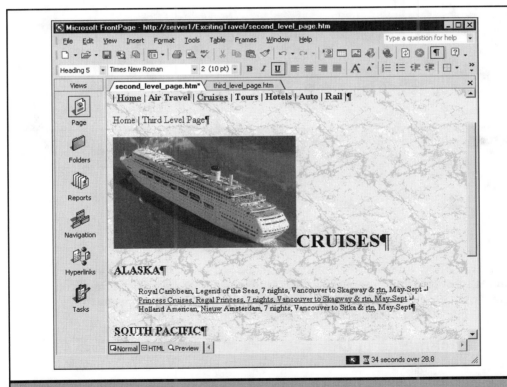

Figure 6-4.   *Links and bookmarks on the Second Level page*

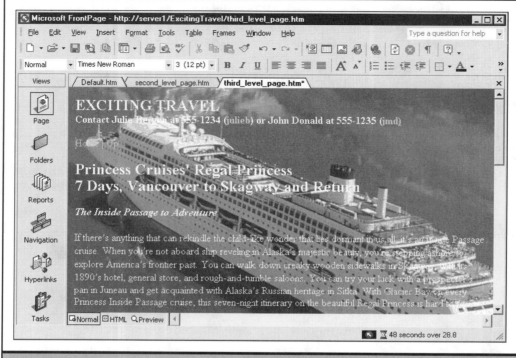

Figure 6-5. *Cleaned up Third Level page with activated link bar*

7. Click Save on the toolbar to save the third page.

8. CTRL+click the word "Home" in the link bar to return to the Home page.

You have now followed the links you established from the first to the second page, from the second to the third page, and from the third page back to the first. You can see that they provide a good means of navigating a web. Later in the chapter, you'll try them out in a browser, where all you'll need to do is click them.

Using Bookmarks in Links

On the Home page, use the two bookmarks you set to create two detail links within the Cruises travel options:

1. On the Home page, scroll the page so you can see the numbered list of travel options.

2. Drag across the word "Alaska" in the list of cruise destinations, as you can see here:

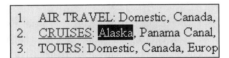

3. Click Link on the toolbar to open the Insert Hyperlink dialog box.

4. Click Second_Level_Page in the list of pages, and then click Bookmark. Your two bookmarks will appear, like this:

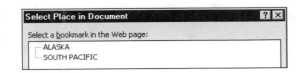

5. Double-click ALASKA to select that bookmark, and then click OK to close the dialog box and establish the link.

6. Drag across the words "So. Pacific" (in the same lines as the Alaska you selected in Step 2 earlier), click Link, select Second_Level_Page, click Bookmark, and double-click SOUTH PACIFIC. The Address in the bottom of the Insert Hyperlink dialog box now includes the bookmark, as shown next:

7. Click OK to close the dialog box and to set the link.

Setting Links to Other Than Web Sites

All of the links that you have created so far have been to other pages within this single web application. Later in this chapter, you'll make a link to another web site and web. FrontPage allows you to make a link to:

- An existing page in the current web
- A new page in the current web
- Another web
- A bookmark in either the current web or another web
- A frame in either the current web or another web
- A file on a local hard disk
- An e-mail address to send e-mail

A link to an e-mail address using the mailto link is commonly found in the footer on a web page. This allows the user to easily contact the webmaster or the page's creator by using e-mail. FrontPage will create a mailto link when you enter text that looks like an e-mail address (two text strings, without spaces, separated by the @ character). In the footer for each page in your Exciting Travel web is the e-mail address webmaster@excitingtravel.com. FrontPage has automatically created the mailto link, as you can with these steps:

1. Scroll to the bottom of the Home page in Page view, so you can see the copyright and other information in the footer.

2. Right-click "webmaster@excitingtravel.com," and then select Hyperlink Properties.

3. In the URL text box on the Edit Hyperlink dialog box you can see that the URL for the hyperlink is mailto:webmaster@excitingtravel.com, as shown next.

4. Click OK to close the Edit Hyperlink dialog box, and then click Save on the toolbar to save the Home page.

You now have a number of links, so it is time to see if they work.

Testing Your Links in a Browser

The only way to know if your links are really working is to try them in a browser:

1. If you didn't save each of the three pages in the preceding steps, do that now by opening the File menu and selecting Save All.

Tip *You can tell if a page has been saved since it was last changed by looking at the tabs at the top of the window. If the page name has an asterisk beside it, it needs to be saved.*

2. Your Home page should still be displayed in Page view. Click Preview In Browser on the toolbar. If you have more than one browser, the Preview In Browser dialog box will open, otherwise your browser will open. If you get the dialog box, select the Browser and Window Size you want to use and click Preview.

Tip *You should always look at your work in both 640×480 and 800×600 resolution. Remember that you have no control over the user's browser resolution, so your work must look good in both resolutions.*

3. If your web browser is already open, you can enter the address or URL for your web in the Address drop-down list. The address should be in the form *servername/webname/*. In FrontPage's Page view, you can find this in the Page

Properties dialog box for any page in a web (right-click the page and choose Page Properties). In Folders or Navigation views, it's in the Properties dialog box (right-click the page and choose Properties). For example, here is the URL for the Home page in its Page Properties dialog box opened from Page view:

| Location: | http://server1/ExcitingTravel/Default.htm |
| Title: | Home Page |

If you include a page filename in the URL when you open a browser, you will open that page, which may not be the home page. You do not need to include the page filename if you want to open a home page.

You can drag across the URL in the FrontPage Page Properties dialog box, press CTRL+C to copy it to the Clipboard, open a browser, click the Address box, and press CTRL+V to paste the URL there.

4. If you have previously opened the Exciting Travel web in your browser, click Refresh on the browser's toolbar to make sure you are using the latest files.

5. Scroll down the page until you can see the Available Travel Options. Move the mouse pointer until it is over the word "CRUISES." The mouse pointer will turn into a pointing hand, and the URL for the second page will be shown in the status bar at the bottom of the window, as you can see in Figure 6-6.

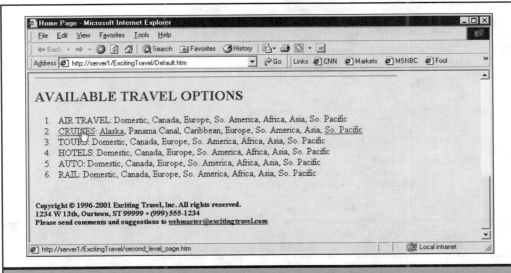

Figure 6-6. *When the mouse pointer is over a hyperlink, its URL is displayed in the status bar*

6. Click CRUISES and your second page will be displayed. Your first hyperlink has now opened the Second Level page.

7. Click Home in either link bar. Your Home page should again be displayed.

8. If you are not already there, scroll down so you can see the Available Travel Options, and then click So. Pacific. The South Pacific heading will be positioned as far up in the window as information below it allows (if there is enough information below the bookmark, the bookmark will be at the top of the window), as shown in Figure 6-7.

9. Click the line beginning "Princess Cruises, Regal Princess." The Third Level page will open.

10. Click Up in the link bar, and you'll be returned to the Second Level page. Notice how the page is positioned at its top.

11. Click Home on the link bar. When the Home page opens, it will be positioned at its top.

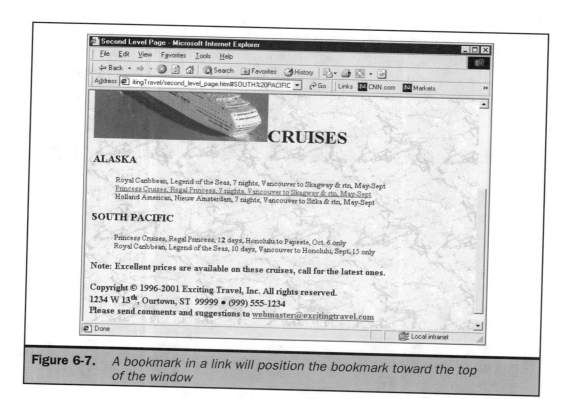

Figure 6-7. A bookmark in a link will position the bookmark toward the top of the window

12. Scroll to the bottom of the Home page, and click the webmaster address. Your e-mail system should start and display a new message window with the webmaster address in the To text box, as you can see in Figure 6-8.

13. Close down your e-mail system without sending a message, and then close your browser and return to FrontPage's Page view.

All of your links should have worked, providing an excellent navigation system around your web. If you find that a link did not work, right-click it in FrontPage Page view, click Hyperlink Properties to open the Edit Hyperlink dialog box, and correct where the link is pointing. Checking your work in a browser not only confirms that your links work as expected, it also gives you a visual check of the page design. You cannot count on the appearance of a page in Page view carrying over to your browsers. Check your work on your browsers often.

Assigning Hyperlinks to a Graphic

Although text makes for good links, graphics have even greater possibilities. You can assign a single link to a graphic, or you can divide a graphic into sections, called

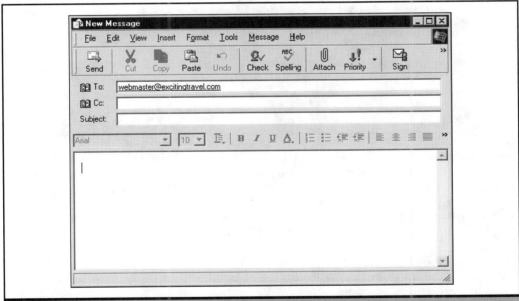

Figure 6-8.   *Clicking a mailto link opens your e-mail new message window*

CREATING
WEB SITES

hotspots, and make each section a separate link. All of the concepts that you learned about with text links also apply to graphics. You can have links to the existing web, both with and without bookmarks. You can have external links to web sites as well as to other types of Internet sites. In addition, you can make either a single graphic that has been divided or multiple graphics into a link bar, and you can test graphic links in your browser.

Making a Graphic a Single Link

Making a graphic a single link is very much like what you did with a piece of text. To do this for a graphic:

1. In Page view, open the Second Level page. Scroll the page down, if necessary, so you can see the picture of the ship.

2. Click the picture so it is selected, showing little boxes in the four corners as well as in the middle of each side, like this:

3. Click Link on the toolbar to open the Insert Hyperlink dialog box, and then double-click the Third Level page (you may need to click Existing File Or Web Page first to see the Third Level page) to establish that as the destination of the link.

Now when you move the mouse pointer over the graphic, you'll see "third_level_ page.htm," the address for the third page, in the status bar.

Linking a Graphic to an External Web

Linking a graphic or text to an external web requires nothing more than specifying the external web's URL in the link:

1. Scroll the Second Level page down so the insertion point is on the blank line just above the footer.

2. Insert a horizontal line (you can use a FrontPage-created line from the Insert menu, as is done here, or you can place a graphics line).

3. If a blank line appears above the horizontal line, delete it. If necessary, add a blank line below the horizontal line.

4. On the next line, type **OUTSIDE SOURCES**, format it as a Heading 2, press ENTER, and type

   Check these additional sources for cruise information:

   Format it as a Heading 4, and press ENTER.

5. Use Insert | Picture | From File to insert two or three small images that can be used for links and center them, as shown in Figure 6-9. (You can use the art on the CD that comes with this book; see \Book\Chap06 folder for this purpose.) You may want to size the images and make the background transparent. If so, click the picture, select Set Transparent Color from the Pictures toolbar, and click the background color you want to get rid of.

CREATING
WEB SITES

Figure 6-9.   *Graphics set up for external links**
*"Carnival" and the "reverse-C" are registered service marks of Carnival Cruise Lines. Used with the permission of Carnival Cruise Lines. "Princess Cruises" and the "Lady with wind-blown hair" are registered trademarks of Princess Cruises. Used with permission of Princess Cruises. "Royal Caribbean" and the "Crown & Anchor" are registered trademarks of Royal Caribbean Cruises Ltd. Used with permission of Royal Caribbean Cruises Ltd.

6. Click one of your images to select it (say the Royal Caribbean logo as an example), and then click Link to open the Insert Hyperlink dialog box. Click the Address text box at the bottom of the dialog box.

7. Type a URL, for example, **http://www.rccl.com/** and click OK. You should see the URL in the status bar when you move the mouse pointer over the graphic.

 If you click the Use Your Web Browser button in the Insert Hyperlink dialog box, locate the web site you want to link to, and then return to the Insert Hyperlink dialog box, the URL will be automatically copied to the Address text box in the Insert Hyperlink dialog box.

To complete this section of the web, given that you used the three images from this book's CD, you would attach the URL **http://www.princess.com/** to the Princess Cruises logo and the URL **http://www.carnival.com/** to the Carnival Cruise Lines logo. Save your page when you are done.

Adding Hotspots to Graphics

FrontPage has a feature that allows you to divide a graphic into sections that can be rectangles, circles, or polygons, and to assign each of those sections a different link. Each linked, or clickable, section is called a *hotspot*. When FrontPage generates the actual web that is downloaded by the user, it creates an *image map* of the graphic and all of its hotspots. To create a graphic with hotspots:

1. Open the Home page of the Exciting Travel web in Page view and, if necessary, scroll down the page until you see the Available Travel Options.

2. Drag across the words "AIR TRAVEL," and click Link on the toolbar.

3. Click Create New Document on the left of the dialog box, type the name **Air.htm**, accept the other defaults, and click OK. This will create a new page in the current web and link it to the selected object. A new page is generated and opened in Page view.

4. Separately, you can copy the title and link bar for the page. For now, enter several blank lines to leave room for the header, and then type

    Click the area of the world for which you want airfares.

    (including the period), format it as Heading 3, and then press ENTER.

5. Open the Insert menu, choose Picture | From File, and from \Book\Chap06\ on this book's CD, double-click World.tif to insert a world map on the page. Select the map and size and center it, as shown in Figure 6-10.

6. With the world map selected, use the tools on the right in the Pictures toolbar, which automatically opens when you click a picture, to draw the hotspots on the map. For example, select the Rectangle tool and draw a rectangle around the United States. When you complete the rectangle

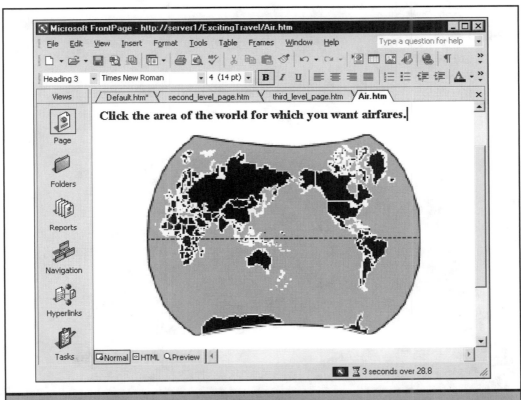

Figure 6-10.   *A new page created with a world map*

and release the mouse button, the Insert Hyperlink dialog box will open. You have all the normal choices for a new link including an existing page, with or without a bookmark, any other site on the Internet, or a new page. If you create a new page, be sure to save it and give it a name that can be used for the link.

7. When you have completed drawing the shapes you want over the various areas of your map, you'll see all of the shapes on your map. The shapes will not be visible in a browser. When you move the mouse pointer over one of the areas, you'll see the URL, absolute or relative, in the status bar, as you can see in the lower left of Figure 6-11.

8. Right-click an area of the map that you have not drawn a hotspot over, choose Picture Properties, and in the General tab Default Hyperlink section's Location

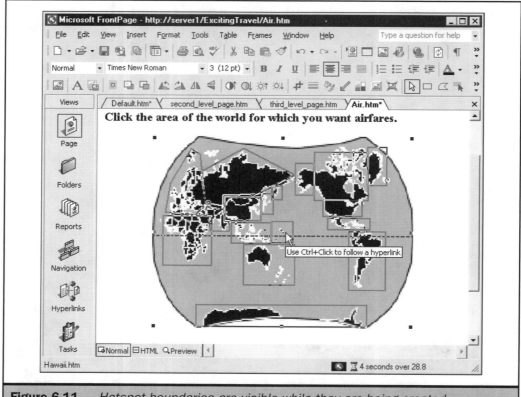

Figure 6-11. *Hotspot boundaries are visible while they are being created*

text box, enter the link that you want used if someone clicks outside of a hotspot, like this:

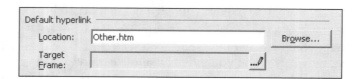

9. Click OK to close the Picture Properties dialog box.

10. To see the hotspots uncluttered by the map, click Highlight Hotspots on the Pictures toolbar. The map will disappear, leaving only the shapes you drew, as you can see here:

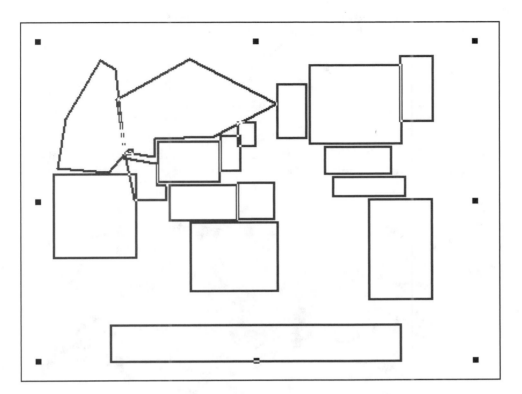

11. Turn off Highlight Hotspots, save your new Air Travel page, save the associated image, return to your Home page, open the File menu, and choose Save All.

Testing Your Graphic Links in a Browser

Once again it is prudent to open your browser and see how your links are working:

1. Open your browser with the Exciting Travel Home page displayed, and click Refresh on the toolbar to make sure you are looking at the most recent copy of your web.

2. Scroll down the Home page until you can see Available Travel Options, and then click AIR TRAVEL. Your new Air Travel page will open and display the map you placed there.

3. Move the mouse pointer around the map to see the various hotspots you created and their URLs in the status bar. Click several to see that they work, using Back to return to the Air map page. When you are done looking at the map, click Back to return to the Home page.

4. Click CRUISES to open the second page, click the image of the ship, and your third page should open (click Refresh if this doesn't work).

5. Click Up on the link bar to return to the second page.

6. Scroll down the page until you can see the two or three graphics you added, one or more of which you assigned a link to an external web.

7. If you are connected to the Internet and entered the Royal Caribbean URL, click it, and the Royal Caribbean web will open, as you can see in Figure 6-12. You have been transported out of your web to the Royal Caribbean web in Miami, Florida. Click Back to return to your web.

8. Close your browser. If you have any problems, edit the links to see what the trouble is. When all your links are working, click Hyperlinks in the Views bar.

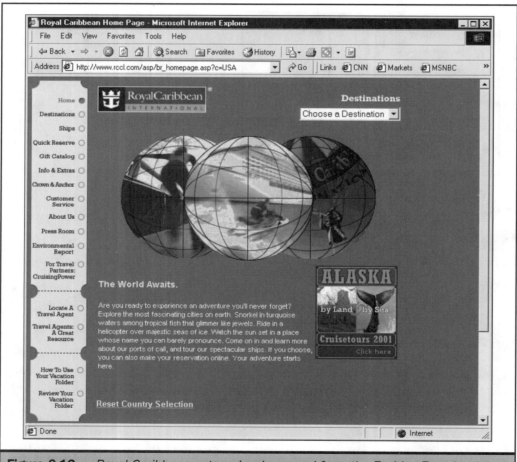

Figure 6-12.   *Royal Caribbean external web opened from the Exciting Travel web**

*Royal Caribbean home page used with the permission of Royal Caribbean Cruises Ltd.

Managing Hyperlinks

The Exciting Travel web displayed in Hyperlinks view now looks very different than it did when you started this chapter, as you can see in Figure 6-13. With this ability to display your links, FrontPage is an excellent tool for managing them. Besides the obvious visual checking that you can do in Hyperlinks view, it has the ability to verify that the link exists through the Verify Hyperlink button on the Reporting toolbar. FrontPage also has a command in the Tools menu that helps you in link management: Recalculate Hyperlinks updates the display of all links as well as the server databases used by the Include and Search components. To check out your links:

1. Click Reports in the Views bar. The Reporting toolbar should open automatically with the Reports view. If it did not open, open the View menu and choose Toolbars | Reporting.

2. Click Verifies Hyperlinks… on the right of the Reporting toolbar. You are given a choice of verifying all hyperlinks or just unknown ones, which are listed behind the dialog box, and given a tip that all open modified pages should be saved. Click Verify All Hyperlinks and click Start. Each of your links is checked (if you are not currently connected to the Internet, your system will attempt to connect if you have

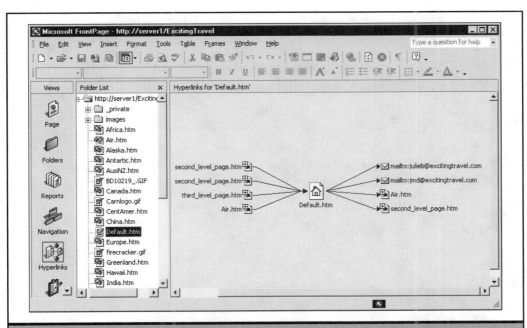

Figure 6-13.   *Hyperlinks view showing the links to and from the home page*

an external link) and, if broken, entered on the Broken Hyperlinks report shown next (I intentionally deleted two of the map links to show broken links).

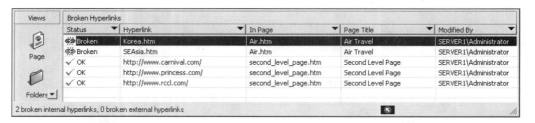

3. Select a broken link and click Edit Hyperlink on the Reporting toolbar. The Edit Hyperlink dialog box will open, as shown next, allowing you to replace the current link with a new one. You can change all pages with this link, or only selected ones.

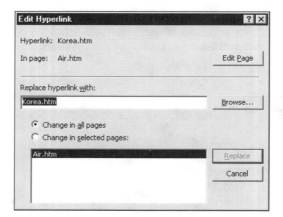

4. If you click Browse in the Edit Hyperlink dialog box, the Insert Hyperlink dialog box will open, although it is called Edit Hyperlink. Here you can select a page in the current web, enter any URL, browse for a site on the Web, search for a file on your disk, or create a new page.

5. When you have fixed all of your broken links, return to Hyperlinks view for your Home page, and select Recalculate Hyperlinks from the fully extended Tools menu. You are told what the process will do, and that the procedure will take several minutes, as shown next. Click Yes to proceed. When the process is complete, your web will be redisplayed in FrontPage with any repairs it was able to do.

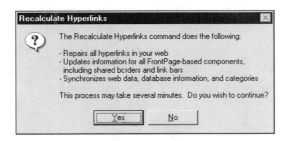

Note *When you have broken a link, the icon for the linked page is broken in the Hyperlinks view of FrontPage, like this:*

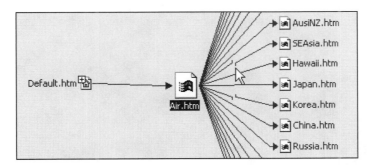

You have seen in this chapter how easy it is to establish links in FrontPage both with text and with graphics, within a web and externally, and how you can manage those links with some powerful tools. Next, we'll look at the great tools FrontPage provides to add and work with tables and frames in your webs.

The Complete Reference

FrontPage 2002

Chapter 7

Using Tables and Frames

So far in this book, you have used the full width of a web page for placing all text and graphics. Good layout designs can be accomplished this way, but it does not allow for text or graphics to be placed in independent columns, and the only way to align text within a line (other than at the ends) is to add spaces with the Formatted paragraph style. FrontPage has two features that allow you to break up some or all of a page into sections that can contain text or graphics. These two features are tables and frames. You can also position page elements using cascading style sheets, which are covered in Chapter 10, but support for style sheets is available only in the latest browsers. Tables and frames are supported in older browsers, which means your design is more likely to appear as you intended.

 Normally, browsers ignore multiple spaces in text; only the first space is displayed. The two exceptions to this are when the spaces are formatted with the Formatted paragraph style and when the nonbreaking space HTML character ( ) is inserted from the Symbol dialog box (the first character in the first row). Using HTML code is covered in Chapter 12.

Designing with Tables

Tables allow you to divide a portion of a page into rows and columns that create *cells* by their intersection. Tables can be used to systematically arrange information in rows and columns, or they can be used to lay out text and graphics on a page. In web design, tables are probably the most important tool for creative page layout. Just a few of the ways that you can use tables are as follows:

- Tabular data display, with and without cell borders
- Side-by-side columns of text
- Aligning labels and boxes for forms
- Text on one side, graphics on the other
- Placing borders around text or graphics
- Placing graphics on both sides of text or vice versa
- Wrapping text around a graphic
- Adding colored backgrounds to text or graphics

When you create a table, you can determine the number of rows and columns in the table, the horizontal percentage of a page that will be used by the table, the percentage of the table's width in each column, and whether the table has a caption. Within the percentage limits set for the table and column, a cell will automatically expand both horizontally and vertically to contain the information placed in it.

Although you can create a table based on a percentage of the screen, with columns as a percentage of the table, there are often problems getting the table to display the way you want. If you use fixed pixel widths based on the minimum 640×480 screen, you'll be able to create a more consistent look. Each method has advantages and you will probably use both, depending on the function of the table.

After a table has been created, you can:

- Add or remove rows and/or columns
- Combine adjacent cells
- Split one or more cells
- Add to or remove from a cell or group of cells any formatting available to the table's contents
- Split the table into two or more tables
- Edit the border of the table
- Enter repetitive information into the table using Fill Right and Fill Down
- Automatically format a table

Displaying Tabular Data in a Table

The classic table, such as you might create in a spreadsheet application, segments text into rows and columns. To build such a table, take the following steps:

1. If it's not already loaded, start FrontPage.

2. In FrontPage, open the File menu and choose New | Page or Web.

3. In the New Page or Web task pane, select the One Page Web option. In the Specify The Location Of The New Web combo box, select your web server and type **Wine** for the title of the new FrontPage web, and then click OK.

4. Click the Folders view in the Views bar, and then double-click the Home Page (Default.htm) in the Contents, or right, pane.

5. Press ENTER to move down the page one line and leave room at the top.

6. Open the Table menu and choose Insert | Table. The Insert Table dialog box will open. Figure 7-1 shows what this book will use as the default values in this dialog box. If your dialog box has different values in it, change them to match the values here and then click Set As Default For New Tables. In the dialog box, take a look at the options available when you create a table; they are described in Table 7-1.

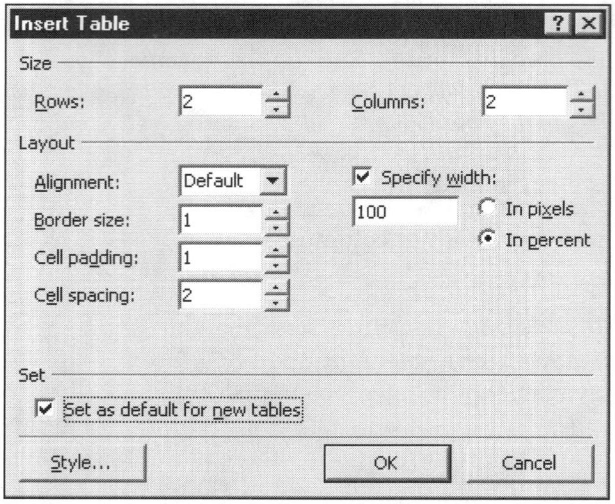

Figure 7-1. *The defaults for new tables*

Option	Description
Rows	Specifies the number of horizontal rows in the table.
Columns	Specifies the number of vertical columns in the table.
Alignment	Aligns the table on the left, center, or right of the page. Default alignment is the same as left alignment.
Border Size	Sets the number of pixels in the border. A 0-pixel border will not appear in a browser, but you'll see a dotted line in FrontPage. The default is 1.
Cell Padding	Sets the number of pixels between the inside edges of a cell and the cell contents on all four sides. The default is 1.

Table 7-1. *Table Options*

Option	Description
Cell Spacing	Sets the number of pixels between adjacent cells. The default is 2.
Width	Sets the overall table width to be a fixed number of pixels or a percentage of the window size, if Specify Width is selected. Otherwise, the table is the sum of the cells, which are individually sized to contain their contents within the size of the window. If the percentage method is selected, each cell is given an equal percentage of the table.

Table 7-1. *Table Options* (continued)

CREATING WEB SITES

7. Click OK. A two-row, two-column (four-cell) table is displayed with the cursord in the first column of the first row. Select the table by pressing and holding SHIFT+CTRL while pressing END (to select everything to the end of the page, see the following Tip), and then remove it by pressing DEL. If the new paragraph character you entered in Step 5 is also removed, press ENTER to place a blank line at the top of the page.

To delete a table with DEL, you must select something outside of the table, like a new line or new paragraph character, in addition to the table itself and delete that something with the table.

8. Click the Insert Table button on the toolbar. In the drop-down table that opens, click the second cell from the left in the second row, as shown next. Another four-cell table appears on your page.

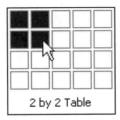

2 by 2 Table

The Insert Table button on the toolbar offers a quick method for creating a table using the defaults, while the Insert Table option in the Table menu allows you to set the properties for the table as it is created.

You can create a table with more rows or columns than shown in the Insert Table drop-down table by dragging past the edge of the list. The box will expand to display the number of rows and/or columns you select.

Working with Table Properties

Table properties affect all of the cells in a table and establish how the overall table will look. To see that for yourself:

1. In the new table that was just created, type **1** in the upper-left cell, press TAB to move to the cell on the right, and type

   This is a longer statement

   Your table should look like the one shown next. The table takes up almost 100 percent of the window's width, and the two cells in each row split that width.

1	This is a longer statement

2. Press the DOWN ARROW twice to move out of the table, and then press ENTER to leave a blank line.

Pressing TAB in the last cell of a table will insert a new row at the bottom of the table.

3. Open the Table menu and choose Insert | Table. In the Insert Table dialog box, click Specify Width to clear it, and then click OK. A second, much smaller table appears.

4. Type **1**, press TAB, and type

   This is a longer statement

5. Press TAB again to move to the left cell in the second row, type **2**, press TAB once more, and type

   This is a statement

   Each column in the table is as wide as the cell in that column with the longest content, as shown in Figure 7-2.

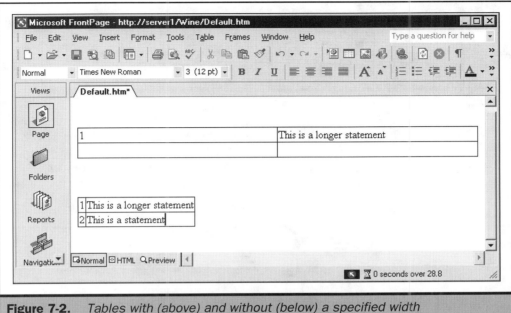

Figure 7-2.   *Tables with (above) and without (below) a specified width*

6. Right-click the second table to open the context menu. You can see that it has both Table Properties and Cell Properties options. Choose Table Properties, opening the dialog box shown in Figure 7-3. Like the dialog box (shown in Figure 7-1) opened with the Insert Table option in the Table menu, it allows you to set the table's Alignment, Border Size, Cell Padding, Cell Spacing, and Width. You can also choose a height for the table, a background picture or color, colors for the table's border, and whether to show both the cell and table borders, or just the table borders. The Float option allows text to wrap around the table by placing the table at the left or right edge of the page. This dialog box does not allow you to specify the number of rows and columns.

7. Change Border Size to **5**, Cell Padding to **6**, Cell Spacing to **8**, uncheck Show Both Cells And Table Borders if it is checked, and click OK. Your table should look like the following one on the left. Reopen Table Properties, choose Show Both Cells And Table Borders, and click OK. The table should now look like the one on the right.

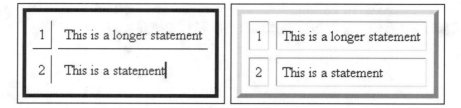

8. Right-click the upper-left cell in the upper table (see Figure 7-2) and select Cell Properties. The Cell Properties dialog box will open, as you can see in Figure 7-4. Take a moment and look at the options it contains. They are described in Table 7-2.

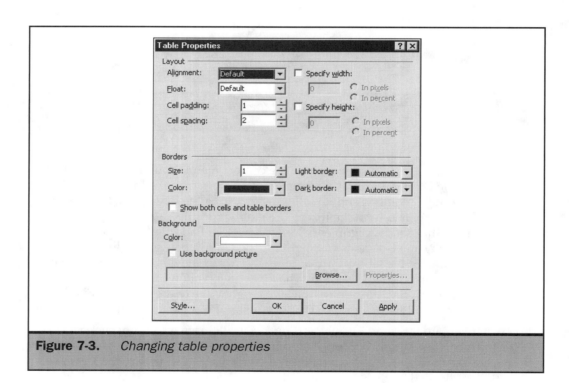

Figure 7-3. *Changing table properties*

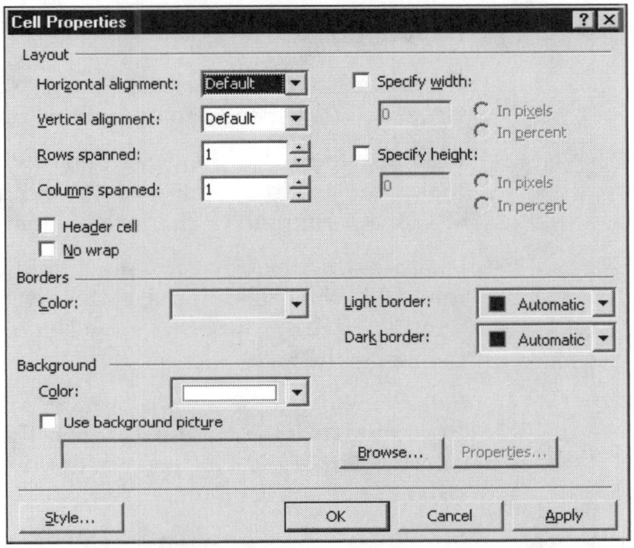

Figure 7-4. *Changing cell properties*

Option	Description
Horizontal Alignment	Horizontally aligns the contents of the cell. It can be Left, Center, Right, Justify, or Default, which is the same as Left.
Vertical Alignment	Vertically aligns the contents of a cell. It can be Top, Middle, Baseline, Bottom, or Default, which is the same as Middle. Baseline aligns the baseline of text in a cell with the baseline of the largest text in the row.
Rows Spanned	Joins adjacent vertical cells to make a single larger cell that spans two or more rows.

Table 7-2. *Cell Properties*

Option	Description
Columns Spanned	Joins adjacent horizontal cells to make a single larger cell that spans two or more columns.
Header Cell	Identifies the cell as the label for a row or column and makes the text in the cell bold. (You can also do this with the paragraph or character formatting options.)
No Wrap	Indicates that the web browser should not wrap the text in the cell; otherwise, the text will be wrapped if the browser window is too narrow to display the text.
Specify Width	Sets the width to be a fixed number of pixels or a percentage of the table size, if Specify Width is selected. Otherwise, the cell width is automatically sized to hold its contents.
Specify Height	Sets the height to be a fixed number of pixels or a percentage of the table size, if Specify Height is selected. Otherwise, the cell height is automatically sized to hold its contents.
Borders	Sets the color used for the border, which can consist of one or two colors. Use the Border drop-down to specify a single-color border, and use any two of the three drop-downs to specify a two-color border, which will have a three-dimensional effect.
Background	Sets the background for a cell. This can be either a picture, for which you can browse and set its properties, or a background color.

Table 7-2. *Cell Properties* (continued)

Applying Cell Properties

Cell properties apply to just the one or more selected cells in a table, as shown in the following steps.

Note | *If you change the cell width, you should do so for an entire column, and you should make sure that the sum of the cell widths in a row does not exceed 100 percent, or you will get unpredictable results.*

1. With the insertion point still in the upper-left cell of the upper table and the Cell Properties dialog box open, change Horizontal Alignment to Center, Vertical Alignment to Top, and click OK. You should see the contents of the cell you selected (a "1") change accordingly.

Note | *Cell padding and spacing may prevent much movement, especially vertically, in a cell when you change the alignment.*

2. Select the bottom row in the upper table by pointing to the border of the table and clicking when the pointer changes to a heavy arrow. Then right-click the selected row, choose Cell Properties, change Columns Spanned to **2**, and click OK. Your table should look as shown next. The leftmost cell does span the two upper cells, but you now have an extra cell on the right (although it might look like an extra column was created, it is actually only an extra cell).

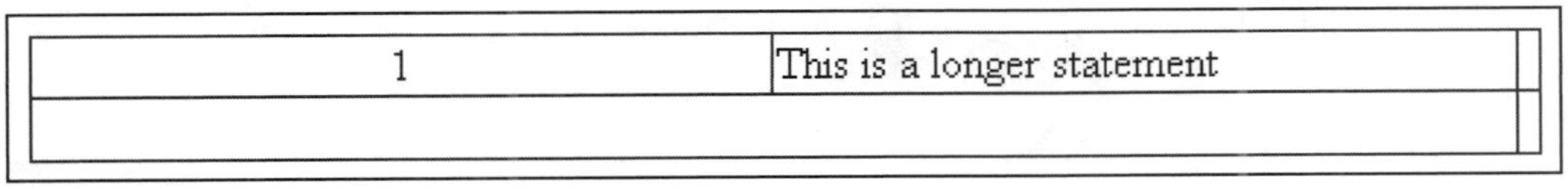

1	This is a longer statement	

Tip | *To select either a row or a column, move the mouse pointer to the outer edge of the table—the left edge for a row, the top edge for a column—until the mouse pointer changes to a heavy arrow, and click. If you drag the heavy arrow, you can select multiple rows or columns.*

Note | *The width of your columns may be different than the illustration due to differences in screen resolution.*

3. Press CTRL+Z or choose Undo Edit Properties from the Edit menu to undo Step 2. In a moment, you'll see another way to do this that is probably closer to what you want.

CREATING WEB SITES

4. Select the top row of the upper table, open the Cell Properties dialog box, increase Rows Spanned to **2**, and click OK. The top two cells come down and push the bottom two to the right, like this:

1	This is a longer statement	

5. Click the Undo button on the toolbar.

6. Select the two cells in the left column, open Cell Properties, uncheck Specify Width, and click OK. Click the top left cell, open the Cell Properties dialog box, click Specify Width and In Percent, type **20** for the width, and click OK. Both of the two left cells (not just the cell you selected) become smaller, as you can see here:

1	This is a longer statement

7. Click Undo, click the bottom right cell, and open the Table menu, extending it to its full length. Look at the options in this menu, which are described in Table 7-3.

Option	Description
Draw Table	Creates a table by enabling you to draw the outside border and then insert columns and rows.
Insert | Table	Opens the Insert Table dialog box, where you can select the properties of a table to place at the current insertion point. If the insertion point is in the cell of another table, a second table is placed in that cell.
Insert | Rows Or Columns	Opens the Insert Rows Or Columns dialog box, where you can select the number of rows or columns above, below, to the left, or to the right of the current selection.

Table 7-3. *Table Menu Options*

Option	Description
Insert | Cell	Inserts a new cell to the left of a selected cell, pushing any cells on the right farther to the right.
Insert | Caption	Inserts a blank line, with an insertion point for typing text, immediately above the active table. This line is aligned with and attached to the table. If you select or delete the table, the caption is also selected or deleted. The initial alignment is for the caption to be centered on the table, but it can also be left- or right-aligned on the table.
Delete Cells	Deletes the selected cells, which must be in whole columns or rows.
Select Table, Cell, Column, or Row	Selects a particular area so that it can be merged, split, or sized. You can also select a cell by pressing ALT while clicking the cell.
Merge Cells	Joins two or more selected cells in a row or column—including an entire row or column—into a single cell that spans the area originally occupied by the cells that were merged.
Split Cells	Opens the Split Cells dialog box, where you can split the selected cell into multiple rows or multiple columns.
Split Table	Splits the table into two separate tables immediately above the current row.
Table AutoFormat	Opens the Table AutoFormat dialog box where you can choose from 31 different table formats and select whether to apply the format to the borders, shading, font, and color of a table.
Distribute Rows or Columns Evenly	Equalizes the width or height of the selected rows or columns.
AutoFit To Contents	Reduces the width of each column in a table to the minimum width needed to display the longest content in the column. This has the same effect as clearing the Specify Width check box in the Cell and Table Properties dialog boxes.

Table 7-3. *Table Menu Options* (continued)

Option	Description
Convert Text to Table	Opens the Convert Text to Table dialog box, where you convert selected text into a table. You should use commas (or another punctuation character) to separate columns, and paragraphs to separate rows. See the Tip in the "Building a Tabular Table" section later in this chapter for a detailed explanation of why you should not use tabs to separate columns.
Convert Table to Text	Converts a table into text with the contents of each cell becoming a separate paragraph.
Fill Down or Right	Repeats the contents of the first cell in the selected cells of a row or column.
Table, Cell, or Caption Properties	Opens the Table, Cell, or Caption Properties dialog box.

Table 7-3. *Table Menu Options* (continued)

Tip *To select multiple cells not in a row or column, press and hold CTRL while clicking the additional cells.*

Employing the Table Menu Options

The Table menu provides some important options for working with tables. To see for yourself:

1. In the Table menu, choose Insert | Table, accept the existing settings in the Insert Table dialog box, and click OK. You should now have a 2×2 table in the cell of your original table, as shown here:

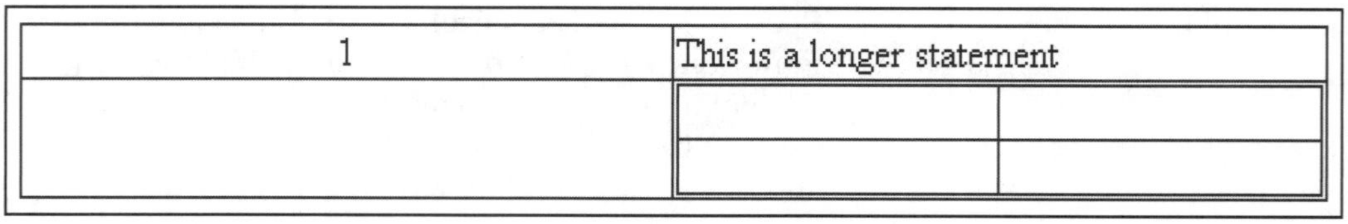

1	This is a longer statement	

2. Click Undo and click the upper-left cell in the same table. Open the Table menu and choose Insert | Rows Or Columns. The Insert Rows Or Columns dialog box will open:

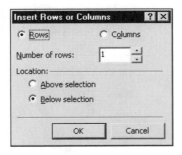

3. Accept the default options, Rows, 1, and Below Selection, and click OK. A new row appears in the middle of the table.

4. Reopen the Table menu and choose Insert | Rows Or Columns again. Click Columns, Left Of Selection, and then OK. A new column appears on the left so that your table now looks like this:

		1	This is a longer statement

5. Open the Table menu and choose Insert | Cell. A new cell appears in the table, pushing the right cell in the row out to the right. The insertion point also moves to the new cell, like this:

		1	This is a longer statement

6. From the Table menu choose Select | Cell, or ALT+click the cell, and then choose Delete Cells from the Table menu. The new cell disappears.

7. From the Table menu, choose Insert | Caption. An insertion point appears above and centered on the table. Type

   This is a Caption

8. Select the bottom row of the first table. Then, from the Table menu, choose Merge Cells. The bottom row now only contains a single cell, as shown next:

This is a Caption		
	1	This is a longer statement

9. Click in the upper-right cell of the first table, and then choose Split Cells in the Table menu. The Split Cells dialog box will open:

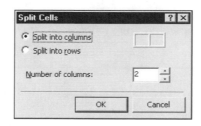

10. Accept the defaults and click OK. Your original cell is now split into two, as shown here:

This is a Caption			
	1	This is a longer statement	

11. Click at the top of the second column, the top cell of which contains "1." From the Table menu, choose Fill | Down. A "1" appears in the other cell that is selected.

12. Click in the bottom cell, open the Table menu, and choose Split Table. The upper table is now two tables, like this:

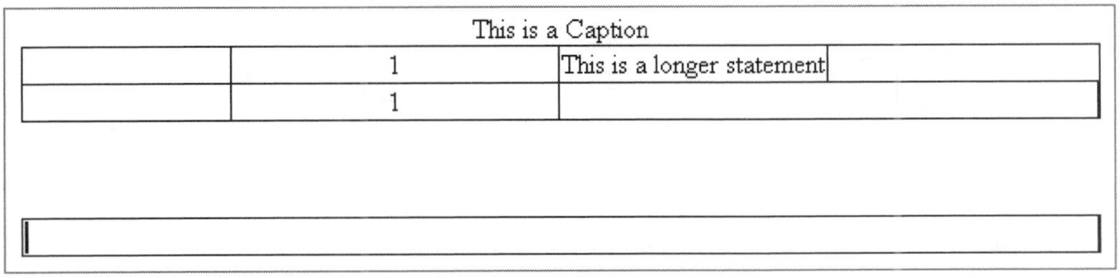

		This is a Caption	
	1	This is a longer statement	
	1		

CREATING
WEB SITES

> **Tip**   *Tables can be selected from the Table menu and by double-clicking in the left margin of the page opposite the table.*

13. With the insertion point in the new single-cell second table, open the Table menu and choose Select | Table. Now press DEL. You'll see nothing happens. Unlike earlier versions of FrontPage this does not delete a table.

14. Move the insertion point to the blank line between the top two tables, press and hold CTRL+SHIFT, press the DOWN ARROW, and then press DEL. The new single-cell table will be deleted.

> **Tip**   *To delete a table, you must select both the table and some object, such as a blank line outside the table, and then press DEL or choose Delete from the Edit menu.*

15. Click in the upper table, open the Table menu and choose Table AutoFormat. The Table AutoFormat dialog box will open, as you can see in Figure 7-5.

16. Select each of the 31 formats to look at them in the Preview area. After looking at them all, select the one you want to use here. Then turn on and off each of the options under Formats To Apply and Apply Special Formats. Select the options you want to use and click OK. The format will be applied and appear on the page. Press CTRL+Z to undo the formatting.

17. Open the Table Properties dialog box and set the Border Size to **0**; then click OK. The table border will become a dotted line. Click Preview. There is now no indication that your text is being formatted by a table, as shown next. Click Normal and then click Undo.

	This is a Caption	
1		This is a longer statement
1		

Drawing a Table

The Table menu and Table Properties dialog box allow you to create complex tables easily, but you can also simply draw a complex table, as described next.

1. Place the insertion point in the blank line between the two tables, press ENTER, and then press the UP ARROW once.

 If you need a blank line between the tables, place the insertion point in the upper-left cell of the lower table and press ENTER.

2. Open the Table menu and choose Draw Table. The Tables toolbar will be displayed, and the cursor turns into a pencil. Table 7-4 describes the Tables Toolbar options.

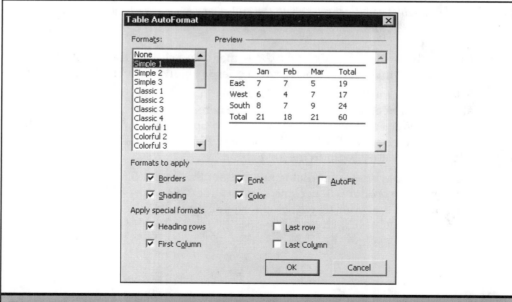

Figure 7-5. *Applying a ready-made format to a table*

Button	Option	Description
	Draw Table	Allows you to draw the overall dimensions of a table, and row and column borders.
	Eraser	Removes rows and columns from a table.
	Insert Rows	Inserts rows without opening the Insert Rows or Columns dialog box.
	Insert Columns	Inserts columns without opening the Insert Rows or Columns dialog box.
	Delete Cells	Deletes the selected cells.
	Merge Cells	Merges the selected cells.
	Split Cells	Opens the Split Cells dialog box.
	Align Top	Aligns the cell's contents with the top of the cell.
	Center Vertically	Centers the cell's contents vertically.
	Align Bottom	Aligns the cell's contents with the bottom of the cell.
	Distribute Rows Evenly	Equalizes the height of the rows in the table.
	Distribute Columns Evenly	Equalizes the width of the columns in the table.
	AutoFit	Reduces the width of each column in a table to the minimum width needed to display the longest content in the column.
	Fill Color	Changes the background color of the selected cell, row, column, or table.

Table 7-4.   *Tables Toolbar Options*

Button	Option	Description
None ▾	Select Format	Choose one of 31 different table formats.
▦	AutoFormat dialog box	Opens the Table AutoFormat dialog box where you can choose from 31 different table formats and select whether to apply the format to the borders, shading, font, and color of a table.
↓	Fill Down	Repeats the contents of the first cell in the selected cells of a column.
→	Fill Right	Repeats the contents of the first cell in the selected cells of a row.

Table 7-4. *Tables Toolbar Options* (continued)

3. Place the pencil-cursor between the two existing tables, and drag it horizontally across the page, and then vertically so that the new table is approximately the height of the second table. The exact dimensions are not important.

4. Place the cursor on the top border of the table approximately in the center. Drag down to the bottom border.

5. Create three rows in the right column by pointing to the column divider you just created and dragging to the right table border twice. Don't worry about the height of the rows.

6. Click Distribute Rows Evenly on the toolbar, and the three rows will be adjusted to equal heights, as shown here:

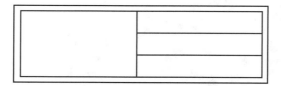

7. Draw a vertical line dividing the second row in the right column into two columns.

8. Draw two vertical lines dividing the third row in the right column into three columns. The second new column will align with the column divider in the row above it, as shown next.

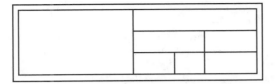

9. Point on the right column border of the first column. The cursor will turn into a double-headed arrow.

10. Drag the column border to the right to make the column wider.

11. Select the Eraser tool in the Tables toolbar, and drag it across the column divider in the bottom row so that the right column of the bottom row is divided into two columns, like this:

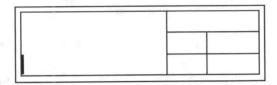

12. Click the Eraser tool to deselect it, and then point on the top border of the table, over the second column. When the pointer turns into a heavy arrow, click to select the column.

13. Press SHIFT and move the pointer to the right, over the column that wasn't selected, and click again. The first column of the table should *not* be selected, and the remaining two columns should be selected.

14. Click Distribute Columns Evenly on the toolbar. Your drawn table should now look similar to this:

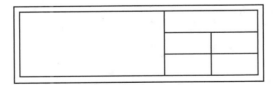

15. Select the table and adjoining space, and then press DEL to remove it.

Through the preceding exercises you saw the incredible flexibility in FrontPage's table capability. And it is all WYSIWYG; you instantly see the table you are building very much as it will appear in a browser. Next, build a real table and then look at all three of your tables in a browser.

Building a Tabular Table

This web was called "Wine" earlier in the chapter because you are about to build a table of wines as might be prepared by a winery. To do so:

1. Click below the bottom table, press ENTER to leave a blank line, and then open the Insert menu and choose File.

2. Open the Insert menu, choose File, and select your CD-ROM drive and the file Wine.txt in the \Book\Chap07 folder. Select Normal Paragraphs With Line Breaks in the Convert Text dialog box and click OK.

Note   *Which option you select in the Convert Text dialog box is determined by the format of the file you are inserting. The Wine.txt file was created in Notepad and is correctly inserted with the Normal Paragraphs With Line Breaks option. Try the various options when importing files to see which works best.*

3. Select all the text that was inserted, open the Table menu and choose Convert | Text To Table.

4. In the Convert Text To Table dialog box, select the Other option button, delete the period in the text box, and type **;** (a semicolon). Click OK. Figure 7-6 shows the table created from the text file. Several of the words in the table have been underlined by FrontPage's spell checker. They are spelled correctly, but the words do not exist in the FrontPage dictionary. Right-click the underlined words and choose Ignore All or Add To Dictionary from the context menu.

Tip   *HTML doesn't support tabs, so if you import a text file that uses tabs to separate (or delimit) each column's contents, the tabs will be removed and the table will not be created correctly. It is best to use a punctuation character that doesn't appear in the text file. The semicolon was used in this example since commas and hyphens appear in the text. In this example, periods could be used instead.*

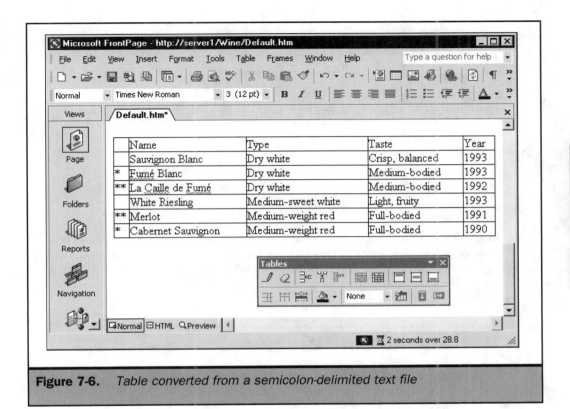

Figure 7-6. *Table converted from a semicolon-delimited text file*

5. If you have one, select the bottom (blank) row of the table and delete it.

6. Right-click the table and choose Table Properties. Choose Center alignment, enter a cell padding of **4**, turn off Specify Width if it is selected, click Show Both Cells And Table Borders, and click OK.

7. Select the top row, right-click a cell in the first row, open the Cell Properties dialog box, click Header Cell and Left Horizontal Alignment, and click OK.

8. From the Table menu, choose Insert | Caption. Click the Bold button and select 4 (14 pt) from the Font Size drop-down list (both on the Formatting toolbar), then type

   Fair Mountain Wines Currently Available

9. Select the first row of the table, then click the down arrow of the Fill Color (Auto) button in the Table toolbar. Select Aqua from the Color drop-down list (the third color square from the left in the second row).

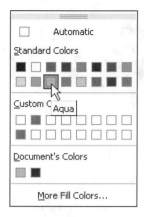

10. Select the remaining rows of the table, and then open the Cell Properties dialog box. Select Yellow from the Background Color drop-down list and click OK. When you are done, your table should look like the one in Figure 7-7. You may have further ideas about how to improve the table. Try them. You can always click on Undo if you don't like a change.

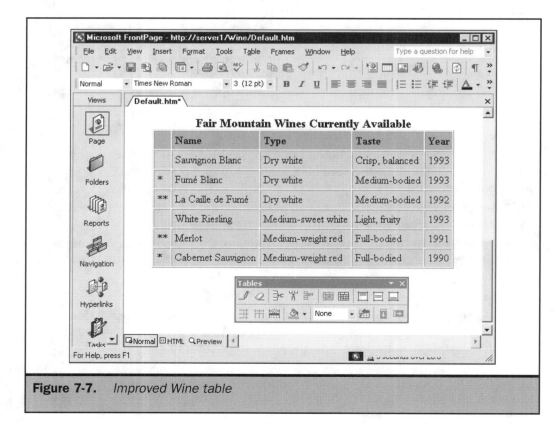

Figure 7-7. *Improved Wine table*

11. Click the Save button to save the tables you have built.

12. Open the File menu and choose Preview In Browser. Select your browser in the Preview In Browser dialog box and click Preview. You should see the Fair Mountain Wines table just like it appeared in Figure 7-7.

13. If you have another browser, open it and view your tables page. Figure 7-8 shows the table in both Internet Explorer 5.5 and Netscape Navigator 6.0. The only differences are Netscape's treatment of the header row and the darkness of

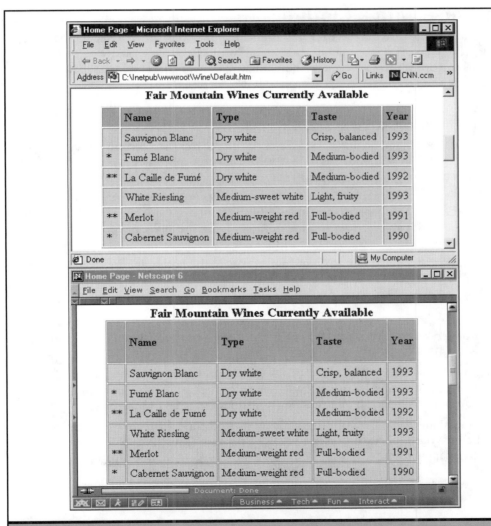

Figure 7-8.   *Wine table in both Internet Explorer 5.5 and Netscape 6.0*

the border lines. Close your Wine web in your browser(s) and in FrontPage when you are done looking at it.

Support for tables has improved greatly in current browsers. There used to be considerable differences in how various browsers display tables—if they even did. You need to view your work in various browsers to decide how these differences affect you. In the Internet arena, Netscape and Microsoft have the lion's share of the market, and both support tables quite well.

Using a Table with a Picture

While tabular tables are the classical way users imagine tables, in web page design, tables are extensively used for some or all of a page's layout. Rarely are you aware that there is a table behind the layout. You can see how this works by using a table to separate and caption a picture and then wrap text around it in your Exciting Travel web:

1. In FrontPage, open your Exciting Travel web, then open the file second_level_page.htm in Page View.

2. Open the File menu and choose Save As. Name the page **second_level_table.htm** and save it in your Exciting Travel web. This prevents any of your changes from affecting your original page.

3. If it isn't already open, select Toolbars | Tables from the View menu and choose the Draw Table tool on the Tables toolbar; then draw a table around the graphic of the cruise ship. When you are done drawing the table, the graphic will be pushed below it.

4. Draw a horizontal line to create a new row at the bottom of the table, as shown in Figure 7-9.

5. Click the Draw Table tool to deselect it, then drag the graphic into the top row of the table.

6. In the bottom row of the table type **The Love Boat** and format it as Heading 3.

7. Open the Table Properties dialog box. Select Left in the Float drop-down menu and choose a Border Size of 0. Click OK. Now the text will wrap around the table, as shown in Figure 7-10 (if "South Pacific" is up next to the picture, add another line before it by pressing ENTER to move it below the picture).

8. Save your work, then open the File menu and choose Preview In Browser. Select your favorite browser and click Preview. Figure 7-11 shows the page in Netscape 6.0.

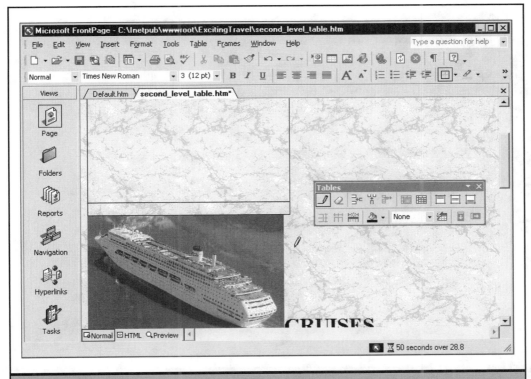

Figure 7-9.   *Adding a two-row table to the Second Level Table page*

9. Close your browser and the Second Level Table page.

Using a table is an easy way to add a caption to an image, as you can see. The importance of tables in web page design is also apparent if you look at the types of pages that can be created from the Page Templates dialog box. Every page type that has more than one column probably uses tables to create the effect.

You may have some other ideas of how to apply tables to this page. Try them. Play with your ideas until you have the look you want—that is how good designs are created. FrontPage's table capability gives you an extremely powerful tool to create what you want.

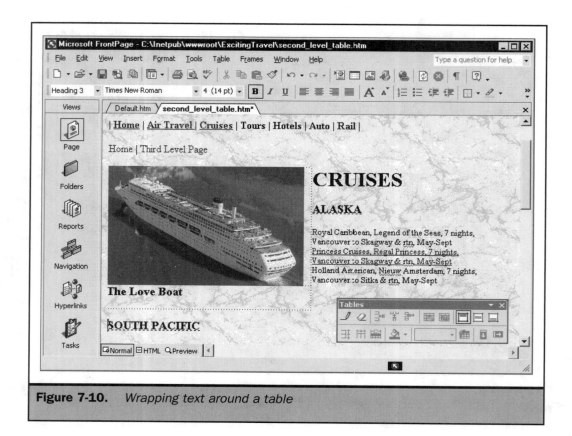

Figure 7-10. *Wrapping text around a table*

Using a Table to Lay Out a Page

A table can be used to lay out all or a large part of a page and therefore be the major influence in how a page will look. Look at how the Home page of the Exciting Travel web would look if a table were used to control the layout of all but the shared bottom border. In this example, you will add a table to an existing page and copy items already on the page to the table. In a normal situation, you would start with a table on a blank or mainly blank page and initially place the items in the table. Here are the steps to use in this example:

1. In your Exciting Travel web, open the file for the Home or Default.htm page in Page View and use Save As to make a copy of the page with the name Home_Table.htm.

2. Press CTRL+HOME to place the insertion point in the upper-left corner (on the left of the web title if the instructions in Chapter 5 were followed). Press ENTER

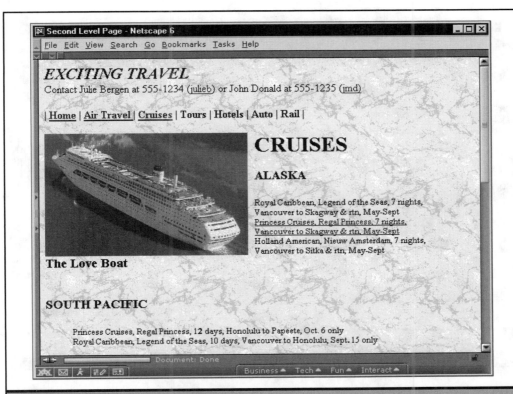

Figure 7-11.   *Text-wrapped table in Netscape 6.0*

to add a blank line at the top of the page and then press the UP ARROW to move the insertion point to the new line.

3. Open the Insert Table icon on the toolbar and choose two columns by four rows. A 2×4 table will appear as shown in Figure 7-12.

4. Select the top row (the top two cells), open the Table menu, and choose Merge Cells. The top row becomes a single cell. Drag the Webtitle.jpg picture to the top row.

5. Select the second row (the second pair of cells), right-click this row, and choose Merge Cells. Drag the pair of lines beginning with "For the latest fares…" and ending with the jmd mailto address to the second row and center it by clicking Center in the toolbar.

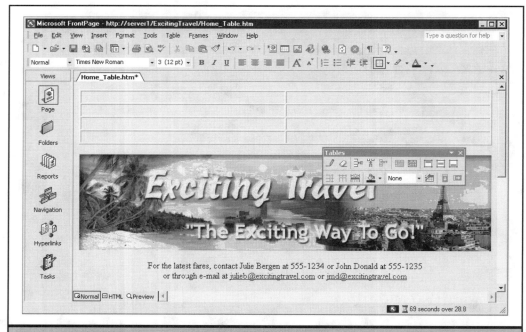

Figure 7-12. *Adding a table to the Exciting Travel Home page*

6. Select the entire Current Specials section down through the parenthetical statement beginning "Some restrictions…" and drag it to the right-hand cell in the third row. If the line separating Current Specials and Available Travel Options was copied into the table, delete it along with any blank lines. Otherwise, delete the line in the body of the page.

7. Select the entire Available Travel Options section down through item 6 and drag it to the right-hand cell in the fourth row.

8. Select the two blank cells on the left in the third and fourth rows and merge the cells. Click in the merged cell, type **Air Travel**, press ENTER, type **Cruises**, press ENTER, type **Tours**, and press ENTER. Format these three lines as Heading 3.

9. Right-click in the left-hand cell spanning rows three and four and click Cell Properties. In the Cell Properties dialog box, open the Vertical Alignment drop-down list, choose Top, in the Specify Width text box enter **15**, and click OK. This should move the three lines to the top of a narrower cell.

10. Select Air Travel, click Link, and double-click Air.htm. Select Cruises, click Link, and double-click Second_Level_Table.htm.

11. Select the two cells on the right of rows three and four, right-click in one of these cells and choose Cell Properties. In the Specify Width text box enter **85**, and click OK.

12. Right-click anywhere in the table, choose Table Properties, change the Borders Size to **0**, and click OK. Save Home_Table.htm and click Preview In Browser. Figure 7-13 shows what you should see.

13. Close your browser and close the Home_Table.htm page, but leave the Exciting Travel web open.

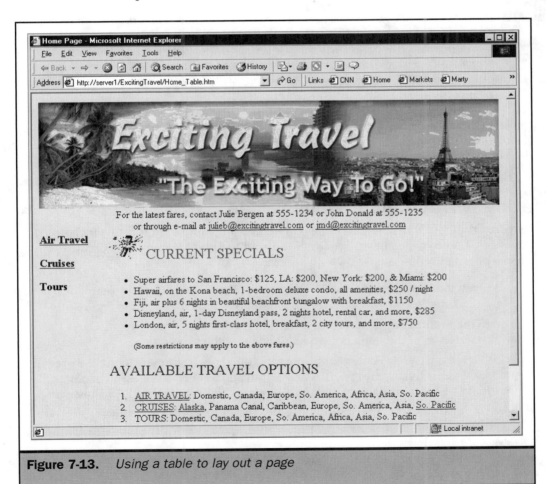

Figure 7-13. *Using a table to lay out a page*

Laying Out with Frames

While both frames and tables divide a page into sections, they do so in very different ways and with very different results. *Tables* are typically a smaller section of a page that has been divided, while traditionally *frames* are actually several pages that have each been allocated a section of a single viewing window. This structure of pages along with the HTML is called a *frames page* or a *frameset*. In FrontPage, frames are built by use of the Frames page templates. The Frames page templates establish a structure of blank pages and the HTML to view them as frames within a single window. This makes the new pages appear as independent segments of a single page.

| Note | *Frame pages created quite a bit of excitement when they were first introduced. This has died down to some extent, and some sources now recommend that they not be used at all. Because frame pages actually load several pages, the total loading time is longer than for a single normal web page. There has also been a tendency to overuse frame pages. Regardless, they are a useful tool for the web designer. They should simply be used with care. Ask yourself if the pages you are creating really benefit from frame pages, and avoid using them simply for a whiz-bang effect.* |

There is a different type of frame called an *inline frame* that is new to FrontPage 2002. It allows you to place a single frame on an existing web page. The inline frame can float or be anchored on the page and displays the contents of another page, which you can scroll. Inline frames are discussed later in this chapter.

Creating a Traditional Frames Page

Explore FrontPage's traditional frames capability and compare it to using tables by building a frames page alternative for your Exciting Travel Home page. Create the frames page with these steps:

1. Open the File menu, choose New | Page or Web, and click Page Templates. In the Page Templates dialog box, click the Frames Pages tab, shown in Figure 7-14.

   In the Frames Pages tab, there is a list of the frames page templates, a description of the template, and a preview of the frames page.

2. Click the Header, Footer, and Contents frame page template icon. The preview shows that this frames page displays four separate web pages: a header, a footer, a contents page, and the main page. Click OK. Figure 7-15 shows the frames page in FrontPage.

Each frame contains two buttons of which you can choose one or the other: Set Initial Page, which you use to choose an existing web page that will be displayed in the frame by default, and New Page, which you use to create a new page to be displayed in the frame.

3. Right-click a frame, and then click Frame Properties. The Frame Properties dialog box shown in Figure 7-16 is displayed. The options are described in Table 7-5.

4. Click the Frames Page button in the Frame Properties dialog box. This displays the Page Properties dialog box that you have used before.

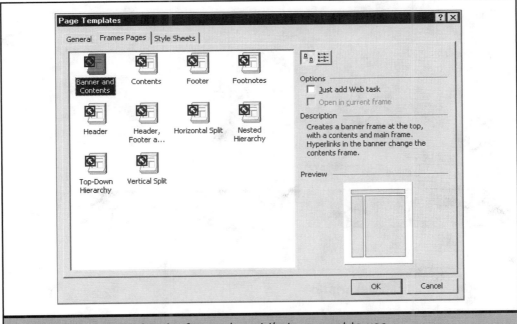

Figure 7-14. *Selecting the frames layout that you want to use*

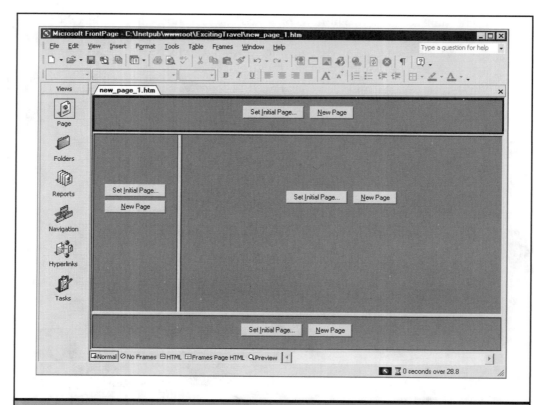

Figure 7-15. *Determining the individual pages that will make up a frames page*

Option	Description
Name	The name of the frame itself, not the page displayed in the frame. This is the name used as a target by hyperlinks in the frame page and the one that determines in which frame a page will be displayed.
Initial Page	The URL of the page that will be displayed in the frame when it is first loaded by the user's browser.

Table 7-5. *Frame Properties*

Option	Description
Frame Size	This has two options, Width and Row Height, that can be set to pixel, percent, or relative values. These function the same way as table dimensions. If your frame contains a graphic, you may want the frame to be no larger than the graphic itself. In that case, you can set the dimensions of the frame to match the graphic using pixel values. The other frames can then use relative or percent values.
Margins	Sets the margins, in pixels, of the selected frame.
Resizable In Browser	Determines if the frame can be resized in the user's browser. If this option is cleared, the user cannot resize the frame.
Show Scrollbars	This has three selections: If Needed, which displays scroll bars if the page content is larger than the space available; Never, which will never display scroll bars regardless of the page content; and Always, which will always display scroll bars. The correct settings for the last two options depend on the page content being displayed in the frame. If it is a menu, you would want the scroll bars to be displayed as needed, and you would probably want the user to be able to resize the frame. If the frame is displaying a header with a graphic, and you've sized the frame to the graphic using the Frame Size options, then you might want to disable both these options.

Table 7-5.   *Frame Properties* (continued)

With a frames page there is an additional tab, Frames, which has two options. The Frame Spacing option is similar to the border width of a table in that it sets the width of the borders between frames in a frame page. The Show Borders check box determines if borders will be displayed between frames. Clearing this check box has the same effect with frames as setting the border width to 0 in a table.

5. Click Cancel to close the Page Properties dialog box; then click Cancel to close the Frame Properties dialog box.

6. In the Top (header) frame, click New Page. A new blank page is opened in the Top frame.

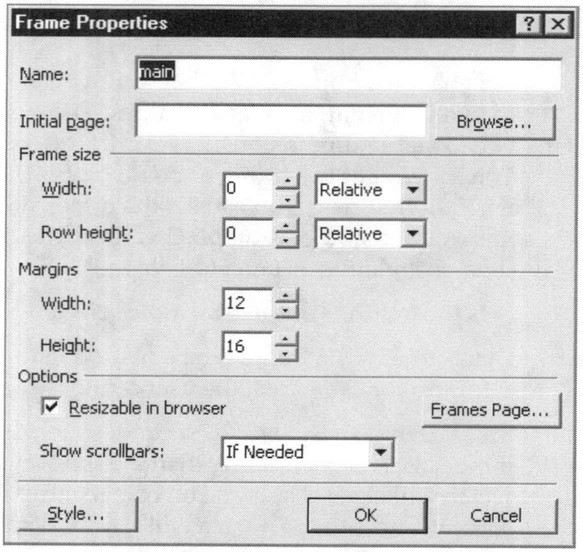

Figure 7-16. *Setting the properties of an individual frame*

7. With the Top frame selected, open the Format menu and choose Shared Borders. In the Shared Borders dialog box, select the Current Page option and then, if it is checked, clear the Bottom check box. Click OK.

> **Tip** *It's usually not a good idea to use shared borders with frame pages. Information may be duplicated and navigation can be complicated by having redundant links. If you are using shared borders in your web, you will usually want to turn off the feature for your frame pages.*

8. Open the Insert menu and choose Picture | From File. In the Picture dialog box, locate the Webtitle.jpg file and double-click it. This will insert the graphic onto the new page.

9. Drag the bottom border of the Top frame down until the entire graphic is visible. Select the graphic and click Center on the toolbar.

10. In the Bottom (footer) frame, click New Page. Open the Format menu and choose Shared Borders. In the Shared Borders dialog box, select the Current Page option and then, if it isn't checked, click the Bottom check box. Click OK. This will create a new page with the Shared Borders footer containing the copyright and other information.

The default page for the Main frame (the right pane in the center of the frames page) will be a variation of the existing home page. Since the Exciting Travel graphic has been placed in the Top frame, you will make a copy of the home page and then remove the graphic, as explained in the following steps.

11. Open the home page (Default.htm) in Page view. Save the page with the filename **Fr_main.htm**. This prevents any changes you make from affecting the home page.

12. Delete the Exciting Travel graphic and any blank lines at the top of the page, then save the page again.

13. Open the frames page in Page view then click Set Initial Page in the Main frame (the right pane in the center of the frames page). In the Insert Hyperlink dialog box that opens, select the modified home page (Fr_main.htm) and click OK.

14. Open the Format menu and choose Shared Borders. In the Shared Borders dialog box, select the Current Page option and then, if it is checked, clear the Bottom check box. Click OK.

15. In the Contents frame (the left frame in the center of the frames page), click New Page.

16. In the Contents frame page type **AIR TRAVEL**, press ENTER, type **CRUISES**, and format both as Heading 3.

17. Select AIR TRAVEL, then click the Link button on the toolbar. In the Insert Hyperlink dialog box, select Air.htm.

18. Click the Target Frame button and, if it isn't already selected, choose Page Default (Main) in the Target Frame dialog box, shown next. Click OK to close the Target Frame dialog box and again to close the Insert Hyperlink dialog box.

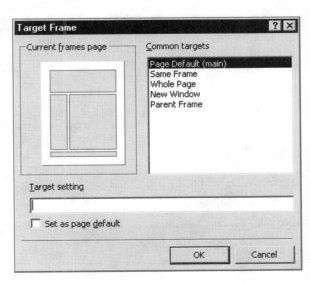

19. Select CRUISES, open the Insert Hyperlink dialog box, select Second_level_ page.htm, make sure that the Target Frame is set to Page Default (Main), and click OK. Your screen should look similar to Figure 7-17.

20. Open the File menu and choose Save As. The Save As dialog box for frame pages opens, as shown in Figure 7-18, and includes an outline of the frames page on the right. This indicates which frame will be saved. To save the frames page itself, there must be a border around the entire page, as shown in Figure 7-18.

21. Click Change Title, enter Frames Page, and click OK. Then enter the File Name Frames.htm and click Save.

22. After the overall frames page is saved, the Save As dialog box will be redisplayed with one of the individual pages in the frame selected. The title and filename you enter will apply to the page in the selected frame.

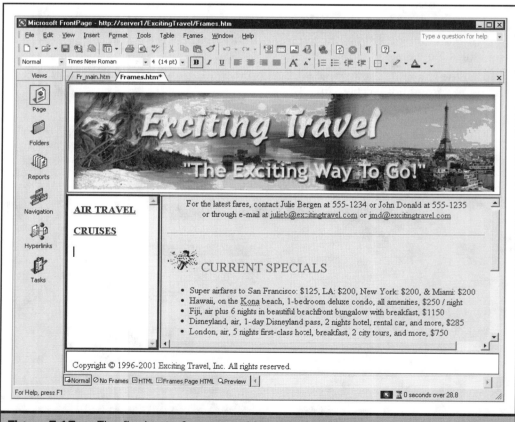

Figure 7-17. *The final set of pages making up a frames page*

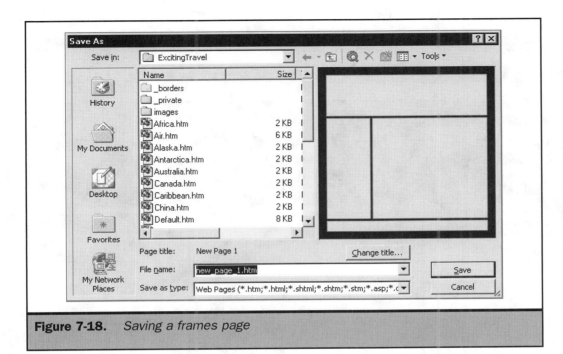

Figure 7-18.   *Saving a frames page*

23. Save the page in the Top (header) frame with the Page Title **Frames Page Header** and the File Name **Fr_header.htm**.

24. Save the page in the Bottom (footer) frame with the Page Title **Frames Page Footer** and the File Name **Fr_footer.htm**.

25. Save the page in the Contents frame with the Page Title **Frames Page Contents** and the File Name **Fr_contents.htm**.

26. Open the File menu and choose Preview In Browser. Figure 7-19 shows the frames page in Internet Explorer 5.5.

27. In your browser, point on the vertical border between the left and right frames in the middle of the page. When the cursor changes into a double-headed arrow, drag the border to the left.

28. Point on the horizontal borders of the header or footer frame. The cursor will not change to a double-headed arrow because, by default in the Header, Footer, and Contents frames page template, these frames cannot be resized.

29. Click the Cruises hyperlink in the Contents frame. The Cruises page (second_level_page.htm) is displayed in the Main frame. Close your browser.

One problem with frame pages is that not all browsers support them. Frames were introduced in Netscape Navigator 2.0, and Microsoft followed suit in Internet Explorer 3.0.

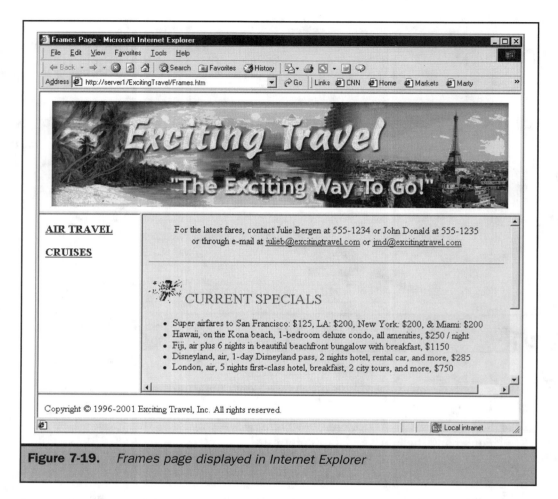

Figure 7-19.   *Frames page displayed in Internet Explorer*

Support for frames was made official with the adoption of HTML 3.2 early in 1997. Older versions of these browsers, as well as other browsers, do not support frames. Some people still use these older browsers, so you must assume a small, but possibly significant, percentage of your audience will not be able to view your frame pages correctly.

This problem is dealt with by creating a No Frames page. If the user's browser does not support frames, the No Frames page is displayed instead. FrontPage will automatically create a No Frames page when a frames page is created, as you can see by clicking the No Frames tab at the bottom of the page when a frames page is open. Figure 7-20 shows the default No Frames page. You can use this page either to direct the user to download a browser that supports frames by creating hyperlinks to Microsoft's or Netscape's browser-download pages on their web sites, or to re-create your frames pages without frames. This is a case where you could use tables to place the categories list in one column and other pages in a second column. Your table could have one row with two columns.

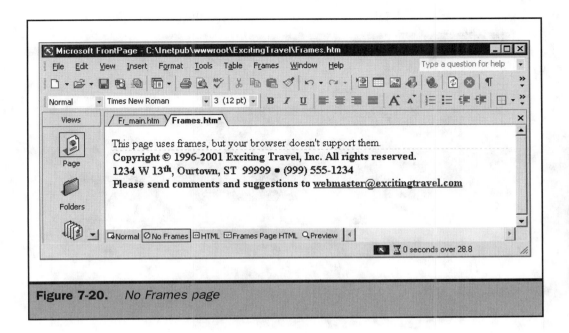

Figure 7-20. *No Frames page*

Frames provide some powerful layout capabilities, in particular the target frame concept and the ability of a frame to scroll. Based on the default target frames, anything that you open by clicking a link in a Contents frame will appear in the Main frame.

Creating an Inline Frame

An inline frame is a single frame on a normal web page. This allows you to have a window on one page that displays the contents of a second page. For example, if the itinerary on the Third Level page of the Exciting Travel web were used in other pages of the web, it would be easier to make changes on a separate itinerary page than on each page where it shows up. By having it as an inline frames page, the reader stays on the current page to see it instead of using a hyperlink to go to a separate itinerary page. See how this is done using the following steps:

1. Open Third_level_page.htm in Page view. Scroll down the page to the Cruise Itinerary heading, place the insertion point at the right end of that line, and press ENTER.

2. Open the Insert menu and choose Inline Frame (you may need to fully open the menu to see it). A frame or window appears on the page, as shown in Figure 7-21.

3. Click New Page. A blank page appears in the frame. Click in the Itinerary table, open the Table menu, and choose Select | Table.

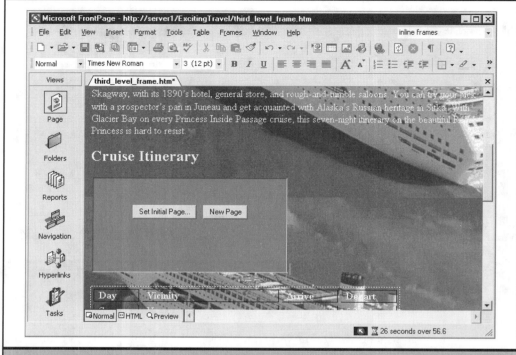

Figure 7-21. *Adding an inline frame to a page*

4. Open the Edit menu and choose Cut. Right-click in the new frame and choose Paste. The table will appear in the frame.

5. Move the insertion point to the upper border of the frame where it becomes a pointer and click to select the entire frame. Selection handles appear around the frame.

6. Drag the lower-right selection handle to size the frame so it nicely fits the table. With the full frame still selected, right-click on the top frame border and choose Inline Frame Properties to open its dialog box, shown in Figure 7-22.

7. Change the frame name to **Itinerary**, change the Width and Height margins to 10, and click OK.

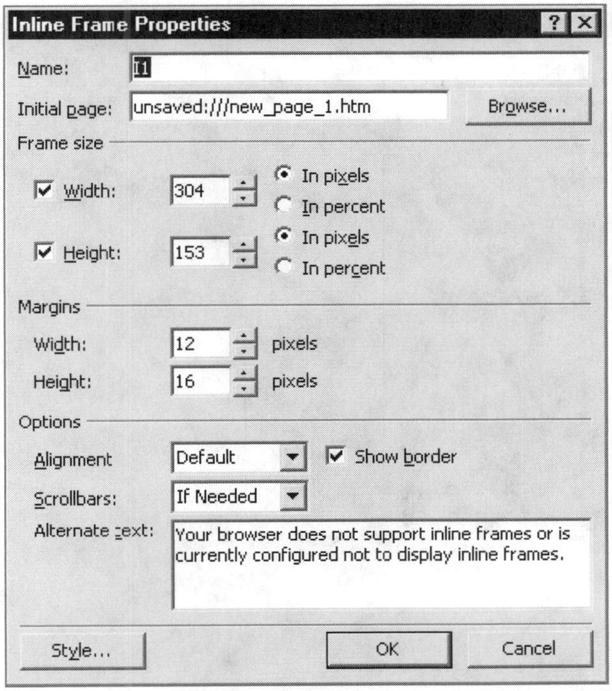

Figure 7-22. *Setting the inline frame properties*

8. Open the File menu, choose Save As and save the page as **Third_level_frame.htm** and click save. After the base page is saved, the Save As dialog box reopens to save the inline frame page. Change the Page title to **Itinerary**, the filename to **Itinerary_frame.htm**, and click Save.

9. Click Preview In Browser. Figure 7-23 shows this scrollable frame within an otherwise normal page.

10. Close your browser and the Exciting Travel web.

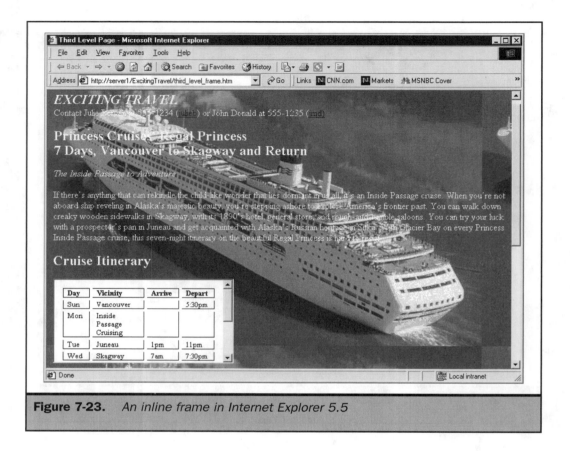

Figure 7-23. An inline frame in Internet Explorer 5.5

Tables and frames add real depth to your ability to create sophisticated, state-of-the-art web pages in FrontPage. You can do it very easily, aided by FrontPage's true WYSIWYG ability that allows you to see the final results.

The
Complete
Reference

FrontPage
2002

Chapter 8

Working with Forms

In Chapters 5 through 7, the focus has been on how to present text and graphic information to users of your web. In this chapter, the tables will be turned—you'll learn how to get information back from users. *Forms* are the obvious mechanism for collecting user input and are the focus of this chapter. Web Components, the focus of Chapter 9, also provide a means for collecting user input and are instrumental in the use of forms. Both forms and Web Components have classically (meaning "last year," in terms of the Web) required either programming or the use of canned programs on a web server. FrontPage has replaced this with its Server Extensions and Components, which save you from any programming or from using canned programs with their arcane HTML calls. FrontPage then goes further by giving you powerful tools to perform these functions in a WYSIWYG environment. See for yourself, starting with using forms.

Using Forms

Forms in a web are very similar to those on paper, as you saw in Chapter 2. You are given boxes to fill in, options to select, and choices to make. The advantages of computer forms over paper forms are that computer forms can be easily modified, you don't have to decipher someone's handwriting, and the data starts out in computer form, so it does not have to be retyped into a computer. As with paper forms, though, the design of a form is very important if you want the user to fill it out willingly and properly. The three cardinal rules of forms are

- Keep it simple.
- Keep it short.
- Make it very clear what the user is supposed to do.

FrontPage provides a comprehensive Form Page Wizard to lead you through the development of a form. In addition, FrontPage has a complete set of tools both in the Forms toolbar and in the Insert menu to allow you to create any form you can dream up. You'll work with both of these in this chapter, beginning with the Form Page Wizard.

Creating Forms with the Form Page Wizard

To create a form, you need to figure out what questions to ask and what fields are necessary for the user to answer them. Go through that process with the idea of creating a questionnaire for prospective project team members. First use the Form Page Wizard to generate the form; then examine and modify the results.

Generating the Form

Like the other wizards you have seen, the Form Page Wizard asks you a series of questions, which it then uses to build a form. To work with the Form Page Wizard, follow these steps:

1. If necessary, start FrontPage.
2. In FrontPage, create a new one-page web and name it **Forms**.

3. Click the arrow to the right of New on the toolbar and choose Page. Select Form Page Wizard in the Page Templates dialog box and click OK. The Form Page Wizard's introductory dialog box will appear telling you about web forms, what the wizard will do, and what you can do with the result. Click Next after reading this.

4. The Form Page Wizard dialog box that opens will eventually show the questions that you are asking on your form. Currently it is blank. Click Add to select the first question.

5. In the next dialog box there is a list of types of questions at the top. Click Contact Information. As you can see in Figure 8-1, a description of the fields that will be placed on the form appears in the middle of the dialog box, and the actual question is displayed at the bottom, where you can change it as you want. Accept the default and click Next.

6. You are then asked to select the specific fields that you want on the form for your first question (see Figure 8-2). All of these are related to an individual contact. For the Name entry you can use one, two, or three fields. Leave the check boxes that are selected as is and click First, Last, which is the two-field choice. Also click Postal Address and Home Phone, and then click Next, leaving the suggested name for the group of variables (Contact) as is.

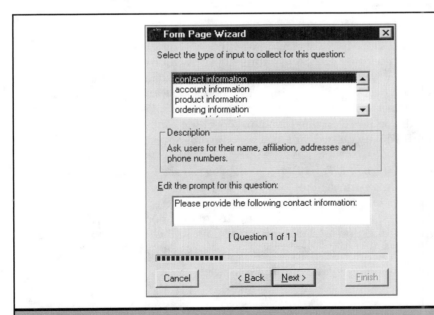

Figure 8-1.   *Choosing the type of questions to be on the form*

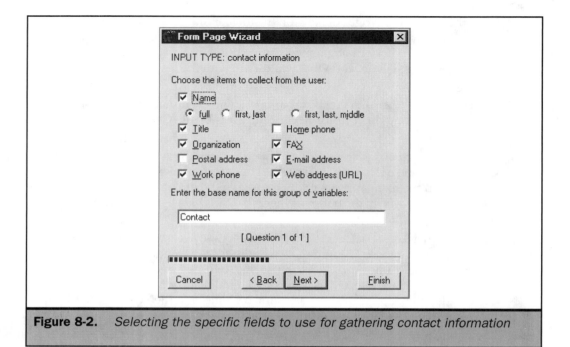

Figure 8-2. *Selecting the specific fields to use for gathering contact information*

7. You are returned to the list of questions, which now shows the contact information question you just selected. Use Steps 5 through 7 to include questions dealing with Account Information and Personal Information. In the dialog box that appears once you choose Account Information, select the As First And Last Names Fields option for the Username, and then accept the other defaults. For the Personal Information dialog box, you don't want to repeat the Name field, so clear the Name check box; but you do want to accept the other defaults.

Note *After you are done using the Form Page Wizard, you can add to, change, and delete what the wizard has produced.*

8. Click Add in the dialog box that shows the list of questions, select the One Of Several Options question, and change the prompt in the lower section of the dialog box to

   Choose the city where you want to be located:

9. Click Next, and enter **New York, Austin**, and **San Francisco** as three separate labels on three lines in the upper list box (press ENTER after the first and second label). Then click Radio Buttons, enter the word **Location** as the variable name, and click Next.

10. Click Add, select the Any Of Several Options question, and change the prompt to

    Select two areas you want to be associated with:

11. Click Next and enter

    Initial Design

    Detail Plan

    Project Management

    Plan Implementation

    Evaluation

    on five separate lines. Enter **PreferredAreas** (without a space) as the name for the group of variables, and click Next.

12. Click Add, select the Date question, change the prompt to

    Enter the date you are available:

13. Click Next, leave the default top date format, enter **Availability** for the variable name, and click Next.

14. Click Add, select the Paragraph question, change the prompt to

    Why do you want to be on this project?

15. Click Next, enter **Why** as the variable name, and click Next. When you are done, your list of questions will look like the one in Figure 8-3.

16. Look at your list of questions. Do you want to change any of them or reposition them in the list? While you can change the finished product, it is easier to change it now, before the form is generated. Click No. 6, the availability date. Click Move Up twice to move the date ahead of the city question. Click any question you want to edit and click Modify. When you are done editing and have returned to the list of questions, click Next to continue with the form creation.

17. You are asked how the list of questions should be presented. Leave the defaults of: As Normal Paragraphs, No Table Of Contents, and Use Tables To Align Form Fields. Then click Next.

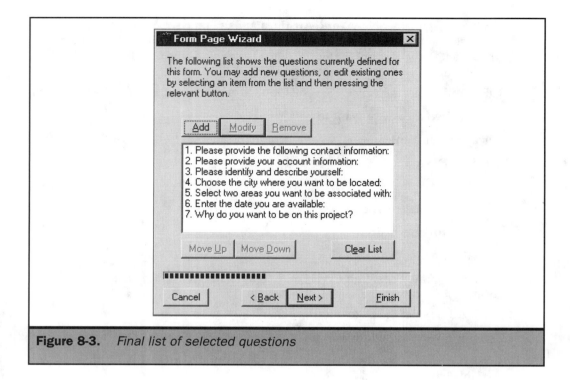

Figure 8-3. *Final list of selected questions*

18. You are asked how you want to save the results of the questionnaire. Choose Save Results To A Text File, enter the filename of **Proj_ans** for the results file, click Next, and then click Finish to generate the form page, which appears as shown in Figure 8-4 (with the Folder List closed). Scroll down the form in Page view to see all the types of form fields created.

19. Save your form by clicking Save on the toolbar, entering the filename of **ProjForm.htm**, changing the page title to **Project Team Questionnaire**, and clicking Save.

Tip *If you want to transfer the results of a web form to a database or spreadsheet, you can use a text file to collect the information. You can choose a comma-, tab-, or space-delimited file (tab probably being the best for exporting from FrontPage since in a database or spreadsheet product you don't have to worry about HTML not supporting tabs as you do when importing into a web page), which is fairly easy to import into most products. In Chapter 19 you will learn how to record the form results directly to a database. In Chapter 11 you will see how database and spreadsheet information can be displayed in web pages.*

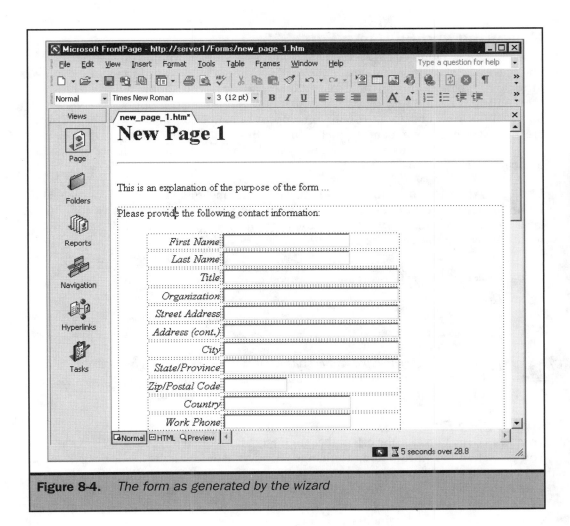

Figure 8-4. *The form as generated by the wizard*

Forms can be formatted by use of either a table or the Formatted paragraph style. The Formatted style was often used in the past for two reasons: it is the only paragraph style that can display more than one consecutive space, which can then be used to align the form fields; and many browsers did not support tables. Most browsers now support tables, and this is now the preferred method for aligning forms. Using tables greatly simplifies aligning the labels and fields in a form, and it allows you to use any available font.

Reviewing and Editing a Form

As with most documents that you create, you'll want to go through your form in detail and make any necessary changes. In the real world, you would need to replace the introductory paragraph with an explanation of the form. This should tell users how the form will be used and why they should fill it out. In this case you might use something like "This form will be used to qualify prospective members of the Project Team. If you are interested in being a member, please fill out this form."

You can customize many areas of the form. The things that you can do are discussed in the following sections.

Changing the Field's Label or Text   Change the label or text on the left of each field by simply typing over or adding to the existing text. This may change the width of the table column. For example, add **& Middle** to the first label, and you'll get the column width change, as shown next. Click Undo to restore your form.

Please provide the following contact information:

First & Middle Name:
Last Name:

If you use the Formatted paragraph style to format your form, changing the label for one field may necessitate adjusting other fields to restore the form's alignment. If you use a table to format the form, the realignment will occur automatically.

Changing the Field's Alignment   Change the alignment by opening the Cell Properties dialog box for the cell and changing the horizontal or vertical alignment. You can select the entire column to change the alignment for all the labels or fields at one time. For example, move the mouse pointer to the top of the label or left column until the pointer is a down arrow, click to select the column, and click Align Left. All the labels will move to the left. Click Undo. If you are using the Formatted paragraph style, you change the alignment by adding or deleting spaces.

First Name
Last Name
Title
Organization
Street Address

*If you use the Formatted style and change the paragraph style on the form fields from
Formatted to any other style, you'll lose all the leading spaces that produce the original
field alignment. This can easily happen if you backspace up to the first paragraph. If this
happens to you, click Undo to quickly recover.*

Deleting a Field   If you want to delete a field and its label, select the table row and
choose Cut from the Edit menu (pressing DEL no longer does this). You can also select
either the label or field individually and press DEL. This leaves the table row available
for placing another label or field. Delete an entire section by selecting the question,
labels, and fields, and choosing Cut from the Edit menu.

Changing a Field's Properties   Right-clicking a field (not its label) and selecting
Form Field Properties opens the field's Properties dialog box, shown next (the dialog
box displayed depends on the type of field selected):

Here you can

- Change the field's name (not the label displayed on the web page)
- Establish an initial value, such as a state abbreviation if most people filling
  out a form are from one state
- Determine if the field contains a password so its contents can be encrypted
- Set the order in which the fields will become active when the user presses
  TAB (this feature doesn't work with all browsers)
- Set the width of the text box, which can also be changed by dragging the end
  of a field, as shown here:

Changing the width of a text box does not affect the maximum number of characters the field can contain. To do that, you use the Form Field Validation dialog box opened by clicking Validate in the Form Field Properties dialog box. For a text field the Text Box Validation dialog box shown in Figure 8-5 is displayed. The Max Length text box displays the maximum number of characters the field will accept, regardless of the width of the field. If the maximum length is greater than the width, the text will scroll in the text box until the maximum length is reached. The other options in the Validation dialog box will be covered later in the chapter in the section "Validating a Form." For now, close all open dialog boxes.

Even if you set the field width and maximum length to the same number, all the text might not fit in the text box without scrolling. This is because the width of a character as determined by the HTML is not always the same as a character displayed on the screen. Test your form fields in a browser by entering the maximum number of characters and setting the width accordingly.

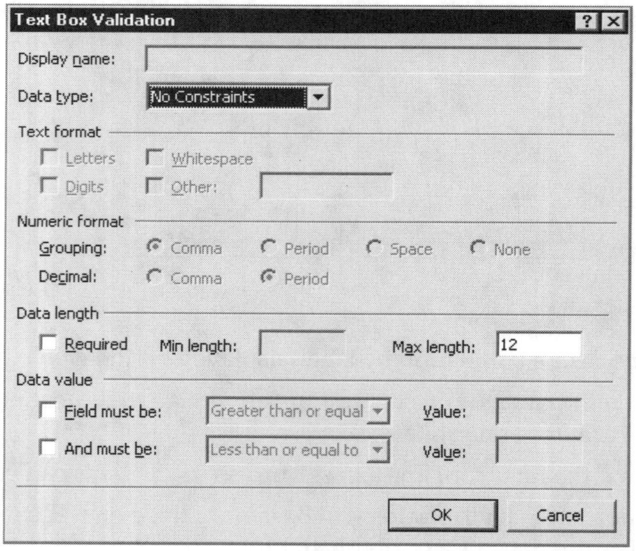

Figure 8-5.   *Validating a text box*

Changing the Field's Placement   The table created with the Form Page Wizard has two columns, each with one label and data entry area on a single line. You may want to have more than one field on a line, such as the State and Zip fields. To do that, you need to split a single cell into multiple cells, like this:

1. Reduce the width of the State/Province field (not the label or the table) to about a third of its original size by selecting it and dragging the right-middle selection handle to the left.

2. With the cursor in the same cell, select the cell by choosing Select | Cell from the Table menu.

3. Right-click the selected cell and select Split Cells. Accept the default Split Into Columns, and then enter **3** in the Number Of Columns spinner and click OK.

4. Cut and paste first the Zip/Postal Code label and then separately cut and paste the Zip/Postal Code form field into the new cells.

5. Right-click the cell containing the Zip/Postal Code label, and open the Cell Properties dialog box.

6. Set the Horizontal Alignment to Right and click OK. Your form fields should look like this:

7. Select the vacated row and select Delete Cells from the Table menu to remove the row.

Validating a Form   Fields in a form often need to be limited to specific types of information, such as allowing only numbers (no letters), or requiring that a field not be left blank. Form validation has traditionally been done on the web server by the form handler (*server-side* validation). This has the disadvantage of requiring the form to be sent to the server, validated, and then sent back to the user if the validation fails. Besides the time involved, server-side validation places a greater demand on the web server's resources. If your web site is receiving a large number of hits each day, this can slow down the server. Validating a form before it's sent (*client-side* validation) has the advantages of speeding up the process and placing less demand on the web server.

Note   *Client-side validation is performed by the web browser. FrontPage generates a JavaScript or VBScript script (see Chapter 15) that is run by the browser to validate the form. JavaScript (the default) is supported by both Netscape and Microsoft, while VBScript is supported mainly by Microsoft. Some browsers do not support either scripting language. If the browser being used does not support the scripting language used, the client-side validation is ignored. This is another reason to encourage visitors to your web sites to upgrade to the latest versions of either Netscape Navigator or Microsoft Internet Explorer.*

Validation criteria for one-line and scrolling text boxes are set by use of the Text Box Validation dialog box that you saw in Figure 8-5. The options are explained in Table 8-1.

Radio buttons or option buttons are validated by use of the Option Button Validation dialog box, shown next, which allows you to make the field required and to set a display name for error messages.

Option	Description
Display Name	Displays the name when an error message is generated. If no name is entered, the contents of the Name field in the form field's Properties dialog box is displayed.
Data Type	Sets the type of data that will be accepted: No Constraints (any characters), Text (alphanumeric characters), Integer (numbers, including "," and "-", without decimals), or Number (numbers with decimal places).
Text Format	Sets the acceptable formats for a text form field: Letters, Digits (numbers), Whitespace (spaces, tabs, returns, and new-line characters), and Other. If Other is selected, you must type the characters (such as hyphens or commas) that will be accepted in the text box.
Numeric Format	Sets both the Grouping and Decimal punctuation characters for numeric fields. Grouping characters can be Comma (1,234), Period (1.234), Space (1 234), or None (1234). Decimal sets the character used as a decimal point: either a Comma or a Period. You cannot use the same character for both Grouping and Decimal.
Data Length	Sets the acceptable length of the data. Required means that the field cannot be left blank. Min Length and Max Length set the minimum and maximum number of characters that can be entered, respectively.
Data Value	Sets a test for the data entered. The value entered in the Value text box is used for the comparison. You can set two tests for each field: Less Than, Greater Than, Less Than Or Equal To, Greater Than Or Equal To, Equal To, or Not Equal To.

Table 8-1. *Text Box Validation Options*

Drop-down lists, or menus, have an additional validation option: Disallow First Choice, as shown next. When this is selected, the first item in the drop-down box cannot be chosen. This enables you to place an instruction or comment, rather than an option, as the first item in the drop-down list.

You can validate all the fields in a form except check boxes and push buttons by right-clicking them, selecting Form Field Properties, and clicking Validate. A dialog box, such as the one shown next, is displayed for each form field that fails the validation criteria, which was generated by making the First Name field required and then submitting the form with the field left blank. In this case, the Display Name field in the Text Box Validation dialog box was set to First name. If the Display Name field had been left blank, the error message would have displayed the form field name "Contact_FirstName."

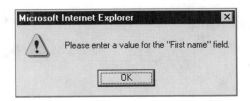

Make the First and Last Name fields required with these steps:

1. Right-click the First Name form field, select Form Field Properties from the context menu, and click Validate.

2. In the Text Box Validation dialog box, select Required for a Data Length, enter **First name** as the Display Name, and click OK twice.

3. Repeat Steps 1 and 2 for the Last Name form field, using **Last name** as the Display Name.

4. Save the page and then open it in your web browser. Without entering any information, click Submit Form. The validation error dialog box just shown is displayed.

5. Click OK to close the validation error dialog box, and then type any characters in the First Name field of the form. Click Submit Form again. The validation error dialog box will now state that a value is needed for the Last Name field.

6. Click OK to close the validation error dialog box; then close your browser.

Changing the Form's Properties   A *form* is a group of fields enclosed within a dashed border on a page. From the context menu of any field in the form or from any open space within the form boundaries, click Form Properties to open the Form Properties dialog box shown in Figure 8-6. This allows you to set the following properties:

- The form handler, labeled Where To Store Results, will return the contents of a form to you. You have a choice of a file (the default), an e-mail, a database, a custom script that you create, and the Discussion or Registration Form Handlers for those types of web forms.

- The Form Name.

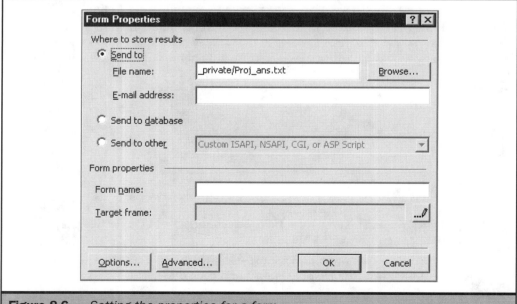

Figure 8-6. *Setting the properties for a form*

- The Target Frame in which you want the form to appear.

- The Options for the form handler. By clicking Options, you open the Saving Results dialog box, shown in Figure 8-7. Here you can change the name and format of the results file, include (or exclude) the field names, and set up a second file to save the results with its format and the selection of fields to be included. The E-mail Results tab allows you to change the address and format of the results e-mail, and to set the Subject and Reply-to Line values. The Confirmation Page tab establishes the URL for a confirmation page to be sent on the receipt of a form and establishes the Validation Failure Page to be displayed if the form fails the client-side validation. In the Saved Fields tab you can select the form fields to be saved and add information to the results file.

If the Send To Other option is selected in the Form Properties dialog box, clicking Options displays the Options For Custom Form Handler dialog box shown next. The Action is the URL of the script that will process the form input. This can either be the default or a custom script. The Method is either Post or Get; Post is the default. The Encoding Type sets how the form data will be encoded; this should be left blank to use the default. You should use the defaults for both the Method and Encoding Type fields unless you have a specific reason for changing them. The finer points of these options relate to the HTTP protocol itself.

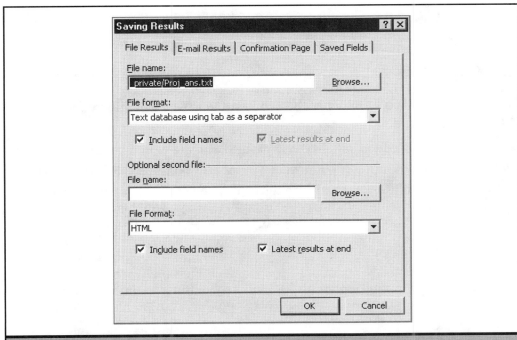

Figure 8-7. Setting options for saving the results of a form

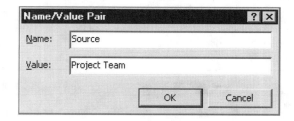

Clicking Advanced in the Form Properties dialog box displays the Advanced Form Properties dialog box, where you can add hidden fields. The hidden fields are information you want to appear in the data collected from the form but not on the form itself.

With the Add, Modify, and Remove buttons, you can add a field name and a value that appear in the data. For example, if you use the same form on several web pages, you could add a field named Source that identifies where this set of data originated, like this:

The lower part of the form that was created by the wizard contains different types of fields, as shown in Figure 8-8. Each of these fields has slight variations in its Properties dialog box. Open each of these in turn and look at their differences. Note the following features:

- The group of option buttons is a single field, and the value is the button selected.

- Each of the check boxes is its own field, and the value is "on" if a box is selected.

- In the scrolling text box, you can select the number of lines as well as the width. The total content, though, can be far greater than you might think by looking at the width and number of lines (five lines of 35 characters, or 175 characters total), since each line can contain up to 256 characters, not just the 35 characters per line used here.

- You can change the label on the push buttons. Push buttons can submit or reset a form (erasing any entries made and not submitting the form) or link the form to a custom script (using the Normal option).

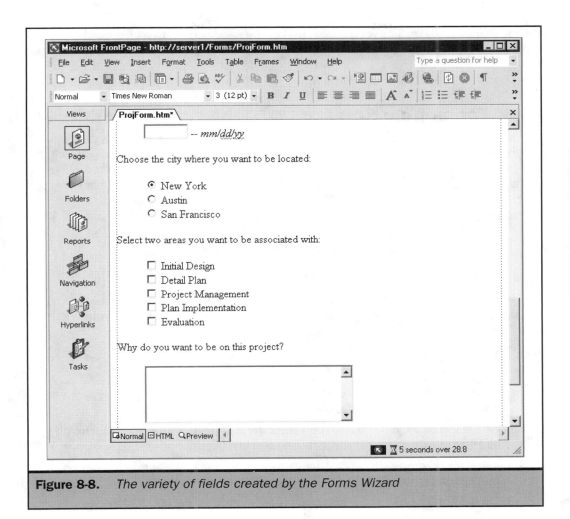

Figure 8-8.   *The variety of fields created by the Forms Wizard*

Note   *The Normal option in the Push Button Properties dialog box is a new feature, supported by HTML 4.0. This option allows the button to call a script, rather than the normal form handler. When the button is clicked, the form data is passed to the script. Scripting is covered in Chapter 15.*

Given the considerable customization that can be done to a wizard-created form, if your form looks anything like a form the wizard can build, it will probably save you time to use the wizard. The wizard also makes the necessary settings for handling the form results that you otherwise would have to remember to do. Next you'll see what it is like to build a form from scratch. Before going to that, close any open dialog boxes and save your project form one more time.

Building Forms from Scratch

As good as the Form Page Wizard is, there will always be the need for forms that are different enough from the standards that it is worthwhile building them from scratch. Now that you're familiar with wizard-created forms, take on the building of a form from scratch, and see the differences in the following exercise using the Form toolbar, shown here. (Display the Form toolbar by choosing Form from the Insert menu and dragging the title bar of the submenu away from the main menu to create a "floating" toolbar.)

Here you will build a request for literature, which could be built with a wizard, but this design calls for it to be laid out with Formatted text quite differently from what the wizard would do.

1. With the Project Team Questionnaire still open in FrontPage, click New Page on the toolbar to open a blank page.

2. Open the Page Properties dialog box by selecting Properties on the File menu, and type **Literature Request** for the title. Click OK to close the dialog box.

3. At the top of the new page, type **Literature Request**, center it, and format it as Heading 1.

4. Insert a horizontal line under the title by use of the Horizontal Line option on the Insert menu.

5. On the first line below the horizontal line, select the Text Box tool from the Form toolbar. A text box will appear within the dashed line representing a form followed by the Submit and Reset form buttons.

6. If it isn't there already, place the cursor to the left of the Submit button, and press ENTER to move the buttons to a separate line.

7. Right-click the text box, and from the context menu, select Form Field Properties to open the Text Box Properties dialog box, type **First** for the name, change the width to **25**, leave the other defaults as shown next, and click OK.

8. Move the insertion point to the left of the new text box, select the Formatted paragraph style, type **First Name:**, and leave a space before the text box.

9. Move the insertion point to the right of the text box, leave two spaces, type **Last Name:**, leave a space, and insert a second text box named **Last** with a width of 25. Press RIGHT ARROW, and then SHIFT+ENTER to start a new line within the form.

10. Type **Company:**, leave four spaces, insert a text box named **Company**, change the width to **66** characters, and press RIGHT ARROW and then SHIFT+ENTER. (The 66 characters make the second line equal to the first line on *my* screen; yours may be different. You can change this number if you want.)

11. Type **Address:**, leave four spaces, insert a text box named **Address1** with a width of **25**. Press RIGHT ARROW, leave two spaces, type **Address 2:**, leave one space, insert a text box named **Address2** with a width of **25**, and press RIGHT ARROW and then SHIFT+ENTER.

12. Type **City:**, leave seven spaces, insert a text box named **City** with a width of **25**, press RIGHT ARROW, leave two spaces, type **State:**, leave a space, insert a text box named **State** with an initial value of **WA**, change the width to **9** characters, press RIGHT ARROW, leave two spaces, type **Zip:**, leave a space, insert a text box named **Zip** with a width of **11** characters, and press RIGHT ARROW and then SHIFT+ENTER.

13. Type **Phone:**, leave six spaces, insert a text box named **Phone** with a width of **25**, press RIGHT ARROW, leave two spaces, type **E-mail:**, leave four spaces, insert a text box named **Email** with a width of **25**, and press RIGHT ARROW and then SHIFT+ENTER.

14. Click Check Box on the Form toolbar, give it the name **Literature**, and accept the defaults shown next. Press RIGHT ARROW, but do not enter a space, and then type

    Click here if you wish literature.

    (include the period). Leave four spaces. (The number of spaces you need in order to make the right end line up may be different.)

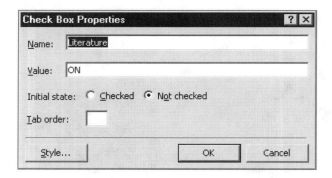

15. Type **Which products?**, leave a space, and click Drop-Down Box on the Form toolbar. In the Drop-Down Box Properties dialog box, type **Lit_Products** for the Name, and click Add to open the Add Choice dialog box. Type **Portable Model** and click Selected as the Initial State, as shown next.

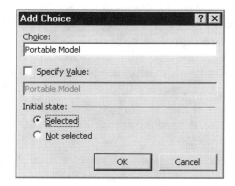

16. Click OK and then click Add twice more to add the choices of **Desktop Model** and **Floor Model**. In both cases, leave the Initial State as Not Selected. In the Drop-Down Box Properties dialog box, click Yes to Allow Multiple Selections, so that your dialog box looks like Figure 8-9.

17. Click OK. Select both the Which products? label and the drop-down box by dragging across them, and press CTRL+C to copy them to the Clipboard. You'll use this twice again. Move the insertion point to the end of the line and press SHIFT+ENTER.

18. Insert a check box named **Use** and accept its defaults. Press RIGHT ARROW and immediately type

    Click here if you use our products.

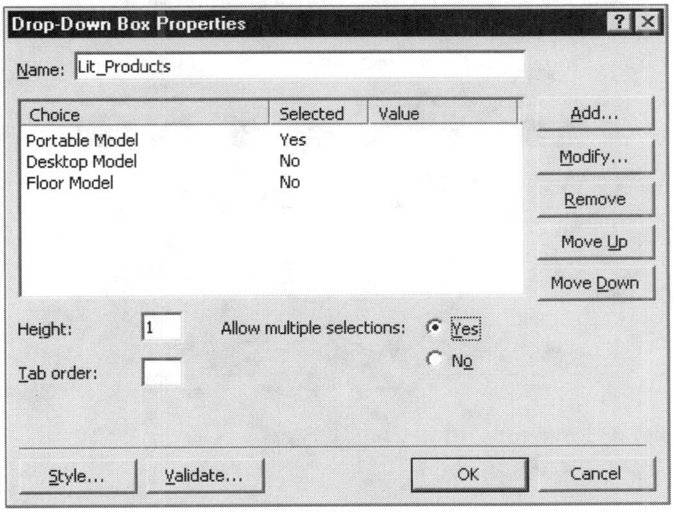

Figure 8-9.   *Setting the options for a Drop-Down Box*

Leave three spaces (the number of spaces you need to align the labels may be different on your system), and press CTRL+V to paste in your "Which products?" label and drop-down box. In the Drop-Down Box Properties change the Name to **Use_Products**. Move the insertion point to the end of the line and press SHIFT+ENTER.

19. Insert a check box named **Plan** and accept its defaults. Press RIGHT ARROW, and immediately type

   Click here if planning a purchase.

   Leave four spaces and press CTRL+V to paste in the Which products? label and drop-down box. Name the field **Plan_Products**, move the insertion point to the end of the line and press SHIFT+ENTER.

Note   *When you right-click a drop-down box, if FrontPage finds any words in the drop-down box text that are not in the dictionary, the Spelling context menu is displayed. Select an option on the context menu for each word found. When the spell-check is complete, right-clicking the drop-down box will display the standard context menu.*

20. On the new line, type

   What is your company size?

21. Leave three spaces, and click Option Button on the Form toolbar. In the Option Button Properties dialog box, enter a Group Name of **Size**, a Value of **Less than 50**, and an Initial State of Not Selected, as shown next.

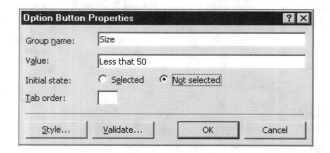

22. Press RIGHT ARROW, and immediately type

    Less than 50

23. Leave three spaces, insert a Not Selected option button with a Group Name of **Size** and a Value of **50 to 500**, press RIGHT ARROW, and immediately type

    50 to 500

24. Leave three spaces, insert a third Not Selected option button with a Group Name of **Size** and Value of **Over 500**, press RIGHT ARROW, type

    Over 500

    and press SHIFT+ENTER.

25. Type

    Please give us any comments you wish:

26. Click Text Area on the Form toolbar, type a Name of **Comments** in the TextArea Box Properties dialog box, and enter a width of **32**, as shown next. Click OK.

27. Right-click the Submit button and choose Form Field Properties to open the Push Button Properties dialog box. Type a Name of **Submit** and a Value/Label of **Submit Form**. Make sure the Button Type is Submit, as shown next, and click OK.

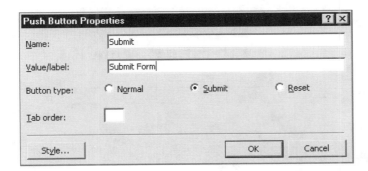

Tip *Push buttons are placed in forms by use of the Push Button button on the Form toolbar.*

28. Right-click Reset and open the Push Button Properties dialog box. Name the button **Reset** with a Value/Label of **Reset Form**, select a Button Type of Reset, click OK, save your form with a File Name of **Literature.htm**, and you're done! The result should look like Figure 8-10.

29. Well, almost done. You still need a handler to process the input from the form. Right-click the form and choose Form Properties. In the Form Properties dialog box, the Send To option button should be selected.

30. In the File Name text box, type **_Private/Literature.txt** for the filename, and then click Options. In the File Results tab of the Saving Results dialog box, select Text Database Using Tab As A Separator for the File Format, and turn off Include Field Names. In the Saved Fields tab, under Additional Information To Save at the bottom click Username, and in the Date Format drop-down list select the first option after None, then click OK twice to get back to your form. Now you are done, so save your form once more.

Note *Much of the spacing and wording in this form was done interactively—in other words, by use of the "try it and see what it looks like" approach. The beauty of a WYSIWYG form editor is that you can immediately see what the form you're building looks like and change it if needed.*

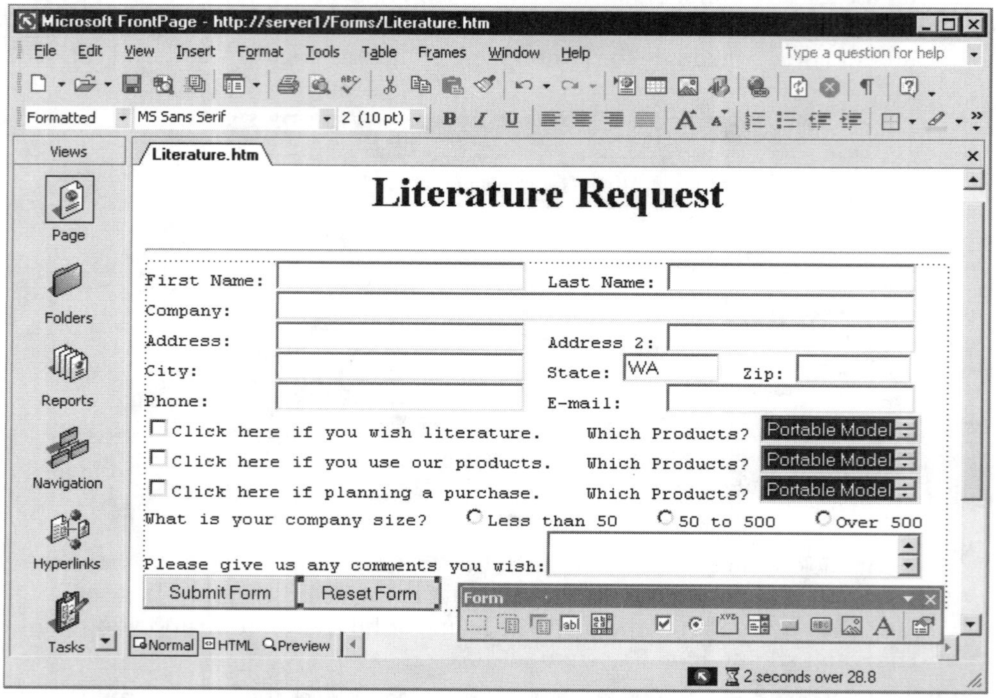

Figure 8-10. *Completed form built from scratch*

Part of the purpose of this "from scratch" example was to see what the Form Page Wizard does for you. You must admit it's a lot. The wizard saves you the hassle of naming, spacing, and layout, not to mention the setup of the form handling. For longer forms like this, the Form Page Wizard offers a lot of advantages.

Handling Form Input

The next step is to look at your forms in a browser. The web called Forms should still be active on your screen and should have three pages: a blank page named Home Page, a Project Team Questionnaire page built with the Form Page Wizard, and a Literature Request form built from scratch. To use the web, you'll need to put some links on the Home page to the two forms. To do that and then try out the forms in a browser, follow these steps:

1. In FrontPage, open the Home Page in Page view. At the top of the page, type **Forms Examples**, format it as Heading 1, and press ENTER.

2. On the next line, type **Form Page Wizard**, format it as Heading 3, select the three words you just typed, and click Link on the toolbar. In the Insert Hyperlink dialog box, select ProjForm.htm, and click OK. Move the insertion point to the end of the line and press ENTER.

3. Type **Custom Form**, format it as Heading 3, select the words, and click Link on the toolbar. In the Insert Hyperlink dialog box, select Literature.htm, and click OK. Your Home page should now look like Figure 8-11. Save this page, put a Home link back to the Home page at the bottom of each form, and save each of them.

4. Open your favorite browser and display the Forms web. Select the Form Page Wizard to open the Project Team Questionnaire, and submit it without filling in the First Name field. Immediately an error message is displayed, as you saw earlier in the chapter.

5. Fill out the form and submit it again. Almost immediately you'll see another benefit of FrontPage—an automatic confirmation form is created for you and is used here to verify your input, as you can see in Figure 8-12. Click the Return To The Form link at the bottom of the confirmation page.

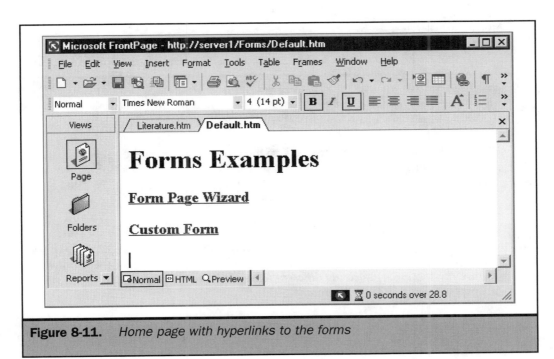

Figure 8-11.   *Home page with hyperlinks to the forms*

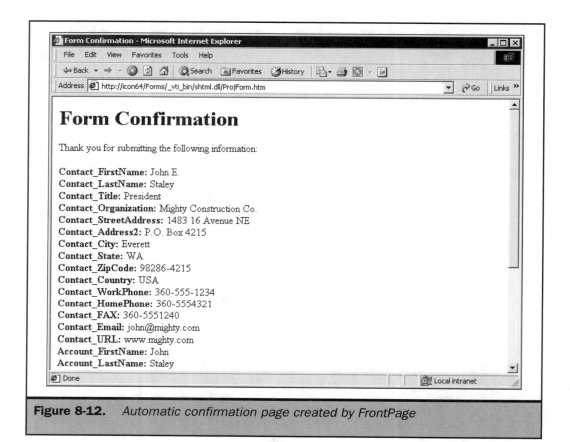

Figure 8-12. *Automatic confirmation page created by FrontPage*

6. Use the Home Page link to get back to the Home page, and then select Custom Form to open the Literature Request form. Fill it out and click Submit Form. Again you'll see the automatic confirmation report. Click Return To The Form, and then close your browser.

> **Note** *The "beautiful" symmetry of the form in FrontPage Page view (previously shown in Figure 8-10) has not totally carried over to the browser, as shown in Figure 8-13. If you look at the form in different browsers, you'll notice different spacing. The user can also change the spacing by selecting different fonts in the browser. In a table, the form's appearance would be much improved.*

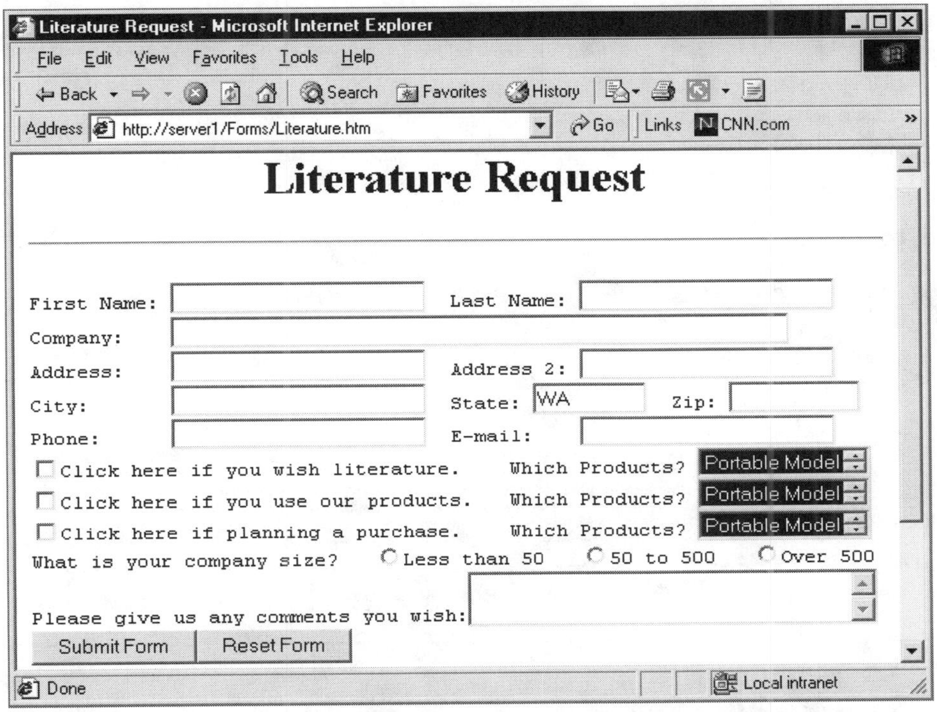

Figure 8-13. *The Literature Request form loses some of its symmetry in a browser*

7. Open the file that was created by the Save Results Component from the Project Team Questionnaire. If you used the default directories when you installed FrontPage, this should be located at C:\Inetpub\Wwwroot\Forms_Private\ Proj_ans.txt. Use Windows Explorer or My Computer to locate it, and then double-click it to open it in Notepad. What you see should look something like this:

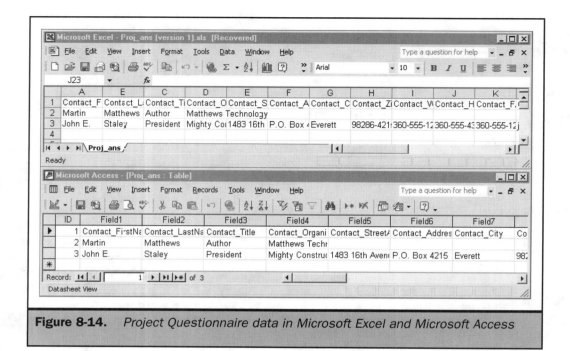

Figure 8-14. *Project Questionnaire data in Microsoft Excel and Microsoft Access*

8. You can also open the files saved from either form in a database program or in a spreadsheet. Figure 8-14 shows the Project Team Questionnaire data in Microsoft Excel and Microsoft Access.

9. Close Notepad and any applications other than FrontPage that you have open. In FrontPage, close your Forms web.

As you can see, FrontPage not only provides significant power for creating a form, but it also does a lot to get the data collected on the form back to you. Also, in the data collection area, a form created with the Form Page Wizard does not necessarily have an advantage over a properly set up custom form. In Chapter 19 you'll learn how to insert the form data directly into a database.

The Complete Reference

Chapter 9

Using Web Components

A s you have read in earlier chapters, a component is a way you can add automation to your web, often to provide interactivity with the user. Some components are buried in other features, such as the form-handling components that you saw in Chapter 8, while others are stand-alone tools that you can use directly. The majority of the stand-alone components are accessed through the Insert Web Component dialog box shown in Figure 9-1 and are briefly described in Chapter 2's Table 2-7.

Web Components are discussed in a number of places throughout this book. Here is where to look for particular component information:

- Dynamic Effects Hover Button, Marquee, and Banner Ad Manager components are covered in Chapter 20.

- Web Search Current Web, Spreadsheets and Charts, Hit Counter, Photo Gallery, Included Content, Table of Contents, and Top 10 List are discussed in this chapter.

- Link Bars are described primarily in Chapter 6.

- List View and Document View, which are used with the SharePoint Team Web Site, are covered in Chapter 24.

- bCentral, MSN, MSNBC, and Additional Components are discussed in this chapter, as is Advanced Controls Confirmation Field.

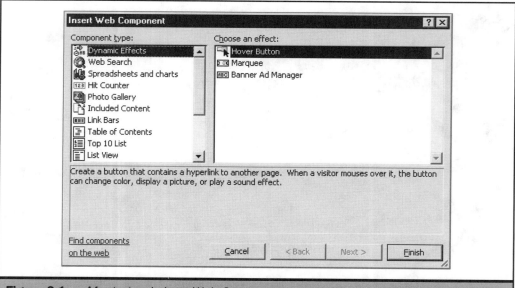

Figure 9-1. *Most stand-alone Web Components are accessed through the Insert Web Component dialog box*

■ Advanced Controls HTML component, which allows you to include HTML commands not modified by FrontPage is covered in Chapter 12. Advanced Controls Java Applet, Plug-In, ActiveX Control, and Design-Time Control are also discussed in Chapter 20.

There are three components that are opened from the Insert menu rather than, or in addition to, opening them from Insert Web Component dialog box. These are the Date and Time component, opened with the Date and Time option; the Comment component, opened with the Comment option; and the Link Bar component, opened with the Navigation option, which just opens the Web Component dialog box at the Link Bar option. The Date and Time and Comment components are described in this chapter.

Note   *In earlier versions of FrontPage, Web Components were referred to most recently as FrontPage Components and before that as WebBots or bots. In some cases Microsoft still uses the term WebBots, and it appears in the code generated by FrontPage. For all practical purposes, the terms* WebBots, bots, FrontPage Components, *and* Web Components *can be used interchangeably.*

Incorporating Components in Your Webs

See how you can incorporate Web Components in your own webs by trying out several of the stand-alone components in the following sections. Begin by opening a new One Page Web named Components and then opening its Home page in FrontPage Page view.

Date and Time Component

The Date and Time component inserts either the date (and optionally, the time) the page was last edited and saved, or the date and time (optional) the page was last automatically updated and saved. A page is edited when someone makes a change and resaves it, while a page is automatically updated when a page's content is changed without direct editing. For example a page is automatically updated when a shared border is changed, even if there were no changes to the active page. To see this, follow these steps:

1. In Page view, open the Format menu, choose Shared Borders, click All Pages, click Bottom, and click OK.
2. Select the words Comment Shared Bottom Border and type

   This page was last edited on

   and leave a space.
3. Open the Insert menu, and choose Date and Time to display the Date and Time dialog box.

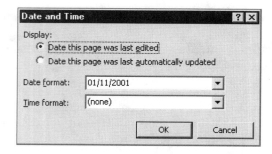

4. Open the Time Format drop-down list, and select the time format that ends with "AM TZ." This means *time zone* and will automatically insert the difference between Greenwich Mean Time (GMT) and the time zone your computer is set to. For example, Pacific Standard Time (PST) is eight hours behind GMT so the date and time are displayed like this:

> This page was last edited on 01/11/2001 08:29:02 AM -0800

5. Click OK. The date and time your page was last edited should appear, as you just saw.

6. Press ENTER, type

   This page was last updated on

   leave a space, again open the Insert menu and the Date and Time dialog box, select Date This Page Was Last Automatically Updated, choose the AM TZ Time Format, and click OK.

7. Save the Home page and click New Page on the toolbar. In the new page that opens, click the left of the top line in the bottom shared border, press ENTER, move up to the new line that is created, and type

   Copyright 2001, Acme Industries

   (You can insert a copyright symbol if you wish by opening the Insert menu, choosing Symbol, double-clicking the copyright symbol, and clicking Close.)

8. Save the new page with the name Newpage1. Reopen the Home page and click Preview in Browser. You should see a difference between the time you edited the footer on that page and the time you made the changes on Newpage1, which, because of the shared borders, updated the footer on the Home page, as you can see next:

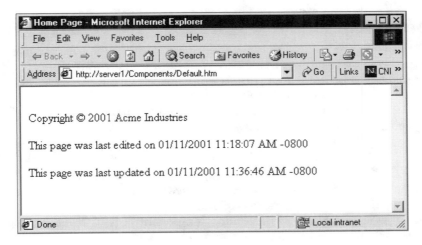

9. Close your browser.

As you have probably observed, the changes in times are not observable in FrontPage, even in Preview mode, unless you close and reopen the web. You have to look at them in a browser. This is often true of Web Components.

Comment Component

The Comment component allows you to insert notes that you want to be visible while the web is in Page view, but invisible or hidden while the web is being viewed in a browser. To see how that works, follow these steps:

1. On the Home page in Page view, click above the shared border, type

   This is normal text.

   (include the period) and press ENTER.

2. From the Insert menu, choose Comment. The Comment dialog box opens. Here you can type any text you want to see in Page view but not in a browser. Type

   This is comment text that should not be visible in a browser.

   (include the period) and then click OK. Press ENTER twice. The comment text will appear in Page view as shown next.

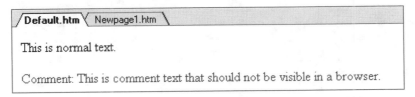

3. Save your web page, open it in a browser, and all you'll see is the normal first line.

Web Search Component

The Web Search Current Web Component creates a form in which users can enter any text that they want to search for in the current web. After users enter such text and click the Search button, the Search Form component carries out the search and returns the locations where the text was found. This is similar to the search forms that are built into FrontPage wizards and templates and described in Chapters 3 and 4. To look at how the Web Search component is used, take these steps:

1. If it isn't already open, open your Components web in FrontPage; then open the Home page in Page view.

2. Leaving at least one blank line beneath the Comment inserted previously, open the Insert menu and choose Web Component. In the Insert Web Component dialog box, select Web Search under Component Type. Current Web should automatically be selected under Choose A Type Of Search.

3. Click Finish. The Search Form Properties dialog box will open, as shown in Figure 9-2. The Search Form Properties tab displays the selections for searching, and the Search Results tab sets how the results are displayed.

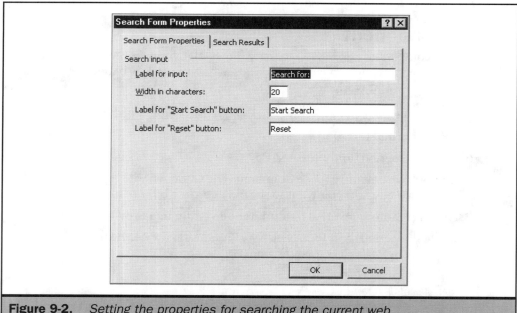

Figure 9-2. *Setting the properties for searching the current web*

4. Accept the defaults in this dialog box and click OK. The search form will appear on the Home page.

5. Save the web page, open the page in your browser, and the search form will appear at the bottom of the page.

6. In the Search For text box, type **home** and click Start Search. In a moment, you will get the results, which should look like Figure 9-3.

Note

On a Windows 2000 or XP computer, if you get the message "Service is not running" when you do a search, it is because the Indexing Service is not started. To get it started, right-click My Computer and choose Manage. Open Services And Applications and select Indexing Service. Open the Action menu and choose Start. Click Yes to begin the Indexing Service when the computer is started. Be aware that it may take a few minutes for the Indexing Service to create an index.

7. Close your browser.

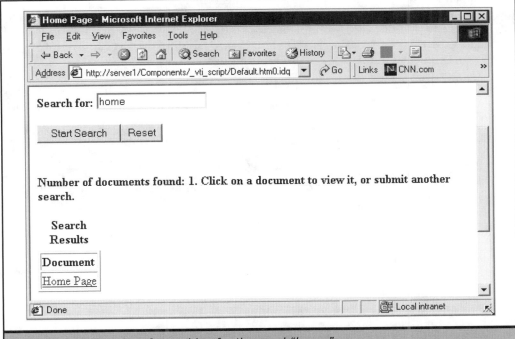

Figure 9-3.   *Results of searching for the word "home"*

If you want certain pages not to be found by the Search Form Component (like style pages and included pages), place the pages in the _private folder of the current web; that folder is not searched. If you're using FrontPage's default folder structure and the Components web, the full path to the private folder for that web is C:\Inetpub\Wwwroot\Components_private.

Web Components represent a high level of sophistication that gives you significant power to build the web you want. Much of the "gee whiz" that you saw in the wizards and templates in Chapters 3 and 4 came from these tools.

Spreadsheets and Charts Components

The Spreadsheets and Charts components allow you to add an Excel spreadsheet, chart, or pivot table to a FrontPage web that allows someone viewing the web page to interactively work with the spreadsheet, chart, or pivot table. In other words, while on the Internet or an intranet, the user of the web page can make a change to the spreadsheet, have it recalculate, and see the result in real time, as if they were in Excel. This is in contrast to inserting an Excel spreadsheet file or cutting and pasting from Excel to a web page in FrontPage, both of which come in as static tables without interactivity. In the following example notice how the various ways of using an Excel spreadsheet work with FrontPage. The file Etearn.xls in the \Book\Chap09\ folder on the CD that comes with this book is used for this exercise.

1. In the Components web that should be open in FrontPage, click New Page to add another page to the web. Press ENTER twice to leave several lines at the top of the page.

2. Move the insertion point to the second line (there should be a blank line both above and below this line). Open the Insert menu and choose File. In Files Of Type, select Microsoft Excel Worksheet, locate the Etearn.xls file in the \Book\Chap09\ folder on the CD that comes with this book, and click Open. The spreadsheet comes into FrontPage as an ordinary table, as you can see in Figure 9-4.

 Depending on how you installed Office, you may be requested to insert the Office installation CD to install the Excel converter.

3. Move the insertion point to the blank line beneath the table that was just created and press ENTER to add another blank line so the insertion point again has a blank line above and below it.

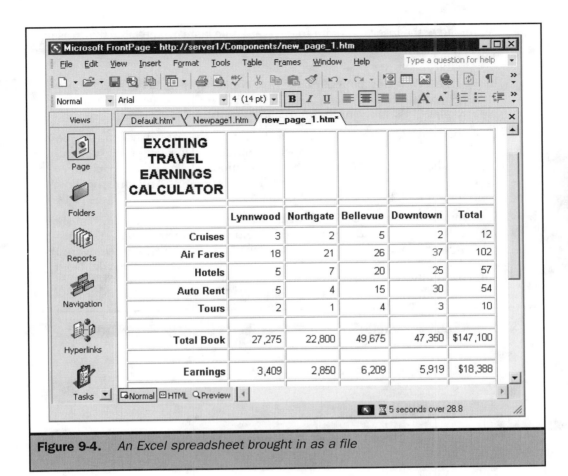

Figure 9-4.   *An Excel spreadsheet brought in as a file*

4. Open Etearn.xls in Excel, select the table, and press CTRL+C to copy it to the Clipboard. Back in FrontPage, click Paste. The spreadsheet comes into FrontPage as a more formatted but still static table, like this:

EXCITING TRAVEL EARNINGS CALCULATOR

	Lynnwood	Northgate	Bellevue	Downtown	Total
Cruises	3	2	5	2	12
Air Fares	18	21	26	37	102
Hotels	5	7	20	25	57
Auto Rent	5	4	15	30	54
Tours	2	1	4	3	10
Total Book	27,275	22,800	49,675	47,350	$ 147,100
Earnings	3,409	2,850	6,209	5,919	$ 18,388

5. Again move the insertion point to the blank line beneath the table that was just created, press ENTER to add another blank line, open the Insert menu, and choose Web Component.

6. In the Insert Web Component dialog box, choose Spreadsheets And Charts | Office Spreadsheet, and click Finish. A small, blank spreadsheet area looking very similar to Excel opens in FrontPage.

7. Click in cell A1 to select it and then click Paste in the spreadsheet area's toolbar. The Exciting Travel spreadsheet opens in the spreadsheet area. Right-click in the spreadsheet, choose Commands And Options, click Advanced, change the Column Width to 10, press ENTER, and close Commands And Options. Your page should look like the one in Figure 9-5.

8. Save your page, naming it **NewPage2**, and then open it in a browser. You should see the two static spreadsheets at the top and the interactive one at the bottom. Try out its interactiveness by changing one of the numbers in the center of the spreadsheet, pressing ENTER, and witnessing the changes in the calculated numbers on the periphery.

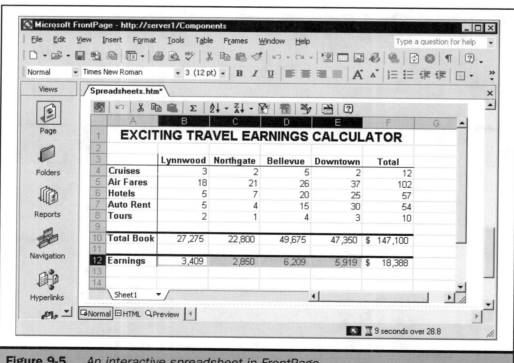

Figure 9-5. *An interactive spreadsheet in FrontPage*

Note *You can also get an interactive spreadsheet in a web by saving an Excel spreadsheet as a web page and choosing Add Interactivity. See Etearn.htm in \Book\Chap09\ on the CD.*

Hit Counter Component

Hit counters have lost much of their popularity because they are not very useful for compiling any real information about traffic on a web site. What they record is *page views*, the number of times a particular web page has been loaded by a browser. Advertisers are generally more interested in *visits*, the actual number of people who access a site. One visit will have a number of page views. If the visitor reloads a page, the hit counter will record it as a separate hit, which is what limits the hit counter's usefulness. Hit counters can be fun to have on a page, though, especially if you don't take them too seriously.

Adding a hit counter to a page requires only a few steps:

1. Open the Home page of the Components web in Page view and move the insertion point to the line just above the shared bottom border.

2. Open the Insert menu, choose Web Component, select Hit Counter as the Component Type, choose a counter style, and click Finish. The Hit Counter Properties dialog box is displayed.

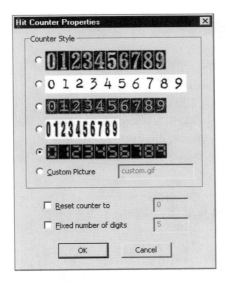

3. In the Hit Counter Properties dialog box, you can again select the counter style to be displayed, the starting number for the counter, and a fixed number of digits to be displayed. Each digit is actually a graphic; you can use the ones included

with FrontPage, download others from the Web, or create your own. The Reset Counter To option lets you set the starting number for the counter. The Fixed Number Of Digits option will always cause the number of digits selected to be displayed. If you accept the default of 5, the first visit will be 00001; when the count reaches 99999, the next visit will roll the counter over to 00000 again.

Tip   *To create your own counter graphic, create a single GIF file with the numbers 0 to 9. Each number is 10 percent of the total width of the graphic. If your graphic is 120 pixels wide, zero would be the first 10 percent of the graphic (12 pixels), one would be the next 10 percent, and so on.*

4. Select any of the Counter Style options and click the Fixed Number Of Digits check box. Accept the default of 5. Click OK. In Page view, a text placeholder is inserted.

5. Save the page and view it in your browser. The hit counter will appear similar to this:

6. Close your browser.

Photo Gallery Component

As you saw with Photo Gallery page template in Chapter 4, the Photo Gallery Component provides an area on which you can display one or more photographs along with their captions. An example of how to do this is described next.

1. In the Components web, open the Newpage1.htm page in Page view. This page should be blank except for the bottom-shared border. With the insertion point in the upper left, add two blank lines and then place the insertion point on the middle line so that a blank line exists both above and below it.

Tip   *As you are working on a web page it is a good idea to always leave a blank line above and below an object that is being inserted so that you can more easily get on either side of it. You can very easily remove the blank lines if desired when you are done with the insert.*

2. Open the Insert menu, choose Web Component, select Photo Gallery as the component type, pick one of the gallery layouts (the vertical arrangement is used here), and click Finish. The Photo Gallery Properties dialog box will open.

3. Click Add | Pictures From Files. Select the pictures that you want from the File Open dialog box. Hold CTRL to select several pictures that are not next to each other, or hold SHIFT to select the first and last of several contiguous pictures. When you are done selecting pictures, click Open. You are returned to the Photo Gallery Properties dialog box.

4. Select each of the pictures you chose and add a caption and/or description while looking at the picture in the preview area of the dialog box, as shown in Figure 9-6.

5. When you have added the captions and descriptions that you want, click OK. Thumbnails of the pictures with their captions and descriptions will appear on your web page, like those in Figure 9-7.

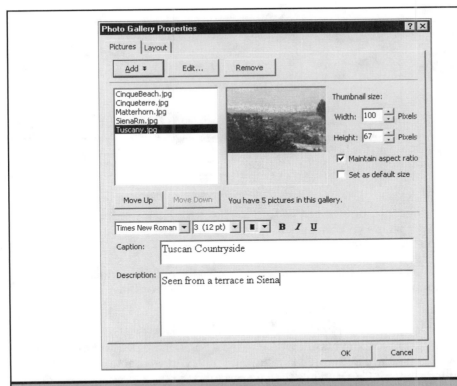

Figure 9-6.   *Add captions and descriptions to a photo gallery*

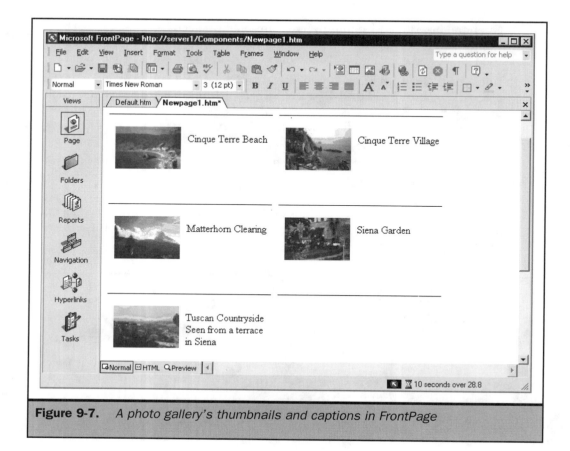

Figure 9-7. *A photo gallery's thumbnails and captions in FrontPage*

6. Save the page including the embedded graphics files you used and display it in a browser where you can click a thumbnail and have it displayed full-size. When you are done looking at your pictures, close your browser.

The Photo Gallery component or template provides the ability to quickly and easily display a number of pictures without using a lot of page space or download time.

Included Content Components

The Included Content components allow you to incorporate repeated web content that you enter once in one place in the web and have it display in several locations. There are five Included Content Components that are described in the following sections:

■ **Substitution component**   Defines variables such as author and URL that may be repeatedly used on the pages of a web.

- **Include Page component**   Allows you to include one page's contents on another page.

- **Scheduled Page component**   Allows you to schedule when one page's contents will be included on another page.

- **Scheduled Picture component**   Allows you to schedule when a picture will be included on a page.

- **Page Banner component**   Allows you to include either a graphic or simple text as the page's heading based on a set of circumstances.

Substitution Component

The Substitution component replaces a value on a web page with a configuration variable when the page is viewed by the user. A *configuration variable* contains specific information about either the current page or the current web. There are four predefined configuration variables, as shown in Table 9-1, and you can define additional variables in the FrontPage Web Settings dialog box Parameters tab, which you can open from the Tools menu. You can see how this works with the following instructions:

Variable	Description
Author	Name that is in the Created By field of the FrontPage current page's Properties dialog box Summary tab (opened by right-clicking a page in Folders view and choosing Properties).
Description	Contents of the Comments scrolling text box of the FrontPage current page's Properties dialog box Summary tab.
Modified By	Name of the person who most recently changed the page, contained in the Modified By field of the FrontPage current page's Properties dialog box Summary tab.
Page URL	Filename in the Location field of the FrontPage current page's Properties dialog box General tab.

Table 9-1.   *Configuration Variables*

1. In the Folders view, while it is still displaying the Components web, right-click the Home page (Default.htm) and choose Properties. The page's Properties dialog box will open with the General tab showing, as you can see in Figure 9-8.

2. If it isn't already open, click the General tab of the page's Properties dialog box so you can see the Location field. Click the Summary tab to see the Created By and Modified By fields and to both see and change the Comments scrolling text box.

3. In the Comments scrolling text box, type

   This is a great web!

   Click Apply and then click OK to close the Properties dialog box.

4. Immediately above the Hit Counter on the Home page in Page view, type

   This page was last modified by

   leave a space, open the Insert menu, choose Web Component, select Included Content, and double-click Substitution. The Substitution Properties dialog box will open.

5. Click the down arrow to see the list of variables shown at the top of the next page. Click Modified By and then OK. You'll see the name of the person who last modified the page appear on the Home page in Page view.

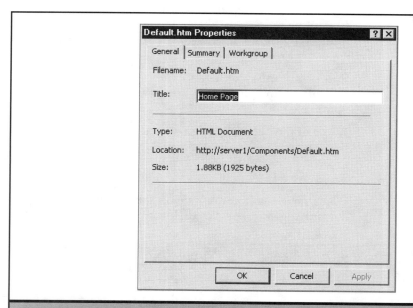

Figure 9-8. A page's Properties General tab Location provides the page's URL

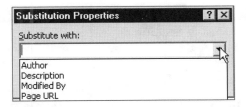

6. Leave a space and then type

   who left these comments:

   leave a space, reopen the Substitution Properties dialog box, choose Description, and click OK.

   The comments you left should appear, as you can see next:

This page was last modified by SERVER1\Administrator who left these comments: This is a great web!

Include and Scheduled Include Page Components

The Include Page component allows you to include one web page on another. For example, if you wanted a section with identical contents on every page, you could put the contents on a web page and then include that page on all others in the web. Future changes to the contents of that page will then automatically appear on all the pages that include the page. The Scheduled Include Page component allows you to include one page on another for a given period. When the time expires, that page is no longer included.

Include Page has been largely replaced with Shared Borders, which provides improved flexibility and control.

To try Include Page, follow these steps:

1. With the Home page of the Components web open in FrontPage's Page view, click New Page on the toolbar to create a new page. At the top of the page, type

   This is a page heading; it should be on all pages.

   (include the period) and format it as Heading 2.

2. Open the Format menu, choose Shared Borders, click Current Page, click Bottom to uncheck it, and click OK. Save this page with the page title Included Header and a filename of Inchead.htm.

3. Return to the Home page, place the insertion point at the top of the page, open the Insert menu, choose Web Component, select Included Content, and double-click Page to open the Include Page Properties dialog box.

4. Click Browse to get a list of pages in the current web.

5. Double-click the Included Header page, and then click OK to return to the web page. You should see the heading appear on this page and the WebBot icon appear when you move the mouse pointer over it, as shown next:

> /Default.htm* \ Newpage1.htm \ Inchead.htm \
>
> ## This is a page heading; it should be on all pages.
>
> This is normal text.
>
> Comment: This is comment text that should not be visible in a browser.

The real beauty of using the Include Page component is that not only are you saved from retyping or copying the heading onto each page, but also changes you make need only be typed once.

The Scheduled Include Page component works like the Include Page component, except that it has a start and stop date and time, as will be demonstrated next, with the Scheduled Picture component.

Scheduled Picture Component

The Scheduled Picture component allows you to display a picture on a page for a fixed period. When the time expires, the picture disappears. To see how this works, take these steps:

1. On the Home page of the Components web in Page view, move the insertion point to the line following the Search form and press ENTER to create a blank line after the Search form

2. Open the Insert menu and choose Picture | Clip Art. In the Insert Clip Art task pane, type **lion** and click Search. Double-click the lion you want to use (the left one in the fourth row is used here). Close the task pane and drag the lower-right-corner sizing handle up to the left to reduce the size to about one-inch square. (If you can't find a lion, you can use Lion.gif in \Book\Chap09 on the CD that comes with this book.)

3. Save the page and, in the process, save the embedded file (the lion) with the name Lion.gif. When the files are saved, select the lion on the Home page and delete it. Once more save the page. Leave the insertion point on the second line below the Search form.

4. Open the Insert menu, choose Web Component, select Included Content, and double-click Picture Based On Schedule. In the Scheduled Picture Properties dialog box, shown in Figure 9-9, click the first Browse to open the Picture dialog box. In the Picture dialog box, select Lion.gif, and click OK.

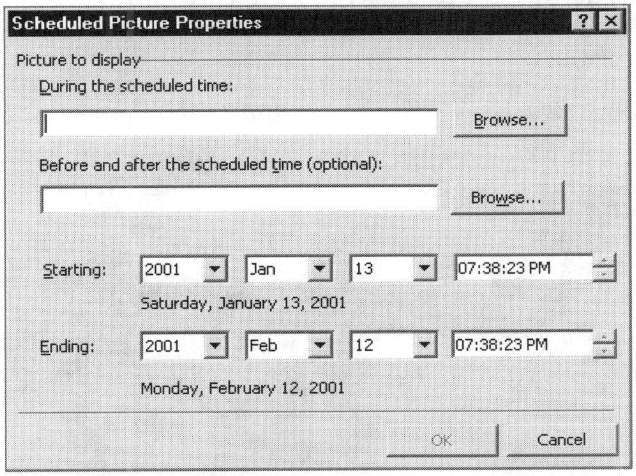

Figure 9-9. *Scheduling when a picture will be displayed*

5. Set the ending time for a couple of minutes past the current time in the Ending date and time spinner. (The default is to display the picture for one month.) Click OK. You should see the picture appear in Page view.

6. Save your web page and open your browser and the Components web. If necessary, click the Refresh button in the Internet Explorer Standard toolbar or the Reload button in the Netscape Navigator Link bar.

7. After the time has expired, go back to FrontPage Page view displaying the Components web Home page and click Refresh on the toolbar or select Refresh from the View menu.

8. The lion graphic will be replaced with the message "[Expired Scheduled Picture]." If you resave the page and return to your browser and refresh it, the graphic will also disappear from there.

9. Close your browser.

Page Banner Component

The Page Banner component is similar to the Include Page component; it allows you to select a picture or text to use as a banner at the top of a web page. Banners are usually larger graphics that identify the site or the page contents.

If the web page does not use a theme or a shared border, then the page title is inserted, and choosing Picture in the Page Banner Properties dialog box has no effect. If a theme has been applied, the theme's banner picture is inserted when Picture is selected. If the page has a top shared border, then a page banner is created automatically.

1. On the Home page in Page view, press CTRL+HOME and then press ENTER. Press UP ARROW if necessary to move the insertion point to the top of the page.

2. Open the Insert menu, choose Web Component, select Included Content, and double-click Page Banner to open the Page Banner Properties dialog box, shown here:

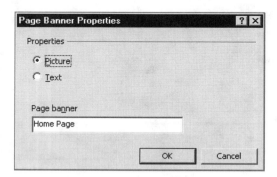

3. Select Text, type **Components Home Page** in the Page Banner text box, and click OK. The page banner text is inserted on the page.

4. Save your work, preview it in a browser, and, when done, close both the browser and the Components web.

Table of Contents Components

FrontPage provides two ways of generating a table of contents: one based on the links that are contained in the web, and one based on categories that you establish. See how both of these work in the next two sections.

Contents Based on Links

The Table of Contents component creates and maintains a table of contents for a web with links to all the pages in the web. Whenever the web's contents are changed and resaved, the table of contents is updated. The Table of Contents component builds the structure of the table of contents based on the links that are on each page. For example, if the home page has three pages directly linked to it and the second page has two other pages linked to it, the structure shown in Figure 9-10 would be built.

If there are pages in the web that are not linked to other pages, they are listed at the end of the table of contents.

Chapters 3 and 4 discuss (and have several examples of) the Table of Contents component as used in web and page wizards and templates. See the "Using the Corporate Presence Wizard" section in Chapter 3 and the "Table of Contents Template" section in Chapter 4.

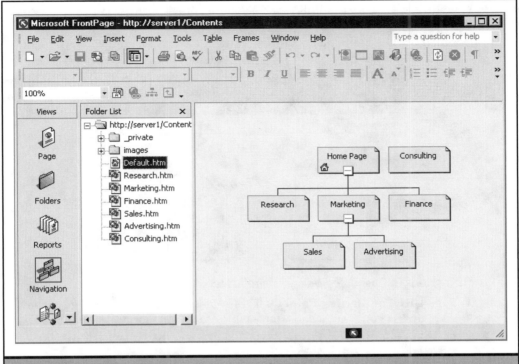

Figure 9-10.   *A web structure for a table of contents*

Note   *When you add the Table of Contents component to a page, you do not see the full table of contents. It is only when you open the page in a browser that the full table is displayed.*

Look at how a table of contents based on links is constructed from scratch. With nothing open in FrontPage, you can do that with these steps:

1. Click the down arrow next to New on the toolbar and choose Web. Select One Page Web, name it Contents, and click OK.

2. Open Navigation view and click New Page three times to place three new pages under the Home page. Then select New Page 2 and click New Page twice more to place two pages under that page. Finally, click New Page again and drag that page up next to the Home page; this will give you the structure that you saw in Figure 9-10.

3. Rename the files, by selecting the name in the Folder List, and the title, by selecting the name in the navigation pane, to the names shown in Figure 9-10.

4. Double-click the Home Page to open it in Page view. Open the Insert menu, choose Web Component, select Table Of Contents, and double-click For This Web Site. The Table Of Contents Properties dialog box will open, as shown here:

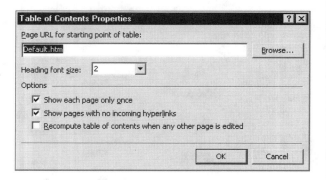

The options in this dialog box are as follows:

- **Page URL For Starting Point Of Table**   Should be the home page of the web, unless you want a subsidiary table of contents for a section of a web.

- **Heading Font Size**   The size of the top entry in the table. Each subsidiary entry is one size smaller.

- **Show Each Page Only Once**   Prevents a page that has links from several pages from being listed under each page.

- **Show Pages With No Incoming Hyperlinks**   Allows unlinked pages to be listed.

- **Recompute Table Of Contents When Any Other Page Is Edited**   Forces the table to be rebuilt if any page in the web is changed. Since this can take a significant amount of time, you may not want to do this. A table of contents is also rebuilt every time the page it is on is saved, which should normally be adequate.

Tip   *Using the Table of Contents component can be a good way to initially establish a link from the home page to all the other pages in the web.*

5. Accept the default entries in the Table Of Contents Properties dialog box and click OK. The initial table of contents entries will appear on the page like this:

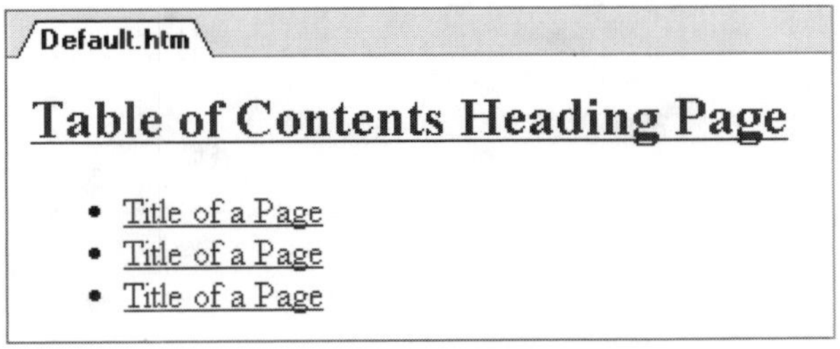

```
/ Default.htm \
```

Table of Contents Heading Page

- Title of a Page
- Title of a Page
- Title of a Page

6. Save the page and then view it in a browser. As you can see next, a full table of contents is generated providing links to all the other pages in the hierarchical structure that you created.

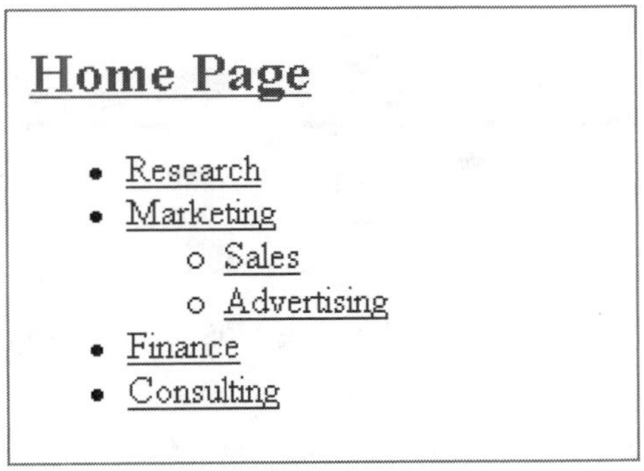

Home Page

- Research
- Marketing
  - Sales
  - Advertising
- Finance
- Consulting

7. Close your browser.

Contents Based on Page Categories

The Page Category component provides an automated method for creating hyperlinks to web pages based on the category that has been assigned to each of the pages. The Page Category component then creates the links to the page based on the assigned category. When a page is added or removed from a category, the hyperlink is also updated. The first step is to create Master Categories for your web:

1. With the Contents web open in Folders view, right-click the Home page (Default.htm) and choose Properties. In the Properties dialog box that opens, select the Workgroup tab, shown in Figure 9-11.

CREATING
WEB SITES

Figure 9-11. *Assigning categories to a page*

2. Click the Categories button to open the Master Category List dialog box, shown next.

3. In the New Category text box, type **Internal Functions** and click Add.

4. Delete any text in the single-line text box, type **External Functions**, and click Add. Delete the other functions except Miscellaneous by selecting them and clicking Remove, then clicking OK and Yes that you want to remove the categories. The Master Categories you created will be displayed in the Available Categories list box on the Workgroup tab of the current page's Properties dialog box.

5. Click the Internal Functions check box to select it and then click OK.

6. In Folders view, right-click first Research.htm and then Finance.htm; for each, choose Properties | Workgroup tab, click the Internal Functions check box to select it, and then click OK.

7. Similarly right-click first Marketing.htm and then Consulting.htm; for each, choose Properties | Workgroup tab, click the External Functions check box to select it, and then click OK.

8. Open the Home Page in Page view. Add two blank lines below the table of contents, type **Internal Functions:** (include the colon), format it as Heading 3, and press ENTER.

9. Open the Insert menu, choose Web Component, select Table Of Contents, and double-click Based On Page Category. The Categories Properties dialog box, shown here, is opened.

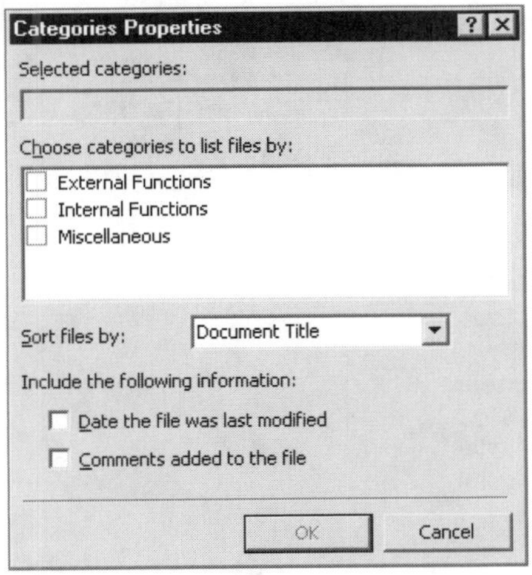

The Categories Properties dialog box displays the Master Categories you created previously and several options for how the hyperlinks will be displayed. Using the Sort Files By drop-down list, you can choose to display the hyperlinks sorted by either the date the page was last modified or by the page title. You can also include the date the page was last modified and/or any comments for the page (comments are added using the Summary tab of the current page's Properties dialog box).

10. Click the Internal Functions and the Date The File Was Last Modified check boxes to select them. Accept the other defaults and click OK.

11. Press ENTER, type **External Functions:** (include the colon), format it as Heading 3, and press ENTER. Open the Insert menu, choose Web Component, select Table Of Contents, and double-click Based On Page Category. The Categories Properties dialog box opens.

12. Click the External Functions and the Date The File Was Last Modified check boxes to select them. Accept the other defaults and click OK.

13. Save the page and then open the Contents web Home page in your browser. Hyperlinks, showing the page title of the web's main pages and the date they were last modified, are displayed in their respective categories, as shown in Figure 9-12.

14. Close your browser and the Contents web.

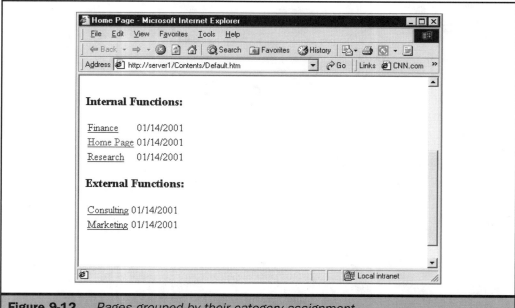

Figure 9-12. *Pages grouped by their category assignment*

There is no reason that a page cannot have more than one category checked and appear in more than one list.

Top 10 List Components

The Top 10 List components provides seven pieces of information that you can gather about visits to the current web site. These are the top 10:

- Visited pages in the current web site
- Referring domains for the current web site
- Referring URLs for the current web site
- Search strings used to find the current web site
- Visiting users for the current web site
- Operating system used to view the current web site
- Browser used to view the current web site

To use any or all of these components, place them on a page of the web as described in the next set of steps.

 To keep the usage statistics to yourself, the page that contains them should probably not be referred to on any other page, and you will have to know the full URL to open the page.

1. Open the Components web that you were using earlier in the chapter, create a new page named **Stats**, and open it in Page view. Place the insertion point at the upper-left corner of the page, press ENTER twice, and then move the insertion point up one line.

2. Open the Insert menu, choose Web Component, select Top 10 List, and double-click Visited Pages. The Top 10 List Properties dialog box will open, as you can see here:

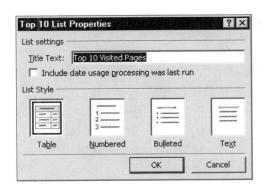

3. Click Include Date Usage Processing Was Last Run and click OK to accept the other defaults. A table will appear with a mock-up of the pages to be reported when viewed in a browser.

4. Save the page and view it in a browser. If your server logs have been recently updated, you will see statistics similar to this:

5. Close your browser and the Stats page but leave the Components web open.

The Top 10 components require that the FrontPage 2002 Server Extensions be installed on an IIS 5 server since the components are simply displaying information in the IIS server logs. By default, server logs are only updated weekly. If you have administrative authority over your server you can change the Usage Analysis settings by clicking Start | Programs | Administrative Tools | Office Web Server Administrator, selecting Administration for the default web site, clicking Go To Site Administration For http://server, and scrolling down and clicking Change Usage Analysis Settings.

Microsoft Site Components

The Microsoft site components are items from various Microsoft web sites that you can include on your site.

- **bCentral Banner Network**   Provides the ability to host a banner ad in exchange for your site appearing in other ads by joining the Banner Network at **http://www.bcentral.com/**.

- **bCentral FastCounter**   Provides a graphic display of the number of unique visits to your web site as explained at **http://www.bcentral.com/**.

- **MSN Stock Quote**   Provides the ability to look up a stock quote through MSN's MoneyCentral.

- **MSN Web Search**   Provides the ability to search the Internet using MSN's search engine.
- **MSNBC Weather Forecast**   Provides a weather forecast from MSNBC on your web page.
- **Visual InterDev Navigation Bar**   Provides a unique navigation bar from Microsoft's InterDev product.

The Visual InterDev navigation bar is currently the only Additional Component, but it is expected that other third-party products will be available in this category, and there may be additional bCentral, MSN, and MSNBC components in the future. These components are very powerful and can really make the difference between an ordinary web site and one that shouts for attention. Look at how a couple of these components are implemented with the following instructions:

1. Open the Components web's Home page in Page view. Place the insertion point on the left end of the included heading ("This is a page heading…"), press ENTER three times, and move the insertion point up one line so there is a blank line above and below it.

2. Open the Insert menu, choose Web Component, select MSN Components, and double-click Search The Web With MSN. A small search form will appear on the page. You will be prompted to connect to the Internet if you are not connected already. Save the page and view it in a browser. The search form in a browser should look like this:

3. Enter some word in the search form (I entered "Autos") and click Search. The MSN Search page will open with the results of your search, as you can see in Figure 9-13.

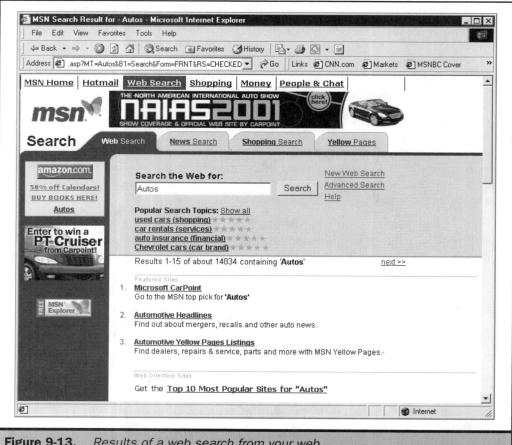

Figure 9-13.   *Results of a web search from your web*

4. Close your browser and return to the Components Home page in FrontPage. Below the MSN search form, add the blank lines and move the insertion point so there is a blank line separating it from the search form and another below it.

5. Open the Insert menu, choose Web Component, select MSNBC Components, and double-click Insert A Weather Forecast. The Insert A Weather Forecast Properties dialog box will open asking you for the name of a city or a U.S. ZIP code.

6. Enter a city name or ZIP code and click Next. The city or ZIP code will be confirmed. Click Finish. A sample weather forecast will appear in FrontPage. Save the page and view it in a browser. The current weather forecast will look like this:

7. Close your browser and the Components web.

Confirmation Field Component

The Confirmation Field component allows you to build a confirmation page that echoes the contents of a web form that has been submitted. Such a page would replace the automatic confirmation form you saw in Chapter 8 (Figure 8-12). To build a confirmation page for your Literature Request form:

1. In FrontPage, open the Forms web you created in Chapter 8, and then open the Literature Request form (Literature.htm) in Page view.

2. In Page view, create a new page. On the new page, create a brief confirmation letter. Begin by putting a heading on the page, such as

   Great Products Company

   formatting it as Heading 1, centering it, and then pressing ENTER.

3. Click Align Left on the toolbar; then at the left margin, type **To:** and press SHIFT+ENTER.

4. Open the Insert menu, choose Web Component, select Advanced Controls, and double-click Confirmation Field. In the Confirmation Field Properties dialog box, type **First**, as shown next, and then click OK.

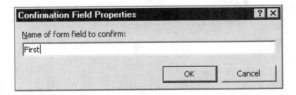

5. Leave a space, again open the Confirmation Field Properties dialog box, type **Last**, click OK, and press SHIFT+ENTER for a new line.

There is no easy way to get a list of field names—you need to either remember them, write them down as you are creating a form, or open the Properties dialog box for each field. Suggestions have been made to Microsoft that a Browse feature be added to the Confirmation Field Properties dialog box.

6. Repeat Step 4 to enter confirmation fields for **Company**, **Address1**, and **Address2** all on separate lines ending with SHIFT+ENTER.

7. Again repeat Step 4 to enter confirmation fields for **City**, **State**, and **Zip** all on one line, with a comma and a space between *City* and *State*, and a space between *State* and *Zip*.

8. Enter two blank lines and type the body and ending of the letter, something similar to that shown in Figure 9-14. Follow this with a link that says **Return to the form** and points to the Literature Request form. When you are done, save

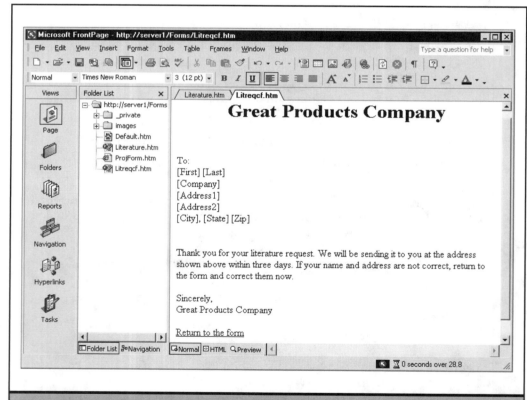

Figure 9-14. *Custom confirmation letter in Page view*

the confirmation letter with a page title of **Literature Request Confirmation** and a filename of **Litreqcf.htm**.

9. Open the Literature Request form, right-click the form, choose Form Properties, click Options, and then click the Confirmation Page tab. Click Browse and double-click Literature Request Confirmation. Litreqcf.htm should appear in the text box. Click OK twice. Save the Literature Request form.

10. In your browser, open the Forms web, click Custom Form, fill out the form, click Submit Form, and you'll see a confirmation letter similar to the one shown in Figure 9-15.

11. Close your browser and your Forms web.

For more on confirmation forms, see Chapter 4.

CREATING
WEB SITES

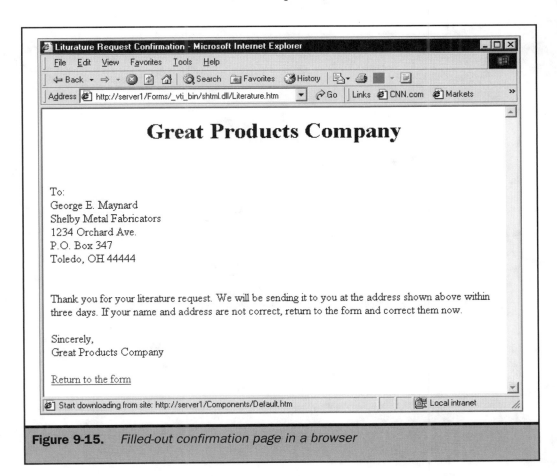

Figure 9-15. *Filled-out confirmation page in a browser*

Chapter 10

Advanced Formatting
Techniques

353

In the preceding chapters you have seen many ways to lay out, format, and enhance a web page. These are, for the most part, classic techniques that have been available to web authors for some time. FrontPage additionally brings you several advanced techniques for doing this. The purpose of this chapter is to cover these advanced techniques, including:

- Customizing existing themes
- Creating and using style sheets
- Positioning and wrapping text around objects
- Easily choosing web-safe colors
- Creating graphics within FrontPage

Customizing Existing Themes

If you have used the themes that are available in FrontPage and looked at the many alternatives, you may have come to the conclusion that while there are many neat elements in a number of the themes, no one theme is exactly the way you would like it to be. You can solve this by customizing one of the existing themes to add your own logo; change the styles, colors, and graphics used; and save the theme with your name. In this way you create your own theme.

Modifying a Theme

You begin the process of creating a customized theme by picking an existing theme, preferably one that is close to what you want, and opening it for modification.

1. With FrontPage open in any view (you don't need to have a web or page open), open the Format menu and choose Theme. The Themes dialog box will appear as shown in Figure 10-1.

2. Click each of the themes in the list and look at them with and without their Vivid Colors, Active Graphics, and Background Picture options.

Tip   *If you cannot find a theme you like and you haven't already done this, you can install additional themes by choosing that option from the top of the themes list (you'll need to have your Office or FrontPage CD in its drive).*

3. Select the theme and accompanying options that come closest to the theme you want to create.

4. Click Modify. An additional set of buttons opens, as you can see next, that allows you to modify the colors, graphics, and text styles in the selected theme and then save the resulting theme with a new name.

You'll see how to change each of these elements in the next several sections.

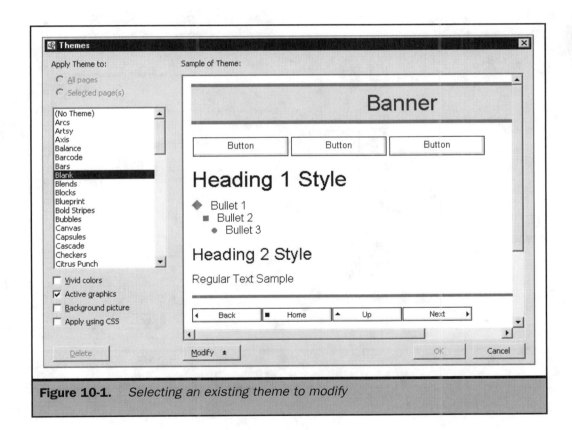

Figure 10-1. *Selecting an existing theme to modify*

Changing the Colors in a Theme

The colors in a theme control the coloration of all parts of a web page including the background, headings, hyperlinks, banner text, and table borders. You can set these with the following steps:

1. Click Colors. The Modify Theme dialog box opens as shown in Figure 10-2. It provides three ways to set the colors used in a theme: readymade color schemes, a color wheel, and custom color selection.

2. With the Color Schemes tab selected, click a number of the readymade schemes and scroll the Sample Of Theme preview box to see how the colors are applied.

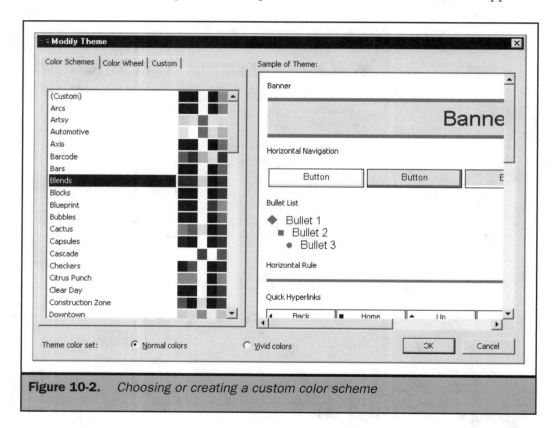

Figure 10-2. *Choosing or creating a custom color scheme*

3. Click the Color Wheel tab. Drag the small circle in the color wheel to see how the color schemes change. Also change the Brightness slider and observe its effects.

4. Click the Custom tab. Click the down arrow under Item and observe the list of items on a web page for which you can set a particular color, as shown here:

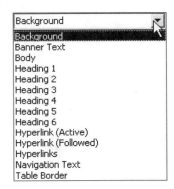

5. Select several of the page items one at a time—say, Background, Heading 1 and 2, and Banner Text—and choose a color to use for each.

6. Click the Color Schemes tab and you will see a new (Custom) scheme with the colors you chose.

As in the Themes dialog box, you can select normal or vivid colors at the bottom of the dialog box.

7. Click OK to close the Modify Theme dialog box.

Replacing the Graphics in a Theme

The graphics that can be used on a page and set in a theme include the background, the banner, bullets, and buttons. You can change any or all of these with the following steps:

1. Click Graphics. The Modify Theme dialog box again opens, but this time it allows you to change the picture and font used for a particular item on the page, as you can see in Figure 10-3.

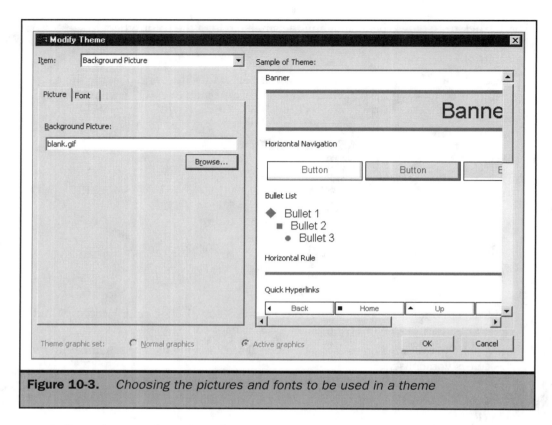

Figure 10-3. *Choosing the pictures and fonts to be used in a theme*

2. Open the Item drop-down list to see the list that can be changed, like this:

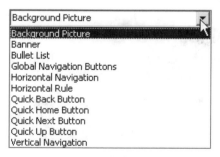

3. Select several items from the drop-down list and look at what you can select a picture for. In some cases—for example, Horizontal Navigation—there are three elements that need pictures (the regular button, the selected button, and the button that is hovered over).

4. Click Browse and find an alternative graphic to use for the selected item. (The items for the current theme are in the \Windows\Temp\FrontPage TempDir\Mstheme*Theme name* folder in Windows 95/98/Me or \Documents and Settings*user*\Local Settings\Temp\FrontPage TempDir\Mstheme\ *Theme name* in Windows 2000 or XP Professional or Server.)

5. When you have selected a graphic to use for an item, click the Font tab. Here you can choose from a variety of fonts and select the style, size, and alignment you want to use. Graphics that don't have text associated with them, such as horizontal rules, have a grayed out Font tab.

6. After the graphics and fonts are the way you want them for all the items you are using on the page, click OK to return to the Themes dialog box.

Applying Different Text Styles to a Theme

As you just saw, the Graphics button allows you to set the fonts, sizes, and font styles (bold, italic) to be used for text on the graphic items in a theme such as banners and buttons. The Text button allows you to do the same tasks for normal text (called "Body") and headings on a web page. You can also create or modify a style sheet related to the theme. Explore theme text modification with these steps:

1. Click Text. The Modify Theme dialog box will open. In this case, you can choose Body or one of the heading types and then select the font you want to use for that particular type of text.

2. Open the Item drop-down list. You can see that you have six levels of headings and Body to choose from:

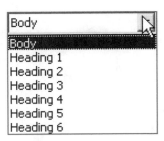

 Body text refers to regular text as well as hyperlinks (regular, followed, and active).

3. With Body selected, scroll the samples until you see Regular Text Sample, and then click several fonts you might like to see how the text looks in the sample area. Once you find a family, look at the weights that are available and decide

how you are going to assign those weights to the body and heading items. For example, here are the assignments I made, as shown in Figure 10-4:

- Heading 1: Arial Black
- Heading 2: Arial Unicode MS
- Heading 3: Arial
- Heading 4: Arial Narrow
- Heading 5: Arial Narrow
- Heading 6: Arial Narrow
- Body (Regular Text): Century Gothic

4. Select a text item (Body or one of the headings) and click a font. Repeat this for all the text items.

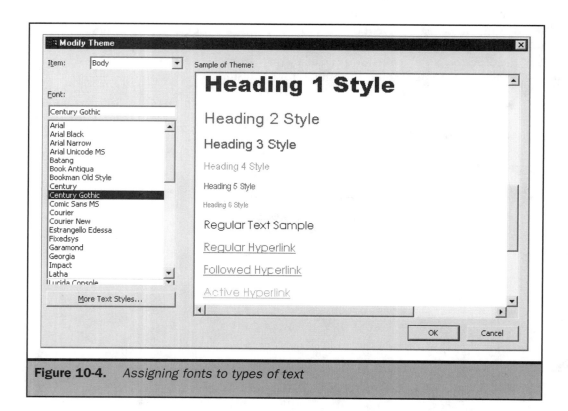

Figure 10-4. *Assigning fonts to types of text*

5. When you have completed selecting the font you want to use for all of the text items, click More Text Styles. The Style dialog box will open, like the one in Figure 10-5.

6. With User-Defined Styles selected in the List drop-down box, click Body in the Styles list. A description of that style will appear along with examples of it.

7. Click Modify to open the Modify Style dialog box and then click Format | Font. Here choose the font style, size, color, and effects that are to be used for the selected style. When you set the characteristics of the style, click OK twice.

Note   *The next section will describe style sheets and how to create them and use them in more detail.*

8. Repeat Steps 6 and 7 for all the styles you want to modify. After defining all the styles, click OK to close the Style dialog box and click OK again to close the Modify Theme dialog box.

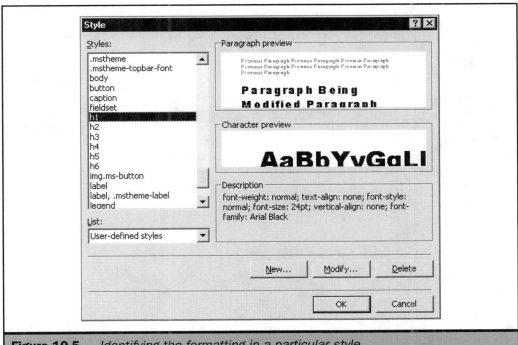

Figure 10-5.   *Identifying the formatting in a particular style*

9. In the Themes dialog box, click Save As to save your changes under a new name. Enter a name and click OK. The new theme name will appear in the list of themes under the Apply Theme To area. Click Cancel to close the Themes dialog box.

10. Apply this theme by opening a new or existing web, open the Format menu, choose Theme, click Apply Theme To All Pages, select your new theme, and click OK. As you build the web pages, select the style you want to use for a particular item (heading, body text, and so on) from the style drop-down list on the left of the Formatting toolbar.

Themes are a very powerful device to maintain a consistent look and feel when a number of people are creating parts of a web site or an intranet.

Creating and Using Style Sheets

Style sheets, which are also called cascading style sheets (CSS), allow you to predefine a number of styles and then consistently apply them throughout a web site. This not only gives a consistent look to your site, it saves you time and allows you to change the entire site by simply changing the style sheet. As you saw previously, you can use style sheets with themes, but you can also define your own style sheets and use them to control the webs you create.

There are two types of style sheets: *embedded style sheets* that apply only to the page on which they reside and *external style sheets* that are linked to and used in a number of pages. How these two types of style sheets are created is different, although their usage is the same.

> **Note** *Early web browsers (before Internet Explorer 3.0 and Netscape Navigator 4.0) cannot use style sheets, and pages that are formatted with them probably will not look as they are intended to. There are two style sheet standards: CSS 1.0, which covers formatting, and CSS 2.0, which covers the positioning and layering of page elements. Internet Explorer 3.0 supports CSS 1.0, and Internet Explorer 4.0 and later and Netscape Navigator 4.0 and later support both CSS 1.0 and 2.0.*

Creating Embedded Style Sheets

An embedded style sheet is created in the page in which it will be used. Follow these instructions to create an embedded style sheet.

> **Note** *If the Style option is dim (not available) in the Format menu, it has been disabled. It can be enabled by opening the Tools menu, choosing Page Options, clicking the Compatibility tab, and clicking CSS 1.0 and CSS 2.0 under the Technologies section.*

1. In Page view, open the page in which you want the style sheet. Then open the Format menu and choose Style. A Style dialog box will open like the one you saw in Figure 10-5.

2. In Figure 10-5 the Styles list shows user-defined styles, while here it shows HTML tags. If you select User Defined Styles in the List box, you will see it is empty. To build a style sheet, you can either choose an HTML tag to attach the style to or you can create a style from scratch. If you choose an HTML tag, the style is automatically applied when the tag is used (for example the Body tag is automatically used in every web page, while the H1 tag is used whenever you use a Heading 1). With user-defined styles, you must manually apply them to the page element you select.

3. Click Body in the Styles list and then click Modify to create a style for the body text on the page (you can also just double-click Body). The Modify Style dialog box opens showing a preview of the style and giving a description of it, which is initially blank.

4. Click Format and choose Font. The Font dialog box opens, as you can see in Figure 10-6. Choose the font, font style, size, color, and effects you want (remember this is the body text, the majority of text on a page).

5. Click the Character Spacing tab. Open the Spacing drop-down list. Here you have expanded and condensed options, and in the spinner to the right you can set the amount of either by 1 point increments. In the Position drop-down list you can raise or lower the text from a normal baseline to subscript and superscript positions or to five other positions above and below the baseline.

6. Click OK to close the Font dialog box and, back in the Modify Style dialog box, again click Format and choose Paragraph. The Paragraph dialog box will open and you can select the paragraph alignment from the drop-down list and set indentation and line and word spacing from spinners.

7. Click OK to close the Paragraph dialog box. In a similar manner, look at the Borders And Shading, Bullets And Numbering, and Position dialog boxes.

8. When you are back in the Modify Style dialog box, click OK to return to the Style dialog box. Notice that you now have Body in your User Defined Styles, and its description is as you defined it.

9. To define styles for other tags, such as H1 (Heading 1), select HTML Tags from the List drop-down box, click the tag in the Styles list, click Modify, and repeat Steps 3 through 7.

10. To define your own style—for example, Red H1 for a red Heading 1—click New, enter the name, such as **h1(red)**, click Format, and follow Steps 3 through 7.

11. When you have defined all the styles you need, click OK to close the Style dialog box, save your page, and close it.

You'll see in a minute how to apply your new styles, but if you want to sneak a peek, open the Style drop-down list on the left of the Formatting toolbar and you'll see the standard styles at the top (Body is Normal) and your custom styles at the bottom of

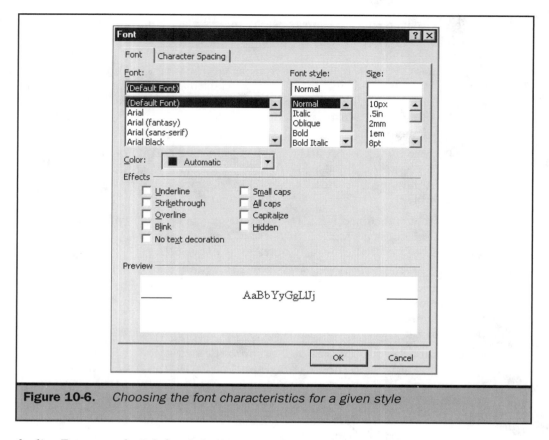

Figure 10-6.   *Choosing the font characteristics for a given style*

the list. For example, I defined the custom styles Special and H1(red), which are shown at the bottom of this Style list:

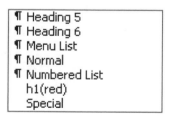

Creating External Style Sheets

An external style sheet gives you the benefit of being able to apply a set of styles to a number of pages, a whole web site, or even several web sites. Then, with a single change in the style sheet you can change all of the pages to which it is linked. External style sheets provide a very powerful means to maintain a consistent look to all of the pages in a site. Here are the steps to create an external style sheet:

1. Click New | Page to open the Page Templates dialog box. Click the Style Sheets tab, which will open as you can see in Figure 10-7. This tab allows you to either create a style sheet from scratch (the Normal Style Sheet) or to start with one of 12 readymade style sheets, which are also used in the themes. The description will give you an idea of the style sheets, but there are no previews available. In any case, you can add to and modify the style sheet you start with.

2. Click Blueprint to see what you have when you start with a readymade style sheet. Note from the description that you should have Century Gothic text and headers, purple hyperlinks, and a bright yellow background.

Tip   *If you open the Page Template dialog box from within an open web, there's an option that is a true procrastinator's dream, Just Add A Web Task, instead of adding a new page, frame page, or style sheet.*

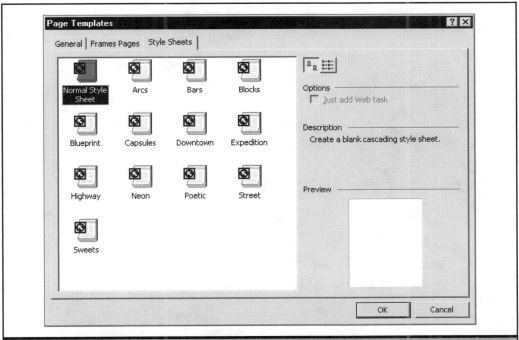

Figure 10-7.   *Selecting a starting point for a style sheet*

3. Click OK. A new page opens in Page view with a .CSS extension and displaying the HTML used in the page, as shown in Figure 10-8. Notice that there are no tabs at the bottom of the page. For this type of page, HTML is the only way you can look at it.

You can edit the style sheet in two ways: you can directly edit and add to the HTML on the page, being sure to follow the rules for writing HTML (see Chapter 12); or you can use the Style option in either the Format menu or the floating Style toolbar.

4. Scroll down the page until you see first the group of heading styles and then the individual heading styles. The group defines the font to be used for all the headings, while the individual styles define their color.

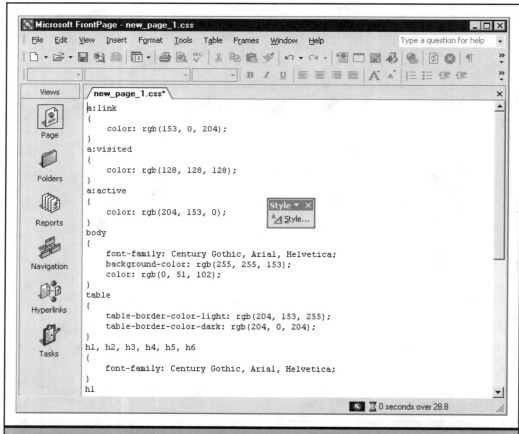

Figure 10-8. *An external style sheet in Page view shows the HTML behind the page*

5. Click Style in the floating Style toolbar. The Style dialog box will open with a number of user-defined styles, as you can see next, which you can add to or modify as you did in the previous section.

6. After you have made the additions and changes that you want to make, click OK to close the Style dialog box. In FrontPage, open the File menu and save the page with a .CSS extension in your root web (C:\Inetpub\Wwwroot\ if you are using Windows 2000 and IIS or if you are using Windows 98 and PWS). Close the web.

Had you used the Normal Style Sheet instead of a readymade one, you would have opened a blank page and a blank style sheet to which you could add your own styles—either for HTML tags or user-defined styles.

Linking to External Style Sheets

For a page to use an external style sheet, it must be linked to the style sheet. Once that is done, the linked style sheet behaves as though it is an embedded style sheet. All the styles in the external style sheet are available in the Style drop-down list in the Formatting toolbar. Here's how to link to an external style sheet:

1. With the page that you want linked to the external style sheet open in Page view, open and fully extend the Format menu and click Style Sheet Links. The Link Style Sheet dialog box will open.

Note   *In the Link Style Sheet dialog box, you can choose to link the style sheet to all the pages in a web or to only the pages you have selected.*

2. If the URL list does not show any style sheets, click Add. The Select Style Sheet dialog box will open, followed almost immediately by the Select File dialog box.

Select the drive and path to the folder in which you stored your style sheet, normally your root web (C:\Inetpub\Wwwroot is the default), and then double-click your style sheet. The Select File and Select Style Sheet dialog boxes will close, and you will see the path to your style sheet in the Link Style Sheet dialog box, like this:

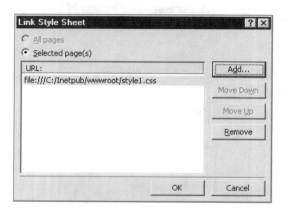

 If your Select File did not open immediately and you are left looking at the Select Style Sheet dialog box, click the Select A File On Your Computer button on the far right of the line with the URL text box.

3. Click the link to select it, and then click OK to close the dialog box. The styles on the external style sheet are now available on the page.

The external style sheet does not have to be on your hard disk, it can be anywhere on your network or your intranet, and theoretically it could be on the Internet. The potential problem of that is that you would have to be connected to the Internet to access the styles.

Using Style Sheets

Using a style sheet, as has been implied, is very easy—you just select the style you want to use from the style drop-down list, like this:

1. Open either the page with an embedded style sheet or the page that is linked to a style sheet in Page view. (The external style sheet just described is used in the steps and figures below.)

2. Open the Style drop-down list on the Formatting toolbar and select Heading 1. Type the heading and press ENTER. The next line should be Normal or Body text. Type a line and again press ENTER.

3. From the style list, select Heading 2. Type the heading and press ENTER. Again, the next line is Normal style.

4. Type some text to be a hyperlink, select the text, click the Hyperlink button on the toolbar, and select a destination to which to link. The line will be formatted as a hyperlink.

5. Try out any other styles you have defined. Using these steps and the linked style sheet, my page looks like Figure 10-9. If you had different styles, yours, of course, will look different.

6. Close your page without saving it.

While it may be a bit of a hassle to set up a style sheet initially, you'll find it more than pays you back for the time you spend.

Positioning and Wrapping Text Around Objects

When you place an object like a picture on a web page with text, the default is for the picture to be flush left and for the text to flow from the bottom right corner of the picture from left to right and top to bottom, as you can see in Figure 10-10. (The pictures and text in this section are from Princess Cruises' 1999 Alaska Catalog and are used with the

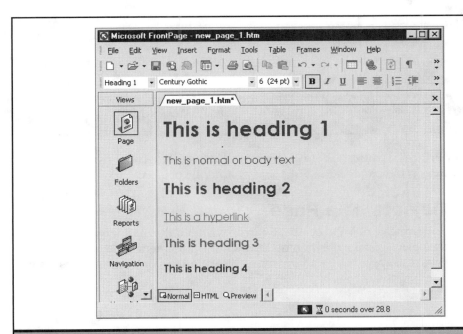

Figure 10-9. *Style sheet styles applied to text on a page*

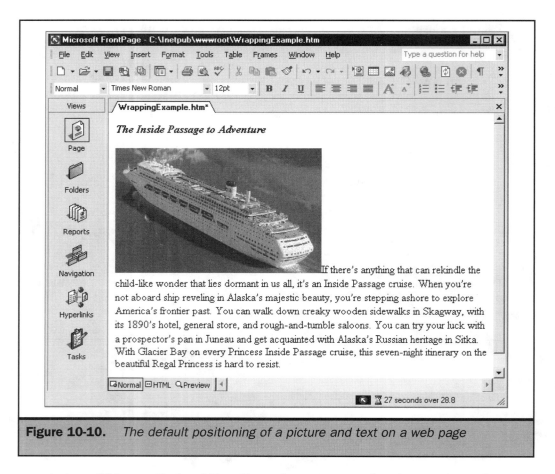

Figure 10-10. *The default positioning of a picture and text on a web page*

permission of Princess Cruises.) FrontPage gives you several tools to position objects in different ways on the page and to wrap text around the objects.

Positioning Objects on a Page

The default positioning of objects on a page can be changed through the positioning properties of the object. Simple positioning through the alignment controls on the Formatting toolbar is supported by all browsers. Use of tables for positioning is also supported by most browsers, but the advanced positioning described here requires web browsers that support CSS 2.0, specifically Internet Explorer 4.0 and above. This advanced positioning can be *relative* to the other objects on the page or *absolute* to a specific set of coordinates and can be assigned a layer or *z-order* in the stack of objects on the page. Advanced positioning is done through the object's Properties dialog box, the Position dialog box, and the Positioning toolbar.

 Advanced positioning may conflict with Dynamic HTML and cause unpredictable results, so the two should not be used together.

Using Absolute Positioning

Absolute positioning allows you to specify the exact pixel position for the upper left-hand corner of an object. You can do that by dragging an object to that position or by specifying that position in either the Position dialog box or Positioning toolbar. When you place an object at an absolute position, it is taken out of the text stream and text will no longer flow around it or be impacted by its position—the text will be either above it or below it on a separate layer. Absolute positioning means that the object is located at a specific set of pixel coordinates independent of the screen resolution and therefore will not change even though the layout of text and other relative objects have changed with a different resolution. So it is important to test a page with absolute positioning on all the common resolutions (640×480, 800×600, and 1024×768), as well as in both Netscape Navigator and Internet Explorer. The following steps demonstrate how absolute positioning works:

1. In FrontPage with nothing else open, open the File menu, choose Open, set the path to the \Book\Chap10\ folder on the CD that comes with this book, and double-click PositioningExample.htm. A page similar to Figure 10-10 will open, but the picture will be on a different line from the text.

2. Click the picture to select it, open the Format menu, and choose Position (you must open the menu all the way to do this). The Position dialog box will open as shown in Figure 10-11.

3. Click Absolute. Notice how the Left and Top location spinners become active. This is the number of pixels from the left edge and from the top edge of the page—its absolute position on the page. You can change that position by changing the numbers.

Figure 10-11. *Controlling the positioning of an object relative to the text on a page*

4. Change the left spinner to 130, and click OK to close the dialog box. The picture will now be on top of the text and in its approximate center, like this:

5. Open the View menu and choose Toolbars | Positioning. The Positioning toolbar will appear showing the position of the selected picture.

6. Move the mouse pointer to the picture, where it becomes a four-headed arrow. Drag the picture around. Notice that it is independent of the text and that the Positioning toolbar shows you your position in pixels, as you can see in Figure 10-12.

7. Save your page as Absolute.htm in your default folder, My Documents or My Webs, then open the File menu, choose Preview In Browser, and double-click Internet Explorer. Internet Explorer will open and display a slightly different positioning than what you had in FrontPage, as shown in the top of Figure 10-13 (compare to Figure 10-12).

8. Return to FrontPage, open the File menu, choose Preview In Browser, and double-click Netscape Navigator. Again, you have a very slightly different positioning from that in both FrontPage and Internet Explorer 5.5, as shown in the bottom of Figure 10-13.

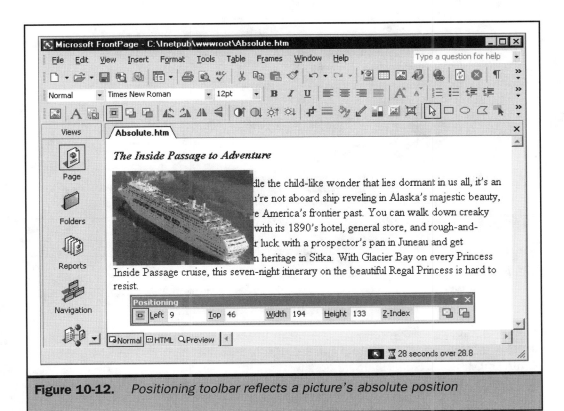

Figure 10-12.   *Positioning toolbar reflects a picture's absolute position*

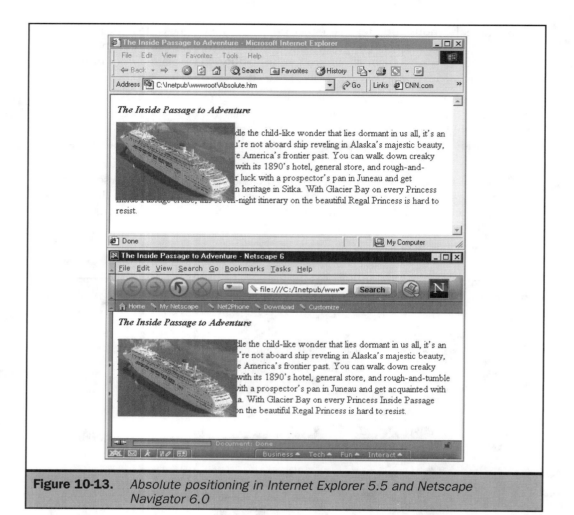

Figure 10-13.   *Absolute positioning in Internet Explorer 5.5 and Netscape Navigator 6.0*

9. Close Internet Explorer, Netscape Navigator, and your current page in FrontPage. Also close the Positioning toolbar.

You should also try different screen resolutions. The preceding figures were shot at 1024×768; when I switched to either 800×600 or 640×480, there did not seem to be a significant difference. But that will not always be the case. You need to test your pages at those resolutions, especially if you are using absolute resolution.

Using Relative Positioning and Wrapping Text

Relative positioning allows you to set the position of an object in relation to other objects on the page, so no matter how the size of the page changes, the objects will remain in the same relative position. This allows you to wrap text around a picture and keep it that way with various screen resolutions. This is demonstrated with the following instructions:

1. In FrontPage with nothing open, open the WrappingExample.htm file from the \Book\Chap10\ folder on the CD that comes with this book. A page will appear with two pictures and two pieces of text all from the Princess Cruises 1999 Alaska catalog (used with their permission).

2. Click the top picture to select it, open the Format menu, and choose Position (you may have to open the menu all the way) to open the Position dialog box you saw in Figure 10-11.

3. Click the Right Wrapping Style, Relative Positioning Style, and click OK. The picture of the boat will move over to the right and the text will move up and to the left of the picture.

4. Click the bottom picture, again open the Position dialog box, choose Left Wrapping and Relative Positioning, and click OK. The picture will stay where it is and the text will move up on the right, as you can see in Figure 10-14 (you may need to drag the pictures up a bit to get this positioning).

5. Save this page as Relative.htm in your default folder and preview the page in both Internet Explorer and Netscape Navigator and in several resolutions. Figure 10-15 shows Internet Explorer and Netscape Navigator at 1024×768.

6. Close both Internet Explorer and Netscape Navigator as well as your page in FrontPage.

In my case, both Internet Explorer and Netscape Navigator displayed the page close to but not exactly the way it was intended to be displayed. You may have a different experience. This demonstrates the need to preview your pages in both browsers.

Note   *The placement of photos and text can also be done with a table, which would ensure that everyone would see it as you intended.*

Easily Choosing Web-Safe Colors

FrontPage brings substantial improvement to applying web-safe colors to graphics, backgrounds, tables, hyperlinks, and text and to picking up existing colors. In HTML, color is specified as a six-character hexadecimal (hex) value that is difficult to use. Early

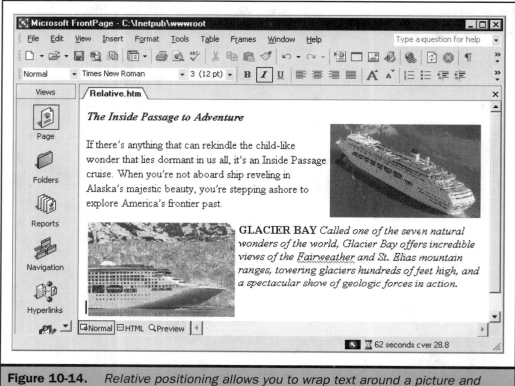

Figure 10-14. *Relative positioning allows you to wrap text around a picture and have it stay there*

versions of FrontPage allowed you to select a color without having to use the hex value but gave you only 48 colors that were web-safe and then a more difficult way to pick any custom color. Later versions of FrontPage give you 134 web-safe colors, a way to pick up an existing color from anything on your screen, even outside of FrontPage—for example, in a browser—and a way to create any custom color. If you create custom colors, they are available throughout FrontPage and are even maintained between editing sessions. Look at where and how color is created in FrontPage in the following instructions:

1. From the \Book\Chap10\ folder on this book's CD, open the Color.htm file in FrontPage. The page that opens gives you some text, a table, a hyperlink, and a horizontal line, plus the background on which to work with color.

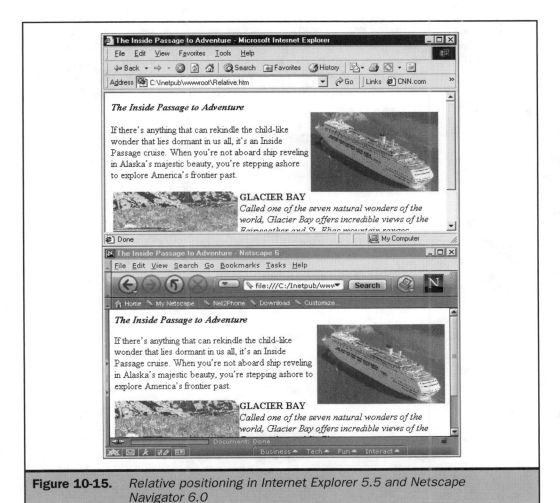

Figure 10-15. *Relative positioning in Internet Explorer 5.5 and Netscape Navigator 6.0*

2. Right-click the heading text and choose Font. In the Font dialog box there is a Color drop-down list. If you click the down arrow, a small color palette opens showing the 16 primary colors and allowing you to choose more colors, like this:

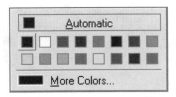

3. Close the Font dialog box, right-click the table, and choose either Table Properties or Cell Properties (the dialog boxes are close to the same; one applies to the entire table, the other to a single cell). The Table or Cell Properties dialog box opens and shows four of the Color drop-down controls—three for the border and one for the background, as you can see next. If you open any of these drop-down lists, you'll see the 16-color palette from the previous step.

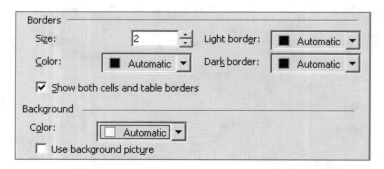

4. Close the Table or Cell Properties dialog box, right-click the horizontal line, and choose Horizontal Line Properties. Again you see the same Color drop-down control, and if you open it you see the 16-color palette.

5. Close the Horizontal Line Properties dialog box, right-click any blank area of the page, and choose Page Properties. In the Background tab you see five Color drop-down controls—three for hyperlinks, one for the background, and one for text, like this:

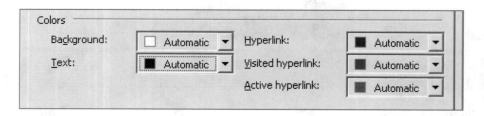

6. Click the Background color drop-down control to display the 16-color palette and then click More Colors. The More Colors dialog box will open, as you can see in Figure 10-16. Here are the 134 web-safe colors (127 in the hexagon and 7 below, since white is in the hexagon). When you click a color either in or below the hexagon, the color's hex value is displayed in the upper-right of the dialog box. If the color has an official color name, it is displayed beneath the hex value.

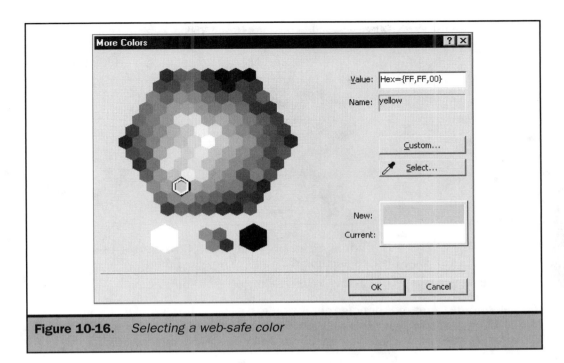

Figure 10-16.   *Selecting a web-safe color*

7. Click the eyedropper Select button. The mouse pointer turns into an eyedropper, and with it you can go anywhere on your screen, including outside of FrontPage. Hovering over a color will cause that color to be identified in the More Colors dialog box; clicking that color will select it.

Tip   *You can press ESC to return the eyedropper mouse pointer to a normal pointer.*

8. Click Custom to open the Color dialog box, which is the same as the Color Selection dialog box in FrontPage 97 and 98, shown in Figure 10-17. Here there are 48 web-safe colors and the ability to pick any color there is by clicking the color matrix and dragging the brightness level, or by choosing one of the numeric color schemes. When you have chosen a custom color, click Add To Custom Colors; it will be displayed in the Custom Colors blocks in the lower left. Close the Color dialog box to return to the More Colors dialog box.

9. Choose a color and click OK to close the More Colors dialog box. You are returned to the Page Properties | Background tab. Open the Text color drop-down palette and specify a color using any of the schemes that have been discussed. Click OK

to close the Page Properties dialog box; you'll see the background color you have chosen on the page. Reopen the font color palette you saw in Step 2, and notice how a new section has been added entitled Document's Colors, like this:

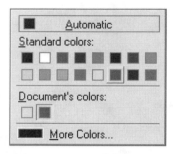

10. Close the open dialog boxes. Open any of the other Color drop-down controls' palettes and see that the document colors are repeated there.

11. Close all dialog boxes and close the Color page without saving it.

The color features of FrontPage allow you to easily define a set of web-safe colors and then use those colors anywhere in a web site. Like the other features in this chapter, the color features significantly enhance your ability to easily produce outstanding web sites.

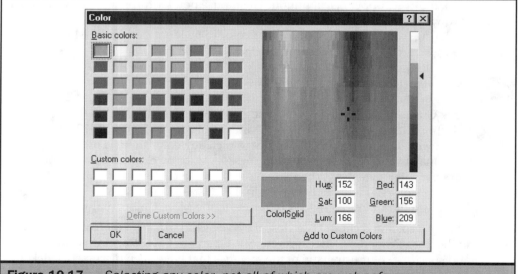

Figure 10-17. *Selecting any color, not all of which are web-safe*

Creating Graphics within FrontPage

While most of the graphics you use to build a web site in FrontPage will be created elsewhere, FrontPage does have a fair capability to directly create some graphics. All of this capability is centered on the Drawing toolbar, shown next, which was described in Chapter 2. Two major components on the drawing toolbar are AutoShapes and WordArt.

Using AutoShapes

AutoShapes are a set of readymade shapes that include basic shapes, block arrows, and flowchart elements, as well as lines, stars, banners, and callouts, as you can see next. Once you have selected the shape, you can place it anywhere on the page by moving the mouse pointer to that area and clicking. In this manner, you can lay down a "normal-sized" object or size it by dragging the mouse. To resize the object once it's on the page, simply select it and drag one of the selection handles in or out. You can also fill an enclosed shape with color and/or change its outline color by using the Fill and Line Color tools.

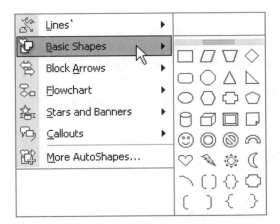

Build a simplified schematic diagram for purchasing airline tickets using AutoShapes and following these steps:

1. Open the Exciting Travel web in FrontPage, and double-click Air.htm. Scroll down so you can see the bottom of the world map and the top of the bottom shared border.

2. Place the insertion point on the bottom-right corner of the map and press ENTER eight or nine times to open up a fair amount of space in which to build the schematic. Place the insertion point on the second line below the map, leaving one blank line above it.

3. Type
Steps in Buying Airline Tickets
Format the line as Heading 2, and press ENTER twice.

4. Open the View menu and choose Toolbars | Drawing. In the Drawing toolbar open AutoShapes, point to Flowchart, and click the upper-left rectangle called Process. The pointer becomes crosshairs.

5. Place the crosshairs under and to the left side of the heading and drag a rectangle that is roughly two inches wide by one inch tall, like this:

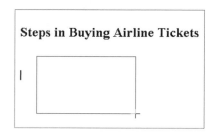

6. From AutoShapes | Flowchart select the diamond, the third shape in the top row, and drag a diamond roughly the same width as the rectangle beneath the rectangle. Click the rectangle to select and press CTRL+C to copy it.

7. Press CTRL+V twice to paste two copies of the rectangle. Drag one rectangle below the diamond and the other to the right of the diamond.

8. From AutoShapes | Lines, choose the single-headed arrow. Drag the arrow from the bottom of the top rectangle to the top of the diamond. Similarly, drag one arrow from the bottom of the diamond to the bottom rectangle and another one from the right of the diamond to the rectangle on the right.

9. In the Drawing toolbar, click the Text Box button and drag a text box just inside the existing top rectangle. Type the following:
Choose the date and time that you want to leave and the date and time you want to return.
This should be formatted as Normal, which is Times Roman size 3 (12 point).

10. Right-click the border of the text box, choose Format Text Box, change the Line Color to No Line, and click OK. In a similar manor, create a text box, turn off the border, and insert the text in the other flowchart objects, including the Yes and No text outside the objects, as shown in Figure 10-18.

11. Save your page and leave it and FrontPage open.

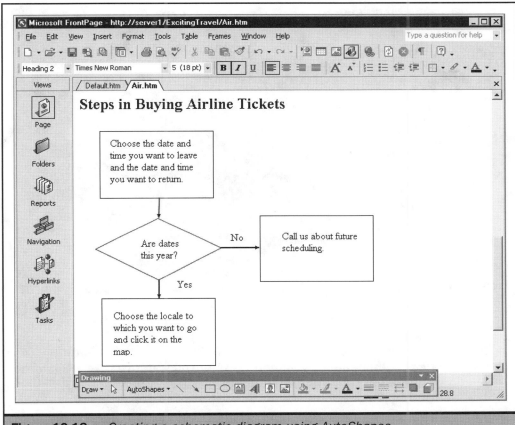

Figure 10-18.   *Creating a schematic diagram using AutoShapes*

Using WordArt

WordArt takes text that you have entered and selected and applies one of 30 effects that you select from the WordArt Gallery. After you have selected the effect, the Edit WordArt Text dialog box opens, allowing you to make any changes to the text you want. When you click OK, the text with the applied effect will appear on your current page. When the text is selected, a WordArt toolbar appears allowing you to edit the text; select a different effect from the gallery; change the color, size, layout, and rotation of the text; make all the characters the same size; make them vertical; change their alignment; and alter their spacing. See how in this final set of steps:

1. In the Air.htm page in Page view, insert three blank lines just above the text immediately above the map, move the insertion point to the middle line you

just created, and type:
AIR TRAVEL

2. Select AIR TRAVEL and click Insert WordArt in the Drawing toolbar. Select a style that you want to use (the second column, third row was chosen here) and click OK twice. The word art will appear on the page with its menu, like this:

3. Save the page and then view it in a browser. The WordArt and the schematic diagram should appear as you saw them in FrontPage.

4. Close the Exciting Travel web and FrontPage.

The Drawing toolbar, AutoShapes, and WordArt have a number of features that are not described here, but they are easy for you to explore on your own. We recommend that you do that.

Chapter 11

Importing and Integrating Office and Other Files

Y ou will probably want to augment your FrontPage web with files imported from other applications—if for no other reason than because the files you want already exist in another format. This is especially true with multimedia files, since FrontPage does not have the capability to create multimedia files. FrontPage has several ways of working with information created outside of it, including importing information onto an existing page, importing information onto a new page, and attaching or linking to a non-FrontPage file from a web. Look at this from the standpoint of Microsoft Office XP and other productivity applications. (Working with multimedia files will be covered in Chapter 21.)

Importing Microsoft Office XP and Other Productivity Files

FrontPage 2002 is part of the Microsoft Office XP family and thus is tightly integrated, and in several editions bundled, with the other Office products. If you use the Office products Word, Excel, PowerPoint, and Access, you can see a definite similarity in the menus, toolbars, and behavior of FrontPage. Of equal or even greater importance, though, is how easy it is to bring files created in the other Office products into FrontPage. Here you'll look at several Office products and see how you can import information they create into FrontPage. If you use other productivity applications, such as those from Corel, WordPerfect, or Lotus, you will find that they are not as tightly integrated as the Office applications, but you can still easily import these files into FrontPage.

| Note | *Microsoft Access is covered in depth in Chapter 19.* |

Using Text from Microsoft Word and Other Word Processors

FrontPage can bring externally created text, especially Microsoft Word text, into a web in a number of ways. Among these are:

- Pasting text from the Windows Clipboard onto an existing page in Page view.
- Inserting a file onto an existing page in Page view. The file can be in any of the file formats listed in Table 11-1.
- Opening a file onto a new page from within Page view. The file can be in any of the file formats listed in Table 11-1.
- Importing a file onto a new page in either HTML format or its native format, if that format has been associated with its native editor in FrontPage. (Microsoft Word's DOC format is an example of this.)
- Dragging and dropping a file into FrontPage.

File Format	Extensions
Hypertext Markup Language	.HTM, .HTML
Hypertext Templates	.HTT
Preprocessed HTML	.HTX, .ASP
HTML Document	.HTM, .HTML, .HTX, .OTM
Lotus 1-2-3	.WK1, .WK3, .WK4
Microsoft Excel Worksheet	.XLS, .XLW
Recover Text from Any File	.*
Rich Text Format	.RTF
Text Files	.TXT
Windows Write	.WRI
Word (Asian Versions) 6.0/95	.DOC
Word 2.x for Windows	.DOC
Word 4.0–5.1 for Macintosh	.MCW
Word 6.0/95 for Windows and Macintosh	.DOC
Word 97/2000/10	.DOC
WordPerfect 5.x/6.x	.DOC, .WPD
Works 4.0/5.0 for Windows	.WPS

Table 11-1.   *File Formats That Can Be Brought into FrontPage in Page View*

To see how these methods differ, you'll need documents from Microsoft Word or another word processing application to use as examples. You can find the Office XP product examples used in this chapter on the CD accompanying this book.

Pasting Text from the Clipboard

Probably the easiest way to bring in a small amount of text from almost any Windows application is through the use of the Windows Clipboard. To see how it works with FrontPage:

1. Place the CD that accompanies this book in your drive. Start Microsoft Word and from the \Book\Chap11 folder on the CD, open the file Word Document Example.doc, as shown in Figure 11-1.

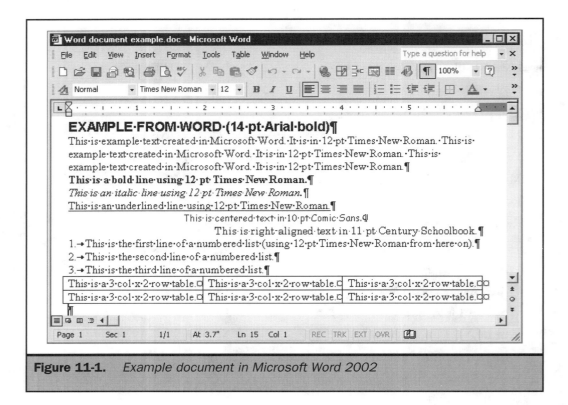

Figure 11-1. *Example document in Microsoft Word 2002*

2. Select all the text (CTRL+A), and copy it to the Windows Clipboard by pressing CTRL+C.

3. Close Microsoft Word and start FrontPage.

4. Create a new One Page Web, name it **Import**, and double-click its home page to open it in Page view.

5. In Page view, press CTRL+V to paste the contents of the Clipboard there. Your result should look like Figure 11-2.

6. Press CTRL+A to select all of the text, and press DEL to get rid of it.

As you can see, most of the formatting is retained when you bring text into FrontPage from the Windows Clipboard. The only significant changes are that the vertical spacing between paragraphs is different, and the Century Schoolbook font has changed to Times New Roman.

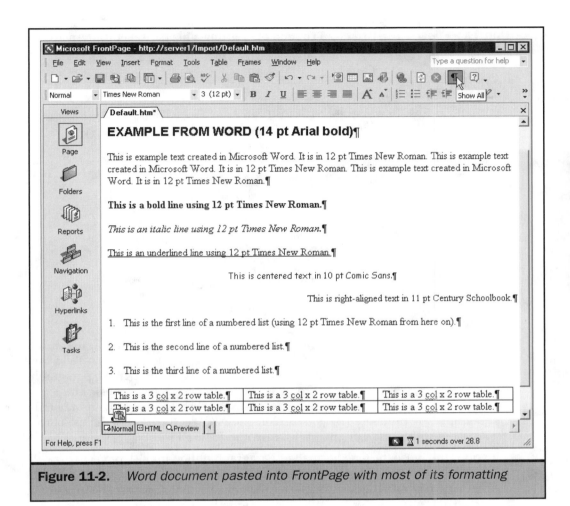

Figure 11-2. *Word document pasted into FrontPage with most of its formatting*

CREATING
WEB SITES

Note

*FrontPage and some browsers support the use of fonts other than the default Times New Roman. However, the font used must be installed on the user's computer to be displayed correctly, even if the browser supports the use of other fonts. More information about using fonts on the Web can be found at **http://www.microsoft.com/truetype/**.*

Inserting a File onto an Existing Page

You can insert a file onto an existing page by using any of the supported file formats. You'll look at the Word DOC, HTML, RTF, and TXT files next. The steps are similar for all the supported formats.

Inserting TXT Files   The Text (.TXT) option of inserting a file has several alternatives. To try them, follow these steps:

1. On the blank home page in Page view, open the Insert menu and choose File. The Select File dialog box will open.

2. Click the DOWN ARROW in the Files Of Type drop-down list box. Here you can see some of the types of files you can bring into FrontPage:

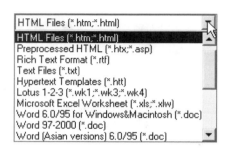

3. Click Text Files, select Word Text Example.txt from the \Book\Chap11 folder on the CD, and click Open.

4. In the Convert Text dialog box, accept the default Formatted Paragraphs, and click OK. The text comes in using the FrontPage Formatted paragraph style, but much of the formatting from Microsoft Word is gone, even though the paragraph breaks remain, which is new to FrontPage 2002. (In previous versions, paragraph breaks were replaced with new-line (SHIFT+ENTER) breaks.) Also, the numbered paragraphs are numbered. If you turn on Show All on the right of the toolbar, you can see the paragraph marks, as shown in Figure 11-3.

   If you were to use the One Formatted Paragraph option in the Convert Text dialog box, you would have no paragraph breaks, only new-line breaks where either new-line or paragraph breaks exist in the original document. With the Formatted Paragraphs option, you get paragraph breaks wherever you had paragraph breaks in the original text.

5. Click Undo, open the Insert menu, choose File, and double-click your TXT file. Select Normal Paragraphs With Line Breaks and click OK. The text comes in using FrontPage's Normal style, with paragraph breaks in the places you had them, multi-line paragraphs wrapped to fit the page, and numbered paragraphs with their designated numbers. All remaining formatting is lost. If you were to use the Normal Paragraphs option, you would still get paragraph or line breaks where you had paragraphs in the original, multi-line paragraphs would still be wrapped, and the numbered paragraphs, as expected, would be numbered.

Tip   *Notice that when you insert the TXT file with Formatted Paragraphs, the first paragraph is one line, or rather it is formatted without word wrap. With the Normal Paragraphs option, the text is wrapped to the width of Page view.*

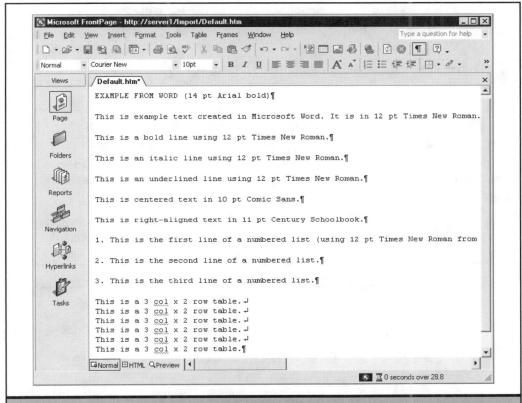

Figure 11-3.   *A Word file in TXT format with formatted paragraphs*

6. Click Undo. Once again open the Insert menu, choose File, and double-click your TXT file. Select Treat As HTML, and click OK. The text comes in as HTML. Since there were no HTML tags in the original text, there is no formatting and no paragraph or line breaks in the places you had them.

7. Click Undo.

The text format does not give you much, unless you want to bring in some plain text in FrontPage's Formatted paragraph style.

Inserting a DOC File   As you saw in Table 11-1, many word processors use the .DOC extension for their files. In this example, a Word 2002 file is used. The steps will be similar for any of the word processors supported by FrontPage.

1. From the blank home page in Page view, open the Insert menu, choose File, and select the Word 97-2002 file type. Open the \Book\Chap11 folder on your CD.

2. Double-click Word Document Example.doc. The file will appear on the open page, as shown in Figure 11-4. Notice that the numbers are again missing on the numbered list.

If this is the first time you are bringing a DOC file into FrontPage, you may be told that you need to install the import filter. In that case, insert your installation CD and follow the directions on the screen.

3. At the left end of the heading that begins "EXAMPLE FROM WORD," type **Inserted DOC** to distinguish this page from others you will create.

4. Open the File menu and choose Save As. Click Change Title, type **Inserted Word DOC File** for the Page Title, click OK, type **Worddoc.htm** as the File Name, and click Save.

An inserted DOC file retains some, but not all, of the formatting in the original document. There are two major differences between the original and this HTML

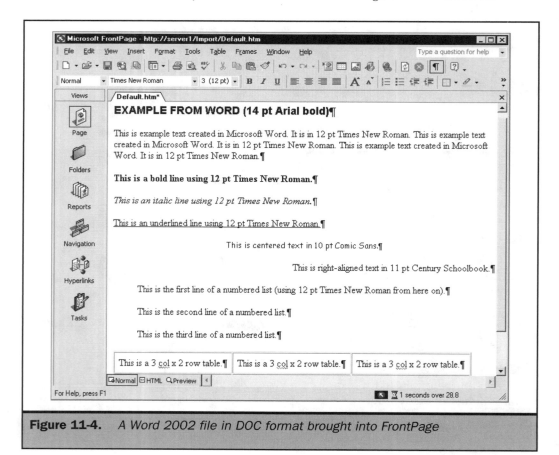

Figure 11-4. *A Word 2002 file in DOC format brought into FrontPage*

version—the numbers are missing from the numbered list, and the originally 11-point right-aligned line is 12 points (because there is no standard HTML size of 11 points; the closest standard sizes are 10 or 12 points). Additionally, it is Times New Roman, not Century Schoolbook.

Inserting an HTML File   An HMTL file (with a file extension of .HTM or .HTML) is the normal format of all text files on the Web, including FrontPage text files. For that reason, it is the default when you insert a new file. The HTML files come into FrontPage nicely, as you can see.

Note   *Microsoft Word 97 through 2002 allows you to save files directly in HTML format (.HTM extension). Microsoft has a free add-in called Internet Assistant you can download for Word 6 or 7/95 that will do the same thing, at **http://www.microsoft .com/downloads/release.asp?ReleaseID=13796**. You may also read about this in the Microsoft Knowledgebase article ID Q153860. Open **http://support.microsoft .com/support/kb/articles/q153/8/60.asp**.*

1. Open a New Normal Page in Page view, open the Insert menu, choose File, and change the file type to HTML Files.

2. In the \Book\Chap11 folder on the CD, double-click Word HTML Example.htm. The file will appear on the open page, as shown in Figure 11-5.

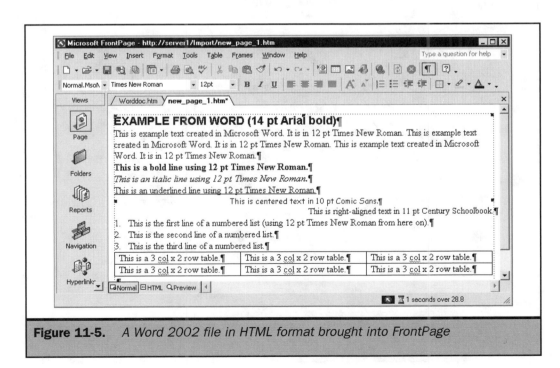

Figure 11-5.   *A Word 2002 file in HTML format brought into FrontPage*

3. At the left end of the heading that begins "EXAMPLE FROM WORD," type **Inserted HTML** to distinguish this page from others you will create.

4. Open the File menu and choose Save As. Click Change Title, type **Inserted Word HTML File** for the Page Title, click OK, type **Wordhtml.htm** as the File Name, and click Save.

The HTML file has maintained more of the original formatting than any other method. The only significant feature missing is the Century Schoolbook font.

Inserting an RTF File   RTF (Rich Text Format) was created to communicate the majority of text formatting. Many applications, not just word processing programs, have the ability to export files in RTF. To see how well FrontPage handles these files, follow these steps:

1. Open a new normal page in Page view, and then, as in the preceding description, prepare to insert a file in the Rich Text Format. Then from the

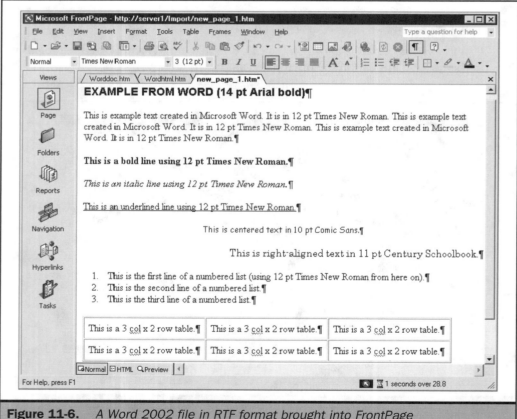

Figure 11-6.   *A Word 2002 file in RTF format brought into FrontPage*

\Book\Chap11 folder on the CD, double-click Word RTF Example.rtf. The file will appear on the new page, as you can see in Figure 11-6.

2. At the left end of the heading at the top, type **Inserted RTF**, select Save As from the File menu, click Change Title, type **Inserted Word RTF File** for the Page Title, click OK, type **Wordrtf.htm** for the File Name, and click Save.

The results of the RTF import are very good—the best of any so far—with the only exception being that the 11-point text is converted to 12 point. Note that the Century Schoolbook font is retained, however.

Opening a File onto a New Page

The third way you can bring text files into a FrontPage web is through Page view's File menu Open command. This yields the Open File dialog box, shown in Figure 11-7, from which you can again select any of the supported file types. To explore this method:

1. Open the File menu and choose Open. In the Open File dialog box that is displayed, select the Word 97-2002 type, open the \Book\Chap11 folder on the CD, and double-click the DOC version of your Word file.

2. Word will open and display the file. Here you can edit the file and then copy and paste it into a web page in FrontPage. The end result is similar to the DOC file you inserted earlier in this chapter, as shown in Figure 11-2.

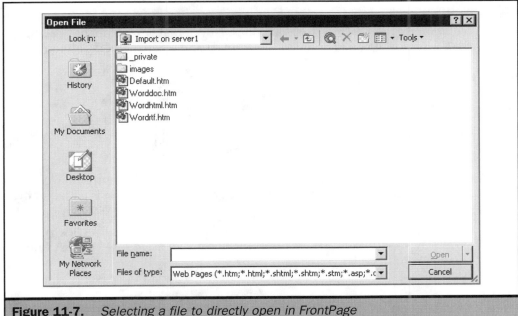

Figure 11-7. *Selecting a file to directly open in FrontPage*

3. In FrontPage, open the File menu, choose Open. In the Open File dialog box, select the Web Pages file type, and double-click Word HTML Example.htm. Microsoft Word will open and the file will be displayed. Again you can edit, copy, and paste it onto a new page in FrontPage. The result is just as you saw earlier in Figure 11-5.

4. Again in FrontPage, choose Open from the File menu, in the Open File dialog box that is displayed, select the Rich Text Format file type, and double-click Word RTF Example.rtf. Again Microsoft Word will open and the file will be displayed. Once more you can edit, cut, and paste it into FrontPage. The result is similar to the RTF page you brought into the web earlier.

5. Close any sessions of Microsoft Word left open on your system.

You can see that the Open command opens the parent application for the file type where you can edit the file and then cut and paste it into FrontPage. In all the examples, the resultant page is as you saw earlier.

Importing a File onto a New Page

The fourth method for bringing text files into FrontPage is to use FrontPage's File menu Import command. Try that next:

1. In FrontPage Folders view, open the File menu and choose Import. The Import dialog box opens. (If you get the Web Site Templates dialog box, you need to create a One Page Web and then try to Import.)

2. Click Add File and the Add File To Import List dialog box opens. Click the down arrow in its Files Of Type drop-down list. Notice that you do not have all the choices here that you had in Page view Insert and Open methods, as you can see here:

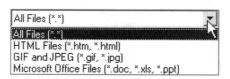

3. Choose HTML Files as the file type, select Word HTML Example.htm from the \Book\Chap11 folder on the CD, and then click Open. The file is added to the Import dialog box.

4. Click Add File again, select All Files as the type, and then double-click Word Document Example.doc, which represents the native Word for Windows format of your Word file.

5. With the top of your Import dialog box looking like the one shown next, click OK.

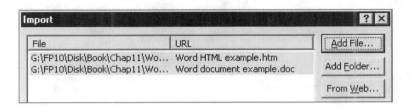

6. Back in Folders view, you will see two new pages. One is the DOC file, Word Document Example.doc (which has the Word icon), and the other is the HTML file with a modified Word icon. Both files are in their native format and have your heading or first line of text as their page title, like this:

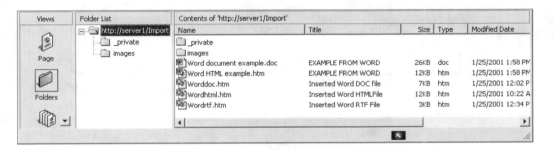

The ability to import a file in its *native format* is very important because it means you don't have to convert it before you use the file. But this process has limitations. You'll see how this works next. Later in the chapter, in the "Bringing Files from Other Productivity Applications" section, you'll also see how this works with other applications.

1. Double-click the file with the Word icon in Folders view of FrontPage. Microsoft Word will load, and the file will be displayed and ready to edit as you saw in Figure 11-1.

2. Close Microsoft Word and double-click the Word HTML icon. Again Microsoft Word will load, and the file will be displayed.

3. The .HTM and .DOC extensions have been associated with Microsoft Word, and that application is opened to edit the file. These extension associations are determined by your Windows Registry.

4. Close Microsoft Word, open FrontPage's Tools menu, and click Options. In the Options dialog box, click the Configure Editors tab, shown next. You can use this dialog box to associate a file extension with the application that FrontPage will open to edit the file.

CREATING
WEB SITES

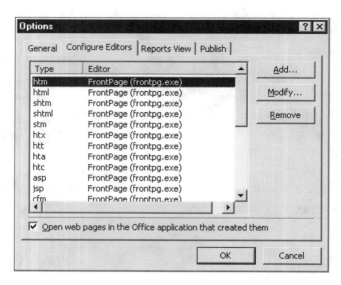

5. Click Add. The Add Editor Association dialog box will open. Enter a new file association that makes sense for you. For example, to add an association between the application CorelDRAW and the extension .CDR, type **cdr** as the File Type, press TAB, type **CorelDRAW** for the Editor Name, press TAB again, and then click Browse and locate the CorelDRAW application, as you can see in the following illustration. Click OK. If you don't have CorelDRAW, use an application that you do have for this example.

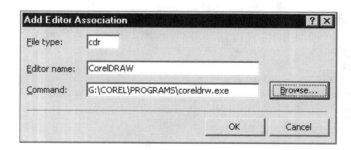

6. Your new application will appear in the Configure Editors tab of the Options dialog box. Click OK to close it.

There is one catch to using a file in its native format in a web—you are assuming that users have the application on their computer so they can view the file. This assumption is best made on an intranet where you can control the desktop environment of your users.

Drag and Drop

Another way to bring files into FrontPage is to drag and drop a file into Folders, Navigation, or Page views. We'll start with the Folders view.

Drag and Drop in Folders View

1. Open Windows Explorer and open the \Book\Chap11 folder on this book's CD.

2. Select Folders view in FrontPage, minimize any running applications besides Windows Explorer and FrontPage, and then right-click an empty portion of the taskbar and click Tile Windows Horizontally. The Windows Explorer window and FrontPage window are arranged so that both are visible on your screen, as shown in Figure 11-8.

3. Select the Word Text Example.txt file in Windows Explorer, and then drag it onto the left pane of FrontPage, on top of the Import folder, as shown next. The pointer changes to an arrow with a plus sign, indicating the selected file will be copied to the new location. Release the mouse button to copy the file to the selected folder.

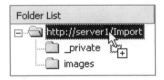

> **Note** *In FrontPage's Folders, Navigation, Hyperlinks, and Page views, if the Folder List is turned on, you can drop the file into the selected folder.*

4. Double-click the Word Text Example.txt file in FrontPage and it opens in Notepad. Close Notepad without changing the file.

Dragging and dropping a file onto FrontPage has the same result as importing a file by use of the Import option on the File menu.

> **Note** *Dropping an HTML file onto FrontPage imports only the HTML page; any images on the page are not imported and must be imported separately.*

Drag and Drop in Page View

You can also use drag and drop to insert files into Page view. The result is the same as selecting File from the Page view Import menu, as you'll see next:

1. Arrange your screen (as is shown in Figure 11-8) so that both the Windows Explorer and Page view windows are visible.

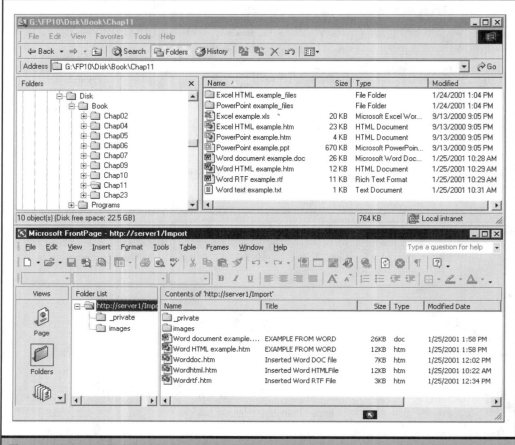

Figure 11-8. *Windows Explorer and FrontPage arranged to drag and drop files*

2. Click New on the toolbar in Page view to open a new page.

3. In Windows Explorer, select the Word Document Example.doc file, and drag it onto the new page in Page view.

4. Type **Dropped DOC** at the left end of the heading, select Save As from the File menu, click Change Title, type **Dropped Word DOC File** for the Page Title, click OK, type **Dropdoc.htm** for the File Name, and click Save.

5. If you have several open pages in FrontPage, close them now.

Bringing Files from Other Productivity Applications

By using HTML, RTF, or a file in its native format (if you think the user can open it), you can bring files from many applications into FrontPage. Now you'll see how this works with Microsoft Excel and PowerPoint files.

Using Microsoft Excel Files

In Microsoft Excel, as in most spreadsheet applications, you can create both tabular information and charts or graphs, as shown in Figure 11-9. When you bring this material into FrontPage, you must use either the native format—which handles both types of data—and hope the user has the product or the viewer, or you must handle the two data types separately. Try this with Excel.

1. In Microsoft Excel, open Excel Example.xls, shown in Figure 11-9, from the \Book\Chap11 folder on this book's CD.

2. In Excel, open the File menu and choose Save As. In the Save As dialog box click My Network Places, select your Import web (or go to the location where you have saved your webs), click Open, and then click Save.

3. Back in Excel again, open the File menu and choose Save As Web Page. The Save As dialog box will open, as shown in Figure 11-10. Here you can save

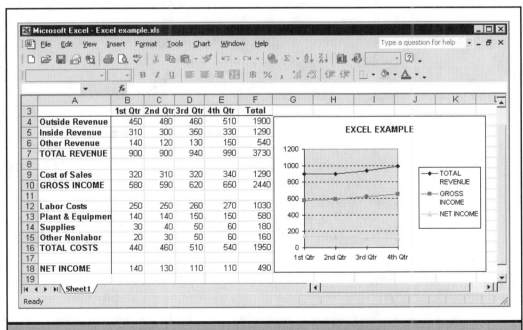

Figure 11-9. *Excel example with both tabular and chart data*

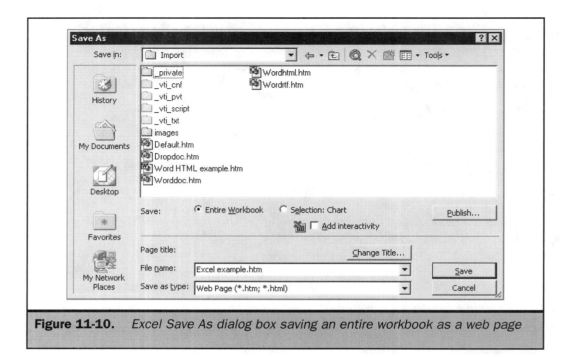

Figure 11-10. *Excel Save As dialog box saving an entire workbook as a web page*

either the current selection or the entire workbook. In the example here, the tabular data and the chart will be saved as one file.

4. Make sure that the Save As Type is Web Page. Click Change Title, type **Excel HTML Example** for the Page Title, and click OK. Change the filename to **Excel HTML example.htm**, and click Save. Close Excel.

5. In FrontPage, click Refresh on the toolbar and the Excel files will appear in Folders view. Double-click the Excel HTML Example.htm file and Excel will open and display the file with both the spreadsheet and the chart. Close Excel.

6. Select the Excel HTML Example.htm file in Folders view and click Preview In Browser. Your browser will open and display the web page complete with its chart, as you can see in Figure 11-11. If you open the native Excel file (Excel Example.xls) in your browser and your browser is Internet Explorer 5 or later, but not Netscape, it will open; open Excel within it and display your workbook as shown in Figure 11-12. (If you try to open the native Excel file in a browser and are told that you are trying to download the file, choose to open it and not save it to disk.)

You can also use the methods of bringing files into Page view discussed earlier in this chapter to insert all or part of your spreadsheet onto a web page in FrontPage.

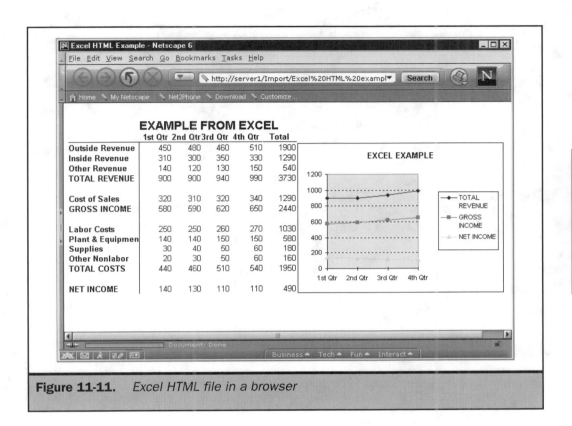

Figure 11-11.   *Excel HTML file in a browser*

Also, both spreadsheet tabular and chart data can be copied to the Clipboard and pasted onto a web page, and the files can be dragged and dropped into Folders view.

When you save an Excel spreadsheet as a web page and choose Selection: Sheet and Add Interactivity, and then open that spreadsheet in a browser, you will get an interactive spreadsheet where you can change the numbers and see both the totals and the chart change without having Excel on the browser machine. This is independent of FrontPage and allows you to save the changed spreadsheet back to Excel.

Bringing in PowerPoint Files

In PowerPoint, like Word and Excel, you have two choices for getting its files on the Internet: in native format and in HTML format. To look at each of these, follow these steps:

1. Load PowerPoint. In the New Presentation task pane under Open A Presentation, choose More Presentations. In the Open dialog box, locate the PowerPoint Example.ppt in the \Book\Chap11\ folder on this book's CD, and click Open.

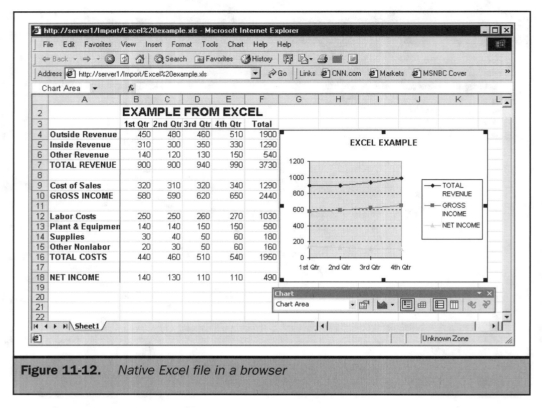

Figure 11-12. Native Excel file in a browser

2. Open the File menu and choose Save As Web Page. The Save As dialog box will open as shown here:

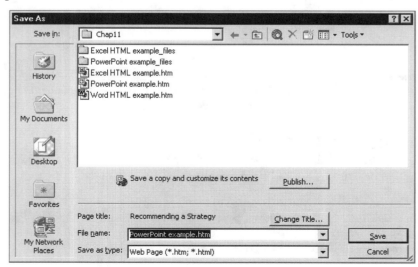

3. Click Change Title, type **PowerPoint HTML Example** for the Page Title, click OK, type **PowerPoint HTML Example.htm** for the File Name, specify the Import folder as the Save In location, and click Save.

4. Using Windows Explorer, open the folder in which you saved the PowerPoint example, then open the PowerPoint HTML Example folder and observe the complete web that has been created (as seen in Figure 11-13). Close Windows Explorer and return to PowerPoint.

5. Open the File menu once more and choose Save As. Again select the Import folder being used in this chapter. Select Presentation (*.ppt) as the Save As Type, name the file **PowerPoint PPT example.ppt**, and click Save. Close PowerPoint.

6. In FrontPage Folders view, click Refresh on the toolbar and you will see both PowerPoint .PPT and .HTM example files.

7. In FrontPage Folders view, double-click the PowerPoint HTML Example.htm file in the Import folder to open it in PowerPoint. What you get is your original presentation, as you do with the .PPT file. Close PowerPoint when you are ready.

8. Again in FrontPage Folders view, select the PowerPoint HTML Example.htm file and click Preview In Browser on the toolbar. You get the browser window shown in Figure 11-14. Close the browser.

9. Once more in FrontPage Folders view, select the PowerPoint PPT Example.ppt file and click Preview In Browser on the toolbar. Now you get just the PowerPoint presentation without the buttons or frames that incorporate the outline. (If you are told that you are trying to download the file, choose to open it and not save it to disk.)

PowerPoint 2002 Save As Web Page

The PowerPoint 2002 Save As Web Page command creates a complete web with a number of files that are placed in their own folder complete with fonts, a page for each slide, and a number of pictures. This web uses frames with an outline of the presentation in the left frame and the current slide and its graphics in the right frame. If you open this web directly in Microsoft Internet Explorer 5 or later, as shown in Figure 11-14, you can see these frames as well as several custom buttons at the bottom of the window. The Outline button on the left turns the outline frame on or off, the next button expands or collapses the outline, then there are two buttons that move the slide show backwards and forwards, and finally on the right a button that expands the slide to fill the screen. In full screen mode, you click the slide to go to the next slide, press BACKSPACE to reach the previous slide, and press ESC to return to the normal browser window. If you right-click the slide, you get a context menu with several options.

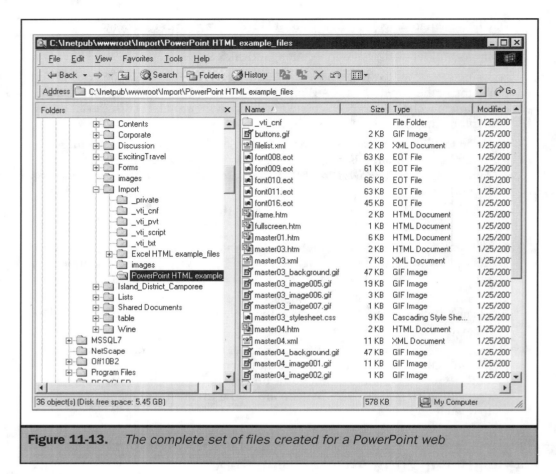

Figure 11-13. *The complete set of files created for a PowerPoint web*

All of the Microsoft Office applications, including Access and Outlook, have the impressive ability to create HTML and other files that are usable in a web and importable with FrontPage. This is a great way to quickly generate web content.

Using Legacy Files on an Intranet

An intranet provides an excellent opportunity to make good use of, or even improve, *legacy* (previously created) files. Manuals and sets of procedures are particularly good examples of this. Instead of maintaining 20 (or 50 or 500!) sets of company manuals that rarely get used except to settle an argument, maintain one set on your intranet. Here people can use a search capability to quickly find what they are looking for, whenever they want and wherever they are.

Manuals and sets of procedures almost surely exist as word processing files that can be easily transferred to FrontPage. Once you do that, you can add the Table of

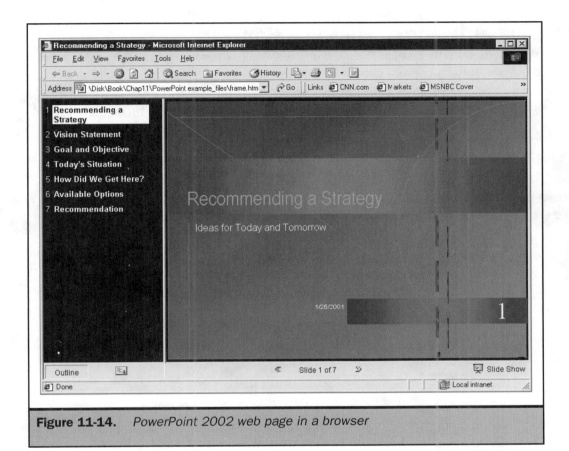

Figure 11-14.   *PowerPoint 2002 web page in a browser*

Contents Component to quickly index the files, the Search Form Component to search all of the text, and the Shared Borders to place headers and footers on each page with link bars, time stamps, and contacts.

Company reports and periodicals are also good candidates for your intranet—current editions and previous issues can be searched and read in one easily accessible place.

The availability of FrontPage's search capability to easily find information on an intranet could be the primary reason for putting information on it. In the same vein, the Table of Contents and Shared Borders can significantly improve usability of existing documents. In other words, putting your legacy documents on your intranet with FrontPage not only gives them a new way to be distributed and read, but features such as the Search, Table of Contents, and Shared Borders also make them substantially more usable, and therefore more likely to be used. Finally, and far from least important, putting information on an intranet ensures that everyone in the organization is getting the same information and the latest version of it.

Looking at Imported Files in a Browser

You have seen how Excel and PowerPoint files look in a browser, but take a peek at how the rest of the Import web you have built looks:

1. Open the very first "Home page" you created for this web in Page view. This should be your Home page with a filename of Default.htm. If you do not find it, use any other page to open Page view and create a new page. In either case, enter a title for the page of **Import Home Page**, format it with Heading 1 and center it, press ENTER, open the Insert menu, choose Web Component, select Table Of Contents | For This Web Site, and click Finish.

Note   *This is a great demonstration of how the Table of Contents FrontPage Component can automatically create links to all the HTM pages and the DOC, XLS, and PPT files.*

2. Accept the defaults for the Table of Contents Properties; this gives you a link to all of the HTM files (although they won't appear until you open the web in a browser), and click OK.

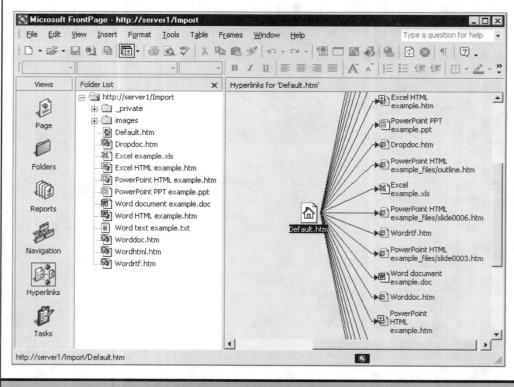

Figure 11-15.   *Hyperlinks created by the Table of Contents component*

3. Save the Home page with the **Import Home Page** Title and the **Default.htm** page File Name. Click Hyperlinks in the Views bar. You should see all of the links for the Import Home Page, as shown in Figure 11-15.

4. Click Preview In Browser on the toolbar. The Import Home Page will appear, as you can see in Figure 11-16.

Note *Links to seemingly duplicate pages are a result of the many secondary files in the PowerPoint example.*

5. Click a number of the links to view the imported (or opened or inserted) files, using the browser's Back button to return to the Import Home page. You will not find many surprises.

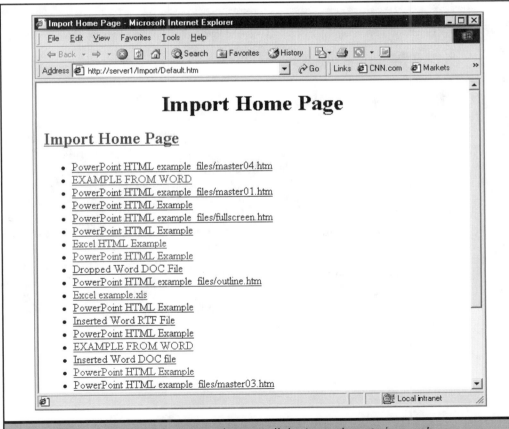

Figure 11-16.   *Table of Contents gives you links to each page in a web*

6. If you have a second browser, open the same web in it and go through each of the links. Note the differences. For example, if you try to open the PowerPoint HTML Example.htm in Netscape Navigator 6, you will get this message:

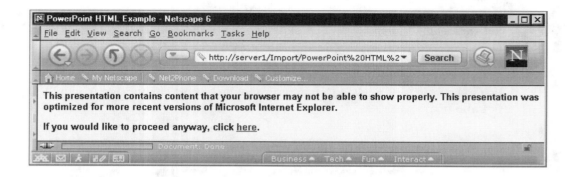

7. Close your browser(s) and close the Import web.

Importing Hyperlinks

One of the better examples of Office integration is the ability of FrontPage to recognize and preserve hyperlinks present in imported files. Not only does FrontPage display the hyperlinks in FrontPage views, but when affected files are moved or renamed within the FrontPage web, FrontPage will update the hyperlink references in the Office files. Figure 11-17 shows an excerpt from Chapter 1 of this book saved as a Word document, including hyperlinks to references of other chapters in the book. After importing the file (Word Hyperlink Example.doc), along with the three chapter files (Chapter 11.doc, Chapter 16.doc, and Chapter 19.doc), into a FrontPage web, the hyperlink relationships are displayed in FrontPage's Hyperlinks view, as shown in Figure 11-18.

Importing files into a FrontPage web—whether they are text, tables, presentations, or databases (covered in Chapter 19)—provides a great deal of ready-made content. When these files are artfully used, they can quickly give a web a lot of depth. As you are building a web site, remember the many existing files available. Their use in a web will further leverage their original investment.

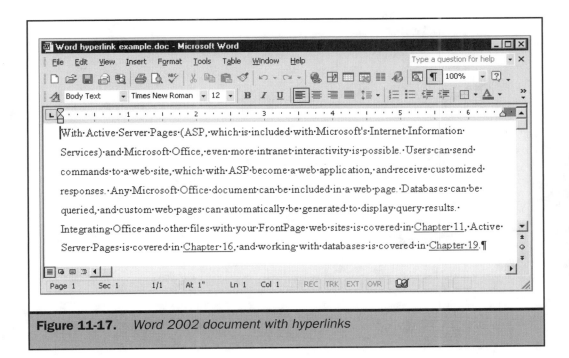

Figure 11-17. *Word 2002 document with hyperlinks*

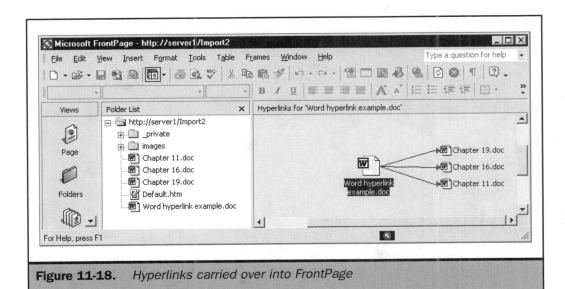

Figure 11-18. *Hyperlinks carried over into FrontPage*

The Complete Reference

FrontPage 2002

Part III

Working Behind the Scenes

In the previous chapters, you've learned how to use FrontPage to build webs without extensive knowledge of HTML or other Web technologies. With FrontPage, you can build great webs without this knowledge, but the Web is an evolving creature with a growing array of new technologies (most of which are still evolving themselves). This section contains the information you need to better understand how your webs work and how to add features that can raise your webs to the next level where web pages have dynamic content and your audience can truly interact with your webs.

Chapter 12 explains Hypertext Markup Language (HTML), the foundation language of the Web. Chapter 13 covers Dynamic HTML (DHTML), the first major evolutionary step in Web languages. Chapter 14 discusses Extensible Markup Language (XML), which enables content and presentation to be treated separately—a major step forward for the Web. Chapter 15 describes scripting for the Web using JavaScript and Visual Basic Script (VBScript), the most common scripting languages used on the Web. Chapters 16 and 17 discuss Active Server Pages (ASP), a technology that empowers you to create truly interactive webs. Chapter 18 looks at Java Server Pages (JSP), an alternative to ASP that is compatible with operating systems other than Windows. Chapter 19 explains how to integrate databases with your webs, a necessity for advanced Web applications, and Chapter 20 discusses how to add active elements (such as animations) to your webs using FrontPage.

Chapter 12

Working with HTML

W ith FrontPage you don't have to learn HTML (Hypertext Markup Language), the foundation programming language of the Web, you can build great web pages without ever learning HTML or even reading this chapter. But for those who either want to go further—to put the last bit of flourish on their web page—or who just want to understand the HTML behind their FrontPage-created web, this chapter will be useful. With access to FrontPage, you probably will not have to create many webs from scratch in HTML, so this chapter will not provide exhaustive coverage of that topic, nor will it cover every nuance of every HTML tag. Both areas are fully covered by sites on the Web, as listed at the end of this chapter. What this chapter will cover is how to understand the HTML that is generated by a FrontPage web and how to add specific capabilities to a FrontPage web with HTML.

Note   *The CD that comes with this book includes Stephen Le Hunte's HTML Reference Library, HTMLib. It is a valuable resource that provides, in Windows Help format, a detailed reference to every HTML tag and its attributes. It is strongly recommended that you install HTMLib and refer to it as you read this chapter.*

Note   *Even though there is a standards body for the Web (the World Wide Web Consortium— http://www.w3.org) compliance with its standards is somewhat voluntary. As a result, you cannot count on all web browsers interpreting your HTML code identically. Some differences are relatively minor, while others are not. It's always best to test your work in the major browsers before publishing it. At the time of this writing, Microsoft's Internet Explorer is the dominant browser, with a market share of over 80 percent. Netscape's Communicator (and Navigator) is a distant second. (There was a time when these positions were reversed.) You also need to be aware of the versions of the various browsers as not everyone updates to the latest versions when they are released. It's reasonable to design for versions 4.0 and later of Internet Explorer and Communicator, but this will not absolutely cover everyone surfing the Web.*

Introducing HTML

HTML is a series of tags that identify the elements in a web page. *Tags* or *markup tags* consist of a tag name enclosed in angle brackets and normally come in pairs. Tags are placed at the beginning and end of an element, generally text, which you want to identify, with the ending tag name preceded by a slash. For example,

```
<TITLE>This is a title</TITLE>
```

uses the Title tag to identify text that will be placed in the title bar of the browser window. Tags are not case sensitive, so they can be all uppercase, all lowercase, or a mixture. Tags are placed around text to control its formatting and placement on a page, to identify a hypertext link, to identify a graphic, sound, or video to be loaded, or to identify a particular area of a web page.

> **Tip** *While HTML is not case-sensitive, this is an exception in the realm of programming languages. For example, both XML (covered in Chapter 14) and JavaScript (Chapter 15) are case-sensitive. Webs today rarely contain only HTML, as you will learn in the following chapters. Treating your HTML as if it is case-sensitive is a good programming habit that will reduce headaches when working with multiple languages.*

In addition to a tag name, a tag may contain one or more *attributes* that modify what the tag does. For example, if you want to center a paragraph on the page, you could use this tag:

```
<P ALIGN="CENTER">This will be a centered paragraph</P>
```

ALIGN="CENTER" is an *attribute* for the Paragraph tag.

> **Tip** *HTML does not require that attribute values be enclosed in quotes, as just shown, but other languages, such as XML, do. Again, it's best to be consistent. In this case, this means enclosing all attributes in quotes.*

> **Note** *In the listings and HTML examples in this chapter, tags are shown in all capital letters and bold, while attributes are just all capital letters. Also, continuation lines are indented from their parents. These conventions are used solely for readability. By default, HTML created by FrontPage is lowercase, indented using spaces, and attribute values are enclosed in quotes. In the HTML Source tab of the Tools | Page Options dialog box, you can change these settings. HTML can also be color-coded for readability when a page is viewed in HTML mode (by clicking the HTML tab at the bottom of the Page view pane) by selecting Show Color Coding from the context menu.*

Using Basic Tags

All web pages must contain a basic set of tags. These tags identify the document as being an HTML document and identify the major parts of the document. With the exception of DOCTYPE, these are the only tags that must be included in a web page to conform to the HTML standard. The Body tag is also used to identify the page defaults, such as the background color or image and the text color. The basic tags, some of which are shown in Listing 12-1, are described with their attributes in Table 12-1.

> **Tip** *On the CD that accompanies this book—in the \Book\Chap12\ folder—there is a folder named HTML that is a web with all of the listings and other files discussed in this chapter.*

Listing 12-1
Basic set
of HTML

```
<!DOCTYPE HTML PUBLIC "-//W3C//DTD HTML 4.0//EN">
<HTML>
  <HEAD>
    <META HTTP-EQUIV="Content-Language" CONTENT="en-us">
    <META HTTP-EQUIV="Content-Type" CONTENT="text/html;
      charset=windows-1252">
    <META NAME="GENERATOR" CONTENT="Microsoft FrontPage 5.0">
    <META NAME="ProgId" CONTENT="FrontPage.Editor.Document">
    <TITLE>Listing 1</TITLE>
    <META NAME="Microsoft Border" CONTENT="none">
  </HEAD>
  <BODY TEXT="#FFFFFF" BGCOLOR="#0000FF">
    <P>This is the text that is the body of this web document.</P>
  </BODY>
</HTML>
```

Note
In HTML (and other programming languages), you will often see numbers written using hexadecimal notation, as in the numerical values for the BODY tag attributes TEXT and BGCOLOR in Listing 12-1. Hexadecimal is a base-16 numbering system where the basic "numbers" are 0 through F and are used in pairs; 0 in decimal notation (base-10) is written 00 in hexadecimal. In HTML, hexadecimal numbers are preceded by a pound sign (#). The section "Using Color" explains how colors are defined using hexadecimal notation.

Note
In the tables of tags and attributes in this chapter, tags are shown with their angle brackets, and attributes are indented from the left.

Tag or Attribute	Description
<!DOCTYPE ...>	Identifies the document as adhering to the given HTML version. This tag is optional and often left off.
<HTML> </HTML>	Identifies the intervening text as being HTML.
<HEAD> </HEAD>	Contains the title and document identifying information. The <TITLE> tag is required in the <HEAD> tag.

Table 12-1. *Basic Set of HTML Tags with Their Attributes*

Tag or Attribute	Description
`<TITLE> </TITLE>`	Identifies the title that is placed in the browser's title bar.
`<META ...>`	Assigns content to an element that can be used by a server or browser and cannot otherwise be assigned in HTML; "Microsoft FrontPage 5.0" is assigned to "GENERATOR" in Listing 12-1. Placed within the `<HEAD>` tag.
`<STYLE> </STYLE>`	Defines a style sheet that prescribes specific styles that are to use certain elements such as normal paragraph (`<P>`) and first-level headings (`<H1>`). See "Style Sheets" later in this chapter.
`<BODY> </BODY>`	Specifies the part of the page that is shown to the user and defines overall page properties.
ALINK	Identifies the color of the active link as either a color name or hexadecimal number representing a color value.
BACKGROUND	Identifies the background image that will be tiled if necessary to fill the window.
BGCOLOR	Identifies the background color that will be used, as either a color name or a hexadecimal number representing a color value. The hexadecimal value for blue is shown in Listing 12-1.
BGPROPERTIES	Specifies that the background image will not scroll with the window if `BGPROPERTIES=FIXED`.
LEFTMARGIN	Sets the left margin for the entire page and overrides any default margin (a margin of 0 will be exactly on the left edge).
LINK	Identifies the color of links that have not been used, as either a color name or a hexadecimal number representing a color value.

Table 12-1. *Basic Set of HTML Tags with Their Attributes* (continued)

Tag or Attribute	Description
TEXT	Identifies the color of text on the page as either a color name or a hexadecimal number representing a color value. The hexadecimal value for white is shown in Listing 12-1.
TOPMARGIN	Sets the top margin for the page and overrides any default margin (a margin of 0 will be exactly on the top edge).
VLINK	Identifies the color of links that have been used as either a color name or a hexadecimal number representing a color value.

Table 12-1.   *Basic Set of HTML Tags with Their Attributes* (continued)

Just because an HTML tag exists doesn't mean you have to use it. As in most other endeavors, the KISS principle applies to the use of HTML.

Using Color

Color names that can be used with ALINK, BGCOLOR, LINK, TEXT, and VLINK, as well as other tags with Microsoft Internet Explorer 2.0 and 3.0 are Black, White, Green, Maroon, Olive, Navy, Purple, Gray, Red, Yellow, Blue, Teal, Lime, Aqua, Fuchsia, and Silver. Microsoft Internet Explorer 4.0 and later, and Netscape Navigator or Communicator 3.0 and later, support 140 named colors (for a complete listing see **http://msdn.microsoft.com/workshop/author/**, click Show Toc, click HTML References then Elements, and select BODY, BGCOLOR, then Color Table). In addition to the named colors, a color value may be used that is a combination of three hexadecimal numbers, one each for Red, Green, and Blue. (This is often called a hexadecimal triplet.) Each primary color can have 256 tones (ranging in value from 0 to 255 decimal or 00 to FF hexadecimal) and these combinations allow a total of over 16 million colors, compared with the 16 or 140 named colors. The video card and monitor must be configured to support High Color (16-bit, which produces over 65 thousand colors) or True Color (24- or 32-bit color, which displays over 16 million colors) to get the full benefit of these colors.

An easy way to convert between decimal and hexadecimal notation is to use the Windows Calculator in Scientific mode. Open the calculator from Start | Programs | Accessories | Calculator then select View | Scientific. Click either the Hex or Dec option, enter a hexadecimal or decimal number, and click the appropriate mode to convert the number. Hexadecimal may seem a bit complicated but it makes a great deal of sense to a computer, which is really using binary (base-2) notation and internally converting all numbers.

In the past, any discussion of color on the Web focused on the Web Safe palette—216 colors that would display correctly on virtually any monitor. One reason the earliest browsers had only 16 named colors was that many systems wouldn't support more than 16 colors. Today, this situation, like everything else connected with the Web, is vastly different. As this is written (in the Fall of 2000) studies show that little more than five percent of the computers surfing the Web are limited to 256 colors. At this point, it makes little sense to adhere to a standard that has been made obsolete by advancing technology. This doesn't mean that named colors should not be used when they fit the application, only that the importance of adhering to this standard has greatly diminished.

One of the best sources for information on color and web browsers is *The DMS Guide to Web Color* at **http://www-personal.umich.edu/~jweise/answers/colorguide/**. This site includes palettes that can be used with Adobe Photoshop and other graphics programs. The CD that comes with this book also has a Color Wizard that is part of Stephen Le Hunte's HTML Reference Library. The Color Wizard gives you three ways to visually create the hexadecimal values for any possible color.

 http://msdn.microsoft.com/workshop/author/ is a comprehensive site on web authoring and is extremely valuable. Along with extensive coverage of HTML, you will find valuable information on many other Web languages and technologies.

Setting Paragraph Styles

Paragraph styles include basic paragraph definition and alignment, headings, the line break, bulleted, numbered, and definition lists, preformatted (called "Formatted" in FrontPage) paragraphs, comments, and horizontal lines or rules. Unless the preformatted style is used, normal line endings, extra spaces of more than one, and tabs are ignored in HTML. Lines simply wrap to fit the space allotted for them unless you use the Paragraph tag. Listing 12-2 shows examples of paragraph styles. This listing is combined with the tags in Listing 12-1 to produce the web page shown in Figure 12-1. Paragraph styles are described in Table 12-2.

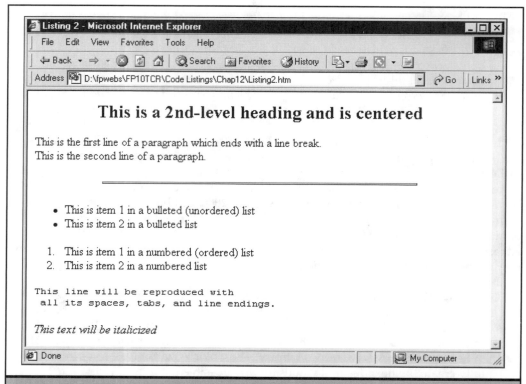

Figure 12-1. *The web page listing resulting from placing Listing 12-2 between the Body tags of Listing 12-1*

Tag	Description
`<P> </P>`	Identifies the start and end of a paragraph and its alignment with `ALIGN=` and `LEFT`, `CENTER`, or `RIGHT`.
`<Hn> </Hn>`	Identifies a heading in one of six heading styles ($n = 1$ to 6) and its alignment with `ALIGN=` and `LEFT`, `CENTER`, or `RIGHT`.
` `	Forces a line break similar to pressing SHIFT+ENTER in FrontPage.

Table 12-2. *Paragraph Style HTML Tags*

Tag	Description
<HR>	Creates a horizontal rule or line where you can specify the alignment, color, shade, size (height), and width across the page.
<OL> </OL>	Contains an ordered (numbered) list.
<UL> </UL>	Contains an unordered (bulleted) list.
<LI> </LI>	Identifies an item in a numbered or bulleted list.
<DL> </DL>	Contains a definition list.
<DT> </DT>	Identifies a term to be defined, displayed on the left of a window.
<DD> </DD>	Identifies the definition of the term that immediately precedes it, indented from the left.
<ADDRESS> </ADDRESS>	Identifies a paragraph of italicized text.
<BLOCKQUOTE> </BLOCKQUOTE>	Identifies a paragraph that is indented on both the left and right, as you might do with a quotation.
<CENTER> </CENTER>	Centers all text and images contained within it.
<!-- --> or <COMMENT> </COMMENT>	Identifies a comment that the browser will ignore and not display. <COMMENT> </COMMENT> is not used in Netscape Navigator .
<DIV> </DIV>	Identifies a division of a page for which the alignment is set with ALIGN= and LEFT, CENTER, or RIGHT .
<PRE> </PRE>	Identifies preformatted text in which all spaces, tabs, and line endings are preserved (called "Formatted" in FrontPage). The maximum number of characters in each line can be set with WIDTH= (generally 40, 80, or 132).

Table 12-2.   *Paragraph Style HTML Tags* (continued)

Listing 12-2
Example
of using
paragraph
style tags

```
<H2 ALIGN="CENTER">This is a 2nd-level heading and
   is centered</H2>
<P>This is the first line of a paragraph which ends with
   a line break.<BR>
This is the second line of a paragraph.</P>
<HR WIDTH="70%" SIZE="3">
<UL>
   <LI>This is item 1 in a bulleted (unordered) list</LI>
   <LI>This is item 2 in a bulleted list</LI>
</UL>
<OL>
   <LI>This is item 1 in a numbered (ordered) list</LI>
   <LI>This is item 2 in a numbered list</LI>
</OL>
<!-- This is a comment, it is ignored by a browser and
   not displayed -->
<PRE>This line will be reproduced with
 all its spaces, tabs, and line endings.</PRE>
<ADDRESS>This text will be italicized</ADDRESS>
```

Tip   *In HTML, it is not always necessary to have a closing tag, for example, the List Item tag <LI> can be used without the closing </LI> tag. It is also not necessary to have a </P> if it would be immediately followed by a <P>. All browsers will assume the last item or paragraph has ended when a new one starts. However, XML does require that every tag be closed. To ensure future compatibility between the languages, FrontPage inserts the closing tags.*

Note   *You can nest lists within lists and get automatic indenting.*

Applying Character Styles

Character styles, which determine how one or more characters will look or behave, come in two forms. *Logical* character styles are defined by the browser and may be displayed in any way that the browser has established. *Physical* character styles have a strict definition that will be the same in all browsers. Examples of character style tags are shown in Listing 12-3, while Figure 12-2 shows how Microsoft Internet Explorer 5.5 and Netscape Navigator 6.0 display them. Note the lack of differences. Table 12-3 describes most character styles.

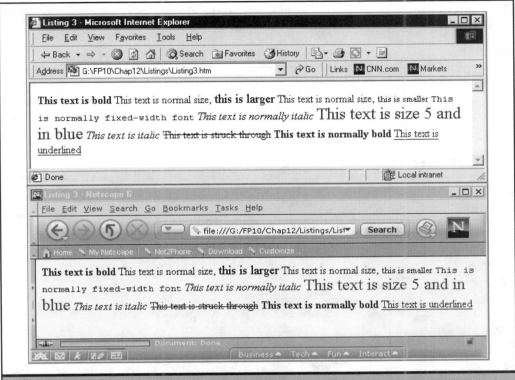

Figure 12-2. *Character style tags displayed in Microsoft Internet Explorer 5.5 and Netscape Navigator 6.0*

Listing 12-3
Examples
of using
character
style tags

```
<B>This text is bold</B>
This text is normal size, <BIG>this is larger</BIG>
This text is normal size, <SMALL>this is smaller</SMALL>
<CODE>This is normally fixed-width font</CODE>
<EM>This text is normally italic</EM>
<FONT COLOR="#0000FF" SIZE="5">This text is size 5 and
   in blue</FONT>
<I>This text is italic</I>
<STRIKE>This text is struck through</STRIKE>
<STRONG>This text is normally bold</STRONG>
<U>This text is underlined</U>
```

Note   *Figure 12-2 demonstrates that browsers ignore line endings unless they are marked with*
<P>, <BR>, or other paragraph styles.

Tag	Description
<B> </B>	Applies the Bold physical character style to the enclosed characters.
<BASEFONT>	Establishes the font size and/or color and/or typeface for a web (<STYLE> is now often used in place of <BASEFONT>; see "Style Sheets" later in this chapter).
<BIG> </BIG>	Makes the enclosed characters one size larger.
<BLINK> </BLINK>	Applies the Blink physical character style to the enclosed characters; introduced by Netscape, this tag is not part of the HTML standard and is not recommended.
<CITE> </CITE>	Applies the Citation logical character style to the enclosed characters; normally italic.
<CODE> </CODE>	Applies the Code logical character style to the enclosed characters; normally a fixed-width font.
<DFN> </DFN>	Applies the Definition logical character style to the enclosed characters; normally italic.
<EM> </EM>	Applies the Emphasis logical character style to the enclosed characters; normally italic.
<FONT> </FONT>	Applies the font size and/or color and/or typeface specified to the enclosed characters; if <BASEFONT> is used, <FONT> size can be relative to the base font size.
<I> </I>	Applies the Italic physical character style to the enclosed characters.
<KBD> </KBD>	Applies the Keyboard logical character style to the enclosed characters; normally a fixed-width font.
<S> </S> or <STRIKE> </STRIKE>	Applies the Strikethrough physical character style to the enclosed characters.

Table 12-3.   *Character Style HTML Tags*

Tag	Description
`<SAMP> </SAMP>`	Applies the Sample logical character style to the enclosed characters; normally a fixed-width font.
`<SMALL> </SMALL>`	Makes the enclosed characters one size smaller.
`<STRONG> </STRONG>`	Applies the Strong logical character style to the enclosed characters; normally bold.
`<SUB> </SUB>`	Applies the Subscript physical character style to the enclosed characters.
`<SUP> </SUP>`	Applies the Superscript physical character style to the enclosed characters.
`<TT> </TT>`	Applies the Typewriter Text physical character style to the enclosed characters; a fixed-width font.
`<U> </U>`	Applies the Underline physical character style to the enclosed characters.

Table 12-3.   *Character Style HTML Tags* (continued)

Displaying Special Characters

HTML defines that the less-than, greater-than, and ampersand characters have special meanings and therefore cannot be used as normal text. To use these characters normally, replace them as follows:

Less-than (<)	< or <
Greater-than (>)	> or >
Ampersand (&)	& or &

All other characters that you can type on your keyboard will be displayed as they are typed. In addition, HTML has defined a number of other characters that can be displayed based on entering an *escape sequence* where you want the character displayed (in FrontPage these characters are also available from the Insert | Symbol window). The escape sequence can take either a numeric or a textual format, as was shown with the three special characters just mentioned. In either case, the escape sequence begins with an ampersand (&) and ends with a semicolon (;). In the numeric format, the ampersand is followed by a number symbol (#) and a number that represents the character. All characters, whether they are on the keyboard or not, can be represented with a numeric

Character	Name	Numeric Sequence	Text Sequence
…	Horizontal Ellipsis	&#133;	&hellip;
•	Bullet	&#149;	&bull;
™	Trademark	&#153;	&trade;
©	Copyright	&#169;	&copy;
Æ	AE ligature	&#198;	&aelig;
Ä	a umlaut	&#228;	&auml;
É	e acute accent	&#233;	&eacute;
Õ	o tilde	&#245;	&otilde;

Table 12-4. *Samples of Character Escape Sequences*

escape sequence. The textual format has been defined only for some characters and excludes most characters on the keyboard. Additional examples of the two formats are shown in Table 12-4.

Note *Unlike the rest of HTML, escape sequences are case-sensitive—for example, you cannot use < for the less-than symbol.*

For complete lists of the escape sequences, see the Microsoft Internet Explorer Specification Character Set at **http://msdn.microsoft.com/workshop/author/**. At that site, click Show Toc, choose HTML References then Character Sets, and select either ISO Latin-1 Character Set or Additional Named Entities for HTML.

Style Sheets

Style sheets, or *cascading style sheets* (CSS), allow you to define and apply paragraph and character styles to an entire document or web. Style sheets can be part of (embedded in) an HTML document within the Head tag using the Style tag, or can be a separate document referenced by the HTML page using the Link tag. Listing 12-4 shows the definition of a simple embedded style sheet that defines two heading and two paragraph styles.

Listing 12-4
Definition and use of a style sheet

```
<HTML>
  <HEAD>
    <TITLE>This is the title</TITLE>
    <STYLE>
```

```
<!--
    H1.red { font-family: Arial; font-size: 18pt;
            font-weight: bold; color: red}
    H1.blue { font-family: Arial; font-size: 18pt;
             font-weight: bold; color: blue}
    P.main { font-family: Times; font-size: 12pt}
    P.special { font-family: Times; font-style: italic;
            font-size: 12pt}
    -->
  </STYLE>
 </HEAD>
 <BODY>
   <H1 CLASS="red">This is a heading in red</H1>
   <P CLASS="main">This is a main paragraph</P>
   <H1 CLASS="blue">This is a heading in blue</H1>
   <P CLASS="special">This is a special paragraph</P>
 </BODY>
</HTML>
```

A style is a set of properties that can be attached to any HTML tag, such as <H1> (level-1 heading). In effect, you can redefine HTML tags. For example, to have all your level-1 heads display as 18 pt Arial bold in blue, you would redefine the level-1 head like this:

```
H1 {font-family : Arial; font-size : 18 pt
    font-weight: bold; color: blue}
```

You can also have classes of styles. For example, if you want some of your level-1 heads to be blue and some red, you could define two styles: H1.blue and H1.red, as shown in Listing 12-4. The HTML to use the red style would then look like this:

```
<H1 CLASS="red">This heading would be in the H1.red style</H1>
```

Style sheets use a single tag, Style, and within that tag define the various styles you want to use. To keep older browsers that do not know how to handle styles from generating an error, comment tags are placed at the beginning and end of the definitions. These are ignored by the more recent browsers and keep the older browsers from choking on the style definitions.

For more information on the HTML related to style sheets, see the Style Sheets Reference section of the HTML Reference Library (HTMLib) on the CD that comes with this book, the Style Sheet resource page at W3C (**http://www.w3.org/Style/**), and

WORKING BEHIND
THE SCENES

Microsoft's web authoring site mentioned earlier (**http://msdn.microsoft.com/ workshop/author/**).

Working with Images and Image Maps

Images are added to a web by use of the Image (`<IMG>`) tag, which specifies the path and filename of the image as well as a number of attributes such as size, positioning, margins, and border. One of the attributes, `ISMAP`, identifies the image as having an image map attached to it. The image map is a separate MAP file used by the server to relate areas of the image to URLs. To use `ISMAP`, you must include the Image tag in an Anchor tag (see the next section, "Adding Hyperlinks and Bookmarks"). A couple of examples are given in Listing 12-5 and shown in Figure 12-3. Many of the Image attributes are described in Table 12-5.

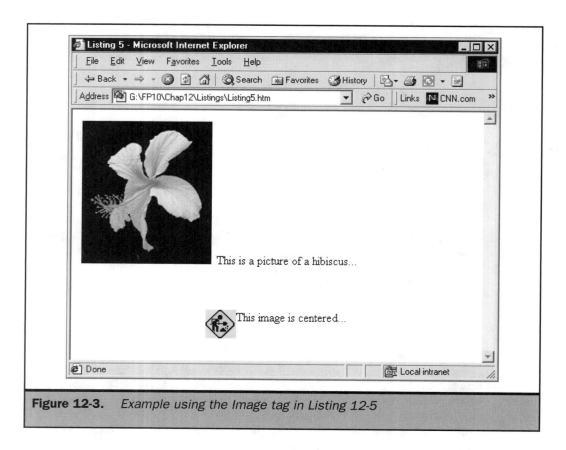

Figure 12-3. *Example using the Image tag in Listing 12-5*

Attribute	Description
ALIGN	Positions text at the TOP, MIDDLE, or BOTTOM of the image, or positions the image on the LEFT or RIGHT of the text.
ALT	Identifies alternative text that is displayed when the mouse pointer is placed on the image or if the image cannot be displayed.
BORDER	Specifies that a border of so many pixels be drawn around the image.
HEIGHT	Specifies the height, in pixels, of the image.
HSPACE	Specifies the blank space, in pixels, on the left and right sides of the image.
ISMAP	Indicates that the image has an image map.
SRC	Identifies the path and filename or URL of the image.
USEMAP	Indicates the name of the image map that is to be used.
VSPACE	Specifies the blank space, in pixels, on the top and bottom of the image.
WIDTH	Specifies the width, in pixels, of the image.

Table 12-5.   *Image Tag Attributes*

WORKING BEHIND
THE SCENES

Note   *The   (which can also be) in Listing 12-5 is a nonbreaking space and is used with the Paragraph tags to create a blank line (paragraph) that HTML will not get rid of.*

Listing 12-5
Examples of
using the
Image tag

```
<P><IMG SRC="hibiscus.jpg" ALT="A picture of a hibiscus"
  ALIGN="bottom" BORDER="2" HSPACE="3" WIDTH="166"
  HEIGHT="190"> This is a picture of a hibiscus ...</P>
<P> </P>
<P ALIGN="center"><IMG SRC="undercon.gif" ALT="Under
  Construction" ALIGN="top" WIDTH="40" HEIGHT="38">
  This image is centered...</P>
```

Specifying the HEIGHT *and the* WIDTH *speeds up loading, because a quick placeholder will be drawn for the image, allowing the text to continue to be loaded while the image is drawn. Without these dimensions, the loading of the text must wait for the image to be drawn and thereby determine where the remaining text will go. Netscape Navigator 3.0 and above and Internet Explorer 4.0 and above will automatically scale the other dimension based on the current aspect ratio of the image if just one of the dimensions (*HEIGHT *or* WIDTH*) is given.*

Adding Hyperlinks and Bookmarks

Hyperlinks provide the ability to click an object and transfer what is displayed by the browser (the *focus*) to an address associated with the object. HTML implements hyperlinks with the Anchor tag (`<A> </A>`), which specifies that the text or graphic that it contains is a hyperlink or a bookmark or both. If the tag is a *hyperlink* and the contents are selected, then the focus is moved either to another location in the current page or web, or to another web. If the tag is a *bookmark,* then another Anchor tag may reference it and potentially transfer the focus to it.

An image used as just described assumes that the entire image is the hyperlink. An image may also be broken into sections, where each section is a link or a *hotspot.* To break an image into multiple links requires an *image map* that is implemented with the Map tag. The Map tag contains Area tags that define the shape of a specific area of the image and the link that it is pointing to.

Listing 12-6 provides some examples of the Anchor, Map, and Area tags, which are shown in Figure 12-4. Table 12-6 describes these tags and their attributes.

Listing 12-6
Examples of hyperlinks and bookmarks

```
<P>This is a link to the <A HREF="default.htm">Home
   Page.</A></P>
<P><A NAME="This ">This </A>is a bookmark.</P>
<P>This <A HREF="#This ">link </A>takes you to the bookmark.</P>
<P><MAP NAME="ComputerMap">
   <AREA SHAPE="POLYGON" COORDS="163, 121, 197, 145, 91, 183, 55,
      157" HREF="#Keyboard">
   <AREA SHAPE="POLYGON" COORDS="6, 90, 147, 87, 148, 115, 46, 145,
      2, 124" HREF="#Processor">
   <AREA SHAPE="RECT" COORDS="30, 6, 124, 70" HREF="#Screen"></MAP>
   <A HREF="computer.map">
      <IMG ALIGN="bottom" SRC="computer.gif" WIDTH="200" ISMAP
         USEMAP="#ComputerMap" HEIGHT="186"></A></P>
```

The pointer in Figure 12-4 is pointing to the hotspot labeled "Screen," as shown at the bottom of the window (.../Listing6.htm#Screen).

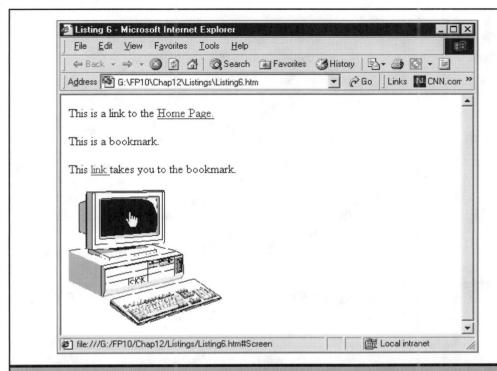

Figure 12-4.   *Hyperlinks and bookmarks defined in Listing 12-6*

Tag or Attribute	Description
`<A> </A>`	Specifies the definition of a hyperlink.
HREF	Identifies the destination URL, which can be a bookmark, page, or web.
NAME	Identifies the bookmark at this location.
TARGET	Identifies a specific frame in the link destination.
TITLE	Identifies a name for a link that is displayed when the mouse passes over the link; otherwise the link address is displayed.

Table 12-6.   *Anchor, Map, and Area Tags and Their Attributes*

Tag or Attribute	Description
<MAP> </MAP>	Specifies the definition of an image map.
NAME	Identifies the name of the image map.
<AREA> </AREA>	Specifies the definition of one image area.
SHAPE	Identifies the type of shape being defined to be CIRC, CIRCLE, POLY, POLYGON, RECT, or RECTANGLE.
COORDS	Identifies the coordinates of the shape being defined using x and y positions in terms of image pixels for each point.
HREF	Identifies the bookmark or URL to which the focus is transferred.
NOHREF	Indicates that a given area causes no action to take place.

Table 12-6. *Anchor, Map, and Area Tags and Their Attributes* (continued)

Note *The SHAPE attribute of the Area tag may be left out, and a rectangular shape will be assumed.*

Defining Forms

A form in HTML is defined by the input fields that it contains. Each input field is defined by its type, name, and potentially a default value. There are a number of field types around which you can wrap text and formatting to get virtually any form you want to define. One example is shown in Listing 12-7 and displayed in Figure 12-5. Table 12-7 describes the tags and attributes related to forms.

Listing 12-7
Example of
a form

```
<H1>This is a form</H1>
<FORM ACTION="saveresults" METHOD="post">
  <PRE>
    Name: <INPUT TYPE="TEXT" SIZE="50" MAXLENGTH="256"
      NAME="Name"><BR>
    Address: <INPUT TYPE="TEXT" SIZE="50" MAXLENGTH="256"
      NAME="Address"><BR><BR>
    Send Data? Yes <INPUT TYPE="RADIO" NAME="Send" Value="Yes">
```

```
     No <INPUT TYPE="RADIO" NAME="Send" Value="No">
   For what product? <SELECT NAME="Product" MULTIPLE SIZE="1">
     <OPTION VALUE="Caribbean" SELECTED> Caribbean Cruise
     <OPTION VALUE="Mediterranean">Mediterranean Cruise
       </SELECT><BR>
   Check if a member <INPUT TYPE="CHECKBOX" NAME="Member"
     Value="TRUE">
   <BR><BR>
   <INPUT TYPE="SUBMIT" VALUE="Send It"> <INPUT TYPE="RESET"
     VALUE="Forget It">
  </PRE>
</FORM>
```

Creating Tables

HTML provides a very rich set of tags to define a table, its cells, borders, and other properties. As rich as the original HTML table specification was, there have been many extensions to it by both Microsoft and Netscape. Since these extensions are not consistent

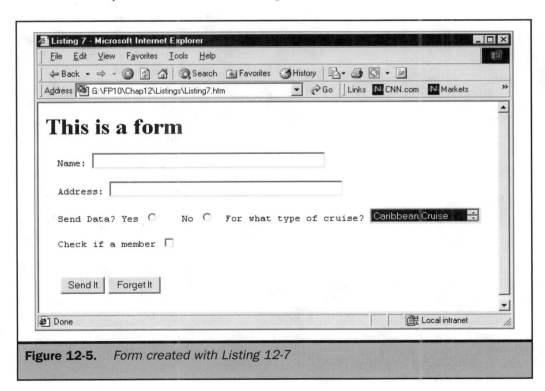

Figure 12-5. *Form created with Listing 12-7*

Tag or Attribute	Description
`<FORM> </FORM>`	Specifies the definition of a form.
`<INPUT>`	Identifies one input field.
`TYPE`	Specifies the field type to be `CHECKBOX`, `HIDDEN`, `IMAGE`, `PASSWORD`, `RADIO`, `RESET`, `SUBMIT`, `TEXT`, or `TEXTAREA`.
`NAME`	Specifies the name of the field.
`VALUE`	Specifies the default value of the field.
`ALIGN`	If `TYPE=IMAGE`, positions text at `TOP`, `BOTTOM`, or `CENTER` of image.
`CHECKED`	If `TYPE=CHECKBOX` or `RADIO`, determines if by default they are selected (`TRUE`) or not (`FALSE`).
`MAXLENGTH`	Specifies the maximum number of characters that can be entered in a text field.
`SIZE`	Specifies the width of a text field in characters, or the width and height in characters and lines of a text area.
`SRC`	Specifies the URL of an image if `TYPE=IMAGE`.
`<SELECT> </SELECT>`	Specifies the definition of a drop-down menu.
`NAME`	Specifies the name of a menu.
`MULTIPLE`	Specifies that multiple items can be selected in a menu.
`SIZE`	Specifies the height of the menu.
`<OPTION>`	Identifies one option in a menu.
`SELECTED`	Specifies that this option is the default.
`VALUE`	Specifies the value if the option is selected.

Table 12-7.   *Form Tags and Attributes*

between the two companies, they need to be used with caution. Listing 12-8 provides an example of the HTML for creating the simple table shown in Figure 12-6. Table 12-8 shows the principal table tags and their attributes.

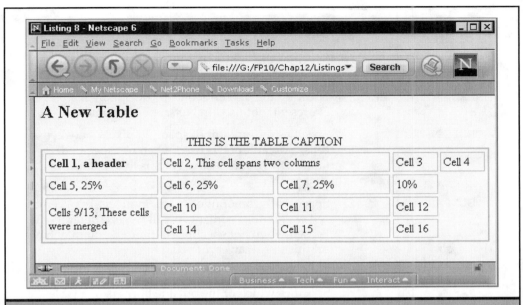

Figure 12-6.   *Table created with Listing 12-8*

Tag or Attribute	Description
`<TABLE> </TABLE>`	Specifies the definition of a table.
`ALIGN`	Specifies that the table will be aligned on the `LEFT` or `RIGHT` of the page, allowing text to flow around it.
`BACKGROUND`	Specifies that a URL containing an image be used as a background; works in Internet Explorer 3.0 and above and Netscape Navigator 4.0 and above.
`BGCOLOR`	Specifies a background color for an entire table.
`BORDER`	Specifies the size, in pixels, of a border to be drawn around all cells in a table.
`BORDERCOLOR`	Specifies a border color if a border is present; works in Internet Explorer 3.0 and above and Netscape Navigator 4.0 and above.

Table 12-8.   *Table Tags and Attributes*

Tag or Attribute	Description
BORDERCOLORLIGHT	Specifies the lighter of 3-D border colors if a border is present; not used in Netscape Navigator.
BORDERCOLORDARK	Specifies the darker of 3-D border colors if a border is present; not used in Netscape Navigator.
CELLSPACING	Specifies the amount of space, in pixels, between cells; a default of 0 is used when not specified (although you may have set this to 2 in an earlier chapter).
CELLPADDING	Specifies the amount of space, in pixels, between the cell wall and its contents on all sides; a default of 0 is used when not specified (although you may have set this to 1 in an earlier chapter).
COLS	Specifies the number of columns in the table.
FRAME	Specifies which of the outside borders of a table are displayed—VOID (none), ABOVE (only the top), BELOW (only the bottom), HSIDES (horizontal sides), VSIDES (vertical sides), LHS (left-hand side), RHS (right-hand side), BOX (all); not used in Netscape Navigator.
HEIGHT	Specifies the height of a table as either a certain number of pixels or a percentage of the window.
RULES	Specifies which of the inside borders of a table are displayed—NONE, BASIC (horizontal rules between the heading, body, and footer sections), ROWS, COLS, ALL; not used in Netscape Navigator.
STYLE	Specifies a style sheet for the table.
WIDTH	Specifies the width of a table as either a certain number of pixels or a percentage of the window.
<TR> </TR>	Identifies the cells in a single row of a table. BACKGROUND, BGCOLOR, BORDERCOLOR, BORDERCOLORLIGHT, BORDERCOLORDARK, HEIGHT, and STYLE are the same as described for <TABLE>.

Table 12-8. *Table Tags and Attributes* (continued)

Tag or Attribute	Description
ALIGN	Specifies that the text in the cells of this row is aligned on the LEFT, CENTER, or RIGHT of each cell.
VALIGN	Specifies that the text in the row can be aligned with the TOP, CENTER, BASELINE, or BOTTOM of the cells; if not specified, text is center-aligned. Not used in Netscape Navigator.
<TD> </TD>	Identifies a single data cell in a table. BACKGROUND, BGCOLOR, BORDERCOLOR, BORDERCOLORLIGHT, BORDERCOLORDARK, HEIGHT, WIDTH, STYLE, and VALIGN are the same as described for <TABLE> or <TR>.
ALIGN	Specifies that the text in this cell is aligned on the LEFT, CENTER, or RIGHT of the cell.
COLSPAN	Specifies the number of columns a cell should span.
ROWSPAN	Specifies the number of rows a cell should span.
NOWRAP	Specifies that the text in the table cannot be wrapped to fit a smaller cell, forcing the cell to enlarge.
<CAPTION> </CAPTION>	Identifies the caption for a table.
ALIGN	Specifies that the caption is aligned to the LEFT, CENTER, or RIGHT of the table; not used in Netscape Navigator.
VALIGN	Specifies that the caption should appear at the TOP or BOTTOM of the table; not used in Netscape Navigator.

Table 12-8. *Table Tags and Attributes* (continued)

Listing 12-8
Table
example

```
<H2>A New Table</H2>
<TABLE BORDER="2" CELLPADDING="3" CELLSPACING="4" WIDTH="100%">
  <CAPTION ALIGN="CENTER">THIS IS THE TABLE CAPTION</CAPTION>
  <TR><TH ALIGN="LEFT" WIDTH="25%">Cell 1, a header</TH>
```

```
    <TD COLSPAN="2" WIDTH="25%">Cell 2, This cell spans two
      columns</TD>
    <TD WIDTH="10%">Cell 3</TD>
    <TD WIDTH="10%">Cell 4</TD></TR>
  <TR><TD WIDTH="25%">Cell 5, 25%</TD>
    <TD WIDTH="25%">Cell 6, 25%</TD>
    <TD WIDTH="25%">Cell 7, 25%</TD>
    <TD WIDTH="10%">10%</TD></TR>
  <TR><TD ROWSPAN="2" WIDTH="25%">Cells 9/13, These cells were
    merged</TD>
    <TD WIDTH="25%">Cell 10</TD>
    <TD WIDTH="25%">Cell 11</TD>
    <TD WIDTH="10%">Cell 12</TD></TR>
  <TR><TD WIDTH="25%">Cell 14</TD>
    <TD WIDTH="25%">Cell 15</TD>
    <TD WIDTH="10%">Cell 16</TD></TR>
</TABLE>
```

Tip	*A table without the BORDER attribute will not have a border, but will take up the same space as if it had a border of 1. Therefore, specifying a border of zero (0) will take up less space.*

Incorporating Frames

HTML frames allow the definition of individual panes or *frames* within a browser window. Each frame contains a separate page that can be scrolled independently of the other frames. HTML defines frames in terms of *frame pages,* which contain Frameset tags, which in turn contain Frame tags. In a frame page, the Frameset tag replaces the Body tag and provides the overall structure of the frames to be created in a browser window. Similarly, the Frame tag is used to define the structure of a single frame. Figure 12-7 shows a simple frame page that was created with the tags displayed in Listing 12-9. (The banner, contents, and main pages are separately defined to contain the information you see.) The tags and attributes related to frames are described in Table 12-9. Because the browser in Figure 12-7 correctly displays frames, the body message "This page uses frames, but your browser doesn't" is not displayed.

Listing 12-9
A frame
page with
Frameset
and Frame
tags

```
<HTML>
  <HEAD>
    <TITLE>Listing 9</TITLE>
  </HEAD>
  <FRAMESET ROWS="12%,*,11%">
    <FRAME SRC="frtop.htm" NAME="top" NORESIZE>
```

```
   <FRAMESET COLS="35%,65%">
     <FRAME SRC="frconten.htm" NAME="contents">
     <FRAME SRC="frmain.htm" NAME="main">
   </FRAMESET>
 <FRAME SRC="frbottom.htm" NAME="bottom" NORESIZE>
 <NOFRAMES>
   <BODY>
     <P>This web page uses frames, but your browser doesn't</P>
   </BODY>
 </NOFRAMES>
</FRAMESET>
</HTML>
```

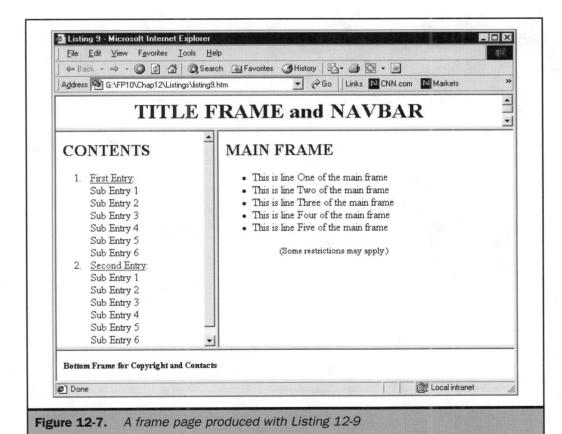

Figure 12-7. *A frame page produced with Listing 12-9*

Tag or Attribute	Description
`<FRAMESET>` `</FRAMESET>`	Specifies the definition of a set of frames.
COLS	Identifies the number of vertical frames (columns) in the frameset and their absolute or relative size (see comments on this attribute).
ROWS	Identifies the number of horizontal frames (rows) in the frameset and their absolute or relative size (see comments on this attribute).
FRAMEBORDER	Turns the border around a frame on (FRAMEBORDER="Yes" or "1") or off (="No" or "0").
FRAMESPACING	Identifies extra space, in pixels, inserted between frames; not used in Netscape Navigator.
BORDERCOLOR	Specifies the color of the frame border; not used in Internet Explorer 3.0, but is in 4.0.
`<FRAME>` `</FRAME>`	Specifies the definition of a single frame.
FRAMEBORDER	Turns the border around a frame on (FRAMEBORDER="Yes" or "1") or off (="No" or "0").
FRAMESPACING	Identifies extra space, in pixels, inserted between frames.
MARGINWIDTH	Identifies the size, in pixels, of the left and right margin in a frame.
MARGINHEIGHT	Identifies the size, in pixels, of the top and bottom margins in a frame.
NAME	Identifies the name of the frame so it can be referred to by TARGET attributes.
NORESIZE	Prevents the frame from being resized by the user.
SCROLLING	Turns the appearance of scroll bars on or off with SCROLLING="Yes"/"No"/"Auto"; Auto is the default.
SRC	Identifies the URL of the web page that will occupy the frame.

Table 12-9. *Frame Tags and Attributes*

Tag or Attribute	Description
BORDERCOLOR	Specifies the color of the frame border; not used in Internet Explorer 3.0, but is in 4.0 and later.
<NOFRAMES> </NOFRAMES>	Specifies HTML that will be displayed by browsers that cannot display frames, but ignored by browsers with frame capability.
<IFRAME> </IFRAME>	Specifies the definition of an inline frame; WIDTH, HEIGHT, HSPACE, VSPACE, and ALIGN are the same as described for <IMG>.

Table 12-9.   *Frame Tags and Attributes* (continued)

Note *If FRAMEBORDER and FRAMESPACING are specified in the Frameset tag, they will automatically apply to all the Frame tags contained within it and only need to be specified for the Frame where a change is desired.*

Note *The TARGET attribute, which you have seen with other tags, is used to load pages into specific frames.*

Internet Explorer 3.0 introduced *inline frames* (also called floating frames). These are individual frames that can be placed anywhere in a standard HTML document. If the browser does not support floating frames, the HTML within the <IFRAME></IFRAME> tags is displayed on the page in the usual manner.

Note *No tags that would be within a Body tag can precede the first Frameset tag, although Frameset tags can be contained within another Frameset tag.*

Within the ROWS and COLS attributes is a list of values separated by commas, one for each horizontal frame ("row") or vertical frame ("column") in the frameset. These values can be:

- The absolute width of a column or height of a row, in pixels. For example,
  COLS="200, 100, 300"
  sets up three columns that, from left to right, are 200, 100, and 300 pixels wide, respectively.

- A percentage of the window's width for a column or the window's height for a row. For example,
  ROWS="15%, 85%"
  sets up two rows, one taking 15 percent of the window and the other, 85 percent.

- A relative value to the other rows or columns. For example,
  COLS="*, 2*"
  sets up two columns, the right one getting twice as much space as the left
  one (this is the same as using "33%, 67%").

- Any combination of absolute, percentage, and relative. For example,
  ROWS="100, 65%, *"
  sets up three rows: the top is 100 pixels high, the middle is 65 percent of
  the window, and the bottom gets the remaining space.

Using absolute pixel values with the ROWS and COLS attributes can result in some weird-looking frames, due to the many differences in screen sizes and resolutions.

Using Multimedia

Multimedia is the inclusion of audio, video, and animation pieces in a web. You can simply offer a user a multimedia file to be downloaded by clicking its link, and then, depending on the availability of players, the file can be automatically or manually played. If you want to make multimedia an automatic part of a web (called *inline* audio or video)—for example, to automatically play an audio piece when a web opens—you must use some extensions to HTML. These include the <BGSOUND> tag for playing inline audio and the DYNSRC attribute for the Image tag to play inline audio-video. Also <MARQUEE>, which is a scrolling bar of text across the window, is included here as a form of animation. Netscape Navigator 3.0 and above support the <EMBED> tag, which allows you to include audio and video files with one of the Netscape plug-ins. Netscape plug-ins for standard audio and video files are included with Navigator 3.0 and above, and more can be found on the Netscape web site (**http://home.netscape.com/ developer/**). Internet Explorer 4.0 (and later) also supports the <EMBED> tag. Listing 12-10 provides some examples of using multimedia with Internet Explorer, and Table 12-10 describes the related tags and their attributes.

Listing 12-10
Examples of
the HTML
to use
multimedia

```
<BGSOUND SRC="all.wav" LOOP=2>
<IMG SRC="hibiscus.jpg" DYNSRC="goodtime.avi" CONTROLS
  START=MOUSEOVER>
<MARQUEE BEHAVIOR=SLIDE, DIRECTION=RIGHT>The marquee will
  scroll this text</MARQUEE>
```

Tag or Attribute	Description
`<BGSOUND>`	Specifies a sound to be played automatically as a page is loaded. Not used in Netscape Navigator.
`SRC`	Identifies the URL of the WAV, AU, or MID file that will be played as soon as it is downloaded.
`LOOP`	Identifies the number of times the sound will play; if `LOOP=-1` or `INFINITE`, the sound will play until the page is closed.
`<IMG>`	Specifies a video or animation clip is to be played.
`DYNSRC`	Identifies the URL of the inline video AVI file to be played. Not used in Netscape Navigator.
`START`	Identifies when the file should start playing (`START=FILEOPEN` or `MOUSEOVER`); `FILEOPEN` is the default, and `MOUSEOVER` means the file will start playing when the mouse is moved over the alternative image.
`CONTROLS`	Specifies that the video player control panel should be displayed.
`LOOP`	Identifies the number of times the video will play; if `LOOP=-1` or `INFINITE`, the sound will play until the page is closed.
`LOOPDELAY`	Identifies how long to wait, in milliseconds, between repetitions in a loop.
`SRC`	Identifies the image to display if the browser cannot play the video.
`<MARQUEE>` `</ MARQUEE>`	Specifies the definition of a scrolling bar of text across the browser window. Not used in Netscape Navigator.
`ALIGN`	Identifies the alignment of the text in the marquee to be at its `TOP`, `MIDDLE`, or `BOTTOM`.
`BEHAVIOR`	Identifies how the text should behave. `BEHAVIOR=SCROLL` means the text will continuously scroll from one side to the other; `=SLIDE` means it will move from one side to the other and stop; `=ALTERNATE` means the text will continuously bounce from one side to the other. `SCROLL` is the default.

Table 12-10.   *Multimedia Tags and Attributes*

WORKING BEHIND
THE SCENES

Tag or Attribute	Description
BGCOLOR	Identifies the background color.
DIRECTION	Identifies the direction that the text will scroll (=LEFT or =RIGHT); LEFT is the default.
HEIGHT	Identifies the height of the marquee in either pixels or percentage of the window.
HSPACE	Identifies the right and left margins of the marquee in pixels.
LOOP	Identifies the number of times that the text will loop; if LOOP=-1 or INFINITE, the sound will play until the page is closed.
SCROLLAMOUNT	Identifies the number of pixels between successive loops of text.
SCROLLDELAY	Identifies the number of milliseconds between successive loops.
VSPACE	Identifies the top and bottom margins of the marquee.
WIDTH	Identifies the width of the marquee, either in pixels or as a percentage of the window.
<EMBED>	Specifies a sound or video file to be played by the appropriate plug-in; SRC, WIDTH, HEIGHT, BORDER, HSPACE, and VSPACE are the same as for <IMG>.

Table 12-10. *Multimedia Tags and Attributes* (continued)

Note *The Image tag attributes in Table 12-10 are in addition to the regular Image tag attributes listed in Table 12-5, which can all be used with video and animation clips.*

Understanding FrontPage-Generated HTML

Many of the example listings in the "Introducing HTML" section have been created with FrontPage and only slightly modified to fit the needs of the section. Let's look at three more examples of increasing complexity and get a feeling for the HTML generated by FrontPage. First, though, we'll explore the ways of looking at FrontPage's HTML.

How to Look at FrontPage HTML

You have at least two ways to look at the HTML generated by FrontPage: in Page view and in your browser. If you have more than one browser, you can look at the HTML in each. Use the following steps to see the differences among the views:

1. Load FrontPage if it's not already loaded. If the New Page Or Web side pane is not displayed, click New in the File menu and choose Page Or Web.

2. In the New Page Or Web side pane, click Web Site Templates.

3. In the Web Site Templates dialog box, select the One Page Web icon, if it's not already selected.

4. In the Specify The Location Of The New Web drop-down, select your default web directory and name the web Simple HTML, then click OK.

5. Open the home page in Page view and enter a heading, a couple of short paragraphs with some formatting, and place an image with text after it, as shown in Figure 12-8. Save the page.

6. Open the View menu and choose Reveal Tags. Figure 12-9 shows the Simple HTML web home page with the HTML tags revealed. You can click a tag to select it and

WORKING BEHIND
THE SCENES

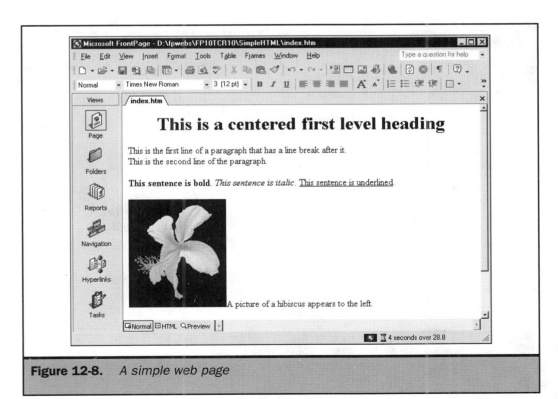

Figure 12-8.   *A simple web page*

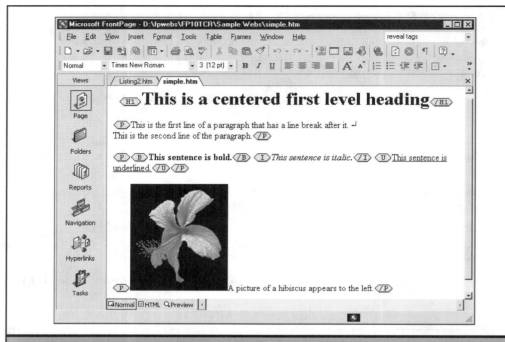

Figure 12-9. *Simple HTML home page with the HTML tags revealed*

its contents, right-click a tag to display a context menu, and double-click a tag to open the tag's property sheet. This method is not as complete as using the HTML view tab. For example, the IMG tag for the graphic is not displayed.

7. Click the HTML tab at the bottom of Page view. The HTML source will appear as shown in Figure 12-10.

8. Click the Normal tab, make some small change to your web page like centering the image, and *without saving* the page, click the HTML tab again and you will see your change, like this:

```
sentence is underlined</U>.</P>
<P ALIGN="center">
<IMG BORDER="0" SRC="images/hibiscus.jpg" WIDTH="166" HEIGHT="190">A picture of
a hibiscus appears to the left.</P>
```

Note   *The highlighting allows you to see the effect on the HTML of the changes you make in FrontPage since the last time you saved the page.*

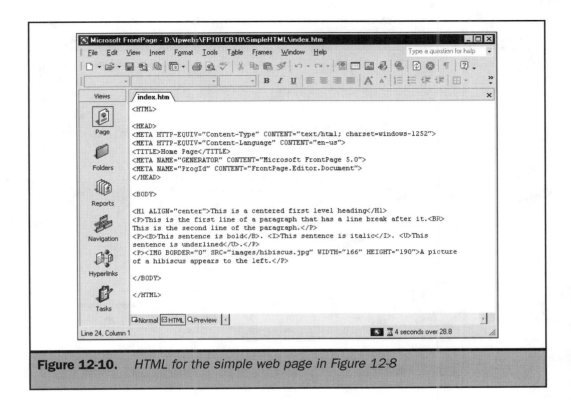

Figure 12-10.   *HTML for the simple web page in Figure 12-8*

9. Close the HTML window and open the Simple HTML web in Microsoft Internet Explorer if you have it. Open the View menu and choose Source. Windows Notepad will open and display the HTML behind the Simple HTML web page, as you can see in Figure 12-11.

10. Close Notepad and Internet Explorer, and open Simple HTML in Netscape Navigator if you have it. Open the View menu and choose Page Source. A Netscape window will open as shown in Figure 12-12. You can see that the Netscape and Internet Explorer source looks very similar.

11. Close the Netscape window and Navigator, and reopen FrontPage Page view.

In the three views in which you have just seen the Simple HTML example, there are no major differences, although you may see some with other pages. In this example, it just depends on your preference and what you want to do with what you are looking at. If you just want to look, Netscape and Internet Explorer offer a quick way to do that. If you want to directly change the HTML, you can do that in FrontPage or Microsoft Internet Explorer with Notepad editor. In all three views you can select and copy the HTML to the Windows Clipboard, copy it to another editor, and then easily move the HTML from both FrontPage and Navigator to, for example, Notepad.

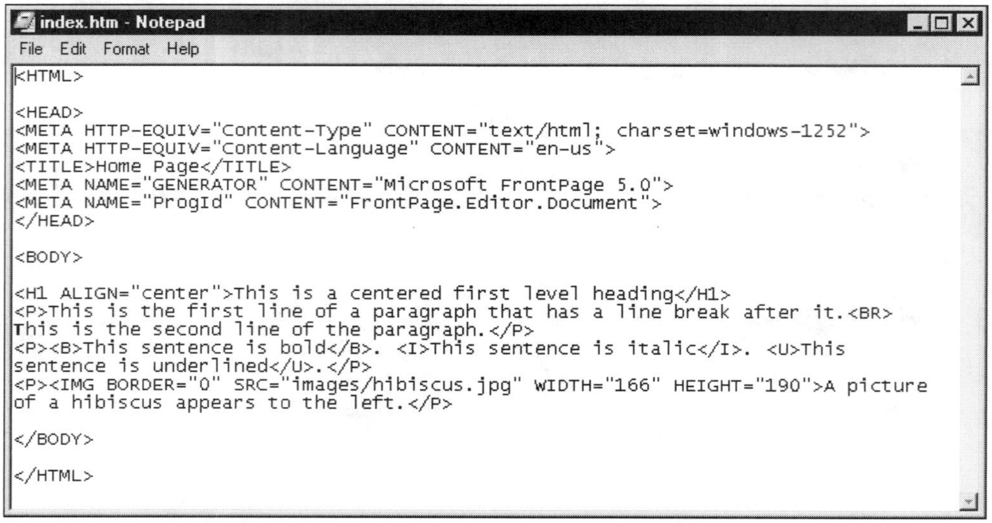

```
index.htm - Notepad
File  Edit  Format  Help
<HTML>

<HEAD>
<META HTTP-EQUIV="Content-Type" CONTENT="text/html; charset=windows-1252">
<META HTTP-EQUIV="Content-Language" CONTENT="en-us">
<TITLE>Home Page</TITLE>
<META NAME="GENERATOR" CONTENT="Microsoft FrontPage 5.0">
<META NAME="ProgId" CONTENT="FrontPage.Editor.Document">
</HEAD>

<BODY>

<H1 ALIGN="center">This is a centered first level heading</H1>
<P>This is the first line of a paragraph that has a line break after it.<BR>
This is the second line of the paragraph.</P>
<P><B>This sentence is bold</B>. <I>This sentence is italic</I>. <U>This
sentence is underlined</U>.</P>
<P><IMG BORDER="0" SRC="images/hibiscus.jpg" WIDTH="166" HEIGHT="190">A picture
of a hibiscus appears to the left.</P>

</BODY>

</HTML>
```

Figure 12-11. *Simple HTML source displayed by Netscape Navigator*

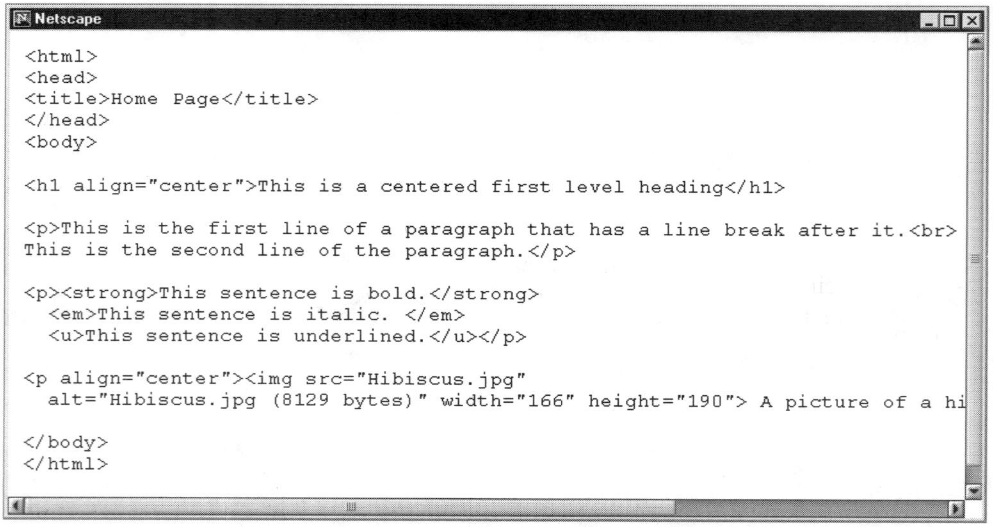

```
Netscape
<html>
<head>
<title>Home Page</title>
</head>
<body>

<h1 align="center">This is a centered first level heading</h1>

<p>This is the first line of a paragraph that has a line break after it.<br>
This is the second line of the paragraph.</p>

<p><strong>This sentence is bold.</strong>
  <em>This sentence is italic. </em>
  <u>This sentence is underlined.</u></p>

<p align="center"><img src="Hibiscus.jpg"
  alt="Hibiscus.jpg (8129 bytes)" width="166" height="190"> A picture of a hi

</body>
</html>
```

Figure 12-12. *Simple HTML source displayed by Netscape Navigator*

In the next several sections of this chapter, you will try all three methods (if you have both browsers). By the end of the chapter, you'll be able to decide which you like best.

Looking at a Simple HTML Example

Take a closer look at the tags and attributes that were created by FrontPage in the Simple HTML example. Listing 12-11 shows the HTML for this example. It was copied to the Clipboard and then pasted in the manuscript for this book. The tags and attributes were put in uppercase letters, the tags were made bold, and tags contained in other tags or lines that were a continuation of the previous line were indented. Otherwise, this listing has not changed from that generated by FrontPage.

Listing 12-11
A simple HTML example

```
<HTML>
<HEAD>
    <TITLE>A Simple Web Page</TITLE>
</HEAD>
<BODY>
    <H1 ALIGN="center">This is a centered first level heading</H1>
    <P>This is the first line of a paragraph that has a line break
       after it.<BR>
       This is the second line of the paragraph.</P>
    <P><B>This sentence is bold.</B>
       <I>This sentence is italic.</I>
       <U>This sentence is underlined.</U></P>
    <P><IMG BORDER="0" SRC="hibiscus.jpg" width="166" height="190">
       A picture of a hibiscus appears to the left.</P>
   </BODY>
</HTML>
```

There are no surprises in Listing 12-11. All of the tags and attributes were discussed in the "Introducing HTML" section earlier in the chapter. There are, however, a few interesting items to note:

■ FrontPage uses the ALIGN=CENTER attributes of Heading and Paragraph tags instead of embedding the tags in a Center tag.

■ The Bold (B) and Italic (I) tags are used; in versions of FrontPage prior to FrontPage 2000, you would see the Strong and Emphasis tags.

■ The HEIGHT and WIDTH attributes are added to the Image tag to establish the area to be occupied by the image and to allow the following text to be displayed while the image is loaded.

WORKING BEHIND THE SCENES

Looking at Exciting Travel HTML

For a second example, close your Simple HTML example and open the Exciting Travel home page you created in earlier chapters. The beginning of the web page is shown in Figure 12-13, and the HTML that creates it is provided in Listing 12-12 (to reduce the bulk and repetition, the FrontPage generated navigation bar, the last two items in the indented bulleted list, and the last two items in the numbered list were removed, as was the bottom-shared border).

Figure 12-13.   *Exciting Travel home Page*

> **Note**   *There is a significant difference between the HTML you see in the HTML tab of Page view and the HTML you see in the browser. The reason is that, in the browser, the FrontPage active Web Components, or formerly "WebBots," have been fully expanded with a significant amount of HTML, whereas in Page view you see only the component itself. Listing 12-12 shows what you see in a browser.*

Listing 12-12
Exciting
Travel
Home Page

```
<HTML>
  <HEAD>
    Style Definitions Code Not Shown
    <META HTTP-EQUIV="Content-Type" CONTENT="text/html;
      charset=windows-1252">
    <META HTTP-EQUIV="Content-Language" CONTENT="en-us">
    <TITLE>Home Page</TITLE>
    <META NAME="GENERATOR" CONTENT="Microsoft FrontPage 5.0">
    <META NAME="ProgId" CONTENT="FrontPage.Editor.Document">
    <META NAME="Microsoft Border" CONTENT="b, default">
  </HEAD>
  <BODY BGCOLOR="#FFFFCC"><!--MSNAVIGATION-->
    <TABLE BORDER="0" CELLPADDING="0" CELLSPACING="0" WIDTH="100%">
      <TR><!--MSNAVIGATION-->
        <TD VALIGN="top">
          <H1 ALIGN="center"><IMG BORDER="0" SRC="Webtitle.jpg"
            WIDTH="750" HEIGHT="180"></H1>
          <P ALIGN="center"><SPAN STYLE="font-weight:normal">For
            the latest fares, contact</SPAN>
          <st1:GivenName><SPAN STYLE="font-weight:normal">
            Julie</SPAN></st1:GivenName>
          <SPAN STYLE="font-weight:normal">Bergen at 555-1234
            or </SPAN><st2:PersonName><st1:GivenName>
          <SPAN STYLE="font-weight:normal">John</SPAN>
          </st1:GivenName><SPAN STYLE="font-weight:normal"></SPAN>
          <st1:Sn><SPAN STYLE="font-weight:normal">Donald</SPAN>
          </st1:Sn></st2:PersonName><SPAN
            STYLE="font-weight:normal"> at 555-1235<BR>or through
            e-mail at <A HREF="mailto:julieb@excitingtravel.com"
            STYLE="font-family: Times New Roman; color: blue;
            text-decoration: underline; text-underline: single">
            julieb@excitingtravel.com</A> or <A HREF="mailto:
            jmd@excitingtravel.com" STYLE="font-family: Times
            New Roman; color: blue; text-decoration: underline;
```

```
          text-underline: single">jmd@excitingtravel.com</A>
        <o:p></o:p></SPAN></P><HR>
        <H2><SPAN STYLE="font-weight:normal">
        <IMG BORDER="0" SRC="00000961.gif" WIDTH="60"
          HEIGHT="43"><FONT COLOR="#FF0000">CURRENT
          SPECIALS</FONT><o:p></o:p></SPAN></H2>
        <UL>
          <LI><SPAN STYLE="font-weight:normal">Super airfares
            to San Francisco: $125, LA: $200, New York: $200,
            &amp; Miami: $200<o:p></o:p></SPAN></LI>
        </UL>
        <BLOCKQUOTE>
        <P CLASS="MsoBodyText"><SPAN STYLE="font-weight:normal">
        <FONT SIZE="2">(Some restrictions may apply to the above
          fares.)</FONT><o:p></o:p></SPAN></P>
        </BLOCKQUOTE>
        <P><SPAN STYLE="font-weight:normal"><IMG BORDER="0"
          SRC="BD10219_.gif" WIDTH="623" HEIGHT="2"></SPAN></P>
        <H2><SPAN STYLE="font-weight:normal"><FONT
          COLOR="#0000FF">AVAILABLE TRAVEL OPTIONS</FONT>
        <o:p></o:p></SPAN></H2>
        <OL>
          <LI><P><SPAN STYLE="font-weight:normal"><A HREF=
            "Air.htm">AIR TRAVEL</A>: Domestic, Canada, Europe,
            So. America, Africa, Asia, So. Pacific</LI></SPAN>
          <LI><P><SPAN STYLE="font-weight:normal"><A HREF=
            "second_level_page.htm">CRUISES</A>: <A HREF=
            "second_level_page.htm#ALASKA">Alaska</A>, Panama
            Canal, Caribbean, Europe, So. America, Asia, …
          </LI></SPAN>
        </OL></span><p><!--msnavigation-->
      </TD>
    </TR><!--MSNAVIGATION-->
  </TABLE><!--MSNAVIGATION-->
<TABLE BORDER="0" CELLPADDING="0" CELLSPACING="0" WIDTH="100%">
  <TR><TD><H5><B STYLE="mso-bidi-font-weight:normal">
  <SPAN STYLE="font-size:12.0pt;mso-bidi-font-size:10.0pt;
    font-family:&quot;Times New Roman&quot;
    ;mso-fareast-font-family:&quot;Times New Roman&quot;
    ;mso-ansi-language:EN-US;mso-fareast-language:
    EN-US;mso-bidi-language:HE">Copyright © 1996-2001
    Exciting Travel, Inc. All rights reserved.<BR>
```

```
    1234 W 13<SUP>th</SUP>, Ourtown, ST<SPAN STYLE=
    "mso-spacerun:yes">  </SPAN>99999</SPAN>
  <SPAN …> (999) 555-1234<BR>
    Please send comments and suggestions to
    <A HREF="mailto:webmaster@excitingtravel.com">
    webmaster@excitingtravel.com</A></SPAN></B></H5>
    </TD></TR><!--MSNAVIGATION-->
  </TABLE>
 </BODY>
</HTML>
```

Looking at the Corporate Presence HTML

The Corporate Presence Wizard (and the web it creates), shown in Figure 12-14, is FrontPage's tour de force. It uses most of the features available in FrontPage, including many of the FrontPage active Web Components. As a result, the HTML has many unusual elements, as shown in Listing 12-13. These elements are used by the FrontPage

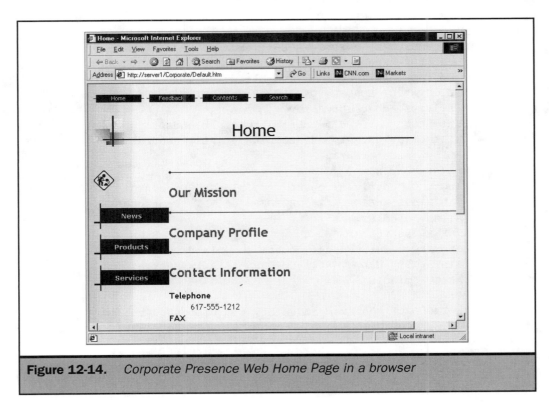

Figure 12-14. *Corporate Presence Web Home Page in a browser*

Server Extensions (which are used with the Microsoft Personal Web Server and Internet Information Services, and other commercial web servers). In Listing 12-13, some repetition has been removed for brevity.

Listing 12-13
Corporate
Presence
Web Home
Page in a
browser

```html
<HTML>
<HEAD>
  <META HTTP-EQUIV="Content-Type" CONTENT="text/html;
    charset=windows-1252">
  <META HTTP-EQUIV="Content-Language" CONTENT="en-us">
  <TITLE>Home</TITLE>
  <META NAME="GENERATOR" CONTENT="Microsoft FrontPage 5.0">
  <META NAME="ProgId" CONTENT="FrontPage.Editor.Document">
  <META NAME="Microsoft Theme" CONTENT="blends 000, default">
  <META NAME="Microsoft Border" CONTENT="tlb, default">
</HEAD>
<BODY BGCOLOR="#FFFFFF" TEXT="#000000" LINK="#993300"
  VLINK="#0000FF" ALINK="#FF9900">
  <!--msnavigation-->
  <TABLE BORDER="0" CELLPADDING="0" CELLSPACING="0" WIDTH="100%">
   <TR>
    <TD><!--MSTHEME--><FONT FACE="Trebuchet MS, sans-serif">
     <P><A HREF="index.htm">
      <IMG SRC="_derived/home_cmp_blends000_gbtn.gif" WIDTH="95"
       HEIGHT="20" BORDER="0" ALT="Home" ALIGN="middle"></A>
     <A HREF="feedback.htm">
      <IMG SRC="_derived/feedback.htm_cmp_blends000_gbtn.gif"
       WIDTH="95" HEIGHT="20" BORDER="0" ALT="Feedback"
       ALIGN="middle"></A>
     <A HREF="toc.htm">
      <IMG SRC="_derived/toc.htm_cmp_blends000_gbtn.gif"
       WIDTH="95" HEIGHT="20" BORDER="0" ALT="Contents"
       align="middle"></A>
     <A HREF="search.htm">
      <IMG SRC="_derived/search.htm_cmp_blends000_gbtn.gif"
       WIDTH="95" HEIGHT="20" BORDER="0" ALT="Search"
       ALIGN="middle"></A>
     </P>
     <P><IMG SRC="_derived/index.htm_cmp_blends000_bnr.gif"
       WIDTH="600" HEIGHT="60" BORDER="0" ALT="Home"><BR></P>
     <P> </P>
     <!--mstheme--></FONT>
    </TD>
   </TR><!--msnavigation-->
```

```
</TABLE><!--msnavigation-->
<TABLE BORDER="0" CELLPADDING="0" CELLSPACING="0" WIDTH="100%">
 <TR>
  <TD VALIGN="top" WIDTH="1%"><!--mstheme-->
   <FONT FACE="Trebuchet MS, sans-serif">
   <P><IMG SRC="images/undercon.gif" ALT="[Under Construction]"
    BORDER="0" WIDTH=40 HEIGHT=38></P>
   <P>
    <A HREF="news.htm"><IMG SRC=
     "_derived/news.htm_cmp_blends000_vbtn.gif" WIDTH="140"
     HEIGHT="60" BORDER="0" ALT="News"></A><BR>
    <A HREF="products.htm"><IMG SRC=
     "_derived/products.htm_cmp_blends000_vbtn.gif" WIDTH="140"
     HEIGHT="60" BORDER="0" ALT="Products"></A><BR>
    <A HREF="services.htm"><IMG SRC=
     "_derived/services.htm_cmp_blends000_vbtn.gif" WIDTH="140"
     HEIGHT="60" BORDER="0" ALT="Services"></A>
   </P><!--mstheme-->
   </FONT>
  </TD>
  <TD VALIGN="top"><!--mstheme-->
   <FONT FACE="Trebuchet MS, sans-serif">
    <P><!--webbot bot="PurpleText" preview=
     "Write an introductory paragraph for your home page here.
     This is like the front door to your home on the Internet.
     Invite visitors to step in and have a look around. "
     --></P>
   <P></P>
   <!--msthemeseparator--><P ALIGN="center">
   <IMG SRC="_themes/blends/blesepd.gif" WIDTH="600"
    HEIGHT="10"></P>
   <H2><!--mstheme-->
    <FONT FACE="Trebuchet MS, Arial, Helvetica"
     COLOR="#330099">Our Mission
    <!--mstheme--></FONT></H2><!--msthemeseparator-->
   <P ALIGN="center">
    <IMG SRC="_themes/blends/blesepd.gif" WIDTH="600"
     HEIGHT="10"></P>
   <H2><!--mstheme-->
    <FONT FACE="Trebuchet MS, Arial, Helvetica"
     COLOR="#330099">Company Profile
    <!--mstheme--></FONT></H2><!--msthemeseparator-->
```

```
<P ALIGN="center"><IMG SRC="_themes/blends/blesepd.gif"
  WIDTH="600" HEIGHT="10"></P>
<H2><!--mstheme-->
 <FONT FACE="Trebuchet MS, Arial, Helvetica"
   color="#330099">Contact Information
 <!--mstheme--></FONT></H2>
<DL>
 <DT><STRONG>Telephone</STRONG></DT>
  <DD><!--webbot bot="Substitution" s-variable="CompanyPhone"
  startspan -->617-555-1212<!--webbot bot="Substitution"
  i-checksum="13173" endspan --></DD>
 <DT><STRONG>FAX</STRONG></DT>
  <DD><!--webbot bot="Substitution" s-variable="CompanyFAX"
  startspan -->617-555-1212<!--webbot bot="Substitution"
  i-checksum="13173" endspan --></DD>
 <DT><STRONG>Postal address</STRONG></DT>
  <DD><!--webbot bot="Substitution"
   s-variable="CompanyAddress" startspan -->
   123 Web Way, Cambridge MA 02138<!--webbot bot=
   "Substitution" i-checksum="64585" endspan --></DD>
 <DT><STRONG>Electronic mail</STRONG></DT>
  <DD>General Information: <A HREF=
   "mailto:someone@microsoft.com">
   <!--webbot bot="Substitution" s-variable="CompanyEmail"
   startspan -->someone@microsoft.com<!--webbot bot=
   "Substitution" i-checksum="52012" endspan --></A><BR>
   Sales: <BR>
   Customer Support: <BR>
   Webmaster: <A HREF="mailto:someone@microsoft.com">
   <!--webbot bot="Substitution"
    s-variable="CompanyWebmaster" startspan -->
    someone@microsoft.com<!--webbot bot="Substitution"
    i-checksum="52012" endspan --></A></DD>
 </DL>
 <!--mstheme--></FONT><!--msnavigation-->
 </TD>
</TR><!--msnavigation-->
</TABLE><!--msnavigation-->
<TABLE BORDER="0" CELLPADDING="0" CELLSPACING="0" WIDTH="100%">
 <TR>
  <TD><!--mstheme--><FONT FACE="Trebuchet MS, sans-serif">
   <P> </P>
```

```
    <P>[ <NOBR>Home</NOBR> ]
    [ <A HREF="news.htm" TARGET=""><NOBR>News</NOBR>
       </A> ]
    [ <A HREF="products.htm" TARGET=""><Nobr>Products</NOBR>
       </A> ]
    [ <A HREF="services.htm" TARGET=""><NOBR>Services</NOBR>
       </A> ]</P>
   <H5><!--mstheme--><FONT FACE="Trebuchet MS, Arial, Helvetica"
     COLOR="#330099"> Send mail to <a href=
     "mailto:someone@microsoft.com">someone@microsoft.com</A>
     with questions or comments about this web site.<BR>
     Copyright © 2000 ACME Industries Inc.<BR>
     Last modified: October 23, 2000
     <!--mstheme--></FONT></H5>
     <!--mstheme--></FONT>
   </TD>
  </TR><!--msnavigation-->
 </table>
</BODY>
</HTML>
```

Some of the major observations in Listing 12-13 are as follows:

■ The HTML uses tags that are unique to FrontPage, commands within comments, <!- - mstheme - - and <! - - msnavigation - - >, to provide instruction to the FrontPage server extensions to implement the use of themes and the navbar.

■ The <! - - webbot bot="PurpleText"…- - > annotation active component provides text that is only visible while authoring—not in the browser.

■ The <! - - webbot bot="Substitution"…- - > active component provides a useful and observable function by being a single source of information, like the company address and phone number, that can be used throughout the web.

If there is one feeling that you should come away with after looking at the HTML generated by FrontPage, it is a much greater appreciation for FrontPage and what it saves you in creating web pages. Just the amount of reduced typing is mind-boggling, but more important are all the automatic features, where you simply don't have to worry about some minutiae that is important to the browser but not to anyone else. For example, the following items are totally handled by FrontPage:

■ The hexadecimal triplet for the custom color in the theme

■ The height and width of images

■ The particular font size for a piece of text

- Making sure you have all the ending tags for your beginning tags
- Translating some characters into their escape sequence

Adding Capability to a FrontPage Web with HTML

Besides understanding the HTML that FrontPage generates, the other reason to learn about HTML is to be able to augment FrontPage when it doesn't provide an HTML-supported function. There is actually very little strict HTML that FrontPage does not support, but the techniques that will be described are still very useful. HTML is no longer the only web language; as you will see in the following chapters. DHTML and other languages can greatly enhance a web and all the features of these languages are not always directly supported by FrontPage.

First, look at how you'd add HTML to FrontPage, and then look at an example of a feature not directly supported in FrontPage: modifying a table.

How to Add HTML to FrontPage

There are three ways to add HTML to FrontPage:

- Directly edit the HTML produced by FrontPage outside of FrontPage and resave it. This technique is strongly discouraged, because it potentially removes the ability to maintain the web with FrontPage, and there is now an excellent way to add HTML within FrontPage.

- Use the HTML tab in Page view, which allows you to see and edit the HTML that describes a given page.

- Use the HTML Web Component, which is available anywhere on a normal page in Page view, by positioning the insertion point where you want to add the HTML, opening the Insert menu, and choosing Web Component | Component Type Advanced Controls | HTML and clicking Finish. The HTML Markup dialog box, shown here, will open and allow you to directly enter HTML.

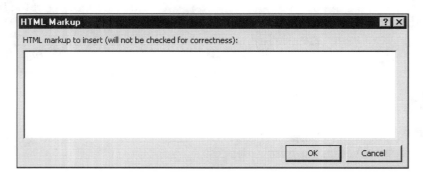

The HTML tab provides much more flexibility and a complete picture of the HTML behind a page. The HTML Web Component allows you to encapsulate the HTML you are adding and keep it separate from the FrontPage-generated-and-checked HTML. You will use the HTML tab in the next section to modify the HTML for a table.

Inserting HTML to Modify a Table

The table that you saw in Figure 12-6 had an outside border or frame around the entire table and individual borders around each cell. In Page view Normal tab, you control how a table looks with the Table Properties dialog box, where the border controls allow you to change the size and color of the border, but not turn off the outer frame while leaving the cell borders. You can do that with HTML. Here you will use the HTML tab to remove the borders of any simple table. For illustration purposes, the table created earlier in this chapter and shown in Figure 12-6 is used, but you can use any table with the following steps.

Note   *In the Page view Normal tab, you can achieve the same effect of cell borders without a table border by first turning off all borders in the Table Properties dialog box by making the Borders Size 0. Then select the cells you want to have borders, open the Cell Properties dialog box, click Style, click Format, choose Border, click Box, make the Width something larger than 0, and click OK three times. The HTML technique is easier!*

1. From FrontPage, either create a new web or open an existing web with a table in it (on this book's CD it is Listing8.htm in the \Book\Chap12\HTML\ folder). In either case, open Page view.

2. If necessary, create a simple 4×4 table with a little text in each cell (like "Cell 1," "Cell 2," and so on).

3. Right-click the table and choose Table Properties. In the Table Properties dialog box, make the Borders Size **0**, close the Properties dialog box, and look at the results in the Preview tab. Reset the border to **2** and then, one at a time, make each of the border colors white (or the same color as the background), and look at the results. You can see that either all the borders are showing or all the borders are not visible. When you are done, return the Table Properties dialog box to its default settings.

4. Open the HTML tab and click between `<table` and `border` to place the insertion point there.

5. Type **frame="void"** (including both quotation marks). Make sure there is a space on either side of the newly typed material.

6. Click Save on the toolbar to save your page, and then click the Preview tab or look at it in a browser. Your result should resemble the table in Figure 12-15.

7. Close your browser and FrontPage.

With the two examples here and the HTML reference earlier in the chapter, you can see how easy it is to make significant additions to your FrontPage webs.

WORKING BEHIND THE SCENES

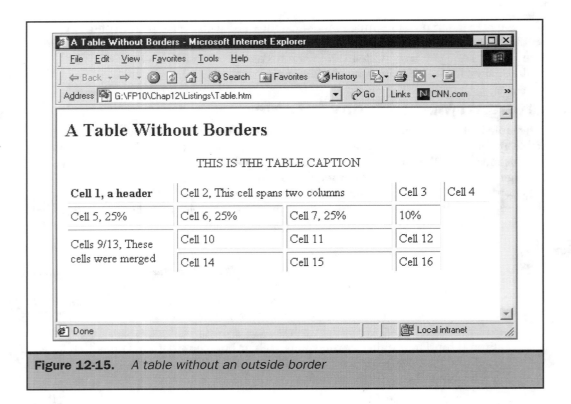

Figure 12-15. *A table without an outside border*

HTML Authoring Resources

There are a number of excellent resources on HTML authoring available on the Web. The following is a list of the ones that are most important. Some of these documents are ancient by Internet standards (anything over a year old), but the basic information is still valid. It is important to understand that HTML has become a mature web language. HTML 4.0, the current version, is also the last version. The future of Web programming is in the languages such as DHTML and XML that will be covered in the following chapters. Nonetheless, a solid understanding of HTML, which these documents will provide, is still the first step.

Note
URLs change very quickly. While every effort was made to get the following URLs correct when this book went to print, some probably will have changed by the time this book reaches the bookstores. If you are having trouble with a URL, drop off right-hand segments, delineated by slashes, until it works. Microsoft's site is changing faster than anybody's, so if one of their URLs isn't working, don't be surprised. The best work-around is to go to **http://msdn.microsoft.com/workshop/author/** *and work forward.*

The following is a list of resources available online:

- *A Beginner's Guide to HTML* by NCSA (the National Center for Supercomputing Applications). NCSA is part of the University of Illinois at Urbana-Champaign, and is home to the original creators of Mosaic, the first of the web browsers from which Netscape Navigator, Microsoft Internet Explorer, and others have descended. Last updated November 9, 1998. The guide can be found at **http://www.ncsa.uiuc.edu/General/Internet/WWW/HTMLPrimer.html**

- *Composing Good HTML* by James "Eric" Tilton (last updated July 13, 1998). Available at **http://www.ology.org/tilt/cgh/**

- *Style Guide for Online Hypertext* by Tim Berners-Lee (the originator of the World Wide Web). Last updated May 1995. Available at **http://www.w3.org/Provider/Style/**

- *Web Etiquette* by Tim Berners-Lee (last updated May 1995). Available at **http://www.w3.org/Provider/Style/Etiquette**

- *A Basic HTML Style Guide* by Alan Richmond (NASA GSFC). Last updated September 16, 1994. Available at **http://guinan.gsfc.nasa.gov/Style.html**

- Microsoft offers a number of documents that provide support of HTML authoring for the Internet Explorer. It is also one of the best sources for the latest developments in Web technologies. Both can be found at **http://msdn.microsoft.com/workshop/author/**

- Netscape's HTML resources for use with Navigator include a number of documents, some also referenced here, indexed at **http://developer.netscape.com/docs/index.html**. Netscape's complete *HTML Tag Reference* (last updated January 26, 1998) at **http://developer.netscape.com/docs/manuals/htmlguid/index.htm**. Netscape's HTML tags, sorted by Navigator release, is also very useful. It can be found at **http://developer.netscape.com/docs/manuals/**

- For those with a technical inclination, there's no better source than the World Wide Web Consortium. A listing of Technical Reports and Publications can be found at **http://www.w3.org/TR/**

- World Wide Web Consortium's (W3C) *HTML 3.2 Specification* (dated January 14, 1997) is available at **http://www.w3.org/TR/REC-html32.html**

- World Wide Web Consortium's (W3C) *HTML 4.01 Specification* (last updated December 24, 1999) is available at **http://www.w3.org/TR/REC-html40**

- One of the most valuable HTML references on the Internet is *The HTML Reference Library* by Stephen Le Hunte. This is a very extensive Windows 3.1 (or alternatively, Windows 95/98) Help System for HTML. It is a gold mine of information and is available on the CD included with this book, or for download from **http://www.htmlib.com/**

- This site is mirrored for North American users at **ftp.clara.net/win/internet/html**

There are also a number of other good books on the Web and HTML authoring. Among them are:

- *HTML: The Complete Reference, Second Edition* by Thomas A. Powell (Osborne/McGraw-Hill, 1999).

- *Web Design: The Complete Reference* by Thomas A. Powell (Osborne/McGraw-Hill, 2000).

- The book that has become the standard for web design is *Designing Web Usability: The Practice of Simplicity* by Jakob Nielsen (New Riders Publishing, 1999).

The Complete Reference

FrontPage 2002

Chapter 13

Using Dynamic HTML

In the previous chapter, you learned how HTML, the foundation language of the World Wide Web, works with FrontPage. In this chapter, you will explore the first real advance of web markup languages: Dynamic HTML (DHTML). DHTML, which, like HTML, is dependent on support from browsers was on the frontier of the Web until version 4 and later of Microsoft's and Netscape's browsers. Since these browsers have moved into the mainstream, DHTML, which offers extended capability for the web developer, is making the days of pure HTML webs an increasingly distant memory.

FrontPage simplifies using DHTML; in fact, many FrontPage features directly available on the menus are actually DHTML based. However, you will need to actually write DHTML code to take full advantage of its potential. This chapter presents an overview of DHTML, looks at FrontPage's built-in support for DHTML, and concludes with how to expand FrontPage's DHTML support by editing your work in the Page view HTML tab.

Dynamic HTML

Dynamic HTML is based on the Document Object Model (DOM), which moves HTML to the next level of functionality by making every object on a web page dynamic and interactive. It's hard to underestimate the impact this technology has on web design. The Document Object Model concept makes each element of a web page an object with properties that can be modified. For example, it allows content to be modified in real time, without the user reloading the page in their browser from the server. Cascading style sheets (CSS), which were introduced in Chapter 12, are also a part of the Document Object Model. In addition to setting styles for text, CSS enables absolute positioning of elements on a web page.

Note *The basic DHTML standard is defined in the HTML 4.01 Recommendation of the World Wide Web Consortium (**http://www.w3.org/MarkUp/**). The Document Object Model is covered in greater detail by the W3C at **http://www.w3.org/DOM/**.*

Unfortunately, as with most other developments on the Web, DHTML support varies by manufacturer. Both Netscape and Microsoft support the W3C Recommendation to some degree, but with some significant differences. Fortunately, DHTML degrades gracefully; that is, pages that use it will appear normal to the user even if their browser doesn't fully support DHTML. They will just lack the interactivity of full DHTML support.

At this time, it appears that Microsoft has developed the better implementation of DHTML. It adheres more closely to existing standards and provides more flexibility. For example, Microsoft's implementation supports both VBScript and JavaScript, while Netscape's supports only JavaScript. Part of this is probably based on Netscape's apparent desire to have as little to do with Microsoft technologies as possible. This is a business decision. As a web developer, you need to be concerned with functionality.

> **Note**   *An area of possible confusion with DHTML is scriptlets—an idea that really didn't win acceptance. The basic concept of a scriptlet is a small, reusable piece of code that can be used throughout a web application. Internet Explorer 4 introduced the concept, but with the release of Internet Explorer 5 Microsoft recommended that DHTML behaviors be used instead.*

In this section you will see how Microsoft has implemented DHTML. This is the version supported by FrontPage and Internet Explorer 5 and later. As a result, the examples you create may not function in Netscape Navigator. This doesn't mean that DHTML cannot be used with Netscape, only that you will need to check your specific DHTML code carefully in the browsers your intended audience uses.

> **Note**   *Recent statistics show that Microsoft has all but won the browser wars with around 86 percent of Web traffic using some version of Internet Explorer. It also appears that Microsoft has been successful in getting its users to upgrade to IE 5 or later, as IE 4's share has fallen to below 15 percent and is falling fast. While the argument can be made that this is not a good thing from the consumer's viewpoint (fewer choices), it does mean that the web developer's job is much easier. Designing for IE 5 means that somewhere around 80 percent of Web users will see your work as you intend and the number can be expected to increase. There was a time when Netscape was king of the hill and Microsoft may well be dethroned in the future. If and when that happens the usurper will have to provide the same feature-rich environment that IE has. This all means that technologies such as DHTML can be used with increasing confidence.*

> **Tip**   *Keeping up with the changing landscape of the Web is easier when you know what it looks like. StatMarket (**http://www.statmarket.com/**), a division of WebSideStory, is an excellent source of information about the Web. They provide both a free e-mail and a more complete subscription service.*

Event Handling

In HTML there is very limited support for handling events, such as moving the mouse pointer over an object. The only event that is really handled is clicking a hyperlink or form button. In DHTML this has been greatly expanded. Table 13-1 lists the names of the mouse events Microsoft's flavor of DHTML supports and the actions that trigger them. Table 13-2 lists the keyboard events and actions.

> **Note**   *The events listed in Tables 13-1 and 13-2 are by no means all the events that can be used with DHTML. To get the most from DHTML, study the documentation at **http://msdn.microsoft.com/workshop/author/default.asp**.*

WORKING BEHIND THE SCENES

Mouse Event	Action Triggered When
onmouseover	The mouse pointer is placed on an object.
onmouseout	The mouse pointer moves off an object.
onmousedown	Any mouse button is pressed.
onmouseup	Any mouse button is released.
onmousemove	The mouse pointer is moving over an object.
onclick	An object is clicked with the left mouse button.
ondblclick	The left mouse button is double-clicked on an object.
oncontextmenu	The right mouse button is clicked on an object (supported by IE 5 only).
ondrag	An object is being dragged with the mouse (supported by IE 5 only).
ondragend	The left mouse button is released after dragging an object (supported by IE 5 only).
ondragstart	The dragging of an object starts (supported by IE 5 only).
ondragenter	An object being dragged enters a specified target area (supported by IE 5 only).
ondragover	An object being dragged is over a specified target area (supported by IE 5 only).
ondragleave	An object being dragged leaves a specified target area (supported by IE 5 only).
ondrop	The left mouse button is released while dragging an object over a specified target area (supported by IE 5 only).

Table 13-1.   *Microsoft-Supported DHTML Mouse Events*

These events are used to trigger actions in the web page. For example, you could change the color or size of an object when the user points to it. FrontPage contains several ways to use DHTML without having to program the event and action, as you will see in the next section.

Keyboard Event	Action Triggered When
onkeypress	A key is pressed and released. Holding a key down will generate multiple onkeypress events.
onkeydown	A key is pressed. Holding the key down will not generate multiple events.
onkeyup	A key is released.

Table 13-2.   *Microsoft-Supported DHTML Keyboard Events*

Animating Text with DHTML

Animating text—making it move on a page—can be done a number of ways. Internet Explorer 4 supports the HTML Marquee tag (covered in Chapter 20), and this is a common use for a Java applet. DHTML does this also, and this is a good place to start your exploration of DHTML in FrontPage. Begin with these steps:

1. In FrontPage, create a new One Page Web named **AdvMarkup**.
2. Open the home page (Default.htm) in Page view and type **DHTML Moves Me**; then format it as Heading 2.
3. Open the Format menu and choose Dynamic HTML Effects. This displays the DHTML Effects toolbar, shown here:

This toolbar allows you to apply DHTML effects to the selected object. In the On drop-down list, you select the event that will trigger the effect. The Apply drop-down list displays the available effects, and the third drop-down list allows you to set any available properties of the chosen effect. You can remove any effect by clicking Remove Effect, and the button at the far right of the toolbar toggles between whether or not the DHTML effect is highlighted in FrontPage.

You can also display the DHTML Effects toolbar by opening the View menu and choosing Toolbars | DHTML Effects.

4. With the cursor still on the same line as your text, click the down arrow in the On drop-down list in the DHTML Effects toolbar and choose Page Load.

Note *The DHTML Effects toolbar provides limited support for DHTML events. To fully utilize DHTML with FrontPage, you will need to manually edit the code using the Page view HTML tab. Chapter 15 introduces web scripting languages, and following chapters provide further examples of web scripting.*

5. Click the down arrow in the Apply drop-down list and choose Zoom.

6. Click the down arrow in the third drop-down list and choose Out. Your page should look similar to Figure 13-1.

7. Save your page and then open it in Internet Explorer. Your text will start out large and then decrease in size.

Figure 13-1. *AdvMarkup web home page in Page view*

8. Repeat Steps 5 through 7, choosing different types of animation from the Apply drop-down list and refreshing the page in your browser after each change.

9. In Page view, with the cursor still on the same line as your heading, select Mouse Over from the On drop-down list in the DHTML Effects toolbar.

10. Select Formatting from the Apply drop-down list, and then select Choose Font from the third (Effects) drop-down list. The Font dialog box, shown here, is displayed.

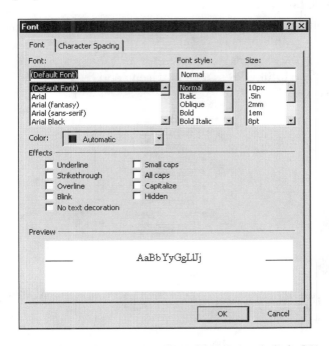

11. Select Arial Black from the Font scrolling list box and click OK.

12. Save your page and then load it in Internet Explorer. The Zoom Out effect runs when the page is first loaded.

13. Point to the heading and the font will change to Arial Black. When you move the mouse pointer off of the heading, it will return to the default font.

As you can see, FrontPage greatly simplifies using DHTML. You do not need to do any programming to add DHTML to your webs. You can also use these DHTML effects with any object, not just text. DHTML is also much more flexible than extended HTML tags, such as the Marquee tag, because it is a script, not a tag with limited predefined attributes. FrontPage support for other DHTML features is enabled in much the same way as animating objects.

Collapsible Lists

Collapsible lists are any type of list (bulleted, numbered, and so on) where the list items below the top level of the hierarchy are not displayed until the user clicks a list item. This next exercise will show you how easy it is to create a collapsible list with FrontPage and DHTML. Begin now with these steps.

1. In Page view, place the cursor on the first line below your heading; then type **A Dynamic List** and format it as Heading 3. Press ENTER.

2. Click Bullets on the Formatting toolbar and type **Item 1**. Press ENTER, type **Description 1**, and press ENTER again.

3. Type **Item 2**, press ENTER, type **Description 2**, press ENTER again, and then type **Another Description**. Press ENTER twice to end the list. Your list should look similar to this:

> **A Dynamic List**
>
> - Item 1
> - Description 1
> - Item 2
> - Description 2
> - Another Description

4. Place your cursor at the beginning of the Description 1 line and click Increase Indent on the Formatting toolbar twice.

5. Place the cursor at the beginning of the Description 2 line and click Increase Indent twice.

6. Place the cursor at the beginning of the Another Description line and press Increase Indent four times. Your list should now look similar to this:

> **A Dynamic List**
>
> - Item 1
>   - o Description 1
> - Item 2
>   - o Description 2
>   - ▪ Another Description

7. Right-click Item 1 in the list and select List Properties. In the List Properties dialog box, select Enable Collapsible Outlines and Initially Collapsed, as shown next. Click OK.

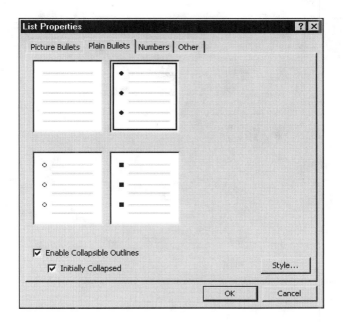

| Tip | *The Enable Collapsible Outlines and Initially Collapsed check boxes are available on all the tabs of the List Properties dialog box.* |

8. Save your page and then reload it in Internet Explorer. The list should appear with two list items: Item 1 and Item 2.

9. Click Item 1 in the list and Description 1 should now be displayed.

10. Click Item 2. When Description 2 is displayed, click it also. This displays the last item in the list, Another Description, as shown in Figure 13-2.

11. Click Item 2 to collapse the items below it in the list hierarchy—Description 2 and Another Description.

DHTML makes adding advanced features, such as dynamically changing text and collapsible lists, extremely easy in your webs. In the next section you'll see how DHTML can be used to "dress up" a form.

Form Group Box

FrontPage now provides a method of grouping form fields by creating a border with a label around the form fields. You will do this with these steps.

1. In FrontPage Page view, place the cursor on the first line after your collapsing list.

2. Open the Insert menu and choose Form | Form. With the cursor to the left of the Submit button, press ENTER, then the up arrow once.

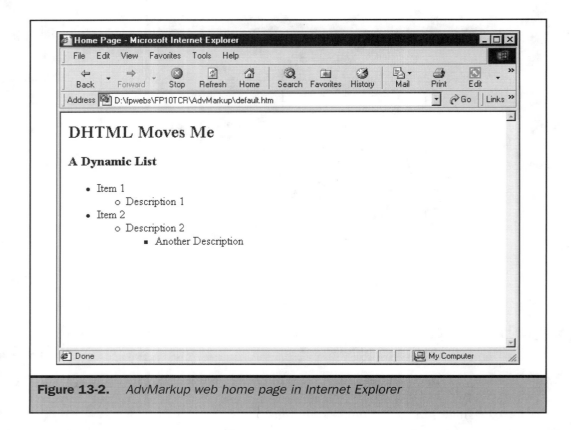

Figure 13-2. *AdvMarkup web home page in Internet Explorer*

3. From the Insert menu, choose Form | Group Box. Your form should look like this:

4. With the cursor placed within the Group Box outline, choose Form | Option Button from the Insert menu. Press SPACE and type **Red** followed by two spaces.

5. Repeat Step 3 to create option buttons for **Green** and **Blue**.

6. Right-click the Group Box and select Group Box Properties to display the Group Box Properties dialog box, shown here.

7. In the Label text box type **Choose a Color** then click OK.

You can also edit the label directly by clicking it as you would with any text in FrontPage.

FrontPage uses the DHTML FIELDSET tag to create the border around the form option buttons. This tag can actually do much more than what FrontPage uses. For example, with FrontPage the FIELDSET tag is only used with forms. If you try to create a Group Box without a form, FrontPage will create the form. In the next section you'll see how to edit your page code in the Page view HTML tab to create a frame around a graphic using the FIELDSET tag.

Adding a Border to a Graphic

While a single-cell table (one row and one column) can be easily used to draw a frame around a graphic, the task is more complicated if you want to have a label, such as a title, as part of the border. At a minimum, a two-row, three-column table would have to be used. With these steps you will use the FIELDSET tag to do this much more simply.

Note *The graphic used here is the Hibiscus.jpg that was used in Chapter 12. It's on the CD that accompanies this book in the folder /Book/Chap12/HTML.*

1. Place the cursor on the line below your form. From the Insert menu choose Picture | From File.
2. In the Picture dialog box select the graphic you want to use and click Insert.
3. Save your AdvMarkup web home page, including the embedded graphic file, and click the Page view HTML tab.
4. Scroll down the page until you find this line of code:

```
<P><IMG BORDER="0" SRC="images/hibiscus.jpg" WIDTH="166"
    HEIGHT="190"></P>
```

Note *Your graphic path and filename, width, and height will be different if you used a different graphic.*

5. Place your cursor between the paragraph tag, `<P>`, and the image tag , `<IMG...>`, and press ENTER.

6. Type **<FIELDSET>**, then place your cursor to the left of the closing paragraph tag, `</P>`.

7. Type **</FIELDSET>** and press ENTER.

8. Save your page and switch to Normal view. There should be a line border that stretches across the page around the graphic.

9. Right-click in the Group Box and select Group Box Properties. The Group Box Properties dialog box, shown previously, is displayed.

10. In the Label text box, type **Hibiscus** then click Style.

11. In the Modify Style dialog box, click Format then select Border from the drop-down menu.

12. In the Borders And Shading dialog box Borders tab, shown next, enter **8** in each of the Padding spinners and click OK three times.

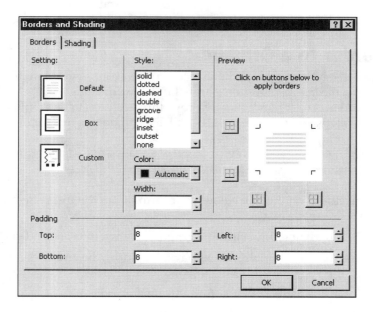

Your Group Box frame around the graphic is almost complete, but it still extends across the entire page. To fix this you will need to add some code manually again.

13. Save your page then click the Page view HTML tab. Find your opening `<FIELDSET>` tag. It should look like this:

```
<FIELDSET STYLE="padding: 8">
```

14. Place your cursor after the 8 and type **;width=182px**. Your tag should look like this:

```
<FIELDSET STYLE="padding: 8;width=182px">
```

The semicolon separates the properties of the Style attribute. The value of 182 pixels for the width is determined by adding the padding (8 + 8) and the width of the graphic (166).

15. Save your page and select the Page view Normal tab. Your graphic with a Group Box should look like this:

This is actually a very simple use of the FIELDSET tag. For a more complete look at what it can do refer to the documentation at **http://msdn.microsoft.com/ workshop/author/dhtml/reference/objects/fieldset.asp**.

In the preceding examples DHTML was used to improve the appearance of the page, but it can also add a great deal of functionality. In the next section you will use DHTML to add clickable form field labels, which make your web pages behave more like an actual Windows application.

Clickable Form Field Labels

In Windows dialog boxes you can select a check box or option button by clicking the label for the box or button. With web forms you have to actually click the check box or option button to select it. You can use DHTML to make web form labels function in the same way as Windows dialog boxes. Do that now with these instructions.

1. On your AdvMarkup web home page in FrontPage Page view, select the label Red and its option button in the form.

2. Open the Insert menu and choose Form | Label.

3. Repeat Steps 1 and 2 for the Green and Blue labels and option buttons.

4. Save your page and then open it in Internet Explorer.

5. Click the label and the option button is selected. Click the label again and the option button is cleared.

Another DHTML effect that adds a dynamic element to your work is page transitions, as you will see next.

Page Transitions

Page transitions are effects that can be applied to a web page when the user enters or exits a page, or when the user enters or exits your site. You apply a page transition to the active page from the Page Transitions dialog box, shown next.

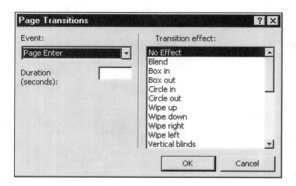

Page transitions can be triggered by four events, selected from the Event drop-down list in the Page Transitions dialog box:

- **Page Enter** invokes the transition when the page is loaded.
- **Page Exit** invokes the transition when the user leaves the page.
- **Site Enter** invokes the transition when the user enters your site by loading any page.
- **Site Exit** invokes the transition when the user leaves your site by loading a page that is not on your site.

You can specify the amount of time for the transition (in seconds) by entering a value in the Duration (Seconds) text box. The transition effect is selected from the Transition Effect scrolling list box.

A very useful DHTML effect that gives you greater control over your pages is the ability to position objects precisely on your page, as you will see next.

Positioning

Tables are often used to position items in relation to each other, but there is little control of where the table is placed on the page. With HTML, tables can be positioned left, right, or center, and the size of the table can be defined, but that is about the limit of what you can do. DHTML extends this by allowing you to place an object, not just a table, at a specific offset from the top left corner of the page. You can also set how text will wrap around the object, much like text is wrapped around a graphic or table using the ALIGN attribute of the IMG or TABLE tags. The following exercise will show you how this works. Begin with these steps.

1. Create a new page in your AdvMarkup web and save it with the Page Title **DHTML Positioning** and the File Name **Position.htm**.

2. Type **This is a picture of a hibiscus** and format it as Heading 3.

3. Press ENTER, then open the Insert menu and choose Picture | File. Select the image you've used in the previous exercises (hibiscus.jpg). The image is placed in the upper-left corner of your page, below your text.

4. Click the image of the hibiscus to select it; then open the Format menu and choose Position. The Position dialog box, shown next, is displayed.

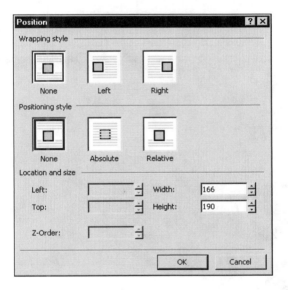

The Wrapping Style options set how text will wrap around the object (the hibiscus graphic in this case). The Positioning Style options allow you to choose no positioning (None), Absolute (an exact location on the page), or Relative (positioned relative to other objects on the page) positioning. When either Absolute or Relative positioning is selected, the Location And Size options become available. Left and Top are used to specify the position of the object from the upper-left corner of the page. Width and Height are the size of the object. The default values are the size of the object in pixels.

Z-Order sets the *layer* of the object. With style sheets, objects on a page can be placed in layers, so that one object can be placed behind or on top of another object. Imagine that each object (text, graphics, and so on) is printed on clear plastic, like an overhead transparency. One sheet contains the text for the page, and another sheet contains the graphic. If the text is the top sheet and the graphic is on the bottom sheet, you will see the graphic behind the text. If you reverse the order, the graphic will cover part of the text. This concept is familiar if you have worked with page layout programs such as Adobe PageMaker, but it is a new concept for the Web.

5. In the Position dialog box, select None for Wrapping Style and Absolute for Positioning Style; then type **50** in the Left Location And Size spinner and **75** in the Top Location And Size spinner. Click OK. Figure 13-3 shows the hibiscus graphic absolutely positioned in Page view.

6. Place the cursor on the line you typed, open the Format menu and choose Position. In the Position dialog box, select Absolute for Positioning Style. Notice that the text has both a width and height, as shown in the Width and Height Location And Size spinners. This is another new concept for a web page; the width displayed is the full width of the page, not just the width of the text.

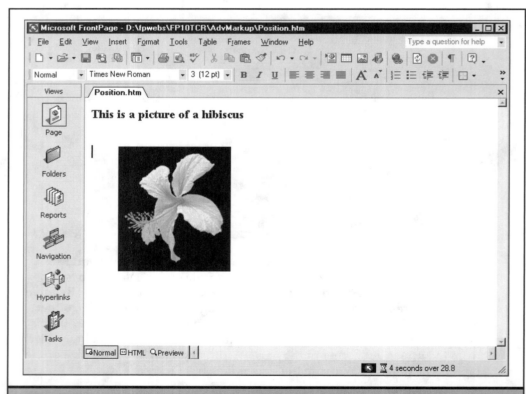

Figure 13-3. *Hibiscus graphic absolutely positioned in Page view*

If you visualize the text as being on a separate piece of paper that is the width of the page and then placed on top of the web page, the concept is clearer.

7. Type **50** in the Left Location And Size spinner and **160** in the Top Location And Size spinner; then type **0** in the Z-Order spinner. Click OK. Figure 13-4 shows what your page should now look like. The text has been absolutely positioned behind the graphic.

Tip *When positioning has been applied to an object and it is selected you can use the arrow keys to move it in one pixel increments.*

8. Select the hibiscus graphic, open the Format menu, and choose Position. In the Position dialog box type **–1** in the Z-Order spinner. Click OK. Your page should look similar to Figure 13-5. The text is on the layer in front of the graphic.

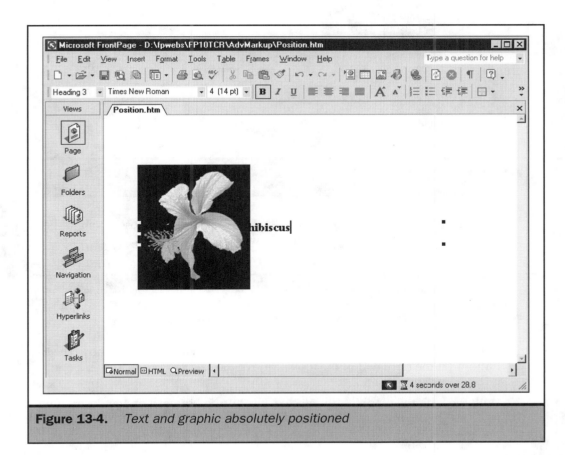

Figure 13-4. *Text and graphic absolutely positioned*

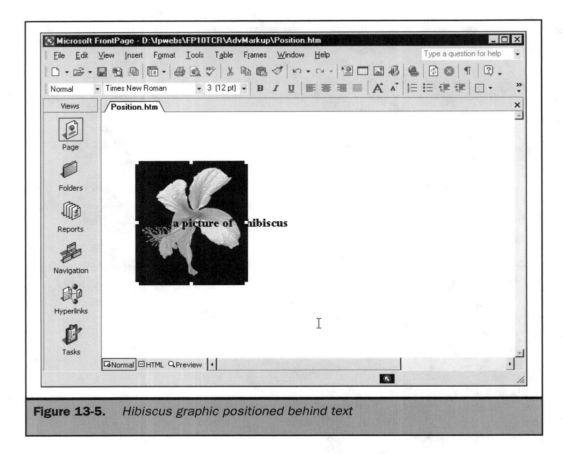

Figure 13-5. *Hibiscus graphic positioned behind text*

9. Click the hibiscus graphic; then open the View menu and choose Toolbars | Positioning. The Positioning toolbar, shown here, is displayed.

This toolbar duplicates most of the functions of the Position dialog box. The two buttons on the right end of the toolbar move the selected object forward one layer or back one layer.

10. With the hibiscus graphic still selected, click Bring Forward on the Positioning toolbar. This changes the Z-Order of the layers and places the text behind the graphic.

11. Save your work, including the embedded graphic, and then open your DHTML Positioning page in Internet Explorer, as shown in Figure 13-6, where you can see the layers effect.

Extending DHTML in FrontPage

While FrontPage allows you to do quite a bit with DHTML, you can do even more by writing your own code in HTML view. In this next exercise you will learn how to extend DHTML in FrontPage using HTML view. You will do this using these steps.

1. Create a new page in your AdvMarkup web and save it with the Page Title **Move Me** and the File Name **Moveme.htm**.

2. Type **Move Me**, format it as Heading 2, and press ENTER.

3. Type **Left | Center | Right** and click the Center alignment toolbar button. Press ENTER.

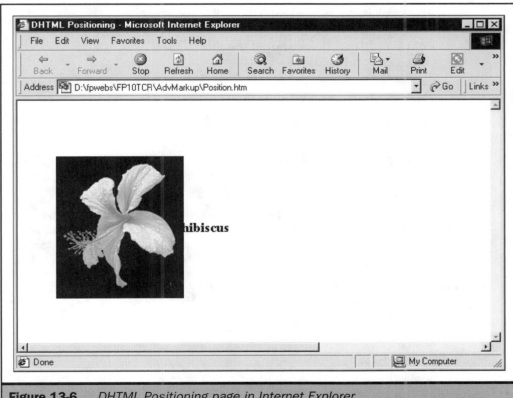

Figure 13-6.   *DHTML Positioning page in Internet Explorer*

4. Open the Insert menu and choose Picture | From File. Insert the hibiscus graphic you used previously and save your page including the embedded graphic.

5. Select the Page view HTML tab. Find the lines of HTML for the graphic. It should look similar to this:

```
<P ALIGN="center"><IMG BORDER="0" SRC="images/hibiscus.jpg"
  WIDTH="166" HEIGHT="190"></P>
```

In the Document Object Model both the paragraph and the image are objects that can be manipulated. You're going to manipulate the paragraph tag, so the first thing to do is give it an identifier that will simplify referencing it.

6. Place the cursor in the opening paragraph tag and select ALIGN="center", then type **ID="imgpara1"**. Make sure there's a space between the P and ID in the tag.

Next you need to modify the Left | Center | Right text to control the paragraph tag which is wrapping the image.

7. Place your cursor between the closing bracket (>) of the opening paragraph and the first letter of "Left" and press ENTER. This is just to make the code easier to work with.

8. Type **<SPAN onClick="imgpara1.align='left'">**, then place the cursor after the word "Left", and type **</SPAN>**.

9. Move your cursor in front of the word "Center" and press ENTER. Your code should look similar to this:

```
<SPAN onClick="imgpara1.align='left'">Left</SPAN> |
Center | Right</P>
```

10. With the cursor in front of the word "Center" type **<SPAN onClick="imgpara1.align='center'">** then move the cursor to the end of the word "Center" and type **</SPAN>**.

11. Move your cursor to the start of the word "Right" and press ENTER. Type **<SPAN onClick="imgpara1.align='right'">**, move the cursor to the end of the word "Right", type **</SPAN>**, and save your page. Your completed code should look similar to this:

```
<SPAN onClick="imgpara1.align='left'">Left</SPAN> |
<SPAN onClick="imgpara1.align='center'">Center</SPAN> |
<SPAN onClick="imgpara1.align='right'">Right</SPAN></P>
<P ID="imgpara1">
<IMG BORDER="0" SRC="images/hibiscus.jpg" WIDTH="166"
  HEIGHT="190"></P>
```

12. Open your Move Me page in Internet Explorer and click Right, then Center, then Left. Your image should move to the appropriate location. Figure 13-7 shows the page after Center has been clicked.

Left, Center, and Right are not hyperlinks so they are not underlined and the cursor does not change appearance when placed on them. They are, under the DOM, objects so they can have events attached to them; in this case, the onClick event.

The align attribute of the paragraph, which is what is being controlled in this example, is referenced in the form *object.property* where "imgpara1" is the object and "align" is the property. Each onClick statement changes the value of the paragraph's align property. Another important point is that the page is not reloaded from the server when the alignment is changed—everything is happening in the browser itself.

Note *This example will not work in Netscape's browsers due to differences in how they interpret DHTML.*

Figure 13-7. *Move Me page in Internet Explorer after Center has been clicked*

Dynamic HTML greatly extends the power of HTML. You can use it without any programming with FrontPage's built-in support or you can expand the functionality with a little hand-coding. In the past, differences in implementation by the various browsers have complicated its use, but that situation is greatly improved. As you will see in the following chapters, webs are becoming very active places, thanks to DHTML and the other advanced markup languages.

Chapter 14

Extensible Markup Language (XML)

W hile FrontPage 2002 offers no real support of XML, it is a subject that should be of interest to every web developer. XML has survived its own hype and is quickly becoming a popular and useful tool for the exchange of all kinds of data. I've heard XML described as "a golden hammer, for which every problem is quickly becoming a nail." This may be a slight exaggeration, but the world has certainly embraced XML as the solution to a variety of problems.

This chapter is in no way a "complete" XML reference or guide, but instead an introduction to XML and some of its uses. The next time someone asks you what XML is, you'll certainly be able to answer them with confidence. We'll cover enough detail to help you get started incorporating XML and related technologies like XSL and DTDs (Document Type Declarations) into your own work. If you decide that XML is your "golden hammer," there are a wide variety of dedicated books and online references available on the subject and I encourage you to seek out these comprehensive resources.

> | Note | *Microsoft's Internet Explorer is currently the only browser that directly supports XML. For this reason, all examples in this chapter that involve a web browser will only work with Internet Explorer version 4.01 or later unless specified.*

What Is XML?

When trying to understand what XML is and what it's used for, it helps to drop the **X** and think of it in terms of another **Markup Language**. By now, you should have a good grasp of what HTML (Hypertext Markup Language) is. In simple terms, it's just a set of structured identifiers (tags) that tell the browser how to format and display the content that resides within. "<b>abcdefg</b>" is differentiated from "abcdefg" by the set of bold tags (<b></b>) that surround the text. That's what HTML is best at, *describing the format of how information should be displayed*.

But what is "abcdefg?" We know that it is the first seven characters in the English language. We know that when surrounded by HTML bold tags, it will display in a web browser as bold text, but what does it mean or refer to? That's what XML is used for, *describing the context and meaning of information (data) in a structured manner*. Like HTML, XML uses tags to mark up textual data. The following example illustrates how XML could be used to mark up information about vacations available through Exciting Travel. This example code is also available on the book's companion CD in the file vacation.xml, located in the \Book\Chap14\ folder.

```
<vacation>
  <cruise>
    <destination>Alaska</destination>
    <price>987.65</price>
  </cruise>
```

```
<cruise>
  <destination>Bahamas</destination>
  <price>475.99</price>
</cruise>
</vacation>
```

While this looks a little like HTML, I doubt you'll ever see a <vacation> or <cruise> tag as part of an HTML standard. That's where the X in XML comes in. XML stands for **E**xtensible **M**arkup **L**anguage. You create your own tags as needed, extending the language to describe and delimit (that is, clearly define the starting and ending points of) our data.

Applying common sense and your understanding of HTML, you can pretty well guess that we're talking about vacations and that everything that lies between the <vacation> and </vacation> tags has something to do with vacations. Taking a step down into the hierarchy, you can ascertain that the information is about two cruises, as there are two sets of <cruise></cruise> tags. Stepping further into the hierarchy, you also see that we have identified the destination and price of each cruise. This has nothing to do with how the cruise data is displayed, but instead gives you a standard by which the hierarchical data can be parsed (read and interpreted). Using your imagination, you can see how this could be useful when sharing information, not only between people, but between different software applications.

XML Data Is Highly Structured

Like HTML, XML uses arrow-bracketed tags to separate markup from data. Start tags begin with the tag name and end tags begin with a forward slash, followed by the tag name (<price>…</price>). In HTML there are also tags that do not require ending counterparts. The line break <br> and horizontal rule <hr> tags are examples of this. Some HTML hackers also intentionally choose to leave out end tags on items like paragraphs (<p>) because they consider them logically unnecessary, and browsers really don't care if you use them or not. Unlike HTML, XML is said to be *well formed* because it *always* requires an end tag for every start tag. Miss an end tag in an HTML page, and the browser will likely be forgiving; miss an end tag in an XML document, and the entire document is broken.

Being well formed also means that tags must follow an ordered structure. While HTML lets you get away with miss-ordered tag placement such as <font>…</font>, XML does not and will cause an XML parser (reader/interpreter program) to give an error if the first opened, last closed order is broken. While this might seem extreme from an HTML standpoint, think of it in terms of a database flat-file such as a comma-separated values (CSV) file to bring the reason for this restriction. For example, a CSV file, an Excel file format, stores data in columns and rows by using a comma to separate each column value and new lines to separate rows (records). Starting a new line means starting a new data record; if you then entered the last column of the previous record, no one would understand what you meant. Like the CSV file format, in XML, structure conveys meaning. For an XML document to be understood, it must be structured with properly opened and closed identifiers.

XML Data Describes Itself

Unlike CSV files, XML allows you to store data in a hierarchical form. Instead of columns and rows, XML uses nested tags to define relational data structures. Looking back at our previous XML example, you see that each cruise tag contains two sets of tags: destination and price. Because these nested tags are placed within a cruise tag, you know that they contain information about the cruise. You also know that since the tags are different, they do not contain the same type of data. The cruise tags are also nested within the vacation tag set, letting you know that each cruise contains information about vacation. Since the cruise tags are the same, you know that they do contain the same type of data.

```
<vacation>
  <cruise>
    <destination>…</destination>
    <price>…</price>
  </cruise>
  …
</vacation>
```

Whether or not you know what a vacation, cruise, destination, or price is, you can still see the relationships between the data. All price tag sets should contain the same type of information that relates in the same way to all cruise tag sets. All destination tag sets should contain the same type of information that relates in the same way to all cruise tag sets. All cruise tag sets should contain the same type of information that relates in the same way to the vacation tag set, even though the price and destination information contained within is different. These inherent relationships, created by the structured placement of specific tags within the data, make XML self-describing. This self-describing nature of XML is further extended by DTDs (Document Type Declarations), which I'll discuss later in this chapter.

XML Data Is Application Independent

I'm reasonably sure that you have at least once run into the problem of file format incompatibility. This often occurs when you try to use a file created by one software application with a different application. Software manufacturers have tried to ease your pain by offering various conversion programs, but file incompatibility still raises its ugly head now and then, usually at the worst possible time—when you're up against a deadline. XML may be the best solution yet to sharing data between different applications.

Instead of saving files in proprietary binary formats, software makers such as Microsoft are starting to allow users to save them in text-based formats, using XML to define special functionality and formatting. Save a Word document as an HTML file. Then open that file in Notepad and look at the code. You'll see XML being used to store the document's properties and options.

```
<xml>
 <o:DocumentProperties>
  <o:Author>Mark Hammock</o:Author>
  <o:Template>Omh.dot</o:Template>
  <o:LastAuthor>Mark Hammock</o:LastAuthor>
  <o:Revision>2</o:Revision>
  <o:TotalTime>308</o:TotalTime>
  <o:LastPrinted>2001-01-19T02:47:00Z</o:LastPrinted>
  <o:Created>2001-01-20T23:37:00Z</o:Created>
  <o:LastSaved>2001-01-20T23:37:00Z</o:LastSaved>
  <o:Pages>7</o:Pages>
  <o:Words>1485</o:Words>
  <o:Characters>7517</o:Characters>
  <o:Company>Osborne/McGraw-Hill</o:Company>
  <o:Lines>159</o:Lines>
  <o:Paragraphs>71</o:Paragraphs>
  <o:CharactersWithSpaces>8931</o:CharactersWithSpaces>
  <o:Version>10.2202</o:Version>
 </o:DocumentProperties>
</xml>
```

Why would you care about this information when viewing the page in a browser? You probably wouldn't. But open the HTML file again in Word and you'll see that this information, which cannot be described in HTML, has been preserved.

Taking things a step further, what if the entire Word document were converted to and saved as XML? Since XML is used to describe data structures, not formatting, you would need to totally separate the data in the document from its presentation. Handling presentation is the work of languages like HTML and CSS and XSL (two topics I'll cover later in the chapter). This may seem strange at first, but looking deeper, it opens up a world of possibilities.

With a common, isolated source of data, it becomes very easy to change the way the data is displayed. It is also equally easy to change the data without having to worry about the presentation aspects. Most media companies, no matter what their primary domain (radio, TV, newspapers, magazines, etc.), now offer information on the Internet. XML provides them with a method of reusing the same data in a variety of formats. The data stays the same; only the presentation method and formatting changes. You may have already experienced similar benefits to this type of separation through the use of linked cascading style sheets (CSS), changing a style and updating the look of an entire web site.

Understandably, businesses are very excited about XML as a method of reusing and exchanging data. In the ever expanding world of e-commerce, both business to business (B2B) and business to consumer (B2C), information needs to be exchanged between online stores, payment services, fulfillment services and manufacturers. These services are often provided by different companies that need a common way to communicate when exchanging data. XML provides a solution to this problem by providing a platform- and application-independent data format for this exchange.

XML Data Structures

We've already discussed how XML is extensible, allowing you to create your own tags to define and structure your data. But there's much more to XML than basic tags. XML tags, which are known as *elements*, can contain *attributes* just like HTML tags. In fact, XML elements sometimes use only attributes, instead of placing data between start and end tags. Let's look at the various components that make up XML. (We've already covered some of this information, but we'll reprise it here for completeness and reference.)

Elements

Elements are used to define the type of data contained within the element. Once used, an element name should be reused for each occurrence of the same data type, but only for the same data type. An element is comprised of a start tag, an end tag, and any data that lies between. Both start tags and end tags are arrow bracketed, with end tags containing a forward slash (/) before the element name.

```
<element>some data</element>
```

If, and only if, the element contains no data, it can also be represented by adding a forward slash to the end of a start tag, eliminating the need for an end tag.

```
<element/>
```

The scope of elements cannot overlap each other. All child elements must be closed before the parent element is closed. For example:

- <vacation><cruise></vacation></cruise> is not valid
- <vacation><cruise></cruise></vacation> is valid

The first element in every XML document must be a unique *root element*. This compares to the <html></html> tags that begin and end every HTML document.

In the case of XML, it should be a name that meaningfully identifies the data contained within the document.

Attributes

An attribute consists of a name/value pair in the form *attribute="value"* with values always enclosed in quotes. Attributes reside in element start tags and can only be used once within an element. They can, however, be used in any order within the element and can be used in different types of elements.

```
<element attribute="value">some data</element>
```

or

```
<element attribute="value" attribute2="value"/>
```

Unlike elements, which are used to define a type of data, attributes are used to provide additional or ancillary information about an element. This information sometimes takes the form of properties, known as metadata, or in other cases can be used to store the element's data.

```
<price offseason="399.99" inseason="899.99"/>
```

Entity References

Entities serve two main purposes in XML: they allow you to use reserved characters, and they let you create shortcut references (abbreviations) to repeatedly used data, both internal and external. In each case, entities always begin with an ampersand (&) and end with a semicolon (;). I'll cover the second case (abbreviations) further along in the DTD section. Here, look at reserved characters.

Just like HTML, XML tags are surrounded with arrow brackets (<>) so these characters are reserved and cannot be used in data. Instead, you use the HTML encoded < and > equivalents. XML uses the same encoding to allow the use of these and other special characters.

Reserved Character	Entity Reference
<	&lt;
>	&gt;
&	&amp;
"	&quot;
'	&apos;

Processing Instructions, Comments, and CDATA Sections

In addition to the data defining structures within XML, there are also nondata-related structures that are used to add additional information to documents. This can take the form of information for the XML parser, human readable comments, or pass-through information that is used by an application other than the parser.

Processing Instructions

Processing instructions (PI) are used to provide information to applications that interpret XML, known as parsers, and are not part of the XML data structure. They begin with a <? and end with a ?>. Unlike elements, processing instructions have no end tag. The *XML declaration* is an example of a processing instruction used in XML documents. It provides applications that process XML with important information about the document and, if included, must be the first line in the document.

```
<?xml version="1.0" encoding="UTF-8" standalone="yes"?>
```

This example tells the application reading the document that it contains XML as specified by the W3C standard 1.0 (**http://www.w3c.org/XML**), that the characters in the document are encoded using the UTF-8 standard, and that the document does not contain any elements, attributes, or entities that are referenced by an external DTD (Document Type Declaration, covered later in this chapter). Minimally, you should always include "xml" and the version number (<?xml version="1.0" ?>). Currently, there's only one version of XML (1.0), but future releases will make version identification important.

Comments

Just like HTML comments, XML comments begin with <!-- and end with -->. Comments can be placed anywhere in the XML document after the XML declaration, except within an element tag, and are used to improve human readability.

```
<!-- this is an XML comment -->
```

CDATA Sections

CDATA (character data) sections are used to prevent an application from trying to interpret the markup contained within the section. They begin with <![CDATA[and end with]]>.

```
<![CDATA[
  This is an XML declaration:
  <?xml version="1.0" encoding="UTF-8" standalone="no" ?>
]]>
```

CDATA sections are primarily used to display code listings without that code being interpreted by the application parsing the data. The only set of characters that cannot be used within a CDATA section is the closing tag]]>.

Syntax

Unlike HTML, XML's syntax is very important and strict. This is part of what makes XML "well formed." Web browsers can make best guesses at how information should be displayed, but XML parsers depend on precise syntax to provide reliable data interpretation. After all, you wouldn't want a bank to guess at the amount you really meant to write on that check, would you?

XML Is Case-Sensitive

XML treats upper- and lowercase letters differently. As a result, *<cruise>*, *<Cruise>*, and *<CRUISE>* are completely different elements. To avoid case-related problems, it's usually a good idea to write all of your elements and attribute names in lowercase.

XML Does Not Ignore Spaces

Unlike HTML, which ignores repeated spaces unless specifically written as nonbreaking spaces ( ), XML retains each space as it appears in the data. You may have noticed that there isn't a nonbreaking space entity. Because XML does not ignore repeated spaces, also known as *whitespace*, there is no need for a nonbreaking space entity.

All Elements Must Be Closed

Being well-formed, each starting element tag in an XML document must have a corresponding end tag. This closing tag can be a matching end tag in the form *<element></element>*, or the shortcut version *<element/>* may be used when the element does not contain data. In XML terms, the element is then considered not to have a *value*, even though it may contain attributes that have values.

All Element Attributes Must Be in Quotes

Unlike HTML, which allows you to not use quotes around numeric attributes (size=2), *ALL* XML attribute values must be enclosed in quotes (name="value"). Failure to do so will cause an XML parser to generate an error.

Formatting XML

Since XML doesn't define the appearance of the data, you must use other technologies to actually display XML data. Starting with Internet Explorer 4, Microsoft has included an XML parser with their browsers. Included with IE 5 and above is the ability to display XML documents in a hierarchical tree view. Figure 14-1 shows the vacation.xml example as it is displayed by IE 5.5. This example file is located on the book's

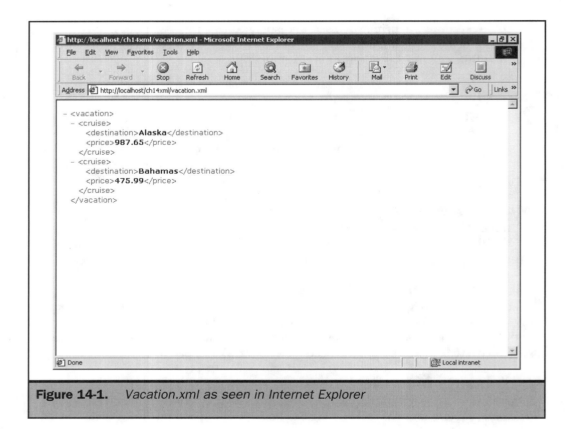

Figure 14-1. *Vacation.xml as seen in Internet Explorer*

companion CD in the \Book\Chap14\ folder. Open this file in IE to follow along with the example.

The first thing you'll notice is that IE's representation of the XML file looks surprisingly like the raw XML. There is a root <vacation> element that contains two instances of the <cruise> element, which each contain <destination> and <price> elements. Color coding has been added and there are minus (–) signs to the left of each element that contains children (lower-level elements). Clicking the minus sign next to the <vacation> element collapses the tree and leaves visible only the <vacation> element and a plus (+) sign to the left. Clicking the plus sign expands the tree, again showing all of the elements and their values. You should already be quite familiar with this interface after working with Windows Explorer and FrontPage folder views.

So how does IE accomplish this? It uses its built-in XML parser to read and interpret the XML source code in vacation.xml. It then applies an internal Extensible Style Language (XSL) style sheet to the data, transforming it into browser-readable HTML. Getting to the actual source code of what is displayed in IE is a little tricky.

If you use IE's View | Source tool, you'll only see the original XML document. To see what's really being displayed by the browser, you must use a debugger to capture the code. The file vacation.htm, located in the companion CD \Book\Chap14\ folder, contains this captured code. We don't have room to cover it here, but if you're curious about the code that IE's parser is generating to display the XML document view, open this file and check out the source HTML. You won't find any XML, just style declarations, standard HTML, and some JavaScript that is used to expand and collapse the tree.

While IE's built-in parser and style sheet offers a great tool for viewing your XML and checking it for errors, its default display falls far short of how you'll want to display your XML data in real world applications. To achieve the desired formatting results, you'll want to create and use your own style sheets.

CSS

Cascading style sheets (CSS) were covered in Chapters 10 and 12 as a method of controlling the look of HTML. In the same way, CSS can also be used to control the display of XML. In CSS, you specify an element by name and then list properties of that element, setting their values as desired. Using CSS with XML works the same way. Instead of specifying HTML tags, you instead use XML element names. Here, destination is the element name and color and font-size are properties of this element for which you are specifying values:

```
destination {color: #FF0000; font-size: 18pt;}
```

CSS style sheets can be *embedded*, that is, contained within the XML document; or *external*, a separate file that is linked to within the document. To embed a CSS style sheet within an XML document, you add an *xml-stylesheet* processor instruction (PI) to the top of the document specifying that the XML parser should use the styles specified within the document when displaying its output. The embedded style sheet processor instruction is as follows:

```
<?xml-stylesheet href="#style" type="text/css"?>
```

Anywhere after this instruction, you can place your style definitions as you would in an HTML file.

```
<?xml-stylesheet href="#style" type="text/css"?>
<style>
  vacation {background-color: #EEEEEE; width: 100%;}
  cruise {display: block; margin-bottom: 20pt; margin-left: 10;}
  destination {color: #FF0000; font-size: 18pt;}
```

WORKING BEHIND THE SCENES

```
    ...
</style>
```

To use a linked CSS style sheet, you simply add an additional attribute (href) to the processor instruction, listing the location of the style sheet that contains your style definitions:

```
<?xml-stylesheet type="text/css" href="vacation.css"?>
```

Linking has several advantages over embedding. You can reuse the same linked style sheet with multiple documents. When you need to make a change, you change it a single time in the style sheet and it is automatically applied to all linking pages. You can also link to multiple style sheets within a single XML document. This is done by simply adding additional xml-stylesheet processor instructions for each additional style sheet you wish to use. This feature allows you to have one style sheet that specifies element layouts, another that specifies sizes, and a third that specifies colors.

Example: Formatting XML Display with a Linked CSS Style Sheet

Located in the \Book\Chap14\ folder on the companion CD are two files named vacation_css.xml and vacation.css. Viewing the source code of the vacation_css.xml file, you see that the earlier vacation.xml example file has been expanded, adding two processor instructions (an XML declaration and an xml-stylesheet instruction) and some additional elements (origin, departs, and returns).

```
<?xml version="1.0" ?>
<?xml-stylesheet type="text/css" href="vacation.css"?>

<vacation>
  <cruise>
    <destination>Alaska</destination>
    <origin>Seattle</origin>
    <price>987.65</price>
    <departs>06/01/2002</departs>
    <returns>06/08/2002</returns>
  </cruise>
  ...
</vacation>
```

Viewing the source of vacation.css, you see that it contains CSS style definitions corresponding to each of the elements in the other example file, vacation_css.xml.

```
vacation {background-color: #EEEEEE; width: 100%;}
cruise {display: block; margin-bottom: 20pt; margin-left: 10;}
destination {color: #FF0000; font-size: 18pt;}
origin {color: #0000FF; font-size: 18pt;}
price, departs, returns {Display: block;
        color: #000000; margin-left: 20pt;}
```

By providing your own CSS style sheet and referencing it with the xml-stylesheet instruction in your XML document, you tell IE that it should use your style sheet instead of its own. Figure 14-2 shows how vacation_css.xml looks in Internet Explorer.

As you can see, CSS style sheets give you some control over how your XML data is displayed. They do not, however, give you nearly the control and power of XSL. This makes them an unlikely choice for future development.

XSL

Providing all the functionality of CSS with greater power and control are XSL (Extensible Style Language) style sheets. XSL combines CSS with *templates* that define

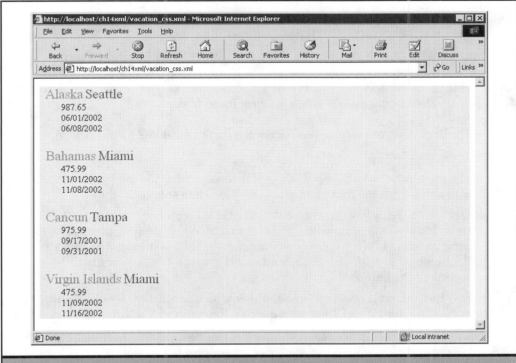

Figure 14-2.   *Linked CSS style sheet display of vacation_css.xml in Internet Explorer*

the format of the resulting code. It also includes powerful searching and filtering capabilities that give you much greater control over exactly how information is formatted. XSL is really made up of three parts:

- **XSLT (XSL Transformations)** Used to transform XML into other types of documents including HTML; it can also be used to reshape one XML document into another.
- **XPath** Used by XSLT to address specific parts and patterns of XML documents.
- **XSL Formatting Objects** Used to define the display of XML elements.

Complete coverage of XSL is well beyond the scope of this chapter. I'll focus on only a small portion of its abilities to format the display of the vacation example.

Unlike CSS, an XSL style sheet is really an XML document itself. Your style sheet will be made up of the following items:

1. The XSL style sheet begins with a standard XML declaration:

```
<?xml version='1.0'?>
```

2. On the next line, an xsl:stylesheet tag identifies the start of the XSL style sheet:

```
<xsl:stylesheet xmlns:xsl="http://www.w3.org/TR/WD-xsl">
```

XML Namespaces (xmlns) are beyond the scope of this chapter. In this case, it identifies the standard to follow in the construction of the style sheet.

3. The beginning of the template is denoted on the third line by the xsl:template tag:

```
<xsl:template match="/">
```

The match="/" attribute tells the XSL processor that the template will be associated with the root element of the XML data source.

4. Once in the template, you can enter any HTML you like, including CSS style declarations or links to CSS style sheets. When creating a template that generates an HTML page, you should always follow standard HTML structure. Begin the page with <html>, <head>, and <body> tags, closing each when their section of the template is complete.

5. End the XSL style sheet as you would any XML document by closing the tags opened in Steps 2 and 3 in reverse order. Remember, XML documents must be well-formed.

Located in the companion CD's \Book\Chap14\ folder are two files named vacation_xsl.xml (XML data source) and vacation.xsl (XSL style sheet). When you view the source of the XSL style sheet (vacation.xsl), you can see that the template is primarily written in standard HTML, which makes up the majority of the code. In fact, there are only a few lines of code that are not straight HTML.

```
<?xml version='1.0'?>
<xsl:stylesheet xmlns:xsl="http://www.w3.org/TR/WD-xsl">
<xsl:template match="/">
  <html>
  <style>
    th {background-color: #000000; color: #FFFFFF;
          font-family: Verdana; font-size: 14pt;}
    td {background-color: #EEEEEE; color: #000000;
          font-family: Verdana; font-size: 12pt;}
  </style>
  <body>
    <table border="1" cellpadding="5" cellspacing="0"
          bordercolor="#000000" bgcolor="#EEEEEE">
      <tr>
        <th>Destination</th>
        <th>Origin</th>
        <th>Price</th>
        <th>Departs</th>
        <th>Returns</th>
      </tr>
      <xsl:for-each select="vacation/cruise">
      <tr>
        <td><xsl:value-of select="destination"/></td>
        <td><xsl:value-of select="origin"/></td>
        <td><xsl:value-of select="price"/></td>
        <td><xsl:value-of select="departs"/></td>
        <td><xsl:value-of select="returns"/></td>
      </tr>
      </xsl:for-each>
    </table>
  </body>
  </html>
</xsl:template>
</xsl:stylesheet>
```

The <xsl:for-each select="vacation/cruise"> tag tells the processor that it should run the code that follows repeatedly for each cruise element in the XML data source document (vacation_xsl.xml). When the </xsl:for-each> end tag is reached, the processor loops back and runs the code again, moving to the next cruise element and repeating the process until there are no cruise elements left. As the code runs each time, the processor reads the contents of the current cruise element and substitutes the value of the specified element in each of the <xsl:value-of select="[some element name]"/>

tags. This is where the data contained in the XML file is inserted into the HTML code that is actually displayed in the browser.

The vacation_xsl.xml file is exactly like the previous example's vacation_css.xml file with one exception. Viewing the source code, you can see that the xml-stylesheet processor instruction has been changed to reference "vacation.xsl" with the type set to "text/xsl".

```
<?xml-stylesheet type="text/xsl" href="vacation.xsl"?>
```

Figure 14-3 shows how vacation_xsl.xml looks in the Internet Explorer.

We've just scratched the surface of the capabilities offered by XSL. Still, you can see that XSL provides much greater power and control over the display of XML compared to CSS. XSL is quickly gaining popularity and will likely become the accepted standard for manipulating and formatting the display of XML.

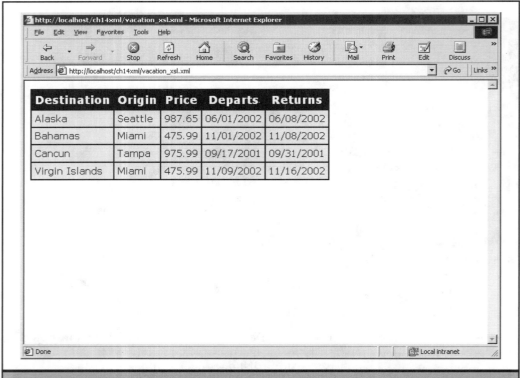

Figure 14-3. *Linked XSL style sheet display of vacation_xsl.xml in Internet Explorer*

Document Type Definitions (DTD)—Valid XML

Earlier in the chapter, I talked about XML's *self-describing* nature. You can look at an XML data structure and see obvious structures and relationships within the elements and data. This is fine when you are the only one working with your data, using XML as a data source to simply display information in a web page. But what if you were counting on someone else to provide your XML data source? Could you really trust them to always create the structure that you are expecting or fill it with the types of data you're counting on? Probably not... This is where DTDs are useful: *to define the logical structure and types of data, including attributes, within an XML document*. When XML is governed by a DTD, it is considered *valid XML*.

Standalone Documents

When no DTD or *schema* is associated with an XML document, it is considered to be a standalone document. I touched on this briefly during our look at processor instructions when I talked about the *XML declaration*. You specify that a document is a standalone document by adding a *standalone="yes"* attribute to this declaration.

```
<?xml version="1.0" encoding="UTF-8" standalone="yes"?>
```

Standalone documents contain no method of validating their structure. As long as the document is *well-formed*, no errors will occur when it is processed by an XML parser. When starting out with XML, these are the types of documents you'll likely be creating. As long as you're not exchanging your XML documents with others (people or applications), you are in control of how your document is structured and the data it contains.

Document Type Declarations

The real beauty of XML lies within its ability to be a universal, self-describing method of transferring data. To accomplish this effectively, you need a way to precisely tell others what is contained in your XML documents and a method of validating the contents. DTDs, sometimes referred to as *traffic cops*, provide a grammar to define constraints on how XML documents must be formed. An XML document is considered valid when it has an accompanying DTD to which it conforms.

DTDs can be contained within an XML document, externally in a referenced file, or both. Adding a standalone="no" attribute to an XML declaration specifies that the document uses a DTD but says nothing about where it is located.

Internal DTDs

An internal DTD begins with a DOCTYPE declaration, which contains the root element name in the form:

```
<!DOCTYPE root_element_name [
```

The opening square bracket ([) at the end of this statement indicates that this is an *internal* DTD and that the definitions will follow. The DTD ends with a closing square bracket followed by a greater than symbol (]>). Within the square brackets, you list all of the markup declarations (elements, attributes, processor instructions, entities, and so on) that will be contained within your XML document.

External DTDs

External DTDs come in two flavors, *private* and *public*, and are referenced within the XML document by a different type of DOCTYPE declaration. Private DTDs are those used by a single person or group of people. A private DTD lists the location (/dtd/filename.dtd, etc.) of the external DTD document and is prefixed by the word SYSTEM as follows:

```
<!DOCTYPE root_element_name SYSTEM "dtd_location">
```

Public DTDs are meant to be used by a larger group or groups of people. The public DTD declaration uses the word PUBLIC to identify this fact and provides both the name of the DTD and a public URL where it may be found. A common DTD declaration you've likely seen, possibly never knowing what it really meant, is

```
<!DOCTYPE html PUBLIC "-//W3C//DTD XHTML 1.0 Transitional//EN"
 "http://www.w3.org/TR/xhtml1/DTD/xhtml1-transitional.dtd">
```

The contents of an external DTD are the same element type declarations as are contained within the internal DTD's DOCTYPE declaration.

Element Type Declarations

Whether within an internal DOCTYPE declaration or an external file, *element type declarations* are used to provide a strict guide to what items will be in an XML document, the order in which they will appear, and the number of times they will appear. These element type declarations take the form:

```
<!ELEMENT element_name allowable_contents>
```

The allowable_contents portion of this declaration lets you specify what will be contained within the element. This can be

- **EMPTY**   The element contains no data.
- **ANY**   The element can contain anything within the constraints of XML's rules.

- **(#PCDATA)** The element contains data, but no child elements. PCDATA stands for *Parsed Character Data*.
- (*Child elements*) The element contains only child elements. These elements are placed in a comma-delimited list within parentheses.
- (*Mixed*) The element contains a mixture of data and child elements.

Putting this all together, the simplest XML document with an internal DTD might look like the following:

```
<?xml version="1.0" standalone="no"?>
<!DOCTYPE myxml [
  <!ELEMENT myxml (#PCDATA)>
]>
<myxml>my data here</myxml>
```

Child Elements

To define the list of child elements contained within an element, you provide a comma-delimited list of the child elements within the element type declaration's allowable_contents section. You then follow that declaration with additional declarations for each of the child elements.

```
<!ELEMENT parent_element (child_element1, child_element2)>
<!ELEMENT child_element1 (#PCDATA)>
<!ELEMENT child_element2 (#PCDATA)>
```

In this example, each of the child elements must appear once and only once within the parent element. To further define the occurrence of variably appearing child elements, you use single character suffixes and separators, as shown in Table 14-1.

Going back to the original vacation.xml example, an internal document type declaration might look like the following:

```
<!DOCTYPE vacation [
  <!ELEMENT cruise (destination, price)>
  <!ELEMENT destination (#PCDATA)>
  <!ELEMENT price (#PCDATA)>
]>
```

Note *The complete code of this example is contained in the file vacation_intDTD.xml within the companion CD's \Book\Chap14\ folder. Use IE's View | Source option to see the complete document type declaration.*

Symbol	Use	Meaning
?	(child_element?)	**Optional** The element may appear once or not at all.
*	(child_element*)	**Optional Repeating** The element may appear many times or not at all.
+	(child_element+)	**Forced** The parent element must contain at least one child element of this type.
|	(child_element1 | child_element2 | child_element3)	**Either Forced** The parent element must contain at least one child element of the types separated by the pipe symbol.

Table 14-1.   *Single-Character Suffixes and Separators*

Entity Abbreviations

As discussed earlier, entities serve two main purposes in XML: they allow you to use reserved characters, and they let you create shortcut references to repeatedly used data, both internal and external. In each case, entities always begin with an ampersand (&) and end with a semicolon (;). I've already covered the use of reserved characters. Now, let's focus on their usefulness when referencing data.

Internal Entity Abbreviations

Internal entities allow you to create abbreviations for repeatedly used data. For instance, instead of repeatedly typing my name, Mark Hammock, in an XML document's author element, I can create an internal entity within a DTD and abbreviate it thereafter. By adding the entity to the DTD, I can simply use the entity whenever I need to reference its value. The format of an internal entity declaration is as follows:

```
<!ENTITY name "entity_value">
```

Located in the companion CD's \Book\Chap14\ folder is a file named entity_example.xml. Viewing its source, you see that the XML document contains an internal DTD which includes an element definition for the author element and an entity definition for the internal entity abbreviation mh. This is followed by a short XML data structure which contains &mh; as data within the author element.

```
<?xml version="1.0" standalone="no"?>
<!DOCTYPE entity_example [
  <!ELEMENT author (#PCDATA)>
  <!ENTITY mh "Mark Hammock">
]>
<entity_example>
  <author>&mh;</author>
</entity_example>
```

In Figure 14-4, you see how Internet Explorer displays this document, replacing *&mh;* with *Mark Hammock*.

External Entity Abbreviations

External entities let you reference files that are outside the XML document. These files can be unparsed (non-XML) or parsed (XML). An image file is a good example of an unparsed entity. The XML parser doesn't need to actually read the binary data that

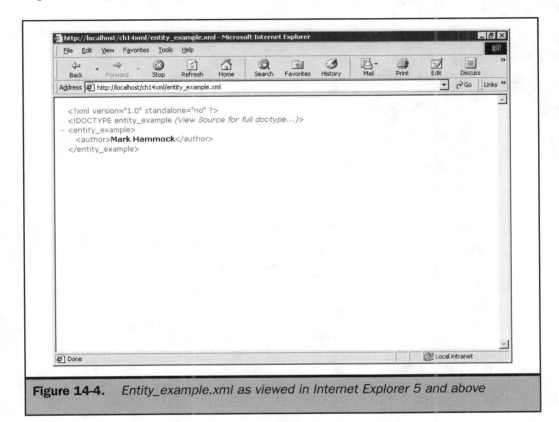

Figure 14-4.   *Entity_example.xml as viewed in Internet Explorer 5 and above*

makes up the image to validate its inclusion. A parsed file might contain commonly used XML data such as copyright information. In either case, using an external entity abbreviation to represent the actual data allows the data to be modified independently without affecting the XML data.

 Adequate coverage of external entities goes beyond the scope of this chapter. They are referenced here only to make you aware of their existence and uses.

XML Data Sources (Using XML in HTML Pages)

Up to this point, we have worked with XML in an XML-specific manner. As stated in the chapter introduction, FrontPage offers no real direct support for XML. But what if you want to include XML data in HTML documents? This can easily be accomplished using a Java applet that Microsoft has provided with Internet Explorer since version 4. The com.ms.xml.dso.XMLDSO.class applet allows you to bind external XML data to HTML elements within your existing pages. FrontPage offers all the tools necessary to insert and use this applet.

In this section, you'll use FrontPage to build a page that uses an XML Data Source Object to pull information from an external XML file and dynamically build nested tables that display the information. You'll accomplish this through a series of short exercises. For the data source, you'll use an XML document named vacation_dso.xml that is included in the \Book\Chap14\ folder on the companion CD.

To prepare for this exercise:

1. Open FrontPage and create a new one-page web named ch14xml.
2. From the File menu, choose Import and, in the Import dialog box, click Add File.
3. In the Add File To Import List dialog box, browse to the file on the companion CD. Double-click it and click OK in the Import dialog box.
4. Open your Default.htm in Page view.
5. Open the Insert Web Component dialog box by clicking the Insert menu and selecting the Web Component option.
6. Scroll down the Component Type list to the Advanced Controls item and select it.
7. Select Java Applet in the Choose A Control list, as shown next, and click Finish to display the Java Applet Properties dialog box.

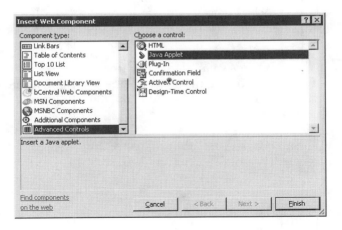

8. In the Applet Source field, type the name of the XMLDSO applet as com.ms.xml.dso.XMLDSO.class.

9. Click the Add button in the Applet Parameters area and type **url** in the Name field. Next, check the Specify Value check box and type **vacation_dso.xml** in the Data field. Click OK to add the parameter to the applet. Your Java Applet Properties dialog box should look like this:

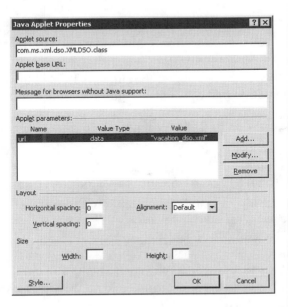

10. Click Style and type **xmldso** in the ID field of the Modify Style dialog box that is displayed. Click OK.

11. Under Size, type a Width and Height of **0** and click OK to insert the applet into your page.

Your page will now contain a small slanted J within a gray square. This is FrontPage's way of visually showing the Java applet. Viewing the page in the HTML tab, you can see that FrontPage has added the following code:

```
<applet width="0" height="0"
          code="com.ms.xml.dso.XMLDSO.class" id="xmldso">
  <param name="url" value="vacation_dso.xml">
</applet>
```

Switch back to the Normal tab to begin the next exercise.

Creating and Formatting HTML Tables to Hold Your Data

Instead of using a CSS or XSL style sheet to format the display of data as you did earlier in the chapter, the XML data source object applet allows you to bind XML data to HTML tags. Use FrontPage's graphical editor to quickly and easily build the HTML framework for a complex, multi-level data representation with these steps:

1. Using FrontPage, press ENTER twice to create some blank space below the JavaScript and create a table that contains two columns and two rows.

2. In the top left cell, type **Vacation Type**, and in the top right cell, type **Destination:** (include the colon).

3. Click the bottom right cell so that the cursor is located there and create another table within that cell containing four columns and two rows.

4. Moving from left to right, type the following in the four cells of the top row in the new table: **Leaves From**, **Departs On**, **Returns On**, and **Price**.

5. Select the entire top row of this nested table, right-click, and select Cell Properties. In the Cell Properties dialog box, check the Header Cell and No Wrap check boxes. Select a dark colored background such as Maroon and click OK.

6. Select the entire top row of the outer table and repeat the instructions in Step 5, selecting the background color Black.

7. Select the entire bottom row of the outer table and set its background color to #FFFFCC (an ivory-like color) by right-clicking the selection and choosing Cell Properties. In the Background area Color list of the Cell Properties dialog box, select More Colors, and enter the hexadecimal color in the More Colors' Value field.

8. Edit the table properties of each table, setting the border size to 1, border color to Black, and cell padding and cell spacing as desired. Click the Style button in each of the Table Properties dialog boxes and type **table** in the ID box for the outer table and **detailtable** in the ID of the inner (nested) table.

9. Open the FrontPage Format menu and click Style. In the Style dialog box Styles list, select *th* and click Modify. In the Modify Style dialog box, click Format and select Font from the displayed list.

10. In the Font dialog box, select Verdana as the Font and set the Font Style to Bold and the Size to 10pt. Change the Color to White and click OK to close the Font dialog box. Click OK again to close the Modify Style dialog box.

11. Change the List drop-down of the Style dialog box from User-defined Styles back to HTML Tags and select *td* in the Styles list. Set the Font to Verdana and the Size to 10pt as you did in Steps 9 and 10.

12. Click Format again and this time select Paragraph from the displayed list. In the Paragraph dialog box, set the Alignment to Center.

13. Click OK in each dialog box until you return to the FrontPage Page view.

Your page should now look something like the one pictured in Figure 14-5.

WORKING BEHIND
THE SCENES

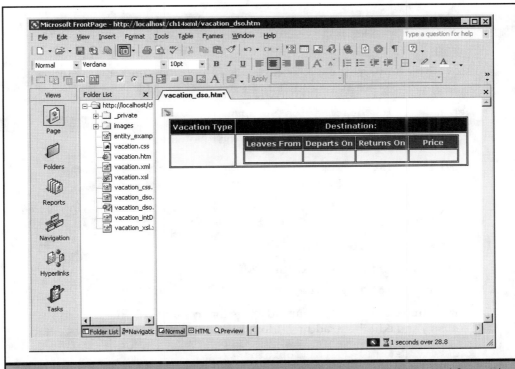

Figure 14-5.   *Home page after inserting a Java Applet, adding tables, and formatting*

Binding the XML Data Source Object to Elements for Display

In the final exercise, you'll work exclusively with the HTML source code to bind the XML data source to page elements. This is accomplished through the use of two attributes: datasrc and datafld. You'll add the datasrc attribute to each of your tables, binding them to your data source object applet. A datafld attribute will be added to the nested table, binding it to the detail level of the XML data source. You'll also add DIV and SPAN tags containing the datafld attribute to cells within the tables, binding them to the actual data that you wish to display.

Switch to the HTML tab to begin this exercise.

1. Locate the first <table> tag and add a datasrc="#xmldso" attribute to that tag. The tag should now look something like the following:

```
<table id="table" datasrc="#xmldso" border="1" cellpadding="3"
            cellspacing="1" width="95%" bordercolor="#000000">
```

2. Locate the second <table> tag and add the datasrc="#xmldso" attribute as in Step 1 and an additional datafld="detail" attribute.

```
<table id="detailtable" datasrc="#xmldso" datafld="detail"
            border="1" cellpadding="2" cellspacing="1"
            width="95%" bordercolor="#000000">
```

3. Moving back up in the code, locate the text *Destination:* and add the following code after the space at the end of this text:

```
<span datafld="destination"></span>
```

The entire <th> should now look like the following:

```
<th width="99%" nowrap bgcolor="#000000">Destination: <span
            datafld="destination"></span></th>
```

4. Move down to the first <td> tag following the next <tr> tag following the "destination" line and insert a <div> as follows:

```
<div datafld="type"></div>
```

This line should now look like this:

```
<td bgcolor="#FFFFCC" align="center"><div datafld="type"></div></td>
```

5. Finally, move down to the four <td> tags that contain only nonbreaking spaces ( ) and edit them, adding <div> tags so they appear as follows:

```
<td><div datafld="detail.origin"></div></td>
<td><div datafld="detail.price"></div></td>
```

```
<td><div datafld="detail.departs"></div></td>
<td><div datafld="detail.returns"></div></td>
```

Save this page and view it in Internet Explorer. Unless you had any typos, it should look like Figure 14-6. Close FrontPage and your browser when through viewing it.

The file vacation_dso.htm in the companion CD's \Book\Chap14\ folder contains an example of the completed page. If you're having problems making your page display properly, compare it to vacation_dso.htm.

Additional XML Resources Online

This chapter provided a glimpse at the power and possibilities offered by XML. As you start implementing XML in your own web sites and applications, you'll likely discover

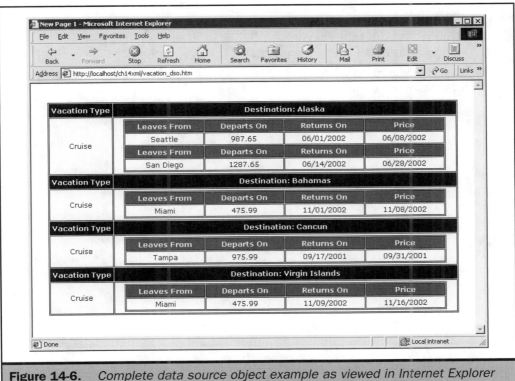

Figure 14-6. *Complete data source object example as viewed in Internet Explorer*

that you need more in-depth and detailed information than can be covered in a single chapter. The following are a few online resources that you may find helpful:

- **http://www.w3.org/XML** The World Wide Web Consortium (W3C) site offers the complete XML 1.0 Specification and links to a variety of book and online resources.

- **http://msdn.microsoft.com/XML** The Microsoft XML Development Center offers information, examples, downloads, and tutorials on all of Microsoft's XML implementations.

- **http://www.w3schools.com** W3Schools.com offers free, web-based e-learning with a variety of tutorials on XML and HTML and related technologies.

- **http://xmlwriter.net/xml_guide/xml_guide.shtml** Wattle Software's XML Guide provides a reference guide based on the W3C's XML Specification 1.0.

- **http://www.biztalk.org** BizTalk, a Microsoft-founded organization supports the rapid adoption of XML technologies.

- **http://www.architag.com/xmlu** archiTAG International's XML University offers XML industry news and tips and promotes their fee-based seminars.

- **http://www.zdnet.com/devhead** ZDNet's Developer offers news, articles, and tutorials on a variety of web-related topics including XML.

- **http://www.xml-zone.com** The DevX XML Zone site offers news, articles, tutorials, newsletters, and forums for the XML developer.

Chapter 15

Web Scripting Languages

The use of scripting languages on the Web is one of the major reasons we now refer to web *applications,* rather than simply web pages or web sites. Scripting languages enable true interactivity in web applications. A *scripting language* is a computer programming language in a simple text format. HTML itself is a scripting language.

The general difference between scripting languages and other programming languages is in how they are treated when executed. Programming languages, like Java and Visual Basic, create a *bytecode* file that is executed by the operating system. (Java and Visual Basic are covered in Chapter 20.) A bytecode file is a binary (all 0's and 1's) file containing instructions that are directly used by the operating system. *Scripts* are text files that are interpreted at the time they are executed and converted into the bytecode the system needs. This explanation is a bit simplified. Java *applets,* for example, are bytecode files compiled from the text source file, but they are still interpreted at run time by the browser's Java interpreter, rather than directly by the computer's operating system. A good working definition is simply that scripts are text files that you can edit directly, unlike a Java applet or an ActiveX control, which must be compiled before it can be used.

JavaScript and VBScript (Visual Basic Script or Visual Basic Scripting Edition) are the two primary scripting languages used on the Web. Perl (Practical Extraction and Report Language) preceded them as the dominant web scripting language but is no longer as popular, for several reasons. Most importantly, it can only be executed on the server, requiring the data to make a round-trip over the Internet and using the server's processing time. This is because current web browsers do not include Perl interpreters. Both JavaScript and VBScript can run on the client (the user's computer), where the transit time and server overhead are eliminated, or on the server. This is an important consideration—client-side processing is much faster for the user. Perl is also primarily a UNIX programming language. This wasn't a problem in the early development of the Web, as most web servers were running the UNIX operating system. Today, Windows servers and Internet Information Services have an ever increasing share of the market. Development of Perl for Windows has always lagged behind Perl for UNIX, making it much less useful for Windows web servers.

Note   *Microsoft has developed its own variant of JavaScript called JScript. Information about JScript can be found at **http://msdn.microsoft.com/scripting/**. An effort has been made to standardize JavaScript under the auspices of the European Computer Manufacturers Association (ECMA) as ECMAScript. Microsoft claims JScript fully conforms to the ECMAScript standard. The examples in this chapter use JavaScript as generated by FrontPage.*

A short time ago these languages were primarily doing simple tasks, such as validating form input (as you'll see in the next section). Their future is much more glorious—they are the glue that binds Java applets, ActiveX controls, and other types of program and data files into powerful web-based desktop applications.

The Web is bursting with an avalanche of products that will allow you to create webs that are completely interactive. Users are able to see web pages tailored to their needs rather than static presentations of information. Data contained in remote databases or other applications can be accessible, not as raw data the user has to wade through, but as concise presentations that can be manipulated on the user's desktop. In Chapters 18, 19, and 20 you will learn how to bring these elements together in your webs.

At the center of these developments are the scripting languages. They accept information from the user, control the flow of data between objects, and prepare the output of the processing. Until recently, JavaScript had greater support than VBScript, due to the fact that Netscape's browsers have supported only JavaScript, while only Internet Explorer has supported both JavaScript and VBScript. Despite Internet Explorer's dominance in the browser market, JavaScript still has the advantage of being cross-platform, that is, it can be used on both Windows and UNIX (or Linux) servers, so that's where we'll start.

JavaScript

JavaScript was developed by Sun Microsystems, Inc., with involvement from the early stages by Netscape. At the time (late 1995), Netscape was developing a prototype scripting language named LiveScript, but chose to abandon the name and combine their efforts with Sun. Support for JavaScript began with Netscape Navigator 3.0 and Internet Explorer 3.0. VBScript is still only supported by Internet Explorer.

The best way to understand JavaScript is to look at some code. FrontPage makes this easy to do, as it will generate either JavaScript or VBScript for you. In the next section you will use FrontPage to generate a JavaScript script that will validate a form.

| Note | *JavaScript and VBScript are the subjects of entire books.* JavaScript Annotated Archives *by Jeff Frentzen and Henry Sobotka (Osborne/McGraw-Hill) and* JavaScript: The Definitive Guide *by David Flanagan (O'Reilly & Associates) are excellent choices for more JavaScript information.* |

Form Validation with JavaScript

Before browsers supported JavaScript, *form validation*, the process of checking the data in each field of a form to be sure it is the correct type, was done on the server using a language such as Perl. This was done through the common gateway interface (CGI). You may be familiar with the term *CGI script* to describe this type of programming. This had the disadvantage of requiring a round-trip over the Internet and of using the server's processing time. With client-side form validation, the process is speeded up because the work is done on the user's computer, rather than on the server.

With FrontPage you use the Form and Field Properties dialog boxes to define the criteria for validation, and the script is created for you—you don't need to know a thing about either scripting language. These steps will take you through the process:

1. In FrontPage, in the New Page Or Web task pane, select One Page Web.

2. In the Web Site Templates dialog box, select One Page Web, name it **Scripting**, and click OK.

3. Open the home page (Default.htm) in Page view.

4. At the top of the page, type **Form Validation** and format it as Heading 1.

5. Move the cursor to the next line and click Text Box on the Form toolbar.

> **Tip**   *You can make the Form menu a floating toolbar by dragging it from the Insert menu. Open the Insert menu, point on Form, and then point on the bar at the top of the Form menu and drag it.*

6. Press HOME to move the cursor to the beginning of the line and type **Enter some text:** (leave a space after the colon). Format the text as Formatted.

7. Press the right arrow one or more times to move the cursor to the end of the text box and before the Submit and Reset buttons. Press SHIFT+ENTER.

8. Click Text Box on the Form toolbar once more and then press HOME.

9. Type **Enter a number:** (leaving two spaces after the colon), press the right arrow, and then press SHIFT+ENTER.

10. Type **Select an option:**, click Option Button on the Form toolbar, type **Option 1**, press SPACE, click Option Button again, type **Option 2**, and then press SHIFT+ENTER.

11. Open the Page Properties dialog box and change the title of the page to **Form Validation**. Click OK and then save your work. Your page should look similar to Figure 15-1.

12. Right-click the first option button and select Form Field Properties. In the Option Button Properties dialog box click Not Selected for the Initial State, then click OK.

Next you will set the form validation criteria, which generates the validation script. First check which scripting language is set as the default.

13. Open the Tools menu and select Web Settings.

14. In the Web Settings dialog box, click the Advanced tab. JavaScript should be displayed in the Default Scripting Language Client drop-down menu, as shown in Figure 15-2. (VBScript and None are the other choices.) All the pages in your web use the default scripting language selected here.

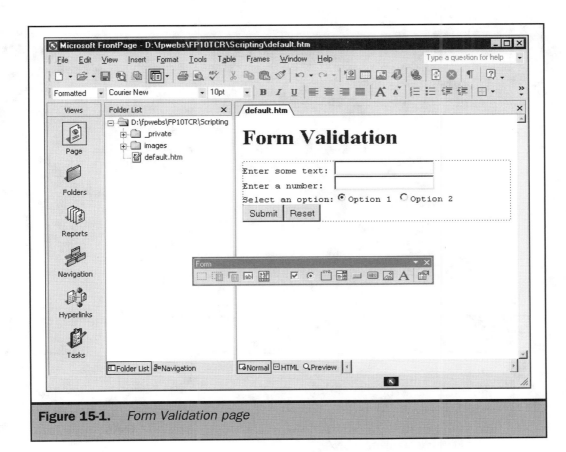

Figure 15-1.   *Form Validation page*

Note *You can run one scripting language on the client (the browser) and another on the server itself. Since only Internet Explorer supports VBScript, JavaScript is the default for client-side scripting. Microsoft's Internet Information Services support both scripting languages, so you can choose either for server-side scripting.*

15. Click OK and then right-click the first one-line text box in the form. Select Form Field Properties from the context menu.

16. In the Text Box Properties dialog box, click Validate. In the Text Box Validation dialog box, select Text from the Data Type drop-down menu, and then click the Letters check box.

17. In the Display Name text box, type **Text Field**. This is the name for the field that will be used in the validation error messages. Click OK twice.

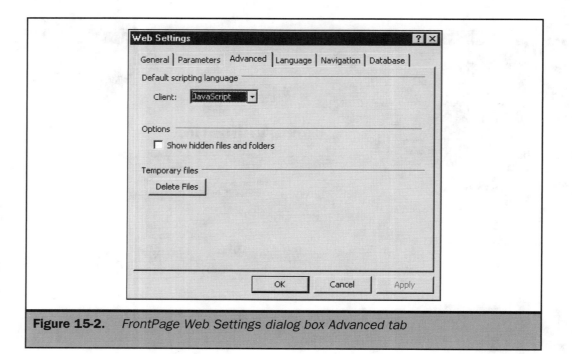

Figure 15-2. *FrontPage Web Settings dialog box Advanced tab*

18. Right-click the second one-line text box, select Form Field Properties from the context menu, and then click Validate.

19. Select Integer from the Data Type drop-down menu and type **Numeric Field** in the Display Name text box.

20. Under Data Value, select the Field Must Be check box and type **5** in the Value text box.

21. Select the And Must Be check box and type **10** in the Value text box. Your Text Box Validation dialog box should look like Figure 15-3. Click OK twice.

22. Right-click the first option button, select Form Field Properties, and then click Validate.

23. In the Option Button Validation dialog box, select Data Required, type **Option Button** in the Display Name text box, click OK twice, and save your page.

24. Open the page in your browser, type **11** in the Enter A Number text box, and click Submit. You should see an error message similar to this:

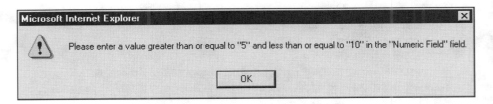

25. Click OK and then select Source from the View menu in Internet Explorer or Document Source from the View menu in Netscape Navigator. At the beginning of the HTML listing, you will see the JavaScript script that generated the error message. The JavaScript portion of the file is shown in Listing 15-1.

Note *Some of the characters may appear as small boxes in the source code listing. This is due to the character set supported by the text viewer displaying the code. If the supported character set doesn't include a character, it is replaced by a small box in the display. This doesn't affect the functionality of the script.*

Figure 15-3.   *Text Box Validation dialog box*

WORKING BEHIND THE SCENES

Listing 15-1
Java Script
Form
Validation

```
<script Language="JavaScript"><!--
function FrontPage_Form1_Validator(theForm)
{
  var checkOK = "ABCDEFGHIJKLMNOPQRSTUVWXYZabcdefghijklmnopqr
    stuvwxyzƒŠŒ Zšœ zŸÀÁÂÃÄÅÆÇÈÉÊËÌÍÎÏÐÑÒÓÔÕÖØÙÚÛÜÝÞßàáâãäåæçèé
    êëìíîïðñòóôõöøùúûüýþÿ";
  var checkStr = theForm.T1.value;
  var allValid = true;
  var validGroups = true;
  for (i = 0;  i < checkStr.length;  i++)
  {
    ch = checkStr.charAt(i);
    for (j = 0;  j < checkOK.length;  j++)
      if (ch == checkOK.charAt(j))
        break;
    if (j == checkOK.length)
    {
      allValid = false;
      break;
    }
  }
  if (!allValid)
  {
    alert("Please enter only letter characters in the \"Text
      Field\" field.");
    theForm.T1.focus();
    return (false);
  }
  var checkOK = "0123456789-,";
  var checkStr = theForm.T2.value;
  var allValid = true;
  var validGroups = true;
  var decPoints = 0;
  var allNum = "";
  for (i = 0;  i < checkStr.length;  i++)
  {
    ch = checkStr.charAt(i);
    for (j = 0;  j < checkOK.length;  j++)
      if (ch == checkOK.charAt(j))
        break;
    if (j == checkOK.length)
    {
```

```
        allValid = false;
        break;
    }
    if (ch != ",")
      allNum += ch;
}
if (!allValid)
{
  alert("Please enter only digit characters in the
    \"Numeric Field\" field.");
  theForm.T2.focus();
  return (false);
}
var chkVal = allNum;
var prsVal = parseInt(allNum);
if (chkVal != "" && !(prsVal >= "5" && prsVal <= "10"))
{
  alert("Please enter a value greater than or equal to
    \"5\" and less than or equal to \"10\" in the \"Numeric
    Field\" field.");
  theForm.T2.focus();
  return (false);
}
var radioSelected = false;
for (i = 0;  i < theForm.R1.length;  i++)
{
  if (theForm.R1[i].checked)
      radioSelected = true;
}
if (!radioSelected)
{
  alert("Please select one of the \"Option Button\"
    options.");
  return (false);
}
  return (true);
}
//--></script>
```

If you've ever done any programming, the JavaScript script in Listing 15-1 will look familiar to you. If you haven't, it may look very strange. The best way to understand what it does is to step through the script and look at each section, as follows.

The JavaScript Form Validation Script

Don't worry if the JavaScript code looks indecipherable. The function of each section of a program is understandable once you begin to understand the type of shorthand it's written in. In this section you will look at each piece of the code and see what it does and how it fits in with the other pieces to make a complete script. In the rest of this section the script has been dissected to explain the purpose of each section of code. In doing so, the formatting has been changed somewhat. Listing 15-1 contains the correct syntax for the script.

Note *Programming, like writing in any language, has a lot of room for style, and programmers tend to develop their own styles. There are rules for good programming, such as adding comments to explain each section, that make code easily understood. The JavaScript code in this section was generated by FrontPage using the rules defined by the team that programmed this feature of FrontPage. This is not the only way the script could have been written, but it is a good example of JavaScript scripting.*

```
<script Language="JavaScript"><!--
```

The script begins by declaring the programming language using the <SCRIPT> tag. The entire body of the script is within the opening and closing <SCRIPT> tags. If the browser doesn't support the scripting language, then the entire script is ignored. The Language property is required to inform the browser which language is being used (either JavaScript or VBScript). There is also an optional property, SRC, which identifies the location of the script (as a URL) if it's not included on the HTML page. This allows you to create a library of scripts that can be used by many web pages without requiring you to include the script on each page. There is also a <NOSCRIPT> tag that is used to define the HTML that will be displayed if the script isn't supported. It is placed after the script in the HTML document.

Note *You will notice a slight shift in terminology used to describe the components of scripting languages as compared to pure HTML. In Chapter 12 we used the terms "tags" and "attributes" to describe the basic HTML commands and their modifiers. Scripting languages approach the terminology of more conventional programming languages, so we use a hybrid set of terms. "Tag" is still used to describe a basic scripting language command, but the term "property" is used to describe how a certain tag can be modified (analogous to "attribute" in pure HTML-speak).*

After the <SCRIPT> tag is an opening HTML comment tag (<!--) matched by the closing comment tag (-->) at the end of the script. Without these tags the entire text of the script would be displayed in browsers that don't support the <SCRIPT> tag. This is a holdover from the old days (pre-version 3 of Netscape's and Microsoft's browsers) and not strictly necessary.

```
function FrontPage_Form1_Validator(theForm)
```

This next line declares the function name and its arguments in the form function *functionName* (*arguments*). In this case the functionName is FrontPage_Form1_Validator, and the single argument is theForm. A *function* is a series of JavaScript statements that performs a task and optionally returns a value. The function statements are enclosed within the { and } brackets. An *argument* is a value that is passed to the function. What this value can be will depend on the purpose of the function. For example, if the purpose of the function was to multiply two numbers, then the two numbers would be the arguments passed to the function. Since the arguments are represented by variables (which can be considered a container for the value), they could be passed from the web page through a form as variables, which is what is being done in this script. The argument theForm refers to the form that is calling the function. This is not the name of the form itself—that is passed with the values you enter in the form text boxes and then submit. The script intercepts the values before the form handler and checks them against the rules established by the function. If they meet the criteria, they are passed on to the form handler; if not, then an error message is generated, as you saw earlier, and the form handler never receives the data. Since the form handler will be on the server, this prevents unnecessary traffic and server time.

Note *Functions cannot be nested, that is, a function cannot be defined inside another function.*

```
{ var checkOK = "ABCDEF...";
   var checkStr = theForm.T1.value;
   var allValid = true;
```

These three lines define the variables that are used by the function to validate the first form field in the format var *variableName* = *variableValue*. Var is the JavaScript keyword followed by the variable name and the value of the variable. The first variable, checkOK, is a text string consisting of all the acceptable characters that can be returned by the first form field. (The list has been shortened here.) The second, checkStr, is the value entered in the first text box, T1. T1 is the default name given to the form field when you created it in FrontPage. If you had given the field a different name, that name would be used in defining the variable. This variable illustrates a JavaScript naming convention—defining an object as a hierarchical string with each level of the hierarchy separated by a period. In this case the hierarchy is the form itself, the field in the form, and the value contained in the field. Each level of the hierarchy is a property of the preceding level, so, in this example, T1 is a property of theForm, which is a variable containing the name of the form that called the function.

This is one method by which data is passed between the HTML page and the script. To the script, the form is an object and so can have properties that can be processed.

JavaScript can also recognize events, such as a mouse click or placing the mouse pointer over a defined area, and execute a function based on the event. The third variable, `allValid`, is a flag that will be used later in the script to determine if the data will be passed to the form handler. It is defined as TRUE, meaning that the script is interpreting the data entered in the first text box as valid. If the data fails to meet the criteria for the field, the value of the variable will be changed to FALSE, which will trigger the error message.

```
for (i = 0;  i < checkStr.length;  i++)
  { ch = checkStr.charAt(i);
    for (j = 0;  j < checkOK.length;  j++)
  if (ch == checkOK.charAt(j))
      break;
    if (j == checkOK.length)
    { allValid = false;
      break; }}
```

Before looking at this section of code in detail, the difference between = and == needs to be understood. In JavaScript the equal sign (=) is the assignment operator. That is, it is used to assign a value to a variable. The double equal sign (==) is the equality operator. It compares the values on each side of it and returns TRUE if they are equal and FALSE if they are not.

This section of the script is the part that does most of the work. The first line is a For-Next loop. The variables i and j are counters that are used to determine which character in the text string is being evaluated. What's happening is that the text string entered in the text form field is being *parsed*; that is, the text string is being looked at one character at a time and compared with the legal characters defined in the `checkOK` variable. At each step each counter is incremented by 1 (i++ and j++) until the last character in each string is reached (i < `checkStr.length`; and j < `checkOK.length`;). The variable `checkStr.charAt(i)` holds the character at position i that has been entered in the text box. The variable `checkOK.charAt(j)` holds the character at position j in the string of legal characters. When the first loop is started, the character at position i in the input string is compared with the character at position j in the string of legal characters. For the first iteration, each of these is 0 (zero), since that is the first position as far as the computer is concerned. (If the input string was ten characters long, the computer would count them as zero to nine, not one to ten.)

The first character in the input string is loaded into the variable ch, and ch is compared with the first character in `checkOK`. If the characters don't match (if the character isn't A), j is incremented (j++) and the first character in the input string is compared with the second legal character (B). This continues, with j being incremented each time, until a match is found or the end of the string of legal characters is reached. If a match is found, the loop stops (`break;`) and i is incremented so that the next character in the input string can be checked. Then the process starts over, with j being reset to zero (j = 0;) so that the entire string of legal characters will be checked.

If no match is found, meaning the character entered in the form field is invalid, the process stops and the value of the variable allValid is changed to FALSE. This happens if the end of the string of legal characters is reached without finding a match (j == checkOK.length). If the character is determined to be invalid, the steps shown next are executed.

```
if (!allValid)
  { alert("Please enter only letter characters in the \"Text
    Field\" field.");
theForm.T1.focus();
return (false);}
```

The first line in the preceding code tests the value of the variable allValid. This line can be read as "If allValid is NOT TRUE, then…" (the exclamation mark is the notation for the logical NOT operator). As you saw in the previous code, allValid is defined as TRUE at the beginning of the script, and the value is changed only if an illegal character is encountered. The "then" is defined by the next line, which causes an alert message box to be displayed, as you saw earlier when you entered the number **11** in the numeric text box and clicked Submit. This is a built-in function of JavaScript, so all you have to do is define the text that will appear in the alert ("Please enter only letter..."). In the alert text, the backslash (\) is an *escape* character. That is, the code needs to understand that the quotation mark (") following the backslash should be interpreted as a character to be displayed, rather than closing the string that is being defined. Text strings must be enclosed within quotes so a method is needed to include quotes as characters within the text string.

The next line contains a very useful JavaScript function, the focus() method, written in the form *object*.focus(). What this does is make the form field where the error occurred in the selected object active (in this case, the cursor is placed in the text box). Once you click OK in the alert message box, your browser will return you to the first form field so you can fix the error. The form field (theForm.T1) is the object. Finally, the script returns the value FALSE (return (false);). This value can be used by the statement that called the function, or it can be ignored. In this case it will prevent the data from being sent to the form handler.

If all the characters inputted pass the test, then the first loop ends when the last character in the checkStr variable has been checked. The script then begins the test for the data entered in the second text box.

```
var checkOK = "0123456789-,";
var checkStr = theForm.T2.value;
var allValid = true;
```

```
var decPoints = 0;
var allNum = "";
```

Like the test for the first form field, this one also begins by defining the variables. There are two additional variables defined in this test, decPoints and allNum. decPoints is a flag that indicates that decimal points are not allowed in the input. It should be noted that this variable isn't actually used after it's defined. Since the validation rule allows only integers (a whole number, that is, a number without a fraction) the decimal point is an illegal character. This is actually dealt with in the variable checkOK, which doesn't define the decimal point as a legal character. This redundancy is a result of the method FrontPage uses to generate the JavaScript code and does no harm. The other variable, allNum, is defined as an empty string. Its function will be explained in the next section of code, where similar loops and tests are started with the new variables.

```
for (i = 0; i < checkStr.length;  i++)
  { ch = checkStr.charAt(i);
    for (j = 0;  j < checkOK.length;  j++)
      if (ch == checkOK.charAt(j))
         break;
    if (j == checkOK.length)
    { allValid = false;
      break; }
    if (ch != ",")
      allNum += ch;
  }
if (!allValid)
{
   alert("Please enter only digit characters in the
      \"Numeric Field\" field.");
   theForm.T2.focus();
   return (false);
}
```

There's one significant difference between this section of code and the validation for the text string. This begins with the line if (ch != ","). This line and the next (allNum += ch;) are saying "If the valid character is NOT a comma (it's a valid number) then add it to the variable allNum." The += operator means "place the value on the right side of the expression in the variable on the left." This is known as *concatenation*. This is not an addition operation; it simply places the character on the right side of the expression in the rightmost position of the string. For example, if allNum equals 12 and ch is 3, the resulting string is 123. It's important to realize that, at this point, the code is treating the values as characters, not numbers. The purpose of these two lines is to create a variable that can be treated as a number by the next section of code, which determines if the number entered is within the range specified.

```
var chkVal = allNum;
  var prsVal = parseInt(allNum);
  if (chkVal != "" && !(prsVal >= "5" && prsVal <= "10"))
  { alert("Please enter a value greater than or equal to
      \"5\" and less than or equal to \"10\" in the \"Numeric
      Field\" field.");
    theForm.T2.focus();
    return (false);
  }
```

This validation check differs from the previous two in that there is a single value to be checked, rather than parsing a string of multiple characters. The work in this section of code is done by the third line. After the second line converts the character string to an integer (var prsVal = parseInt (allNum) ;), three checks are performed: is it a null value (was a value entered), is it equal to or greater than five, and is it equal to or less than ten? The second line is necessary because the program can interpret a number in two ways: as a text string and as an actual number. This line converts the text to a number so that it can be used for the tests that follow. The != operator is the logical NOT EQUAL, so that the expression could be read as "is the value in the form field NOT EQUAL to null." The && operator is the logical AND. The third line could be read as "if the number is NOT equal to null AND it's not equal to or greater than five AND it's not equal to or less than ten, then display the alert error message." Focus would then be returned to the second form field box.

The next section of code validates the option buttons, one of which must be selected.

```
var radioSelected = false;
  for (i = 0;  i < theForm.R1.length;  i++)
  {
    if (theForm.R1[i].checked)
        radioSelected = true;
  }
  if (!radioSelected)
  {
    alert("Please select one of the \"Option Button\"
      options.");
    return (false);
  }
```

Unlike the first two validation tests, this begins by defining the status variable (radioSelected) as FALSE. This actually simplifies the remaining code since the validation rule is that one of the option buttons must be selected. This routine looks at every option button in the form field, and it needs to be understood that the form field is comprised of all the option buttons. In other words, option buttons are very similar to the choices in a drop-down list. The list itself is the form field, and the choices in the list are the possible values of that form field, as each option button is a possible value and all the option buttons together comprise the form field.

If the status were assumed to be TRUE, the value of radioSelected would have to be changed if an option button wasn't selected. This means that if the first option button were selected then the loop would have to break since checking the second option button would change radioSelected to FALSE. This obviously can be done, but it would add a few lines of code to the routine. Simplicity can be a good thing in writing code, which this example illustrates. In the first two validation tests it was easier (the code was less convoluted) to assume the status was TRUE until an illegal character was encountered. In checking the option buttons the opposite creates less convoluted code.

```
return (true);
}
//--></script>
```

These last two lines clean up and end the script. If all the values have passed all the tests, the value TRUE is returned, and the data is sent to the form handler. The last line contains three elements: the // is the JavaScript Comment tag, which is required at the end of the JavaScript script; the --> is the HTML closing comment tag; and finally the HTML </SCRIPT> tag ends the script.

Once a script has been created, there also has to be a method for calling the script. For the form validation script, the call is contained in the <FORM> HTML tag. This next line of code shows how the JavaScript validation script is called by the form:

```
<form method="POST" name="FrontPage_Form1"
onsubmit="return FrontPage_Form1_Validator(this)" … >
```

The HTML form code should look reasonably familiar to you (Chapter 12 contains an explanation of the HTML used for forms). The JavaScript validation script is called with the JavaScript command onsubmit, like this: onsubmit="return FrontPage_Form1_Validator(this)".

The value of the onsubmit attribute is the name of the JavaScript function, defined at the top of the JavaScript script. The argument being passed to the script (in the parentheses at the end of the function name) is this, which indicates the active form. In this manner, it's possible for multiple JavaScript forms on a single page to use the same validation script, provided the field names are identical.

Tip	*JavaScript is case-sensitive, so form and field names must be exact, including upper- and lowercase letters, in both the form and the script itself.*

You'll be using the Form Validation page again with VBScript, so leave your current FrontPage and browser windows open. You can close Notepad or your text viewer.

VBScript

VBScript is similar to JavaScript. It is based on Microsoft's Visual Basic programming language, which gives Visual Basic programmers a bit of a head start. The problem with VBScript is lack of support among browsers. Currently only Microsoft's Internet Explorer includes support for VBScript, and it's unlikely that Netscape will add support anytime soon, so, even though Internet Explorer is currently the dominant browser, your client-side VBScript scripts will have a limited audience. VBScript could be your first choice if you are planning an intranet and you can specify Internet Explorer as the browser everyone must use. Otherwise it's hard to see why you shouldn't simply go with JavaScript for client-side scripting. There are enough differences in the languages to make learning both of them a burden.

For server-side scripting, VBScript offers advantages if your web server is Windows server based. Visual Basic is more tightly integrated with Windows than Java and so could be a better choice for more advanced programming. That statement will bring howls from Java programmers, with good reason, as it ignores the fact that there are many criteria that should go into choosing a programming language. For the purpose of this chapter, which is an introduction to scripting languages, since VBScript is a subset of Visual Basic and VBScript is easier for the novice to understand, the learning curve is reduced. If you're using an operating system other than a Windows server, Java and JavaScript should be your choice for server-side programming, since Visual Basic is not supported by other operating systems. (You can also use other languages like C++, but those languages are beyond the scope of this book.) As you can see, there are several factors that must be considered in choosing a scripting language, and the reality is that you need to have a basic knowledge of both.

You can see some of the differences in the two languages by changing the scripting language in the Advanced tab on the Web Settings dialog box. Do that now with these instructions:

1. In FrontPage, open the Tools menu and select Web Settings.

2. In the Web Settings dialog box, click the Advanced tab and select VBScript from the Default Scripting Languages Client drop-down menu. Click Apply. The FrontPage dialog box shown next will be displayed.

WORKING BEHIND
THE SCENES

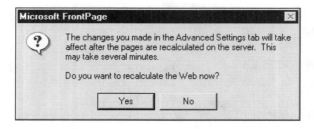

3. Click Yes. After the Scripting web is recalculated, click OK (the OK button will be inactive until the recalculation is done).

4. Load the Form Validation page in your web browser, and select Source or Page Source from the View menu, depending on which browser you are using.

Listing 15-2 shows the same form validation script as Listing 15-1, except that it is now written in VBScript. The flow of the script is pretty much the same, but the syntax has changed. You should still be able to follow what the script is doing.

Listing 15-2
VBScript
Form
Validation

```
<script Language="VBScript"><!--
function FrontPage_Form1_onsubmit()
  Set theForm = document.FrontPage_Form1
  checkOK = "ABCDEFGHIJKLMNOPQRSTUVWXYZabcdefghijklmnopqrstuv
    wxyzƒŠŒ šœ ŸÀÁÂÃÄÅÆÇÈÉÊËÌÍÎÏÐÑÒÓÔÕÖØÙÚÛÜÝÞßàáâãäåæçèéêëìí
    îïðñòóôõöøùúûüýþÿ"
  checkStr = theForm.T1.value
  allValid = True
  validGroups = True
  For i = 1 to len(checkStr)
    ch = Mid(checkStr, i, 1)
    If (InStr(checkOK, ch) = 0) Then
        allValid = False
        Exit For
    End If
  Next
  If (Not allValid) Then
    MsgBox "Please enter only letter characters in the ""Text
      Field"" field.", 0, "Validation Error"
    theForm.T1.focus()
    FrontPage_Form1_onsubmit = False
    Exit Function
  End If
  checkOK = "0123456789-,"
```

```
checkStr = theForm.T2.value
allValid = True
validGroups = True
decPoints = 0
allNum = ""
For i = 1 to len(checkStr)
  ch = Mid(checkStr, i, 1)
  If (InStr(checkOK, ch) = 0) Then
      allValid = False
      Exit For
  End If
  If (ch <> ",") Then
    allNum = allNum & ch
  End If
Next
If (Not allValid) Then
  MsgBox "Please enter only digit characters in the
    ""Numeric Field"" field.", 0, "Validation Error"
  theForm.T2.focus()
  FrontPage_Form1_onsubmit = False
  Exit Function
End If
If ((checkstr <> "" And Not IsNumeric(allNum)) Or
    (decPoints > 1) Or Not validGroups) Then
  MsgBox "Please enter a valid number in the ""T2""
    field.", 0, "Validation Error"
  theForm.T2.focus()
  FrontPage_Form1_onsubmit = False
  Exit Function
End If
prsVal = allNum
If ((prsVal <> "") And (Not (prsVal >= 5 And
    prsVal <= 10))) Then
  MsgBox "Please enter a value greater than or equal to
    ""5"" and less than or equal to ""10"" in the ""Numeric
    Field"" field.", 0, "Validation Error"
  theForm.T2.focus()
  FrontPage_Form1_onsubmit = False
  Exit Function
End If
```

```
radioSelected = False
For i = 0 to theForm.R1.length - 1
  If (theForm.R1.item(i).checked) Then
      radioSelected = True
  End If
Next
If (Not radioSelected) Then
  MsgBox "Please select one of the ""Option Button""
    options.", 0, "Validation Error"
  FrontPage_Form1_onsubmit = False
  Exit Function
End If
FrontPage_Form1_onsubmit = True
End Function
--></script>
```

Some of the differences in the languages can be seen in how For-Next loops are constructed. In the JavaScript validation the syntax is

```
for (i = 0;  i < checkStr.length;  i++)
```

With VBScript the syntax is

```
For i = 1 to len(checkStr)
```

The first thing to notice is that VBScript starts counting at one (1) while JavaScript starts with zero (0). For nonprogrammers, starting at one may make sense, but most programming languages accept zero as the first number and the place where you start counting. If you use both JavaScript and VBScript this can be a point of confusion. Another point of difference is that with VBScript it is assumed that the loop increments by one in each iteration, while JavaScript explicitly defines that value. These values can be specified in VBScript; it just isn't necessary if the default values are used. As you can also see, VBScript is easier to read if you don't know what the JavaScript operators mean (such as i++). On the other hand, JavaScript is more concise, which many programmers like. With JavaScript, for example, it is not necessary to explicitly close each If-Then statement or For-Next loop. This is handled by the structure of the code, while VBScript has End If and Next statements. Another example of the differences is JavaScript's use of single characters, such as the exclamation mark (!) as the logical NOT operator, while VBScript tends to use words, or at least parts of words (such as len for length).

Despite the differences, the overall structure and flow of both examples is very similar. Once the syntax differences are understood you can work in either language without much difficulty.

The Microsoft Script Editor

The examples in the previous sections used scripts created with the Text Field Validation dialog box and generated by the FrontPage Server Extensions. This is a good method if all you want the script to do is validate a form. Both languages are much more useful than that, as you will see in the following chapters.

There are two methods you can use to add scripts to your webs. The first is to use FrontPage to generate the script, as you did in the previous sections. The advantages of this method are that the script can be easily modified from within FrontPage, and you do not need to be a proficient JavaScript or VBScript programmer to create scripts. The second method is to create the script manually using either the Script Editor, shown in Figure 15-4, or by writing the script using the HTML tab of FrontPage's Page view. The advantage with this method is that the page will use slightly less server resources when it is called, as the WebBot code doesn't need to be interpreted.

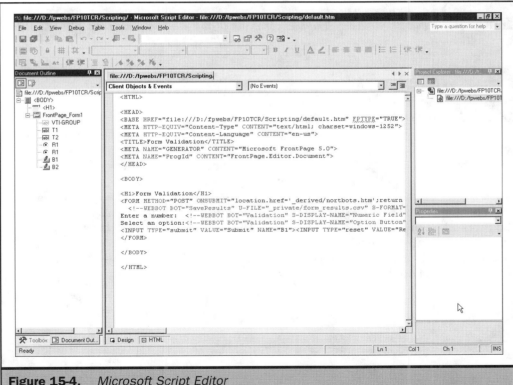

Figure 15-4. *Microsoft Script Editor*

Which method you use will depend on how comfortable you are with writing scripts manually and how often you expect the code to be modified. You can combine the benefits of each method by using FrontPage to generate the script, opening it using your browser's View | Source option, and then copying and pasting it into your page, overwriting the FrontPage WebBot code. The script will no longer be editable from within FrontPage (except by using the HTML tab in Page view), but it will use slightly less server resources.

The Script Editor allows you to edit HTML and Active Server Pages (ASP) files, much like the FrontPage Page view. (Active Server Pages are the subject of the next two chapters.) In this section, only the script editing functions of the Script Editor will be covered. To see how the Script Editor works, follow these steps:

1. With your Form Validation page still open in Page view, open the Script Editor by opening the Tools menu, pointing on Macro, and then clicking Microsoft Script Editor.

The Script Editor may not be installed on your system. In that case, a dialog box will be displayed stating that the Script Editor is not installed and asking if you want to install it now. Click Yes.

In Figure 15-4, the leftmost pane of the Script Editor displays the Script Outline window. (If the Script Outline isn't displayed, click the Document Outline tab at the bottom of the window, then the Script Outline button at the top of the pane.) The Script Outline window shows the objects and scripts on a page. This pane can also display the HTML Outline window by selecting the HTML Outline button at the top of the window or the Toolbox by selecting the appropriate tab at the bottom of the window.

The center pane is the Text or Code Editing window. When the Source tab is selected, this displays the source code of your page. This view is similar to FrontPage when the HTML tab is selected in Page view. The upper-right pane is the Project Explorer window. This window displays the outline of the current project. Below it is the Properties window where the available properties and values of the selected object are displayed and can be edited.

In the Client Objects & Events folder in the Script Outline window, shown in detail here, each object on the page is listed.

2. In the Script Outline window, click the plus sign (+) to the left of the FrontPage_Form1 object to expand the tree. This displays a list of the available events for the object. Expanding the tree for an object will display a list of events available for that object.

Note   *The Script Editor uses the default scripting language selected within FrontPage. In this case, that is VBScript. The events listed in the expanded tree are VBScript events. If JavaScript were set as the default scripting language, the available JavaScript events would be listed.*

3. If you double-click an event, the basic scripting code for the event is inserted into your page. Scripts are usually placed just before the closing </HEAD> tag. Double-click onsubmit in the event list for the FrontPage_Form1 object. The following code will be inserted in the page:

```
<SCRIPT ID=clientEventHandlersVBS LANGUAGE=vbscript>
<!--
Sub FrontPage_Form1_onsubmit
End Sub
-->
</SCRIPT>
```

This is the basic code for the event handler. It does not define the action to be taken when the event occurs; it only creates the skeleton code for your subroutine. The name of the VBScript function is FrontPage_Form1_onsubmit. You must write the VBScript script that defines the action to be executed when the form is submitted. This code goes between the VBScript Sub (after the name of the function) and End Sub statements.

WORKING BEHIND
THE SCENES

4. Open the Edit menu and choose Undo or press CTRL+Z to remove the onsubmit code from your page. In the Code Editing window you can see that the VBScript validation script is not present (which you saw using your browser's View | Source option). What is on the page is the FrontPage WebBot code that the FrontPage Server Extensions use to generate the validation script when the page is requested.

5. Click the Form tag in the Code Editing window. The Properties window (in the lower-right corner of the Script Editor) will display the properties and their values for the form, as shown next.

You can edit any of the properties using the Properties window. For the Action property (shown selected in the preceding illustration), clicking the small box with the ellipsis (...) displays the Open dialog box so that you can select a file for the output of the form.

6. Select Method in the Properties window. A downward-pointing arrow appears in the value cell for the Method property. This opens a drop-down menu displaying the two choices for Method, either Post or Get.

7. Select Name in the Property window. Since this property is a user-defined value, there are no choices or dialog boxes presented. You simply enter the name of the form in the value cell for the property.

8. Close the Script Editor without saving any changes to your page.

To make the most of the Script Editor requires an advanced knowledge of the selected scripting language. If you do choose to write your own scripts, rather than having them generated by FrontPage, you will find it a valuable tool. For example, the Script Editor also contains extremely useful script debugging tools. You can insert *breakpoints* in your script that stop the execution of the script so that you can identify where errors are occurring. You can also view the values of your variables during execution. These features make debugging a script much easier.

Each of the technologies covered in this chapter could easily fill a book of its own, and, in fact, each does. The purpose here is to give you an overview of them so that you can make an informed decision about which technologies you want to add to your own webs. At a minimum, a working knowledge of JavaScript will be beneficial to web designers. If you plan to use server-side scripting on Windows NT and 2000 servers, VBScript is also a must. If you want your webs to stand out in the crowd, these tools are part of your future.

WORKING BEHIND
THE SCENES

Chapter 16

Active Server Pages

T he Web is no longer just a collection of static, unchanging web pages. It has become a truly interactive medium, with input from users controlling the information that is displayed in their browser. Scripting languages were the first step in bringing this shift about, and Active Server Pages (ASP) has taken the concept to the next level.

Active Server Pages is a server-side scripting environment that includes built-in objects and components. These objects and components enable a degree of interactivity that was extremely difficult, if not impossible, to achieve previously. Using ASP effectively requires more hands-on programming than other features of FrontPage, but, as you will see in this and the following chapters, there are many benefits to using this technology to bring true interactivity to your webs.

Note   *ASP is not the last step in the evolution of an interactive web environment—ASP.NET (formerly called ASP+), part of Microsoft's new .NET framework (**http://msdn.microsoft.com/net/**) and the subject of Chapter 17, offers even more features and functionality. As this is being written, ASP.NET is still in beta. ASP and ASP.NET can coexist on your web server, though there are some issues you should be aware of that will be covered in Chapter 17. ASP.NET does not make ASP totally obsolete. For example, ASP.NET is designed to use compiled languages such as Visual Basic and C# (pronounced "c sharp," Microsoft's latest variant of the C programming language) as well as scripting languages such as VBScript, while ASP is designed primarily to use scripting languages. This can make it easier to get started using ASP rather than ASP.NET. ASP can also be used with operating systems other than Windows (such as UNIX and Linux) with Chili!ASP, an ASP clone available from Chili!Soft, Inc. (**http://www.versicom.com**), while ASP.NET is strictly a Windows technology.*

Active Server Pages Overview

ASP is a combination of *objects*, that is, programming code and data that are treated as a single element, and *components*, programs that perform common tasks. ASP components are actually ActiveX components (see Chapter 20). You can also create your own ActiveX components to use in your webs with ASP, or acquire them from other vendors. Using objects and components greatly simplifies normally complex tasks. Active Server Pages files have an .ASP file extension, rather than .HTM or .HTML.

Tip   *Extensive ASP documentation can be installed with IIS. The functionality possible with ASP means that there is a certain amount of complexity that goes with it. If you intend to use ASP to any extent, you should become very familiar with the documentation. The examples in this chapter tend to use the minimum amount of code required to demonstrate the concepts and don't always follow the best rules of programming. For example, variables in the VBScript examples are not declared using the VBScript DIM statement, which should be used in the real world.*

A scripting language, such as VBScript or JavaScript, holds all the pieces together and controls the program flow of the web page. These scripts are normally executed on the server, though you can use a combination of client-side and server-side scripting on a web page. Typically, you would use server-side scripting to create the web page and client-side scripting for tasks such as form validation, as you saw in the previous chapter.

Note *Although either VBScript or JavaScript can be used as the primary scripting language, the examples in this chapter use VBScript as the default language. In the case of server-side scripting, VBScript offers the advantage of being tightly integrated into the Windows 2000 and IIS operating environment. This is the default web server environment assumed in this book. Also, Visual Basic is one of the primary languages for creating ActiveX components. Since VBScript is a subset of Visual Basic, staying within the Visual Basic family reduces your learning curve. JavaScript is still the preferred choice for client-side scripting, since only Microsoft's browsers support VBScript.*

An ASP application is the root directory of the web application and all the files and subdirectories in the root directory. In addition, the root directory must be a virtual directory (see Chapter 5 for an explanation of virtual directories). By default, FrontPage will create most of the required virtual directories and set the proper permissions when you create a new FrontPage web. There are still a few settings that will have to be made manually, but most of the work is done for you.

Note *When talking about permissions on Windows 2000–based web servers, there are two sets that must be considered. First, Windows 2000 itself has permissions that are applied to the directories and files. Second, the web server software also has permissions that must be set. Setting Windows 2000 permissions is beyond the scope of this book and is itself the subject of entire books. Two excellent references are Tom Sheldon's* Windows NT Security Handbook *(1996) and* Microsoft Internet Information Server 4: The Complete Reference *(1998), both published by Osborne/McGraw-Hill. This chapter will focus on configuring only the IIS permissions.*

In an ASP web application, any ASP page that is requested must be processed by the ASP library on the server before it is sent back to the requesting browser. In other words, the ASP file must be executed. This is where the "Active Server" part comes in. The ASP library interprets the scripting code and outputs a standard HTML page that is then sent in response to the browser's request. If the root directory of the ASP application is not a virtual directory and the scripts or execute permission isn't set, the ASP web application will not work. In that case your browser will display an HTTP error page, as shown in Figure 16-1.

Note *Since ASP webs require server-side processing, they have to run on a web server. They cannot be disk-based webs.*

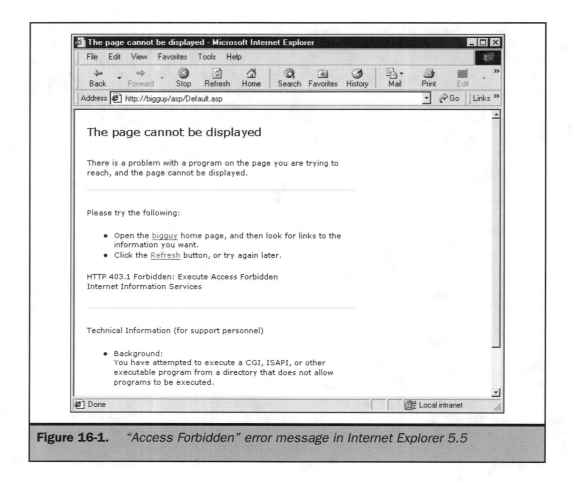

Figure 16-1. *"Access Forbidden" error message in Internet Explorer 5.5*

Before actually creating an ASP web, you need to make sure ASP support is enabled in FrontPage.

1. Open FrontPage if it's not already open, choose Tools | Page Options, and click the Compatibility tab. The Page Options dialog box shown in Figure 16-2 will be displayed.

2. At the bottom of the Page Options dialog box is a list of technologies that FrontPage can support. By default these are all selected, giving the maximum support in FrontPage for current web technologies.

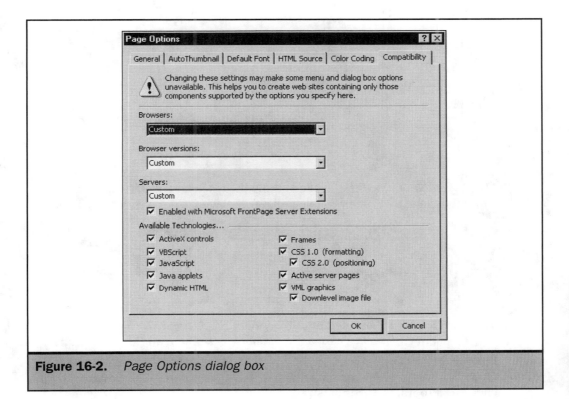

Figure 16-2.   *Page Options dialog box*

3. Check that the Active Server Pages check box is selected; if not, select it. Click OK to close the dialog box.

4. Create a One Page Web and name it asp. The location of the ASP web should be in the default web created with the installation of IIS. This will normally be C:\Inetpub\Wwwroot, and the URL will be http://*computer_name*/. The URL to access this web will be http://*computer_name*/asp/. The default web is a virtual directory and so meets the requirement that the root of an ASP web be a virtual directory.

5. In Folders view, right-click Default.htm and choose Rename.

6. Rename the Default.htm file Default.asp. The dialog box shown here, confirming you want to change the name of your home page, will be displayed. Click Yes.

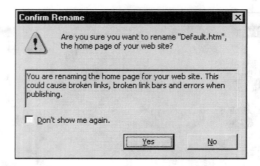

7. Next, a dialog box warning that changing the extension of a filename may cause the file to become unusable will be displayed. Click Yes.

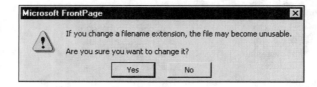

There are two additional settings you should check before actually starting work on your ASP web. These are the default document and the permissions applied to the ASP web.

8. Open the Internet Services Manager by clicking the Start menu button and choosing Programs | Administrative Tools | Internet Services Manager.

9. In the Internet Services Manager, expand the tree for your web server and then expand the tree for the default web. Your Internet Services Manager should look similar to Figure 16-3.

10. Right-click the ASP folder and choose Properties, then click the Documents tab. This displays the default document filenames for the web. If Default.asp isn't displayed, add it by clicking Add, typing **Default.asp** in the Add Default Document dialog box, and clicking OK.

11. Next, click the Directory tab, shown in Figure 16-4. The Read check box should be selected and Scripts Only should be selected for Execute Permissions.

    For a web with only HTML pages, only the Read permission needs to be selected. Since ASP pages contain server-side scripts, the Scripts execute permission also needs to be selected.

12. If you made any changes to the ASP Properties dialog box, click Apply. Click OK to close the dialog box, and then click the Internet Services Manager's Close button.

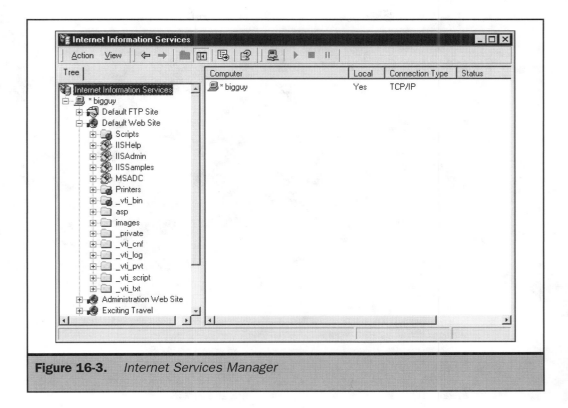

Figure 16-3. *Internet Services Manager*

Now that your web server is properly configured for ASP web applications, you're ready to unleash their interactivity.

ASP Objects

Active Server Pages contains seven built-in objects, described in Table 16-1. These allow you to handle events such as triggering an action to take place the first time a user loads a page from the web, getting information from a user, or setting properties for the user's session.

ASP objects and components can have collections, events, methods, properties, and parameters associated with them. Individual objects and components will have one or more of these, but not all of them. *Collections* are data associated with a particular object. *Events* trigger an action by an object. *Methods* define the action that will be performed by the object. *Properties* are attributes of the object or component. *Parameters* are usually the name of an object that is the target of an action. Each of these will be explained in detail throughout this chapter.

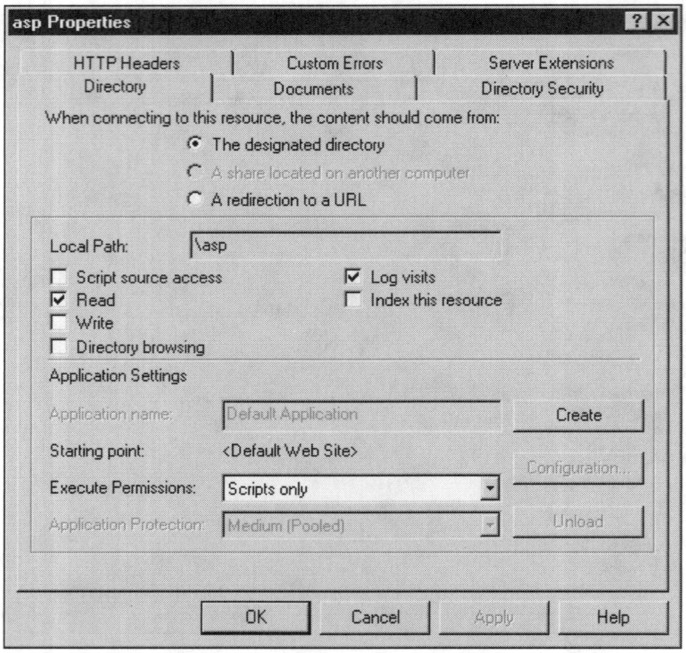

Figure 16-4. ASP Properties dialog box Directory tab

Object	Description
Application	Sets properties or information that is shared by all users accessing the web application.
ASPError	Returns information about any errors generated by the ASP application.
ObjectContext	Commits or aborts a transaction started by a script on an ASP page. The transaction itself is handled by the Microsoft Component Services (formerly Transaction Server).
Request	Handles information passed from the browser to the server.
Response	Sends information from the server to the browser.

Table 16-1. ASP Objects

Object	Description
Server	Provides access to server-side properties and operations.
Session	Sets properties or information for a single user accessing the web application. A session starts when users load the first page from the web and ends when they leave the web or the session time-out value is reached.

Table 16-1.   *ASP Objects* (continued)

In ASP applications you use variables to hold values that are used in the web application. A *variable* is simply a name that serves as a reference to the value assigned to it. For example, you can assign the text string "Hello World" to a variable named "Heading." When you reference the variable Heading in a web page, the text string "Hello World" will be displayed on the web page. Using variables to hold values allows you to set a value used in many places in your web in a single reference. To make a change that affects all the pages in your web, you only have to make a single change to the page where the variable is defined. Variables also allow you to pass values between web pages or between objects. In the following sections you will see how these are applied to ASP objects and components.

Application and Session Objects

In an ASP web application you may want to set values that apply either to every user or to a single user. These values are set by use of the Application and Session objects. The Application object sets properties or information that is shared by all users of a web application. These are any *global* values, or variables you want to set for the entire web application, and are said to have *application scope*. Session objects set *local* values, or variables restricted to a single user, and are said to have *session scope*.

Note   *Session state is maintained only for browsers that support cookies; if cookies are not supported, a new session starts every time the user loads a page in the web. See the section "The Cookies Collection" for more information about cookies.*

Application objects are set by use of the Global.asa file, an optional text file that is placed in the root directory of the web application. Session objects can be set in the Global.asa file or on an ASP web page. The next step in building your ASP web application is to create a Global.asa file for it.

The .ASA extension used by the Global.asa file stands for "Active Server Application."

The Global.asa File

The Global.asa file is unique to ASP web applications. It is optional, but you cannot use Application objects without it. The Global.asa file is not visible to users; it is only used to store Application and Session objects. The file must be named Global.asa; there can be only a single Global.asa file for an ASP web application; it must be in the root directory of the web application; and the root directory must be a virtual directory with Scripts permission. The Global.asa is a text file, and FrontPage uses Notepad as the default editor.

You can use any text editor to create and edit your Global.asa files. However, you cannot use a word processor unless you save the files as text only.

Create your Global.asa file with these steps:

1. Open Notepad by clicking Start | Programs | Accessories | Notepad.
2. Type the following:

```
<script language=VBScript runat=server>
Sub Application_OnStart
   Application("Heading") = "Hello World"
End Sub
</script>
```

3. Open the File menu and choose Save. Select the root directory of your ASP application (C:\Inetpub\Wwwroot for the ASP web). In the Save As dialog box, select All Files (*.*) in the Save As Type drop-down list and change the File Name to Global.asa, then click Save.

You will not be able to open the Global.asa page in your browser. This is a unique file and IIS will not allow it to be opened by a browser. This is a security measure, as this file will usually contain information about your server's configuration that you do not want the public to see.

4. In your FrontPage ASP web, double-click Default.asp to open it, if it's not already open. Click the Page view Normal tab.
5. Press CTRL+HOME to place the cursor at the top of the page.
6. Select Heading 2 from the Style drop-down list.
7. Click the HTML tab in Page view. The cursor should be on the line `<H2> </H2>`.

8. Delete the nonbreaking space (` `) and type **<%= Application("Heading")** **%>** between the `<H2>` and `</H2>` tags.

9. Save your page, open the File menu, and choose Preview In Browser. Select your preferred browser and click Preview. In your browser the words "Hello World" are displayed.

10. Still in your browser, view the source of the page. In Internet Explorer, open the View menu and choose Source. In Netscape Navigator, open the View menu and choose Page Source. Between the body tags (`<BODY>` and `</BODY>`) in the page source you will see the line

    ```
    <H2>Hello World</H2>
    ```

11. In the Page view HTML tab, look at the source for the Default.asp page. Between the body tags you will see the line

    ```
    <H2><%= Application("Heading") %></h2>
    ```

    In your Global.asa file you created an Application object (a variable) named "Heading" and gave it the value "Hello World." When your browser requested the Default.asp page, ASP looked up the value of the Heading Application object and inserted it into the web page before it was sent to your browser. This is the key to how ASP works. When an ASP page is requested, the server processes any code (ASP objects, components, and scripts) and generates a normal HTML page that is then sent to the requesting browser. Since the script is processed on the server, the browser does not need to support the scripting language used.

Note   *The "<%" and "%>" in the Page view HTML tab source code are VBScript delimiters. These define the code between them as a VBScript script that is to be executed on the server.*

12. In Notepad, change the line "Hello World" in the Global.asa file to **"Hello Brave New World"** and save the file.

    Changes to the Global.asa file are recognized by the web application when the file has been recompiled. This happens when the file is changed and saved or when the web application is first started, either by booting the server or stopping and starting the web application. Before the file is recompiled, all existing requests will be processed and no new requests will be accepted. This usually happens without any users being aware of it.

13. In your browser, click the Refresh (Internet Explorer) or Reload (Netscape) button. The heading in your browser will now reflect the change you made to the Global.asa file.

WORKING BEHIND
THE SCENES

As you can see, an Application object allows you to set values that are shared by all users of your web application. You can use the script `<%=Application("Heading")%>` on any page in your web application and format it with any HTML tags. You have a single place to change any application value or property, which greatly simplifies the maintenance of your web.

Application Object Methods, Collections, and Events

The Application object has four methods, two collections, and two events that trigger it. The methods are Contents.Remove, Contents.RemoveAll, Lock, and Unlock. The syntax for using the methods is

```
Application.method
```

The Lock method prevents more than one user from changing an Application object value at one time, while the Unlock method allows other users to change the value. If Unlock is not called, the Application object is unlocked when the ASP file finishes executing or the server time-out value is reached. Contents.Remove and Contents.RemoveAll are used with the Contents collection and are covered in the discussion of collections later in this section.

Note
*Throughout this chapter you will be given the syntax for the ASP objects and components. In these syntax statements, words in bold (including opening and closing parentheses) are used exactly as written. Words in italic indicate that, in actual use, the word is replaced with a value. In the preceding example, the actual use of the methods would be **Application.Lock** or **Application.Unlock**. When a vertical bar (|) is used in the syntax statement, such as **Session.**property | method, it indicates "or." That is, the correct syntax is either **Session.**property or **Session.**method, not **Session.**property.method. Optional elements are enclosed in square brackets, as in **Request.Cookies(**cookie)[(key) | .attribute], which indicates that the key and attribute parameters are optional. Unlike HTML created in FrontPage, your scripts will not be automatically checked for syntax errors, so it is very important to understand and use the correct syntax.*

The Application object events are Application_OnStart and Application_OnEnd. In the Global.asa file, you created a VBScript subroutine that used the Application_OnStart event to assign the text string Hello World to the Application object Heading.

The first line of the script,

```
<script language=VBScript runat=server>
```

identifies what follows as a VBScript script that is executed on the server. The next line,

```
Sub Application_OnStart
```

uses the SUB (subroutine) VBScript statement and the ASP Application_OnStart Application event to declare that what follows is a subroutine that is to be executed the first time any page in the web is requested by any user. This will be the first page loaded after the web application is started (normally web applications start by default when the computer is started). The following line creates the Application object and assigns its value:

```
Application("Heading") = "Hello World"
```

Finally, the subroutine and the script are closed with the END SUB VBScript statement and the closing HTML Script tag:

```
End Sub
</script>
```

Note   *In creating ASP web applications, you will be using at least three different programming languages: a scripting language, HTML, and ASP. This can make for interesting debugging, as you first have to determine which language is causing the problem. When you are working with databases (see Chapter 19), you will also have SQL statements to contend with.*

The Application_OnEnd event is used in a similar manner. The action defined in the subroutine is executed when the web application is shut down. This can be caused either by stopping the web server software, or by turning off or rebooting the computer. For example, if you used the Application_OnStart event to open a file for writing, you would need to close the file when the application shuts down. In that case you would create one subroutine to open the file and a matching subroutine to close the file. The subroutine to close the file would be triggered by the Application_OnEnd event.

The two Application object collections are Contents and StaticObjects. The Contents collection contains all the items that have been added to the Application object using script commands, as you did in your Global.asa file. The syntax for the Contents collection is

```
Application.Contents(key)
```

where *key* is the name of the item to retrieve. In your Global.asa file there is a single object in the collection: Heading with a value of Hello World. You displayed this value on your ASP page using

```
<H2><%= Application("Heading") %></h2>
```

You could also write this as

```
<H2><%= Application.Contents("Heading") %></H2>
```

The methods Contents.Remove and Contents.RemoveAll are used to remove objects from the Application.Contents collection. Contents.Remove deletes a single item, specified by its key value, and Contents.RemoveAll deletes all the objects in the collection.

The StaticObjects collection contains the items added using the <OBJECT> tag. This tag is usually used to embed ActiveX controls in a web page. (Chapter 20 will cover ActiveX controls.) In the Global.asa file it is used to create objects with either application or session scope. The <OBJECT> tag is not used within a script; it is a self-contained tag. The use of the <OBJECT> tag itself is explained in Chapter 20. The syntax for the StaticObjects collection is:

```
Application.StaticObjects(key)
```

As with the Contents collection, *key* is the name of the item being referenced.

The Session Object

A Session object is available to a single user. A session begins when the user first requests a page from the web application and ends when the user abandons the session (by requesting a page outside the web application) or the session times out (there is no activity for a specified period). A session can only be maintained by a browser that supports cookies. A *cookie* is a small file that is written to the user's hard drive to identify the client to the web server. A more in-depth explanation of cookies is in the section "The Cookies Collection."

Reading and writing cookies from an ASP web application is covered in the sections "Request Object" and "Response Object."

Session Object Properties, Collections, and Methods

The Session object has four properties, two collections, and three methods. The properties are CodePage, LCID, SessionID, and Timeout, and the methods are Abandon, Contents.Remove, and Contents.RemoveAll. The collections are Contents and StaticObjects. These collections are the same as for the Application object, with session, not application, scope. The methods Contents.Remove and Contents.RemoveAll are also the same as for the Application object except with session scope. The syntax for the Session object is

```
Session.collection|property|method
```

The CodePage property sets the character set that the web application will use. These character sets are called *codepages*. A codepage contains all the characters, punctuation, etc., for a character set. The CodePage property can be set to any valid codepage on the web server but will normally be left set to the system default. In North America and Europe this is usually ANSI codepage 1252. In Japan you would use OEM codepage 932 to display Kanji. The syntax for the CodePage property is

```
Session.CodePage(=codepage)
```

where *codepage* is the numeric value of the codepage.

The LCID property is the Locale ID. This is used to localize the content to a specific country. The syntax for the LCID property is

```
Session.LCID(=lcid)
```

where *lcid* is a valid Locale ID. For example, the LCID for the United States is L0409. A list of Locale IDs can be found in the Windows 98 Resource Kit (available from Microsoft Press at **http://mspress.microsoft.com/Books/1340.htm**).

The SessionID property is the unique numeric identifier that is created the first time a user loads a page from the web (the start of their session). To place the value of the SessionID property in the variable lngSID, you would use the syntax

```
lngSID = Session.SessionID
```

You can see how this works by displaying the Session ID on your ASP home page.

1. Open your Default.asp file in the Page view Normal tab and press CTRL+HOME.

2. Press DOWN ARROW once and type **The Session ID is**.

3. Click the HTML tab. The cursor should be in the line that you just entered in the Normal tab, which should look like this

```
<P>The Session ID is</P>
```

4. Move the cursor to the end of the line, but before the closing paragraph tag, type a space and then type **<%= Session.SessionID %>**. The line should look like this

```
<p>The Session ID is <%= Session.SessionID %></p>
```

5. Save the page and view it in your browser. You may have to refresh or reload your page. Figure 16-5 shows the ASP home page in Internet Explorer 5.5.

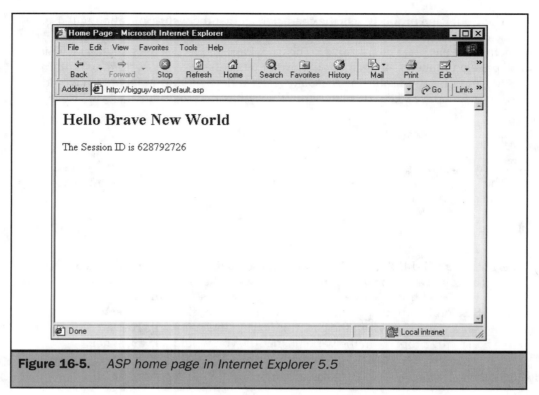

Figure 16-5. *ASP home page in Internet Explorer 5.5*

The Timeout property is the time, in minutes, that the application will wait for user activity before abandoning the session. The default is 20 minutes. To change the time-out value to 10 minutes, you would use the syntax

```
Session.Timeout = 10
```

in your code.

The Abandon method is used to explicitly end a session. You can use this to free up system resources rather than waiting for the time-out value to take effect. All running scripts are completed before the session is abandoned.

ObjectContext Object

The ObjectContext object is used to commit or abort transactions that are called from an ASP page using the Microsoft Component Services. It has two methods, SetComplete and SetAbort, and two events, OnTransactionCommit and OnTransactionAbort. The syntax is

> **ObjectContext**.*method*

Microsoft Component Services is an environment for managing components on a server. A component is an application on a server that is shared by all the web applications. Component Services enable *multi*tier applications, that is, applications that have a client component and a server component. A *transaction* is a process that succeeds or fails as a whole; there cannot be a half-completed transaction.

An accounting example shows why this can be critical for web applications. Say you want to move a sum of money from one account to another. For the transaction to be complete, one account must debit the amount and the other must credit it. If either fails, the transaction is incomplete. However, if one account was debited correctly and the process failed to credit the other, you have an accounting headache. When this procedure is performed as a transaction, all the steps must be completed before the transaction is committed. This prevents the situation where one account is changed and the other is not.

The SetComplete method is used in a script to declare that the script is unaware of any reason for the transaction to fail. If all the components agree, then the transaction is committed. The SetAbort method will abort the transaction. These can be used as part of the logical test in the script. For example, the script can test for a condition and then branch to SetComplete or SetAbort, depending on the results of the test.

The OnTransactionCommit event is triggered when the transaction is committed. As you did with the Application_OnStart event, you can control a subroutine that will run when the transaction is committed. The OnTransactionAbort event is triggered if the transaction is aborted.

Request Object

When a user's browser sends a request to the web server, a great deal of information can be contained in the HTTP header. Along with the URL of the page that is being requested, the header will contain a text string that identifies the browser making the request. The HTTP header may also contain values from an HTML form, values appended to the URL, cookies, and information about the client certificate (if the request is being made over a secure connection). Secure connections over the Internet are covered in Chapter 22.

Request objects have five collections, listed in Table 16-2. These collections give you a great deal of control over a user's experience on your web. The syntax for the Request object is

> **Request**[.*collection*|*property*|*method*] (*variable*)

The Request object has a single property, TotalBytes, and a single method, BinaryRead. The TotalBytes property is read-only and contains the total number

Collection	Description
ClientCertificate	Contains information about the user's client certificate
Cookies	Contains the values of the user's cookies
Form	Contains the values sent by an HTML form
QueryString	Contains additional information stored in the URL string
ServerVariables	Contains information from the HTTP header sent by the requesting browser

Table 16-2.   *Request Object Collections*

of bytes being sent by the client in the body of the request. The BinaryRead method returns the data sent as part of a POST request (used with the FORM tag). Normally you would use the Form collection to retrieve data sent using a POST request (see the section "The Form Collection"); the BinaryRead method retrieves the raw data in an array, rather than a name/value pair.

   If you first call the BinaryRead method, calling Request.Form will generate an error. Conversely, if you call Request.Form first, calling BinaryRead will create an error.

In the following sections you will see how you can use these in your own webs.

   If the collection name is omitted, all the collections will be searched for the named variable. This uses server resources unnecessarily and should be avoided.

The ClientCertificate Collection

The ClientCertificate collection is not extensively used at this time. The user needs to have obtained a certificate from an issuing body, such as VeriSign, Inc. (**http://www.verisign.com**). The issuing body confirms that you are who you say you are and then issues you a certificate. This is a *personal ID certificate,* while servers will have *server IDs.* One valuable use of a personal certificate is that it can ensure that e-mail sent by the certificate holder is not a forgery. This can be important if the e-mail is business related. You can expect that the use of personal certificates will grow, particularly in the business world. The syntax for the ClientCertificate collection is

```
Request.ClientCertificate(key[subfield])
```

where *key* is the name of the certificate field to retrieve and *subfield* is a single field in the Subject or Issuer key. Table 16-3 lists the certificate fields, and Table 16-4 lists the individual fields in the Subject and Issuer keys.

The Cookies Collection

Properly used, cookies are a valuable tool for both the user and the webmaster. Improperly used, they can be a major problem for both.

Cookies have received a lot of publicity in the popular press, most of it bad. Some would have you believe that cookies can extract all sorts of personal information about a user and are a serious threat to the user's privacy. There's no question that cookies can be abused, but they are not magic. They cannot extract any information that the user doesn't supply. They are intended to simply identify the client to the web server. A typical cookie generated by an ASP session looks like this:

ASPSESSIONID=NTPHQYWDDUXWFNFO

As you can see, in its simplest form, a cookie is simply a long string of characters. Cookies can also contain a great deal more information, if the webmaster so chooses.

WORKING BEHIND THE SCENES

Key	Description
Certificate	A string containing all the certificate information.
Flags	Provides additional information about the certificate. There are two keys: ceCertPresent, which indicates a client certificate is present, and ceUnrecognizedIssuer, which indicates the issuer for the most recent certificate is unknown.
Issuer	A string containing all the information about the issuer of the certificate.
SerialNumber	The certificate serial number.
Subject	A string containing all the subfield values for the certificate.
ValidFrom	The starting date of the certificate.
ValidUntil	The expiration date of the certificate.

Table 16-3. *ClientCertificate Collection Keys*

SubField	Description
C	The country of origin
CN	The user's common name (Subject key only)
GN	A given name
I	A set of initials
L	The locality
O	The company or organization name
OU	The name of the organizational unit
S	The name of a state or province
T	The title of a person or organization

Table 16-4. *SubFields for ClientCertificate Issuer and Subject Keys*

Tip   *On Windows computers, cookies are saved in the Windows folder in a folder named Cookies (usually C:\Windows\Cookies with Windows 98 and C:\Documents and Settings\login name\Cookies with Windows 2000). Cookies are text files, so you can view them in any text editor, such as Notepad. You can also delete them from a hard drive if you desire. Cookie filenames are usually in the form user@domain, so a cookie generated for someone named Sally who visited Microsoft's web site would be sally@microsoft.txt.*

Since cookies have become controversial, you should understand why they are used. In the first chapter, HTTP was described as stateless protocol, meaning that each request from a client to the server is a separate entity. When the same client makes another request (such as opening another page in a web), the server has no way of knowing that it is the same client. By writing a cookie to the user's computer, the web server can read it when the request is made and identify the client. It won't be able to tell who the user is unless the user has given personal information at some point. That information can be kept in a database and analyzed to see how users are using the web (how often they visit, how long they stay, what pages they view, and so on). Anonymity is highly prized by many web users, and cookies can be seen as a threat to that.

Note *The current versions of both Netscape and Internet Explorer allow the user to disable cookies. In Internet Explorer 4.0, open the View menu, choose Internet Options, and select the Advanced tab. Under Security there are three options: Always Accept Cookies, Prompt Before Accepting Cookies, and Disable All Cookie Use. In IE 5.5, open the Tools menu, choose Internet Options, select the Security tab, and click Custom Level. In the Security Settings dialog box you can set cookies to Enable, Prompt Before Accepting, or Disable. You can apply these settings to temporary cookies (which are not stored on the computer's hard drive) and stored cookies. In Netscape Navigator, open the Edit menu, choose Preferences, and click Advanced. There are four options: Accept All Cookies, Accept Only Cookies That Get Sent Back To The Originating Server, Disable Cookies, and Warn Me Before Accepting A Cookie.*

Cookies can also make the users' lives easier. For example, users can request a custom home page that has the areas of a site that the users are most interested in. The Microsoft site (**http://www.microsoft.com**), especially if you use Internet Explorer, makes extensive use of cookies. It will even automatically create a custom home page based on your page requests. This may offend some people—and that has to be considered in your own cookie use—but if you're visiting the site for information or downloads, it makes life easier.

Tip *A good source of information about cookies, both technical and philosophical, is Cookie Central at **http://www.cookiecentral.com**.*

The syntax for the Cookies collection is

```
Cookies(cookie)[(key)|.attribute]
```

The functions of the parameters are

- **Cookie** The name of the cookie.
- **Key** An optional parameter that identifies values in a cookie *dictionary*, a collection of cookie values.
- **Attribute** Contains information about the cookie itself. Currently there is a single attribute, HasKeys. This is a read-only value that indicates whether the cookie has key values.

Since a cookie first has to be written to a client, using cookies will be covered in more detail in the section "The Response Object Cookies Collection."

The Form Collection

The Request object Form collection provides a method to handle the responses the user enters in an HTML form. FrontPage itself provides several methods for processing form input, but using the Request object Form collection gives you basically unlimited options for doing the same thing.

The syntax for the Form collection is

```
Request.Form(name)[(index)|.Count]
```

The functions of the parameters are

- **Name**   The name of the form element
- **Index**   An optional number used if the form element has multiple values to determine which value is being referenced
- **Count**   The total number of values for a parameter

Using the Form collection can be demonstrated by adding a form to your ASP home page. Do that now with these steps (the ASP web should still be open in FrontPage):

1. In Normal view, press CTRL+END to move the cursor to the bottom of your ASP web home page.

2. Open the Insert menu and choose Form | Form.

3. Press SHIFT+ENTER then UP ARROW to create a blank line in the form and to place the cursor on it.

4. Type **Enter Your First Name:** leaving a space after the colon, then open the Insert menu and choose Form | Textbox. Press SHIFT+ENTER.

5. Type **Enter Your Last Name:** leaving a space after the colon, then open the Insert menu and choose Form | Textbox.

6. Right-click the first text box (first name) and choose Form Field Properties. In the Text Box Properties dialog box, type **FirstName** in the Name text box, then click OK.

7. Right-click the second text box (last name) and choose Form Field Properties. In the Text Box Properties dialog box, type **LastName** in the Name text box, then click OK.

8. Right-click the form and choose Form Properties. In the Form Properties dialog box, select the Send To Other option button. Custom ISAPI, NSAPI, CGI, Or ASP Script should be selected in the Send To Other drop-down. Click Options.

9. In the Options For Custom Form Handler dialog box, shown next, type **Form_rsp.asp** in the Action text box. Make sure the method is Post, then click OK twice. Save the page.

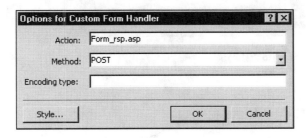

10. Create a new page, and then click Save on the toolbar.

11. In the Save As dialog box, type **Form_rsp.asp** for the File Name and **Form Response Page** for the page title. Click Save.

12. Type **Form Response Page** at the top of the page and format it as Heading 2.

13. Press ENTER and type **Your first name is:** (leave a space after the colon).

When you are instructed to type a line that ends with a period or comma, do not include it unless specifically noted. If the line ends with a colon, always leave a space after the colon.

14. Click the HTML tab. The cursor should be at the end of the line you just typed in the Normal tab.

15. Position the cursor after the space at the end of the line and type **<%= Request.Form("FirstName") %>**. The complete line should look like this

```
<P>Your first name is: <%= Request.Form("FirstName") %></P>
```

16. In the Normal tab, move the cursor to the first blank line on the page and type **Your last name is:**.

17. Click the HTML tab and type **<%= Request.Form("LastName") %>** at the end of the line you just typed. The complete line should look like this:

```
<P>Your last name is: <%= Request.Form("LastName") %></P>
```

18. Save the Form Response Page.

19. Open the ASP home page in your browser, fill out the First and Last Name fields on the form, and then click Submit. The Form Response Page will open with your form entries displayed, as shown in Figure 16-6.

This example basically duplicates part of the Confirmation page you can create for a form in FrontPage. However, using ASP is much more flexible. You have total control

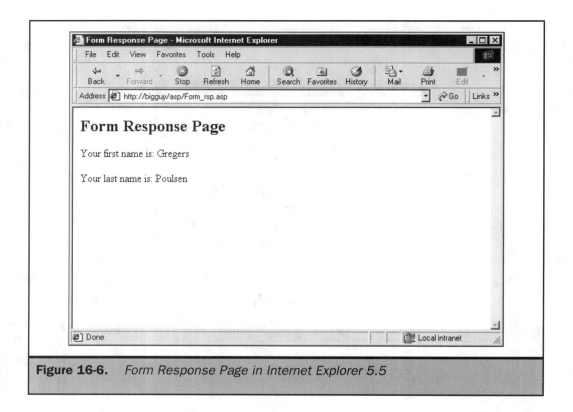

Figure 16-6. *Form Response Page in Internet Explorer 5.5*

over the layout of the page and can pass the values to another application or even to the same page. In the next section, "The QueryString Collection," you will see how you can allow the user to modify the page that contains the script.

The QueryString Collection

With the Request object QueryString collection, it is possible to pass values to a page in the URL itself. These values are separated from the basic URL by a question mark (?). The QueryString collection has the same basic syntax as the Form collection:

```
Request.QueryString(variable)[(index)|.Count]
```

 The QueryString collection is also used when a form uses the Get rather than Post method to send form data. With the Get method, the data is appended to the URL instead of being included in the HTTP header.

This next example will demonstrate how the user can customize a page—in this case, the same page that contains the script.

1. Create a new page in your ASP web and click Save on the toolbar.

2. In the Save As dialog box, type **Backgrounds.asp** for the File Name and **Backgrounds** for the page title. Click Save.

3. With the cursor at the top of the page, type **Would you like a blue background or a yellow background?** and format it as Heading 3.

4. Select the word "blue" and then click Insert Hyperlink on the toolbar.

5. In the Insert Hyperlink dialog box, click Backgrounds.asp. The filename will be copied to the Address drop-down list box.

6. Click the Address drop-down box and then press END. Type **?color=blue**. (Do not include the period.) Your Insert Hyperlink dialog box should look like this:

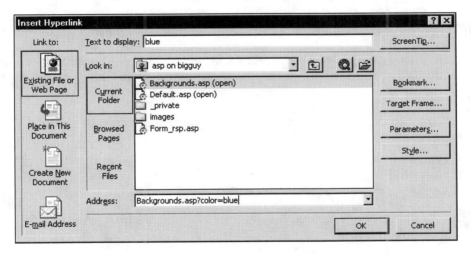

7. Click OK and then select the word "yellow."

8. Open the Insert Hyperlink dialog box again and click Backgrounds.asp.

9. Click the Address drop-down box and then press END. Type **?color=yellow**. (Do not include the period.) Click OK.

10. Save the page.

11. In the next steps you are going to use a combination of VBScript, ASP, and HTML to allow the user to select a background color for the Backgrounds page. To do this, you will create two body tags for the page, one for the blue page and

one for the yellow page. You will use the VBScript Select Case statement to test the value of the color variable being passed in the URL to determine which body tag is used. FrontPage will not allow multiple body tags so you need to have a single body tag with the attributes determined by the VBScript script. You will do this by creating a text string that will be appended to the body tag. Click the HTML tab and place the cursor on the line between the closing head tag and before the body tag.

12. Type **<% Select Case Request.QueryString("color")** and press ENTER.

13. Type **Case "blue"** and press ENTER.

14. Type **strBody = "bgcolor=blue text=yellow link=yellow"** and press ENTER.

15. Type **Case "yellow"** and press ENTER.

16. Type **strBody = "bgcolor=yellow text=blue"** and press ENTER.

17. Type **End Select %>** and press ENTER.

> **Tip**
>
> *You could also use the VBScript If… Else… statements rather than Select Case. Select Case is a better choice if there are more than two choices, as the If… Else… statement can get complicated. If there are more than two choices, or if you think that there may ultimately be more than two choices, you should use the Select Case statement. Planning ahead can save you from rewriting your code later.*

18. Place the cursor in the body tag at the end of the word "body" and press the SPACEBAR.

19. Type **<%= strBody %>**. (Do not include the period.) The complete body tag should look like this

    ```
    <body <%= strBody %>>
    ```

20. Your Backgrounds page code should look like Figure 16-7. Save the Backgrounds page.

21. Open the page in your browser and click the "blue" hyperlink. The page is displayed with a blue background and yellow text.

22. Click the "yellow" hyperlink. The page is now displayed with a yellow background and blue text.

If you load the Backgrounds page without a color specified (the URL doesn't include the question mark and either color=… value), both Case tests fail and strBody is an empty string. In this case the default body tag is used. If you look at the source for this page in your browser, you will see how the body tag is modified when a color is specified. This is an important concept, as it allows the page to degrade gracefully. That is, it doesn't self-destruct if a color value isn't specified. Whenever you are using ASP objects or scripting, you have to deal with what happens in all cases, such as if a browser doesn't support a feature you are trying to use.

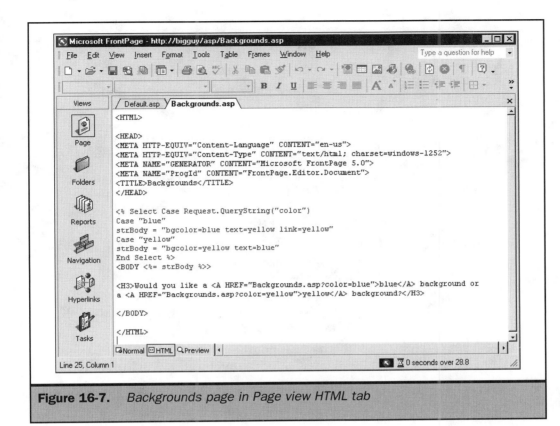

Figure 16-7. *Backgrounds page in Page view HTML tab*

These examples just scratch the surface of what is possible by using the Request object's Form and QueryString collections. With a little imagination, you can add a great deal of interactivity and customization with them.

The ServerVariables Collection

The ServerVariables collection gives you access to a plethora of information about the server environment. The syntax is straightforward:

```
Request.ServerVariables(variable)
```

The variables available in the ServerVariables collection are listed in Table 16-5. They are very useful for examining the server environment, but you will probably not use them as often as the Cookies, Form, or QueryString collections.

Variable	Description
ALL_HTTP	Contains all the HTTP headers sent by the browser.
ALL_RAW	Contains all the HTTP headers without processing. When ALL_HTTP is used, each header name is prefaced with HTTP_. With ALL_RAW, the headers appear exactly as sent.
APPL_MD_PATH	The metabase path for an ISAPI application (a DLL file). The metabase is where Windows stores the configuration information for your web server (IIS or PWS).
APPL_PHYSICAL_PATH	The physical path corresponding to the metabase path. This is the actual location of the file on your hard drive.
AUTH_PASSWORD	Contains the password entered in the browser's authentication dialog box. This variable is only available with Basic authentication.
AUTH_TYPE	The authentication method used by the server. This is set in the Internet Services Manager.
AUTH_USER	The raw authenticated username.
CERT_COOKIE	A unique ID for the client certificate.
CERT_FLAGS	Flags set to indicate if a client certificate is present and if it was issued by a valid authority.
CERT_ISSUER	Contains the information for issuer of a client certificate.
CERT_KEYSIZE	The number of bits in the Secure Sockets Layer (SSL) key. This is 128 bits for domestic browsers and 40 bits for international browsers.
CERT_SECRETKEYSIZE	The number of bits in a server certificate private key.
CERT_SERIALNUMBER	The serial number of the client certificate.
CERT_SERVER_ISSUER	The issuing authority for the server certificate.

Table 16-5.   *Request Object ServerVariables Collection Variables*

Variable	Description
CERT_SERVER_SUBJECT	The contents of the subject field in the server certificate.
CERT_SUBJECT	The contents of the subject field in the client certificate.
CONTENT_LENGTH	The length of the content requested.
CONTENT_TYPE	The type of the content, such as Post or Get.
GATEWAY_INTERFACE	The version of the CGI (common gateway interface) on the server.
HTTP_*HeaderName*	Extracts values not included in the default variables. An example is HTTP_UA_PIXELS, which returns the user's screen resolution. Not all variables are returned by all clients.
HTTP_ACCEPT	Contains the MIME types the browser can accept.
HTTP_ACCEPT_LANGUAGE	A text string specifying the language content should be displayed in.
HTTP_USER_AGENT	The type of browser making the request.
HTTP_COOKIE	The cookie value returned by the browser.
HTTP_REFERER	The URL of the original request when a redirect has occurred. "Referer" is misspelled, but that's the way the specification is written.
HTTPS	Contains ON or OFF depending on whether or not the request came through a secure channel.
HTTPS_KEYSIZE	The number of bits in the SSL key.
HTTPS_SECRETKEYSIZE	The number of bits in the server certificate private key.
HTTPS_SERVER_ISSUER	The issuing authority for the server certificate.
HTTPS_SERVER_SUBJECT	The contents of the subject field in the server certificate.

Table 16-5.   *Request Object ServerVariables Collection Variables* (continued)

Variable	Description
INSTANCE_ID	The ID for the current IIS instance of the client request.
INSTANCE_META_PATH	The path in the metabase for the current instance of the client request.
LOCAL_ADDR	The address of the server that received the request.
LOGON_USER	The Windows 2000 user account that is used for the request. By default this is IUSR_*computername*. This account is created when IIS is installed on Windows 2000.
PATH_INFO	The virtual path information contained in the request.
PATH_TRANSLATED	Maps the virtual path to the physical path.
QUERY_STRING	All the information after the question mark in a request. This is the same information that is in the QueryString collection, but it is not parsed into separate elements.
REMOTE_ADDR	The IP address of the remote host.
REMOTE_HOST	The name of the remote host.
REMOTE_USER	The username string sent by the client without any filtering.
REQUEST_METHOD	The request method, such as Post, Get, and so on.
SCRIPT_NAME	The virtual path of the script being executed.
SERVER_NAME	The web server's name, DNS (Domain Name System) alias, or IP address.
SERVER_PORT	The server's port number handling the request. For web services this is normally port 80. A *port* is a reference to a process on the server, not a physical port.

Table 16-5. *Request Object ServerVariables Collection Variables* (continued)

Variable	Description
SERVER_PORT_SECURE	A flag (either 0 or 1) that indicates if the request is secure. A 1 indicates a secure port is being used to handle the request.
SERVER_PROTOCOL	The name and version of the protocol processing the request.
SERVER_SOFTWARE	The name and version of the server software.
URL	The base portion of the URL.

Table 16-5.   *Request Object ServerVariables Collection Variables* (continued)

Many of these server variables are used with Secure Sockets Layer (SSL) transactions, which require both a server certificate and a client certificate. Certificates and SSL are covered in Chapter 22. This next set of instructions will create a simple web page that displays some of the server variables:

1. In your ASP web, create a new page, and save it with the File Name Server.asp and the page title Server Variables.

2. Type **Server Variables** at the top of the page and format it as Heading 2.

3. Press ENTER, open the Table menu, and choose Insert | Table.

4. In the Insert Table dialog box, specify 6 Rows, 2 Columns, a Cell Padding of 4, and clear the Specify Width check box if it is selected. Click OK.

5. In the first cell of the first row, type **VARIABLE**, press TAB, and type **VALUE**.

6. Press TAB and type **PATH_INFO**.

7. Press DOWN ARROW and type **PATH_TRANSLATED**.

8. In the remaining three cells of the first column, type **SERVER_NAME**, **SERVER_PROTOCOL**, and **SERVER_SOFTWARE**, pressing DOWN ARROW between each entry. Your table should look like Figure 16-8.

9. Click the second cell of the second row and click the HTML tab.

10. The cursor should be in the table cell underneath the cell containing PATH_INFO. Delete the nonbreaking space ( ) and type **<%= Request.ServerVariables("PATH_INFO") %>**. (Do not type the period.) The completed code for the table row should look like this:

```
<TR>
  <TD>PATH_INFO</TD>
```

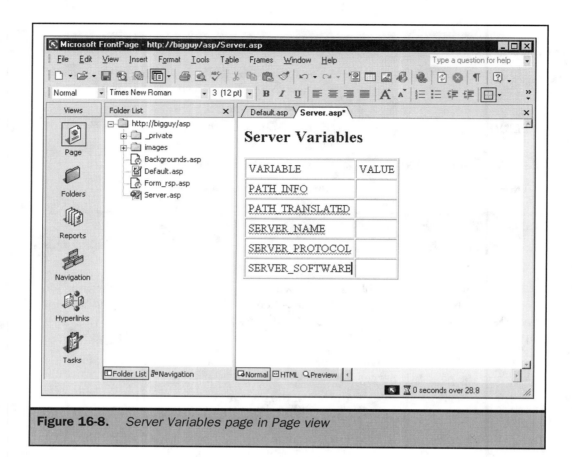

Figure 16-8. *Server Variables page in Page view*

```
<TD><%= Request.ServerVariables("PATH_INFO") %></TD>
</TR>
```

11. Move the cursor to the table cell underneath the cell with the PATH_TRANSLATED label and type

    <%= Request.ServerVariables("PATH_TRANSLATED") %>.

12. Move the currsor to the next cell with a nonbreaking space (under the SERVER_NAME label), delete the nonbreaking space, and type

    <%= Request.ServerVariables("SERVER_NAME") %>.

13. Move the cursor to the next cell with a nonbreaking space (under the SERVER_PROTOCOL label), delete the nonbreaking space, and type

    <%= Request.ServerVariables("SERVER_PROTOCOL") %>.

14. Move the cursor to the next cell with a nonbreaking space (under the SERVER_SOFTWARE label), delete the nonbreaking space, and type

<%= Request.ServerVariables("SERVER_SOFTWARE") %>.

Your page should look similar to Figure 16-9.

15. Save your Server Variables page, and then open it in your browser.

Figure 16-10 shows the Server Variables page in Internet Explorer. Some of the values in your table will be different, reflecting your server setup.

The Request object and its collections allow you to handle a great deal of input from the user. This is the key to creating truly interactive web applications. In the next section you will see how to use the Response object and its collection, properties, and methods to send output to the user.

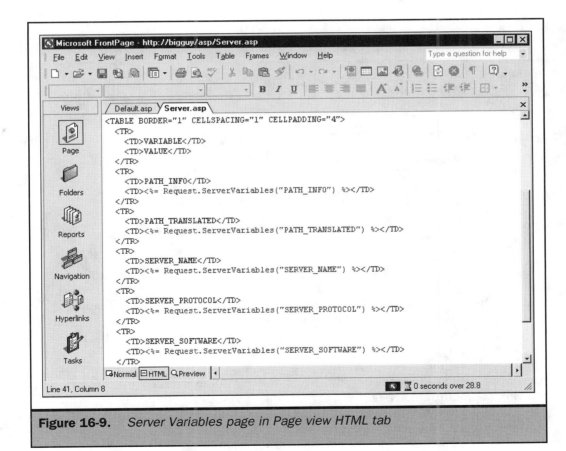

Figure 16-9. *Server Variables page in Page view HTML tab*

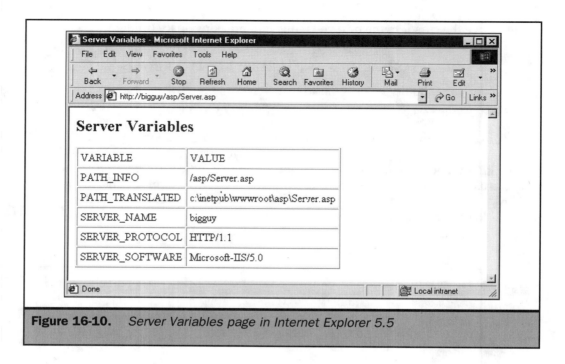

Figure 16-10. *Server Variables page in Internet Explorer 5.5*

Response Object

The Response object is the complement to the Request object. The syntax is

Response.*collection*|*property*|*method*

The Response object has a single collection, Cookies; nine properties, listed in Table 16-6; and eight methods, listed in Table 16-7.

Of the various properties and methods in the Response object, the Redirect method is one of the most useful. It allows you to control what page is sent to the user's browser based on some form of input, such as a selection in a form. For example, earlier in this chapter you created a page to display data entered in a form. What if you wanted to prevent users from seeing that page unless they had entered all the data in the form? With the Redirect method you could send users to the form page if any of the form fields were empty.

In actual use, forms normally use a JavaScript form validation script to prevent users from leaving any required fields blank, but this doesn't prevent users from entering the confirmation page URL in the browser's Address box and going to the page. With the Redirect method, you could test for a valid value in the form field and send users to the form if there weren't one.

Property	Parameters	Description
Buffer	[=*TRUE* | *FALSE*]	When set to TRUE, the server does not send any output to the client until all the scripts on the page have been processed. When set to FALSE (the default), the output of each script on the page is sent as soon as it processed.
CacheControl	[= *cache control header*]	Determines if a proxy server will cache ASP files.
Charset	(*charset*)	Specifies the character set of a page where *charset* is the name of the character set.
ContentType	[=*content type*]	Specifies the type of data being sent to the client. The default content type is text/HTML. Other possible values include image/GIF and image/JPEG.
Expires	[=*minutes*]	Sets the length of time in minutes a page will be cached on the user's browser. If the user reloads the page before the Expires value is reached, the cached file is displayed. When the Expires value has been exceeded, the page will be reloaded from the server.
ExpiresAbsolute	[=[*date*][*time*]]	Sets a date and time a page is flushed from the user's browser. If a date is specified but not a time, the page expires at midnight.
IsClientConnected		A read-only property that indicates whether or not the client is still connected.
Pics	(*PICSlabel*)	Inserts a PICS (Platform for Internet Content Selection) label to the response header. PICS is a system for rating Internet content.
Status	[=*status description*]	Sets a three-digit error code and a brief explanation, such as "403 Access Forbidden," as shown in Figure 16-1.

Table 16-6.   *Response Object Properties*

Method	Parameters	Description
AddHeader	*name, value*	Adds an HTML header to a page. This method is not recommended for use if another Response method will do the job.
AppendToLog	*string*	Adds the string value to the web server log for the request. The string cannot contain commas and has a maximum length of 80 characters.
BinaryWrite	*data*	Sends data to a browser without any conversion—for example, a graphics file.
Clear		Clears any buffered output. If this method is called, Response.Buffer must first be set to TRUE or an error will be generated.
End		Stops the processing of an ASP file. The current results are sent, and the rest of the scripting is ignored.
Flush		Sends any buffered output immediately. If this method is called, Response.Buffer must first be set to TRUE or an error will be generated.
Redirect	*URL*	Loads the page in the user's browser specified by the URL parameter.
Write	*string*	Sends the data specified in the string parameter. This can be any valid data type for your scripting language.

Table 16-7. *Response Object Methods*

You will see an example of the Response.Redirect method in the next section.

The Response Object Cookies Collection

Earlier in this chapter you had an overview of cookies. In this section you will learn how to use them. The syntax for the Response object Cookies collection is

```
Response.Cookies(cookie)[(key)|.attribute]=value
```

The functions of the parameters are

- **Cookie**   The name of the cookie
- **Key**   An optional parameter that identifies a value in a cookie *dictionary*, a collection of cookie values
- **Attribute**   Information about the cookie itself
- **Value**   The actual value of the cookie

The Attribute parameter has five possible values, listed in Table 16-8. As you can see, you have a great deal of control over just what is in a cookie.

The best way to understand cookies is to start using them. In the following exercise, you'll create a form page for the user to enter the cookie values, a page to write out the cookie, and a page to display the cookie values. You will also use the Response.Redirect method to move the user seamlessly from the form page to the page that displays the cookie values. Do that now with these steps:

Note   *Your browser has to be set to accept cookies for this exercise to work correctly.*

1. In your ASP web, create a new page, and save it with the File Name Createcookie.asp and the page title Create a Cookie.
2. In the Page view Normal tab, type **Enter Cookie Values**, and format it as Heading 2.
3. Press ENTER and then insert a one-line text box from the Insert | Form menu or the Form toolbar.

Name	Type	Description
Expires	Write-only	Sets the date on which the cookie will expire.
Domain	Write-only	Sets the domain to which the cookie is sent. This is usually the domain where the web page is located, but some advertisers require the cookie be sent to their domain, rather than to the issuing domain. Netscape allows the user to block this type of cookie.
Path	Write-only	Sets the path that the cookie will be sent to. If this value is not set, the application path is used.
Secure	Write-only	Indicates whether the cookie is secure.
HasKeys	Read-only	Indicates whether the cookie has a dictionary.

Table 16-8.   *Response Object Cookies Collection Attribute Parameter Values*

4. Press HOME and type **Enter your name:** (leave seven spaces after the colon). Format the text as Formatted.

5. Press RIGHT ARROW to move the insertion point between the text box and the Submit button, and then press SHIFT+ENTER to move the Submit and Reset buttons to the next line.

6. Insert another one-line text box, press HOME, and then type **Enter a favorite food:** (leave a space after the colon).

7. Press RIGHT ARROW and then press SHIFT+ENTER. Your page should look similar to Figure 16-11.

8. Right-click the first form field and choose Form Field Properties. In the Text Box Properties dialog box, type **Name** in the Name text box and then click OK.

9. Right-click the second form field and choose Form Field Properties. In the Text Box Properties dialog box, type **Food** in the Name text box and then click OK.

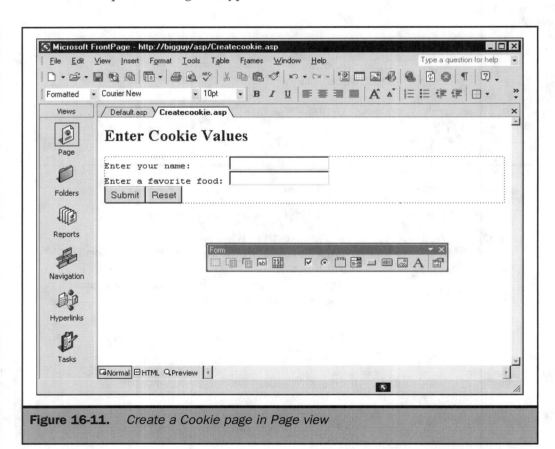

Figure 16-11. *Create a Cookie page in Page view*

10. Right-click the form and choose Form Properties. In the Form Properties dialog box, select Send To Other, and then click Options.

11. In the Options For Custom Form Handler dialog box, type **Writecookie.asp** in the Action text box, make sure Post is the Method selected and click OK twice.

12. Save the page.

13. Open Notepad or your favorite text editor. You have to create this next page in a text editor, as the page cannot have the normal HTML Head and Body tags for Response.Redirect to work correctly. FrontPage will add these tags to your page if you create it in it. This also means you cannot open this page in FrontPage.

14. Create a new page, and save it with the filename **Writecookie.asp** in your ASP web directory. In Notepad be sure that All Files is selected in the Save As Type drop-down or Notepad will give it a TXT extension.

15. Type

```
<% name = Request.Form("Name")
food = Request.Form("Food")
Response.Cookies("theCookie")("Name") = name
Response.Cookies("theCookie")("Food") = food
Response.Redirect "Readcookie.asp" %>
```

This script assigns the values entered in the Name and Food form fields to the variables name and food, respectively. It then assigns the values in the name and food variables to the keys Name and Food for the cookie theCookie. Finally, it redirects the user to the ASP page that will read and display the values for the cookie theCookie. If the script is executed properly, the user will never see the Writecookie.asp page.

16. Save the page.

17. Create a new page in FrontPage and save it with the File Name Readcookie.asp and the page title Read a Cookie.

18. In the Page view Normal tab, type **Your Cookie Values Are:** and format it as Heading 2. Press ENTER.

19. Type **Name =** (leave a space after the equal sign), click the HTML tab and type **<% Request.Cookies("theCookie")("Name") %>** after Name = and on the same line. There should be one space after Name = and before the VBScript delimiter.

20. Click the Normal tab, move the cursor to the line below Name = , and type **Food =** (again, leave a space after the equal sign).

21. Click the HTML tab, and type **<% Request.Cookies("theCookie")("Food") %>** after Food = (and on the same line).

22. Save the page.

23. Open the Create A Cookie page (Createcookie.asp) in your browser.

24. Fill out the form and then click Submit. Your browser should display the Read A Cookie page as shown in Figure 16-12.

Cookies can be very useful to the webmaster, but you must also remember that not every browser will support them, either by design (an older browser that doesn't support cookies) or choice (the user has disabled them). If your web contains features that depend on cookies (such as user preferences or customizable web pages), it might be better to keep the user preferences in a database on your server and to have users log in when they visit your site.

Both methods have advantages and disadvantages, so you will have to decide what works best for your site.

Server Object

The Server object provides one property and seven methods (listed in Table 16-9) that primarily provide utility functions. The syntax is

```
Server.method
```

The MapPath method functions much the same way as the Request object PATH_TRANSLATED ServerVariable, converting a virtual path to a physical path. The CreateObject method is primarily used with ASP components and will be covered in the section "The Server.CreateObject Object and ASP Components." The GetLastError

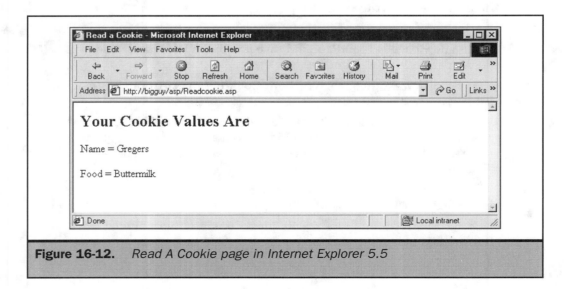

Figure 16-12. *Read A Cookie page in Internet Explorer 5.5*

Method	Description
CreateObject	Creates an instance of an ASP component.
Execute	Calls an ASP file and executes as part of the calling ASP script.
GetLastError	Returns an ASPError object describing any errors that occurred while executing an ASP file.
HTMLEncode	Encodes a text string into HTML so that reserved characters, such as < and >, are displayed correctly.
MapPath	Converts a virtual path to a physical path.
Transfer	Sends all the data, including Application and Session objects, from one ASP file to another.
URLEncode	Encodes a text string so that it conforms to URL encoding rules.

Table 16-9.   *Server Object Methods*

method will be covered in the section "ASP Error Handling." The remaining methods will be covered in the following sections.

The Server Object ScriptTimeout Property

The single Server object property is ScriptTimeout, and the syntax is

```
Server.ScriptTimeout = seconds
```

This value sets the length of time, in seconds, that the server will process a script before abandoning it. This is needed because an error in a script may cause it to run forever without ending, a situation sometimes known as an *infinite loop*. Obviously, this is not a good thing. The ScriptTimeout value prevents this from happening.

 The Windows Registry (a special system file that contains defaults for the operating system and applications) contains the default ScriptTimeout value, which is usually 90 seconds. The Server object ScriptTimeout property overrides the Registry setting for the script that calls it, but it cannot be set to a value shorter than the Registry entry.

The Server Object Execute Method

When building a large ASP web, you'll often find that you need to use the same ASP code on a number of pages. If you placed the code on each page where it was required, any changes made to that code would have to be made on each and every page where it was used. This is a maintenance headache. The Execute method allows you to create a single copy of the ASP code and then reference on each page where it's needed. This is very similar to the *procedure call* available in most programming languages. The syntax is

```
Server.Execute(path)
```

The path can either be absolute (the fully qualified path) or relative. In either case the file must be in the same ASP application as the calling ASP file. The path can include a query string, which means that values can be passed to the ASP file and be processed, and the resulting values will be returned to the calling ASP file.

The Server Object Transfer Method

The Transfer method is similar to the Response Redirect method with an important difference. With the Response Redirect method, none of the state information—the values of objects and variables—is passed from the source page to the target page. With the Server Transfer method, all these values are included. This makes the Server Transfer method much more useful. The syntax is

```
Server.Transfer(path)
```

As with the Execute method, the path can be either relative or absolute, and the files must be in the same ASP application.

The Server Object HTMLEncode and URLEncode Methods

The HTMLEncode and URLEncode methods are handy utilities for converting text strings so they display correctly on web pages and can be included in URLs.

HTML uses certain characters, such as < and >, to define HTML elements. These are known as *reserved characters*. If you attempt to use them as text characters in a web page, HTML will interpret them as HTML coding. The HTMLEncode method converts the reserved characters in the text string to special characters that will display correctly and not be interpreted as part of the HTML coding.

FrontPage will automatically convert reserved characters when they are entered on a page in Page view or are in an imported text file.

The URLEncode method provides a similar function for text strings that are to be included in a URL. As you saw with Request.QueryString, you can attach information to a URL and then use it to control actions on an ASP page. If the extended information contains spaces or other special characters, these will not be interpreted correctly.

You can easily create an ASP page that demonstrates how these two methods work with these instructions:

Note *When you are instructed to type a line that ends with a period or comma, do not include it unless specifically noted. If the line ends with a colon, always leave a space after the colon.*

1. Create a new page and save it with the File Name Encode.asp and the page title HTML and URL Encoding.

2. Type **HTML and URL Encoding** at the top of the page, and format it as Heading 2.

3. Press ENTER and then insert a one-line text box from the Insert | Form menu or the Form toolbar.

4. Press HOME and type **Enter some text:**.

5. Press RIGHT ARROW and then press ENTER.

6. Right-click the form field and choose Form Field Properties.

7. In the Form Field Properties dialog box, type **Text** in the Name text box, and set the Width In Characters to 40. Click OK.

8. Right-click the form and choose Form Properties.

9. In the Form Properties dialog box, select the Send To Other option and then click Options.

10. In the Options For Custom Form Handler Action text box, type **Encode.asp** and click OK twice.

11. Click the HTML tab. In the first blank line after the form code, type

    <% strText = Request.Form("Text") %>.

12. Click the Normal tab, move the cursor to the first line under the form, and type **Your text HTML encoded:**.

13. Press ENTER and type **Your text URL encoded:**.

14. Click the HTML tab and locate the line <P>Your text HTML encoded: </P>, and type **<%= Server.HTMLEncode(strText) %>** before the closing paragraph tag.

15. Move the cursor to the line <P>Your text URL encoded: </P> and type **<%= Server.URLEncode(strText) %>** before the closing paragraph tag. Your code should look like this:

```
</FORM>
<% strText = Request.Form("Text") %>
<P>Your text HTML encoded: <%= Server.HTMLEncode(strText) %></P>
<P>Your text URL encoded: <%= Server.URLEncode(strText) %></P>
</BODY>
```

16. Save the page and then open it in your browser.

17. Type **Some text <P> <h3>** in the form text box and click Submit. Your browser should look similar to Figure 16-13.

If you look at the source for the HTML page displayed in your browser, you will see how the text was encoded for both HTML and the URL. For HTML, the text is written

Some text <P> <h3>

For the URL encoding it is written as

Some+text+%3CP%3E+%3Ch3%3E

In the HTML-encoded example, the less-than (<) and greater-than (>) symbols have been replaced with "<" and ">". For the URL-encoded example, the less-than and greater-than symbols have been replaced with "%3C" and "%3E," and spaces have been replaced with plus signs (+). The percent symbol (%) is used as an escape character, which indicates that what follows is the number of the ASCII character in hexadecimal.

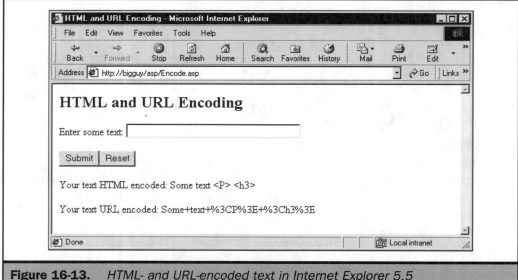

Figure 16-13.   *HTML- and URL-encoded text in Internet Explorer 5.5*

ASP Error Handling

It's inevitable that errors will occur as you build large ASP applications. Prior to IIS 5.0, debugging these errors in ASP used to be less than fun. Basically, the only tool the programmer had was to liberally use Response.Write statements throughout their code to display variable and state values. The situation is much improved thanks to the ASPError object and the Server GetLastError method. The properties of the ASPError object are listed in Table 16-10. The syntax for the Server GetLastError method is

 `Server.GetLastError()`

The Server GetLastError method returns the ASPError object that can then be displayed in your browser. These next steps show you how to do this.

1. Create a new page and save it with the File Name Createerror.asp and the page title Create an ASP Error.
2. Type **This Page Is Error Free** at the top of the page, and format it as Heading 2.

Property	Description
ASPCode	The error code returned by IIS
Number	The standard COM error code
Source	The source code of the line that caused the error
Category	Describes whether the error was caused by ASP, the scripting language, or an object
File	The name of the ASP file that was being processed when the error occurred
Line	The number of the line where the error occurred
Column	The column position in the line that caused the error
Description	A short description of the error
ASPDescription	A more detailed description of the error, if it is ASP related

Table 16-10.   *ASPError Object Properties*

3. Click the HTML tab and place the cursor after the line containing the heading and before the closing body tag.

4. Type

<% For i = 0 to 1
Net %>

5. This line will create a script compilation error since "Next," which is required in a For... Next loop, is misspelled. Your code should look like this:

```
<H2>This Page Is Error Free</H2>
<% For i = 0 to 1
Net %>
</BODY>
```

6. Save your page and then open it in your browser. Figure 16-14 shows the error message that should be displayed. This is the default page for displaying errors that is installed with IIS. You can view the code on this page by opening it in a text editor. By default, the page is located at C:\WINNT\Help\iisHelp\common\500-100.asp (or C:\Windows\Help\iisHelp\common\500-100.asp in Windows 98). The code on this page is a good example of ASP programming.

7. Correct the spelling of Next on your error page, save it, and then refresh your browser. The page should now load without errors.

You can create your own custom error pages, but this requires configuring IIS on your web server. Your error page can be either a file or a URL. This next exercise shows how to configure your custom error page as a file.

1. On your Create an ASP Error page, in HTML view, recreate the error by misspelling "Next." Save your page and reload it in your browser.

2. Create a new page and save it with the filename Displayerror.asp and the page title Display Page Error.

3. Type **The Error Is**, format as Heading 2, and press ENTER.

4. Open the Table menu and choose Table | Insert. In the Insert Table dialog box, specify 10 Rows, 2 Columns, a Cell Padding of 4, and clear the Specify Width check box if it is selected. Click OK.

5. In the first cell of the first row, type **Property**, press TAB, and type **Value**.

6. Press TAB and type **ASPCode**.

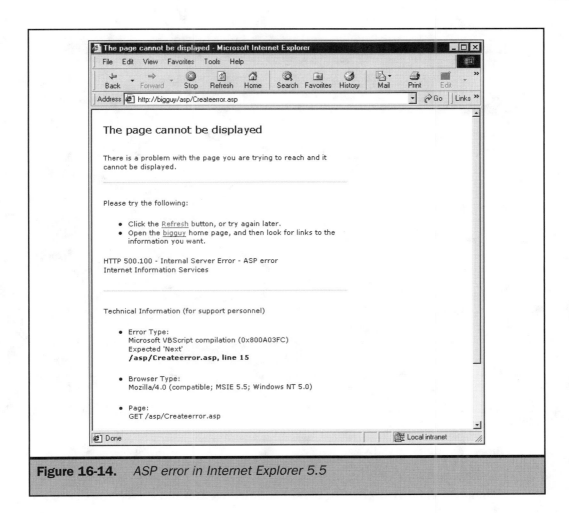

Figure 16-14.   *ASP error in Internet Explorer 5.5*

7. Press DOWN ARROW and type **Number**.

8. In the remaining cells of the first column, type **Source**, **Category**, **File**, **Line**, **Column**, **Description**, and **ASPDescription**. Your table should look like Figure 16-15.

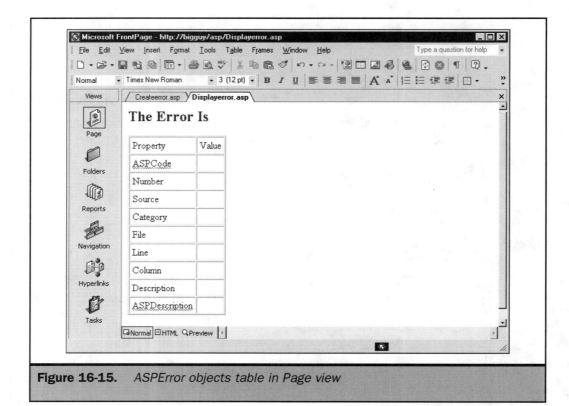

Figure 16-15. *ASPError objects table in Page view*

9. Click the HTML tab and place the cursor on the line immediately below the opening body tag.

10. Type **<% Set objASPError = Server.GetLastError %>** and save your page.

11. Still in HTML view, locate the nonbreaking space ( ) in the second cell of the second table row. The text in the first cell of the second row will be ASPCode.

12. Delete the nonbreaking space and type **<%= objASPError.ASPCode %>**. Your code should look like this:

```
<TR>
  <TD>ASPCode</TD>
  <TD><%= objASPError.ASPCode %></TD>
</TR>
```

13. In the third row, delete the nonbreaking space in the second column and type **<%= objASPError.Number %>**.

14. In the fourth row, delete the nonbreaking space in the second column and type **<%= objASPError.Source %>**.

15. In the fifth row, delete the nonbreaking space in the second column and type **<%= objASPError.Category %>**.

16. In the sixth row, delete the nonbreaking space in the second column and type **<%= objASPError.File %>**.

17. In the seventh row, delete the nonbreaking space in the second column and type **<%= objASPError.Line %>**.

18. In the eighth row, delete the nonbreaking space in the second column and type **<%= objASPError.Column %>**.

19. In the ninth row, delete the nonbreaking space in the second column and type **<%= objASPError.Description %>**.

20. In the tenth row, delete the nonbreaking space in the second column and type **<%= objASPError.ASPDescription %>**.

21. Save your page.

Now you need to configure your web server to display your custom error page instead of the default error page.

22. In Windows 2000 Professional click Start | Settings | Control Panel | Administrative Tools, and click Internet Services Manager. In Windows 2000 Server click Start | Programs | Administrative Tools, and click Internet Services Manager.

23. In the Internet Services Manager, expand the directory trees until your ASP directory is displayed.

24. Right-click your ASP directory and choose Properties. In the ASP Properties dialog box click the Custom Errors tab.

25. Scroll down the Error Messages For HTTP Errors list box until you see the 500;100 HTTP error, as shown next.

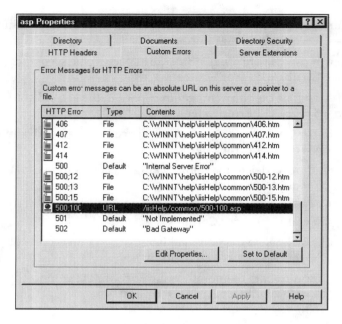

26. Click Edit Properties. In the Error Mapping Properties dialog box select URL in the Message Type drop-down, then type **/asp/Displayerror.asp** in the URL text box. Your Error Mapping Properties dialog box should look this:

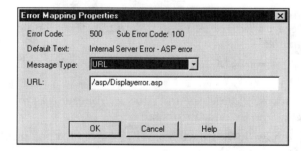

27. Click OK, then click Apply and OK.

28. Open your Create An ASP Error page in your browser. It should look similar to Figure 16-16. (It may be necessary to click Refresh to have it display properly.)

Because the error is a VBScript error and not an ASP error, not all of the properties have values. There are some differences you should notice between your error page and the default error page. One is the actual error number that is displayed. On the default error page it is 0x800A03CF (a hexadecimal number), while your error page displays it as –2146827268. This doesn't provide much information since the standard

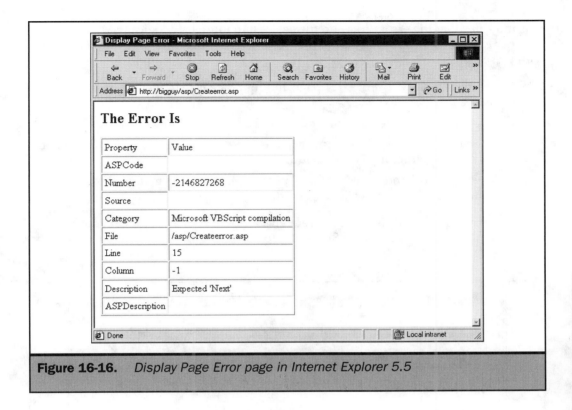

Figure 16-16. *Display Page Error page in Internet Explorer 5.5*

and all the help files available are based on a hexadecimal number. In the following steps you'll modify your Display Page Error page to display the error number as a hexadecimal number.

1. On your Display Error Page in FrontPage HTML view, locate the line that displays the Number property. This is the second cell of the third row.

2. Place your cursor immediately after the opening <TD> tag and type **0x**.

3. Move your cursor to the left of objASPError.Number and type **Hex(**.

4. Place your cursor to the right of objASPError.Number and type **)**. The line should now look like this:

```
<TD>0x<%= Hex(objASPError.Number) %></TD>
```

5. Save your page and refresh your browser. The error number will now be displayed in hexadecimal format.

The change you made converts the error number to hexadecimal format using the VBScript Hex operator. Another point to note is the –1 for the Column number field.

This indicates that the error did not return a column number; a logical FALSE. Another example will show an ASP error rather than a VBScript error. You'll do that with these steps.

1. On your Create An ASP Error page, in FrontPage HTML view, correct the misspelling of "Next."

2. Save the page and reload it in your browser. It should now display correctly.

3. In the HTML tab, move the cursor to the line after your existing VBScript code and type **<!--#Include File="include.inc"-->**.

4. Save your page and refresh your browser. The error information shown in Figure 16-17 should now be displayed.

The error is generated since the file referenced doesn't exist (include files are covered in the section "The Server-Side Include Statement").

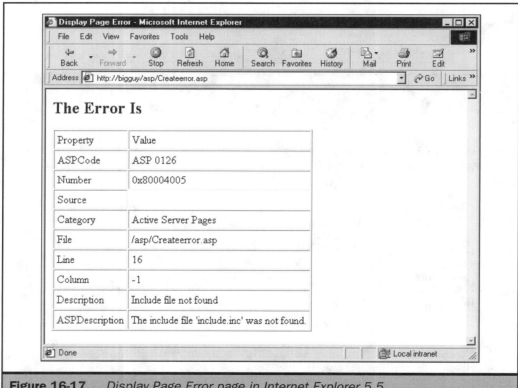

Figure 16-17. *Display Page Error page in Internet Explorer 5.5*

The Active Server Page objects are extremely flexible and powerful. The examples given here have just scratched the surface of what you can do with them. ASP would be a great boon to the web builder even if the objects covered so far were all there was to it, but there's more. The ASP components covered in the next section will show how ASP is an open-ended structure for interactive web applications.

ASP Components

Active Server Pages components differ from the objects that have been covered so far in that they are really ActiveX components. (An explanation of ActiveX components can be found in Chapter 20.) ASP creates the structure to use these components on the server. You are not limited to the components included with ASP; you can integrate any ActiveX components. This is what makes ASP an open-ended system for interactive web applications.

There are 12 components included with IIS. Additional components are available from Microsoft and other sources. Table 16-11 provides a brief description of the default components. In this chapter you will use the Ad Rotator, Browser Capabilities, and Content Linking components. The Database Access Component is the subject of Chapter 19 and will not be covered in this chapter. These should give you a good understanding of how ASP components function.

The Server.CreateObject Object and ASP Components

The components included with ASP are all objects that must be *instantiated* before they can be referenced. This simply means that an instance of the component must be created. This is done with the Server.CreateObject method by creating a variable that references the component. An example of the syntax is

```
Set objComponent = Server.CreateObject([Vendor.]Component[.Version])
```

The Set statement is required in Visual Basic and VBScript when assigning a variable to an object.

*In creating variables, it is a good practice to use a three-character prefix that identifies what type of variable has been created. In the preceding example, objComponent, the prefix "obj" indicates that the variable references an object. Common prefixes are listed in Table 16-12. More information can be found at **http://msdn.microsoft.com/scripting/**.*

By default, instances of objects have page scope. This means that they exist from the time they are created until the script on a page is completely processed. They can also be explicitly destroyed by setting the object variable to Nothing, for example: *objComponent =*

Component	Description
Ad Rotator	Automates the rotation of ad banners
Browser Capabilities	Determines the features of the user's browser
Content Linking	Links pages in a web application and creates tables of contents
Content Rotator	Automates the rotation of HTML content
Counters	Creates an object that can control any number of individual counters
Database Access	Provides connectivity to ODBC-compliant databases
File Access	Provides methods for accessing the computer's file system
Logging Utility	Provides methods for accessing the web server log files
MyInfo	Contains personal information
Page Counter	Tracks page hits
Permission Checker	Checks user permissions to access files
Tools	Provides utilities such as a random number generator that you can add to your ASP pages

Table 16-11. *Active Server Pages Components*

Variable Type	Prefix
Boolean	bln
Byte	byt
Date/Time	dtm
Double	dbl
Error	err
Integer	int

Table 16-12. *Prefixes for Variable Names*

Variable Type	Prefix
Long	lng
Object	obj
Single	sng
String	str

Table 16-12. *Prefixes for Variable Names* (continued)

Nothing. Instances of objects can be given session or application scope by creating them in the Global.asa file with the <OBJECT> tag. In the examples in this section, the objects will be used with page scope.

In the following sections, you will see exactly how Server.CreateObject is used with ASP components.

The Ad Rotator Component

Ad banners have become quite common on web sites. These banners are graphics that usually provide links to the advertiser's web site. Ad banners are typically sold by number of impressions or page views or by click-throughs. *Impressions* are the number of times an ad banner is actually loaded by users. *Click-throughs* are the number of times users click the banner and jump to the advertiser's site.

Once you begin selling ad banners on a site, you have to manage them. Unless an advertiser buys all the impressions for a particular page, each page may have several ad banners, and you will need to rotate them constantly. Even if an advertiser does buy all the impressions for a page, they may have several banners that they want rotated. This would be a full-time job if done manually, which is why the Ad Rotator Component is so useful. It automates the process of rotating banners and even apportions impressions between them so that one banner can get 50 percent of the impressions and the remaining 50 percent can be shared equally by two other banners.

The Ad Rotator Component uses a text file, the Rotator Schedule file, which contains the banner file information and schedule. You can also use a script, the Redirection file, which can be used to capture information when a user clicks a banner before redirecting the user to the advertiser's site.

There are three properties and a single method for the Ad Rotator Component; the properties are described in Table 16-13. The syntax for this method is

```
GetAdvertisement (schedule file)
```

Property	Description
Border	Sets the width of the border around the ad graphic
Clickable	Sets whether the ad graphic is a hyperlink
TargetFrame	The name of the frame in which to display the ad, if used on a frame page

Table 16-13.   *Ad Rotator Component Properties*

Creating a Rotator Schedule File

The first step in using the Ad Rotator is to create a Rotator Schedule file. This is a text file that contains some basic information about all the ad banners and specific information about each banner. You create the schedule file in your text editor.

The syntax for the file is

```
Redirect URL
Width PixelsWidth
Height PixelsHeight
Border PixelsBorder
*
```

These first four items are the optional global values for the Rotator Schedule file. If they are not included, the first line of the file will contain a single asterisk (*) and the default values will be used. The function and default value of each parameter is described in Table 16-14.

Parameter	Default	Description
Redirect		URL of the file that redirects users when they click a banner and captures any information, such as click-throughs
Width	440	Width in pixels of the ad banners
Height	60	Height in pixels of the ad banners
Border	1	Width in pixels of the border around each banner

Table 16-14.   *Rotator Schedule File Global Parameters*

After the asterisk, you enter the information about each ad banner. The syntax is

```
BannerURL
AdvertiserURL
AltText
Impressions
```

The BannerURL is the location of the ad banner graphic; AdvertiserURL is the URL of the web page that is the target of the banner hyperlink; AltText is the alternate text for the banner graphic; and Impressions is the percentage of impressions the banner will receive. The actual value for the Impressions parameter is a number between 0 and 4,294,967,295. In determining the percentage of impressions for each banner, the component totals all the values for all the banners and then calculates the percentage. For example, if you had three banners with impressions values of 6, 3, and 3, the total would be 12. The first banner would get 6/12 of the impressions, or 50 percent, and the remaining two would get 3/12, or 25 percent, each.

 The Rotator Schedule file must be available on a virtual path on the web server.

Create a Rotator Schedule file with these steps:

 In your Schedule Rotator file, substitute the name of your computer for servername. *In the examples shown here, the computer name is* bigguy.

1. Open Notepad or your favorite text editor. In a new page, type

   > **Redirect /scripts/Adredirect.asp**
   > **Width 468**
   > **Height 60**
   > **Border 1**
   > *****
   > **images/banner1.gif**
   > **http://***servername*/**asp/default.asp**
   > **FrontPage 2000**
   > **1**
   >
   > **images/banner2.gif**
   > **http://***servername*/**asp/default.asp**
   > **FrontPage 2000**
   > **1**

2. Save the file in your ASP directory with the name Adsched.txt.

3. In your ASP web, create a new page. At the top of the page, type **Ad Banner Rotation** and format it as Heading 2.

4. Save the page with the page title Ad Banner Rotation and the File Name Banners.asp.

Creating an Instance of the Ad Rotator Component

On the Banners.asp page, you need to create an instance of the Ad Rotator Component and then use the GetAdvertisement method to display a banner. Do that now with these steps:

1. In the Page view Normal tab, move the insertion point to the line below the heading.

2. Click the HTML tab, check that the cursor is on the line below your heading, and type

   ```
   <%
   Set objRotator = Server.CreateObject("MSWC.AdRotator")
   Response.Write(objRotator.GetAdvertisement("Adsched.txt"))
   %>
   ```

3. Figure 16-18 shows the Ad Rotation script in the FrontPage HTML tab.

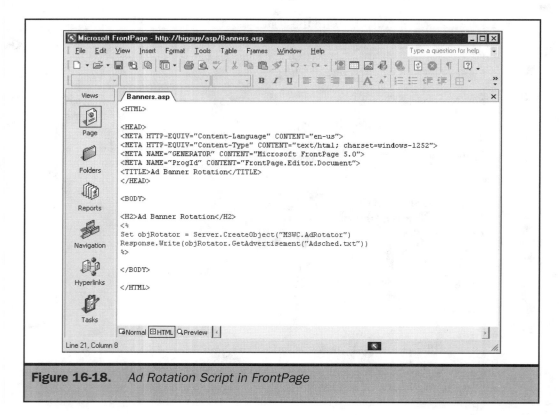

Figure 16-18. *Ad Rotation Script in FrontPage*

4. Save the page.

In your script you use the Response.Write object to write out the value returned by the GetAdvertisement method. You will see the results of this later in this exercise.

5. Click Folders in the Views bar, and in the FrontPage Folder List, double-click the Images folder to open it. Then open the File menu and choose Import.

6. In the Import dialog box, click Add File.

7. In the Add File To Import List dialog box, select your CD-ROM drive, and open the Chap16 folder on the included CD.

8. Click the file Banner1.gif, then press and hold CTRL and click Banner2.gif. Release CTRL, click Open, and then click OK.

9. Open the Banners.asp page in your web browser. It should look similar to Figure 16-19.

10. Click your browser's Refresh (Internet Explorer) or Reload (Netscape) button until the ad banner changes.

> **Note** *Even with two ad banners set to receive 50 percent of the impressions each, every refresh will not always change the banner displayed. On average, over a period of time, each banner should receive 50 percent of the impressions.*

11. View the source of the page in your browser.

By looking at the source, you can see the HTML code that is created by the Ad Rotator Component and written to the web page by the Response.Write object. Two HTML tags

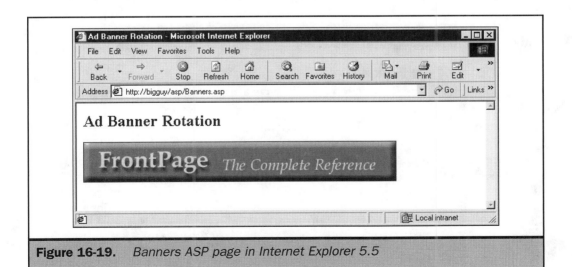

Figure 16-19.   *Banners ASP page in Internet Explorer 5.5*

are used: the < HREF> tag, which creates a hyperlink, and the <IMG> tag, which displays the graphic. Your hyperlink source should look similar to this (depending on which banner is being displayed):

```
<A HREF="/scripts/Adredirect.asp?url=http://servername/asp/
    default.htm&image=images/banner1.gif">...</>
```

The hyperlink will not take you directly to the advertiser's web page; it first takes you to the Redirection file, which you will create in the next part of this exercise. You will use the Request.QueryString object to parse the URL for the final destination and then use the Response.Redirect object to send the user there. First, though, the function of the FrontPage Scripts directory, where the Redirection file will be placed, needs to be explained.

The FrontPage Scripts Directory

In the examples of working with cookies, you created an ASP page, Writecookie.asp, which processed data from one page, Createcookie.asp, and then sent the user to another page, Readcookie.asp. When you're working with ASP files, this situation is not uncommon. You can create ASP pages in FrontPage, complete with HTML headers, to handle these tasks, but you will always have the problem you experienced earlier if you use the Response.Redirect object. A better way is to use the Scripts directory created by default as a virtual directory with Execute and Scripts permission when you install IIS.

The default path for the Scripts directory is C:\Inetpub\Scripts. As a virtual directory, it can be accessed from any page in any of your webs with the virtual path /scripts. For security, this directory does not have Read permission set. This is to prevent users from seeing any of the files located there. Without the Read permission, users cannot load any of the files in the Scripts directory in their browser. This is where you will save the Adredirect.asp Redirection file.

The Redirection File

In its simplest form, the Redirection file will have a single line:

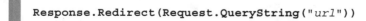

```
Response.Redirect(Request.QueryString("url"))
```

However, you can use this file to do much more. For example, you can record each click-through in a database. Another use is to use the VBScript Select Case statement to expand the URL provided by the Rotator Schedule file. Many advertisers use complicated URLs for their banner ads. Often they will include identifiers for the site hosting the banner and write out the information to their own databases. To avoid passing these long URLs between the Rotator Schedule file, the ASP page, and the

Redirection file, you can use a single, short text string in the schedule file that is expanded to the complete URL in the Redirection file. To do that, follow these steps:

1. Open the Adsched.txt file in your text editor.

2. Change the URL for the first banner to Banner1, and then change the URL for the second banner to Banner2.

3. Save the file and open a new file in your text editor.

4. Type

```
<%
Set AdUrl = Request.QueryString("url")
Select Case AdUrl
Case "Banner1"
AdUrl = "http://servername/asp/default.asp"
Case "Banner2"
AdUrl = "http://servername/asp/default.asp"
End Select
Response.Redirect AdUrl
%>
```

5. Save the file in the Scripts directory (C:\Inetpub\Scripts) with the name Adredirect.asp.

6. Reload the Banners.asp page in your browser and click the ad banner. You will be taken to the ASP web home page you created earlier in this book.

7. Close the Banners.asp page in FrontPage.

The Ad Rotator Component is very flexible, and you don't have to use it just to rotate ad banners. You could rotate graphics with links to pages in your own site or any other graphic content.

The Browser Capabilities Component

There is a great variety of browsers currently in use on the Internet, not just Microsoft and Netscape browsers. Many of the online services, such as AOL and EarthLink, use either proprietary or licensed browsers that are tailored to their needs. Even among Netscape and Microsoft you will find many different versions in use, and each version supports different features.

Microsoft supplies a text file, Browscap.ini, which lists the features of many different browsers. The default path for this file is C:\WINNT\System32\Inetsrv\ Browscap.ini. It is worth opening this file in your text editor, as shown in Figure 16-20, just to get an idea of how many variations exist.

Tip   *An even more extensive Browscap.ini file is available from cyScape, Inc. (http://www.cyscape.com/browscap/).*

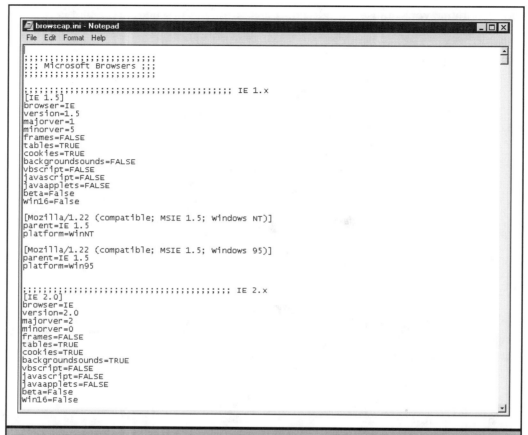

Figure 16-20.   *Browscap.ini file in Notepad*

The latest browsers offer features that are unsupported by earlier versions, and some are only supported by specific browsers. For example, only Internet Explorer supports client-side VBScript scripting. The problem for web designers is to decide which features to include in their webs. There's a tendency to want to use the latest and greatest, but what happens when the site is visited by a browser that doesn't support the features used?

The Browser Capabilities Component and the Browscap.ini file address this problem directly. Every browser identifies itself in the HTTP header sent by the browser (the USER_AGENT) when it requests a file from a web server. You can read this header, extract the browser and version, look up which features it supports in the

Browscap.ini file, and tailor your web pages to the users' browser (or tell them to get an update).

Tip   *It can be very educational to record in a database the browser types and versions visiting your web site so you can analyze the data. If the majority of your users are using browsers that don't support frames, for example, then it's a good idea not to use them. If your audience is technically literate, you will probably find more current browsers than if your site is aimed at the general public.*

In this next exercise, you will create an ASP page that displays some of the major capabilities (or lack thereof) of the browser that has loaded it. Create the page with these steps:

Note   *When you are instructed to type a line that ends with a colon, always leave a space after the colon.*

1. Create a new page in FrontPage, and save it with the page title Browser Capabilities and the File Name Browsers.asp.

2. At the top of the page, type **Your Browser's Capabilities** and format it as Heading 2. Press ENTER.

3. Type **The HTTP User Agent is:** and press ENTER.

4. Type **Your browser is:**, then type **version #** and press SPACE.

5. Press ENTER, open the Table menu, and choose Insert | Table.

6. In the Insert Table dialog box, select 4 Rows, 4 Columns, Center Alignment, and a Cell Padding of 4. The Specify Width check box should be cleared. Click OK.

7. In the first cell of the first row of the table, type **Platform** and press TAB twice.

8. Type **VBScript** and press TAB twice.

9. Type **Cookies**, press TAB twice, type **JavaScript,** and press TAB twice.

10. Type **Tables**, press TAB twice, type **ActiveX Controls,** and press TAB twice.

11. Type **Frames**, press TAB twice, and type **Java Applets**.

12. Save your page. It should look similar to Figure 16-21.

In the next steps, you will use the Page view HTML tab to enter the ASP scripting on the page. You must make sure that each script matches the labels on the page.

13. Click the HTML tab, then place the cursor on the first line after the body tag and type **<% Set objBrowser = Server.CreateObject("MSWC.BrowserType") %>**.

14. Place the cursor at the end of the line The HTTP User Agent is: but before the closing HTML paragraph tag (<P>).

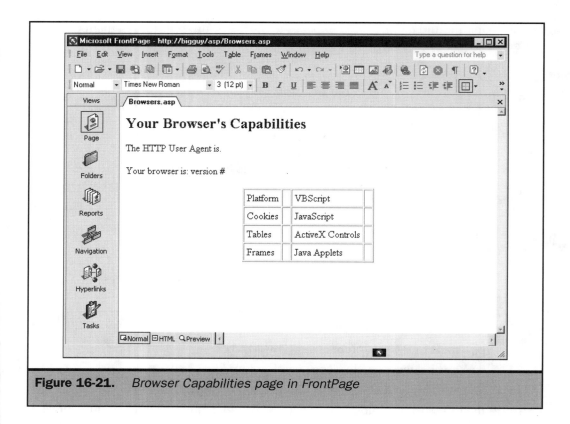

Figure 16-21. *Browser Capabilities page in FrontPage*

15. Type **<%= Request.ServerVariables("HTTP_USER_AGENT") %>**.

16. Place the cursor one space after the colon in the line Your browser is: and type **<%= objBrowser.Browser %>**. Leave a space between your script and the word "version."

17. At the end of the same line (before the closing paragraph tag), type **<%= objBrowser.Version %>**.

The remaining scripts will be placed in the appropriate HTML code for the table cells.

18. Place the cursor in the table row beneath the row with the label Platform. Delete the nonbreaking space ( ) and type **<%= objBrowser.Platform %>**.

19. In the table cell below the label VBScript, delete the nonbreaking space and type **<%= objBrowser.VBScript %>**. At this point, the first row of your table should look like this:

```
<TR>
  <TD>Platform</TD>
  <TD><%= objBrowser.Platform %></TD>
  <TD>VBScript</TD>
  <TD><%= objBrowser.VBScript %></TD>
</TR>
```

The remaining rows of the table will be filled out in the same manner: deleting the nonbreaking spaces and entering the script in the cell below the label in the HTML tab.

20. In the table cell below the label Cookies, type **<%= objBrowser.Cookies %>**.

21. In the table cell below the label JavaScript, type **<%= objBrowser.JavaScript %>**.

22. In the table cell below the label Tables, type **<%= objBrowser.Tables %>**.

23. In the table cell below the label ActiveX Controls, type **<%= objBrowser .ActiveXcontrols %>**.

24. In the table cell below the label Frames, type **<%= objBrowser.Frames %>**.

25. In the table cell below the label Java Applets, type **<%= objBrowser .Javaapplets %>**.

26. Save your page. It should look similar to Figure 16-22.

27. Open the Browser Capabilities page in all your browsers. Figure 16-23 shows the page in Internet Explorer 5.5.

If your browser displays "Unknown" in the table fields, it means that your browser is newer than your Browscap.ini file. You can get an updated file at **http://www.cyscape.com/browscap/.**

Both Internet Explorer and Netscape identify themselves as Mozilla, though Internet Explorer also says "compatible." Mozilla was the code name of Netscape's original browser. The name remains a part of Internet lore for backward compatibility.

The Content Linking Component

The Content Linking Component is used to generate tables of contents for a web. It uses a Content Linking List, a text file containing the URLs of the pages, to accomplish this. This method is more cumbersome than the navigation features in FrontPage, which don't require you to create a text file listing all the pages. However, FrontPage's navigation features are of limited use with ASP pages (Navigation view doesn't support Active Server Pages), so it is a viable method for navigation.

As usual, you create an instance of the Content Linking Component using the Server.CreateObject statement. The syntax is

```
Set objLinks = Server.CreateObject("MSWC.Nextlink")
```

Once the object is instantiated, each method is called with the URL of the Content Linking List passed as a parameter, for example, **GetListCount**(*listURL*). Where an index number is required, the syntax is

```
GetNthDescription(listURL, i)
```

where *i* is the index number. The methods for the component are explained in Table 16-15.

The Content Linking List is a simple text file. Each line of the file contains the URL of the page, a description of the page, and an optional comment. Each item is separated by a tab (this allows you to use spaces within the description and comment), and each

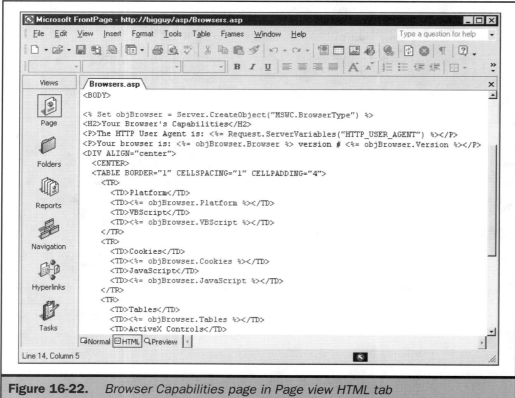

Figure 16-22.   *Browser Capabilities page in Page view HTML tab*

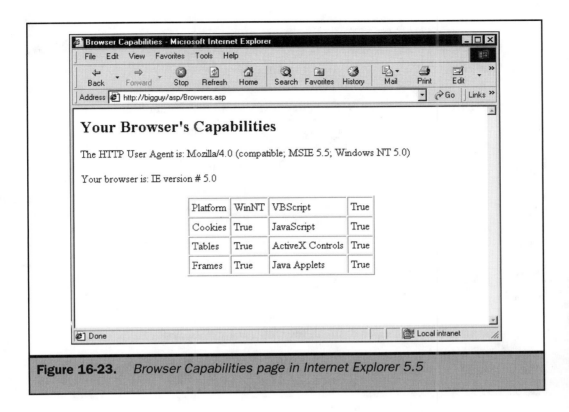

Figure 16-23. *Browser Capabilities page in Internet Explorer 5.5*

line ends with a carriage return. The URL can be a relative or virtual path, but it cannot be an absolute URL. An absolute URL would begin with http:, //, or \\.

You will see how this works in this next exercise. Begin by creating a Content Linking List for your ASP web.

1. In your text editor, create a new document.

2. Type **Backgrounds.asp**, press TAB, type **User Input Changes Page Background Color**, press TAB, and type **This is a comment**.

3. Press ENTER, type **Banners.asp**, press TAB, and type **Rotate Ad Banners Using ASP**. Press ENTER.

4. Type **Browers.asp**, press TAB, and type **Check Your Browser's Features**. Press ENTER.

5. Type **Createcookie.asp**, press TAB, and type **Create A Cookie**. Press ENTER.

6. Type **Encode.asp**, press TAB, and type **HTML- and URL-Encode Text**. Press ENTER.

Method	Description
GetListCount	Returns the number of items in the Content Linking List.
GetNextURL	Returns the next URL in the Content Linking List.
GetPreviousDescription	Returns the previous description in the Content Linking List.
GetListIndex	Returns the number in the Content Linking List for the current page. The first page is number 1.
GetNthDescription	Returns the description of the item with the specified index in the Content Linking List.
GetPreviousURL	Returns the URL of the previous item in the Content Linking List.
GetNextDescription	Returns the description of the next item in the Content Linking List.
GetNthURL	Returns the URL of the item with the specified index in the Content Linking List.

Table 16-15. *Content Linking Component Methods*

7. Type **Server.asp**, press TAB, and type **View Your Server Variables**. Press ENTER.

8. Save your text file in your ASP directory (C:\Inetpub\Wwwroot\ASP\ by default) with the filename Links.txt, and then close your text editor.

9. If it's not already open, open your ASP home page (Default.asp) in FrontPage and click the HTML tab.

In the next part of this exercise, you will create a VBScript loop that uses the Content Linking methods to read your links file and create a hyperlink to each page.

10. Place your cursor at the beginning of the line containing the closing body tag (</BODY>) and press ENTER and then UP ARROW.

11. Type **<UL>** and press ENTER. This will display the index as a bulleted list.

12. Type

```
<%
Set objLink = Server.CreateObject("MSWC.NextLink")
intCount = objLink.GetListCount("Links.txt")
```

```
i = 1
Do While (i <= intCount)
%>
```

This first section of the script instantiates the Content Linking Component; it then reads the number of records in the Content Linking List (Links.txt) and places the number in the local variable intCount. The variable *i* is then initialized with the number one. The value of *i* will be incremented by one in each iteration of the Do While loop. When *i* exceeds the value of intCount, the loop will end. Each iteration of the loop will write a hyperlink to a page listed in Content Linking List. Continue with these steps:

13. Type

```
<LI><A HREF="<%= objLink.GetNthURL(("Links.txt"), i) %>">
<%= objLink.GetNthDescription(("Links.txt"), i) %></A></LI>
```

This script first formats the output as a list item (<>); it then writes URL as the target of the hyperlink and Description as the displayed text from the item in the Content Linking List that corresponds to the value of *i*. When the value of *i* is 1, the first item in the Links.txt file, the URL, and description for your Backgrounds.asp page will be written to your home page. You will finish the loop and the bulleted list in the next step:

14. Type

```
<%
i = (i + 1)
Loop
%>
</UL>
```

15. Save your work and then open your ASP home page in your browser. Figure 16-24 shows the page in Internet Explorer.

The Content Linking Component is not as flexible as Navigation view, but it does provide a useful alternative.

The Server-Side Include Statement

Active Server Pages have one other element that duplicates to some extent a FrontPage feature: the Include statement. It functions much the same as the FrontPage Include Page Component. It has two methods, Virtual and File. The syntax is

```
<!--#nclude method = "filename"-->
```

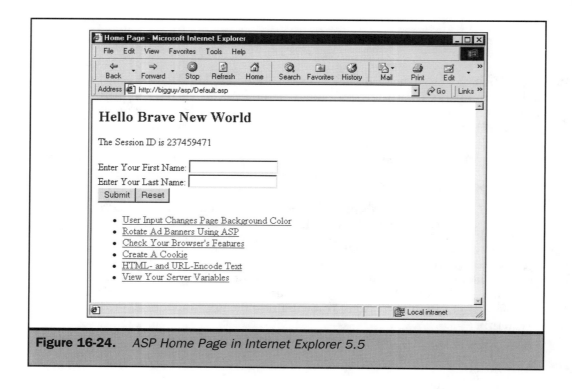

Figure 16-24. *ASP Home Page in Internet Explorer 5.5*

With the Virtual method, the filename is a virtual path; the File method requires an absolute path to the file.

Included files are generally given the extension .INC to indicate how they are to be used, but this is not required.

Active Server Pages are a huge leap forward in bringing true interactivity to web applications. In the next chapter, you will see how this functionality has been improved with ASP.NET and can be used to create state-of-the-art web applications.

The Complete Reference

FrontPage 2002

Chapter 17

Introducing ASP.NET

The features of Active Server Pages you explored in the previous chapter enable you to add quite a bit of functionality to your web applications, but the next generation of ASP, ASP.NET, offers even more functionality. Rather than an evolutionary step from ASP, ASP.NET is revolutionary.

When this book was written, ASP.NET (formerly called ASP+) was still in beta, but it should be available by the time you read this. There may be minor changes between the beta version described in this chapter, and the final release version, however.

As powerful as ASP is, it still suffers from some limitations. Perhaps the biggest difference is that ASP.NET is a compiled, rather than a scripting, environment. As you saw in the previous chapter, ASP can be used with either VBScript or JavaScript. Components can be built using other programming languages, but they are referenced through scripts. Simply going to a compiled environment, plus the ability to use languages such as Visual Basic and C# (Microsoft's latest variant of C—pronounced "C sharp"), offers significant performance increases. ASP.NET also fits nicely into the .NET Framework, Microsoft's latest effort to improve the functionality and performance of web applications.

Note *VBScript is not supported in ASP.NET. The supported languages in Beta 1 are Visual Basic, C#, and JScript (Microsoft's version of JavaScript which complies with the ECMAScript standard). Since Visual Basic (being a compiled language rather than a scripting language) offers significant advantages over VBScript, this is not a serious loss. ASP pages written in VBScript will still work under ASP.NET but they will have to be converted to a supported language to take full advantage of the ASP.NET Framework.*

Tip *Complete information about the .NET Framework can be found at* **http://msdn.microsoft.com/net/**.

This chapter can only provide an overview of ASP.NET, with some of the fundamental differences between ASP and ASP.NET being explored. One thing to note is that ASP.NET files have their own set of file extensions to differentiate them from ASP files. Basically, an "x" is added to the existing ASP extension so that .asp becomes .aspx and .asa becomes .asax.

Note *ASP.NET is compatible with ASP so you can use both in the same web application and even on the same web page. This means ASP.NET won't break any of your existing ASP applications. If ASP.NET is used, then the proper file extension (aspx or asax) must also be used.*

The .NET Framework SDK

If you want to write ASP.NET applications, you will need to download and install the .NET Framework SDK (Software Development Kit). This is a 111-megabyte download (either a single download or 11 smaller downloads), so you may prefer to order the CD from Microsoft instead. The SDK can be installed on Windows ME, 98, NT 4.0, and 2000, so Internet Explorer 5.5 and Microsoft Data Access Components (MDAC) 2.6 are required. Microsoft also warns that the SDK should not be installed on a production machine, as it does for all beta software, with good reason. Beta software can be unpredictable.

With all these requirements and warnings, you may wonder why you would want to install the SDK. It's not necessary to install it to benefit from this chapter, but you won't be able to get any hands-on experience without it. Unless you're planning on doing serious web application development, and have a spare computer on which to install it, it could be more trouble than it's worth. On the other hand, this is the price of staying current with technology, and the issues surrounding the install of SDK will still apply with the final release version. The SDK also contains the documentation for the .NET Framework of which ASP.NET is a part. Ultimately, this is the web technology Microsoft is betting on and it does offer a great deal of potential.

If you decide to download and install the .NET Framework SDK, you need to check the versions of your database drivers and Internet Explorer. First, check your version of IE with these steps.

1. In Internet Explorer, open the Help menu and choose About Internet Explorer. If the version number displayed in the About Internet Explorer window does not begin with 5.5 you will need to update it.

2. If you need to update IE, type **http://www.microsoft.com/windows/ie/** in your browser's address bar and press ENTER. If you already have IE 5.5, proceed to checking your database drivers.

3. On the Internet Explorer home page, find and click the link to download the latest version of IE and the current service pack. The page that opens should have instructions for installing the update, which will vary based on your operating system.

4. Select your language in the drop-down list box and click Download Now.

5. Select Run This Program From Its Current Location in the File Download dialog box and click OK. The file will download and a Security Warning dialog box will be displayed.

6. Click Yes in the Security Warning dialog box. A License Agreement will be displayed. Select I Accept The Agreement and click Next if you want to proceed.

7. After the setup initializes, a dialog box will display what the setup program will download and install. Click Next.

8. Select a Download Site and click Next. When the installation is complete, you will need to restart your computer. Save all your work, then click Finish.

Checking your ODBC (Open Database Connectivity) drivers is a little more involved than updating Internet Explorer. The exact steps depend on your operating system, as explained in the next set of instructions.

1. In Windows 98/Me, click Start, point on Settings, and then click Control Panel. In the Control Panel, double-click ODBC Data Sources (32Bit).

2. In Windows 2000 Professional, click Start, point on Settings, then Control Panel, then Administrative Tools, and click Data Sources (ODBC).

3. In Windows 2000 Server, click Start, point on Programs, then Administrative Tools, and click Data Sources (ODBC).

4. In the ODBC Data Source Administrator dialog box, select the Drivers tab.

   This displays all the ODBC drivers installed on your system and their version numbers. If you are using Access, the version number should be 4.00.5303.01 or greater. For SQL Server, it should be 2000.80.140.00 or greater.

5. Click Cancel to close the ODBC Data Source Administrator dialog box.

With MDAC 2.6, Microsoft is no longer including the Jet database engine components. This is the database engine used by Access. If you plan on using Access as your database, and your drivers need updating, you may need to install a separate download to update the Access ODBC driver. These next steps will install the MDAC 2.6 download and then the Jet 4.0 download. Begin with these steps.

1. In your browser, open Microsoft's Universal Data Access site at **http://www.microsoft.com/data/**.

2. In the left pane of your browser, click Downloads.

3. On the downloads page, find the MDAC 2.6 RTM link (Release To Manufacturing). There may be a newer version by the time you read this, so you want to select the most current one.

4. Click Read The MDAC 2.6 Release Details, then click Download MDAC 2.6 RTM and follow the instructions on the download page.

5. Select Save This Program To Disk in the File Download dialog box and click OK, then select a location on your hard drive for the file and click Save.

6. Locate the saved file and double-click it to start the installation.

7. Accept the terms of the License Agreement and click Next to continue with the installation, then click Finish. When the installation is complete, click Close.

Now install the Jet update. At the time this was written, the current version was Jet 4.0 Service Pack 5 (SP5). There are three different versions of the update, one for Windows 95, 98, or NT 4.0, one for Windows 2000, and one for Windows ME.

8. Open the Knowledge Base page **http://support.microsoft.com/support/kb/articles/Q239/1/14.asp** in your browser. This page contains download links for all three versions.

9. Click the link for the appropriate version for your operating system.

10. Select Save This Program To Disk in the File Download dialog box and click OK, then select a location on your hard drive for the file and click Save.

11. Locate the saved file and double-click it to start the installation.

12. When the installation is complete, you will need to restart your computer. Save your work and click OK.

Now that the prerequisites are completed, download the NET Framework SDK using these steps.

1. In your browser, open the .NET Framework home page, **http://msdn.microsoft.com/net/**.

2. In the left pane, click .NET Downloads. The page that's opened contains download instructions as well as a link for ordering the CD instead of downloading the files.

3. Click either Full Download (111 MB) or Part 1 Of 11 (10.6 MB). Instructions for a multiple-part download are below the download links if you choose that option.

4. An End-User License Agreement will be displayed. After reading it, click Yes if you want to proceed.

5. Select Save This Program To Disk in the File Download dialog box and click OK, then select a location on your hard drive for the file and click Save.

6. Locate the saved file and double-click it to start the installation. If you chose the multiple-part download, follow the instructions on the download page for assembling the installation file.

7. When the Microsoft .NET Framework SDK Setup dialog box is displayed, click Next.

8. Read and accept the License Agreement if you wish to proceed. Click Next three times.

9. When the installation is complete, click OK.

Your computer is now configured to explore ASP.NET. When the .NET Framework is released and you want to start using it with your production webs, you will have to be sure your ISP has their web servers properly configured also.

ASP.NET Web Forms

As with every new technology, ASP.NET has its own jargon. What were once web pages are now *web forms* in an ASP.NET application. At the most basic level a web form is a text file, just like ordinary HTML and ASP pages, with a filename extension of aspx. There's much more of course. This name change also signifies a fundamental change in the way a web page is processed. With ASP, a page is interpreted on the web server when a browser requests it. This means that the page is run through the script engine each time it is requested, which requires a certain amount of server resources. With ASP.NET, the web form is compiled to a .NET Framework class object the first time it is requested. Each additional request uses the existing class, saving resources and time.

The best way to learn the differences between ASP and ASP.NET is to create an ASP.NET web form, which you will do with these next steps.

Note *As with the ASP web you created previously, ASP.NET webs cannot be disk-based webs—they must run on a web server. Also, the correct server permissions and FrontPage support for ASP must be enabled, as described in Chapter 16.*

1. In FrontPage, create a One Page Web and name it **net**. The location of the NET web should be in the default web created with the installation of IIS. This will normally be C:\Inetpub\Wwwroot and the URL is http://*computer_name*/. The URL to access this web will be http://*computer_name*/net/. The default web is a virtual directory and so meets the requirement that the root of an ASP.NET web be a virtual directory.

2. In Folders view, right-click Default.htm and choose Rename.

3. Rename the Default.htm file Default.aspx. Click Yes in the Confirm Rename dialog box, then click Yes again in the dialog box warning that changing the extension of a filename may cause the file to become unusable.

   At this point, FrontPage still doesn't know what to do with an aspx web form. You need to configure FrontPage to be the default editor for web forms before FP can edit them.

4. Open the Tools menu and select Options. In the Options dialog box, select the Configure Editors tab and click Add.

5. In the Add Editor Association dialog box, type **aspx** for the File Type, **FrontPage** for the Editor Name, and **frontpg.exe** for the command, as shown here. Click OK twice.

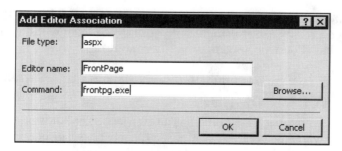

6. Double-click Default.aspx to open it for editing. A dialog box, shown here, may be displayed. Click Yes if it is. FrontPage will install the converter it needs and then open the page for editing.

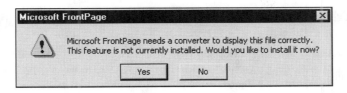

There are two additional settings you should also check before actually starting work on your NET web. These are the default document and the permissions applied to the NET web.

7. Open the Internet Services Manager by clicking the Start menu button, pointing on Programs, then Administrative Tools, and clicking Internet Services Manager. (In Windows 2000 Pro, the Administrative Tools are located in the Control Panel.)

8. In the Internet Services Manager, expand the tree for your web server then expand the tree for the default web.

9. Right-click the NET folder and choose Properties, then click the Documents tab. This displays the default document filenames for the web. If Default.aspx isn't displayed, add it by clicking Add, typing **Default.aspx** in the Add Default Document dialog box, and clicking OK.

10. Next, click the Directory tab. The Read checkbox should be selected and Scripts Only should be selected for Execute Permissions.

11. If you made any changes to the NET Properties dialog box, click Apply. Click OK to close the dialog box then click the Internet Services Manager's Close button.

With your web server and FrontPage configuration complete, you're ready to venture into the brave new world of ASP.NET. A good place to start is to duplicate the functionality of the ASP Form Response page you created in Chapter 16 as a web form. Do that with these steps:

1. In FrontPage, your Default.aspx page should be open in Normal view. Type **It's An ASP.NET World** at the top of the page and format it as Heading 2.

2. Press ENTER, then open the Insert menu and choose Form | Form.

3. Press SHIFT+ENTER, then UP-ARROW to create a blank line in the form and to place the cursor on it.

4. Type **Enter Your First Name:** (leaving a space after the colon), then open the Insert menu and choose Form | Textbox. Press SHIFT+ENTER.

5. Type **Enter Your Last Name:** (leaving a space after the colon), then open the Insert menu and choose Form | Textbox.

6. Right-click the first textbox (first name) and choose Form Field Properties. In the Text Box Properties dialog box, type **FirstName** in the Name textbox, then click OK.

7. Right-click the second textbox (last name) and choose Form Field Properties. In the Text Box Properties dialog box, type **LastName** in the Name textbox, then click OK.

8. Right-click the form and choose Form Properties. In the Form Properties dialog box, select the Send To Other option button. Custom ISAPI, NSAPI, CGI, Or ASP Script should be selected in the Send To Other drop-down. Click Options.

9. In the Options For Custom Form Handler dialog box, type **Form_rsp.aspx** in the Action text box, make sure the method is Post, and then click OK twice. Save the page.

10. Create a new page, then click Save on the toolbar.

11. In the Save As dialog box, select All Files (*.*) for the Save As Type, type **Form_rsp.aspx** for the File Name and **Form Response Page** for the Page Title. Click Save.

12. Type **Form Response Page** at the top of the page and format it as Heading 2.

13. Press ENTER and type **Your first name is:** (leave a space after the colon), then save the page.

14. Click the HTML tab. The cursor should be at the end of the line you just typed in the Normal tab.

15. Position the cursor after the space at the end of the line and type **<%= Request.Form("FirstName") %>**. The complete line should look like this:

```
<P>Your first name is: <%= Request.Form("FirstName") %></P>
```

16. In the Normal tab, move the cursor to the first blank line on the page and type **Your last name is:**.

17. Click the HTML tab and type **<%= Request.Form("LastName") %>** at the end of the line you just typed. The complete line should look like this:

```
<P>Your last name is: <%= Request.Form("LastName") %></P>
```

18. Save the Form Response Page.

The next set of steps is where things start to get interesting. You will use a *server control* to do all the work.

Server Controls

Server controls are a large part of what makes ASP.NET so promising. On the server, they generate the HTML that is sent to the requesting browser. Besides using server resources more efficiently, they simplify browser compatibility issues and make your code easier to write and maintain. The next set of instructions will show you how they work.

1. Open your Default.aspx page in the FrontPage HTML tab.

2. Place your cursor at the end of the opening Form tag, just to the left of the closing bracket (>).

3. Press space and type **runat="server"**. The Form tag should look like this:

```
<FORM METHOD="POST" ACTION="Form_rsp.aspx" runat="server">
```

By specifying `runat="server"` the form tag is now a server control rather than a simple HTML tag. At run time (when the server processes the user request), the appropriate HTML will be generated on the server and sent to the browser. An important aspect of this is that a server control maintains any user-entered values on the round-trip to the server without any further work on your part. Previously this could be maintained by using hidden form fields, which you would have to write and maintain.

4. Select all the text between the brackets in the first Input tag. This is the one that defines the FirstName form textbox.

5. Press DELETE and type **asp:textbox id="FirstName" runat="server"/**. The tag should now look like this:

```
<asp:textbox id="FirstName" runat="server"/>
```

Note that the XML style closing attribute (/) is used. You could also use </asp:textbox> to close the tag but, in either case, the tag must be closed, unlike regular HTML. The single forward slash (/) is generally easier to use. Select all the text between the brackets in the second Input tag. This is the one that defines the LastName form textbox.

6. Press DELETE and type **asp:textbox id="LastName" runat="server"/**. The tag should now look like this:

```
<asp:textbox id="LastName" runat="server"/>
```

7. Select all the text between the brackets in the Submit Input tag, shown here:

```
<INPUT TYPE="submit" VALUE="Submit" NAME="B1">
```

8. Press DELETE and type **asp:button text="Submit" runat="server"/**. The tag should now look like this:

```
<asp:button text="Submit" runat="server"/>
```

9. Save your work, then select the Normal tab. The text boxes for your form are no longer displayed in FrontPage. This is because they won't exist until ASP.NET creates them on the server in response to a browser request.

Note *Depending on your Page Option HTML Source settings, FrontPage may convert your tags to uppercase when you save the page. This won't affect its operation.*

10. Open your home page (Default.aspx) in your web browser. Enter your first and last names in the textboxes and click Submit. Your Form Response page should be displayed with the information you entered.

WORKING BEHIND
THE SCENES

11. Click your browser's Back button to reload your form page, then click Reset to clear the form.

12. View the HTML source of your form page, shown in Listing 17-1, by opening the View menu and selecting Source (in Internet Explorer).

Listing 17-1
HTML
Source for
Default.aspx

```
<HTML>
<HEAD>
<META HTTP-EQUIV="Content-Type" CONTENT="text/html;
    charset=windows-1252">
<META HTTP-EQUIV="Content-Language" CONTENT="en-us">
<TITLE>Home Page</TITLE>
<META NAME="GENERATOR" CONTENT="Microsoft FrontPage 5.0">
<META NAME="ProgId" CONTENT="FrontPage.Editor.Document">
</HEAD>
<BODY>
<H2>It's An ASP.NET World</H2>
<form name="ctrl1" method="POST" action="Form_rsp.aspx"
    id="ctrl1">
<input type="hidden" name="__VIEWSTATE"
    value="YTB6NTQ3ODg0MjcyX19feA==5725bd57" />
<P>Enter Your First Name:
<input name="FirstName" type="text" id="FirstName" /><BR>
Enter Your Last Name:
<input name="LastName" type="text" id="LastName" /><BR>
<input type="submit" name="ctrl6" value="Submit" />
<INPUT TYPE="reset" VALUE="Reset" NAME="B2"></P>
</form>
<P> </P>
</BODY>
</HTML>
```

By looking at the HTML source, you can see how ASP.NET generated the appropriate HTML from your source code. Of particular interest are the opening Form tag and the hidden input tag. The only modification you made to the Form tag was to add the `runat="server"` attribute. ASP.NET expanded this to

```
<form name="ctrl1" method="POST" action="Form_rsp.aspx"
    id="ctrl1">
```

by generating its own Name and Id properties.

Much more interesting is the __VIEWSTATE hidden form field. This generated code maintains any page values that would normally get discarded on trips to the server. The benefit to you is that there is no code for you to maintain. The Hidden attribute of the Input tag has been around for a long time and is often used in HTML for the same function—to maintain page information when a page is reloaded or redirected. But now this is done without any additional effort on your part. All you had to do was use the ASP.NET server controls <form runat="server">, <asp:textbox>, and <asp:button>.

Another point to note is that there's nothing "magic" about this process. That is, no client-side scripts, ActiveX controls, or Java Applets (see Chapter 20) are being used. There also isn't any state being maintained on the server. It all ends up being pure HTML. This is another way ASP.NET saves server resources.

ASP.NET server controls come in two flavors, HTML Controls, listed in Table 17-1, and Web Controls, listed in Table 17-2. HTML Controls are used to render HTML, while Web Controls are more complex objects that offer more programming options. You can also create your own controls fairly easily, as opposed to creating COM objects (such as ActiveX controls). At first glance many of the HTML controls may seem to offer little advantage over plain HTML, but they all allow their properties to be set programmatically, unlike plain HTML. This means that their values can be determined by user input and this is a very significant advantage. ASP also allows you to do this but requires a great deal more programming.

HTML Control	Function
HtmlAnchor	Controls the <A> tag and its properties.
HtmlButton	Controls the HTML 4.0 <BUTTON> tag.
HtmlForm	Controls the <FORM> tag and its properties.
HtmlGenericControl	Controls tags for which a specific server control doesn't exist, such as the <BODY> tag.
HtmlImage	Controls the <IMG> tag and its properties.
HtmlInputButton (Button)	Controls the Form <INPUT TYPE="BUTTON"> tag and its properties.
HtmlInputButton (Reset)	Controls the Form <INPUT TYPE="RESET"> tag and its properties.
HtmlInputButton (Submit)	Controls the Form <INPUT TYPE="SUBMIT"> tag and its properties.
HtmlInputCheckBox	Controls the Form <INPUT TYPE="CHECKBOX"> tag and its properties.
HtmlInputFile	Controls uploading a file from the client to the server. This is supported by HTML 3.2 and later.

Table 17-1.   *ASP.NET Beta 1 HTML Controls*

HTML Control	Function
HtmlInputHidden	Controls the Form <INPUT TYPE="HIDDEN"> tag and its properties. Also used by ASP.NET to preserve Viewstate information.
HtmlInputImage	Controls graphical buttons, which can be used to trigger events.
HtmlInputRadioButton	Controls the Form <INPUT TYPE="RADIO"> tag and its properties.
HtmlInputText (Password)	Controls the Form <INPUT TYPE="PASSWORD"> tag and its properties.
HtmlInputText (Text)	Controls the Form <INPUT TYPE="TEXT"> tag and its properties.
HtmlSelect	Controls the Form <SELECT> tag and its properties.
HtmlTable	Is used with the HtmlTableRow and HtmlTableCell controls to create HTML tables.
HtmlTableCell	Controls the Table <TD> tag and its properties.
HtmlTableRow	Controls the Table <TR> tag and its properties.
HtmlTextArea	Controls the Form <INPUT TYPE="TEXTAREA"> tag and its properties.

Table 17-1.   *ASP.NET Beta 1 HTML Controls* (continued)

Web Control	Function
AdRotator	Rotates ad banners, much like the ASP Ad Rotator component. Uses an XML file to determine the ads to rotate and other properties.
Button	Is used to post a web form (an ASP.NET web page) to the server.
Calendar	Displays a month calendar that will post selected dates back to the server. The user can select a day, week, month, or date selection can be disabled.

Table 17-2.   *ASP.NET Beta 1 Web Controls*

Web Control	Function
CheckBox	Functions like a form check box, but can also trigger posting its value to the server if its AutoPostBack property is set to TRUE.
CheckBoxList	Generates a multiple-choice list either vertically or horizontally within a table.
CompareValidator	Compares the values of two controls and returns TRUE if they are equal and FALSE if they aren't.
CustomValidator	Compares the values of two controls using a custom comparison function. The function can either be server-side or client-side. On the client, the function can be written in any supported scripting language (usually JavaScript).
DataGrid	Displays information in a table format. The information is usually from a database (see Chapter 19).
DataList	Displays information in a list format with one or more columns, which is determined by a template.
DropDownList	Generates a single-selection drop-down list.
HyperLink	Generates a hyperlink.
Image	Generates an image tag.
ImageButton	Is similar to the Button control, but uses an image as the button and can be used with image maps.
Label	Displays text on a web form.
LinkButton	Is similar to the Button control but can also be used with text.
ListBox	Is similar to the DropDownList control but also allows multiple selections.
Panel	Is a container for other controls. This allows you to group controls and set their visibility.
RadioButton	Allows you to place radio buttons within other content on a web form.

Table 17-2. *ASP.NET Beta 1 Web Controls* (continued)

Web Control	Function
RadioButtonList	Generates a list of radio buttons either vertically, horizontally, or within a table.
RangeValidator	Tests to see if the input values fall within a predefined range.
RegularExpressionValidator	Tests to see if the input value matches a predefined expression. Regular expressions perform pattern matching, which is useful for testing e-mail addresses, etc., which must be in a specific format. For example, e-mail addresses must contain a single @ symbol.
Repeater	Displays information in a repeating list, similar to the DataList control. A template is used to define the layout. Unlike the DataList control, there are no predefined styles so all HTML formatting must be defined.
RequiredFieldValidator	Checks if all required fields in a form contain data.
Table	Generates a table using the TableRow and TableCell controls.
TableCell	Generates cells for a table row.
TableRow	Generates rows for a table.
TextBox	Generates a single- or multi-line text box.
ValidationSummary	Displays a summary of validation errors for a form.

Table 17-2.   *ASP.NET Beta 1 Web Controls* (continued)

Using the Calendar Web Control

A good example of the functionality provided by Web Controls can be seen in the Calendar server control. This next exercise will set up a calendar and display the date you select. Do this now with these steps.

1. In FrontPage, create a new page and click Save.

2. In the Save As dialog box, change the Page Title to **ASP.NET Calendar**, select All Files in the Save As Type drop-down, and type Calendar.aspx in the File Name text box. Click Save.

3. Open your Calendar page in Normal view and type **Using the Calendar Web Control**. Format it as Heading 2 and open your page in HTML view.

4. Place your cursor to the left of the closing </HEAD> tag and press ENTER then UP-ARROW.

5. Type **<script language="VB" runat="server">** and press ENTER. This defines the programming language as Visual Basic.

6. Type **Sub Selected_Date(sender As Object, e As EventArgs)** and press ENTER. This is the first line of a Visual Basic subroutine named Selected_Date which has two arguments, or variables: sender and e. Unlike VBScript, which treats every variable the same unless told otherwise, Visual Basic has *strongly typed* variables. This means the type of variable must be specified when the variable is declared. The arguments contain the data the subroutine will process.

7. Type **Label1.Text = "You selected " + Calendar1.SelectedDate.ToLongDateString** and press ENTER. This line defines the text that will be displayed when you select a date from the calendar by setting the Text property of the Label1 object (an instance of the Label Web Control).

8. Type **End Sub**, press ENTER, and type **</script>**. This ends the subroutine definition and closes the script.

9. Place your cursor at the beginning of the first line after the heading.

10. Type **<p><form runat="server">** and press ENTER.

11. Type **<asp:Calendar id="Calendar1" onSelectionChanged="Selected_Date" runat="server"/></p>** and press ENTER. Note the forward slash (/) used to close the ASP tag. This instantiates the Calendar Web Control, which displays the calendar, and sets the Visual Basic subroutine you defined in the previous steps as the action to be taken when a date is selected.

12. Type **<p><asp:Label id="Label1" runat="server"/></p>**, press ENTER, and type **</form>**.

13. Save your page. FrontPage will probably rearrange your code a bit, but this shouldn't affect its functionality.

14. Open your Calendar web form in your browser and select a date, as shown in Figure 17-1.

15. In FrontPage, with your Calendar web form still in HTML view, add **SelectionMode="DayWeek"** to your Calendar Web Control definition. It should now look like this:

```
<asp:Calendar id="Calendar1" SelectionMode="DayWeek"
onSelectionChanged="Selected_Date" runat="server"/>
```

16. Save your Calendar web form again and reload it in your browser. You can now select a single date by clicking it, or an entire week by clicking the ≥ on the left side of each week.

17. View the source of your Calendar web form in your browser.

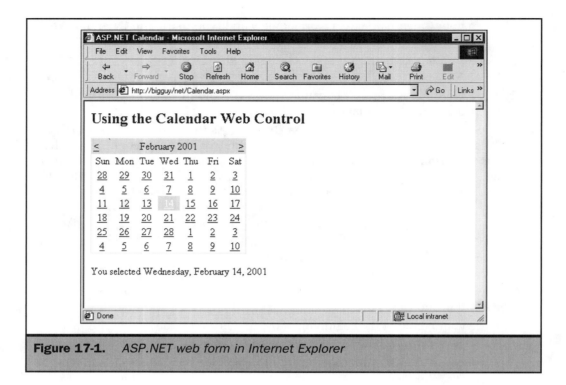

Figure 17-1. *ASP.NET web form in Internet Explorer*

Notice that ASP.NET converted the necessary client-side script to JavaScript and created the table necessary to display the calendar. All from your few lines of code. Another point to notice about the Calendar Web Control is that it is not dependant on any features that a browser may or may not support, such as an ActiveX control or a Java applet, either of which would have to be downloaded from the server to the browser. It's pure HTML with a little bit of JavaScript. This code is also much easier to maintain. To switch from single date mode to day or week mode only required setting one property of the Calendar Web Control. The control also has a number of options for controlling the appearance of the calendar.

18. Close FrontPage and your browser.

Configuring ASP.NET

Another feature of ASP.NET that's a boon to web application developers is application configuration. With ASP you can use the Global.asa file but ASP.NET adds a much more powerful feature with its Config.web files. The Global.asa file or its ASP.NET equivalent, Global.asax, can still be used, but the Config.web file can control many more configuration parameters. There are two things to note with the Config.web file. The first is that it is hierarchical; the second is that it is an XML file. By being an XML file, the Config.web can be created in any text editor or XML parser. This greatly simplifies creating and editing the file.

Hierarchical means that you can have Config.web files at different levels, each controlling the directory it's in and its subdirectories. The server has a Config.web file that sets overall parameters for the server. Then you can have another Config.web file in the application root directory that can override most of the settings of the machine Config.web file, and Config.web files in subdirectories of the application root that override settings in the application root Config.web. Except for the server Config.web, the files are optional. If the application root doesn't have a Config.web, for example, then the settings are inherited from the server Config.web.

| Note | *By default, in .NET Framework Beta 1 the path of the server Config.web file (on Windows 2000 Server and Windows 2000 Professional) is C:\WINNT\ Microsoft.NET\Framework\v1.0.2204\Config.web. You can expect this to change slightly in the production release.* |

ASP.NET Resources

Currently the best way to learn more about ASP.NET and the .NET Framework is on the Web, though you can expect a number of books to be released in the coming months. The following is a list of sites that are particularly useful.

- **http://msdn.microsoft.com/net/** The best place to start is at Microsoft's .NET Framework site. Along with ASP.NET, information on the entire .NET Framework and their new C# programming language is available, including code samples.

- **http://www.aspfree.com/** A comprehensive ASP.NET resource, this site also has the ASP.NET Quickstart samples (included with the .NET Framework SDK) online, which means you don't have to download the SDK and install them to see how ASP.NET works.

- **http://www.aspng.com/** ASP Next Generation offers a number of tutorials and an excellent e-mail discussion group.

- **http://www.asp101.com/** Primarily devoted to ASP programmers, ASP 101 offers a growing collection of information related to ASP.NET.

- **http://www.4guysfromrolla.com/** 4GuysFromRolla.com has a number of articles on web technologies including ASP.NET.

■ **http://www.devx.com/** Another source for a variety of technical information relating to web technologies, DevX covers just about everything.

This chapter has barely scratched the surface of the potential of ASP.NET. With FrontPage you will need to use the HTML view to gain its benefits, as is the case with ASP, but the potential for integrating ASP.NET into FrontPage is greater than with ASP. For technical reasons (that are beyond the scope of this book) integrating ASP into a WYSIWYG editor like FrontPage presents a number of problems, many of which ASP.NET resolves. If you choose to embrace ASP.NET you can expect future releases of FrontPage to offer a great deal of support.

Chapter 18

JavaServer Pages

In the previous two chapters, you've seen how you can greatly expand the interactivity of web applications using Active Server Pages and the new ASP.NET (part of Microsoft's .NET Framework). As useful as these technologies are, they do have a drawback. They are both Microsoft technologies and work best (or only) on Microsoft web servers.

In the real world, not every web server is running Microsoft software. There are a large number of web servers running some flavor of UNIX or Linux, often with Apache web server software (**http://www.apache.org/**). FrontPage Server Extensions are available for every major operating system, so FrontPage webs are not limited to Microsoft web servers. So how can FrontPage users whose webs are not hosted on Microsoft web servers gain the benefits of technologies such as ASP?

The answer is JavaServer Pages (JSP), Sun Microsystem's (**http://java.sun.com/**) solution for dynamically generated web content. This chapter will cover the basics of JavaServer Pages and how to build the same type of interactivity into your webs that you were able to do with ASP. Unfortunately, FrontPage and JSP do not work as seamlessly as ASP and FrontPage. ASP is an integral part of IIS (Internet Information Services), while JSP is not—it relies on an interpreter outside of IIS that processes the JSP page. The interpreter is not as tightly integrated with IIS as ASP or even the FrontPage Server Extensions (from FrontPage's perspective). However, a basic understanding of JSP may be useful to you even if you choose not to use the technology. That basic understanding and the issues regarding FrontPage and JSP is the focus of this chapter.

JavaServer Pages Overview

JavaServer Pages are based on the Java programming language. Since Java is a cross-platform (operating system) language, JSP webs easily migrate from Windows to UNIX. As a developer, this gives you more options in selecting an ISP to host your webs. However, JSP support should not be assumed just because an ISP is running UNIX servers. Unlike ASP, which is an integral part of IIS, JSP requires the installation of a Java programming environment and support for JavaServer Pages. You will need to install and configure these applications on your development server in order to use JSP. This will be covered in the section "Configuring JavaServer Pages."

Note *The name UNIX is used to refer to all flavors of the UNIX operating system, including Linux.*

In Chapter 16, you were introduced to ASP objects, which are ActiveX components (see Chapter 20). With JSP, this functionality is provided by JavaBeans. JavaBeans are reusable components written in Java, which makes them platform-independent. They are used in much the same way you used ASP components in the previous chapters. There are a large number of JavaBeans commercially available, so you are not limited to a predefined set. In addition, JSP uses *servlets*, which are server-side modules written in Java. These are used to extend the capabilities of the web server to support JSP.

ASP or JSP?

Since Active Server Pages and JavaServer Pages are actually very similar and share many features, which one is better? Like most such questions, the answer is "it depends." JavaServer Pages' greatest advantage is that it's platform-independent. Sun's trademarked slogan "write once, run anywhere™" applies to JSP as well as the Java language. If you want active web pages on a UNIX server, or need to support both UNIX and Windows servers, JSP has clear advantages. While you can use a third party ASP interpreter under UNIX, will your ISP be willing to install and maintain it?

If you plan to only use Windows servers, the advantages of JSP aren't as clear. It should be pointed out that finding Windows-based ISPs is not a problem, so there is no significant market advantage to UNIX-based ISPs. (Of course, arguing the relative advantages of each platform keeps network administrators warm on many a cold night.) If you do decide to use JSP you are making a strong commitment to the Java programming language. Java has had a reputation in the past of not being as fast as some other languages, but each new release of the Java virtual machine improves on this, so this isn't a "killer argument" for ASP. In fact, except for platform-independence, there is no killer argument for either system. It comes down to what languages you are willing to learn, and what platform you prefer. In the context of FrontPage, you can expect that the support for ASP (and ASP.NET in future releases) will always be greater than for JSP.

A Simple JSP Example

A quick example shows the basic differences between the systems. In Chapter 16, you created two ASP pages. The first was a simple HTML form where you entered your name, and the second used the ASP Request object to display the information you entered in the form. In ASP, the code you used on the second page (Form_rsp.asp) was

```
Your first name is: <%= Request.Form("FirstName") %>
```

In JSP, the same functionality looks like this

```
Your first name is: <%= request.getParameter("FirstName") %>
```

Note *Remember that JavaScript and Java are case-sensitive, unlike VBScript and Visual Basic.*

As you can see, both use the same script delimiters (<% and %>), the equal sign (=) to indicate the line is an expression (a value is returned), and both ASP and JSP have a Request object. In fact, the only difference in this example is that ASP uses the Request object Form collection and JSP uses the Request object getParameter() method. Table 18-1

Method	Description
getCookies()	Returns the values of the user's cookies
getHeader(*name*)	Returns the value of the specified request header as a string
getAttribute(*name*)	Returns the value of the specified attribute
getAttributeNames()	Returns all the attribute names in the request
getHeaderNames()	Returns all the header names in the request
getHeaders(*name*)	Returns all the values of the specified request header
getMethod()	Returns the HTTP method (GET, POST, or PUT) used to make the request
getParameter(*name*)	Returns the value of the specified request item
getParameterNames()	Returns the names of all the parameters in the request
getParameterValues(*name*)	Returns the value(s) for the specified parameter
getQueryString()	Returns the value of the query string from a request
getRequestURL()	Returns the request URL (not including the query string)
getServletPath()	Returns the portion of the request URL that calls the servlet
setAttributes(*name, Java object*)	Sets an attribute and its value for the request

Table 18-1. *JavaServer Pages Request Object*

lists the methods of the JSP Request object. Compare these to the ASP Request object in Table 16-2 in Chapter 16. With JSP objects and methods the syntax is:

```
request.method(variable)
```

By comparing the JSP Request object and the ASP object you can see that the differences relate more to syntax than actual functionality. Which isn't to say that syntax is the only difference between ASP and JSP. You'll see some of the deeper differences in the following sections.

Object	Description
application	Sets properties or information that is shared by all users accessing the web application
config	Contains information that is passed to a servlet when it is called
exception	Contains information about errors when they occur
out	Defines an object for writing to the JSP page's output stream, such as a line of text
pageContext	Contains information relating to a specific JSP page
request	Retrieves values passed from the client
response	Sends information to the client
session	Sets properties or information for a single user accessing the web application

Table 18-2.   *JavaServer Pages Objects*

JSP Objects

Objects, which allow you to handle events, get information from a user, or set properties, are fundamental to both ASP and JSP. In the previous section, you looked at the JSP Request object in some detail. In Table 18-2, all the JSP objects are listed. You can compare these to the ASP objects in Table 16-1 in Chapter 16.

Each object has one or more methods, as shown for the Request object in Table 18-1.

JSP Syntax

JSP syntax can be divided into three elements: directives, scripting, and actions. Each of these is covered in the following sections. In addition, JSP pages are similar to ASP pages in that they are a combination of HTML and scripting. With ASP, these are VBScript and/or JavaScript scripts, as well as ASP objects and components. With JSP, these are JavaScript scripts and JSP objects and servlets. As you saw in the earlier example, where the ASP form response page from Chapter 16 was converted to JSP, in some cases there is little or no difference, other than following the syntax rules of the scripting language. For example, the script opening and closing tags (<% %>) are identical for both systems. The syntax rules for JavaScript, though, are quite a bit different than for VBScript so your code will look quite a bit different as well.

JSP Directives

Directives are used to set properties for a JSP page. Again, these are very similar between the systems—for example, the directive for setting the scripting language. In ASP, you set the language like this:

```
<%@ language="VBScript" %>
```

In JSP, it would be:

```
<%@ page language="javascript" %>
```

The only real difference is that JSP uses the Page directive. The JSP directives are listed in Table 18-3. You can also include *tag libraries* in your JSP pages. A tag library is a collection of custom server-side tags. Tag libraries give you increased control over your documents and their appearance.

JSP Scripting Elements

Your actual JSP code is contained with scripting elements, which you are familiar with from the previous examples. Table 18-4 lists the JSP scripting elements. These are basically identical to ASP, with the exception of the Declaration element.

JSP Actions

Actions are used to implement JavaBeans and set their properties, create objects, and modify the page. JavaBeans are reusable components written in Java. In ASP, these are simply called components, such as the Ad Rotator component you used in Chapter 16. Table 18-5 lists the JSP actions.

Directive	Syntax	Description
page	`<%@ page attribute="value" %>`	Sets attributes that apply to the entire page
include	`<%@ include file="file" %>`	Inserts the named file in the JSP document
taglib	`<%@ taglib uri="tag library URI" prefix="tag prefix" %>`	Includes the specified tag library in the document

Table 18-3. *JavaServer Pages Directives*

Element	Syntax	Description
declaration	`<%! declaration %>`	Sets page scope definitions, such as variables
expression	`<%= expression %>`	Contains an expression that is evaluated on the server with the result being returned to the client
scriptlet	`<% code %>`	Contains your scripting

Table 18-4.   *JavaServer Pages Scripting Elements*

Configuring JavaServer Pages

Since IIS doesn't offer native support for JSP, you will need to download and install the files needed to run JSP webs. These will also provide detailed Help files and tutorials, which describe JSP features and syntax in much more detail than provided here.

Before embarking on this process you should consider the benefits to yourself or your organization of JavaServer Pages. As mentioned previously, the greatest benefit of JSP is its ability to work on both Windows and UNIX platforms. In addition, if you are already proficient in Java, then JSP plays to your programming skills. If you have no

Action	Description
jsp:useBean	Defines an instance of a JavaBean.
jsp:setProperty	Sets the value of bean properties.
jsp:getProperty	Returns the value of a bean property.
jsp:include	Calls one JSP page from another, then returns control to the calling page.
jsp:forward	Calls one JSP page from another. Control is passed to the page being called.
jsp:param	Adds parameters to the HTTP header as name/value pairs.
jsp:plugin	Enables the instantiation of an applet on the client.

Table 18-5.   *JavaServer Pages Actions*

WORKING BEHIND THE SCENES

compelling reason to support UNIX servers and are not proficient in Java, then JSP will require much more learning, and a bigger investment of your time, than ASP. In addition, ASP is tightly integrated with IIS, while JSP is not. Configuring your development web server for JSP can present difficulties, as you have to have a much greater knowledge of the nuts and bolts of the system than with ASP. In short, JSP requires a greater investment of your resources than ASP. Unless you need to support UNIX servers, it's hard to see what advantages JSP has over ASP, or especially ASP.NET, that warrants this expenditure.

At a minimum, you will need the Java Runtime Environment (JRE) and a JSP server, such as Allaire's (**www.allaire.com**) JRun Server. If you are installing JSP on a UNIX server with the Apache web server, you can use Tomcat (**http://jakarta.apache.org/tomcat/**), Apache's reference implementation of the Java Servlet and JavaServer Pages specifications. Since the focus of this book is on Windows servers, only installation with IIS will be covered. Begin by downloading and installing the Java Runtime Environment, as described here.

Note *The JRE is the minimum Java implementation you need to run JSP. If you are going to do any real work with Java, you need one of Sun's Java software development kits (SDK), such as the Java 2 Platform available at **http://java.sun.com/products/**. Chapter 20 covers using Sun's Java SDK.*

Note *The applications must be installed in the order given to function properly.*

1. Open a browser and load Sun Microsystem's JRE download page at **http://java.sun.com/j2se/**.

Note *The hyperlinks may change by the time you read this. You can find the appropriate links by starting on Sun's Java home page (**http://java.sun.com/**).*

2. Click the Java Platform Runtime Environment link.

3. Click the appropriate link for your operating system.

4. Choose whether to download one large file or multiple smaller files and then click Continue. If you choose to download multiple files, read the instructions for assembling the files once they're downloaded.

5. Read and then accept the licensing agreement if you chose to continue.

6. Select your download site and save the file(s) to your hard drive.

7. Double-click the downloaded file. This will extract the files and start the installation process.

8. Read the license agreement and click Yes if you accept it. Click Next to accept the default installation folder. The installation will proceed.

In the next set of instructions, you will download the Allaire JRun Developer Edition. This is a feature-limited version of the JRun Server that you can use for development. It is not licensed for production use, but it is free.

> **Note** *Allaire has merged with Macromedia (**http://www.macromedia.com**) and JRun is now also known as Macromedia JRun. At the time this was written (Spring 2001), the links in this chapter to the Allaire web site function as described here. If you have any problems with the Allaire links, go to the Macromedia home page and follow their links to download JRun.*

> **Note** *In Chapter 19, Working With Databases, you will be introduced to the concepts of data-driven webs, where content is drawn at run time (when a page is requested) from a data source (generally a database). While JSP has the potential for data-driven webs using JDBC (Java Database Connectivity), this feature is not enabled in the JRun Developer Edition.*

1. Open Allaire's download page at **http://www.allaire.com/download/** and click JRun Evaluation.

2. Click Allaire JRun Server 3.0 Developer Edition for Windows. In order to download the product, you are required to create a user account, if you don't already have one.

3. Click New Account if you need to create an account.

4. Fill out the Enter Personal Account Information form and click Submit.

5. When your account is created, click Next. You will be asked to complete a user survey. When done, click Submit.

6. The download should begin automatically. Save the file to your desktop. This is a large file (approximately 12MB) so this could take a while if you don't have a fast Internet connection.

7. When the download is complete, close all your open applications.

8. Stop your web publishing services before installing JRun Server. In Windows 2000 Professional, open the Start menu and select Settings | Control Panel | Administrative Tools | Services. In the Services console select World Wide Web Publishing Service and click Stop Service in the toolbar, or open the Action menu and select Stop. In Windows 2000 Server, open the Start menu and select Programs | Administrative Tools | Services. In the Services console, select World Wide Web Publishing Service and click Stop Service in the toolbar, or open the Action menu and select Stop.

9. Double-click the JRun icon on your desktop to begin installation.

10. When the JRun Setup dialog box Welcome screen is displayed, click Next.

11. Read the license agreement and click Yes if you choose to continue.

12. The next dialog box is for entering a serial number. A serial number is not required for the Developer Edition. Click Next.

13. Accept the default installation folder by clicking Next.

14. Select Full installation (the default) in the Setup Type dialog box. This installs the documentation as well as sample JSP webs. Click Next twice.

15. In the Install JRun Services dialog box, clear the Install JRun Services check box. For development it's recommended that JRun Server not be installed as a service, though for a production web server it should be. This means you will have to manually start JRun after you reboot your computer. Click Next.

16. In the Select A Java Runtime dialog box, the JRE you installed in the previous steps should be listed. The default location is C:\Program Files\JavaSoft\ JRE\1.3 (your version number may be different). Select your installed JRE and click Next.

17. The JVM Advisor dialog box will be displayed. This checks the version of the Java Virtual Machine you have installed. If your JVM version is greater than the version required by JRun (version 1.2 at the time of this writing), click Next. If it isn't, you will need to update your JRE before you can install JRun.

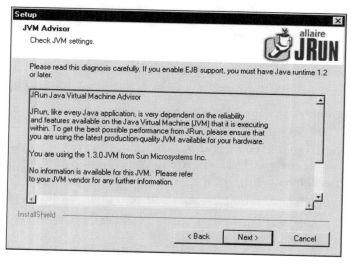

18. The JRun Management Console dialog box is displayed. This dialog box allows you to set a port for the JRun Management Console. A port is a logical connection for a specific application. For example, port 80 is used for HTTP connections. This is a *well-known* port and does not have to be specified. If you open a web page using localhost as the address (127.0.0.1 is the established IP address for localhost), you are actually connecting to localhost:80 (which resolves to 127.0.0.1:80), where the colon indicates the port number. The JRun Management Console needs its own port number on your web server's IP address. By default, this is port 8000 and you should accept this value. Click Next.

19. You must select a password for the JRun administrator account. The administrator username is "admin" and a simple password, such as "password," is recommended for your development environment. Enter your password in the JRun Admin Password and Confirm Password text boxes and click Next.

20. Next, you are asked if you want to receive Allaire's newsletter and product updates by e-mail. If you choose to, enter your name and e-mail address and click Next. If not, clear the check boxes and click Next.

21. In the JRun Setup Complete dialog box, accept the default option, Configure JRun To Connect To My External Web Server Now, and click Finish. A small dialog box with JRun Server Start/Run options will open. Ignore this dialog, as it will close itself in a few moments. Next, the JRun Management Console Login page, shown in Figure 18-1, will be displayed.

22. Type **admin** in the Username text box and your password in the Password text box, and then click Login. The first of four Connector Wizard pages will be displayed, as shown in Figure 18-2. These will take you through configuring your web server and JRun.

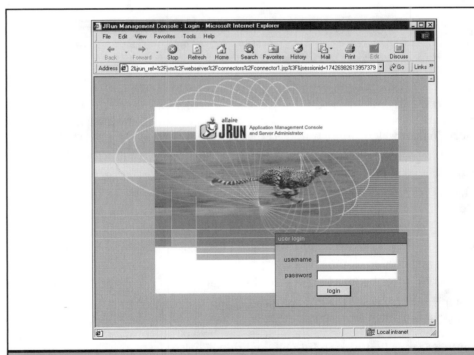

Figure 18-1.   *JRun Management Console Login page*

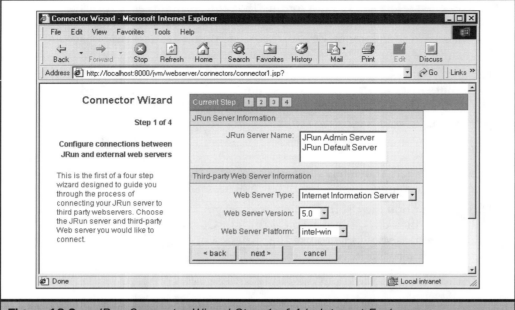

Figure 18-2.   *JRun Connector Wizard Step 1 of 4 in Internet Explorer*

23. Open the Internet Services Manager. In Windows 2000 Professional, open the Start menu and select Settings | Control Panel | Administrative Tools | Internet Services Manager. In Windows 2000 Server, open the Start menu and select Programs | Administrative Tools | Internet Services Manager.

24. In the Internet Services Manager, expand the directory tree in the left pane, right-click your server name, and select Properties.

25. Select WWW Service in the Master Properties drop-down (if it's not already selected), and click Edit.

26. Click the Home Directory tab in the WWW Service Master Properties dialog box, then select Scripts And Executables in the Execute Permissions drop-down.

27. Click Apply. The Inheritance Overrides dialog box will be displayed. Click OK twice, then close the Internet Services Manager.

28. In Step 1 of the Connector Wizard, select JRun Default Server in the JRun Server Name list box, then select Internet Information Server in the Web Server Type drop-down. The Web Server Version should be 5.0 (under Windows 2000) and the Web Server Platform should be intel-win. Click Next.

29. In Step 2 of the Connector Wizard, use the default JRun Server IP Address of 127.0.0.1 (localhost) and type **51000** in the JRun Server Connection Port text box. This is the JRun default connection port. Click Next.

30. In Step 3 of the Connection Wizard, enter your web server's scripts directory. By default, this is C:\Inetpub\Scripts\. Leave the Install As A Global Filter check box selected and click Next.

31. You must restart your web server before you can run JSP webs. In Windows 2000 Professional, open the Start menu and select Settings | Control Panel | Administrative Tools | Internet Services Manager. In the Internet Information Services console, select your web server and click the Start Item button in the toolbar, or open the Action menu and select Start. In Windows 2000 Server, open the Start menu and select Programs | Administrative Tools | Services. In the Services console, select World Wide Web Publishing Service and click Start Service in the toolbar, or open the Action menu and select Start.

32. When your web service has restarted, click Done in Step 4 of the Connection Wizard. The JRun Management Console should open in your browser. In addition, the JRun Quick Start Product Tour may also open.

These resources offer a great deal of information about JSP. The JRun Quick Start Product Tour details the features of JRun Server and is a good place to start learning about the system. The JRun Management Console allows you to configure the Admin and Default servers, access the documentation and examples, and access online resources.

The JRun Management Console is started by opening the Start menu and selecting Program Files | JRun 3.0 | JRun Management Console. The JRun Admin Server has to be running before you can access the JRun Management Console. You also open the JRun documentation and demos from the JRun 3.0 menu.

JavaServer Pages and FrontPage

Once you have correctly configured the JRun server, you create JSP pages in the way that worked with ASP previously. You can create the basic page layout in the FrontPage Normal view and add the JavaScript code in HTML view. In addition, you must make sure that both FrontPage and JRun can access the web. By default, JRun places its webs deep within the Program Files folder, at C:\Program Files\Allaire\ JRun\servers\default\. This isn't where FrontPage expects to find any webs and may not allow you to create a web in that directory due to permission and server extension issues. Nor is this a good place to publish webs.

The purpose of the following exercise is to create a very simple JSP page in FrontPage. You will create a folder in your default web and use the JSP Request object to read and display a value entered in an HTML form. Your default web should already be a FrontPage web and the folder must also be configured as a JRun Web Application. Begin now with these steps.

Note *Java and JavaScript are case-sensitive. In the context of JSP, this means that even your filenames are case-sensitive. A page named Default.jsp is not the same as a page named default.jsp to the JSP server.*

1. In FrontPage, open your default web. By default, the path is C:\Inetpub\ wwwroot\ and the URL is http://localhost/.

2. Create a new folder and name it **jsp**.

3. Create a new page in the folder and save it with the Page Title **JSP Home** and the File Name **default.htm**.

4. At the top of your JSP Home page, type **My First JSP Page** and format it as Heading 2.

5. Press ENTER and insert a text box from the Insert | Form menu or Form toolbar.

6. Press SHIFT+ENTER and then UP ARROW. Type **This is my favorite food:** (leave a space after the colon).

7. Right-click the form and choose Form Properties. In the Form Properties dialog box, select Send To Other and then click Options.

8. In the Options For Custom Form Handler dialog box Action box, type **form_rsp.jsp** and click OK twice.

9. Right-click the form text box and choose Form Field Properties. In the Text Box Properties dialog box Name box, type **Food** and then click OK. Save your page.

10. Create a new page in your jsp folder and save it with the Page Title **JSP Results Page** and the File Name **form_rsp.jsp**.

11. At the top of your JSP Results Page, type **JSP Form Results** and format it as Heading 2. Press ENTER.

12. Type **Your favorite food is** (leave a space after "is") and select HTML view.

13. In HTML view, the cursor should be immediately to the left of the closing paragraph tag. Type **<%= request.getParameter("Food") %>**.

14. Save your page. Open your browser and type **http://localhost/jsp/default.htm** in the Address bar. Press ENTER.

This will generate a 500 Internal Server Error and quite a few lines of error code. The reason for this is that your JSP folder has not been configured as a JSP web application in the JRun Default Server. You will configure this in the next set of instructions.

15. Click your browser's Back button to reload your JSP home page.

16. Open the JRun Management Console by opening the Start menu and selecting Program files | JRun 3.0 | JRun Management Console. The JRun Admin Server must be running for the Management Console to be available. If the JRun Admin Server is not running, open the Start menu and select Program files | JRun 3.0 | JRun Admin Server. In the JRun Admin Server dialog box, shown here, click the Administrator Start button.

17. Log in to the JRun Management Console and expand the JRun Default Server tree in the left pane. Click Web Applications under JRun Default Server.

18. In the right pane, click Create An Application. The Web Application Information form, shown next with the correct information, will be displayed.

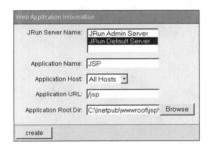

19. Select JRun Default Server in the JRun Server Name list box, then type **JSP** in the Application Name text box. The Application Host should be All Hosts.

20. Type **/jsp** in the Application URL text box and type **C:\Inetpub\wwwroot\jsp** in the Application Root Dir text box. Click Create.

21. Click JRun Default Server in the left pane, then click Restart Server.

22. In your browser, reload your JSP home page. Enter a favorite food in the text box and click Submit. The JSP Form Results page should correctly display the food name you entered.

As you have seen, there are more steps involved in creating a JSP web application using FrontPage than with an ASP web application. If you need to support UNIX web servers and also want to create active webs, these steps may be necessary. If not, you are probably better off using ASP.

In the next chapter, you will learn how to connect databases to your web applications. This is probably the greatest advantage of active web applications using ASP or JSP. Database connectivity does away with the limitations of static content and enables a great deal of functionality and flexibility.

WORKING BEHIND
THE SCENES

The Complete Reference

FrontPage 2002

Chapter 19

Working with Databases

Up to this point, you have learned how to create webs containing information that is basically static. In the previous chapters, you learned how to integrate the capabilities of Active Server Pages (and, to a lesser extent, Java Server Pages) to greatly expand the interactivity of your webs, but the content was still mainly static. In this chapter, you will see how to take your webs to the next level—using databases to provide the information displayed on your web pages. This is a tremendous advantage over traditional webs.

Webs that are database driven, where the content is coming from a database rather than static pages, allow for a great deal of user interactivity while simplifying the task of the web administrator. For example, an e-commerce site needs to display information about products and prices. If the web is static, a price change requires you to manually find all the pages that contain the old price and change it to the new one. If the web is database driven, the price is updated in the database and all pages will show the new price the next time the page is loaded. Using a database to provide content also reduces the number of pages in a web. If a company's product line contains 100 items, and each one is displayed on a single page, there would be 100 pages to maintain. With the content being drawn from a database, there would only be a single page, which would be a template for displaying the information about the selected product.

The focus of this chapter is to provide you with an understanding of databases and how to add them to your webs using FrontPage and Active Server Pages. Each of these subjects really requires a book of its own. The information here, however, will give you an overview of how the pieces fit together and show you how to get started using databases with your webs. The first step is to understand what a database is.

Understanding Databases on the Web

A *database* is an organized collection of information. This can be a simple list of names and telephone numbers, or a complete collection of all the information about a company—its products, salespeople, sales, and inventory. In a database, all the information about one item, such as the name and telephone number for one person, is a *record.* Each record is made up of a number of *fields* or *columns.* In a list of names and telephone numbers, each name is one field, and the telephone number associated with the name is another field in the record. A collection of records is a *table.* A simple *flat-file* database is made up of one table, while a *relational* database has two or more tables with one or more relationships, or *links,* between fields in the tables. In the database table shown here, there are four records, each consisting of five fields. Each row in the table is a record; each column is a field. At the top of each column is the field name for that column. The CustomerID field provides a unique number to identify each record. You may have customers with the same name, or in the same city and state, so you need a way to uniquely identify each customer. There should be at least one field in each record that contains a unique value to identify that record. This field is the *primary key* for the table.

CustomerID	CustomerName	CustomerAddr	CustomerCity	CustomerState
1	Honeymoon Island Hardware	1010 CR 1	Palm Harbor	FL
2	Tom's Tools	2714 Ocean Ave.	Ventura	CA
3	Bulldog Hardware	3609 Bulldog Lane	Athens	GA
4	Bloomfield Hardware	3787 Meadow Road	West Caldwell	NJ
AutoNumber)				

Tip

With many databases, the names displayed at the top of the column, as shown in the previous illustration, do not have to match the actual field name. This can cause confusion if the displayed name and the actual field name are different. Your database queries must use the actual field name, not the displayed name if it is different. The FrontPage Database Results Wizard, described in the section of the same name, will display the correct field names. In Access, you can also find the actual field names by looking at the table in Design view.

Simple flat-file databases are of limited use. Relational databases, on the other hand, can contain millions of records that can be sorted and organized by use of complex criteria. Relational databases get their name from the fact that relationships are created between fields in two or more tables. Figure 19-1 shows the relationships between the tables in the North Beach Tools database that will be used in this chapter. This is a very simple relational database whose purpose is to introduce you both to relational databases and to integrating a relational database into a web.

The North Beach Tools database contains four tables, described in Table 19-1. The Orders table has a relationship with fields in each of the other three tables. These are one-to-many relationships, which means that the contents of a field must be unique in one table, but can appear many times in the other table. In Figure 19-1, this is shown by a 1 next to the field with the unique value and by the symbol for infinity (∞) next to the field that can have many occurrences of the same values. For example, the Customers

Table	Description
Customers	Contains the information relating to individual customers
Products	Contains the information describing each product
SalesReps	Contains the information relating to each salesperson
Orders	Contains the information for each order

Table 19-1. *Tables in the North Beach Tools database*

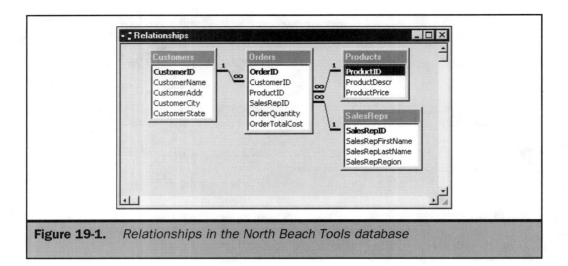

Figure 19-1. *Relationships in the North Beach Tools database*

table contains a unique CustomerID to identify each customer. This is the "one" side of the relationship. The Orders table contains a record for each order the customer places, so there can be a number of records for each customer. This is the "many" side of the relationship. There can also be one-to-one relationships, but these are less common.

The benefit of a relational database is that by linking a unique field in one table to a field in another table, all the information in the first table is made available to the second table without having to be entered each time. The North Beach Tools database illustrates this. The database has tables for customers, products, sales representatives, and orders. In a simple flat-file database, each record in the Orders table would have to contain all the information about the customer, the product, and the salesperson, as well as the information about the order itself. In a relational database, each record in the Orders table would contain only the information unique to the order. The information about the customer, product, and salesperson is collected from the appropriate table as needed. This greatly reduces the size and complexity of the database. For example, to record a price change for a product, only one field in one table (the ProductPrice field in the Products table) needs to be changed. From that point on, every new record in the Orders table will reflect the new price. Relational databases also reduce the total size of the database by avoiding the duplication of information, an important consideration when the database contains thousands or millions of records.

There are two primary database programs that you would use with FrontPage in creating webs. These are Microsoft Access and Microsoft SQL Server. Access (included with Office XP Professional Edition) is an excellent database for applications where the number of queries is limited. If the database will be queried often (more than a few hundred times a day), or will contain thousands of records, Access is not up to the task. SQL Server, on the other hand, is a robust, full-featured client/server database application that can handle millions of records.

*You can use any Open Database Connectivity (ODBC) compliant database with your webs. These include Microsoft's Visual FoxPro and Oracle Corporation's (**http://www.oracle.com**) Oracle databases. ODBC is covered in the section "Open Database Connectivity (ODBC)" later in this chapter.*

Microsoft Access

If you are new to relational databases, Access is an excellent place to start. It contains a number of features, such as wizards, that guide you through the process of creating relational databases. Access is a good choice for a small office intranet. You can also use Access to develop your databases and then upsize them to SQL Server using its Upsizing Wizard. Access 2002 was used to develop the database that will be used in the examples in this chapter. Access is still a desktop database, however, designed for single users. It is not a real client/server database, like SQL Server, so it is of limited use for web applications.

A few excellent resources for learning more about Access are Access 2002: The Complete Reference *and* How to Do Everything with Access 2002, *both by Virginia Andersen (Osborne/McGraw-Hill, 2001).*

Microsoft SQL Server

SQL Server is a *Structured Query Language (SQL)* database. SQL (pronounced "sequel") is a programming language for creating, managing, and querying large relational databases. A brief overview of SQL itself is provided in the section "Structured Query Language Statements." SQL Server can easily handle millions of records and tens of thousands of queries per day. For large corporations, this is a common scenario. It lacks Access's interface and is not so user-friendly. However, you can use Access as a front end to SQL Server tables (the back end). This gives you the best of both worlds.

*A good example of SQL Server in action can be found at **http://terraserver .microsoft.com/**, an online database of aerial photographs and maps of the United States. On an average day, over 45,000 people visit the site and more than 4.5 million database queries are generated. The current peak day had over 233,000 visitors and 12 million database queries.*

A detailed discussion of SQL Server is beyond the scope of this book, nor is it necessary in order to understand how to integrate databases into your webs. You should understand, though, that any serious database work requires a serious database programmer. Large databases, such as SQL Server, are complex applications, and while the basic concepts of relational databases are easy to understand, in actual use the design of the database structure can be quite complex. This is an important point. Poor relational database design will haunt you, and, as more records are added to the database, the problems will become harder to resolve. Just as a building has to have a properly constructed foundation, so must your database.

You can learn more about SQL Server and other large relational databases, as well as ways to gain a better understanding of how to design relational databases, from SQL: The Complete Reference, *by James R. Groff and Paul N. Weinberg (Osborne/McGraw-Hill, 1999).*

Open Database Connectivity (ODBC)

The Open Database Connectivity standard was developed as a way to allow databases to be accessed by different programs—not just the database program that created the data. For example, by using ODBC, you can access a database file using Microsoft Word. This is an important feature for organizations that have data in a number of different database formats, as well as for using databases on the Web. In effect, the ODBC driver is an interpreter between the data stored in the database and the program that is querying the data.

To use an ODBC-compliant database on the Web or with a database program other than the one that created the database itself, the proper ODBC driver must be installed. In the case of web-based databases, the ODBC driver for the database being used must be installed on the web server. To run the examples you will create in this chapter, you will need the Access ODBC driver installed on your computer. This driver, along with ODBC drivers for other popular database programs, can be found on the Windows CD, and on Microsoft's web site at **http://www.microsoft.com/data/download.htm**.

It's important to use the latest ODBC drivers and to make sure you test your application with the same versions as are on the server. Patches and security updates should also be installed when released.

How the Web Server Handles a Request

When a web browser makes a database request (by requesting a page with a database call), a number of things happen before the data is returned and displayed by the browser:

1. The request for a database page is sent by the browser to the web server.
2. The web server reads the requested page and passes the name of the data source and the SQL statement to the ODBC driver.
3. The ODBC driver executes the SQL statement on the specified data source.
4. The data source returns the results of the SQL statement to the ODBC driver.
5. The ODBC driver passes the query results to the web server.
6. The web server formats the query results and sends the file to the web browser.

With a properly configured server with adequate resources, the delay introduced by this process is unnoticeable to the user. This is one reason Microsoft's Access database and other desktop databases are unsuitable for large-volume web sites—they cannot process multiple database queries fast enough. Another bottleneck is the server's hard drive. Database work involves numerous database file reads. Slow hard drives will also be unable to process requests quickly enough for the process to remain transparent to the user when the server is experiencing high traffic volumes. If at all possible, use a client/server database, such as SQL Server, and fast hard drives, such as Fast-Wide SCSI drives. This doesn't mean Access can't be used, only that you should be aware of its limitations and be prepared to upsize it if traffic warrants.

Data Source Name (DSN)

A *Data Source Name* (*DSN*) allows a user with the correct permissions to use a database over a network. This can be an intranet, extranet, or the Internet. The DSN contains the location and type of the database, the time-out and other system values, and the username and password. There are three types of data source names:

- **User**   Allows a single user on the local computer to access a data source.
- **File**   Allows all users with the same ODBC drivers installed to access a data source.
- **System**   Allows all users to access a data source.

The File DSN is a plain text file, which is easily transported between computers. This makes it useful while you're developing applications.

There are several ways you can define a DSN to use a database with FrontPage. If you import a database file into a FrontPage web, you will be prompted for a DSN as part of that process. You can also set a DSN, using the Windows Control Panel. You will see how both of these methods work in the following sections.

Note   *In FrontPage, a DSN is also called a database connection. These terms are used interchangeably in this chapter, but in general use, DSN is preferred.*

A web application does not care where the database is physically located or what type of database it is as long as it has a valid DSN and the correct ODBC drivers are installed. Depending on the database program you are using, you may not be able to import the file into your FrontPage web. Access databases can be easily moved around, but this is much harder to do, if not impossible, with a database program such as SQL Server. With Access, a database is a single file that can be copied and moved like any other file. With SQL Server, a database is a collection of files that cannot be moved easily, similar to an application. With larger web sites, the database program may be running on its own server, creating a situation where it's physically impossible to have the database itself as part of the FrontPage web.

There's also the question of accessing the database for updates and maintenance. For a small web with a few hundred visitors a day, an Access database that is part of the FrontPage web is a viable solution. The database can be maintained on a local computer and uploaded to the server as needed. As the web grows, and traffic increases, this solution may start to provide unacceptable results. It may then be necessary to upsize the database to a more robust database program. This creates its own problems since it may require access to the server that your web presence provider, for valid security reasons, is unwilling to provide. This could add a step between you and your database, requiring you to go through your provider for certain database tasks. These issues will have to be resolved with your web presence provider.

One of the benefits of the DSN system is that these changes will not necessarily mean major changes to your web application. Since the database is referenced through the DSN, not its physical location or type, only the DSN properties would need to be updated.

The FrontPage Database Results Wizard

Now that you've learned the basics of how databases are integrated into webs, it's time to put theory into practice. In this section, you will import the files you need to get started into your root web. Create your database web with these steps:

1. Open your default web in FrontPage. This cannot be a disk-based web and must be opened using the URL. The URL should be http://localhost/ or http://*computer_name*/. By default, the path is C:\Inetpub\wwwroot\.

2. In the Folder List, select the root folder (http://*computer_name*), open the File menu, and choose New | Folder. Name the folder **nbt**.

3. Open the File menu again and choose Import. In the Import dialog box, click Add File.

4. In the Add File To Import List dialog box, select your CD-ROM drive; then open the \Book\Chap19\ folder. There are two subdirectories, Access 2000 and Access 2002. Open the correct folder for your version of Access and select **NorthBeachTools.mdb**. Click Open and then OK. The Add Database Connection dialog box, shown here, is displayed.

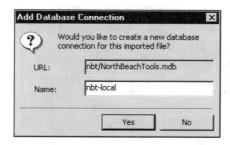

5. Type **nbt-local** in the Name text box and then click Yes.

   The function of the Add Database Connection dialog box is to create a DSN (or database connection) for the database. FrontPage does this by adding the DSN properties to the Global.asa file. (If you open your Global.asa file, you will see the changes made.) This method has the advantage of being very simple for the user to implement. The disadvantage is that the DSN is only valid for the web application that uses that Global.asa file. This can create a problem if you need to access the database using a DSN from outside the web application. This situation may arise in a network environment where the database may be accessed from several workstations. A System DSN is a better choice in this case. How to do this is explained in the section "Defining a System DSN."

6. A message box is displayed recommending that your database be stored in the folder "fpdb", which FrontPage creates automatically (if it doesn't already exist) when you import a database file. Click Yes.

   The fpdb folder is the preferred location for file databases (such as Access; SQL Server cannot be stored in a single file) in a FrontPage web. The only difference between this folder and any other folder you might create is the default permissions assigned to it. When you create a new folder, such as the NBT folder you created in Step 2, the default permissions allow scripts to be run and allow the contents of the folder to be browsed. You can see this by checking the properties of the folder.

7. Right-click the NBT folder and choose Properties.

   In the NBT Properties dialog box, the Allow Scripts To Be Run and Allow Files To Be Browsed check boxes are selected. New folders inherit the permissions of their root folder. In this case, the root folder has both script and browsing permissions, so the NBT folder inherits them. This dialog box allows you to change the permissions for a folder.

Tip   *On your local computer, the Allow Files To Be Browsed check box can be selected, but your production web should not allow file browsing. File browsing permits Internet users to read the file structure of your web server. It's a significant security issue, and one you should be aware of.*

   Your database folder, however, should not allow either of these permissions. You want to keep your database itself as far from the public as possible. This is one reason you may not want your database to be included in your FrontPage web if at all possible. When FrontPage creates the fpdb folder, by default it will not allow either script or browsing permissions. You can check this by looking at the properties of the fpdb folder.

8. Click Cancel to close the dialog box.

When a file has been placed on a CD, such as the North Beach Tools database, it is given Read-only permission by Windows. Before you can modify the database, which you will do later in this chapter, you must change this.

9. In Windows Explorer or My Computer, locate the NorthBeachTools.mdb file (C:\Inetpub\wwwroot\fpdb\NorthBeachTools.mdb by default). Right-click it and choose Properties.

10. In the General tab of the NorthBeachTools.mdb Properties dialog box, clear the Read-only check box and click OK.

Defining a System DSN

The DSN you created for the North Beach Tools database when you imported it into your root web is similar to a file DSN. The properties of the database connection are added to your Global.asa file. This means you can access your database from within the web application that the Global.asa file belongs to. However, this connection isn't valid outside the web application.

Creating the DSN from within FrontPage is not the only method, or always the best method. Nor will you always want to or be able to import a database into your FrontPage web. Moving an Access database around is fairly simple, but the same is not true for other databases, such as SQL Server. A System DSN is often the best choice. Define a System DSN for the North Beach Tools database with these steps:

1. Open the Windows Start menu and select Settings | Control Panel | Administrative Tools | Data Sources (ODBC) (Windows 2000 Professional) or Programs | Administrative Tools | Data Sources (ODBC) (Windows 2000 Server).

2. Select the System DSN tab in the ODBC Data Source Administrator dialog box, as shown in Figure 19-2.

Note   *You may have System DSNs already defined, including one for the Northwind database, a sample database application included with Access 2002. It is not installed by default with Access, but it's a good idea to install it on your own. If you're new to databases, it's an excellent starting point for learning. If you do have any System DSNs configured, they will most likely be configured by an application you have installed. Changing a DSN will prevent the application from running properly.*

The ODBC Data Source Administrator dialog box is used to set User, System, and File Data Source Names, to display information about the installed ODBC drivers, and to configure the Connection Pooling and Tracing options. *Connection Pooling* improves performance by reusing idle database connections, rather than creating a new connection for each user. In this way, the minimum number of database connections will be open at any time. Since each open connection uses server resources, pooling the connections

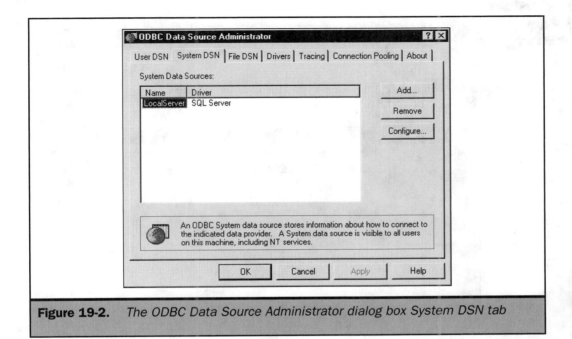

Figure 19-2. *The ODBC Data Source Administrator dialog box System DSN tab*

reduces the server's workload. *Tracing* creates a log of database calls, which is useful for debugging. Tracing is disabled by default, as it can generate very large files.

    3. In the System DSN tab, click Add. The Create New Data Source dialog box, shown next, is displayed.

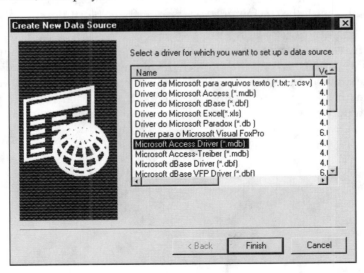

You may have different drivers in your dialog box, depending on which drivers are installed on your system or server. You must have the Access driver installed to use the North Beach Tools database.

4. Select the Microsoft Access Driver and click Finish. The ODBC Microsoft Access Setup dialog box, shown next, is displayed.

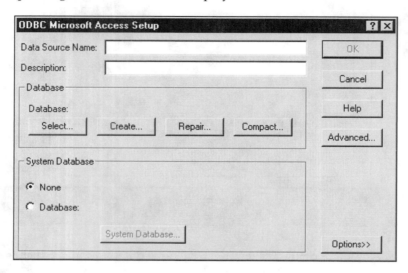

5. Type **nbt** in the Data Source Name text box, press TAB, and type **North Beach Tools Access database** in the Description text box.

6. Click Select, locate your sample database in the Select Database dialog box (the path should be C:\Inetpub\wwwroot\fpdb\NorthBeachTools.mdb), and click OK.

7. Click Advanced to open the Set Advanced Options dialog box, shown next. If your database is password protected, enter the account information in the Login Name and Password text boxes. (To keep things simple, there is no login name or password required to use the North Beach Tools database.) The properties of the DSN are displayed in the Options scrolling list box. Click OK twice.

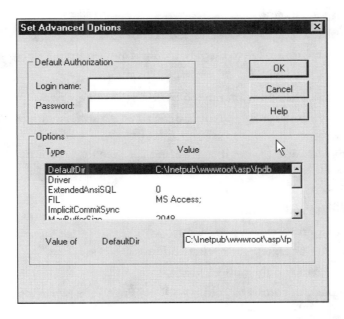

8. The System DSN tab in the ODBC Date Source Administrator dialog box will now display the North Beach Tools System DSN (nbt).

9. Click the Connection Pooling tab, then double-click the Microsoft Access Driver in the ODBC Drivers list box. The Set Connection Pooling Attributes dialog box, shown next, is opened.

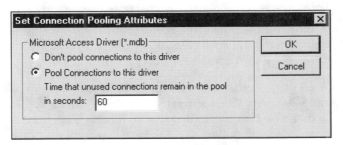

10. Select the Pool Connections To This Driver option, leave the default time-out at 60 seconds, and click OK. The Connection Pooling time-out value is the length of time a connection can be idle before it will be closed.

11. Click Apply and then OK.

The North Beach Tools database now has a System DSN, which you will use to access the database from the web page.

Creating a Web Page from a Database

The next step is to create a page to display the information from a database. First create a home page for the NBT folder:

1. In FrontPage, click New on the toolbar to create a new page.

2. At the top of the page, type **North Beach Tools** and format it as Heading 1. Press ENTER.

3. Type **Products** and format it as Heading 2. Move the cursor to the next line and click Bullets on the toolbar.

4. Type **View All Products** and press ENTER.

5. Type **Find a Product** and press ENTER.

6. Type **Add a Product** and press ENTER.

7. Type **Modify or Delete a Product** and press ENTER.

8. Click Bullets to end the bulleted list.

9. Save the page in your NBT folder with the Page Title **North Beach Tools** and the File Name **Default.asp**.

Next, you will create a page for the Database Results Region. This page will display in a table all the products in the North Beach Tools database.

1. Create a new page in the NBT folder and save it with the Page Title **All Products** and the File Name **Allprod.asp**.

2. At the top of the page, type **North Beach Tools Product Line**, format it as Heading 2, and press ENTER.

3. Open the Insert menu and select Database | Results. The first dialog box of the Database Results Wizard is displayed.

This dialog box allows you to select the type of DSN you want to use. The first option, Use A Sample Database Connection (Northwind), can be applied with the Northwind sample database if you installed it with Access. The second option, Use An Existing Database Connection, lists any database connections in your Global.asa file. Your nbt-local DSN is displayed in the drop-down list. The third option is Use A New Database Connection.

4. Select the Use A New Database Connection option, and then click Create. The Web Settings dialog box Database tab is opened. The nbt-local connection is listed along with a question mark in the Status column. The question mark is displayed until the connection has been verified.

5. Select the nbt-local connection and click Verify. The question mark should change to a green check mark. This indicates that the database connection has been verified.

6. Click Add. This opens the New Database Connection dialog box, shown next.

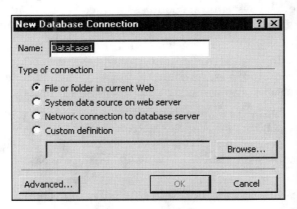

There are four options for selecting the location of the database. File Or Folder In Current Web allows you to use a file or folder in the current web that you haven't already created a data connection for. If you select this option, you would also click Browse to select the file or folder for the data connection. Selecting System Data Source On Web Server allows you to use any DSN that has been configured on the web server. Network Connection To Database Server allows you to use a DSN for a database that exists on a server other than the web server, where your FrontPage web would be located. The fourth option, Custom Definition, allows you to establish a connection using a text file, such as a file DSN. There are obviously a number of ways to establish a data connection, but in actual use you will not need or use all the available options. The next steps will look at how each of the first three options work, but you will use System Data Source On Web Server for the rest of the exercise.

7. Select the File Or Folder In Current Web option, and then click Browse. The Database Files In Current Web dialog box is displayed. Here you can select the file or folder containing the database, and FrontPage will create a data connection for that database in the current web.

8. Click Cancel, then select Network Connection To Database Server and click Browse. The Network Database Connection dialog box is displayed. This dialog box allows you to use a connection to a database located on a server on the network. This is a common scenario for large databases. A database program, such as SQL Server, can require a great deal of server resources. Putting both a large web application, or several web applications, and the database program on the same server can create bottlenecks in the delivery of your content.

Note *Much of the configuration of your web and database will depend on your web presence provider. You will need to know which database programs they support, their policies regarding user access, and the configuration of their servers.*

WORKING BEHIND
THE SCENES

9. Click Cancel, select the System Data Source On Web Server option, and then click Browse. The System Data Sources On Web Server dialog box is displayed. In this dialog box, you should have the NBT System DSN you created earlier.

10. Select nbt and click OK. Click Advanced. This displays the Advanced Connection Properties dialog box. Here you can set the username and password for the database, if required, and the connection and command time-out values. You can also set other parameters that your database supports.

11. Click Cancel. In the New Database Connection dialog box, select the existing text and type **NBT** in the Name text box and click OK. Even though you selected the nbt DSN in the New Database Connection dialog box, you can rename the connection using the Name text box in the New Database Connection dialog box.

12. In the Web Settings dialog box, select the NBT connection and click Verify. After the connection is confirmed (the question mark changes to a green check mark), click Apply and then OK.

13. In the Database Results Wizard dialog box, the NBT database connection should be displayed in the Use An Existing Database Connection drop-down list. Click Next.

14. Select the Record Source option if it's not already selected, and then select Products in the drop-down list. Click Next. After the database is connected, a list of the fields in the selected table, Products, is displayed.

15. Click Edit List. The Displayed Fields dialog box appears. You use this dialog box to select the fields in the database table to be displayed in the results set (also referred to as a *recordset*), and the order in which they will be displayed. You will present all the fields in this example, and use the default order, so click Cancel.

16. Click More Options to display the More Options dialog box. Here you can set the criteria for the database query, the field that will be used to order the returned records, set defaults for the search criteria, limit the number of records that are returned, and create a message to be displayed if no records are returned by the query.

17. Click Ordering, which displays the Ordering dialog box, shown here. Select ProductDescr in the Available Fields list; then click Add. The results set will be sorted on the values in the ProductDescr field of the Products table. By default, this will be an ascending sort (A–Z) as indicated by the yellow triangle pointing up next to ProductDescr in the Sort Order list. You can change the sort order to descending by selecting the sort order field and clicking Change Sort. The yellow triangle would then point down.

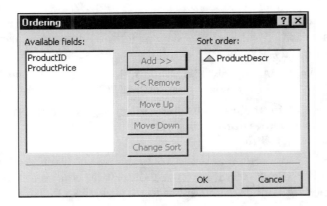

18. Click OK; then type **There were no matches for your search** in the Message To Display If No Records Are Returned text box. Click OK and then click Next.

In the Database Results Wizard – Step 4 Of 5, you can now select how to display the results set, either as a table, a list, or a drop-down list. The options displayed are determined by the formatting option selected. You will use the Table option, but first look at the List options.

19. Select List – One Field Per Item in the Choose Formatting Options For The Records Returned By The Query drop-down list. You can choose whether or not to have labels for all field values and whether or not to have a horizontal rule as a separator between records. In the List Options drop-down list, you can choose how to format the list—with paragraphs, line breaks, bullets, and so on.

20. Select Drop-Down List – One Record Per Item in the Choose Formatting Options For The Records Returned By The Query drop-down list. This option allows you to populate a drop-down list from the database query. In the Display Values From This Field drop-down list, you select the field whose contents will be displayed. You then select the value to be returned in the Submit Values From This Field drop-down list. This allows you, for example, to display a product description to the user and return the product's ID number in the form.

21. Select Table – One Record Per Row in the Choose Formatting Options For The Records Returned By The Query drop-down list.

22. Clear the Expand Table To Width Of Page check box. The other two options, Use Table Border and Include Header Row With Column Labels, should be selected.

23. Click Next. The final page of the Database Results Wizard dialog box allows you to group the records returned. You can either display all the records returned by the query or break them into smaller groups. The option you select will depend on how many records you expect to be returned by the query. The North Beach Tools database contains only a few records in each table, so no

results set will be very large. If you expect the query to return more records than can be easily displayed on a web page—no one wants to scroll through dozens of records—you should break the results set into smaller groups.

24. Select the Display All Records Together option and click Finish. Save your page. Figure 19-3 shows what your All Products page should now look like.

25. Change the title for the first column by selecting ProductID and typing **Product Number**. Change the second column heading to **Description** and the third column heading to **Price**.

26. Right-click the table cell that will display the price of each item (this is the cell with <<ProductPrice>> in it as a placeholder) and choose Cell Properties. Change the Horizontal Alignment to Right and click OK.

27. Place the cursor on the first line after the Database Results region and type **NBT Home**, then select it and click Hyperlink on the toolbar.

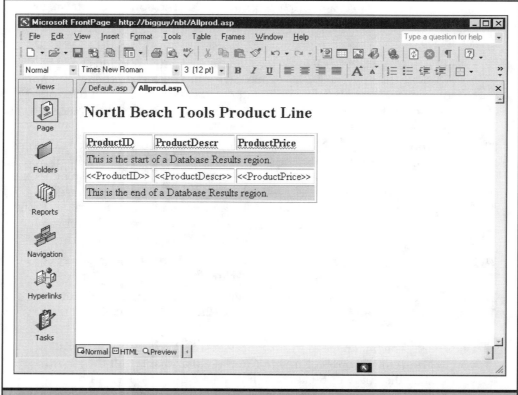

Figure 19-3. *All Products page with Database Results region inserted*

You will have to manually create the hyperlinks for your ASP pages as FrontPage's Navigation view will not create links for Active Server Pages.

28. In the Insert Hyperlink dialog box, open the NBT folder, if necessary, and select Default.asp. Click OK, then save your page.

29. Open the File menu and choose Preview In Browser. Figure 19-4 shows the All Products page in Internet Explorer 5.5.

In FrontPage, you saw placeholders for the selected fields. In your browser, the actual data in the database table is displayed. You can format the table in Page view, as you did by changing the horizontal alignment in the Price cell. The Database Results region will automatically create as many rows as are required to display the results set.

In this case, all the records and all the fields in each record were read by the query. More often you will want to select a specific record or group of records based on some criteria. You will do this next, but first look at the SQL query created by FrontPage.

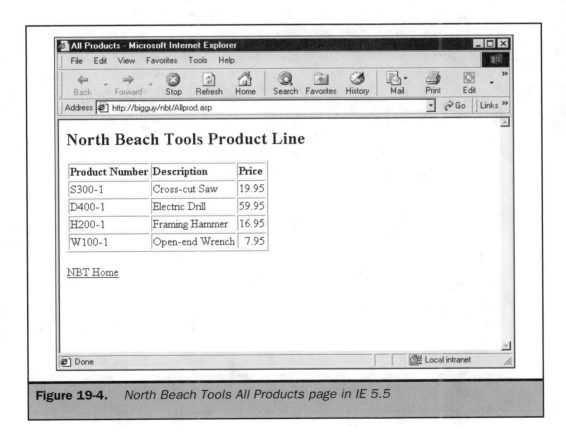

Figure 19-4. *North Beach Tools All Products page in IE 5.5*

Structured Query Language Statements

SQL is the language you use to query and maintain your database. It consists of about 30 commands, but you can accomplish quite a bit with just a few main commands. Table 19-2 describes the principal SQL commands used to query and maintain a database.

Every SQL statement begins with a SQL command followed by the database fields that are the target of the command and, optionally, selection criteria. To see how this works, look at the SQL query you created for the All Products page.

1. In FrontPage Page view, with the All Products page open, click the HTML tab. As you can see, FrontPage generated quite a bit of code to read the database and display the results set.

2. Scroll down the page until you reach a section of code between opening and closing VBScript delimiters (<% and %>), as shown in Figure 19-5.

3. The first line of code in this section should be

```
fp_sQry="SELECT * FROM Products ORDER BY ProductDescr ASC"
```

This line of code assigns the SQL query to a local variable, fp_sQry. The query itself is a text string, as indicated by the quotes around it. This string is passed to the database through your data connection (DSN), which is assigned to the local variable fp_sDataConn in the fourth line of the VBScript code.

The words in all caps are SQL keywords. SELECT defines the operation—to return the fields specified from the database table. In this case, all the fields in the table are selected by using the asterisk wildcard. FROM identifies the table (the Products table) that is the target of the SELECT command. ORDER BY identifies the field (ProductDescr) that will set the sort order, and ASC sets an ascending sort.

SQL Command	Description
SELECT	Retrieves from a database the records that meet the specified criteria
INSERT	Creates a new record in the database
DELETE	Removes an existing record
UPDATE	Modifies an existing record
FROM	Identifies the database table that is the object of the query
WHERE	Identifies the criteria for the query

Table 19-2.   *Principal SQL Database Statements*

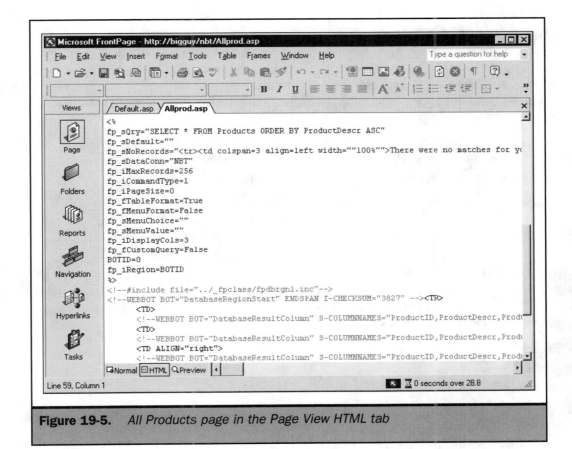

Figure 19-5. *All Products page in the Page View HTML tab*

WORKING BEHIND
THE SCENES

Note *In SQL, it's a good practice to use the syntax* **table.field** *to identify a field in a table, even though FrontPage doesn't do this. The SQL statement could be written as* SELECT Products.* FROM Products ORDER BY Products.ProductDescr ASC. *The example here is about as simple as a SQL query can be. When building complex queries where you join several tables, the table.field syntax will make your life easier.*

FrontPage does a good job of keeping you from actually having to write SQL statements. Using dialog boxes and wizards, it will create most of the SQL queries you need. It is important, however, to understand how the queries work. Advanced queries, drawing from multiple tables, will require you to do some programming manually. You will get firsthand experience writing SQL statements later in this chapter.

Using Search Criteria

One of the benefits of using a database with your web is the ability to create custom searches of your data. FrontPage greatly simplifies this task by allowing you to use a value entered in an HTML form in the SQL query it creates. In this next exercise, you will use this technique to select a single North Beach Tools record. Do that now with these steps:

1. Create a new page, then type **Search North Beach Tools** at the top of the page and format it as Heading 2. Press ENTER.

2. Open the Insert menu and choose Form | Textbox.

3. Press HOME and type **Description:** (leave a space after the colon). Press RIGHT ARROW and then ENTER.

4. Right-click the Description text box and choose Form Field Properties.

5. In the Text Box Properties dialog box, type **SearchWord** in the Name text box, then click Validate.

6. In the Text Box Validation dialog box, select Required for the Data Length, type **24** in the Max Length text box, and then type **Description** in the Display Name text box. Click OK twice.

> **Note**   *The maximum number of characters allowed in the Description field of the North Beach Tools database Products table is 24. This determines the maximum number of characters allowed in the search form.*

7. Right-click the form and choose Form Properties. Select the Send To Other option, and then click Options.

8. In the Options For Custom Form Handler dialog box, type **Results.asp** in the Action text box. Click OK twice.

9. Save the page in your NBT folder with the Page Title **Search North Beach Tools** and File Name **Search.asp**.

10. Create a new page, type **Search Results** at the top of the page, and format it as Heading 2. Press ENTER.

11. Open the Insert menu and choose Database | Results.

12. In the first page of the Database Results Wizard, select the Use An Existing Database Connection option, and then select NBT from the drop-down list. Click Next.

13. Select the Record Source option then select Products from the Record Source drop-down list. Click Next.

14. Click More Options. The More Options dialog box is displayed.

15. Click Criteria. In the Criteria dialog box, click Add. The Add Criteria dialog box shown next is displayed.

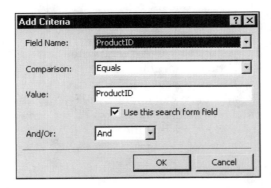

16. In the Add Criteria dialog box, select ProductDescr from the Field Name drop-down list, then select Contains from the Comparison drop-down list.

The Comparison drop-down list contains the types of comparison operators that can be used in your database query. For example, Equals allows you to find exact matches to your search criteria while Not Equals allows you to exclude records that match your criteria. The Contains comparison, which you are using in this exercise, allows partial matches. For example, using the search string "boat" would match "sailboat," "boating," and so forth. If you wanted to limit the search to exact matches, you would use Equals in place of Contains.

17. Type **SearchWord** in the Value text box. This is the name of the form field you created on your Search page that will contain your criterion.

18. Select the Use This Search Form Field check box, if it's not already selected. You are using a single criterion in this exercise so you can ignore the setting in the And/Or drop-down list. Click OK. The Criteria dialog box now contains the criterion for your Search Results page, as shown here. Click OK.

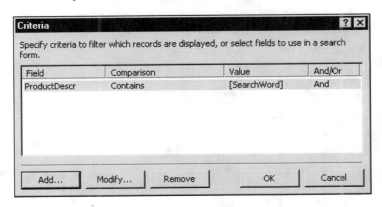

19. In the More Options dialog box, type **There are no records to display.**, including the period, in the Message To Be Displayed If No Records Are Returned text box.

20. Click Defaults to display the Defaults dialog box.

Setting a default for the parameter will ensure that the parameter variable is replaced by a value in the SQL query. You are not going to enter a default value for the parameter as the only link to the Search Results page will be from the form on the Search page. In other words, the Search Results page will not be displayed unless a parameter is first entered in the Search form. Later in this exercise, you'll see, using the ASP Response object Redirect method, how to ensure that the Search Results page can't be opened without a valid search parameter.

21. Click OK two times, then click Next.

22. Select List – One Field Per Item in the Choose Formatting Options For The Records Returned By The Query drop-down list. Both the Add Labels For All

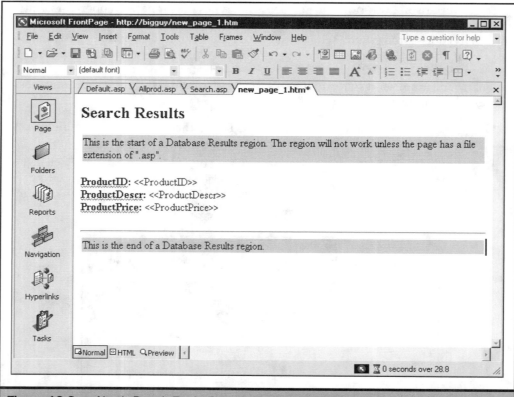

Figure 19-6. *North Beach Tools Search Page in Page view*

Field Values and Place Horizontal Separator Between Records check boxes should be selected.

23. Select Line Breaks in the List Options drop-down list and click Next.

24. Clear the Add Search Form check box, if it's selected, and click Finish. Your Search Results page should look similar to Figure 19-6.

25. Select ProductID and type **Product Number**. Select ProductDescr and type **Description**. Select ProductPrice and type **Price**.

26. Place the cursor on the first line after the Database Results region and type **NBT Home**, then select it and click Hyperlink on the toolbar.

27. In the Insert Hyperlink dialog box, open the NBT folder, if necessary, and select Default.asp. Click OK.

28. Save your page with the File Name **Results.asp**, and then open it in your browser. Figure 19-7 shows the page in Internet Explorer 5.5.

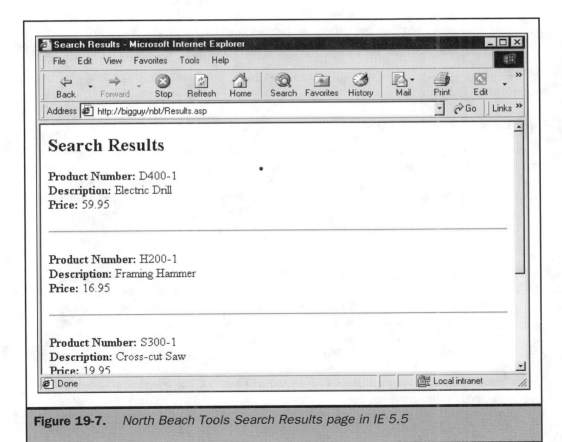

Figure 19-7. *North Beach Tools Search Results page in IE 5.5*

Since you didn't specify a search phrase before loading the Search Results page, all the records are displayed. This is the same result, with different formatting, as your All Products page. This page is designed to display only the records that match specified search criteria, which are entered in the form on your Search page.

29. In FrontPage, click the HTML tab and press CTRL+HOME. Press ENTER and then UP ARROW. The ASP code must be before the <HTML> tag or the redirect will not work. You cannot redirect to another page after the HTML header is written.

30. Type
    <% if Request.Form("SearchWord") = "" Then
    Response.Redirect "Search.asp"
    End If %>

31. Save your page, then refresh the Search Results page in your browser. You will be redirected to the Search page.

32. In the search form text box, type **saw** and then click Submit. The Results page will open and display the information for the cross-cut saw, the only item in the database that matches the search criteria.

33. Close your browser and the open pages in FrontPage.

FrontPage greatly simplifies the task of creating parameterized queries, as this exercise has shown.

Writing to a Database

There are a number of scenarios in which you would want the user to be able to write to a database on your web server—for example, a user survey where the user answers a series of questions. By writing their responses directly to a database, the results can be easily compiled and analyzed. An organization may have a number of remote staff people who need to access and update a database. This might be a business where salespeople need to record sales data from remote locations, such as the customer's place of business.

Note   *Allowing a user to write to a database on your web server raises some serious security concerns. Authorized users, such as employees, can be given this type of access with methods that are more secure than using a web interface. One simple method using the Web is to have the database that is written to located separately, with its own DSN, rather than in the main database. At regular intervals the two databases could be synchronized. How to do this will depend on the database application. If no public access to the database is required, there are network methods that use the Internet without a web interface, such as a Virtual Private Network (VPN). These techniques are beyond the scope of this book, however. Chapter 22, though, will cover security on the Web in more detail.*

In this next exercise, you will create a page that allows the user to add a product to the North Beach Tools database. Security issues will be kept to a minimum; the purpose here is to learn how FrontPage's database tools work. The Internet user account, IUSR_*computername* by default, must be given write permission in order for a web user to be able to write to the database. Do that now with these steps.

1. In Windows Explorer, locate your North Beach Tools database. The location will be C:\Inetpub\wwwroot\fpdb\NorthBeachTools.mdb unless you installed it in another location.

2. Right-click NorthBeachTools.mdb and choose Properties.

3. In the NorthBeachTools.mdb Properties dialog box, select the Security tab, shown in Figure 19-8. The server Administrators group has full control of the file.

Note   *The permission settings explained here are for Windows 2000 Professional and Windows 2000 Server with NTFS formatted drives (rather than FAT32) and without Active Directory configured. The permissions on Active Directory servers are configured differently, though the results are similar.*

4. Click Everyone in the Name list. This group has much less permission than the Administrators group, as shown in the Permissions list.

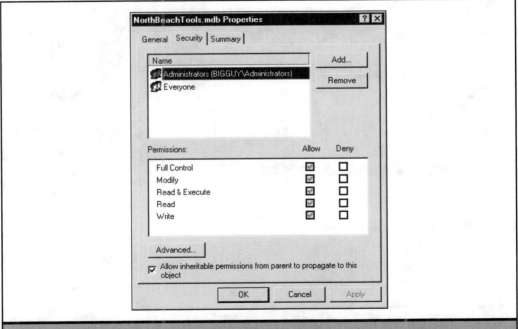

Figure 19-8.   *NorthBeachTools.mdb dialog box Security tab*

The database is accessed through the Internet Guest Account (IUSR_*computername*) when it's connected to a web application. This is a default account configured by the system during installation of IIS. For the purpose of this exercise, you will give this account permission to write to the database file. In real life, it will be up to your ISP to correctly configure database permissions as configuring permissions requires Administrator permission.

5. Click Add. The Select Users, Computers, Or Groups dialog box, shown in Figure 19-9, is displayed.

6. Scroll through the list of accounts until you find the IUSR_*computername* account. Select it, click Add, and then click OK.

7. In the NorthBeachTools.mdb Properties dialog box select the Internet Guest Account if it's not already selected. In the Permissions list, the Read & Execute and Read permissions should be selected.

8. Click the Write check box to select it, then click Apply, and then OK.

9. In FrontPage, create a new page, then type **Add a Product** at the top of the page and format it as Heading 2. Press ENTER.

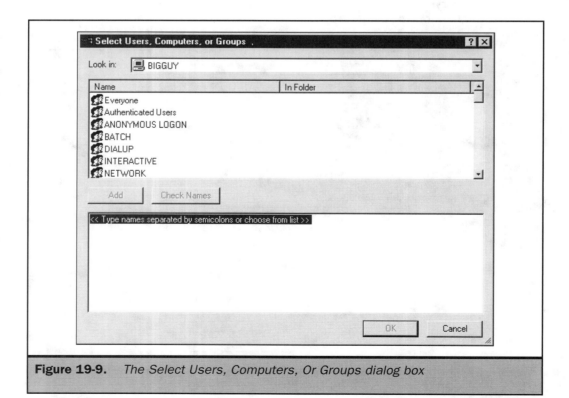

Figure 19-9. *The Select Users, Computers, Or Groups dialog box*

10. Save the page in your NBT folder with the Page Title **Add a Product** and the File Name **Addprod.asp**.

11. Open the Insert menu and choose Form | Textbox.

12. Press HOME and type **Product ID:** with two spaces after the colon. Format it as Formatted, press RIGHT ARROW, and then press SHIFT+ENTER.

13. Type **Description:**, with one space after the colon, and insert a text box. Press SHIFT+ENTER.

14. Type **Price:**, with seven spaces after the colon, and insert a text box. Press ENTER.

15. Right-click the first text box (Product ID) and choose Form Field Properties.

16. In the Text Box Properties dialog box, type **ProductID** in the Name text box and then click Validate.

17. In the Text Box Validation dialog box, select Text from the Data Type drop-down list, and select Required for Data Length.

18. Type **4** in the Min Length text box and **8** in the Max Length text box, then type **Product ID** in the Display Name text box. Click OK twice.

Note *Eight characters is the maximum length allowed in the ProductID field of the North Beach Tools database Products table.*

19. Right-click the second text box (Description) and choose Form Field Properties. Type **Description** for the Name, then click Validate.

20. In the Text Box Validation dialog box, select Text from the Data Type drop-down list, and select Required for Data Length.

21. Type **4** in the Min Length text box and **24** in the Max Length text box, then type **Description** in the Display Name text box. Click OK twice.

22. Right-click the third text box (Price) and choose Form Field Properties. Type **Price** for the Name and then click Validate.

23. In the Text Box Validation dialog box, select Number from the Data Type drop-down list, and select Required for Data Length.

24. Type **Price** in the Display Name text box and click OK twice.

Note *This is the minimal validation for the form. When creating your own databases and forms, you will want to have client-side validation that will trap all possible errors. It is much easier to deal with form validation than arcane error messages returned by the ODBC driver.*

25. Right-click the form and choose Form Properties. In the Form Properties dialog box, select Send To Database, and then click Options. The Options For Saving

Results To Database dialog box Database Results tab, shown in Figure 19-10, is opened.

26. Select NBT from the Database Connection To Use drop-down list. FrontPage will connect to the database and populate the Table To Hold Form Results drop-down list.

27. Select Products in the Table To Hold Form Results drop-down list. Leave the URL Of Confirmation Page and URL Of Error Page text boxes blank for this exercise. In actual use, you would probably want to specify both pages.

28. Click the Saved Fields tab. Select Price in the Form Field column of the Form Fields To Save list box, and then click Modify. The Modify Field dialog box is displayed.

29. Select ProductPrice from the Save To Database Column drop-down list, then click OK.

Note *A field in a database table can be referred to as either a column or field. The term used will depend on the database.*

30. Select Description, click Modify, select ProductDescr from the Save To Database Column drop-down list, and click OK.

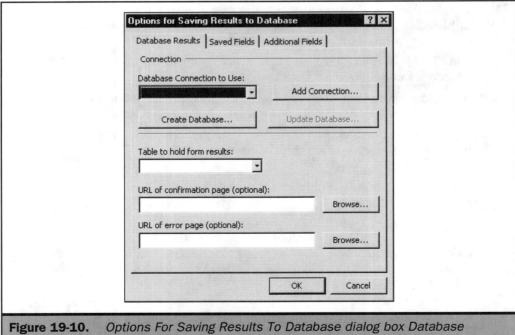

Figure 19-10. *Options For Saving Results To Database dialog box Database Results tab*

31. Select ProductID, click Modify, select ProductID from the Save To Database Column drop-down list, and click OK.

32. Select the Additional Fields tab. Here you can select additional information, such as a time stamp, to also be written to the database. The North Beach Tools database Products table doesn't contain fields to hold any of these values, so you will leave them blank. You should remember this feature, however, when designing your own databases as they can be very useful.

33. Click OK twice. Place the cursor on the first line after the form and type **NBT Home**, then select it and click Hyperlink on the toolbar.

34. In the Insert Hyperlink dialog box, open the NBT folder, if necessary, and select Default.asp. Click OK.

35. Save your page, then open it in your browser.

36. In your browser, type **S400-1** in the Product ID text box and press TAB.

37. Type **Radial-arm Saw** in the Description text box and press TAB.

38. Type **129.75** in the Price text box and click Submit. The default Form Confirmation page will open in your browser.

39. Open the North Beach Tools database in Access, then open the Products table. You will see that the information you entered in the form has been added to the Products table, as shown here.

⊞ Products : Table			
	ProductID	ProductDescr	ProductPrice
▶ +	D400-1	Electric Drill	59.95
+	H200-1	Framing Hammer	16.95
+	S300-1	Cross-cut Saw	19.95
+	S400-1	Radial-arm Saw	129.75
+	W100-1	Open-end Wrench	7.95
*			0.00

Record: ◄ ◄ 1 ► ►► ►* of 5

40. Close the North Beach Tools database and Access. Open the North Beach Tools All Products page in your browser. Your new entry is now displayed in the list of all the North Beach Tools products.

This illustrates one of the prime advantages of a database-driven web—a change made to information in the database will appear on your web pages the next time they are loaded without any further human intervention.

The FrontPage Database Results Wizard can create most of the code you need to work with databases. However, to really master database and web integration, you need to understand how FrontPage and ASP are working together. FrontPage's database tools are based on the Active Server Pages Database Access Component, so mastery begins with understanding how it works.

WORKING BEHIND THE SCENES

The ASP Database Access Component

The Active Server Pages Database Access Component uses ActiveX Data Objects (ADO) to manipulate information in a database. The actual version used in ASP and FrontPage is ADODB, a version of ADO optimized for Microsoft's OLE DB drivers. ADO is an extremely powerful tool for integrating databases and webs.

 This section will introduce this technology, but it cannot be a thorough explanation of it. For more information, visit Microsoft's Universal Data Access web site (http://www.microsoft.com/data/).

Since ADODB is an ASP component, it is used in much the same way as the ASP components you worked with in previous chapters. There are three primary ASP objects for working with databases:

- **Connection object** provides the connection to the database.

- **Command object** provides the instructions for the data source specified by the Connection object.

- **Recordset object** contains the results of the Command object. This can be single or multiple records.

With these objects you can open a database connection, execute a query against the database, and store the results of the query. Listing 19-1 is the minimal code required to open a database, execute a command, and handle the results. The parts of this listing are explained in the following sections.

Listing 19-1
Minimum ASP code for reading a database

```
Set objConnection = Server.CreateObject("ADODB.Connection")
objConnection.Open ConnectionString
Set Recordset = objConnection.Execute("SQL Statement")
objConnection.Close
```

The remaining objects are:

- **Error**   Returns errors from an ADO operation.

- **Field**   Allows you to work with data from a single column of a recordset.

- **Parameter**   Used to hold values for queries and stored procedures.

- **Property**   Contains information about dynamic characteristics of ADO objects. ADO objects have built-in and dynamic characteristics—built-in characteristics are set by ADO, and dynamic characteristics are contained in the specific ADO object.

The Connection Object

The Connection object is used to handle communication between the data source and the web server. The connection must be opened before the data source can be accessed and should be closed when the operation is completed. The methods used with the Connection object are listed in Table 19-3, and the properties are listed in Table 19-4.

As with all the Active Server Pages components, you must create an instance of the Connection object before you can use it (the first line in Listing 19-1). Once the Connection object is created (or *instantiated*), you can use it until you close it or it times out. Each open connection uses system resources, so you generally want to close your connections as soon as the database operation is completed, as shown in the last line of Listing 19-1.

The Open Method

When you call the Open method, the database and its parameters (such as login name and password) are specified. You generally do this with either a DSN or with the ConnectionString property. The ConnectionString property can be either defined when the database is opened, or created as a Session object in the Global.asa file. The parameters of the ConnectionString property are listed in Table 19-5.

Method	Description
BeginTrans, CommitTrans, RollbackTrans	Used for database transactions. A *transaction* is a group of related changes to tables, so that any changes are made to all the tables at the same time. BeginTrans creates a new transaction, CommitTrans makes any changes and closes the transaction, and RollbackTrans cancels any changes and closes the transaction.
Close	Ends the connection.
Execute	Runs the specified query or procedure.
Open	Creates the connection to the data source.
OpenSchema	Returns the database *schema* information. A schema is like a blueprint of the database.

Table 19-3. *Connection Object Methods*

WORKING BEHIND
THE SCENES

Property	Description
Attributes	Contains attributes of an object. With the Connection object, it is used with CommitTrans and RollbackTrans to determine if a new transaction is started when they are called. This feature is not supported by all databases.
CommandTimeout	The time, in seconds, the command will wait to be executed. The default is 30 seconds. If this value is exceeded, the command will return an error message.
ConnectionString	The properties of the connection being created.
ConnectionTimeout	The time, in seconds, the connection will wait to be executed. The default is 15 seconds. If this value is exceeded, the Connection object will return an error message.
CursorLocation	Allows either a client-side or server-side cursor. A cursor marks the current position in a multirecord recordset.
DefaultDatabase	Sets the default database for the connection.
IsolationLevel	Used with the BeginTrans method to set how transactions interact with each other—for example, whether uncommitted transactions are visible to all users. Also, higher isolation levels can be given priority over lower isolation levels.
Mode	Sets permissions for using the database.
Provider	The name of the connection provider. With ASP, this is usually ADODB. By default, it is MSDASQL (the Microsoft ODBC provider for OLE DB).
State	Returns the current state of an object, either open or closed.
Version	The ADO version number.

Table 19-4.   *Connection Object Properties*

Parameter	Description
Provider	Name of the ODBC driver used for the connection.
Data Source	Name of the data source being opened.
User ID	Username for the data source connection.
Password	Password for the login account.
Filename	Name of a file to open. If a file is specified, the Provider attribute is not used; the appropriate provider will be opened by the specified file.

Table 19-5. *ConnectionString Property Parameters*

The ConnectionString is written as a series of name=value pairs separated by semicolons, similar to this:

```
DSN=NBT;DBQ=C:\Inetpub\wwwroot\nbt\fpdb\NorthBeachTools.mdb;
DriverId=25;FIL=MS Access;MaxBufferSize=512;PageTimeout=5;
```

For security, you should create a user account for the database that has read-only permission, and use this account for all web-based queries. If it is necessary for the user to write to the database, you should consider creating a separate database with read-write permission. You can then synchronize the databases offline. The time and money spent creating and populating a database application is usually very significant. Obviously, you want as much security as possible for your investment.

Note *In this chapter, discussion of security has been kept to a minimum to focus on database connectivity and because setting up user accounts is more a function of the database and server, not FrontPage or ASP. In the real world, you should use the maximum amount of security practical with your database.*

The Command Object

The Command object is used to define the command that will be applied to the data source. It has two methods, CreateParameter and Execute. CreateParameter is used to create a new parameter for the Command object and assign values to it. As with the Connection object, the Execute method is used to run the command against the data source. In fact, you can often use the Connection.Execute object to perform the same function as the Command.Execute object. The third line of Listing 19-1 uses the Connection object, rather than the Command object, to execute the query. The Command object is more flexible and so should generally be used.

The Command object has seven properties, listed in Table 19-6.

| Note | *ASP SQL statements are passed to the ODBC driver as text strings. The ODBC driver converts them into the proper syntax for the data source. Commonly used queries can be defined as stored procedures, which are part of the database. Calling a stored procedure is faster than passing a text SQL statement. Consult your database documentation to see how to create stored procedures.* |

You can also use the Command object without first opening the Connection object by setting the ActiveConnection property of the Command object to a valid connection string. This method is not recommended if you are making more than one call per page, because it opens a new connection for each command, rather than reusing an existing connection.

The Recordset Object

Most SQL queries in your web will return some form of data, such as one or more fields from one or more records. (SQL statements that insert or update a record will return a value indicating success or failure.) With FrontPage and ASP, the Recordset

Property	Description
ActiveConnection	The active data source connection for the command.
CommandText	The query, *stored procedure* (a precompiled query), or a database table name that will be run against the data source.
CommandTimeout	The time, in seconds, the command will wait to be executed. The default is 30 seconds. If this value is exceeded, the command will return an error message.
CommandType	The type of command (text, table name, stored procedure, or unknown). Specifying a CommandType speeds up the command execution.
Name	Assigns or returns the name of an object.
Prepared	Determines whether to compile the command before executing it. This will slow the first execution of the command, but will speed up subsequent executions.
State	Returns the current state of an object, either open or closed.

Table 19-6. *Command Object Properties*

object is used to store the information returned by executing the SQL query. Because the Recordset object is used for holding the records returned by a database query, it has a large number of methods and properties. These are needed so that you can manipulate the data in the recordset. The Recordset methods are listed in Table 19-7, and the properties are listed in Table 19-8.

Method	Description
AddNew	Creates a new record in the recordset, but doesn't write it to the database until the Update or UpdateBatch method is called.
CancelBatch	Cancels a batch update.
CancelUpdate	Cancels any changes made to a record before calling the Update method.
Clone	Creates a copy of a Recordset object.
Close	Used to close an open recordset.
Delete	Removes the current record from a recordset.
GetRows	Places the selected fields from multiple rows in an array.
Move	Changes the position of the current record in a recordset.
MoveFirst	Makes the first record in the recordset the current record.
MoveLast	Makes the last record in the recordset the current record.
MoveNext	Makes the next record in the recordset the current record.
MovePrevious	Makes the previous record in the recordset the current record.
NextRecordset	Closes the current recordset and opens the specified recordset.
Open	Opens a cursor in the specified recordset. Cursors are described in the section "Recordset Cursors."
Requery	Updates the recordset by rerunning the query on the database.
Resync	Refreshes the current recordset from the database.
Supports	Indicates if the recordset supports a certain type of functionality. The recordset functionality is determined by the type of cursor used.
Update	Saves the current record to the database.
UpdateBatch	Saves all pending updates to the database.

Table 19-7. *Recordset Object Methods*

Property	Description
AbsolutePage	Specifies the page to move to. A *page* is a group of records in a recordset. If the recordset contains ten records, it could be divided into two pages with five records on each page.
AbsolutePosition	Makes the specified record in the recordset the current record. The first record is numbered as 1.
ActiveConnection	Sets the Connection object or connection string for the recordset.
BOF and EOF	Returns a True or False value, indicating you are moving before the first record or after the last record in the recordset.
Bookmark ·	Used like bookmarks in a word processor to identify a record. You can then make the bookmarked record the current record by using the bookmark.
CacheSize	Determines the number of records in a recordset that are cached in memory locally.
CursorLocation	Allows either a client-side or server-side cursor. A cursor marks the current position in a multirecord recordset.
CursorType	Sets or returns the cursor type being used in the Recordset object.
EditMode	Indicates if the record is being edited and if any changes have been saved.
Filter	Used to apply additional criteria to a recordset so that only a subset of the recordset is used.
LockType	Sets or returns the type of lock on a recordset. Locks are covered in the section "The LockType Property."
MaxRecords	Specifies the number of records to return in a recordset. By default, this value is 0, which returns all the records. If the query is very general, the number of records returned may be excessively large. Setting the MaxRecords value to a reasonable number will prevent the recordset from becoming unmanageable.
PageCount	Indicates the number of pages in a recordset.

Table 19-8. *Recordset Object Properties*

Property	Description
PageSize	Returns the number of records per page in a recordset.
RecordCount	Returns the number of records in a recordset.
Source	The source of the recordset, which can be a Command object, SQL statement, table name, or a stored procedure.
State	Returns the current state of an object, either open or closed.
Status	Used during batch updating to determine the status of records affected by the update.

Table 19-8. *Recordset Object Properties* (continued)

Recordset Cursors

A cursor in a recordset is a pointer to the current record. There are four types of cursors you can use. They are listed in Table 19-9.

Cursor Type	Description
Dynamic	Allows full movement through the recordset and allows the user to see additions, changes, and deletions made by other users.
Keyset	Allows full movement through the recordset, but prevents you from seeing other users' additions and prevents other users from deleting your records. All changes are still visible.
Static	Creates a copy of the records in the recordset. This is useful for searching the data and creating reports. Full movement is allowed, but additions, deletions, and changes are not visible.
Forward-only	The default; this is identical to the Static cursor, except that only forward movement is allowed. This is the fastest method for reading a single pass through a recordset.

Table 19-9. *Recordset Object Cursors*

The Forward-only cursor (the default) is used when you expect a single record to be returned in the recordset (for example, when you are selecting a record based on a field that contains a unique value), or you don't need to move backwards through a recordset (you are only making a single pass through the recordset). The Static cursor is used when the user needs to be able to move freely through the recordset. On the Web, these are the cursors you will use most often. If the user is allowed to modify the database, you will need to use either the Dynamic or Keyset cursors.

The LockType Property

Locks are placed on database records to prevent the user from performing certain actions—for example, to prevent the user from modifying data in the recordset. The types of locks available are shown in Table 19-10. You should always use the ReadOnly lock, unless the user specifically needs to be able to update a database record.

The Adovbs.inc File

Both cursor types and lock types are usually passed to the database as numeric values. This makes the resulting code hard to read, unless you've memorized the numeric values for each cursor and lock type. Microsoft provides a file with ASP that maps these numeric values to text strings you can use in your code. This file is named Adovbs.inc, and you can use it with your ASP pages by including it on each page using the ASP Server-Side Include command. Table 19-11 lists the cursor and lock types, their numeric values, and the text string you can use in your code.

Note   *There is also a comparable file if you are using JavaScript as the default server-side scripting language. The filename is Adojavas.inc.*

In the next section, you will see how the Connection, Command, and Recordset objects, along with some of their methods and properties, are used to create database-based web pages.

Lock Type	Description
ReadOnly	Prevents the user from modifying the data
Pessimistic	Locks a record as soon as it starts being edited
Optimistic	Locks a record being edited when the Update method is called
BatchOptimistic	Used like the Optimistic lock when doing batch updates

Table 19-10.   *Recordset Object Lock Types*

Cursor or Lock Type	Value	Text String
Forward-only cursor	0	adOpenForwardOnly
Keyset cursor	1	AdOpenKeyset
Dynamic cursor	2	AdOpenDynamic
Static cursor	3	AdOpenStatic
Read-only lock	1	adLockReadOnly
Pessimistic lock	2	adLockPessimistic
Optimistic lock	3	adLockOptimistic
Batch Optimistic lock	4	adLockBatchOptimistic

Table 19-11.   *Cursor and Lock Numeric and Text Values*

Using ASP to Create Web Database Pages

Previously you used the FrontPage Database Results Wizard to integrate database information on a web page. You can do the same thing using ASP objects and VBScript. The advantage to this is that you can tailor your code to your application. The Database Results Wizard generates generic code that works fine most of the time, but doesn't allow you to change the code in any way. (If you change the FrontPage-generated code, FrontPage overwrites your changes the next time the page is saved.) The disadvantage is that entering the code by hand is slower and you will have to also create any error checking needed.

Note   *In the following exercise, there is a minimum of error checking. This is to focus on the core functionality of using ASP's database connectivity. In actual use, you would need to check for error conditions and deal with them.*

This next exercise will introduce you to the process of creating a database web page using ASP. You will create pages that allow you to modify and delete a record in the database. You will also learn how to populate a form from a database. Begin now with these steps:

1. Open a new page in FrontPage, then type **Modify or Delete a Record** and format it as Heading 2. Press ENTER.

2. Insert a form text box and press HOME. Type **ProductID:** (leave a space after the colon).

3. Press RIGHT ARROW and then ENTER. Right-click the ProductID text box and choose Form Field Properties.

4. Type **ProductID** in the Name text box, then click Validate.

5. Select Text in the Data Type drop-down list, then select Required for Data Length.

6. Type **8** in the Max Length text box, and then type **ProductID** in the Display Name text box. Click OK twice.

> **Note** *The ProductID field is the primary key for the Products table. This means that it is a unique value, while both Description and Price allow duplicate values. That is, many records may have the same price or the same description, but each ProductID must be unique. This is enforced by the database itself. You want this form to send a unique value that will be inserted into the SQL query so that only a single record will be returned.*

7. Right-click the form and choose Form Properties.

8. Select Send To Other, then click Options. Type **Modify2.asp** in the Action text box. Click OK twice.

9. Save your page in your NBT folder with the Page Title **Modify or Delete a Record** and the File Name **Modify.asp**.

10. Open the File menu and choose Import.

11. Click Add File and locate the Adovbs.inc file. The default location is C:\Program Files\Common Files\System\ado\adovbs.inc.

> **Note** *If you don't have the Adovbs.inc file installed, you can use the appropriate numeric values from Table 19-11 in the following exercises.*

12. Select the Adovbs.inc file in the Add File To Import List dialog box, click Open, and then click OK.

13. Create a new page, click the HTML tab, and press CTRL+HOME to move the insertion point to the top of the page.

14. Type **<!--#Include File="Adovbs.inc"-->** and press ENTER.

> **Note** *You could also place the Adovbs.inc file in a virtual directory and use <!--#Include Virtual="/virtual_directory/Adovbs.inc"--> This would allow you to have a single copy of the Adovbs.inc file that can be referenced by all your webs that include the virtual directory.*

15. Click the Normal tab. With the cursor at the top of the page, type **Record to Modify or Delete**, and format it as Heading 2. Press ENTER.

16. Insert a text box, press HOME, type **ProductID:** (with three spaces after the colon), and format it as Formatted.

17. Press RIGHT ARROW and then SHIFT+ENTER. Type **Description:** (with one space after the colon), and insert a text box.

18. Press SHIFT+ENTER, type **Price:**, with seven spaces after the colon, and insert a text box. Press ENTER.

19. Right-click the ProductID text box and choose Form Field Properties.

20. Type **ProductID** in the Name text box, then type **Placeholder** in the Initial Value text box, and click OK.

> **Note**
>
> *You will not use any validation for this form because you will be entering code in the HTML tab later in this exercise. Not having the validation code will make it easier to locate the correct placement for the code. This form will be used to collect data to be written to the database, so in actual use you would have client-side validation. The validation rules would be determined by the database structure.*

21. Right-click the Description text box and choose Form Field Properties. Type **ProductDescr** in the Name text box, type **Placeholder** in the Initial Value text box, and click OK.

22. Right-click the Price text box and choose Form Field Properties. Type **ProductPrice** in the Name text box, type **Placeholder** in the Initial Value text box, and click OK.

23. Right-click the form and choose Form Properties. Select Send To Other and click Options.

24. Type **Modify3.asp** in the Action text box and click OK twice.

25. Right-click the Submit form button and choose Form Field Properties.

26. In the Push Button Properties dialog box, type **Action** in the Name text box, and then type **Update Record** in the Value/Label text box.

27. Check that the Submit Button type option is selected and click OK.

28. Right-click the Reset form button and choose Form Field Properties.

29. Type **Action** in the Name text box, type **Delete Record** in the Value/Label text box, and then select the Submit Button Type option. Click OK.

30. Save your page in the NBT folder with the Page Title **Record to Modify or Delete** and the File Name **Modify2.asp**.

In the next section of this exercise, you will enter VBScript and ASP code to populate the form you created in the previous steps. It is very important that this code be placed in the correct location on the page and that the syntax be correct. The pages are included on the CD in the \Books\Chap19 folder. Check your own work against these pages if you encounter any errors.

1. With your Modify2.asp page still open in FrontPage, click the HTML tab.

2. Place the cursor on the first line after the opening <BODY> tag and type

```
<%
strProductID = Request.Form("ProductID")
SQL = "SELECT Products.* FROM Products WHERE Products.ProductID = '" & strProductID & "'"
Set objConnection = Server.CreateObject("ADODB.Connection")
objConnection.Open "NBT"
Set objCommand = Server.CreateObject("ADODB.Command")
Set RS = Server.CreateObject("ADODB.Recordset")
objCommand.CommandText = SQL
objCommand.CommandType = adCmdText
Set objCommand.ActiveConnection = objConnection
RS.Open objCommand, , adOpenForwardOnly, adLockReadOnly
%>
```

Because the SQL statement is a VBScript text string, it has to be formatted by use of VBScript's rules for formatting text strings. First, the entire string must be contained within double quotes ("). The ProductID value for the WHERE clause will be passed by the form on the Modify.asp page and so must be inserted into the SQL text string. It is easiest to assign this value to a local variable, strProductID, before inserting it into the SQL string.

The variable strProductID must then be *concatenated* with the SQL string. Concatenation joins two strings into a single string. The ampersand (&) is the VBScript operator that does this in the second line of the code you entered. The type and placement of the single and double quotes around the concatenated string are critical. In the section of the SQL string '" & strProductID & "'" there is first a single quote (') and then a double quote ("). When the SQL string is interpreted, there must be single quotes around the text. This is the purpose of the single quote. The double quote ends, or delimits, the first part of the SQL string.

Next comes the concatenation operator, then the strProductID variable, followed by another concatenation operator, a double quote, a single quote, and the final double quote. There are really three strings that are being concatenated into a single string. If the value of the strProductID variable was ABC, the final concatenated SQL string passed to the ODBC driver would be "SELECT Products.* FROM Products WHERE Products.Product.ID = 'ABC'". ABC is enclosed in single quotes and the entire string is enclosed in double quotes.

If the variable was numeric, rather than text, you would not use the single quotes. This is because anything in single quotes is interpreted as text, and anything without single quotes is interpreted as a number.

The remaining code establishes the parameters of the data connection. In actual use, it is easier to have this code in an Include file. This simplifies maintenance by creating a single source. In the Include file you could either use the numeric values for the cursor and lock parameters, or map just the ones you need to text strings (shown in Table 19-11). It would not be necessary to include the Adovbs.inc file in that case.

3. Find the HTML for the first form text box. The line will look like this:

```
<input type="text" name="Product" size="20" value="Placeholder">
```

You will replace the text "Placeholder" with the value returned for ProductID by the SQL query.

4. Select the word Placeholder, but not the quotes around it. Type **<%= RS("ProductID") %>**. The line should now look like this:

```
<input type="text" name="Product" size="20" value="<%= RS("ProductID") %>">
```

5. Replace the text Placeholder in the HTML for the Description form text box with **<%= RS("ProductDescr") %>**.

6. Replace the text Placeholder in the HTML for the Price form text box with **<%= RS("ProductPrice") %>**.

7. Place the cursor on the blank line between the closing </BODY> and </HTML> tags and type
<%
RS.Close
Set RS = NOTHING
%>

This closes the recordset and frees up the server resources it was using.

8. Save your page and then check your work so far by opening the Modify.asp page in your browser.

9. Type **S400-1** in the ProductID text box in your Modify or Delete a Record page in your browser, then click Submit. Figure 19-11 shows the Record To Modify Or Delete page with the data for the record with the ProductID of S400-1.

This page will generate an ODBC driver error if you enter a ProductID that doesn't exist in the database. The error message will state, "ADODB.Field (0x80020009) Either BOF or EOF is TRUE, or the current record has been deleted. Requested operation requires a current record." BOF is Beginning of File and EOF is End of File. Either one indicates there are no current records. You will add the code to deal with this error condition with the following steps.

10. Back in Modify2.asp, in the Page view HTML tab, place the cursor at the end of the heading line, <H2>Record to Modify or Delete</H2>, and press ENTER.

11. Type **<% If NOT RS.EOF Then %>**.

12. Move the cursor to the line after the closing form tag, </FORM>, type **<% Else %>,** and press ENTER.

WORKING BEHIND THE SCENES

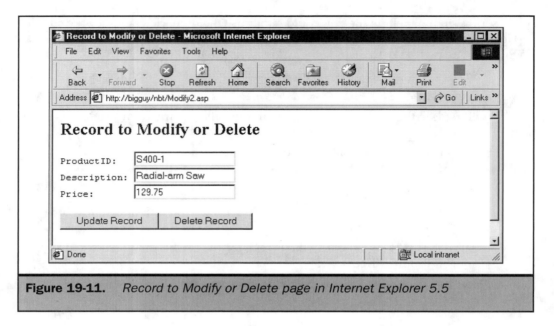

Figure 19-11. *Record to Modify or Delete page in Internet Explorer 5.5*

13. Type **<H3>There was no matching record</H3>** and press ENTER.

14. Type **<% End If %>**, press ENTER, and save your page.

15. Open the Modify Or Delete A Record page (Modify.asp) in your browser, and type **123** in the ProductID text box. Click Submit. The Record To Modify Or Delete page now displays the No Matching Record message.

The first line you entered checks for an End Of File (EOF) in the recordset. This condition exists when there are no records returned in the recordset or the last record has been read from the recordset (the database cursor is after the last record). If EOF is NOT TRUE (there is a record in the recordset), then the form is displayed. If EOF is TRUE (there are no records in the recordset), then the form code is skipped and the error message is displayed.

Next, you will create the page that will update or delete the selected record. This page will contain the SQL statements that will update or delete the record; which one is executed will depend on which Submit form button was clicked on the Modify or Delete a Record page.

16. In FrontPage, create a new page and then click the HTML tab. Press CTRL+HOME then type **<!--#Include File="Adovbs.inc"-->** and press ENTER.

17. Place the cursor on the first line after the opening <BODY> tag and type

    <%
    strProductID = Request.Form("ProductID")

```
strDescription = Request.Form("ProductDescr")
sngPrice = Request.Form("ProductPrice")
If Request.Form("Action") = "Delete Record" Then
strAction = "D"
Else
strAction = "U"
End If
If strAction = "U" Then
SQL = "UPDATE Products SET Products.ProductDescr = '" & strDescription & "',
Products.ProductPrice = " & sngPrice & " WHERE Products.ProductID = '" &
strProductID & "'"
Else
SQL = "DELETE Products.* FROM Products WHERE Products.ProductID = '" &
strProductID & "'"
End If
Set objConnection = Server.CreateObject("ADODB.Connection")
objConnection.Open "NBT"
Set objCommand = Server.CreateObject("ADODB.Command")
Set RS = Server.CreateObject("ADODB.Recordset")
objCommand.CommandText = SQL
objCommand.CommandType = adCmdText
Set objCommand.ActiveConnection = objConnection
RS.Open objCommand, , adOpenForwardOnly, adLockOptimistic
If strAction = "U" Then
%>
<h2>Record <%= strProductID %> Updated</h2>
<% Else %>
<h2>Record <%= strProductID %> Deleted</h2>
<% End If %>
```

18. Click the Normal tab. Your page should look similar to Figure 19-12. Both messages are displayed because FrontPage is not interpreting the VBScript code that controls which will be displayed in actual use.

19. Press CTRL+END and type **NBT Home**, then select it and click Hyperlink on the toolbar.

20. In the Insert Hyperlink dialog box, open your NBT folder and select Default.asp. Click OK.

21. Save your page in the NBT folder with the Page Title **Update Or Delete Record** and the File Name **Modify3.asp**.

Now it's time to test your work.

22. Open your Modify Or Delete A Record page (Modify.asp) in your browser and type **S400-1** in the ProductID text box. Click Submit. Your Record To Modify Or

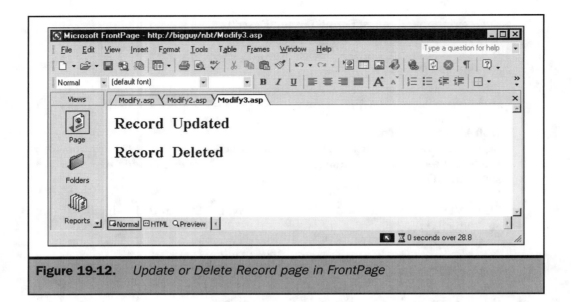

Figure 19-12. *Update or Delete Record page in FrontPage*

Delete page should open, displaying the details for the radial-arm saw with a price of 129.75.

23. Change the Price to **149.75** and click Update Record. The confirmation page should open in your browser displaying Record S400-1 Updated.

Your North Beach Tools web is almost finished. All that needs to be done is to create hyperlinks from the North Beach Tools home page to the other pages in the web. When that is completed, you will test your Modify or Delete pages more thoroughly.

24. Open your North Beach Tools home page (Default.asp) in FrontPage.

25. Select View All Products and click Hyperlink on the toolbar. Select Allprod.asp and click OK.

26. Select Find A Product and click Hyperlink on the toolbar. Select Search.asp and click OK.

27. Select Add A Product and click Hyperlink on the toolbar. Select Addprod.asp and click OK.

28. Select Modify Or Delete A Product and click Hyperlink on the toolbar. Select Modify.asp and click OK.

29. Save your page and then open it in your browser.

30. Click View All Products. Your browser should display the complete North Beach Tools product line.

31. Click NBT Home and then click Find A Product. Type **saw** in the Description text box and click Submit. Your Search Results page should display all the saws in the database. Click NBT Home.

32. Click Add A Product. Type **S400-2** in the Product ID text box and press TAB.

33. Type **Circular saw** in the Description text box, press TAB, type **74.95** in the Price text box, and click Submit.

34. Click Return To The Form and then click NBT Home. Click View All Products. The circular saw should be included in your list of all North Beach Tool products. Click NBT Home.

35. Click Modify Or Delete A Product, then type **S400-2** in the ProductID text box and click Submit. The details for the circular saw should be displayed in your Record To Modify Or Delete page.

36. Change the Cost to **79.95** and click Update Record. Your Update Or Delete Record page should display the Record S400-2 Updated message.

37. Click NBT Home and then click View All Products. Your product list should display the updated price for the circular saw. Click NBT Home, then click Modify Or Delete A Product.

38. Type **S400-2** in the ProductID text box and click Submit. Click Delete Record, then click NBT Home.

39. Click View All Products. The circular saw will no longer appear in your product list.

The examples in this chapter have barely scratched the surface of what you can do with FrontPage, ASP, SQL databases, and the Web. It has been an introduction designed to give you some ideas about the possibilities of integrating databases into your webs. FrontPage streamlines the task of creating ASP database pages, but a thorough knowledge of a scripting language, SQL programming, and relational database theory are still essential. These subjects are beyond the scope of this book, however. For example, you haven't been introduced to the joys of inner, outer, right, and left joins, which are essential for creating SQL queries involving multiple tables, not to mention unions. If you don't have these skills yourself, consider finding a good relational database programmer who can help make your ideas a reality. More and more, the creation of world-class web sites is becoming a team effort.

The Complete Reference

FrontPage 2002

Chapter 20

Activating Your Webs

The World Wide Web has come a long way since the ability to create hyperlinks between documents was a revolutionary technology. Today's web browsers support animation, video, and audio files integrated into webs, but even these advances have been overshadowed. You've seen how JavaScript, VBScript, and Active Server Pages produce true interactivity on the Web. Java and ActiveX further expand your horizons. Java applets and ActiveX controls are computer programs that can be downloaded to and then executed on your computer by your web browser, or can be run on the server in the same manner as server-side scripting. These technologies are truly revolutionary and are the future of world-class web sites.

In this chapter, you will first learn how current web browsers support HTML features such as *marquees* (text that scrolls across a web page) that do more than statically display information, and how these are different from Java applets and ActiveX controls. Then you will learn how to use these newest web technologies in your own webs. This is the frontier of the World Wide Web.

Active Browser Features

As you've learned in the previous chapters, a web page is a text file containing HTML instructions. Your web browser loads the HTML file and creates the web page displayed in the browser by interpreting the HTML instructions. In Chapter 21, you will see how to add multimedia to your web pages by using some of the newest HTML tags. However, these features only work with web browsers that support these HTML tags. This means that there often needs to be a cycle of browser upgrades before the features are widely supported. Even after browser support is available, not everyone downloads the latest version of his or her favorite browser promptly (particularly as browser downloads have become quite large). This all means that you use these features at your own risk—in other words, only a small portion of your audience may see your webs the way you intended.

Java, ActiveX, JavaScript, and VBScript are fundamentally different. If a browser supports these programming languages, as both Netscape Navigator and Microsoft Internet Explorer do to some extent, what you can do on a web page is limited only by your imagination. This frees the web designer from waiting for browser upgrades to begin using the latest web features. The resulting stability is essential as the Web grows. One of the biggest problems in creating webs is the dependence on the user's web browser. Almost every current browser can support the standard HTML features, such as displaying tables, to one degree or another, but support of multimedia varies greatly. Since Netscape and Microsoft offer conflicting HTML tags, the situation will not resolve itself soon.

With Java and ActiveX, the problem is simply sidestepped. You can either write your own applets and controls (which requires a good knowledge of computer programming), or download them from a number of sources on the Web.

Note   *Support for these technologies in current browsers is less than perfect. This situation is rapidly changing, and you can expect that most web users will soon be able to see your activated webs exactly as you intended.*

Adding a Scrolling Marquee

A good example of how an HTML tag (interpreted by a browser) differs from a Java applet (a stand-alone executable computer program) can be seen by adding a marquee to a web page. This is an HTML tag currently only supported by Microsoft's Internet Explorer. If you use this feature, it will be lost on anyone using Netscape Navigator. By creating the same effect with a Java applet, you can make it possible for more of the people visiting your web site to see your pages as you intended. To understand the differences, first create a web page with a marquee in FrontPage using the Marquee HTML tag with these instructions:

1. Open FrontPage if it's not already open, and then create a new One Page Web and name it **Active**.

2. At the top of the home page, type **Welcome To the World of Active Web Pages**, and format it as Heading 2.

3. Select the text and open the Insert menu, then choose Web Component. In the Insert Web Component dialog box select Dynamic Effects in the Component Type list and Marquee in the Choose An Effect list, then click Finish. The Marquee Properties dialog box, shown next, will be displayed. The selected text is shown in the Text text box.

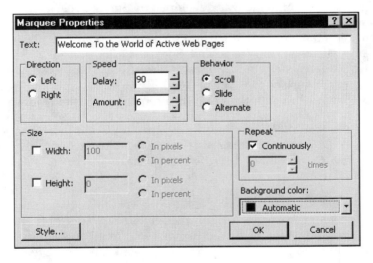

In the Marquee Properties dialog box, you specify the text to be displayed; the direction, speed, and type of movement of the text; the number of times it repeats; the width and height of the marquee box; and the background color of the marquee.

4. Accept the defaults and click OK.

5. Save your page with the Page Title of **Active Web Home Page** and the File Name **Default.htm**.

6. Open your Active Web Home Page in Microsoft Internet Explorer. The text you entered previously will scroll from the right side of the page to the left and repeat continuously.

7. Open Netscape Navigator and load the Active Web Home Page into it. The text simply sits at the top of the page since the Marquee tag is not supported by Netscape's browser.

8. In FrontPage, right-click the marquee text and select Marquee Properties.

9. In the Marquee Properties dialog box, select the Alternate Behavior option and click OK. Save the page again.

10. In Internet Explorer, click Refresh on the toolbar. The marquee will now travel back and forth between the left and right margins of the page.

As you can see, the Marquee tag can add a little life to a web page, but only if it is supported. Since only Internet Explorer currently supports the tag, this is a feature of limited use. In the next section, you will find other ways to activate your webs that have better cross-platform support.

Java

The Java programming language was developed by Sun Microsystems, Inc., and initially released in Fall, 1995. Netscape was an early licenser of Java, and Microsoft soon followed. With the release of Microsoft's Internet Explorer 4.0, the uneasy alliance between Sun and Microsoft came to an end. Sun sued Microsoft for alleged violations of their licensing agreement, which Microsoft denied. Sun claimed that Microsoft changed certain core interface components in violation of the agreement. Microsoft Sdid make the changes, but maintains that the licensing agreement allowed them to.

Note *In early 2001, Sun and Microsoft finally reached a settlement in which Microsoft was granted the license to continue distributing their existing versions of Java with current products, provided all future product versions "conform to and pass Sun's compatibility tests."*

Java's proponents see it as a replacement for the Windows operating system. At the current level of development this is a bit of wishful thinking. Microsoft probably wishes Java would go away so everyone would use ActiveX. In all probability, neither side will get what it wants. Regardless of the growing pains the language is experiencing, it is, and will, continue to be an important language for many network and web applications.

Object-Oriented Programming

Java is an *object-oriented* programming language very similar to C++, one of today's standard programming languages. An object-oriented programming language defines an *object* as a process that accepts information, processes it, and then outputs the result of the processing. The format of the input is always clearly defined, as is the output. One object may receive its input from the output of another object. For example, an object may be a simple program that accepts a text string and then converts the text to all capitals. The input is the text string, regardless of case, and the output is the same text string converted to all uppercase. The object is the code that performs the conversion. Java applets are built by combining a number of objects (each performing a relatively simple task) into a computer program that can carry out complex operations. This concept is very powerful, as you will learn in the following sections.

> **Note** *Programming your own Java applets is a complex subject, well beyond the scope of this book. Two excellent resources for learning more about object-oriented programming and Java are* Java 2: A Beginner's Guide *by Herbert Schildt (Osborne/McGraw-Hill, 2000) and* Java 2: The Complete Reference *by Herbert Schildt (Osborne/McGraw-Hill, 2001). There are many preprogrammed Java applets available on the Web, so programming your own applet is not necessary for you to add Java applets to your web. The examples in this chapter will use readily available Java applets.*

By its very nature, Java offers several features besides object orientation that make it suitable for programming on the Web. It's safe, robust, interactive, platform-independent, and offers high performance.

Safe

Since Java applets are computer programs downloaded and executed on the user's computer, what's to stop the unscrupulous programmer from sending a destructive applet over the Web to wreak havoc on thousands of computers? With the rapid growth of the Internet, this has become a leading concern for many, including the creators of Java. Their solution was to strictly limit what a Java applet can do. Java applets cannot access or misuse operating system resources, which leaves little room for vandalism. It is possible, for example, to write an applet that will slow down your computer by monopolizing resources, but this does not cause permanent damage.

Robust

With millions of users around the world connected to the Internet, any program written for use there must be able to function flawlessly on many different computers with unique configurations. By Java's very nature, these problems are kept to a minimum. Provided the browser includes support for the Java language, properly coded applets can usually be depended on to function properly.

Interactive

Many web sites today display information passively; that is, the content is defined by the web author and displayed by a browser in much the same way as a page in a magazine is produced. In Chapter 19, you saw how databases could be integrated in webs so that information could be presented dynamically. Java and the other technologies covered in this chapter take the process a step further. As you will see in the examples in this section, Java applets, because they are computer programs running on the user's computer, can accept input from the user, process it, and display the output on a web page. All this can be done locally (on the user's computer) and so leaves the web server free to handle other tasks.

Platform Independent

On the Internet (and intranets), computers running Windows, Apple's Macintosh operating system, and UNIX (and its variants such as Linux) can coexist along with a few other minor operating systems. One of the beauties of HTML and the Web is that all these systems can access and display the same web pages. Java extends this platform independence by creating code that does not rely on a specific operating system. Each browser that supports Java applets contains a Java interpreter that handles the interaction between the applet itself and the computer operating system. In this way, a single Java applet will function properly on a Windows PC, a Mac, or a UNIX computer. This is a capability with far-reaching implications. Up to this point, computer programs were written to run on only a single operating system. With Java, it is now possible to write complex applications that can run on any operating system for which an appropriate browser is available.

 Though Sun's "write once, run anywhere" Java motto has often been rephrased to "write once, debug everywhere," it is still a quantum leap forward in platform independence.

High Performance

All the features of Java applets mentioned so far would be of limited use if the applets were not high performance. Almost every computer user has experienced the frustration of slow response times when running some applications. Java's creators made sure the Java code would work efficiently even on older, slower computers. Also, both Netscape and Microsoft have worked to make the Java interpreters in their web browsers as fast as possible.

The features just described combine to make Java the first of a new generation of programming languages created to work efficiently and flawlessly across the Internet or a company intranet. Now that you have some understanding of just what Java is and can do, it's time to add an applet to your web.

Banner Ad Manager Component

You need look no farther than FrontPage's Insert menu to find your first Java applet. The Banner Ad Manager is a Java applet at heart. In Chapter 16, you learned how to use the ASP Ad Rotator Component to rotate ad banners on your site. The FrontPage Banner Ad Manager performs a similar task with different options. Add your first Java applet to your Active home page by first importing the graphics to display from the included CD.

1. In the Folder List, select your Images folder in your Active web.

2. Open the File menu and choose Import. In the Import dialog box, click Add File.

3. In the Add File To Import List dialog box, select your CD drive and then open the Chap20 folder. Select Banner1.gif, press and hold SHIFT, then select Banner2.gif. Release SHIFT and click Open, and then OK.

4. In Page view, place your cursor on the first line below your Marquee text, then open the Insert menu and choose Web Component.

5. In the Insert Web Component dialog box that is displayed, select Dynamic Effects in the Component Type list and then Banner Ad Manager in the Choose An Effect list.

6. Click Finish and the Banner Ad Manager dialog box (shown here) is displayed.

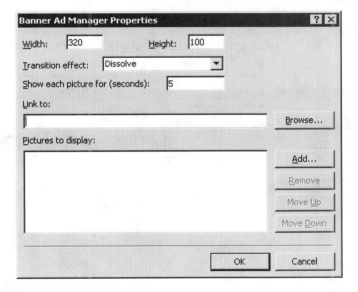

In the Banner Ad Manager dialog box, you set the size of the graphics to display, the transition effect to be used to change the graphic displayed, the length of time to display each graphic, a hyperlink for the graphics, and select the graphics to be used.

7. Type **468** in the Width text box and **60** in the Height text box.

8. Select Dissolve in the Transition Effect drop-down list, and accept the default of 5 seconds in the Show Each Picture For (Seconds) text box.

9. In the Link To text box, type **http://www.osborne.com/programming_webdev/ programming_webdev.shtml**. (Do not include the period.)

10. Click Add to add the graphics to display in the Pictures To Display list box.

11. In the Add Picture For Banner Ad dialog box, open your Images folder. Select **Banner1.gif** and click Open.

12. Click Add, then select **Banner2.gif** and click Open, then OK.

13. Save your work and then open your Active web home page in your browser. Figure 20-1 shows the page in Netscape Navigator in mid-transition.

14. In FrontPage, right-click the graphic and select Banner Ad Manager Properties.

15. Select Blinds Horizontal from the Transition Effect drop-down list and click OK.

16. Save your page and then reload it in your browser to see the effect.

The key difference between the ASP Ad Rotator Component and the FrontPage Banner Ad Manager Component is that the ASP component rotates banners each time the page is loaded (server-side) and the FrontPage component rotates them continuously because it is running in the browser (client-side). Another difference is that the ASP component is an ActiveX control, while the FrontPage component is a Java applet. Since only Internet Explorer supports ActiveX

Figure 20-1. *Active web home page in Netscape Navigator 6*

controls in the browser, it's necessary to use Java applets when you need cross-browser support. On an intranet, where you can control the browser in use, you could use ActiveX controls on the client. On the Web, this is impossible unless you don't care about the user experience for a large portion of your audience.

The transition effects you see are possible with both technologies; so, in that respect, neither offers a significant advantage over the other (though you will find programmers in both camps who disagree). The Java applet also limits you to a single URL for the hyperlink, while the ASP component allows a separate URL for each graphic to link to. This is not an inherent limitation of the Java language, however. It is simply how the applet was written.

17. In FrontPage Page view, click the HTML tab. Here you see the HTML that displays the Banner Ad Manager applet, as shown in Figure 20-2.

The <APPLET> tag is used to identify the Java applet using the parameters listed in Table 20-1. There will usually be a series of <PARAM> tags between the opening and closing <APPLET> tags. These are name-value pairs that contain the values passed to the applet. The correct names and the types of values are determined at the time the applet is written, so there are no standard names. The values that can be passed to the applet should be explained in the applet's documentation. In this case, using the FrontPage Banner Ad Manager, the parameters are exposed in the Banner Ad Manager dialog box.

FrontPage contains another Java applet accessible in the Insert Web Component dialog box. This is the Hover Button, which you will use in the next section.

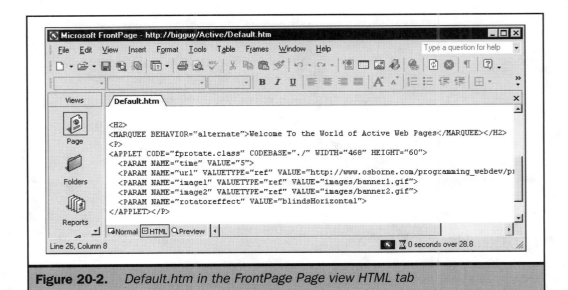

Figure 20-2.   *Default.htm in the FrontPage Page view HTML tab*

Property	Description
Align	Specifies the alignment of the applet. The values are the same as for the <IMG> tag.
Alt	The alternative text displayed for the applet. It's used in the same manner as the Alt property for the <IMG> tag.
Archive	The location of a compressed file containing the applet and any other files it needs, such as multimedia files. This property is Netscape-specific.
Class	Identifies a style sheet to use with the applet.
Code	The name of the applet. The location is relative to the Codebase.
Codebase	The URL of the directory that contains the applet.
Datafld	The column name from a data source that the applet is bound to.
Datasrc	The data source that the applet is bound to.
Height and Width	The height and width in pixels of the applet's display area.
Hspace and Vspace	The horizontal and vertical space around the applet in pixels.
ID	A unique identifier used with a style sheet or to reference it in a script.
MayScript	A flag that indicates if the applet can be scripted using JavaScript functions.
Name	A unique name for the applet that can be used by other applets on the same page to interact with the applet.
Src	A URL that can point to resources used by the applet.
Style	Identifies any inline styles to be applied to the applet.
Title	A title for the applet. This is Internet Explorer-specific and is displayed as a Tool Tip when the applet is pointed to.

Table 20-1. *Applet Tag Properties*

Creating a Hover Button

A *hover* button is one that changes in some way or that controls an action triggered when the user moves the mouse pointer over it. The easiest way to understand how it works is to create one. Do that now with these steps:

1. Click the Page view Normal tab and place the insertion point on the third line (under the banner image).

2. Open the Insert menu and choose Web Component.

3. In the Insert Web Component dialog box displayed, select Dynamic Effects in the Component Type list and then Hover Button in the Choose An Effect list.

4. Click Finish and the Hover Button Properties dialog box shown next is displayed.

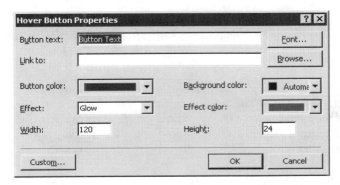

In this dialog box, you can set the button's text, its hyperlink, its colors and size, and the effect. Clicking Custom displays the Custom dialog box (shown next) where you can set a sound to be played, or a custom image to be displayed when the mouse pointer moves over the button.

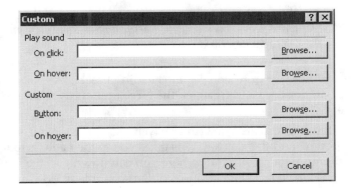

5. Accept the defaults in the Hover Button Properties dialog box by clicking OK.

6. Save your page, refresh it in your browser, and move your mouse pointer over the Button Text graphic to see the effect of the applet.

This example shows how easily a Java applet can be used. You can look at the HTML for the Hover button in the HTML tab to see the similarities between it and the Banner Ad Manager. The next step is understanding how Java applets are created. First, you need to download and install some Java development tools.

Finding Java Applets

Unless you're an experienced C++ programmer, your first Java applets will probably be ones you download from the Web. There are a growing number of web sites that have applets available for downloading. The first step, then, is to get onto the Web and find some Java applets. A good place to start is Sun Microsystems' Java home page. The following steps will take you there.

Note   *Web sites that offer Java applets change often as new applets are added. The descriptions of the web sites in this book reflect their status in the first quarter of 2001 (when this book was written).*

Tip   *The current versions of both Netscape Navigator and Internet Explorer support Java, but there are differences. The ongoing turf war between Sun and Microsoft has made it even more important to have the latest versions of Netscape's Navigator and Microsoft's Internet Explorer browsers and to test your applets with both the newest and older browser versions.*

1. Make sure your Internet connection is functioning, and open your browser.
2. In the Location or Address text box, type **java.sun.com/applets/** and press ENTER. In a few moments the web page shown in Figure 20-3 should be displayed in your browser.

Tip   *Web sites change often, and URLs sometimes become outdated. If the URLs used in this chapter no longer work when you try them, start from the home page and follow the hyperlinks to the resources described.*

3. Scroll down the page until you see the heading Freebie Applets. In the first paragraph under the heading, click the "free applets available for use" hyperlink.
4. When the Freebie Applets You Can Use web page is displayed, scroll down to the Clock hyperlink and then click it. This takes you to the page (**http://java.sun.com/ openstudio/applets/clock.html**) where you can download the applet's files, as shown in Figure 20-4. This page also contains sample HTML code for using the applet and lists the applet's parameters.

Note   *The file you will download will be compressed and you will need to extract the individual files using a Zip utility such as WinZip from WinZip Computing, Inc., an evaluation copy of which is available on the CD packaged with this book, or from http://www.winzip.com/.*

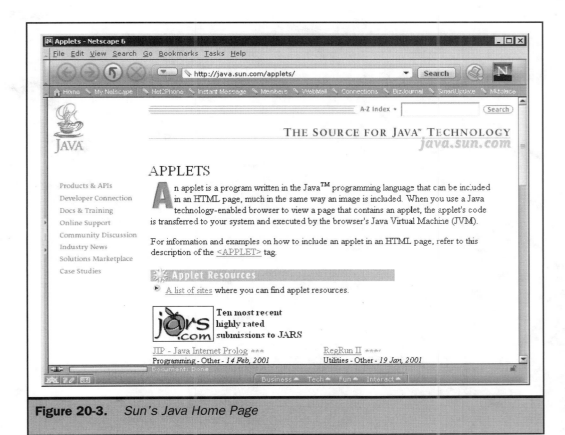

Figure 20-3. *Sun's Java Home Page*

5. Click Download Now. If your browser prompts you to open the file or save it, choose to save it to disk. Select a work folder on your hard drive to save the file. You will have to unzip the download in this folder and then place the necessary files in your Active web. The compressed file actually contains several sample applets you can use, but this exercise will focus exclusively on the Clock applet.

6. When you have finished downloading the compressed applet file, you will need to unzip it. Do this in the work folder where you saved the download. When the compressed file is unzipped, it will create a folder named Demo that will contain subfolders for the Clock applet as well as the other sample applets.

7. In FrontPage, import the Clock applet to your Active web by opening the File menu and choosing Import.

8. In the Import dialog box, click Add Folder. In the File Open dialog box, locate the folder that contains the Demo folder created when you unzipped the file.

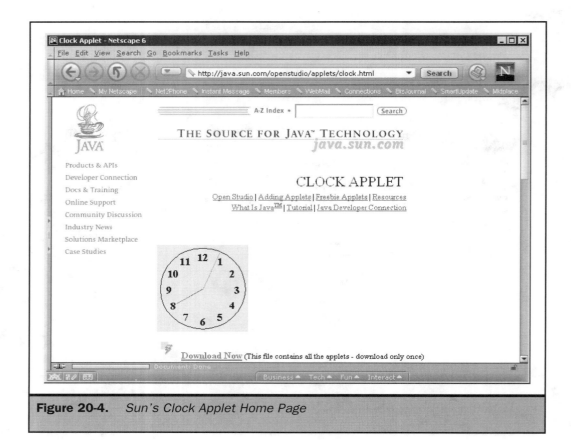

Figure 20-4.   *Sun's Clock Applet Home Page*

9. Open the Demo folder; then select the Clock folder and click Open and then OK. This will import more files than you absolutely need for this exercise, but it is easier at this point than selecting the individual files. When the folder is imported, your Active web should have a folder named Clock that contains two subfolders, Classes and Src, as shown in Figure 20-5.

The Classes folder contains the compiled Java applet files that have a .CLASS file extension. These are the files you will use when you add the applet to your page. The Src folder contains the source code for the applets, and these have a .JAVA file extension. You will learn more about the source files and how to use

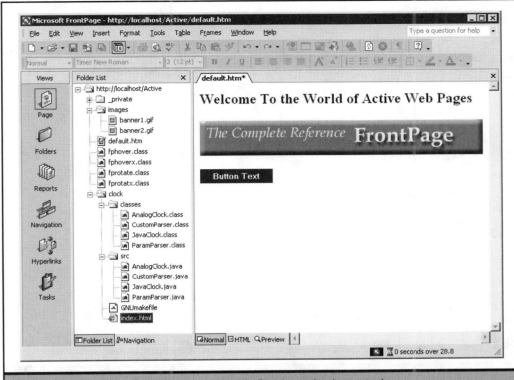

Figure 20-5.   *FrontPage Folder List with Clock applet imported*

them in the section "Compiling Java Applets" later in this chapter. Two other files were also imported in the Clock folder. GNUmakefile is a batch file used to create the .CLASS files. You will not use this file. The other file is a web page (Index.html) that displays the Clock applet. Figure 20-6 shows this page in Netscape Navigator.

10. In your Folder List, select the file GNUmakefile and press DEL. In the Confirm Delete dialog box, click Yes.

11. In Page view, place your cursor on the line below your Hover button.

12. Open the Insert menu and choose Web Component.

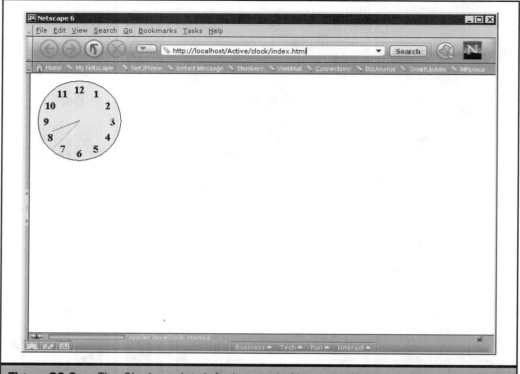

Figure 20-6. The Clock applet default page in Netscape Navigator

13. In the Insert Web Component dialog box displayed, select Advanced Controls in the Component Type list and then Java Applet in the Choose A Control list.

14. Click Finish and the Java Applet Properties dialog box, (shown in Figure 20-7) appears.

15. Type **JavaClock.class** in the Applet Source text box, then type **Clock/Classes** in the Applet Base URL text box. Click OK. This is the minimum information FrontPage needs to properly display the Clock applet. Figure 20-8 shows the page in FrontPage Page view. FrontPage displays a graphic placeholder for the applet.

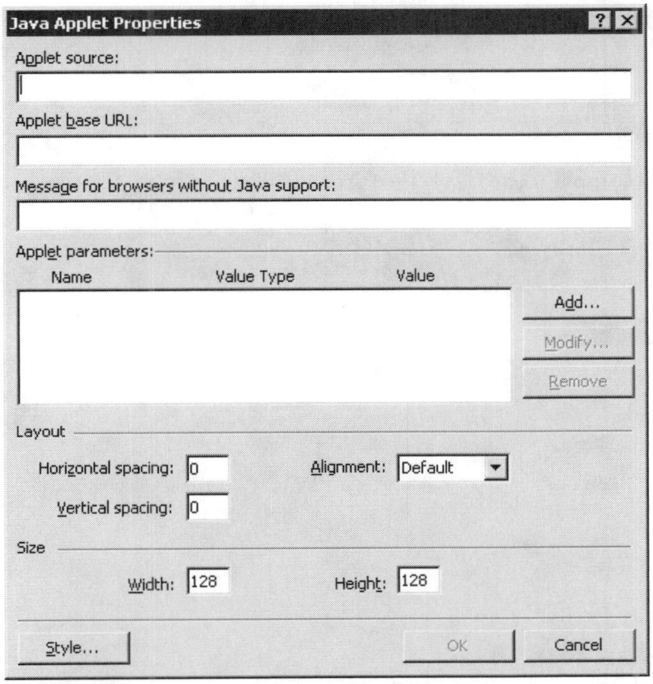

Figure 20-7.   *The Java Applet Properties dialog box*

16. Save your page, then open it in your browser. Figure 20-9 shows the page in Netscape Navigator.

    Most applets accept additional parameters that control their appearance and/or functionality. The parameters the Clock applet accepts are listed in Table 20-2. In the remainder of this exercise, you will use the Java Applet Properties dialog box to set some of these parameters. The applet will use default values for any parameters that are not specifically set.

Figure 20-8. The Active web home page with Clock applet in Page view

Parameter	Description
bgcolor	The RGB background color, in hexadecimal, for the applet.
border	The width in pixels of the space around the clock's face.
ccolor	The RGB color, in hexadecimal, of the clock's face.
cfont	The text string containing the font, style, and point size of the numbers on the clock's face. Each element is separated by the	("pipe") character.
delay	The refresh rate in milliseconds for the applet.

Table 20-2. Clock Applet Parameters

Parameter	Description
hhcolor	The hour hand RGB color, in hexadecimal.
link	The optional URL if the clock is to be a hyperlink.
mhcolor	The minute hand RGB color, in hexadecimal.
ncolor	The RGB color of the numbers, in hexadecimal.
nradius	The radius, in pixels, where the numbers will be drawn.
shcolor	The second hand RGB color, in hexadecimal.

Table 20-2.   *Clock Applet Parameters* (continued)

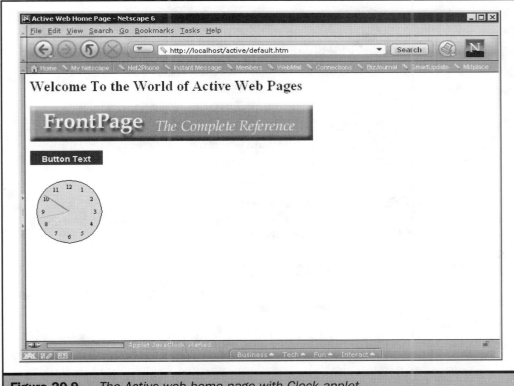

Figure 20-9.   *The Active web home page with Clock applet*

17. In FrontPage Page view, right-click the Clock applet and choose Java Applet Properties.

18. In the Java Applet Properties dialog box, click Add. This displays the Set Attribute Value dialog box shown next. You will enter the name of the parameter in the Name text box and a value for the parameter in the Data text box. The Specify Value check box should be checked and the Data option selected.

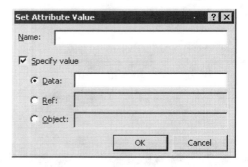

19. Type **bgcolor** in the Name text box, then type **0000FF** in the Data text box. This will give the clock a blue background. Click OK.

20. Click Add, then type **cfont** in the Name text box and **Arial I Bold I 18** (there are no spaces in this text) in the Data text box. The vertical bar (the "pipe" character) is entered by pressing SHIFT+\. Click OK.

21. Type **150** in both the Width and Height text boxes and click OK.

22. Save your work and then reload your Active web home page in your browser. Figure 20-10 shows the page in Netscape Navigator.

For any applets you have that are compiled (you have a file with a .CLASS extension), this is basically all you need to do to add a Java applet to your FrontPage webs. The next step is understanding how Java applets are created. First, you need to download and install some Java development tools.

The Sun Java Development Kit

Java applets are often distributed as source code that must be compiled before it can be used in your webs. This provides an additional measure of security. Rather than downloading an executable applet that may or may not perform as advertised, you download a text file that is compiled into the executable. This helps ensure the applet will do what it's advertised to do and nothing more. There are several sources for Java toolkits. Formerly known as the JDK, the Java 2 Software Development Kit, Standard Edition (J2SE™ SDK), available from Sun Microsystems' web site (**http://java.sun.com/ j2se/**), is the one you will use in the following sections. It contains the source code for a number of sample applets as well as a Java compiler for converting the Java source

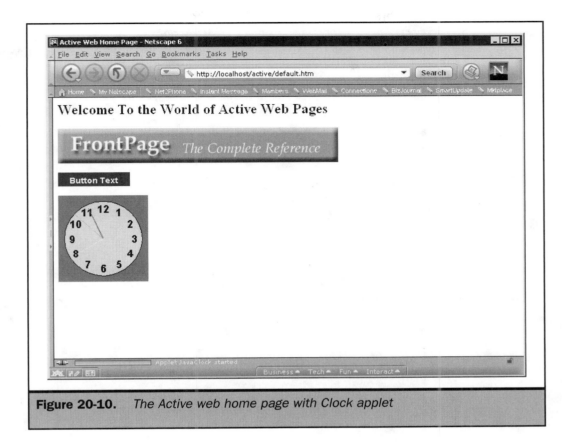

Figure 20-10.   *The Active web home page with Clock applet*

code into Java applets that can be included in your webs. Another useful toolkit is the Microsoft Software Development Kit (SDK) for Java (**http://www.microsoft.com/ java/sdk**). If you plan on really working with Java, you should download both toolkits. They contain extensive documentation that will make working with Java much easier.

Note   *There are also a number of other Java tools, such as WebGain's VisualCafé and Borland's JBuilder, that simplify the process of creating Java applets. If you decide to write your own applets, you should investigate these products. Probably the best place to start looking is Sun's Java Solutions Guide at* **http://java.sun.com/solutions/**.

All the basic tools you need for working with Java code are included with Sun's Java 2 SDK, Standard Edition (J2SE). The J2SE includes example Java applets, both as source code and compiled applets, one of which you will use in the exercises in the following sections. The documentation files are in HTML format, and the demos also include HTML pages. Begin your exploration of Java by downloading the J2SE package.

Note   *The J2SE package is a hefty download (just under 31MB for the SDK and another 22+MB for the documentation), but the tools provided are necessary if you really want to work with Java. A full installation of the J2SE SDK will require about 52MB of hard drive space, without the documentation.*

1. In your web browser, go to Sun's J2SE home page at **http://java.sun.com/j2se/**.

2. Under Current Releases, find the link for the J2SE SDK. At the time this was written, the link text was **Java™ 2 SDK, Standard Edition, v 1.3 (SDK)**. Click this hyperlink.

3. On the following page, click the Microsoft Windows link. This will load the first page of the download, shown in Figure 20-11 (you will have to scroll down the page to see these links), where you can choose to download the JDK as a single large file or several smaller files.

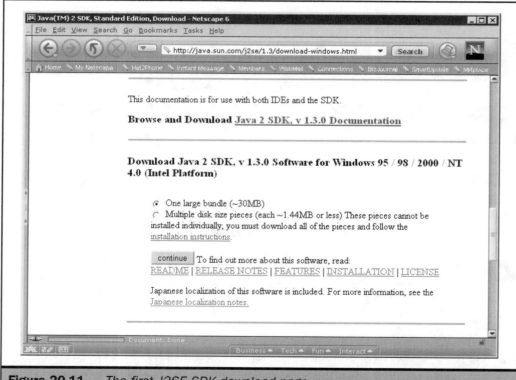

Figure 20-11.   *The first J2SE SDK download page*

> **Note**
>
> *You can choose to download the J2SE SDK as a single download or as several smaller ones. Choose whichever is easier for you. If you download the J2SE SDK as several smaller files, you will need to concatenate them into a single file after download. Instructions for concatenating the files are included on the Download page.*

4. Select how you want to download the files and then click Continue. This will load the second page for the download, which contains the Sun J2SE SDK license agreement.

5. After reading the license agreement, click Accept if you accept the terms of the agreement. This will take you to the final page where you can choose to download the J2SE SDK using either the FTP or HTTP protocol. Using FTP will probably be somewhat faster, but you may have difficulties if you are behind a firewall. In that case, use the HTTP protocol.

6. You will be prompted for a location to save the J2SE SDK to. This should be your Temp or work folder. Select the location to save the file(s) and click OK.

> **Note**
>
> *At the time this was written (March of 2001), the most recent release of Sun's J2SE SDK was version 1.3. By the time you read this, there may be a newer version. If so, the filenames will have changed.*

7. Next, download the documentation. The link to the documentation download page is located two pages back. Click your browser's back button twice to return to the first download page. You may be prompted as to whether you wish to repost form data after clicking back the first time. If prompted, click OK and then click the browser's Back button again.

8. You should then see a text hyperlink above the SDK download options, "Browse and Download Java 2 SDK, v 1.3.0 Documentation," as seen back in Figure 20-11. Click this hyperlink. This opens the J2SE SDK 1.3 documentation view, search and download the page.

9. Scroll down the page until you see the heading Download JavaTM 2 SDK Docs - HTML Format. In the drop-down list box that displays Please Select Format, select *ZIP format* and click your preferred Continue button.

> **Note**
>
> *You can choose to download the file as a single download or as several smaller ones. Choose whichever is easier for you. If you download the documentation as several smaller files, you will need to concatenate them into a single file after download. Instructions for concatenating the files are linked to the Download page.*

10. A page similar to the SDK license agreement page will be displayed. After reading the license agreement, click Accept if you accept the terms of the agreement. This will take you to the final page where you can choose to download the J2SE SDK Documentation using either the FTP or HTTP protocol. As with the SDK download, using FTP will probably be somewhat

faster, but you may have difficulties if you are behind a firewall. In that case, again use the HTTP protocol.

11. Click either FTP Download or HTTP Download. When prompted, select the same folder you saved the J2SE SDK to for the documentation download.

The J2SE SDK file is self-extracting, but the documentation files require a compression utility, such as WinZip.

12. After the files are downloaded, open the folder in Windows Explorer where you saved the J2SE SDK program file (j2sdk1_3_0_02-win.exe) and double-click it. A dialog box will be displayed indicating the files are being unpacked; then the installation program will start.

13. When the setup Welcome dialog box is displayed, click Next. The next dialog box will display the license agreement.

14. After reading the license agreement (use the vertical scroll bar or PAGE DOWN to see more of it), click on Yes if you agree to the terms. (If you do not agree, the software will not be installed.)

15. In the next window, you can select the folder in which to install the J2SE SDK. Accept the default (C:\Jdk1.3_02) by clicking Next. You may also change the drive letter if you prefer to install the J2SE SDK on another drive.

16. In the Select Components dialog box select all the components and click Next. The J2SE SDK installation on your system will begin.

17. When the files are installed, the Setup Complete dialog box will be displayed. Clear the Yes, I Want To View The Readme File check box and click Finish.

18. Open the Readme file in your browser by locating the file in Windows Explorer (C:\Jdk\1.3.0_02\Readme.html by default) and double-clicking it. The Readme file contains general information about the J2SE SDK. Review the file.

19. In Windows Explorer, double-click on the documentation file (j2sdk-1_3_0-update1-doc.zip). If you have installed and associated an application for Zip-compressed files, the application will open.

20. Unzip the files to the Jdk1.3.0_02 folder. You must unzip the documentation files to the same folder structure as when they were originally compressed. In WinZip, you do this by selecting the Use Folder Names check box.

21. To save space on your hard drive, you can now delete the original compressed files in the temp folder you downloaded the J2SE SDK and documentation to. If you have room, you may want to save the original compressed SDK and documentation files in case you need to reinstall them.

You now have the tools needed to compile Java applets from the source code files. In the next section, you will use these tools to compile a sample applet included with the J2SE SDK.

Compiling Java Applets

While the Java 2 Software Development Kit contains some precompiled applets as well as the complete HTML pages that demonstrate them, knowing how to compile a Java applet from source code is a necessary skill for web designers who intend to use Java in their webs. Even if you never intend to write your own applets, you will probably still need to compile the applets you download from the Web, many of which are available only as Java source code. The process is relatively straightforward, but it does require using the Command Prompt interface included in Windows and a basic knowledge of using MS-DOS command syntax. The following steps will take you through the process:

1. Create a temporary folder on your hard drive for the source code file. Name the folder **Javawork**.

2. Copy the TicTacToe.java file (C:\Jdk1.3.0_02\Demo\Applets\TicTacToe\ TicTacToe.java if you used the default folder structure) to the Javawork folder.

3. Open WordPad (Start | Programs | Accessories | WordPad), and then select Open from the File menu. In the Open dialog box, select All Documents (*.*) from the Files Of Type drop-down menu.

Note | *Notepad is not suitable for opening or editing the Java source code files included with the J2SE SDK. These files contain characters that do not display properly in Notepad.*

4. Open your Javawork folder from the Look In drop-down menu and then the file and folder list, and double-click TicTacToe.java. The TicTacToe.java source code file will be displayed.

   The source code includes a number of comments that describe the function of each Java statement in the file. Comments are all the text between the /* (or /**) and */ markers. For example, in the lines

   ```
   /**
   * White's current position. The computer is white.
   */
   int white;
   ```

   The comment (White's current position...) explains that the Java statement `int white;` is an integer that represents the current grid position of white's move. The variable name, white, contains the integer value. This variable is used to pass the current position of white to other functions in the applet. It is an axiom of programming that one of the best ways to learn a new programming language is to study other people's code. This is equally true of Java. If you are familiar with programming languages such as C++, the Java code will look familiar to you.

5. Close WordPad without changing the file.

6. Open a Command Prompt by selecting Start | Programs | Accessories | Command Prompt. If you're running Windows 98, this will be listed as MS DOS Prompt under the Start menu's Programs menu.

7. At the C:\> prompt in the Command Prompt window, type **cd \Javawork** (or use the path where you created the Javawork directory), as shown here, and then press ENTER. CD is the DOS command for Change Directory. This will make the Javawork directory the current directory, and the prompt will read "C:\Javawork>."

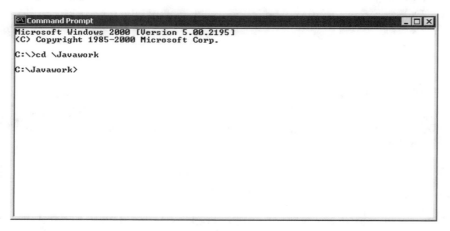

> **Note** *If you created the Javawork directory on another drive, such as D:, you will first need to change to that drive before issuing the CD command. To change drives, enter the drive letter, followed by a colon and press ENTER (i.e., D:).*

8. Type **dir** and press ENTER. This is the command to display the contents of the current directory. Your Command Prompt window should display a listing similar to this:

```
Command Prompt                                          _ □ X
Microsoft Windows 2000 [Version 5.00.2195]
(C) Copyright 1985-2000 Microsoft Corp.

C:\>cd \Javawork

C:\Javawork>dir
 Volume in drive C has no label.
 Volume Serial Number is 1763-1A06

 Directory of C:\Javawork

02/27/2001  10:50p      <DIR>          .
02/27/2001  10:50p      <DIR>          ..
06/02/2000  01:11p               8,020 TicTacToe.java
               1 File(s)          8,020 bytes
               2 Dir(s)     151,126,016 bytes free

C:\Javawork>_
```

Note   *If running Windows 95, 98, or Me, the directory listing will display two names for each file. On the left will be the DOS name of the file in 8.3 format, in this case TICTAC~1 JAV, and on the right, the long filename supported by Windows, TicTacToe.java.*

9. Compile the TicTacToe.java source file by typing **C:\Jdk1.3.0_02\bin\javac TicTacToe.java** at the C:\Javawork> prompt and pressing ENTER. The name of Sun's Java compiler is javac. The command you entered instructed it to convert the source file TicTacToe.java into the executable applet TicTacToe.class.

10. When the C:\Javawork> prompt reappears in the Command Prompt window, type **dir** and press ENTER. In the listing that is displayed, you will see there are now two files in the Javawork directory—the original source file and TicTacToe.class, the executable applet.

In the preceding steps you used the simplest form of the javac command to generate the applet. There are also a number of options you can use with javac to control the compiling or to generate messages. In the next step, you will use the -verbose option to generate a list of all the steps the compiler is taking to generate the applet. This will overwrite the applet you just created.

11. At the C:\Javawork> prompt type **C:\Jdk1.3.0_02\bin\javac -verbose TicTacToe.java** and press ENTER. As each step is executed, the compile event and the time it takes to compile are displayed.

A complete listing of the options for the javac compiler can be found in the documentation web pages at **C:\jdk1.3.0_02\docs\tooldocs\win32\javac.html**. You can open this page and find information about the other tools included with the J2SE SDK. You open the documentation home page (**C:\jdk1.3.0_02\docs\index.html**) and click the Tool Docs hyperlink. This takes you to the Java 2 SDK Tools and Utilities documentation index. Scrolling down the page and clicking Basic Tools opens the Basic Tools page, shown in Figure 20-12, which contains a brief description of each tool and a hyperlink to the page where the tool is explained in detail.

12. Close the Command Prompt window by typing **exit** at the C:\Javawork> prompt and pressing ENTER.

The final step in compiling a Java applet is to test it on a web page. Do that now with these instructions:

1. In FrontPage, open your Active web home page in Page view (if it isn't already open).

2. Create a new folder in your Active web with the name **TicTacToe**. Make sure the folder is selected.

3. Open the File menu and choose Import. In the Import dialog box, click Add File.

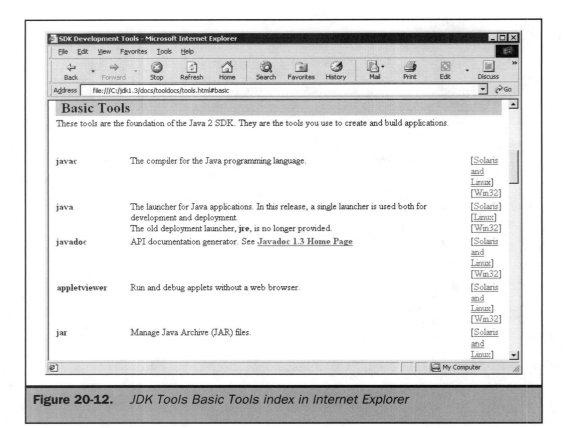

Figure 20-12. JDK Tools Basic Tools index in Internet Explorer

4. In the Add File To Import List dialog box, select your Javawork folder in the Look In drop-down list. Select TicTacToe.class and click Open.

5. With the Import dialog box still selected, click Add Folder.

6. In the Browse For Folder dialog box, select the folder in the J2SE SDK that contains the sound files the applet uses. The default path is C:\Jdk1.3.0_02\ Demo\Applets\ TicTacToe\Audio. Click Open to add this folder to the import list.

7. Repeat Step 6 to select the folder containing the graphic files the applet uses. The default path is C:\Jdk1.3.0_02\Demo\Applets\TicTacToe\Images.

8. Click OK in the Import dialog box to add the selected files and folders to your web.

9. In Page view, place the cursor on the line below your Clock applet.

10. Open the Insert menu and choose Web Component.

11. In the Insert Web Component dialog box that is displayed, select Advanced Controls in the Component Type list and then Java Applet in the Choose A Control list. Click Finish to display the Java Applet Properties dialog box.

12. In the Java Applet Properties dialog box, type **TicTacToe.class** in the Applet Source text box and **TicTacToe** in the Applet Base URL text box.

13. Type **150** in both the Width and Height text boxes, and then click OK.

14. Save your work. In Page view, your Active web home page should look similar to Figure 20-13.

15. Open the page in your browser. Figure 20-14 shows the TicTacToe applet in Netscape.

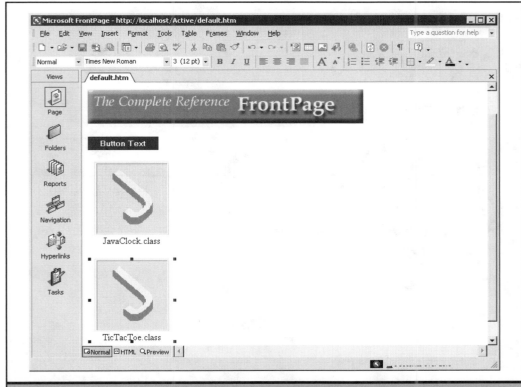

Figure 20-13.   *The Active web home page in Page view with the TicTacToe applet added*

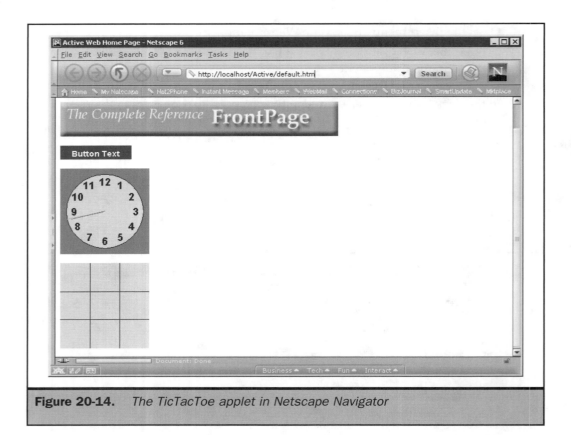

Figure 20-14. *The TicTacToe applet in Netscape Navigator*

16. Start the game by clicking in any empty cell. An X will be placed in that cell, and the applet will counter by placing an O in a cell that will block you, as shown here.

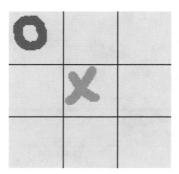

This has been only a brief trip through the world of Java. It is a powerful programming language that opens new doors for the web designer. Because Java is a true programming language, it also requires a comprehensive knowledge of the language and its capabilities to be used effectively. If you are a C++ programmer, the transition will be smooth. If Java is your first real programming language, you will have to devote a significant amount of time and energy to learning it. It is a language that is playing a significant role in web design, so your time may be well spent. If you don't want to learn a programming language, you can find a great number of precompiled Java applets on the Web. The information in this section has presented the basics you need to download and use applets you find on the Web.

In the next section, you will learn about ActiveX, Microsoft's technology that is designed to offer even more advantages to the web designer than Java.

ActiveX

Java is a new technology. In a sense, its designers began with a clean sheet of paper. (An interesting personal history of Java is included in *The Java Handbook* (Osborne/McGraw-Hill, 1996) by Patrick Naughton, one of the original team members at Sun that created the language. This book is currently out of print, but you can find copies in used book stores and online.) ActiveX is more evolutionary, having its roots in Microsoft's OLE (object linking and embedding) technology.

Note   *By this point, you already have experience using ActiveX controls on the Web. All the ASP components you've used in the previous chapters are ActiveX controls.*

OLE was developed as a method of sharing text and graphics, generally called objects, between applications on a computer. If an object was linked between documents, a pointer was created in the receiving document pointing to the object in the original document. When the original object was updated, the linked object was also updated. For example, you could link a spreadsheet to a word processing document. When the data in the spreadsheet changed, it would be reflected in the word processing document. When an object was linked, it actually existed only in the original document. The receiving document only contained a pointer to the original. When an object was embedded, an actual copy was placed in the receiving document.

While this method worked fine when both documents were on a single computer, it had its shortcomings in a networked environment. This led Microsoft to develop new technologies, such as Component Object Model (COM), Distributed Component Object Model (DCOM), and OLE Control Extensions (OCX).

Essentially, ActiveX is object-oriented programming for the Web. In the section of this chapter on object-oriented programming, the concept of objects was introduced. An object was defined as a process that accepts information, processes it, and then outputs the result. ActiveX brings the same modular concept to a web page, with the addition that an object can also be a data file. This is a greatly simplified explanation of the technology, but it avoids turning this chapter into a programming handbook, rather than a guide for web designers who want to add the latest features to their FrontPage webs.

The ActiveX equivalent of a Java applet is an ActiveX control. Because ActiveX has evolved from OLE, ActiveX controls can be used with many different programming languages, including all the Microsoft programming and database languages. This means you can use the same control with your Access database as you do with your web page. This is also an area where ActiveX differs from Java.

ActiveX is a very useful technology, but it does have its drawbacks. In particular, it is a Windows-based technology. This leaves Mac and UNIX users out of the picture, at least for the present. If and when support is added for these platforms, the code will need to be compiled separately for each. This would lead to maintaining separate web pages for each operating system. Of course, Windows computers make up the majority of the market, and with corporate intranets, the operating system can be controlled. It also is less secure than Java, which is balanced by the fact it is potentially more powerful.

> **Note** *Neither Java nor ActiveX is totally secure. Creative programmers can almost always find a way to get around security safeguards. When implementing any web technology, you must use caution and pay attention to what is happening on your web site.*

These issues are not new to computing. At every stage of growth in the industry, the question of features versus compatibility has arisen. Often, as with ActiveX, compatibility has suffered in order to increase the usefulness of software. These are simply issues you need to consider before using ActiveX with your webs.

Since ActiveX controls are commonly written in Visual Basic, this section will not go into writing your own controls. Instead, you will use ActiveX controls included with FrontPage and readily available on the Web. Additional information about ActiveX and other Internet technologies can be found on the MSDN Online Web Workshop (**http://msdn.microsoft.com/workshop/**).

The next section will show you how to use ActiveX with your FrontPage webs.

ActiveX and FrontPage

FrontPage comes with a number of ActiveX controls you can add to your webs, as you will see next. Your Active web home page should still be open in FrontPage.

1. In Page view, move the cursor to the line below your TicTacToe Java applet.

2. Open the Insert menu and choose Web Component.

3. In the Insert Web Component dialog box that is displayed, select Advanced Controls in the Component Type list and then ActiveX Control in the Choose A Control list. Click Next to display a list of available ActiveX controls, shown here.

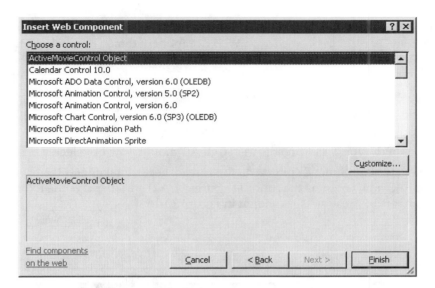

This looks like quite a collection of ActiveX controls, but there are actually more.

4. Click Customize in the Insert Web Component dialog box. The Customize ActiveX Control List dialog box shown next is opened.

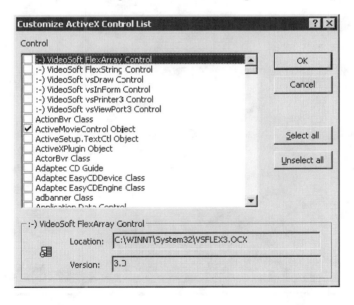

5. Click Cancel to close the Customize ActiveX Control List dialog box. In the ActiveX control list of the Insert Web Component dialog box, select Microsoft Office Spreadsheet 10.0 and click Finish. A functioning spreadsheet is placed on your page, as shown in Figure 20-15.

6. Save your page and then open it in Internet Explorer.

7. In Internet Explorer, scroll down until the ActiveX spreadsheet is visible. In cell A1, type **2**, then press DOWN ARROW.

8. In cell A2, type **2** and press ENTER. Cell A3 should now be selected.

9. Click the AutoSum (Σ) button on the spreadsheet's toolbar and then press ENTER. Cell A3 now contains the formula =Sum(A1:A2) and displays the total of the numbers in those cells, as shown in Figure 20-16.

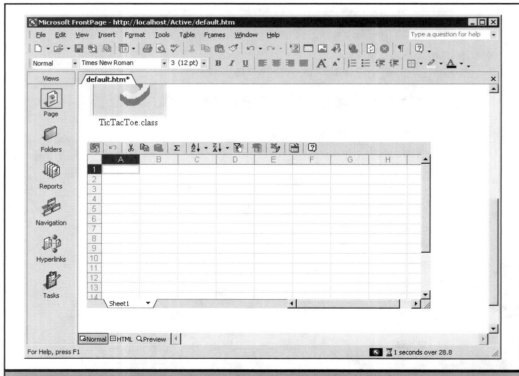

Figure 20-15. *The Microsoft Office Spreadsheet 10.0 ActiveX control in FrontPage*

10. In FrontPage Page view, right-click the spreadsheet ActiveX control in an area
    outside of the cell matrix and select ActiveX Control Properties. This opens the
    ActiveX Control Properties dialog box, shown here.

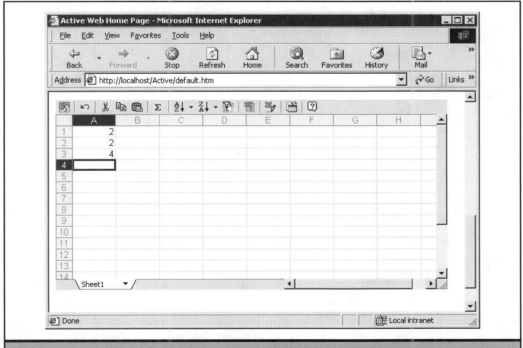

Figure 20-16.   *The Spreadsheet ActiveX control in Internet Explorer*

The options available in the ActiveX Control Properties dialog box will depend on the specific ActiveX control. As you can see, the Microsoft Office Spreadsheet 10.0 ActiveX control has quite a few options. The choices shown here in the Object Tag tab will be available for most controls.

1. In the HTML Alternative Representation text box, type **<H1>This browser doesn't support ActiveX.</H1>** and click OK.

2. Save your page and then open it in Netscape Navigator, as shown in Figure 20-17.

The preceding example illustrates one of the problems with ActiveX controls—Netscape Navigator doesn't support them without a separate plug-in. Microsoft still doesn't own the browser market so using ActiveX controls may limit some people from getting the full effect of your web site. On an intranet, if you can control the browsers used, this limitation doesn't apply.

The Microsoft Office Spreadsheet ActiveX control is one of a number of ActiveX controls that are included with FrontPage. All the ActiveX controls installed on your

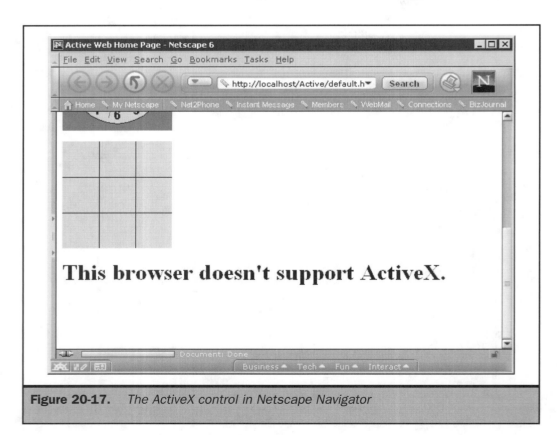

Figure 20-17. *The ActiveX control in Netscape Navigator*

system (both those included with FrontPage and those you download and install separately) are displayed in the Customize ActiveX Control List dialog box. The controls selected in the Customize ActiveX Control List dialog box are also available in the Insert ActiveX Control dialog box.

Each of the technologies covered in this chapter could easily fill a book of its own, and in fact each does. The purpose here was to give you an overview of them so you could make an informed decision about which technologies you want to add to your own webs. Both Java applets and ActiveX controls require programming that is not for the faint of heart. If you already program in C++, the step up to these new languages will not be difficult. The Sun (**http://www.sun.com**), Netscape (**http://home.netscape.com**), and Microsoft (**http://www.microsoft.com**) web sites all have a variety of programming tools, documentation, and examples to get you started.

These technologies continue to advance—if you want your webs to stand out in the crowd, these tools are part of your future.

The
Complete
Reference

FrontPage
2002

Part IV

Extending Your Web Site

In earlier sections you learned how to do a large number of things
with your webs, some simple and some very sophisticated. In
Part IV, you'll learn how to add some frosting to your web cake.
In Chapter 21, you'll see how to add multimedia, especially sound,
to a web. Chapter 22 looks at how to manage the security of your

webs, while Chapter 23 discusses how to set up an e-commerce site. Chapter 24 describes how to set up an intranet, including the SharePoint Team Web Site, and Chapter 25 looks at publishing and promoting web sites.

The Complete Reference

FrontPage 2002

Chapter 21

Adding Multimedia to Your Webs

The World Wide Web started off silent and motionless. Those days are over. Audio is becoming commonplace, and video and sophisticated animation are establishing a strong foothold. In webs you'll see links to WAV audio files and AVI and QuickTime (MOV) video files. There are also links to audio and video files like RealNetworks' (**http://www.real.com**) RealAudio and RealVideo and Microsoft's (**http://www.microsoft.com**) NetShow. Animation has also moved beyond the capabilities of animated GIFs with the introduction of Macromedia's (**http://www.macromedia.com**) Flash technology, as well as dynamic HTML. The possibilities are exploding for web developers. Audio, video, and animation capabilities are changing very quickly. RealNetworks, Microsoft, and Macromedia are the major players, but there are a lot of others fighting for a piece of this pie.

Audio and video files used to have to be completely downloaded before they could be played and, because they are very large files, the download time is much longer than the playing time. This put audio and video in the category of cool but not very useful. RealNetworks changed that in 1995 when they released the first streaming audio player. With *streaming* audio you don't have to download the entire file to listen to it—about ten seconds of the file downloads and then it starts playing. This broke the time barrier, and now there is no limit to the length of the file being played.

Streaming audio not only allows longer pieces to be put up on the web, but it also allows live webcasting. Soon after the introduction of streaming audio, radio stations began broadcasting on the web 24 hours a day. Now live concerts appear on the web. And in early 1997, RealNetworks launched RealVideo, which brought streaming video to the web on a large scale. Microsoft was not far behind with streaming audio and video using their NetShow product.

Video still has its limitations on the web because of insufficient bandwidth. Streaming video over a 56K modem is pretty limited because the image is small and it's not full-motion video. Although it is amazing how good it actually is over slower modems, it is still in the cool but not very useful category. The availability of larger bandwidth connections will change this. As ISDN (Integrated Services Digital Network), cable modems, and DSL (digital subscriber line) technology become widely used there should be an explosion of streaming video. Intranets generally are not as bandwidth limited and can make good use of this technology today.

Creating video content is not for the faint of heart or those with small pocketbooks. The equipment is more expensive than the equipment for recording sound. The software to edit video is also more expensive, and there are many more elements to consider in editing and creating video. You have all the elements of audio to deal with plus the more complex visuals. There is more to video than can be covered in a chapter, so this chapter will focus on audio.

Technology like Macromedia's Flash can provide some very sophisticated animations, but animation is also a very specialized field so it will not be covered in this chapter. If you want to do simple animations, look at using GIF Construction Set

Professional from Alchemy Mindworks (**http://www.minworkshop.com/alchemy/**) to produce animated GIFs or dynamic HTML, as described in Chapter 13.

Audio can be included in a web site using equipment that most people already have. A computer with a sound card, a CD player, a tape recorder, and/or a microphone allow you to put audio files on your web: streaming and nonstreaming, live, or on demand. Whether it is a baby's first cry or a live musical performance from your living room, you can put those sounds on the web for your friends, family, and the world to hear.

The rest of this chapter will tell you how to capture sound and use both nonstreaming and streaming files to deliver that sound in your web applications.

Capturing the Sound

The first step is to capture the sound in a digital format on your computer—to record it digitally through your sound card and create a WAV file that can be edited and saved. This includes identifying the source, connecting the source to your computer, and actually doing the recording.

The RealAudio encoder RealProducer has the capability to encode a RealAudio file directly from a sound source without first producing a WAV file. Producing the WAV file first, though, allows you to edit the WAV file to delete any silent spots in the beginning and end of the selection, as well as make any other desired changes to the file.

The Sound Source

The source can be any playback device such as a CD player, tape recorder, MIDI player, or phonograph. The source can also be live from a microphone or several microphones using a mixing device. If you can get an audio signal to your sound card, you can digitally record it on your computer.

Connect the Sound Source to the Sound Card

You've got the sound source and a sound card. The question is, how do you connect them? There are two things to consider: the connectors and where to put them.

Connectors

Anyone who has set up a stereo has dealt with this. There are all those wires coming out of the back that go to speakers and to the tape deck or CD player. At the end of the wires are the connectors. Life would be simple if there was only one connector, but life is not simple. The wires coming out of your stereo generally do not have the connector that will fit into your sound card.

There are two types of connectors you are dealing with: the 1/8-inch miniplug and the RCA plug, which are shown next.

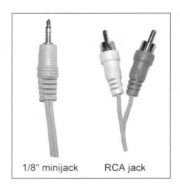

1/8" minijack   RCA jack

"Jacks" are female and are in the hardware being connected. "Plugs" are male and are on the ends of the cables being plugged in.

A stereo commonly has RCA jacks, which needs the corresponding RCA plug for connecting, and your sound card uses a 1/8-inch minijack, which needs a 1/8-inch miniplug. If you have a source that uses an RCA jack, you will need to get an adapter. Radio Shack is an excellent place to get these adapters, or you can get a cable with a pair of RCA plugs on one end and a 1/8-inch stereo miniplug on the other end.

Sometimes you may run into another type of connector. If you do, go back to Radio Shack because they have adapters and combinations that will fit most requirements.

Where to Put the Connectors

Where you plug in the sound source connector is very important. You always want to connect a line-out to a line-in. Generally you should not use a speaker output or the headphone output. These are amplified signals that are difficult to control and may overpower your sound card. The line-out is not amplified. You connect the line-out on your sound source (tape deck, CD player, or mixer) to a line-in on your sound card.

It helps to visualize where the signal is going. Let's use the stereo receiver/amplifier connected to a tape deck as an example. When you put a tape into the tape deck and play it, the signal is going from the tape deck to the receiver/amplifier. It is going from the line-out on the tape deck to the Tape line-in on the receiver/amplifier. When you record something, it is going from the Tape line-out on the receiver/amplifier back to the line-in on the tape deck.

Some stereo manufacturers confuse the issue by using Play and Record designations where you plug Play to Play and Record to Record. In these cases, the Play on the tape deck is the line-out and the Play on the receiver/amplifier is the line-in. This gets confusing. Fortunately, if you connect them wrong, nothing will be hurt. You just won't get any sound. If this happens, just switch them around.

Similarly, if you are recording from a tape recorder or stereo, you go from the line-out on the source to the line-in on your sound card. This may be the most difficult part of this process because you will have to crawl behind your computer, find the jacks on your sound card, and decipher the miniscule hieroglyphics to tell where to plug in the cable from your sound source.

Check the documentation that came with your sound card for a schematic showing the positions of the jacks. This little bit of research may save you a lot of frustration behind your machine.

Record the Sound Digitally

Now that your source is attached to the sound card, you are ready to create a digital recording. There are two elements used in recording: a mixer and a digital audio editor. A mixer adjusts the incoming audio levels from several sources, and a digital audio editor edits and then creates the digital file. These elements are usually programs, which come with your sound card. How much capability they have can vary. The more expensive sound cards have programs with quite a few controls; the less expensive cards have fewer controls. There are also some very good digital audio editors available as shareware with a reasonable registration. One such editor is included on the CD that is packaged with this book: GoldWave 4.21, which is available from GoldWave, Inc. at **http://www.goldwave.com**. Several other digital audio editors are available for download on the Web including Cool Edit 2000, which is available from Syntrillium Software Corporation at **http://www.syntrillium.com**.

Mixer

A *mixer* adjusts the level of the sound going into the sound card—the input volume. If the sound level is too high, it will be distorted. If it is too low, it will be hard to hear. A mixer lets you adjust it to the right level. A mixer can be an external hardware soundboard or a software program that comes with your sound card. Here you can see the mixer controls that come with the Sound Blaster PCI128 sound card:

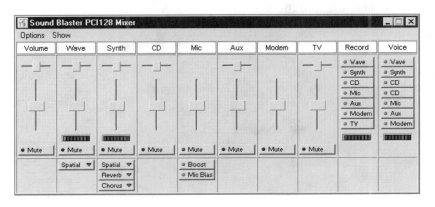

The vertical slider bars control the volume of the sound coming into the sound card. Moving the slider bar up increases the volume of the audio signal, and moving it down decreases the volume. At the top of each section is a balance control that adjusts the sound between left and right. On the right and at the bottom are switches as marked.d

Digital Audio Editor

A *digital audio editor* edits and records sound. The examples shown in this book use both GoldWave 4.21 and Cool Edit 2000 digital audio editors. Different digital audio editors work fundamentally the same. The steps to get a finished audio (WAV) file are as follows:

1. Set the recording levels.
2. Select the recording settings.
3. Record the sound.
4. Edit the sound.
5. Save the sound.

Set the Recording Levels   The first step is to view the recording levels using the digital audio editor and to use the mixer to set the levels. Figure 21-1 shows the GoldWave 4.21 digital audio editor ready to record with the mixer also showing. Start playing what you are going to record. The left and right channel bars in the Device Controls show the recording level. You want to check it with a loud section of what you are recording. The bars move from right to left indicating the level. When the bar is all the way to the right, you are starting to get distortion or clipping. You want it to just fill up the bar at the loudest sections of the piece you are recording. Slide the appropriate slider up and down until the levels look the way you want them. Other digital audio editors may look a little different, but they use the same principles.

Select the Recording Settings and Record the Sound   There are several recording settings that need to be set. Here are the common settings that are available (this dialog box is from Cool Edit 2000):

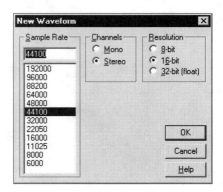

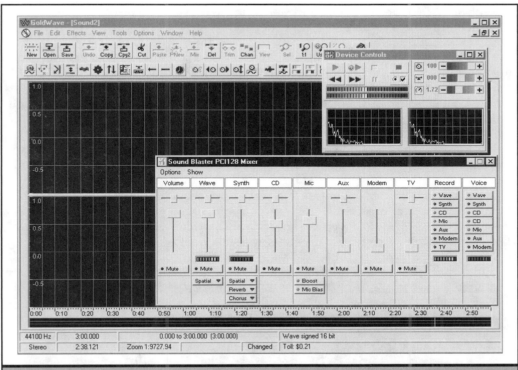

Figure 21-1.   *Setting the recording levels with GoldWave 4.21 and the Sound Blaster PCI 128 Mixer*

- **Mono or stereo (channels)**   Mono will give you smaller files, but you lose the stereo effect.
- **Sampling rate**   A "sample" is a digital snapshot. When these samples are close together in time, they produce a smooth sound. CD quality is 44,100 Hz (hertz or cycles per second). The higher the sampling rate, the bigger the file.
- **Sampling size (resolution)**   8-bit, 16-bit, or 32-bit. The bigger the sampling size, the bigger the file, but also the higher the quality.

A 44,100 Hz sampling rate at 8 bits for a mono recording will give you the same sound quality as a 44,100 Hz sampling rate at 16 bits for stereo.

If your final product is going to be a WAV file that the user will download, you might consider making the file as small as possible while still giving you the minimum quality you want. If you are going to compress the file for RealAudio, or any other compression, you can afford to increase the size some to improve the quality.

With all the settings made, start the recording and, when the piece to be recorded is finished, stop the recording.

Edit the Sound   Figure 21-2 shows what a recorded sound looks like in both channels using Cool Edit 2000. If this were mono, there would only be one channel showing. The beginning shows just a thin line. This indicates that no audio was recorded. The line expands as the audio begins. The thickness of the line indicates how loud it is. When the thickness fills the frame, there is maximum volume. Where the sound crosses the threshold lines on either side, it is distorting or clipping. A little bit of clipping might be all right, but listen to those sections carefully. You may have to record again with the recording levels turned down a little. You can play the digital recording and listen to it with the controls in the digital audio editor.

Most editors provide a lot of functions for editing an audio file. You select a point of time or a section of time visually. To select a point of time, place the mouse pointer where you want and click. A vertical line appears that shows the point of time selected. This is useful if you want to insert something at that point.

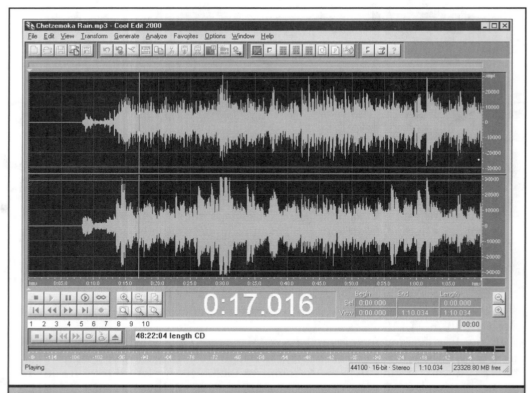

Figure 21-2.   *A recorded sound in Cool Edit 2000*

To select a section of time or a sound segment, drag the mouse across it to indicate the section you want. In Figure 21-3, the beginning section is selected for deletion using GoldWave 4.21. Use the Delete or Cut command to delete the section that is selected.

Copying and pasting is very similar. To copy and paste, you select the section of the audio you want to copy, press CTRL+C to copy, select a point where you want to insert it, and press CTRL+V to paste. In more elaborate digital audio editors, you have a lot of control over the sound. The example shows the basic steps to edit your audio file.

Save the Sound   When you have the audio file the way you want it, you need to save it either as a WAV file or in one of the compressed formats, the most popular of which is Motion Pictures Experts Group (MPEG) Layer-3 (MP3). WAV files are the most common and the easiest for your users to play, since all recent browsers can open WAV files. At the same time, WAV files can be very large. A one-minute WAV file recorded at 44,100 Hz, 16-bit stereo, is over 10MB. If you are going to put a WAV file in a web, try to keep the size down by making it very short or by using lower-quality recording settings. *MPEG Layer-3 (MP3)* is a new audio compression that will give you

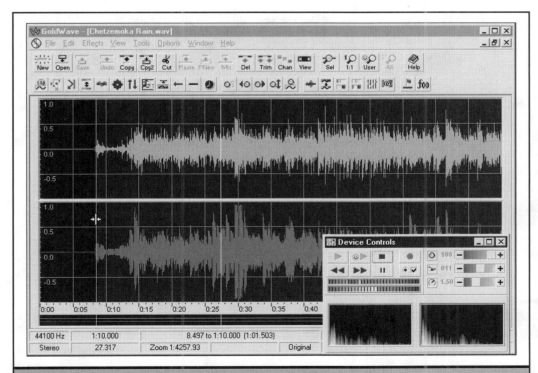

Figure 21-3.   *Selecting a section of sound to delete*

near-CD quality while compressing the WAV file to about one-tenth its original size (a 10,835KB WAV file compresses down to 1,095KB with MP3). The same 10MB WAV file, if it is recorded in 8-bit mono at 22,500 Hz will only take 1,293KB.

Using Nonstreaming Audio Files

Nonstreaming audio files are simpler to handle than streaming files and don't require special software. Let's look at using both standard WAV files and compressed MP3 nonstreaming files.

Using Standard WAV Files

When you want to link to a WAV file, you need to import the file into your web and create a hyperlink to it on your web page. This is done in the same way you would create a hyperlink to any other object. Here are the steps to do that using a 60-second segment from "Chetzemoka Rain" by David Michael on this book's CD:

1. With FrontPage loaded and the page on which you want the audio file open in Page view, select File | Import. The Import dialog box will open.

2. Click Add File. Open the \Book\Chap21\ folder on the CD that comes with this book, and double-click Chetzemoka Rain.wav. Click OK in the Import dialog box. The WAV file will be imported into your web.

3. On your web page, select the word, phrase, or picture to which you want to attach a hyperlink to the WAV file, and click Hyperlink on the toolbar.

4. Double-click Chetzemoka Rain.wav and save your page.

5. View the page in FrontPage's Preview mode and select the link to the WAV file. Your default audio player will load and play the audio clip as shown in Figure 21-4.

"Chetzemoka Rain" is composed and copyrighted 1993 by David Michael and is played by David Michael and Randy Mead. It is taken from their CD Keystone Passage. *You can reach David Michael through Purnima Productions, P.O. Box 317, Port Townsend, WA 98368, 800-646-6523, 360-379-9732, harp@olympus.net, or on his web site* **www.acousticdogma.com**. *The piece is used with his permission.*

Tip *By importing the WAV file, it becomes part of the web and will be uploaded when you publish the web. If you use an FTP program to upload your files, remember to upload the WAV file, too.*

Compressing the WAV File with MP3

MP3 is a relatively new and very popular format, and its usage is increasing rapidly because of the quality and small size of its compression. Listening to an MP3 file requires an MP3 player. The Windows Media Player 6.4 in Windows 98 SE and

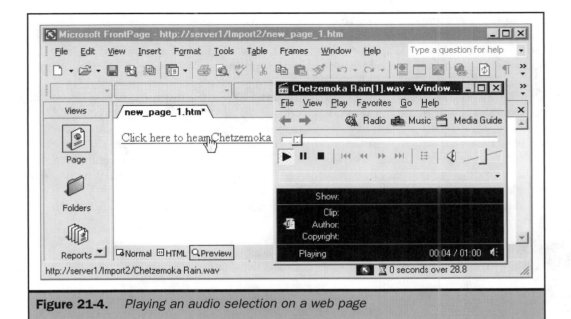

Figure 21-4. *Playing an audio selection on a web page*

Windows 2000 handles MP3 files, as does Windows Me's Windows Media Player 7 even more elegantly. RealPlayer 8 Plus from RealNetworks, Inc. (**http://www.real.com**) is an excellent alternative that can be downloaded for free and then, if desired, registered for $29.95. Also, the web site **http://www.mp3.com** has links to several MP3 players that are free. Probably the best and one of the most popular is Winamp 2.72 from Nullsoft, Inc. (**http://www.winamp.com**). Many bands are using MP3 files for promotional purposes because they can provide a CD-quality song with a relatively small file size. These files are still relatively large. The Band released a three-minute and 56-second song as an MP3 file that came out to 3.61MB. While a number of the bands using MP3 are unknown, many larger recording labels are also now using the MP3 format. MP3.com is an excellent site from which to download copies of many of the songs that have been saved in MP3 format.

> **Note** *It is also easy to copy music from CDs that are copyrighted. This is illegal. Always be sure the material doesn't belong to someone else, or that you have the owner's permission to use or copy it.*

To record a file into MP3 you must have an encoder. Some encoders are built into products, but most shareware and free products require that you purchase an encoder separately. Recent U.S. software patents granted on MP3 encoding have complicated the picture. Some encoders are focused on recording from CDs and are called "rippers." When searching for an encoder, look for one that encodes WAV files to MP3. MP3.com lists a number of encoders that are usually shareware or demoware and that you will eventually need to purchase. One of the more interesting encoders is BladeEnc by Tord Jansson (**http://bladeenc.mp3.no**). This is not a pretty-looking program, but it is small and works in a very interesting way. You go into Windows Explorer, or My Computer, and open the folder that has the BladeEnc program. Then simply drag the WAV you want to encode onto the BladeEnc program, and a DOS window appears that gives you the progress of the encoding. When it is complete, press ENTER to exit, and your MP3 file is on your desktop. BladeEnc comes from Europe, so it does not have the patent problems (yet—the European Union is working on software patents), and it is also truly freeware; there is no charge for it. If you want a prettier front end, you can get MP3 Strip_It! Digital from DigitalCandle, Inc. (**http://digitalcandle.com**), which uses the BladeEnd encoder, but it requires a $25 registration fee.

When you have an MP3 file you want in a web, you need to import it and create a hyperlink to it on your page as you did with a WAV file.

If you put an MP3 audio file on your web, you are assuming that your web's users have an MP3 player. Depending on your audience, this may or may not be a good assumption. Most young people do, and most people with recent operating systems do. As a precaution, you might include a link to MP3.com or Real.com where users can download a player if they don't have one.

Using Streaming Audio Files

With streaming audio, you don't need to be concerned about the length of the audio clip. The user will click your link, the player will load, and after a short period the clip will start to play. The two major streaming audio technologies are RealNetworks RealAudio and Microsoft's NetShow. The RealAudio tools are more developed, and about 85 percent of the streaming audio and video on the Web is RealAudio. As a result, this chapter focuses on creating streaming audio with RealAudio.

How RealAudio Works

Before you get into the nuts and bolts of doing RealAudio, it helps to understand how the system works. Following a system description, there will be step-by-step instructions on how to implement streaming RealAudio in your own web. This section describes the primary components and how they work together.

Components of a RealAudio System

The RealAudio system is a client/server system. RealServer provides the content, the RealAudio file, over a network (the Internet or an intranet), and RealPlayer then plays it.

RealPlayer   RealPlayer 8 (see Figure 21-5) is the latest client that lets you listen to RealAudio files and watch RealVideo files. There are two players: RealPlayer 8 Basic

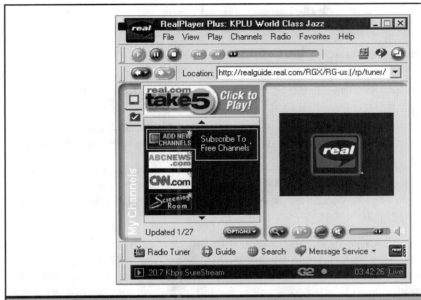

Figure 21-5. *RealPlayer 8 Plus for playing RealAudio and RealVideo files streamed over the Internet or an intranet*

which is a free download, and RealPlayer 8 Plus that costs $29.99 and has additional features. You can download the players from the RealNetworks web site (**http://www.real.com/player/**). On both players, the controls at the top under the menus let you play, pause, stop, and move to any spot in the RealAudio file. The bottom area gives information about the RealAudio or RealVideo being played and is also on both players.

RealAudio Encoder   The encoder is the program that creates a RealAudio or RealVideo file from digitized audio or video file or a live audio or video signal. RealNetworks has two versions of the encoder, RealProducer Basic 8.5 and RealProducer Plus 8.5. They are available from the RealNetworks web site (**http://www.realnetworks.com/products/ producer/**).

RealProducer Basic 8.5 is free and can be used for creating RealAudio or RealVideo files from recorded and real-time sources. RealProducer Plus 8.5 is required for creating live streams and has other advanced capabilities. The current price for RealProducer Plus 8.5 is $149.95. The use of RealProducer Plus 8.5 is described later in this chapter, where you will also see what it looks like.

RealServer   RealServer is the program that delivers the RealAudio and RealVideo files over a network. One RealServer can deliver many RealAudio files to many

RealPlayers at the same time. Each file being delivered is referred to as a *stream*. RealNetworks has several RealServers with different prices and capabilities:

- **RealSystem Server Basic**   Free. Can serve 25 on-demand or live audio or video streams.

- **RealSystem Server Plus**   Costs $1,995 at this writing. Includes extra tools and can serve 60 streams.

- **RealSystem Server Professional**   Aimed at Internet service providers. Currently starts at about $8,000 for a 100-stream server and goes up from there.

These servers are available from the RealNetworks web site (**http://www.realnetworks .com/products/server**). The prices and capabilities change regularly as the technology advances and there are many variables, especially at the upper end, so check the RealNetworks web site for the latest information.

While RealSystem Server Basic is free and RealSystem Server Plus is reasonably priced, the limitation will be the bandwidth available to you. Even a 256 Kb DSL line will only support around ten streams. If you will only need limited streaming, this may work, or you may need to go to an Internet service provider with a RealSystem Server Professional and large available bandwidth.

RealAudio Files and Metafiles

There are two file types that are commonly used in the RealAudio system: the RealAudio file (.ra) and the RealAudio metafile (.ram). RealMedia technology has added the capability to include pictures and animation with audio to create synchronized multimedia presentations using the RealMedia file format (.rm). Here, though, we will focus on the older and more common RA and RAM files.

RealAudio Clip (.ra)   The RealAudio Clip is an audio file encoded in the RealAudio format. The file is created with the RealProducer encoder and delivered by the RealSystem Server.

RealAudio Metafile (.ram)   If you linked directly to the RealAudio file, it would download like a WAV file. The RealAudio system uses a metafile that contains the location of the RealAudio file and is the file that is linked to from the web page.

How the RealAudio File Is Delivered

Figure 21-6 shows the RealAudio components and how they deliver the RealAudio file. The numbers in the figure match the following steps.

1. At the request of a web browser, the web server delivers a page to the browser that has a link to a RealAudio metafile.

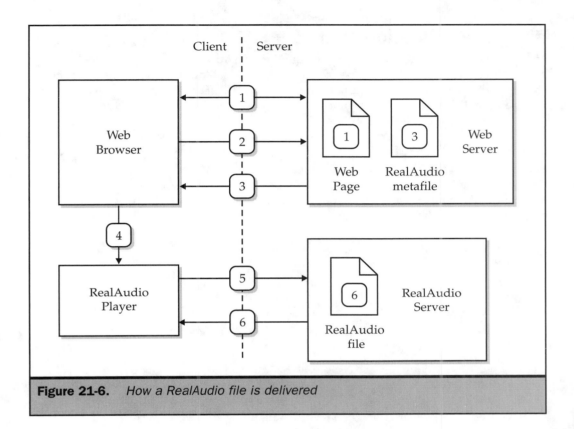

Figure 21-6.   *How a RealAudio file is delivered*

2. If the user clicks the link, the web browser requests the metafile from the web server.

3. The web server delivers the metafile to the web browser. Based on the .ram file extension, the web server sets the MIME type (defined later under "Creating a RealAudio Metafile") of the file to *audio/x-pn-realaudio*.

4. Based on the MIME type, the web browser starts RealPlayer as a helper application and passes it the metafile.

5. RealPlayer reads the URL from the metafile and requests the RealAudio file from the RealServer.

6. RealServer begins streaming the requested RealAudio file to RealPlayer.

Note   *RealPlayer does not require a web browser to function. The user can enter the URL of a .ra or .ram file directly into RealPlayer or use the Preset or Scan buttons on RealPlayer Plus.*

EXTENDING YOUR
WEB SITE

Creating a RealAudio File

The first step in using RealAudio is to create the RealAudio file. This is for on-demand and not live streams, which will be covered shortly. RealAudio files are created with the RealProducer encoder that is shown in Figure 21-7. The following sections will focus on the different parts of the encoder and how they are used to produce a RealAudio file for on-demand streaming.

Set Up RealProducer

Begin setting up RealProducer by loading it. By default in version 8.5 a New Session dialog box automatically opens. If this is not the case, select File | New Session. In either case, the New Session dialog box will open, as shown next, allowing you to select the recording wizard that you want to use.

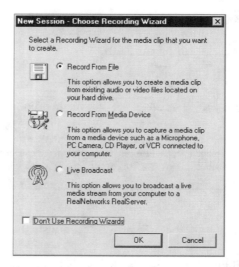

The choices that you have for recording wizards are Record From File, Record From Media Device, or Live Broadcast. If you select Record From Media Device, you can create a RealMedia file from devices such as microphones, a CD player, a radio or television in or connected to your computer, or a digital video camera. If you select Record From File, you can create a RealMedia file from an existing file in another format. If you choose Live Broadcast, you can take a live audio and/or video stream coming into your computer and feed it to a RealServer. Once you have selected the recording wizard that you want to use, click OK.

If you choose Record From File, you are asked to enter the filename and then click Next. If you choose Record From Media Device, you are asked to select the audio and video capture devices that you want to use and then click Next. Then you are asked to enter the RealMedia Clip Information.

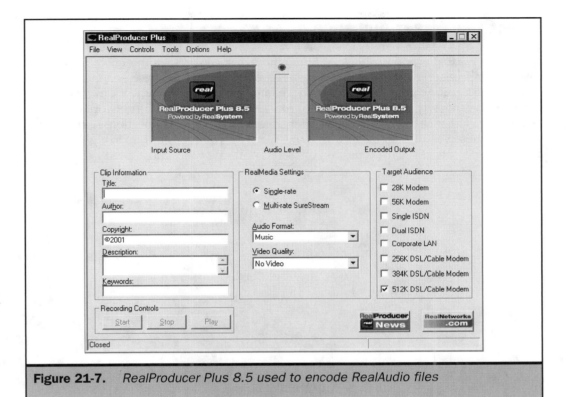

Figure 21-7. *RealProducer Plus 8.5 used to encode RealAudio files*

Note *Live Broadcast will be covered in the section on live RealAudio.*

Enter the RealMedia Clip Information

The RealMedia Clip Information area of RealProducer allows you to enter the title, author, copyright, description, and keywords that are displayed in RealPlayer when the RealMedia file is played. This is how ownership and copyright information is recorded in a RealMedia file.

Select File Type Option

The next option to select in RealProducer is a choice between Multirate SureStream for RealServer and Single Rate For Web Servers. SureStream is the RealNetwork technology that allows RealServer to provide a stream that can be used by both slower and faster modems. If you believe that there will be multiple modem speeds in your target audience, and you are using a RealSystem Server, then you will need to pick the Multirate SureStream selection to enable that capability. If you have selected only one modem speed, or you are using an older RealServer, pick the Single Rate selection.

Select the Target Audience

One of the better features of RealNetwork's technology is that you can create an encoded RealAudio file that is optimized for different modem speeds. When this encoded file is streamed from a server, the server determines the encoding to use based on the available bandwidth. If a fast connection becomes bogged down because of network traffic, the server will seamlessly switch to a lower bandwidth encoding until the network clears. The Target Audience dialog box, shown here, has four different connections selected. If you have chosen Multirate SureStream as the file type, you can select up to eight. If you choose Single Rate as the file type, you can select only one connection speed.

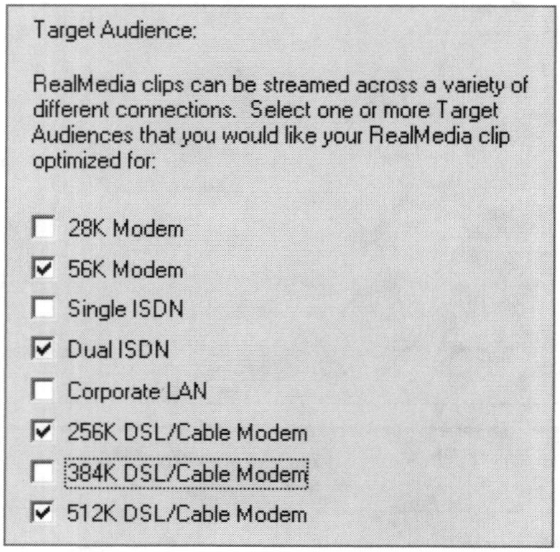

```
Target Audience:

RealMedia clips can be streamed across a variety of
different connections.  Select one or more Target
Audiences that you would like your RealMedia clip
optimized for:

☐  28K Modem
☑  56K Modem
☐  Single ISDN
☑  Dual ISDN
☐  Corporate LAN
☑  256K DSL/Cable Modem
☐  384K DSL/Cable Modem
☑  512K DSL/Cable Modem
```

Select the Audio Format

The next step is to select in the Audio Format dialog box the type of format or codec that the encoder will use, as shown next.

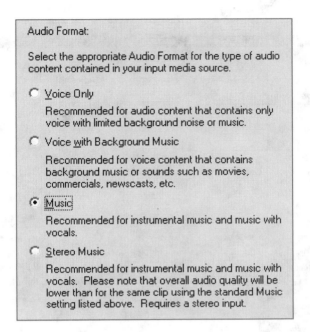

Codecs (short for compressor/decompressor) are listed by the type of sound being encoded; they control the degree of compression used in the RealAudio file created. The degree of compression can be changed by opening the RealProducer's Options menu and choosing Target Audience Settings | For Audio Clips. When you do that, the Target Audience Settings—Audio Clips dialog box opens, as you can see in Figure 21-8. Here you can assign codecs to each selection.

If you open one of the drop-down boxes, as shown here, you will see all the codecs available for the selection.

EXTENDING YOUR
WEB SITE

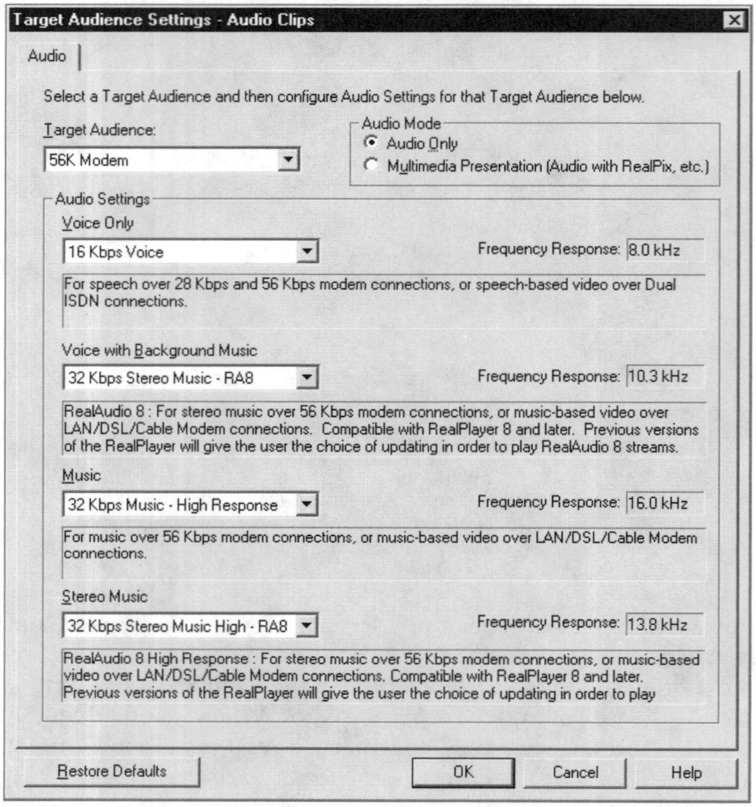

Figure 21-8. *Assigning codecs for each type of audio content*

RealAudio provides a wide selection of codecs so that you can tailor the compression to the bandwidth available to your users. The largest compression, resulting in the smallest file size but lowest quality, is the 5 Kbps voice codec. The smallest compression, resulting in the largest file size and highest quality, is the 352 Kbps stereo music codec. Stereo codecs sacrifice audio quality by reducing the frequency response to allow for two channels of sound. Below each codec selection there is a description for the best use of that codec.

The default selections in this dialog box are driven by the selection in the Target Audience box at the top of the dialog box. If that selection is changed to a different speed, the default codecs change also.

The smallest file size resulting from the most compression is used for a 28 Kbps modem and is a codec that gives a 20 Kbps stream. The 8 Kbps difference between the modem capability and the stream allows for the overhead of network traffic.

If your users are having network congestion problems, you might select a codec that will send out a smaller stream even if they have a faster modem. For example, most people today have at least a 56 Kbps modem, but if you believe that there will be a fair amount of network congestion between you and your users, you might still use a 20 Kbps stream.

Finishing Setting Up RealProducer

After selecting the Audio Format and clicking Next, you are asked to enter the output file path and name. Click Save As to browse for the path you want to use or an existing file if you want to replace it. Click Next again to see a summary of the selections you have made, as you can see next. If you see one or more that are not correct, click Back and correct it. When you are ready, click Finish. The RealProducer itself reappears with the settings you have chosen, like those in Figure 21-9.

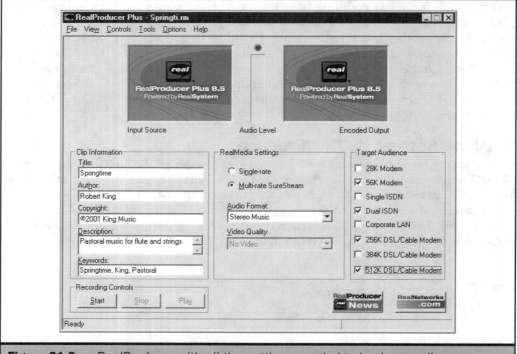

Figure 21-9. *RealProducer with all the settings needed to begin encoding*

Select Preferences

There are a few additional options to set for encoding. Select Options | Preferences to open the Preferences dialog box, which has six tabs. The first one is the General tab shown next.

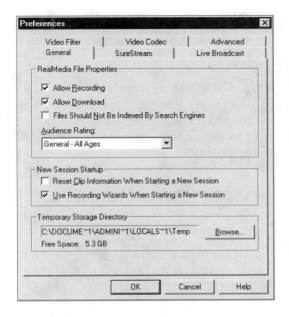

In the RealMedia File Properties area of the General tab, you can set the streams so they can be listened to but not recorded or downloaded by the user. If you want to allow recording or downloading, check the appropriate selection. Next, you can turn off the default recording wizards that were discussed previously (although I believe they are helpful) and reset the clip information each time a new session is started (whether or not you choose this depends on how different your sessions are). The Temporary Storage Directory defines the location for three temporary files RealAudio uses in creating its files.

The SureStream tab allows you to choose that your file be compatible with the older RealPlayer 5.0. Single Rate files do not support RealPlayer 5.0. If you want to have the backward compatibility, select Add 5.0 Compatibility and use SureStream. Emphasize Audio/Video is for use with Video clips. If you are not using video, keep the default Emphasize Audio.

The Live Broadcast tab allows you to choose how you will connect to the server, and the remaining three tabs deal with video settings, which are beyond the scope of this book.

Turn On the Volume Control

Depending on the source of what you are encoding, you may want to turn on either the Windows or your sound card's Volume control. You may be able to do this using the icons in the system tray on the bottom-right of the screen, but RealProducer will also start the Windows Volume control. You can do this by choosing Options | Audio Capture Settings | Volume Control. The Windows Volume control will open like this:

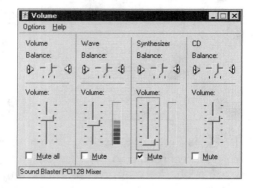

Encode the WAV file

The final step is to start the encoding. The lower-left area of RealProducer has the recording controls shown next.

When the encoding is in progress, you can check the audio levels from the Audio Level bar in the center top of RealProducer.

If you are encoding a WAV or other file, the end of the file will automatically stop the encoding. If you are encoding either a live stream or some other continuous source, you'll need to click Stop to conclude the encoding. When the encoding concludes, the Processing Complete dialog box will open and allow you to view the Statistics dialog box, a sample of which is shown in Figure 21-10. The most useful statistics are the Real Time Performance figures. These tell you how much of your computer's capacity you are using to produce the streams that you asked for. If you are getting close to 100% you are about to use all the capacity you have and you will get the error message shown next. The upper Real Time Performance number is approximately the sum of the streams below, so if you are running out of capacity, discontinue one or more of the streams.

 You can view the statistics while you are encoding by opening the View menu and choosing Statistics.

HTTP Streaming vs. Network Streaming

There are two types of streaming available for RealAudio files. Although you have seen that you need a RealServer to stream RealAudio files, you actually can stream files without RealServer. This is called *HTTP streaming*; streaming from a RealServer is called *network streaming*.

Many Internet service providers don't have a RealServer, and HTTP streaming is useful if you are being hosted with one that doesn't. The downside is that, while it will deliver multiple streams, HTTP streaming is not as robust or efficient. With network streaming you can move ahead to any point in the file, but with HTTP streaming you cannot—you can only move backward to a point in the file that has already played. The

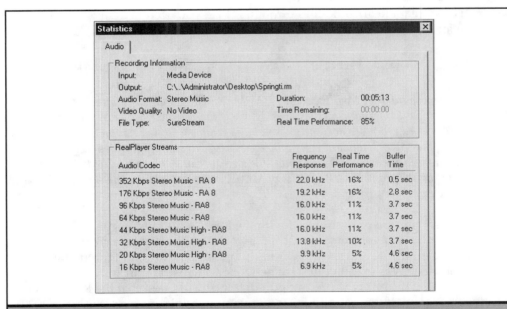

Figure 21-10. *The Real Time Performance and other encoding statistics*

EXTENDING YOUR
WEB SITE

downside of streaming using a RealServer is that, since the Internet service provider has paid for RealServer, that cost could be passed on to you in additional fees for use of RealServer.

If you are dealing with longer RealAudio files—15 minutes or more—or plan to have a lot of usage, it is recommended that you use a RealServer. If you use shorter files that will not be streamed by a lot of users at once, use the HTTP streaming.

The RealAudio file has to be copied to a server either locally for an intranet or remotely at your Internet service provider. If you are using HTTP streaming, you will copy it to the web server. If you are using network streaming, you will copy it to RealServer.

Creating a RealAudio Metafile

The RealAudio metafile is a one-line text file to which a web page is linked. The metafile starts RealPlayer and then passes the location of the RealAudio file to RealPlayer. The RealAudio metafile is usually automatically created when Real Producer encodes a RealAudio or RealMedia file. The metafile can also be created using a text editor like Notepad. A word processor can be used, but you must save the file as a pure text file without formatting.

An HTTP Streaming Metafile

Before you can stream RealAudio files through HTTP, you need to define the following MIME type for your web server:

```
Audio/x-pn-realaudio (files with .ra, and .ram file extensions)
```

 Note   *Multipurpose Internet Mail Extensions (MIME) is the standard for attaching nontext files to standard Internet mail messages. Nontext files include graphics, spreadsheets, formatted word processor documents, sound files, and so on. In addition to e-mail software, the MIME standard is used by web servers to identify the files they are sending to web clients; in this way, new file formats can be accommodated simply by updating the browser's list of pairs of MIME types and appropriate software for handling each type.*

Some web servers are preconfigured with the RealAudio MIME type. There are three ways to find out if your web server is one of these. The first is to create a link to an HTTP streaming file and see if it works. If the server is not configured, it won't work. The second way is to call your local network administrator or Internet service provider and ask if the server is preconfigured. If it isn't, request that the RealAudio MIME type be set up. If you are administering your own IIS server on Windows 2000 or XP Server or Professional you can check this for yourself as a third way. To do that on Server, open the Start menu and choose Programs | Administrative Tools | Internet

Services Manager. On Professional, open Start and choose Settings (not in XP) |
Control Panel | Administrative Tools | Internet Services Manager. In either case,
right-click your server, and choose Properties. At the bottom of the Internet Information
Services tab in the area labeled Computer MIME Map, click Edit. Scroll down the list of
Registered File Types and look for the RealAudio RA and RAM file types. If they are not
there, installing either RealPlayer or RealProducer will put them there.

You should have already copied the RealAudio file to the web server because you
need to use the path and the filename of the RealAudio file in the metafile. The metafile
will have a single line with the following form:

```
http://hostname/path/file.ra
```

Hostname is the name of your web server. Here is a listing of a typical metafile,
which you would save with a .ram file extension:

```
http://www.whidbey.net/rafiles/matthews/media/summertime.ra
```

Network Streaming Metafile

If you copied your RealAudio file to RealServer for network streaming, you will use
the path name and the filename of the RealAudio file in the metafile. The metafile will
take one of two forms depending on if it is a RealSystem Server or an older version
of RealServer, or if you are targeting RealPlayer 3.0 to 5.0 or RealPlayer 8. The older
RealServers and RealPlayers use the PNM protocol as shown here:

```
pnm://hostname/path/file.ra
```

Hostname is the name of your RealServer. Again, the file is saved with a .ram extension.
The primary protocol for RealServer is RealTime Streaming Protocol (RTSP), so the
metafile would appear like this:

```
rtsp://hostname/path/file.ra
```

RAM files for network streaming are identical to RAM files for HTTP streaming
with the exception that they use PNM or RTSP as the protocol instead of HTTP.

Linking to the Metafile

Use FrontPage to import the RealAudio metafile to your web, and then create a
hyperlink to it the same way you imported and created a hyperlink to an audio
segment earlier in this chapter. When you do that, your web page will stream your
RealAudio file when a user clicks the link to the metafile.

Live RealAudio

All the audio in the previous sections has been on-demand. Anyone can select the audio file at any time and listen to it from the beginning of the file. But RealAudio also can play in real-time, such as a radio broadcast or a live show. While a radio broadcast may be playing prerecorded material, it is still going out real-time, so if someone selected the link after the show had started, they would join it somewhere in the middle in real-time.

Producing live RealAudio is very similar to on-demand streaming. One difference is that live RealAudio requires the use of a RealServer because HTTP streaming only works with on-demand material. Another difference is that with on-demand RealAudio you create a WAV file from an audio signal and then encode the WAV file into a RealAudio file. With live RealAudio, you bypass the WAV file step and encode the audio signal on-the-fly.

Start with a Live Audio Signal

The first step is having a live audio signal. This signal is delivered to the sound card the same way you delivered a signal to record a WAV file. The signal can be prerecorded material from a CD or tape recorder, or it can be live going from a microphone to the sound card. If you are using multiple microphones, you will need a mixing device, such as a soundboard or mixer-amplifier, to combine the different microphone signals into one signal for the sound card.

Set Up the RealAudio Encoder for Live Streaming

The RealProducer encoder is uniquely set up for live streaming. In the initial New Session dialog box you select Live Broadcast. The Live Broadcast Recording Wizard starts and asks for the Input Source similar to what you saw when choosing Record From Media Device or Record From File. Next, enter the RealMedia clip information, file type, target audience, and audio format as you did for an on-demand stream.

You are then asked for the Media Server that you want to use. This is the RealServer from which you will be broadcasting your live stream. Enter its name, which may be as simple as **Server1** for a server on an intranet, or something like **www.whidbey.net** for an ISP. Next, enter the server port, which is the port that has been set up on the physical server for RealServer. Port 4040 is the RealAudio default, but 7070 is also used. Finally, enter the filename, which is the name of the stream that you will use in the RealAudio metafile, and the username and password needed to use the RealServer. If you desire, you can also archive the broadcast in a file on the local disk by checking the associated box and entering the path and filename. When you are done, your Media Server dialog box will look something like Figure 21-11.

Encode the Audio Signal for a Live Stream

After completing settings necessary for the media server, click Next, review and correct as necessary all of the settings, as shown in the settings summary, and then click Finish. Then all you need to do is click Start in the Recording Controls section of the primary

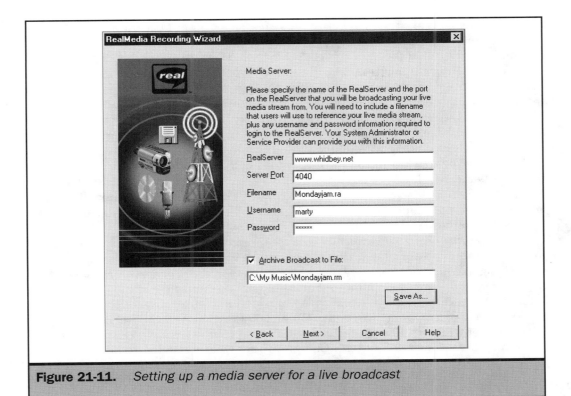

Figure 21-11. *Setting up a media server for a live broadcast*

RealProducer dialog box. Keep track of the signal in the Audio Level bar the same way you would for creating on-demand RealAudio files. Use the mixer to control the sound level as you did for recording a WAV file, and possibly keep Statistics turned on as you did in encoding a WAV file.

Live Webcasts

There is a lot of live streaming audio and video on the web today, including concerts, sports events, and radio programs. These are called "webcasts" and range from large-budget professional productions to small-budget shows done in a living room, basement, or garage. Many of the large-budget events treat web broadcasting as they do radio and TV broadcasting, with lots of equipment and people and similar formats. Some of the smaller ones, though, are experimenting with the technology and the format to produce something different.

One such low-budget experimental show is *TestingTesting* (**http://www.electricedge .com/testingtesting/**), which is a biweekly live 30-minute performance of interactive improvisational Internet music done in the producer's living room. The show has two regular musicians and a special guest musician, or musicians, each week. Because of the living room atmosphere, the performers are relaxed, and it becomes much more fun than a more formal performing space. One of the differences between this show and radio or TV is that they use a guest book on their web site in which the Internet audience can enter comments during the show. Those comments are read to the performers during breaks in the music. This changes the direction of the show, making the Internet audience a part of it. The show is advertised as being 30 minutes long, but it often runs 35 to 40 minutes and sometimes longer. There are no rules. Each show is saved and is available for those who were not able to be there live. The guest book comments are saved along with digital pictures taken during the show.

TestingTesting is broadcast on the Internet using the procedures in this chapter. The format is being developed as the producer and performers experiment with this new medium. This is like the early days of radio or TV. The audience for a show like this isn't measured in millions, it is measured in dozens—dozens that become personally involved with those on the show.

TestingTesting uses a music format because the people involved with it are mostly musicians and there are a lot of talented players in the area where they live. But webcasting like this could use any number of formats. It could be used for talk shows or other live programs like old radio shows but with an interactive element from the Internet audience. Or someone could play music from their record collection that others might like to hear but can't on commercial radio. This is niche webcasting on a low budget with an audience that talks back. Use your imagination in this new medium. Join the *TestingTesting* crew in figuring out what it can do.

The
Complete
Reference

Chapter 22

Security on the Web

Y ou have surely seen discussions in the media regarding security risks on the Web. You've probably heard stories about how someone has done something to compromise someone else's security on the Internet or has gotten through to a company's servers or a private intranet. These stories appear infrequently for two reasons: the occurrences are rare, and people don't like to report that their security has been breached. The vast majority of stories are about university or private research efforts that, with much work and a lot of computer power, have broken through the security in some obscure area of a given Internet program. A lot is made of the weakness found, the manufacturer rushes to fix it, and few if any people ever experience a loss or misuse of their Internet information. The impact is negligible because current security measures on the Internet are very good, and because of the sheer volume of transactions on the Web. Only a tiny percentage of those transactions has value to others and therefore has any potential to be misused. However, the number of transactions that users would like to keep private is growing rapidly. If you are a regular user of the Web, chances are that you have purchased merchandise, ordered a service, or transferred some confidential information about yourself over the Internet. Fortunately, security measures are also growing in their ability to protect us.

Security Needs

Look at all the activity on either the Internet or intranets now, and more importantly, consider what will be taking place in the future. Ask yourself in what areas security is an issue. The Internet, which, grossly simplified, looks something like Figure 22-1, has millions of users connected to hundreds of thousands of interconnected computers. Added to this are a growing number of intranets connected to the Internet. As information is transferred between two users on the Internet, it is routed through a large number of intermediary computers under the independent control of many different entities. There is no way to control where the information may be routed or limit who controls the computers it is routed through. Also, for the modest price of an Internet account, anyone can get on the Internet and do what they wish. Consider what is happening on the Internet:

- E-mail is being sent, routed, and received. It can contain anything from "Hi, how are you?" to very sensitive trade secrets or large monetary transactions.

- Web sites are being accessed to read, print, or download their information. On the majority of sites, access is unlimited and free, but on others, access is limited (by a password or other means) for various reasons.

- In an already large and growing number of web sites, goods and services are being sold, purchased by way of credit card or other payment forms.

- Newsgroups are being read and contributed to, again generally with unlimited access, although occasionally access is password controlled.

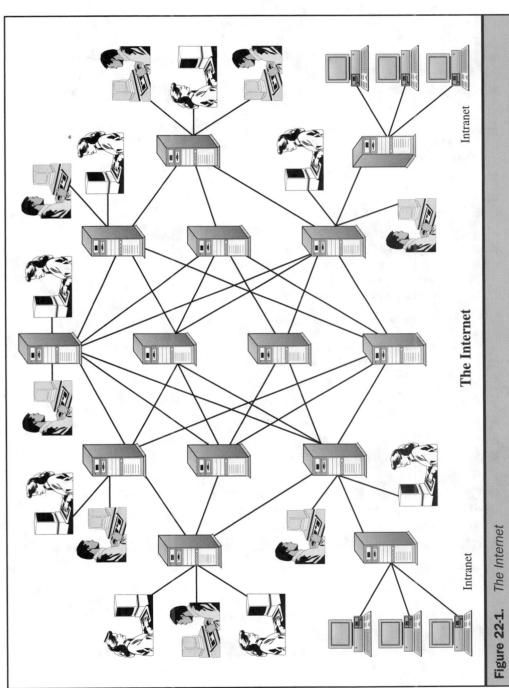

Intranet

The Internet

Intranet

Figure 22-1.   The Internet

- Direct real-time audio and video communications, which today are a moderate part of the Internet traffic, will grow as the bandwidth of the Internet expands. For the most part the communications are not sensitive in nature, but there may be charges for its receipt.

- Telnet, Gopher, and other classical Internet services remain barely alive and will soon disappear.

- Web servers are being maintained; web pages are being added, revised, and removed; user IDs and passwords are being changed; and scripts are being worked on.

- Increasingly, people on intranets are gaining access to the Internet.

- More slowly but increasingly, people on the Internet are gaining limited access to intranets through the use of extranets that allow businesses and corporations to conduct much of their work with off-site business partners.

- A large portion of the computer population, especially its younger members, are sharing music and other files using a peer-to-peer file sharing system first developed by Napster where you can go through a directory computer to reach and copy files that are on my computer.

Where are the risks in this Internet activity? There are, of course, many, but among them are:

- Interception and misuse or misdirection of e-mail

- Creation and transmission of e-mail from a misrepresented source

- Accessing a controlled-access web site without the appropriate permission

- Interception and misuse of credit card or other financial information during an Internet business transaction

- Misrepresentation on the part of a buyer or seller in an Internet business transaction

- Gaining unauthorized access to the administrative functions of a web server to misuse the user IDs and passwords, or to otherwise upset the operation of the server

- Gaining unauthorized access to a web server and changing web pages or scripts

- Gaining unauthorized access to an intranet for whatever reason

The primary security goals, then, are just three:

- Limiting access to web pages, web servers, and intranets to only those with proper authorization

- Securing the transmission of information, whether sensitive e-mail, credit card data, or financial information

- Authenticating the sender, the receiver, and the data transferred

Controlling Access

"Controlling access" has at least two different connotations:

- Limiting access to all or part of a web site to only a certain group, such as subscribers to an electronic publication or administrators on the web site

- Securing an intranet site from access via the Internet by setting up a computer, software, or other device called a *firewall,* which controls entry to and possibly exit from the intranet

Limiting Access to a Web Site

Limiting access to a web site means that you have a specific list of people or groups of people to whom you have granted some type of permission to access your site. When you install FrontPage on your computer, you (really your computer) are automatically given permission to access the web pages you create. Also, a default *root web* (containing your home page) is automatically created, and, on Windows 98 with PWS and Windows 2000 Professional with IIS, the world (everyone) is given permission to access it. By default, all the web pages you create are given the same permission as the root web, meaning that if your administrator has done nothing to limit permission, everyone will be able to access all the pages you've built.

If you publish your web to IIS, running on Windows NT 4.0 or Windows 2000 Server, the default permissions are more limited and have probably been further limited by a network administrator. You still have some latitude in setting permissions for those who visit your web site, however.

You cannot establish permissions in FrontPage if you are working with a web you have not published (that exists only on your hard disk), or a web that is published on the Microsoft Personal Web Server.

As a default, you set the level of permission for the root web (home page), and all subwebs under it will automatically have the same level of permission. If you are directly working on your server, this is http://localhost, or the server name, like http://www.myserver.com. If you want, though, you can separately set the level of permission for any or all of the subwebs, such as http://localhost/excitingtravel or http://www.myserver.com/excitingtravel.

Note

To use permissions with Windows NT 4.0 or Windows 2000 and IIS, the webs must be stored in an NTFS (NT file system) partition and not a FAT (file allocation table) partition. This is because the permissions depend on Access Control Lists (ACLs) that are implemented with NTFS. Also, your Web presence provider (WPP) must create an NT user account on the web server you will use to access your files.

Creating Subwebs

On your local computer or server, a subweb like Exciting Travel has been formally set up as a web in its own folder. In this case, it is easy to open that subweb and establish permissions. But what if you wanted to establish a second-level subweb within Exciting Travel, so, for example, you could let everyone (anonymous users) browse many of the pages in the web, but have some pages in a subweb that only travel agents could access. To do this you must create a folder, move the pages you want into it, and then make that folder a separate web. To do this, follow these steps:

1. Load FrontPage and then open the Exciting Travel web you created earlier in this book. This must be the copy of the Exciting Travel web that is running on a Windows NT, 2000, or XP Server with IIS, not a local copy using PWS.

   If you want, you can use the copy of the Exciting Travel web on the CD in \Book\ Chapter 22\Exciting Travel\.

2. In Folders view and in the Folder List, click the primary folder for the Exciting Travel web (on my server, this is http://server1/excitingtravel, as you can see next).

3. Open the File menu and choose New | Folder (you may have to extend the New menu). Type **AirTravel** for the folder name. Drag Air.htm and the other geographic pages, as well as World.gif, into this new folder.

4. Right-click the new folder and choose Convert To Web. A message is displayed telling you the penalties of converting the folder to a new subweb. You need to determine if these penalties are worth having a separate set of permissions. In most cases, the warning is worse than the actual consequence. Note how it works here.

5. Click Yes. The AirTravel folder gets a new icon showing it is a subweb and in the contents pane you are told you can no longer view the files without opening the subweb. This allows you to set separate permissions for it.

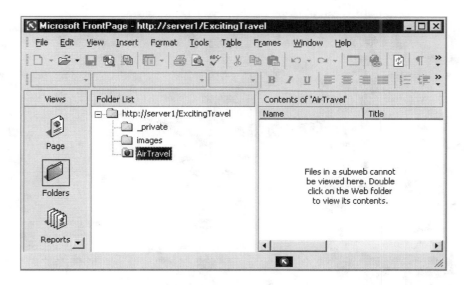

6. Double-click the AirTravel folder. Another instance of FrontPage is opened with the AirTravel subweb, as shown in Figure 22-2.

7. Double-click Air.htm to open it in Page view. Look at the page; it should look pretty much the same as the original page except that the bottom shared border is missing.

8. Click Preview In Browser. Again look at your page. Click the map and see that it still works as intended. Click Home in the link bar. Your Exciting Travel home page will open. Scroll down and click the AirTravel link. You are returned to the AirTravel page. All the links work.

9. Close your browser and the copy of FrontPage displaying the AirTravel subweb. The original instance of FrontPage, which displays the home page of Exciting Travel, should remain open.

Note   *The only penalty in creating a subweb was that the shared border was lost and must be manually copied to the subweb.*

With your AirTravel pages separated into a subweb, you can now set the permissions you want for both the parent web Exciting Travel and the subweb.

EXTENDING YOUR
WEB SITE

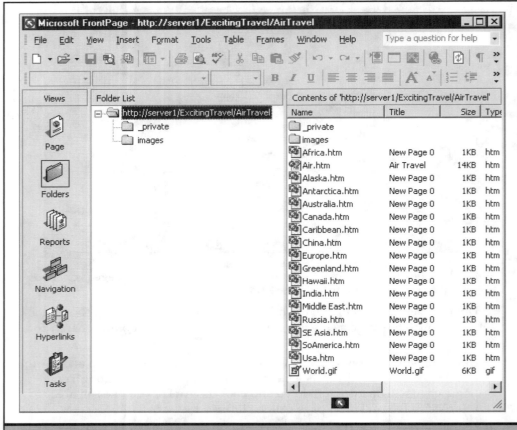

Figure 22-2. *A separate AirTravel subweb*

Setting Permissions

In Windows NT, 2000, and XP using NTFS, permissions are set for users and groups in terms of the roles assigned to each. In many situations people come to a web site as anonymous users. In other words, they don't sign on to the site with a username and password, so you don't know who they are. Your first task in setting permissions, then, is to set the permissions you want to give an anonymous user, or really to the group of all people who are anonymous users. You can also identify specific users with a username and password and determine the permissions or roles you want these users to have. Finally, you can establish the roles, and the permissions inherent in those roles, you want available to assign to people, anonymous or otherwise.

How permissions are set in FrontPage depends on the server environment on which the webs have been published—whether you are using the latest Windows 2000 or XP, IIS 5, SharePoint, and FrontPage 2002 Server Extensions or not.

Setting Permissions with the Latest Server Software

With the latest software and extensions on the server hosting the web page for which you want to set permissions, FrontPage opens an interactive HTML page in a browser that allows you to perform the necessary administrative tasks. To see how this is done with the home page of the Exciting Travel web displayed, open the Tools menu and choose Server | Permissions. The Permissions Administration page will open, as shown in Figure 22-3.

Your Permissions Administration page may look different than the one in Figure 22-3 due to what users, roles, and permissions have already been set for the server and web you are looking at.

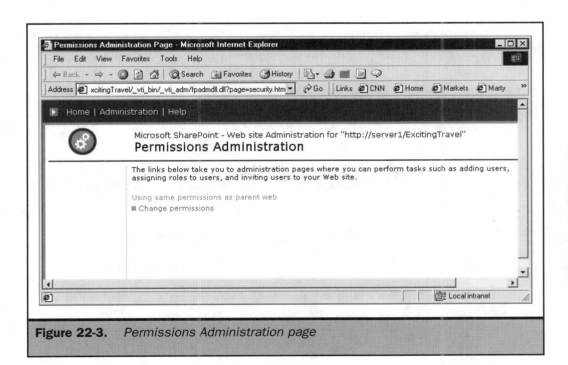

Figure 22-3.   *Permissions Administration page*

EXTENDING YOUR
WEB SITE

Initially it is assumed that the Exciting Travel web is using the same permissions as the parent web, in this case the server. If you click Change Permissions, select Use Unique Permissions For This Web Site, click Submit, wait a minute, and click Cancel, you get a new set of permissions that allow you to:

- Set or change anonymous access
- Set or change unique permissions
- Set up and manage named users
- Set up and manage the roles that are available for both anonymous and named users
- Invite people to join a SharePoint web

Anonymous Access Settings   The first step in granting permission to your web site is to determine if you want to allow anonymous users to the site, and what roles or permissions you want to give them. Do that now and see how you begin the process of permission setting.

1. Click Change Anonymous Access Settings. The page of that name opens and allows you to turn anonymous access on or off and to assign a role to those users, as shown in Figure 22-4.

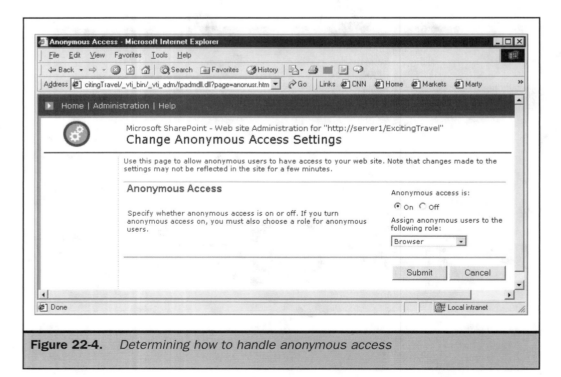

Figure 22-4.   *Determining how to handle anonymous access*

2. Open the drop-down list of roles, as shown next. These roles, which you can change as you'll see in a moment, have the following default definitions:

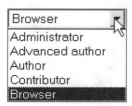

- **Administrator** can view, add, and change all server content, and manage server settings and accounts.
- **Advanced Author** can view, add, and change pages, documents, themes, and borders, and recalculate hyperlinks.
- **Author** can view, add, and change pages, as well as documents.
- **Contributor** can view pages and documents, and view and contribute to discussions.
- **Browser** can view pages and documents.

3. Make the anonymous access settings that are correct for you and click Submit. You are asked if you are sure you want to change the security of your site.

4. Click OK and you'll be sent to a Site Administration page where you can set users and roles as well as a number of other web administration functions both for the root web and the subwebs it contains.

Note *The roles you will see in the Anonymous Access page will depend on how the network administrator has configured your web on the web server she or he manages. If you get an error message in the Change Anonymous Access Settings page saying you can't change roles for this web because it inherits the access control of the parent web, open Tools | Server | Administration Home and change the permissions for the Exciting Travel subweb from inherit to unique permissions from its parent.*

Changing Subweb Permissions   Changing subweb permissions is what you did initially where you have a choice between using the same permissions as the parent web or not.

Here, we're talking of Exciting Travel as a subweb of http://servername. The Change Subweb Permissions we refer to for Exciting Travel. But then Exciting Travel also has its own subweb, AirTravel, which is addressed in the Subwebs section of the Web Site Administration page.

Adding and Managing Users   The Manage Users option allows you to add named users, give them usernames and passwords, and assign them roles. Here are the steps to do that:

1. Click Manage Users. The Manage Users page will open like this:

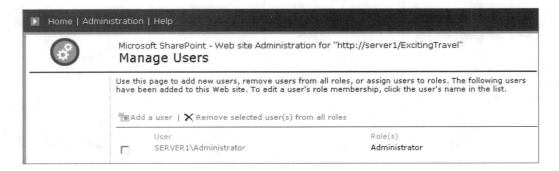

2. Click Add A User. Enter a username, password, and select a role for the user as shown in Figure 22-5. When you are done, click Add User. Another user will be added to the list.

3. Click the new user you just added. The Edit User Role Membership page opens. Here you can change the role of a user, but not the username or password; those require you delete the name and re-add it. Click Cancel to return to the Manage Users page.

4. Click the check box next to your new user and then click Delete Selected User(s) From All Roles. Click OK when asked if you are sure you want to delete this user.

5. Click Administration at the top of the page to return to the Web Site Administration page.

The Send An Invitation option invites a person who you have just added in Manage Users to use a SharePoint team collaboration web site and communicates to them their username and password. SharePoint is discussed further in Chapter 24.

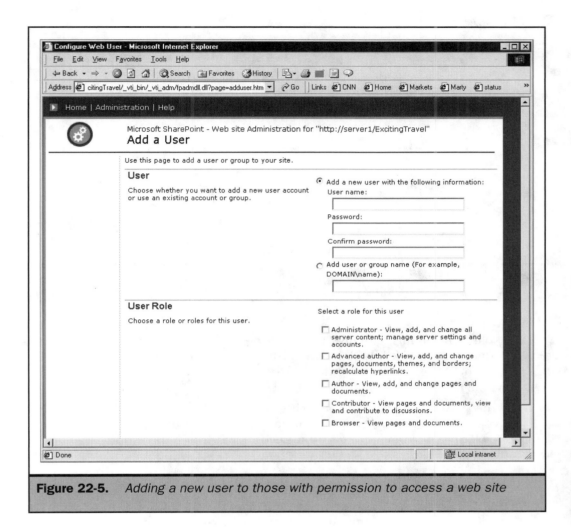

Figure 22-5.   *Adding a new user to those with permission to access a web site*

EXTENDING YOUR
WEB SITE

Adding and Managing Roles   With both anonymous and named users, you give them permissions by assigning them predefined roles. The Manage Roles option on the Permissions or Web Site Administration pages allows you to add, change, and delete roles and the permissions that are attached to them. Look at how this is done next.

1. On the Web Site Administration page, click Manage Roles. The page shown in Figure 22-6 opens, displaying the five default roles and their permissions.

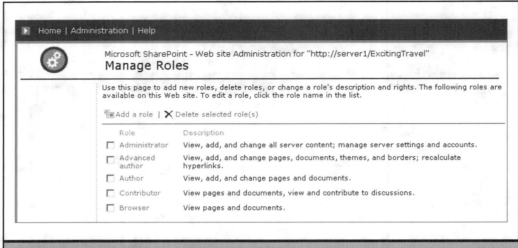

Figure 22-6. *Managing the roles that can be assigned to users*

2. Note that Administrator does not have a description and then click Administrator. The Edit Role Administrator page opens. Here is a detailed list of rights or permissions that can be assigned to a role. Scroll down this list to see all that are available.

3. When you are done looking at the list, click in the Description text box and type: **All web design, team contributor, and web administration rights**. Scroll to the bottom of the page and click Submit. The Administrator now has a description.

4. Click Add A Role. Type **Manager** as the Role Name, **Manage Contributions** as the Description, and click Author Pages, FrontPage Browse, Manage Tasks, Edit Tasks (automatically selected), and all of the Team Contributor Rights (a number of which are automatically selected). When you are done your page should look like Figure 22-7.

5. Scroll down to the bottom of the page and click Create Role. You will see Manager appear in the list of roles in the Manage Roles page.

6. Click the check box opposite Manager, click Delete Selected Role(s), and click OK that you are sure you want to delete a role.

7. Click Home to open the Home page of your web. Here you can try out any changes you made in users, roles, and permissions. When you are done, close your browser, the Exciting Travel web and FrontPage.

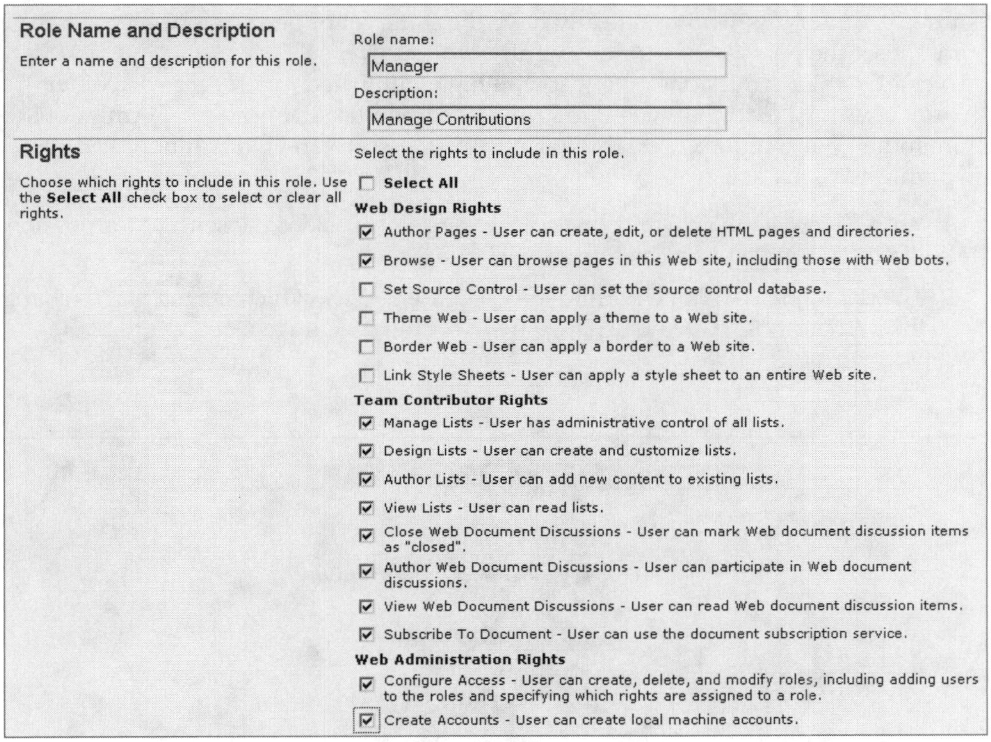

Figure 22-7. *Creating the role of Manager*

Setting Permissions with Legacy Server Software

If the server hosting the web for which you want to set permissions does not have SharePoint and the FrontPage 2002 Server Extensions, then the process of setting permissions looks different. If you open that web in FrontPage, you can establish three levels of permissions:

- **Browse**, which allows the user to look at, read, and navigate the web site
- **Author**, which allows the user to change as well as browse the site
- **Administer**, which allows the user to set permissions as well as to author the web site

Like the newer server software, you can set the permissions for the root web and all subwebs under it will automatically have the same set of permissions or you can separately set the permissions for any or all of the subwebs.

To change the permissions on a web you have published to a server with older software, you must load that web into FrontPage, then use the Server | Permissions option in the Tools menu, as you did with the newer software. Do that now and see how permissions are set.

1. With a web displayed, and Tools | Server | Permissions chosen, the Permissions dialog box will appear, as shown in Figure 22-8.

2. The default is Use Same Permissions As Parent Web, which means that to change the permissions, you must change them for the parent web.

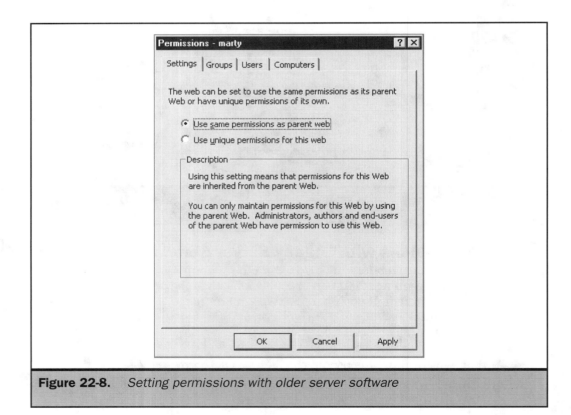

Figure 22-8. *Setting permissions with older server software*

3. First click the Users tab, where you should see, at a minimum, that an administrator or possibly you, have Administer, Author, and Browse permissions. If you click the Groups tab, you'll see that Everyone has been granted Browse permission, and the Administrators group has full control, like this:

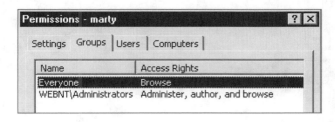

The groups you will see in the Groups tab of the Permissions dialog box will depend on how the network administrator has configured your web on the server.

4. Return to the Settings tab, click Use Unique Permissions For This Web, and click Apply (if you don't click Apply, you won't be able to open the Users and Groups tabs).

5. Click the Users tab and then your account name in the user list, then click Edit. (If Edit is dimmed, click OK to close the dialog box and then reopen it.) In the Edit Users dialog box, click Browse This Web, like this:

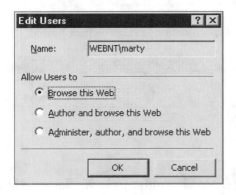

6. Click OK to return to the Users tab of the Permissions dialog box.

7. Click Add to open the Add Users dialog box. If you have a list of names on the left (this is the list of User accounts on the network of which the web server is a member), double-click one that you want to have some level of permission with this web.

8. Click the permission level you want for this person, as shown in Figure 22-9. (Given that Everyone has Browse permission, the person you're adding should have a higher-level permission.)

Add Users   ? ✕

O̲btain list from:
WEBNT   ▾

N̲ames:
carmen
carroll
cats
caunint
cbk
cbm
cbmdist
cecilia1

Add names̲:
WEBNT\cbm;

A̲dd >>

Allow users to

○ B̲rowse this web
◉ A̲uthor and browse this web
○ Ad̲minister, author, and browse this web

OK   Cancel

Figure 22-9. *Assigning a role to a new user*

9. Click OK. Your Users tab should now resemble this:

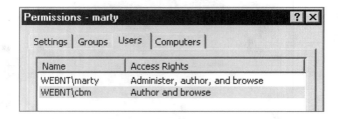

Permissions - marty   ? ✕

Settings | Groups | Users | Computers

Name	Access Rights
WEBNT\marty	Administer, author, and browse
WEBNT\cbm	Author and browse

10. Click Groups and then click Add. Again, you can double-click an entry on the list on the left or type a new group on the right. Select the permission level desired, and then click OK to close the Add Group dialog box. Then click OK again to close the Permissions dialog box. You can also close your web and FrontPage.

Note   *In addition to users and groups, you may also be able to set permissions for computers, so anyone using that computer can access your web. Permissions can be set for a single computer by giving it a complete IP address, or for groups of computers based on an IP mask, as shown next. This is particularly useful for limiting access to just those people in a particular company.*

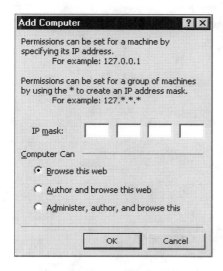

Setting up Users, Groups, and Computers   The users, computers, groups, and members of groups to whom you grant permission to access your web are established within the server outside of FrontPage and are maintained in *Access Control Lists* (ACLs), which are referenced by FrontPage. The individual users are assigned IDs and passwords that they must use to gain access, while computers are assigned IP addresses. The users and computers may also be assigned to one or more groups. FrontPage can then reference the users and computers either individually or by group. The process of setting up users and computers and establishing groups is handled by the network or server administrator and is a function of the operating system.

Controlling Access to a Web Server

The permissions you set for the web pages you create are used by the web server to implement the access controls you want. If your server or that of your Internet service provider (ISP) is not Windows NT 4.0, 2000, or XP Server or Professional with IIS, then you must work with your network administrator or ISP to set up the access controls you want by using the services available on the web server. Most web servers have a multiple-level permission scheme set up by user, group, and/or computer that allow you to implement an access scheme similar to FrontPage's older Browser, Author, Administrator scheme. In fact, most servers go beyond this.

Windows NT 4.0, 2000, or XP Server with IIS provide at least four security mechanisms, each of which give you one or more levels of access, as you can see in Figure 22-10. These four mechanisms, which can be implemented in any combination by IIS, are:

- Internet Protocol (IP) address control
- User account control

- Virtual directory control
- Windows NT File System (NTFS) control

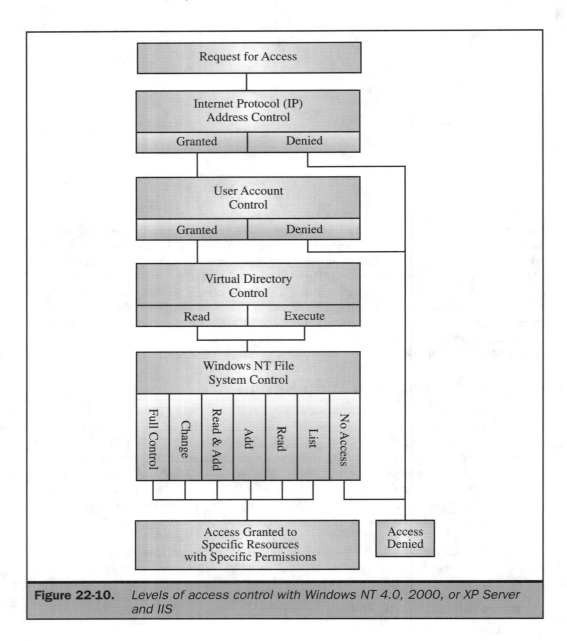

Figure 22-10. *Levels of access control with Windows NT 4.0, 2000, or XP Server and IIS*

IP Address Control

The IP address control checks the *source* IP address (where the data is from) on every packet of data received by the server and compares it against a list of IP addresses that contains predefined actions to be applied to packets with that address. The packet is then handled in accordance with the predefined actions. IP address control is useful for either blocking or accepting major groups of users, like everyone from a particular company or organization within a company. This is the principal mechanism used by firewalls (discussed later in this chapter). The major limitation in IP address control is that you cannot identify particular directories that can be accessed by a given IP address.

User Account Control

A standard part of Windows NT/2000/XP security is user account control, which requests a user ID and password when accessing the server or specially designated directories. Such access can be over a LAN or over the Internet, so part of the IIS security that is implemented can include user account control. To make user account control simpler, define an anonymous account allowing access to nonsensitive directories with limited privileges—normally read-only—for anyone who makes it through the IP address control. For additional access and privileges, users are asked to enter their user ID and password. These are checked for validity by use of either *Basic* or *Challenge/Response* user authentication. The difference between these two authentication schemes is in the way that the ID and password are returned to the server. In the Basic scheme, the user ID and password are simply encoded in a manner that is not terribly hard to decode by someone intercepting it on the Internet. The Challenge/Response scheme never requires that the password be transmitted, but rather uses a cryptographic challenge sequence to authenticate it. The Challenge/Response scheme only works on Microsoft Internet Explorer 2.0 and above.

Virtual Directory Control

With IIS, you can define an alias for a directory path on the server and then use that path in a URL (the uniform resource locator, which is an address on the Internet). This alias is called a *virtual directory*. For example, the default path for a web site called ExcitingTravel on a server named Server1 is C:\Inetpub\Wwwroot\ ExcitingTravel. If you define the alias for this path to be /excitingtravel, then the URL for the web site would be **http://server1/excitingtravel**, which you have seen on many figures and illustrations throughout this book.

When you define an alias, you can give it one of two access privileges, Read or Execute, used for the defined path and all files and folders within it. The Read privilege allows the user to read and download the contents. The Execute privilege only allows the user to execute the contents—not to read or download them. The Execute privilege is used for scripts and applications.

Windows NT File System (NTFS) Control

The Windows NT File System (NTFS) control in both Windows NT 4.0, Windows 2000, and Windows XP is what associates a user account (name and password) with specific directories, files, and folders, as well as other server resources. This association is accomplished through the Access Control List (ACL) for each server resource. The ACL for a particular resource—say, a directory—will have a list of users and groups of users and a set of permissions, which, for Windows 2000 Server and Professional using NTFS are shown in Figure 22-11. The permissions for both Windows NT 4.0, Windows 2000, and Windows XP are described in Table 22-1.

 Windows 2000 and Windows XP have slightly different names for their levels of permission than does Windows NT.

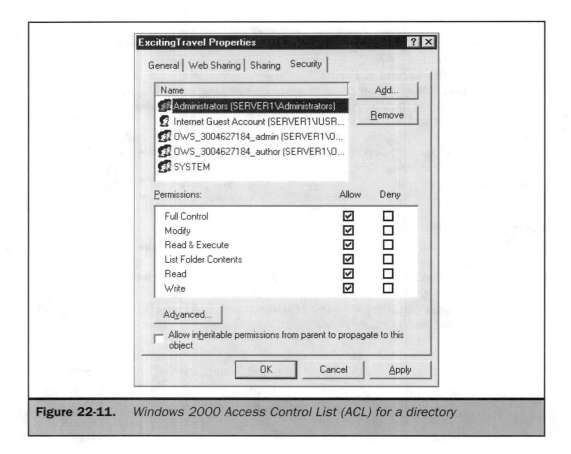

Figure 22-11.   *Windows 2000 Access Control List (ACL) for a directory*

Permission Level Windows NT / 2000 or XP	Description
No Access / No Access	Prevents any access to the directory and its files.
List / List Folder Contents	Allows the listing of filenames and subdirectory names and the changing of the subdirectories. Prevents access to file contents.
Read / Read	Allows listing filenames and subdirectory names, changing subdirectories, viewing data files, and running applications.
Add / Write	Allows adding files and subdirectories to directories, but does not allow viewing data files or running applications.
Add & Read / Read & Execute	Allows listing filenames and subdirectory names, changing subdirectories, viewing data files, and running applications, as well as adding files and subdirectories to directories.
Change / Modify	Allows add and read permission, as well as changing data in files, and deleting the directory and its files.
Full Control / Full Control	Allows change permission for the directory and its files, and takes ownership of the directory and its files.

Table 22-1.   *Descriptions of ACL Levels of Permissions*

Limiting Access to an Intranet Site

One type of access control that is not handled by FrontPage is limiting access to an intranet web site. This is the situation in which you have an intranet that you want to connect to the Internet. It may be that you want to just allow your intranet users access to the Internet. Alternatively, you may want to allow people on the Internet—for example, your own employees who are traveling—to get onto your intranet. This is done with several schemes, but the most common is a firewall, which is a separate computer through which all traffic to and from the Internet must pass, as shown in Figure 22-12. At the simplest level, a firewall works by *packet filtering,* which checks each packet of information that is transferred, either outbound or inbound, through the firewall and makes sure that its IP address is acceptable.

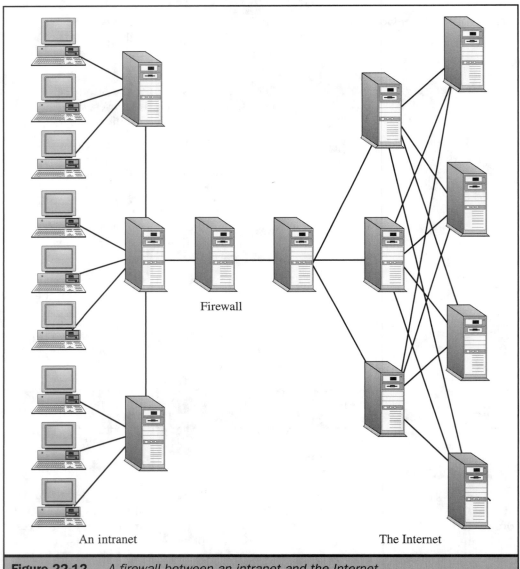

Firewall

An intranet

The Internet

Figure 22-12. *A firewall between an intranet and the Internet*

To add a further level of protection and in some cases speed up this process, the firewall computer may be set up as a *proxy server*. A proxy server, which is simply software running in a computer acting as a firewall, acts as a relay station between your intranet and the Internet. It acts like an "air lock" between the two. Requests to servers on either side of the firewall are made to the proxy server, which examines them, and if they are appropriate, sends a proxy on to the addressed server to fulfill the request.

Securing Transmission

Transmission security means the *encryption* or concealment of the information being transmitted so it cannot be read and misused without the ability to *decrypt* or reveal it. Encrypting of information is probably as old as the human race and has really blossomed with the advent of computers. Data encryption has become so sophisticated that the U.S. government, worried that they won't be able to decrypt the data (can you imagine that!), won't allow the technology to be exported (although this is changing). Several encryption schemes for securing Internet transmissions are in use. They are private key encryption, public key encryption, and combinations of the two.

Private Key Encryption

Private key encryption, or *symmetric cryptography*, is relatively old and uses a single key to both encrypt and decrypt a message. This means that the key itself must be transferred from sender to receiver. If this is done over the phone, the Internet, or even a courier service, all someone needs to do is get hold of the key, and he or she can decrypt the message. Private key encryption, though, has a major benefit in that it is much faster (as much as 1,000 times faster) than the alternatives. Private key schemes are therefore valuable in situations where you do not have to transfer the key or can do so securely—for example, personal use such as encrypting the contents of your disk or sending information to someone that you first meet face to face. There are several private key encryption schemes being used with the Internet, including the U.S. government's Data Encryption Standard (DES) and the private RC2 ("Rivest Cipher" or "Ron's Code" [for Ron Rivest] 2) and RC4 from RSA Laboratories.

Public Key Encryption

Public key encryption, or *asymmetric cryptography*, was developed in the mid-1970s and uses a pair of keys—a public key and a private key. The public key is publicly known and transferred, and is used to encrypt a message. The private key never leaves its creator and is used to decrypt the message. For two people to use this technique, each generates both a public and a private key, and then they openly exchange public keys, not caring who gets a copy of it. They encrypt their messages to each other using the other person's public key, and then send the message. The message can only be decrypted and read by using the private key held by the recipient. The public and private keys use a mathematical algorithm that relates them to the encrypted message. By use of other mathematical algorithms, it is fairly easy to generate key pairs, but with only the public key, it is extremely difficult to generate the private key. The process of public key encryption is relatively slow compared to private key encryption. Public key encryption is best in open environments where the sender and recipient do not know each other. Most public key encryption uses the Rivest-Shamir-Aldman (RSA) Public Key Cryptosystem, called "RSA" for short, developed and supported by RSA Laboratories.

*You can encrypt your e-mail in newer versions of Outlook, Outlook Express, and other e-mail programs using features built into the programs, or in any e-mail program using the Pretty Good Privacy (PGP) software that uses RSA public key encryption and is available from Network Associates at their web site **http://www.pgp.com/** (select Encryption under their Products heading).*

Combined Public and Private Key Encryption with SSL

Most encryption on the Internet is actually a combination of public and private key encryption. The most common combination was developed by Netscape to go between the Hypertext Transfer Protocol (HTTP) used in servers and browsers on the Web and Transmission Control Protocol/Internet Protocol (TCP/IP) used in both local and wide area networks (including the Internet) and is called Secure Sockets Layer (SSL). It provides a fast and highly secure means of both encryption and authentication (see "Authenticating People, Servers, and Data" later in this chapter).

Recall that private key encryption is very fast, but has the problem of transferring the key. And public key encryption is very secure but slow. If you were to begin a secure transmission by using a public key to encrypt and send a private key, you could then securely use the private key to quickly send any amount of data you wanted. This is how SSL works. It uses an RSA public key to send a randomly chosen private key for either a DES or RC4 encryption, and in so doing sets up a "secure socket" through which any amount of data can be quickly encrypted, sent, and decrypted. After the SSL header has transferred the private key, all information transferred in both directions during a given session—including the URL, any request for a user ID and password, all HTTP web information, and any data entered on a form—is automatically encrypted by the sender and automatically decrypted by the recipient.

There are several versions of SSL, with SSL version 3 being the most commonly used as of this writing (spring 2001). Compared to earlier versions, SSL 3 is more secure and offers improved authentication. Microsoft also has its own improvement of SSL called Personal Communications Technology (PCT). Both SSL 3 and PCT have been proposed to the World Wide Web standards committee (W3C) as security standards.

Internet Explorer 5 has added another encryption standard called TLS 1 for "Transport Layer Security," which is an open security standard similar to SSL 3.

Implementing SSL

You may be thinking that SSL sounds great, but it also sounds complex to use. In fact, it's easy to use. All that's required is a web server that supports SSL, such as the Netscape Commerce Server or the Microsoft IIS, plus a supporting web browser such as Netscape Navigator 3.0 or Microsoft Internet Explorer 3.0 and their respective later releases. From the browser, simply begin the URL you want with "https://" in place of "http://." SSL will then kick in, and without you even being aware that it's happening, the browser and server will decide whether to use DES or RC4, use RSA to transfer a private key, and then use that key and the chosen private key encryption scheme to encrypt and decrypt all the rest of the data during that session. The only thing you see is a message saying you are about to use a secure connection, similar to this:

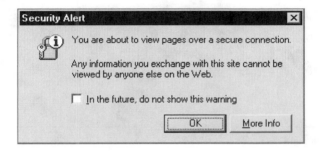

 Once you are connected using SSL, your browser will indicate that a secure connection is established. Netscape and Microsoft display an icon of a padlock in the browser's status bar.

 Even though the combination of public and private encryption is relatively fast, it is still significantly slower than no encryption. For that reason, it is recommended you only use SSL when you send sensitive information such as financial or credit card data.

FrontPage and SSL

FrontPage implements SSL in several ways. You can specify whether a new web is to use SSL by selecting Secure Connection Required (SSL) in the Web Site Templates dialog box, as you can see in Figure 22-13. Also, FrontPage automatically (without you doing anything) uses SSL for all communications between the FrontPage client and the server. This provides protection when you are transferring a web page to the server and when you are doing remote web authoring. To use SSL, you must publish the web on a server that supports SSL, such as Windows NT 4.0, 2000, or XP Server and Professional with IIS (the Microsoft Personal Web Server does not support SSL).

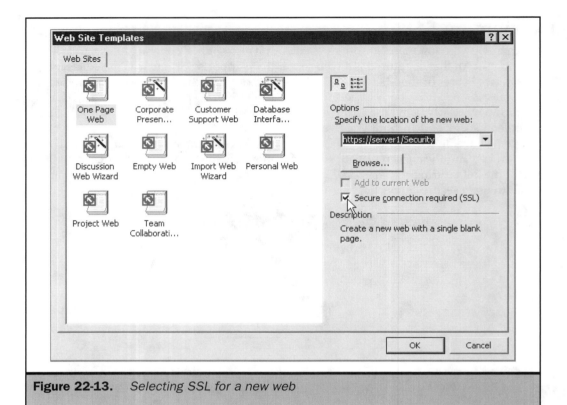

Figure 22-13.   *Selecting SSL for a new web*

Authenticating People, Servers, and Data

SSL is designed to do double duty. Not only does it provide a secure method of data transmission, but it also provides the authentication of the data and the server, and with SSL 3 it provides authentication of the user. Authentication is important for three reasons:

- To make sure that senders are who they say they are, and to prevent them from denying that they are the sender. This is authentication of the client or sender.

- To make sure that recipients are who they say they are, and to assure that they received the information. This is authentication of the server or recipient.

- To make sure that the data being sent has not been modified before it was received. This is authentication of the data.

SSL addresses each of these areas of authentication with the following steps:

1. A *message digest* is generated for the data being sent through use of a sophisticated algorithm that is very sensitive to changes in the data. This is equivalent to computing a checksum or a cyclical redundancy check (CRC) for a large number.

2. The message digest is encrypted with the sender's private RSA key to produce a *digital signature*.

3. The recipient uses the sender's public key to decrypt the digital signature that came with the data exposing the message digest. If the public key works, then the sender is who she said she was and in fact sent the data.

4. The recipient then recomputes a new message digest using the data that was received. If the two message digests are the same, then the data has not been altered in transit.

5. The recipient next encrypts the new message digest using the recipient's private RSA key to create a new digital signature and sends it to the original sender.

6. The original sender uses the recipient's public key to decrypt the second digital signature. If the public key works, then the recipient is as claimed, and if the two message digests are the same, then the original data was received by the recipient.

This sounds complicated, but if you are using SSL, it is all done automatically, and you only know if there is a problem. There is one flaw in this security scheme—how can either the sender or the recipient be sure they have the public key of the other and not of someone masquerading as the other person? In this situation, the false person would be able to use the private key that went with the false public key to decrypt and misuse the data. To counter this flaw, a public key can be enclosed in a *certificate*. A certificate uses the private key of a *certifying authority* to encrypt both a message digest of the human-readable name of the sender and the sender's public key. Then, by using the public key of the certifying authority, you can get the public key along with the name of the owner. Of course, you must trust that the public key of the certifying authority is legitimate! A prominent certifying authority, where you can obtain a certificate for yourself, is VeriSign, Inc., at **http://www.verisign.com/**.

What's Coming for Internet Security

Recognizing the reluctance of the public to use the Internet as a trusted medium for transferring financial and other confidential data, Microsoft and other software leaders have developed, or are developing, several features to ease security concerns. These range from *security zones*—where you can adjust the level at which you allow active content to be run on your computer and data to be copied to your computer—to *safe houses*, where you can securely store data on your computer or removable media.

In Internet Explorer 4.0 and later, you have four zones, as shown in Figure 22-14. In each of the zones, you can select the level of security from among four defined levels (three levels in IE 4.0) and one customizable level. You can then assign web sites to the zones. The zones and levels are shown in Table 22-2 (note that all levels apply to all zones).

Due to the potential to allow damaging content in the Internet and Restricted Sites zones, you are given a warning, such as shown here, when you select a security level that may be too low.

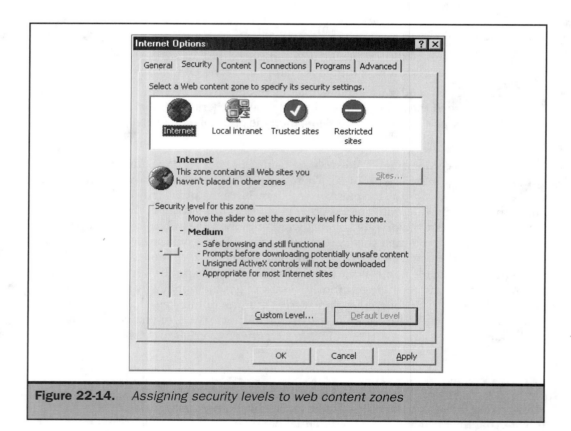

Figure 22-14. *Assigning security levels to web content zones*

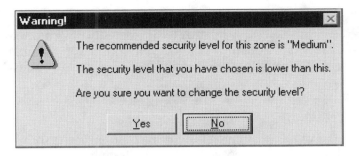

In Internet Explorer 4.0 and on, the security zone features are available from the Security tab of the Internet Options dialog box. The security zone you are currently using is displayed in the browser's status bar.

Today you can use certificates and the Microsoft Profile Assistant options available in the Content tab of the Internet Explorer 5.0 or later Internet Options dialog box, to provide safe and easily retrievable access (for those you want to have access) to personal verification and data. On the horizon is support for conducting business using smart cards and Internet cash, where you electronically move "money" from one silicon repository to another.

Security Zones	Levels of Security
Internet is a catch-all of those sites that haven't been placed in other zones.	*High* provides the most predefined security measures. It prevents damaging content from being downloaded.
Local Intranet includes fully trusted sites behind a corporate firewall.	
Trusted Sites are frequently visited web sites, such as the web site of a business partner that you trust will not adversely affect your computer.	*Medium* provides a warning message for content that may damage and won't download unsigned ActiveX controls.
Restricted Sites are those that could adversely affect your computer.	*Medium-low* doesn't provide warning messages, but won't download unsigned ActiveX controls (not in IE 4).
	Low provides no warning for content that has the potential for damage.
	Custom allows you to select specific security settings.

Table 22-2. *Security Zones and Levels of Security*

EXTENDING YOUR WEB SITE

Like it or not, much of how we conduct our daily lives in the future will be through the Internet in some capacity. As with other technologies that we may have initially approached reluctantly but now fully embrace, the security on the Internet will be refined and improved because too much will depend on it to do otherwise.

Bibliography

There are mountains of information on Internet and intranet security issues. Listed here is a sampling of documents, as well as two books on the subject. Most of the Internet sites mentioned had many more related documents.

Computer Security Institute, publishers of the *Computer Security Journal*, and other publications on Computer security, **http://www.gocsi.com/**

Library of Congress, *Computer and Internet Security, A Library of Congress Internet Resource Page*, 4/26/2000, **http://lcweb.loc.gov/global/internet/security.html**

Microsoft Corporation, *Microsoft Privacy and Security Fundamentals*, **http://www.microsoft.com/privacy/safeinternet/**

National Security Institute, *Connecting to the Internet: Security Considerations*, CSL Bulletin, July 1993, **http://www.nsi.org/Library/Compsec/intersec.txt**

National Security Institute, *Security Issues in WWW*, **http://www.nsi.org/Library/Internet/security.htm**

Netscape Communications Corporation, *Netscape Security Center*, **http://home.netscape.com/products/security/index.html**

NT Bug Traq (**http://www.ntbugtraq.com**) offers a mailing list to keep you informed of the latest security issues regarding Windows NT and 2000 Server, and a web site where you can locate the latest fixes.

Redmond, Frank III, *Making Sure Your Server's Secure*, Microsoft Interactive Developer, 11/96, **http://www.microsoft.com/mind/1196/iissecurity.htm**

RSA Laboratories, Inc., *Frequently Asked Questions about Today's Cryptography*, Version 4.1, 2000, **http://www.rsasecurity.com/rsalabs/faq/**

RSA Laboratories, Inc., *Public-Key Cryptography Standards (PKCS)*, **http://www.rsasecurity.com/rsalabs/pkcs/**

Stein, Lincoln D., *The World Web Security FAQ*, Version 2.0.1, 3/24/2000, **http://www.w3.org/security/faq/**

Rutstein, Charles B., *Windows NT Security*, 1997, Computing McGraw-Hill

The Complete Reference

FrontPage 2002

Chapter 23

Doing E-Commerce

What is electronic commerce? There are many different answers to this question. E-commerce is buying a book, an airplane ticket, or a computer online. E-commerce is also an airline ordering aircraft parts for a Boeing 747 electronically, and it is a bank sending a financial transaction to another bank electronically. It can also be any aspect of buying and selling online, which could include marketing, order taking, or customer service.

E-commerce, in this chapter, is when someone offers a product for sale on the Web and someone else buys it. This sounds simple, but a lot of different things must be considered to make that sale over the Web. Many of those considerations are similar to what the traditional physical storefront deals with. You are offering products for sale and they must be marketed, sold, paid for, and delivered. The details are different for e-commerce, but, whether the store is a physical or electronic storefront, you are still running a store and your web storefront must meet many of the same requirements of a physical storefront to be successful.

The e-commerce market is also growing rapidly. Predictions of how big the e-commerce market will be are many, but all agree it is growing rapidly and will be enormous. A University of Texas study reports 1999 revenue generated from e-commerce sales at $171.47 billion, a 72 percent increase from 1998's revenue of $99.81 billion (**http://www.internetindicators.com**). In a June 2000 release, International Data Corporation reported that the "growth of Internet commerce is accelerating and shows no signs of letting up." They estimate that 29 percent of Internet users purchased a product or service online in 2000 and expect that percentage to increase to 38 percent by 2003, generating a worldwide revenue of $1.6 trillion (**http://www.idc.com/Internet/press/PR/NET0060500PR.stm**). And the ranks of online users are growing. IDC predicts that by 2004, 210 million Americans will go online (**http://www.idc.com/eBusiness/press/EBIZ082500pr.stm**).

More and more companies are jumping into this market. These include Internet-only companies like Amazon.com, Priceline.com, and eBay, traditional bricks-and-mortar retailers like K-Mart, Barnes and Noble, and JC Penney, and offline electronic retailers like the Home Shopping Network and QVC. Large companies with physical storefronts and catalog sales are moving onto the Web. But the move to the Web is not just with large companies. In 1995, Amazon.com opened an Internet storefront selling books that was created and run with software they developed themselves. Today the potential web storeowner has many off-the-shelf options that can be used to create an e-commerce store. Some of these options do everything from creating the pages to handling all the ordering and payment; others rely on tools like FrontPage to create the pages while depending on software running on the server to add features for ordering and payment. The prices for various software options also vary quite a lot, but they all provide a much less expensive solution than starting from scratch like Amazon.com.

While putting a store on the Web is easier than ever, putting a successful store on the Web is not easy. It is no easier, in fact, than establishing a successful physical store. After all, long before your grand opening, there is plenty to do in the way of setting up a retail store. Thankfully, a wealth of advice for such ventures is available on the Web. Several publishing companies have web sites with information on e-commerce.

For instance, ZDNet's E-business (**http://www.zdnet.com/icom/e-business**) offers news, reports, and information about e-commerce and doing business over the Web. ZDNet also has a site devoted to more general small business concerns called Small Business Advisor (**http://www.zdnet.com/smallbusiness**). The Microsoft bCentral (**http://www.bcentral.com**), meanwhile, offers tips and advice to e-business entrepreneurs along with a heavy mix of service offerings ranging from domain name registration to site hosting, to shopping cart systems and advertising services. Internet.com's E-commerce Guide (**http://ecommerce.internet.com**) is another site devoted to e-commerce. Even software companies that want to sell you e-commerce software will often have sections of their site devoted to general information of e-commerce and doing business on the Web.

Factors Important to E-Commerce

While the primary focus of this chapter is the creation of a web store, before that discussion begins, it is useful to talk about other factors important to e-commerce: security, payment options, and designing for success.

Security

In e-commerce, security is a major issue, as it is in any transfer of money. Since Chapter 22 discusses security on the Web, you might want to review the sections on encryption, private and public keys, Secure Sockets Layer (SSL), and authenticating servers. These subjects are essential to creating and maintaining a secure e-commerce site. This section will go into more detail describing how security is implemented and some options you have regarding digital certificates.

Sending data over the Internet is much more secure than the uninformed scare stories passed on by the popular media. But the reality of security and the perception of security by your customer are two different things. When a customer gives out personal or credit card data at a physical store, or through a mail-order catalog, that customer is basing their trust on a variety of visual clues as to the professionalism with which your data will be handled. A customer at a high-end store like Nordstrom does not question the security of their credit card data when they hand it over to a sales clerk. That same customer may think twice about handing it over to someone on the Internet he or she knows nothing about. You need to show you are taking care of the customer's data as it crosses over the Internet and that you will be handling it responsibly once you receive it.

The key to secure transactions (both actual and perceived) is the *digital certificate*. VeriSign (**http://www.verisign.com**) is the leading issuer of digital certificates. Before issuing a digital certificate, VeriSign reviews the applicant's credentials, such as the Dun & Bradstreet number, articles of incorporation, or business license, and takes several other steps to ensure the organization is what it claims to be and not an imposter. VeriSign then issues the digital certificate, which is your electronic credential.

VeriSign's price for this service currently starts at $349. A lower-cost alternative is another VeriSign company, Thawte Certification (**http://www.thawte.com**), who offers SSL certificates starting at $125.

Not only does the digital certificate identify the owner of the web store, but it also enables Secure Sockets Layer (SSL) to establish secure communications between your server and the customer's browser. SSL provides the following components for online commerce:

- **Authentication**   By checking the digital certificate, your customer can verify that the web site belongs to you and not an imposter.

- **Message privacy**   SSL encrypts all traffic between your web server and the customer's computer using a unique session private key. To securely transmit the session key to the customer, the server encrypts it with the customer's public key, automatically sent to the server by the customer's computer. Each session key is used only once, during a single session with a single customer.

- **Message integrity**   When a message is sent, the sending and receiving computers each generate a code based on the message content. If even a single character in the message is altered, the receiving computer will generate a different code, and alert the recipient that the message is not legitimate. If not alerted, both parties will know that what they are seeing is exactly what the other party sent.

When you open a web page that is secure, you will get a Security Alert box like this:

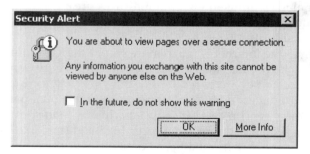

When SSL has been enabled, and the secure web page loaded, Internet Explorer shows a small, closed padlock at the bottom of the browser. The padlock does more than tell you that the connection is now secure. It also gives you access to information about the digital certificate. When you double-click the padlock, the Certificate box appears as in Figure 23-1. The General tab has the name of the owner of the digital certificate and the time period of its validity. Selecting the Details tab gives you the details about the digital certificate, such as the serial number and dates between which it is valid. Selecting the Certification tab then tells you who issued the digital certificate and its current status.

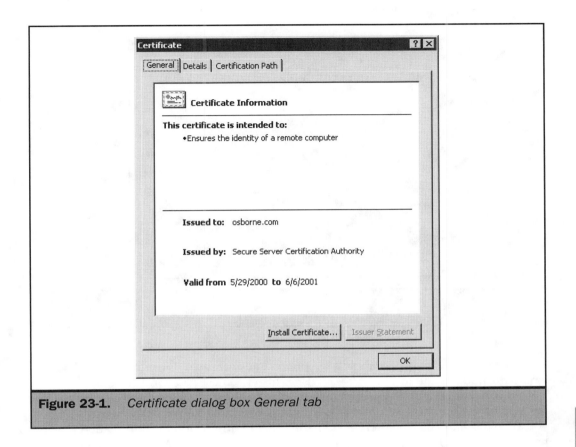

Figure 23-1. *Certificate dialog box General tab*

There are a couple of options for getting digital certificates. The first is to get one from a certificate issuer (VeriSign, Thawte, etc.) in the name of your company. The second is to use the digital certificate of the Web presence provider (WPP) who is hosting your site, if they offer that service. If you are using a simple form that is on one page, you can use the second option if your Internet service provider (ISP) (who is acting as the WPP) has a secure server with a digital certificate. The secure page would be on a secure server, and you would access it with the HTTPS protocol.

The problem with the second option is that the customer may receive notification that a name other than the one they expect is on the digital certificate as seen in Figure 23-2. This will cause many to hesitate, and they may not go on. The best long-term solution is to get your own digital certificate.

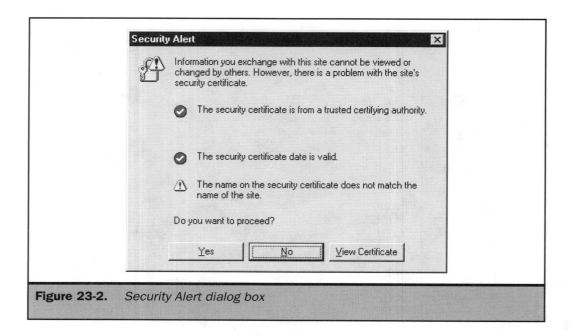

Figure 23-2.   *Security Alert dialog box*

Some e-commerce programs process orders and then use a form-mail program to e-mail the information to you. If your WPP is also your ISP and handles your e-mail as well as your secure server, the information is probably going from the secure server to the mail server to you via their network and not over the Internet. If the secure server you are using and your mail server are in different locations, and the information is being passed on via the Internet, you need to explore securing the e-mail data, too. Some e-commerce packages recognize this and provide ways to secure that data. Some e-mail programs can use SSL, and there are other encryption schemes available such as PGP (Pretty Good Privacy). Contact your WPP to see what they have to secure your e-mail data if it is going over the Internet. Another low-cost alternative is to store the customer and order information in an online database, accessible to the business owner using their browser over a secure connection. FrontPage provides you with the tools required to do this and we'll further investigate this low-cost alternative later in this chapter.

When you receive sensitive data, you should also have a way to keep it secure in your offline environment. Only trusted people should have access to your customer's credit card information, so it needs to be kept locked up with password protection on your server and you need to control access to any paper copies you might make. Leaving other people's credit card information lying around is like leaving their money lying around. It may get picked up.

Payment

Cash is not an option for paying online, but there are a number of other ways to transfer funds. Some are familiar and others are specific to the Internet. They include:

- Credit cards
- Checks
- Electronic cash
- Smart cards

Credit Cards

Credit cards are the preferred method of payment for online customers. They are easy to use, and consumers are familiar with them. Credit cards also have an advantage for the customer since they limit the customer's liability. Customers can cancel the transaction if they wish, and if credit card fraud is involved, they are only liable for $50 if they meet the card company's requirements for reporting the incident.

In any sale, you are trying to make it as easy as possible for the customer to buy. Credit cards are the easiest way for the customer. All they have to do is fill out the credit card information and submit the order. What makes it easy isn't just that credit is involved. Debit or check cards are included here too because they act just like credit cards, but the funds are deducted from the customer's checking account. What makes it easy is the existing card company and banking infrastructure that processes the credit, or debit, card.

The Credit Card Process The basic process for using a credit or debit card is that the customer submits the credit card number to the merchant and the merchant sends the merchandise to the customer. The merchant also sends the credit card number and amount to a *merchant processor*. The merchant processor transfers the money into the merchant's account, usually within 48 hours, and begins the process of billing the customer. The merchant's account is a bank account, set up to automatically receive these funds. An easy way to sign up with a merchant processor is to go to your bank and ask for a merchant account. Not all banks offer this service, but many do. Their rates vary for this service, so shop around. Costco (**http://www.costco.com**) also sets up merchant accounts through NOVA Information Systems (**http://www.novainfo.com**), a leading merchant processor, for very reasonable fees.

In the preceding scenario, the question is, how does the e-commerce merchant get the credit card transaction to the merchant processor? The answer is that you can either automate the process with online processing or use the historical manual processing.

Online Processing To do online processing, you can use a service like PayPal (**http://www.paypal.com**) that handles the acceptance of the customer payment. You simply place a customized link on your site, which takes the customer to PayPal, returning them to your site after they have submitted the payment. The downside to this type of online processing is that you have no automated way of telling whether the customer completed the payment transaction other then e-mail verification from PayPal or checking your account's transaction history. To do truly automated online processing, you need both an e-commerce package that will submit an online order to a merchant processor and a merchant processor that will receive it. The middleman between you and the merchant processor can be CyberCash (**http://www.cybercash.com**), which offers online credit card processing for merchant processors. Many of the e-commerce software packages are set up to tie into CyberCash, and many merchant processors use CyberCash, including NOVA Information Systems. One of the things that online processing can do is quickly verify that the credit card is valid and provide authorization in real time at the time of the purchase.

Online processing with CyberCash does add another step in the process that also adds to the cost of the transaction over manual processing. If you have a small web store with a small number of transactions, it might be better to use a payment service like PayPal or manual processing. Manual processing has its costs also, so you will have to figure out what is best for you. But be sure to look at manual processing.

Manual Processing   Manual processing is done with the Point-of-Sale (POS) terminal. When you swipe your credit card at a store, it is at a POS terminal. Taking credit card numbers over the Internet means you can't swipe the card, but you can key in the number. This is how mail-order companies process the credit card numbers they receive. You may find that there is a higher processing charge for key-in over swiping. Terminals can be leased or purchased from the merchant processor. Leasing starts around $30 to $40 a month and purchasing the terminal starts around $250. There are also software programs that allow you to process the numbers with your PC. NOVA charges $450 for their PC Transacted for Windows processing software. Again, shop around with different merchant processors because you need to add in the cost of the POS terminal or software along with the service charges.

Checks

Not everyone has a credit card, and even though most can get a debit card with their checking account, many people aren't able to, or choose not to. Most small businesses can't afford to turn away paying customers, so you need to decide if you want to handle check orders.

There are several ways to handle check orders. The first is to have the customer print out the order form and mail it in with the check. If the customer fills out the online form and prints it out, the entries may or may not print, so it may be easier on the check customers to create a separate snail-mail form to print out and fill in with pen or pencil or provide them with a plain-text printable version once they have filled out the form. The second way is for the customer to fill out the online form and submit it electronically with Check being selected as the method of payment. Then you hold the order until the check arrives, at which time you can process it. The customer has to do less this way. A third method of accepting check payments is to use a check acceptance service like E Commerce Group's Speedpay (**http://www.ecommercegroup.com**). Speedpay allows customers to make payments by debiting their checking account, similar to the way a check card works. Whichever method makes sense for your business, always make it as easy as possible for the customer and be ready to accept as many methods of payment as you can.

Electronic Cash

Some items are too inexpensive to purchase with a credit card. Nobody uses a credit card to buy a newspaper, which is why a number of companies are working to find a way to charge customers for items costing $5 or less. These inexpensive things are not worth the service charges with credit cards. These *micropayment* methods are not doing well with players like CyberCash and DigiCash abandoning their efforts. They require the customer to install and learn new software. With few merchants participating, acceptance has been very low. Services like PayPal, which allows individuals to make these minute payments using pre-funded accounts, seem to be gaining greater acceptance, however.

Smart Cards

Smart cards are plastic cards into which consumers can digitally download money. They are popular in Europe, but haven't caught on in the U.S. yet. Smart cards are efficient, secure, and easy to use in both real and virtual stores. Many banks and tech firms, including Microsoft, are working on smart card systems for the U.S. eCash Technologies, Inc. (**http://www.ecash.net**) has gained a level of acceptance by partnering with well-known sites such as Martha Stewart, Timex, and Mrs. Fields. Still, this is a technology whose time has yet to come.

Web Design Tips for a Web Store

Chapter 1 goes into detail on designing a web application, but there are some additional considerations with web stores:

- **Make first-time buyers comfortable**   Give them tips on shopping at your site, and possibly offer incentives for their first purchase. First-time buyers are reluctant to order online, so make sure your phone, fax, and e-mail information are listed prominently at strategic locations throughout the site. If buyers don't have a positive experience the first time, they probably won't be back.

- **Make the process fast**   Not only make it fast to load by reducing heavy graphics, but make the buying process simple from start to finish. Don't put any barriers in the way, like making them download plug-ins or filling out forms so they can shop in your web store.

- **Make it easy to find the products**   Pay attention to navigation and searching so the customer can easily find what you have to sell.

- **Make all your products available**   Provide a good selection, particularly if it is a web store that has a real-store counterpart. Customers expect to see everything online that they see in the physical store or catalog.

- **Make it easy for the customer to give you their money**   Don't hide the cash register. Make it clear how to get to the checkout stand, and make it easy to go there.

- **Make it clear what the customer is paying**   Don't hide shipping, handling, or any other extra charges. The order summary should show exactly what the customer is paying.

- **Make communication important**   Send e-mails letting your customers know their order has been received, shipped, and delivered.

- **Make it hard for your customers to leave**   Don't put links to non-shopping pages on your product pages.

Web Store Options

E-commerce sites can range from a one-page web store to major outlets like Amazon.com. These extremes use very different software packages. It doesn't take complex software to offer four or five items on a single page, but it does to offer millions of books, CDs, and videos. This section will look at the range of options available based on the size and budget of the web store.

There are two basic approaches: the simple form for web stores with just a few items, and the shopping cart site for web stores with more items than can fit on a single page. The shopping cart site uses a shopping cart metaphor to collect all the customer's choices. Then it adds up all the subtotals and extra charges, such as shipping and taxes, and sends the information to the merchant.

A Forms-Based Web Store

Form construction is covered in detail in Chapter 8. This section will show how a form can be used in a simple e-commerce site. This works when there are just a few items because the form limits it to one page. In that page, you have to put all the items for sale as well as payment and shipping information. If the page starts getting long and requires a lot of scrolling, or there are too many items to put on a single form, consider using a shopping cart site, covered later in this chapter.

In this exercise, we'll look at a simple, yet fully functional form-based store. Customers will enter their order on a single-page form. When they submit the form, the information will be stored in an Access database within the site and a custom confirmation page will display their submitted order, allowing them to print it for their records. We'll use the new Database Interface Wizard to create a secure order retrieval and maintenance area for Exciting Travel's use. While a real airfare sales transaction would require much more information, this example in the spirit of the Exciting Travel site, illustrates a simple order entry form web store system.

Importing the Form

Both the working files and completed source for this exercise can be found on the book's companion CD in the \Book\Chap23\ folder. Use the following steps to create a web and either: import the exercise files and build a form-based web store, or import the completed web to just follow along with the exercise. Step 4 will provide you with this option.

1. Create a new web named **chap23** using the FrontPage Import Web Wizard. This wizard can be found by clicking File | New | Page Or Web and selecting Web Site Templates.

2. After selecting a location and name for your new web, start the wizard by clicking OK.

3. In the Choose Source dialog box, select the From A Source Directory… option and check the Include Subfolders check box.

> **Note** *Make sure you click Include Subfolders or you won't get most of the detail behind the web site.*

4. Browse to the Exercise web folder on the CD and click Open, or type in its location in the Location field. To build the form-based web store, use the \Book\Chap23\Exercise folder. To simply follow along with the exercise using the completed code, use the \Book\Chap23\Complete folder.

5. Click Next twice and then Finish to complete the wizard, importing the example files into your web.

6. Open the Tools menu and click Web Settings to open the Web Settings dialog box.

7. Click the Database tab and select the *orderform* database connection in the list.

8. Click Verify to initialize the database connection in FrontPage and make sure it is working properly, signified by a check mark in the Status column next to its name.

9. Click OK to close the Web Settings dialog box.

Refer to Chapter 3 for more information on the Import Web Wizard.

In your new web, locate and open the page orderform.asp. As the name implies, this is our order form page. Part of this page showing the products for sale can be seen in Figure 23-3. Customers will select their departure and arrival locations and the number of passengers that will be traveling. When they enter a number and move off the Passengers field, the page will automatically calculate the subtotals and total order amount. We'll accomplish this by adding a little JavaScript and some hidden form fields to the page.

EXTENDING YOUR WEB SITE

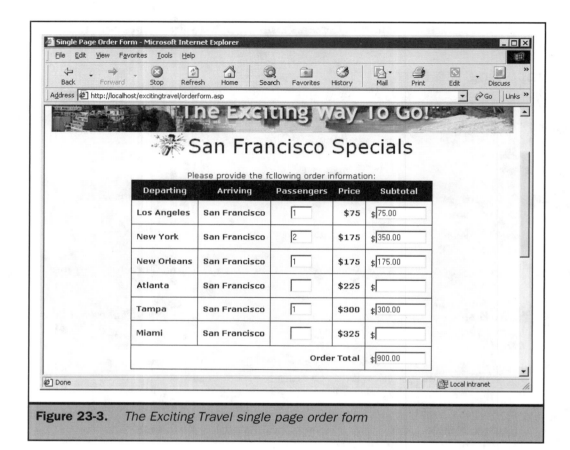

Figure 23-3.   *The Exciting Travel single page order form*

Figure 23-4 shows the second half of the page. After selecting the fares they would like to order, the customer fills in their billing and customer information and submits the form. We'll try to make sure the customer has entered all the necessary information to place the order and politely ask them to fill in any missing information before allowing them to submit the form.

How the Form was Constructed

Before adding additional functionality to our simple web store's order form, let's take a closer look at how this form was constructed using techniques covered in previous chapters. The techniques that are relevant to our exercise are as follows:

- Data Validation (Getting Good Information)
- Saving Orders (Building the Database)

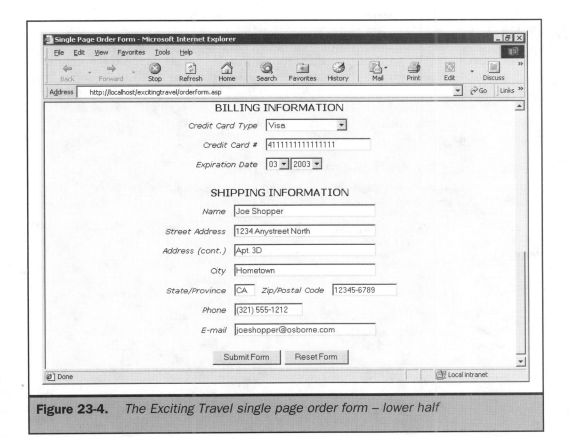

Figure 23-4. *The Exciting Travel single page order form – lower half*

Data Validation (Getting Good Information)   The page contains a form with the necessary form fields. For more information on creating forms, refer to Chapter 8, "Working with Forms." After creating the basic form, validation and constraints were added to define the information that a customer may enter. For example: the Passengers fields only accept integers and are not required; the State field accepts only text and requires exactly two characters to be entered. By setting these rules for each field on the form, we help insure that the customer will give us the information we need, reducing expensive customer service calls. We also help FrontPage create a well-designed database by telling it what kind of data will be stored. Detailed information on form validation can be found in Chapter 15, "Web Scripting Languages."

Note   *Special form field naming conventions were also used, which will be covered later as we discuss their use.*

Saving Orders (Building the Database) Our page has also been configured to save its results to an Access database within the site. As discussed in Chapter 19, "Working with Databases," FrontPage has the ability to not only save a form's information to a database, but to actually create the database for us, based on the fields in the form. This feature was also available in FrontPage 2000, but the database connection information was visible in the client-side source code, providing a major security risk. FrontPage 2002 now puts the database connection information in server-side ASP code that is not available to client browsers.

Completing the Web Store Order Form

To make our form customer-friendly and avoid math errors that might require additional customer service inquiries, we need to add a little JavaScript to perform our calculations.

1. Using Folder view in your web, open the file **javascript.txt** by double-clicking it to open the code in Notepad.

2. This file contains three JavaScript functions within <script> tags. Copy the entire contents of the page by pressing CTRL+A (to select all) and CTRL+C (to copy) and close the file.

3. Back in FrontPage, open orderform.asp in Page view and switch to the HTML view of the page. As you can see, there's lots of server-side script that FrontPage has added to handle saving the form results to the database. Scroll down the page until you find the <body bgcolor="#FFFFCC"> tag.

4. Place the cursor at the end of your <body bgcolor="#FFFFCC"> tag line, press ENTER, and paste the copied code. Listing 23-1 shows the complete script source.

Listing 23-1
JavaScript
code pasted
from
Javascript.txt
into
Orderform.asp

```
...
<body bgcolor="#FFFFCC">
<script language="JavaScript">
function getSubTotal(itemNum) {
  var frm = document.FrontPage_Form1.elements;
  var qty = parseInt(frm['Qty' + itemNum].value,10);
  var price = parseFloat(frm['Price' + itemNum].value);
  if (!isNaN(qty))
    frm['SubTotal' + itemNum].value =
      formatDollar(parseFloat(qty * price));
  else
    frm['SubTotal' + itemNum].value = '';
  getTotal(6);
}
function getTotal(itemCount){
  var i;
```

```
    var sub = 0;
    var total = 0;
    var frm = document.FrontPage_Form1.elements;
    for (i=1;i<=itemCount;i++) {
        sub = parseFloat(frm['SubTotal' + i].value);
        if (!isNaN(sub))
          total = parseFloat(total + sub);
    }
    frm['OrderTotal'].value = formatDollar(total);
}
function formatDollar(Val) {
  Val=''+Val
  if (Val.indexOf(".", 0)!=-1) {
    Dollars = Val.substring(0, Val.indexOf(".", 0));
    Cents = Val.substring(Val.indexOf(".", 0)+1,
      Val.indexOf(".", 0)+3);
    if (Cents.length==0)
      Cents="00";
    if (Cents.length==1)
      Cents=Cents+"0";
  }
  else {
    Dollars = Val;
    Cents = "00";
  }
  return (Dollars+"."+Cents);
}
</script>
<p align="center"><font face="Verdana">
...
```

Script Functions   The purpose of this part of the exercise is to show how scripting can be used to add automated calculating functions to an order form. Therefore, we won't spend a lot of time on the script, but take a quick look at the three functions and what they do:

■ **getSubTotal(itemNum)**   This function takes a single argument, the item number, and concatenates that number with static field names to resolve the proper field names used in the form ("price" + "1" = "price1" – we'll use # to represent the item number for the sake of discussion). It then multiplies the contents of the Qty# field with the Price# field to get the SubTotal# field's contents, provided that the Qty# field contains a number. After calculating the subtotal for the specified item, the function then calls the getTotal() function. *Note: The price# fields are hidden form fields that will be added in a later step.*

■ **getTotal(itemCount)**   This function also takes a single argument, the number of items on the form. It then loops through all of the subtotal fields in the form and adds their values to get the order's total. Since we want to maintain an accurate order total at all times, this function is called by getSubTotal each time an item quantity is changed.

■ **formatDollar(Val)**   This function takes the value passed to it (our order subtotals and total), turning it into the standard U.S. currency form with two numbers to the right of the decimal. This conversion is strictly for cosmetic purposes and adds a touch of professionalism that our customers expect.

Implementing the Script   Implementing this script is quite easy as we only need call the getSubTotal() function when the customer changes any of the Passengers fields (named Qty#). It does, however, require some manual source code editing:

1. Switch to the Normal tab, click the first field in the Passengers column and then switch back to the HTML view. On the right of the highlighted line should be the following code:

```
<input type="text" name="Qty1" size="2">
```

2. Add an **onchange** event handler to this field, providing the corresponding item number as the argument of the getSubTotal() function call:

```
<input type="text" name="Qty1" size="2" onchange="getSubTotal(1);">
```

3. Locate the "Qty2" field lower in the page and add another **onchange** event handler, passing it the number of this Qty# field. (You can copy what you type above and change the 1 to a 2.)

```
<input type="text" name="Qty2" size="2" onchange="getSubTotal(2);">
```

4. There are a total of six Qty# fields in the form. Locate each of the other four and add the **onchange** event as you did in the previous step, incrementing the number passed to the getSubTotal() function to match the item number.

Adding Hidden Form Fields   Now that we've added the event handlers that will call on our JavaScript, there's still one step left to make our form auto-total. We need to add some hidden form fields that contain our item prices. While these fields can be placed anywhere within the form, lets add them at the bottom:

1. Looking at the source code in HTML view, locate the closing form tag by searching for "</form>".

2. Placing the cursor before this tag, press ENTER to start a new line in the source code and add the following code starting on the new line:

```
<input type="hidden" name="Price1" value="75">
<input type="hidden" name="Price2" value="175">
<input type="hidden" name="Price3" value="175">
<input type="hidden" name="Price4" value="225">
<input type="hidden" name="Price5" value="300">
<input type="hidden" name="Price6" value="325">
```

3. Save the page and switch to the Preview tab within FrontPage.

Testing the Form   To test our auto-totaling form, enter a number in one of the text boxes within the Passengers column and press TAB. The total of the number you entered times the corresponding price should be displayed in the subtotal field. As you enter numbers in other boxes within the Passengers column and tab off, or move away from the field, you should see the subtotal of the current item update as well as the total for the entire order. Pretty cool, huh?

> **Note**   *Don't try out the rest of the form and submit it yet. It still needs a couple of items.*

There's really only one problem with this form in its current state. To see for yourself, move to a subtotal field and change its contents. Oops, our form's information is now invalid. To prevent users from making a similar change, we want to keep anyone from manually changing the subtotal fields. To do this we can use one of two methods: adding a read-only attribute to the subtotal <input> tags or calling the JavaScript blur() function whenever the cursor enters one of the fields. While adding the read-only attribute is the cleanest and easiest way, this method only works with Internet Explorer (Netscape browsers ignore this attribute entirely). For this reason, we'll use the blur() function.

1. Switch to the Normal tab and click the first subtotal field.

2. Switch to the HTML tab and add an **onfocus** event handler as follows (the *onfocus* event is triggered each time the cursor is placed in the corresponding field):

```
<input type="text" name="SubTotal1" size="8" onfocus="blur();">
```

3. Repeat Steps 1 and 2 until the six SubTotal# fields and the OrderTotal field all have an onfocus event handler.

4. Save the page and switch back to the Preview tab. You can no longer directly alter the contents of the subtotal or total fields, and more importantly, neither can your customers.

Custom Confirmation Form

While FrontPage will provide an auto-generated confirmation page for you, there's no way of formatting the page or what information it provides. So, to keep our simple web store looking professional, we'll create our own confirmation page. Formatting this page will be very simple because the order form page already contains all the information we'll be displaying.

We start by telling FrontPage that we'll be using a custom confirmation page:

1. In the Normal tab, open the Form Properties dialog box by right-clicking the form and selecting Form Properties from the context menu.

2. Click Options to display the Options For Saving Results To Database dialog box.

3. In the URL Of Confirmation Page text box, type **confirmation.asp**. This will be the name of our confirmation page. Your dialog box should look like this:

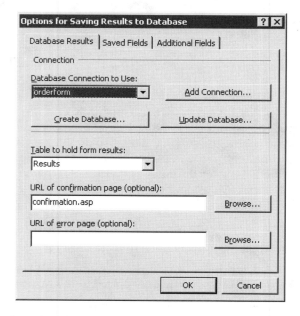

4. Click OK to close this dialog box. FrontPage will display a warning that confirmation.asp doesn't exist in the current web. Click Yes to create the hyperlink anyway, close this dialog box, and continue (we'll create this page next).

5. Click OK again to close the Form Properties dialog box and save the page.

Creating a New Confirmation Page   Next, we need to create the new confirmation.asp page.

1. Without closing the order form page, create a new page and save it with the name **confirmation.asp** and the title **Order Confirmation**.

2. At the top of the page, add the following text:
   Thank you for submitting your order. Please print this page for your records.

3. Switch back to the order form page, click the top table, open the Table menu and choose Select | Table, and press CTRL+C to copy the table.

4. Switch back to the new page, press ENTER twice to create some space below the title and press CTRL+V to paste the copied table.

5. Repeat Steps 3 and 4 for the remaining two tables, pasting each of them below the preceding table.

Adding Confirmation Fields   Now we have a page that looks like our order form. To turn this into a functioning confirmation page, we need to replace each of the form fields with a FrontPage web component called a Confirmation Field component. Starting with the field named Qty1, we need to replace each form field with a corresponding Confirmation Field:

1. Click the first Qty# form field (in the Passengers column) to select it.

2. Open the Insert menu and choose Web Component to open the Insert Web Component dialog box.

3. Scroll to the bottom of the Component Type list and select Advanced Controls.

4. In the Choose A Control listing, select Confirmation Field as seen here and click Finish.

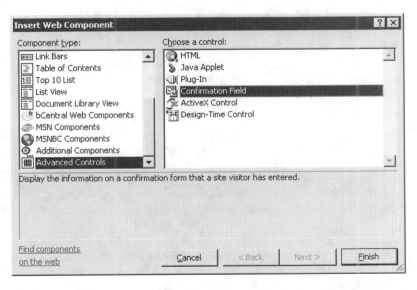

5. In the displayed Confirmation Field Properties dialog box, type **Qty1** and click OK.

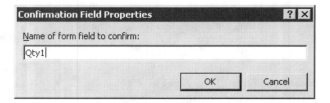

Notice that the single-line textbox form field has been replaced with [Qty1], which signifies the Confirmation Field web component in design mode. Because FrontPage has this component buried deep within its menu structure, we'll reuse the first component by copying and pasting it in place of each of our other form fields for speed and convenience.

6. Click the [Qty1] component and copy it by pressing CTRL+C (or using the copy method of your choice).

7. Moving down to the Qty2 form field below, click that field and press CTRL+V to paste the copied web component.

8. Double-click the inserted Confirmation Field web component to display the Confirmation Field Properties dialog box.

9. Edit the Name Of Form Field To Confirm entry to read Qty2 and click OK to apply the change.

Note *If you're not sure of the starting form field's name, double click it to display the Text Box Properties dialog box where its name is displayed in the Name field.*

10. Repeat Steps 2 through 4 for each of the form fields on the page, with the exception of the Credit Card Number field, until you have replaced each with a Confirmation Field component with each component set to the original form field's name.

11. For security reasons, the one field you don't want to display is the credit card number. Instead of pasting in a Confirmation field, replace the form field with repeated x's (*xxxxxxxxxxxxxxxx*). Your page should now look something like Figure 23-5.

Note *Be sure and complete converting all of the form fields to confirmation fields. If you leave some of the form fields with validation code in them, it will cause a problem later in this exercise.*

The final Confirmation Field web components that need to be inserted are price fields, which will display the value of the hidden price fields. We could leave the visible price information as is, but that would require that we edit the confirmation page if we made a price change. To avoid this, we'll add components to display the price.

1. Select the text of the first price, not including the dollar sign (*75, not $75*).

2. Paste the Confirmation Field web component over the price text.

3. Double-click the component and type **Price1** in the Name Of Form Field To Confirm field.

4. Repeat Steps 1 through 3 for each of the other five prices.

5. Save your completed page.

We now have a confirmation page that looks like our order page and is easily printable. Figures 23-5 and 23-6 show the page in FrontPage and in use, respectively. When a customer submits an order, the order information will now be saved to the database and redisplayed to the customer for printing. Go ahead and test your order form and confirmation page by opening orderform.asp in your browser, filling out the form and submitting it.

Note   *In a real-world application, you'd also want to add additional navigation links to your pages.*

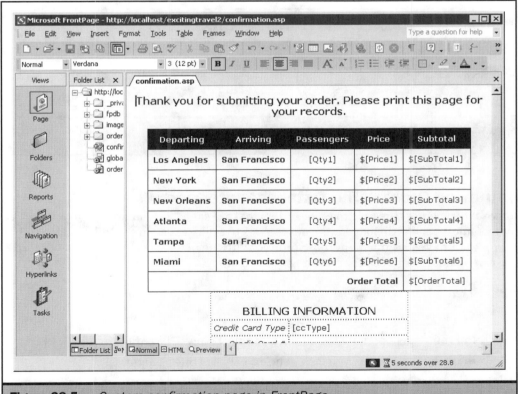

Figure 23-5.   *Custom confirmation page in FrontPage*

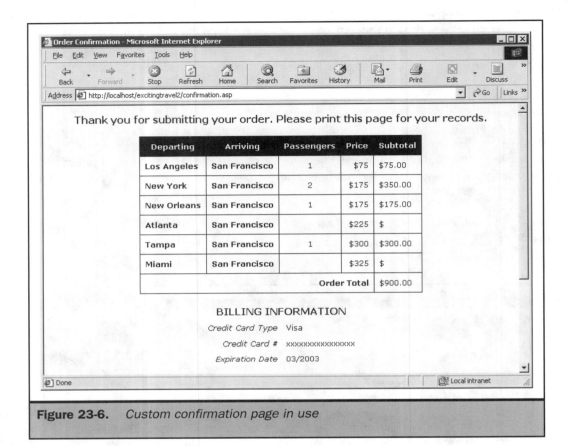

Figure 23-6. *Custom confirmation page in use*

Retrieving Orders (The Database Interface Wizard)

Now that customers are able to enter orders that are saved to a database and a confirmation page is displayed, the next step is to build a system that allows Exciting Travel to retrieve and maintain those orders. With the new Database Interface Wizard, this can be done without programming.

For detailed coverage of this wizard, see Chapter 19, "Working with Databases."

1. In FrontPage, open the File menu and select New | Page Or Web.
2. In the New Page Or Web task pane, select Web Site Templates....
3. Select the Database Interface Wizard in the Web Site Templates dialog box and check the Add To Current Web check box.

4. Click OK to open the wizard.

5. The first step of the wizard lets you create a new database or use a variety of existing data sources. We have already created our database and therefore select the Use An Existing Database Connection option. Our single existing database connection, Orderform, is selected by default.

6. Click Next to move to the table/view selection step. Our database only has one table, Results, so that table is automatically selected.

7. Click Next again to move to the third step where we can select which table columns (fields) to use in the wizard-generated pages.

8. We want all of the information the customer sent and can proceed to step four without changing the field list. Click the Next button to continue.

9. All we really care about is the Database Editor portion of the wizard for this example. Check this check box and uncheck the others. Click Next to proceed to the final step.

10. We definitely want our order information secure, so enter a Username and Password that will be required to access our orders in the database. For this example, type a Username of **secure** and a Password of **password**. Of course, you'd want to be a little cleverer in an actual application. Confirm the password and DO NOT check the Don't Protect... check box.

11. Click Finish to start the wizard's page generation, building the Database Interface.

12. The files created by the wizard are placed in a new folder called orderform_ interface/results/editor. Expand the Folders view to display these files.

Creating a Quick List   Almost done, we still need to edit a couple of pages to clean things up. The order list/selection page, named List.asp, includes more information that we likely want to display when selecting an order.

1. Open that page for editing and delete all of the table columns except ID, OrderTotal and TimeStamp, making sure to delete both the heading columns and the Database Results Region columns.

Tip   *You can easily select all of these columns by moving the mouse pointer to the top of the column you wish to select where it changes to a down arrow. To select multiple columns, either click and drag the arrow across the columns or hold down the CTRL key and click on each of the columns you wish to select. To delete the selected columns, right-click the selection and choose Delete Cells.*

2. When finished, your page should look something like Figure 23-7. Save this page and close it.

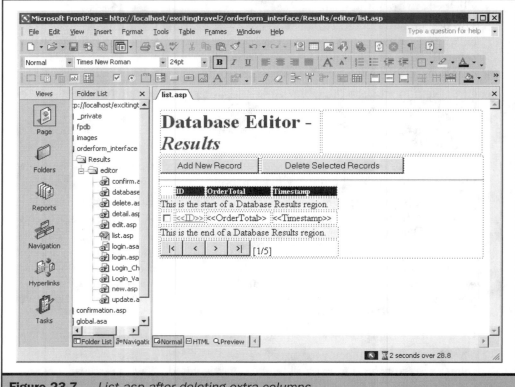

Figure 23-7. *List.asp after deleting extra columns*

Using the Form for Order Display   The other page we want to edit is the actual order display page named Detail.asp. Go ahead and open this page in FrontPage. While the wizard-generated page displays the complete order information, the default formatting looks nothing like our order form. To customize this page's look, we'll employ the same trick we used with the confirmation page.

1. Click anywhere within the Comments code at the top of the page. Press the DOWN ARROW key and then the RIGHT ARROW key. Your cursor should now be at the end of the top yellow bar of the Database Results Region.

2. Press ENTER a few times to add some space between this bar and the table below.

3. Select all but the last row of the table listing the database fields, making sure not to select either of the yellow bars or the final table row containing the Edit and Delete buttons.

4. Delete these table cells by opening the Table menu and selecting Delete Cells.

5. Switch back to the confirmation page, click the top table, open the Table menu, choose Select | Table, and press CTRL+C to copy the table.

6. Switch back to detail.asp, click on the first blank line following the top yellow bar and press CTRL+V to paste the copied table.

7. Repeat Steps 5 and 6 for the remaining two tables, pasting each of them below the preceding table.

8. Edit the Table Properties of each of the three-pasted tables setting their Alignment to Center. After doing so, your screen should look something like Figure 23-8.

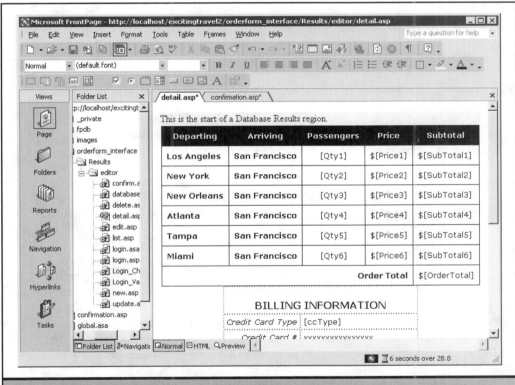

Figure 23-8. *Detail.asp after replacing results table with three tables from the confirmation page*

After pasting the confirmation page tables, we need to change all of our Confirmation Fields to Column Value fields. To do so:

1. Select the [Qty1] Confirmation Field, open the Insert menu, and choose Database I Column Value option.

2. Each time you insert a Column Value field, you are prompted to select the Column To Display from a drop-down list. Select Qty1 and click OK to replace the existing field. Note the design display of the new Column Value field, which now looks like <<Qty1>>.

3. Repeat Steps 1 and 2 until you have replaced each Confirmation Field web component with the corresponding Column Value field.

4. Differing from the confirmation page, we do want to display the customer's credit card number on this page. Select the x's that we used to represent this information on the confirmation page and replace them with a credit card number (ccNum) Column Value field.

5. Save the page.

Note	*Be sure to replace all of the confirmation fields with column value fields, or your order retrieval page may not function properly.*

After replacing each Confirmation Field, your page should look like Figure 23-9.

To open the new order retrieval system in your browser, load the page database_editor.asp in the orderform_interface/Results/editor folder. After successfully logging in, you are presented with the Results - Home frameset page as seen in Figure 23-10. Orders are displayed by clicking an order ID hyperlink. When you are done looking at your order retrieval system, close your browser, the Chap23 web, and FrontPage.

This exercise has shown how Exciting Travel can set up a simple form-based order system to take order information over the Internet. Before putting this example into production, we would also need to obtain and install a digital certificate, enable SSL and use the HTTPS protocol when sending customers to the order page or accessing the order retrieval system. Even with password protection preventing unauthorized access to the Database Interface, we still owe it to our customers to protect their information when sending it across the Internet. Our example system shows that creating a form-based order system in FrontPage is relatively simple to do. This system might work for you if you only need to offer a few items. If the number of items grows and the page starts getting very long, it becomes time to consider going to a shopping cart-based web store.

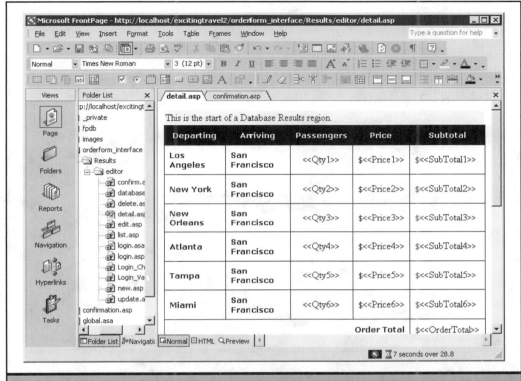

Figure 23-9.   *Order Retrieval page after replacing confirmation fields with column value fields*

Shopping Cart Store

One hundred years ago, stores were very different than they are now. Clerks brought the merchandise from the product display to you and then added up the totals. Over the last century that all changed with customers now going through the product displays and getting their own merchandise, loading it into their shopping cart, and then going to the check-out stand for the total to be added up. The early successful e-commerce sites took the shopping cart metaphor and successfully brought it into cyberspace. This has served e-commerce sites well in providing a familiar way for customers to select and purchase products.

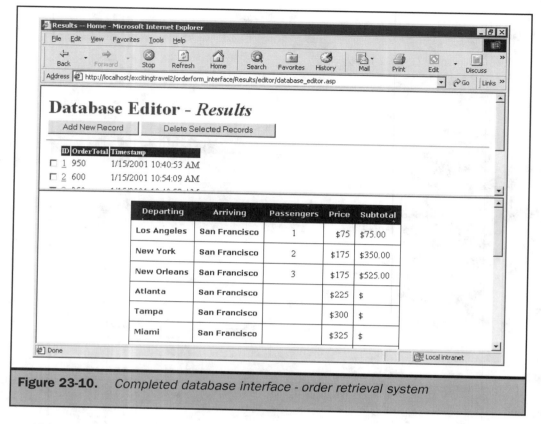

Figure 23-10. *Completed database interface - order retrieval system*

Although the shopping cart metaphor rules in the online stores, there are a number of different shopping cart programs available that all do things a little differently. All of them, though, provide the same four elements to a shopping cart store:

1. Getting the shopping cart

2. Viewing the product displays

3. Putting the items into the shopping cart

4. Buying the products at the checkout stand

This section will look at these four different elements and then explore some of the options available to you with software packages for putting that shopping cart into your web store.

To see how it works, we'll enter the fictional Exciting Travel Store site, a store set up to sell vacations. Figure 23-11 shows the store's home page, which links to the day's featured vacation. This page is the front door to the web store. The next step is to go into the store and get the shopping cart.

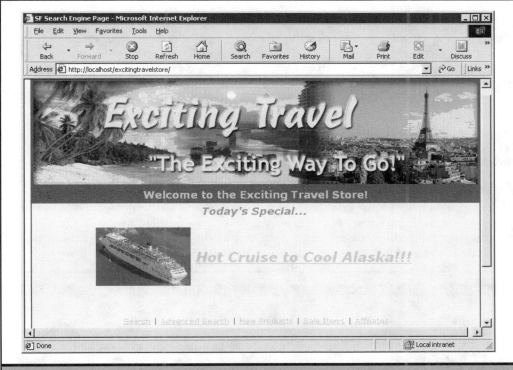

Figure 23-11.   *Exciting Travel Store Home page*

Getting the Shopping Cart

The shopping cart is the metaphor for the parts of the e-commerce program that keep track of who you are and what you have decided to purchase. Computers are very good at keeping track of items. That is not the tricky part of the online shopping cart. The tricky part is keeping track of who you are.

Keeping track of who you are involves the concept of *state*. Maintaining state is when a constant connection is maintained, like with a telephone. Even if there is no conversation, the line is still open and the connection is maintained. That doesn't happen with the Web and HTTP. When you click a link and your browser requests a page, a connection is made with the web server. The web server passes the page back to the browser, and the connection is broken. When you click another link that asks for a page from the same web server, the web server has no clue that it has ever sent you anything in the past.

When you are in a web store, and you put something in your shopping cart, how does the web server know it is still you when you go to another page and select something else? There are a lot of ways of doing that, but one of the most common ways is the use of cookies. A *cookie* is a file the e-commerce program puts on your local machine. When you are in the web store, it looks for the cookie to see who you are, so it knows which shopping cart is yours. Cookies are explained in more detail in Chapter 16.

There are other ways to do the same thing. Some systems embed a unique identifier into all the links and forms when it sends a page back to the browser. That way, when a page is requested from a link, or the contents of a form is sent, the identifier is returned to the e-commerce program and it knows who it came from and re-embeds that identifier into the page it sends back to the browser.

Viewing the Store's Wares

From the home page of our store, you click the link to the featured vacation or search functions and suddenly you are in the online store, shown in Figure 23-12. From here you can view the product displays. Only after you add a product to your basket are you actually given a shopping cart and the system starts tracking who you are.

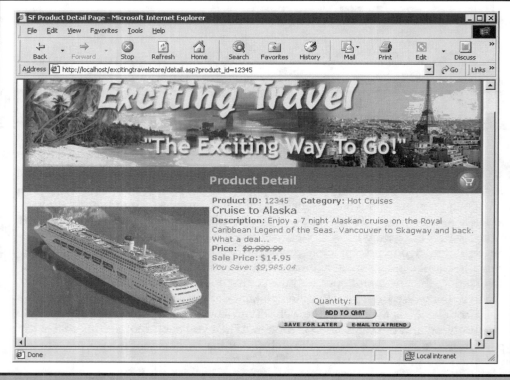

Figure 23-12.   *Product page*

Organizing and presenting the products are web design issues discussed in Chapter 1. You might want to review Chapter 1 and make sure all your products are easy to find, and that it's easy to move around in your site. It is at this point that your customer is being sold on the product, so do your best. On an actual travel site you would likely have the opportunity to view information about the cruise's ports of call, ship's accommodations, and a detail schedule of cruise dates.

Putting the Products into the Shopping Cart

Looking at our Hot Cruise to Cool Alaska example, you'll see that it contains a text box and an Add To Cart button, along with an automated bookmark and e-mail forwarding options. The customer simply puts a quantity in the text box and clicks Add To Cart to add the cruise to the shopping cart.

It is also important to be able to handle options. When selling clothing, you may want to let the customer specify size and color. Cruise fares are often priced differently, depending on when you choose to travel. Figure 23-13 shows our Alaskan cruise order page with different price options. It has a drop-down box that displays the options for the customers to choose from and add to the shopping cart.

Figure 23-13.   *Product Page with Options*

There's only one item on this page, unlike our form-based web store discussed earlier. We don't have to list all of our products on the same page because you can go to any page in the store and add items to the same shopping cart. In fact, if you don't want to purchase an item at that moment, but would like to leave it in your cart for later, you can save your cart.

At the top of every page in the Exciting Travel Store is a Cart image button that lets you look in the shopping cart. When you click Cart, you are shown a web page like Figure 23-14 with all the items you have selected.

Sometimes, in a physical store, you change your mind and take something out of the cart, putting it back on the shelf. Your e-commerce program should allow you to do the same thing. Not only does the shopping cart show you what you've selected, but it also allows you to change the quantity, delete items or save the cart for a later visit. The Recalculate Order button updates your cart after you have changed the quantity. Other e-commerce programs may have different ways of doing this, but they should allow the same basic functionality.

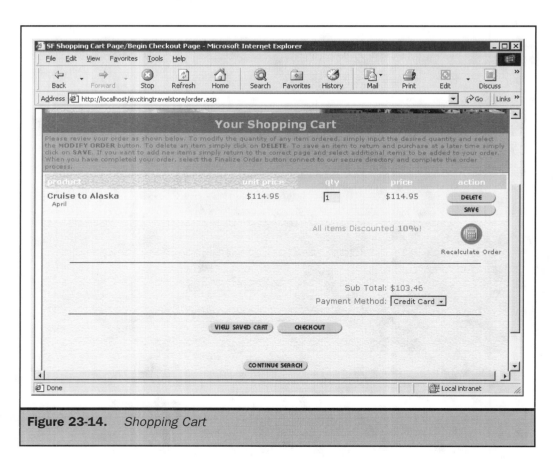

Figure 23-14.   *Shopping Cart*

Buying the Products at the Checkout Stand

When you have selected all the items and adjusted the quantities, it is time to go to the checkout stand. At the bottom of the cart page is a Checkout button. Selecting it opens a web page that requests your payment, billing, and shipping information, as shown in Figure 23-15.

Since we want to encourage repeat customers, we make it easy for them to check out by allowing them to log in, retrieving all of their billing and shipping information. New shoppers fill in this information once and never have to again, provided their information hasn't changed. As you scroll down the page, you'll have the same type of information for the customer to fill out as you did in our simple form-based store. There is a Verify button at the bottom that lets the customer review all of their information one final time before sending the order to the e-commerce program, which then responds with a web page confirming the order and then sends an e-mail to the store owner with the order information.

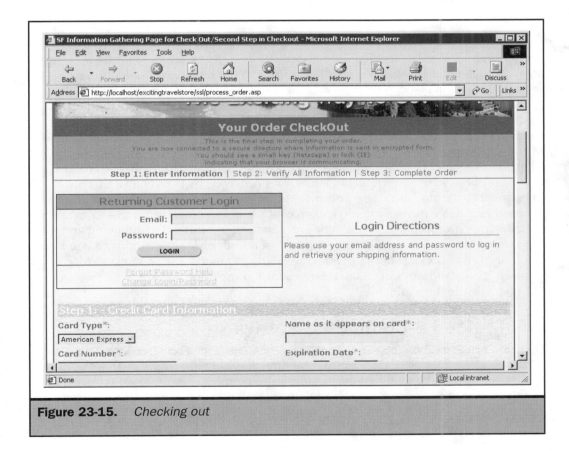

Figure 23-15.   *Checking out*

E-Commerce Packages

While it would be possible to program your own shopping cart system, there are a number of excellent, thoroughly tested systems available to you. The look and feel, as well as the functionality of the site are often determined by the e-commerce package you choose. Some of the packages offer a lot of flexibility in how you build your site, while others take you down a narrower path with fewer options for laying out and organizing your site. A lot depends on your budget and how much effort you want to put into your web store.

There are a number of companies offering e-commerce solutions that integrate with FrontPage. The following examples are only to illustrate what is available in each category. Each package offers different features, of which we only have space here to scratch the surface. The e-commerce field is changing fast, so it is important to do your research before committing to an e-commerce package. Check out the manufacturers' web sites for a complete list of features and, in many cases, comparisons with competing products.

Free FrontPage E-Commerce Software

There is free software available to run FrontPage web stores. FrontCart (**http://www.frontcart.com**) builds Perl script-driven carts. It integrates into FrontPage by adding a FrontCart menu. It features a dialog box-driven site setup and maintenance, but being a beta product, it still has a few rough edges, including lack of documentation. FrontCart will run on any Perl-enabled web server and requires little additional server setup. This product is not for the faint of heart, but looks very promising and is definitely worth watching.

AddSoft's StoreBot 2000 Standard (**http://www.addsoft.net/storebot**) is a FrontPage Web Component-driven product that generates ASP code by simply inserting a web component (bot) into your page. This means that once created, your pages can use standard FrontPage themes and navigation controls. StoreBot uses an Access database to store site configuration, as well as product and order information, allowing you to configure and maintain the site from any browser. Order processing must be handled manually as this package does not integrate with automated processing systems. StoreBot 2000 Standard is included on this book's companion CD in the \Programs\Addsoft\ folder.

Low-Mid Priced E-Commerce Software

There are places on the Web that let you build your site from a browser with online-only solutions. These sites do not integrate with FrontPage, but are pretty easy to set up. One of the larger ones is Yahoo!Store (**http://store.yahoo.com**). Yahoo!Store uses predefined templates that you choose. You upload your information and pictures, which are plugged into the templates, and you are online in minutes. Yahoo!Store provides online malls to which you can link your store. There are no web developers or WPPs to deal with. Pricing is by the month. A web store of up to 50 items is $100/month. A store with up to 1,000 items is $300/month. Check them carefully to see just what you can get.

LaGarde Inc. offers a full-featured, FrontPage integrated e-commerce system called StoreFront 5.0 (**http://www.storefront.net**). Our example Exciting Travel Store site was built using StoreFront 5.0 SE and I have to say this is my personal favorite. StoreFront integrates with FrontPage as an AddIn, inserting a new toolbar that provides access to their Web Creation Wizard, site configuration utility, reports site maintenance, and a well written online help system. Clicking the Web Creation Wizard, you answer a few questions and StoreFront creates an entire store, including Access database and DSN. Site customization and setup of the database-driven site is primarily handled through dialog boxes, although the full ASP code is available for editing as well. StoreFront fully integrates with a long list of payment processing systems or can be set to send orders via e-mail. StoreFront 5.0 SE is available at a cost of $279 and the higher end StoreFront 5.0 AE, which supports a SQL Server back end, is available for $679.00.

AddSoft offers Professional and Enterprise versions of its StoreBot 2000 package that work the same way as their Standard product, offering an increasing line of features. The professional package provides additional reporting and configuration options, and is probably the minimum version you'll want to use in this product. StoreBot 2000 Professional sells for $199. A full-featured trial version of StoreBot 2000 Professional is included on the companion CD in the \Programs\Addsoft\ folder. StoreBot 2000 Enterprise includes all the features found in the professional version and also includes support for a SQL Server back end. StoreBot 2000 Enterprise sells for $999, however, readers of this book will be offered a 25 percent discount if they enter the code OMFP10 when they order from the AddSoft site (**http://www.addsoft.net/ storebot**).

Rounding out the list is ComCity's SalesCart™ (**http://www.comcity.com**). Like the other low-medium priced packages, SalesCart comes in three flavors: SalesCart, SalesCart Pro, and SalesCart SQL. SalesCart offers a wizard-driven interface for creating completely ASP-driven stores and integrates with most payment processing systems and offers both customer and merchant e-mail verifications. SalesCart sells for $180 and the Pro version, which offers additional configuration and management features, sells for $399. SalesCart SQL supports a SQL Server order database back end and sells for $650. A 30-day trial version of SalesCart is also included on the companion CD in the \Programs\ComCity\ folder.

Higher-Priced E-Commerce Software

The mid-high end packages start at just under $5,000 and can support the most demanding web store. Microsoft's Commerce Server 2000 (**http://www.microsoft.com/**

commerceserver) and IBM's WebSphere Commerce Suite (**http://www.ibm.com/ software/webservers/commerce/**) are in this category. These provide robust capabilities for database integration and multi-server hosting, and can link to enterprise order and fulfillment systems. They require experienced programming support to use their functionality.

Marketing Your Web Store

Once your web store is up and running, you need to market it. The types of promotion mentioned in Chapter 25 are essential for your web store, but there is an additional type that many business sites are using. It is often the case that a business going onto the Web already has a customer base and a customer snail-mail list. Take advantage of this. Do a snail-mailing using a postcard inviting your customers to check out your new web site. On the front of the card have your business logo and your web site address. On the back of the postcard you can have any additional message. Check out your local printer to see if they do postcards. Five hundred four-color postcards should cost between $95 and $100 to print and another $150 for postage. This is an effective way to let people who are already familiar with your business find out about your web store.

Keep Them Coming Back

Once customers have come to your web store, you want them to return. A very effective way to remind customers that you are still there and let them know about ongoing sales and specials in your web store is through the e-mail list. Set up a form on your web store to gather e-mail addresses, then send periodic announcements of web store activities to keep your customers coming back.

Don't forget your e-mail manners. Let your customers know how you plan to use their address. You will be more successful in getting addresses if you tell them that the addresses are to be used only for your store's communications and will not be sold. You are also asking your customers to give you something of value: their address. Offer them something in return. It could be a simple gift or a discount on future purchases.

The E-Commerce Future

The e-commerce revolution is still just beginning. The large companies have already staked out their claims on the Internet, huffing and puffing about how great they are on every web page they turn out. Still, the Internet lets the small business be heard, too, and may benefit them the most. After all, the entry costs are very low to have access to a market the size of the Internet. No doubt, as more people turn to the Internet for their shopping, it will be the nimble who profit on the Web. Join the fun (and hopefully profit).

The Complete Reference

FrontPage 2002

Chapter 24

Setting Up an Intranet Web Site

Like the Internet with its World Wide Web, LANs and intranets are an exploding phenomenon. As this growth increases, many expect the use of intranets to exceed that of the Internet. The competitive success of a company often depends on internal communication and the ability to quickly share information—two major benefits of intranets. As with any new technology, however, there are and will be many opportunities to stumble. How a company implements an intranet may be even more important than the decision to do so.

This chapter will look at intranets—what they are, why they are needed, and how to set them up—both in terms of the hardware and software needed to make them function, and the content they should provide. You will see how intranets can help your business or organization, and how to create an intranet by using FrontPage. Finally, this chapter will discuss how to set up a SharePoint Team Web Site on an intranet.

What Is an Intranet?

An *intranet* site is a web site that is viewable only to those within an organization's network. Although based on the same protocols as the World Wide Web, an intranet is protected from the outside world either by not being connected to the outside or through a series of hardware and software obstacles known as a firewall.

Focusing on the World Wide Web and on connecting to the world over the Internet (a wide area network, or WAN), some people overlook the fact that the same protocols and technology can be used over a local area network (LAN). With a LAN, Windows 98, and the Microsoft Personal Web Server (PWS), or Windows 2000/XP Professional and Microsoft Internet Information Server (IIS), you can create your own web to link computers in an office. With Windows NT 4.0/2000/XP Server, IIS, and a LAN or private WAN, you can set up an intranet within a large office, between buildings, or even among company sites around the world.

An intranet may be as simple as two computers networked in a home office, or as complex as a network linking the offices of a global corporation. In the latter case, an intranet could link the computers within regional segments of the organization, while the Internet could be used to connect the various intranets—this is referred to as an *extranet*.

Networking computers to share information is, of course, not a new concept. Networked computers can be found in virtually every medium-to-large business and in many smaller ones. When networked, the resources on any computer can be shared by any other computer on the network. With Windows, the addition of a network interface card can turn any PC into either a network server or a workstation. For larger networks, specialized software, such as Novell's NetWare, or Windows NT/2000/XP Server, is required to effectively allow computers to share information.

Classical networking involves the sharing of files and some hardware devices such as printers. More recently it has included the use of e-mail. An intranet that uses the technology of the Web significantly enhances the functionality of a LAN or a corporate

WAN by adding the ability to read and interact with a large set of documents that are easily created and kept up to date. Almost as important, many of these documents already exist as word processing, spreadsheet, and database files. With FrontPage they can be easily converted to interactive web pages.

Tip   *Existing word processing, spreadsheet, and database files can be easily converted for use on an intranet by importing them into FrontPage. In the classic example of the company procedures manuals, the web's ready availability, search tools, and easy maintenance and updating are powerful incentives to having an intranet.*

As was explained in Chapter 1, the Internet and the World Wide Web are built upon three software technologies:

- **TCP/IP** (Transmission Control Protocol/Internet Protocol), which is the underlying technology of the Internet for the exchange of information and the identification of parts of the network

- **HTTP** (Hypertext Transfer Protocol), which handles the actual transmission of web documents

- **HTML** (Hypertext Markup Language), which is the programming language of the Web

These same technologies are used to implement an intranet, and they must be added to the networking software that is already in place. HTTP and HTML are used only by the web server and the browser, and do not affect the classical networking software. TCP/IP, on the other hand, directly competes with classical networking protocols such as IPX/SPX or NetBEUI on Intel-based computers. TCP/IP can be used instead of or in addition to other protocols, and setting it up can be a headache. The objective, of course, is to have the protocols operate in harmony to perform all of the necessary networking functions.

One of the problem areas with classical networking was linking different types of computers, such as PCs, Macintoshes, Sun, and various UNIX- and Linux-based computers. Each operating system (or platform) requires its own specialized software, which isn't always compatible between systems. An intranet built with TCP/IP, HTTP, and HTML doesn't have the compatibility problems of other networking systems. The early support of the U.S. government ensured the widespread adoption of TCP/IP as a network protocol, and HTTP servers and HTML browsers are available for virtually every platform. For organizations that have acquired a variety of computer hardware, creating an intranet is not difficult. While a simple file-sharing network allows files to be accessed between computers, the three Internet technologies allow much greater interactivity by use of hypertext links, searches, forms, and discussion boards. Some of these features are available with products such as NetWare, but at greater cost and complexity, and without the hardware flexibility. A FrontPage-created intranet, especially with SharePoint, presents a much superior solution for sharing and collaboration within an organization.

 *For a case study of an intranet that uses the Microsoft's Office family, visit the Microsoft Office web discussion of how the Providence Health System used an intranet at **http://www.microsoft.com/frontpage/studies/phs.htm**.*

Why Have an Intranet?

The reasons for having an intranet are as varied as the organizations creating it, but the common purposes are to communicate among the members of the organization and to involve them in improving their effectiveness and collaboration. An intranet that is carefully planned and implemented can significantly improve overall productivity in the organization, and reduce costs involved with communication, such as costs for phone calls, faxes, and paper, not to mention the costs of missed opportunities, missed meetings, or misunderstandings.

Communication

The intranet can replace newsletters, reports, lists of job openings, manuals, procedures, employee guidelines, meeting schedules, details of benefit plans, and lunch menus. Almost anything that is written or graphic and has an audience of more than a few people is a candidate for the intranet. The benefits of using the intranet are substantial:

- An intranet document can be put up when convenient for the creator, and read when convenient for the reader.

- Readers can keep and conveniently file an intranet document, or they can just read it and discard it, knowing the source document will be there for some time.

- The documents can be simple text or full multimedia. By including multimedia, you can make documents more inviting to open and read.

- The communication can be one-way, from the creator to the reader, or it can include forms and discussion boards to let the reader communicate back to the creator or to other fellow readers.

- The documents can be easily indexed and searched, making the information they contain easier to find and use.

- The cost of printing, distributing, and maintaining manuals, procedures, and guidelines is reduced, as are some fax and delivery expenses.

- Information can be shared over many different computers and workstations, not just PCs. The Internet protocols and technology have been implemented on most computers, giving them the ability to attach to an intranet.

One of the biggest benefits, though, and the second major reason for using an intranet, is that it facilitates the involvement of more members of the organization in the organization's activities. The reasoning is that if you make it easier to locate, read, excerpt, file, and dispose of documents, more people will use them and acquire the knowledge they contain. If you make it easier to comment on and participate in the creation of something that can be put on an intranet, more people will. If you provide easy access and easy use of indexing and search capabilities, end users will directly seek more archival information. If you add multimedia and color graphics and thereby make a document more fun and interesting, more people will read it. If you allow many different types of computers and workstations to connect to an intranet, more people will be able to participate.

Simply stated, an intranet greatly facilitates the dissemination of information within an organization, as well as the communication and involvement of its members.

Productivity

An intranet can greatly increase productivity. When critical documents are located in a central place, people can find them easily. Historically, many hours are lost in just trying to locate information within a company. Often one of the first applications built for intranets is a central repository of forms, in electronic format, so that users can find the form they need quickly, and print it at their convenience.

Cost Reduction

Several significant cost reduction studies have been performed on organizations using intranets. With intranets, you can easily track the change in copy and fax paper used per month and in telephone costs. If you communicate to users that the intranet can be used in place of the telephone (for discussion or collaborative-based communication) and in place of the printer (for on-demand information such as employee phone lists, chart of accounts information, and forms), you can begin to monitor other uses of communication within the company.

Employee Involvement

But the most important reason to have an intranet is that it enables greater employee involvement in the company. If the intranet is perceived as a team effort, and everyone is given the chance to participate, they will use it often and take pride in its growth.

What Do You Put on an Intranet?

The decision regarding what to put on an intranet is one of the most difficult; much depends on the character and philosophy of the organization. How open does your organization want to be, and how much security do you need? What does the company want to do with their intranet? Disseminating relatively simple information, such as newsletters, administrative manuals and procedures, and lunch menus, is not a problem; doing so with financial information, marketing reports, and corporate plans may well be more difficult.

Conducting a Needs Analysis

A *needs analysis* is by definition an analysis of what users need on the intranet in order to meet the intranet's objectives. If those objectives are to increase communication across the company and boost productivity, an analysis of how that might be accomplished must take place. There are many strategies you can take, depending on the overall objective of your company. First, of course, you must talk with the members of your organization who will authorize your intranet project.

Before you begin collecting information, a policy needs to be set on how open the company wants to be with its employees. This broad policy then needs to be translated into specific examples of documents in each of the major areas of the company (marketing, production, finance, and so on) that are allowed on the intranet and those that are not. It is very easy to gloss over this issue in the crush of all the other issues, but unless this is clearly thought through and then delineated, problems can occur.

Once the policy is established, specific documents and their priority have to be identified. This is best done by a committee of users and providers. A *user* is, obviously, a person or persons who will be using the intranet. The *providers* are the people who will be providing the content of the intranet. In an intranet scenario, the providers can be either a small group set up for this purpose or a number of independent people, depending on the kind of intranet structure you are building. There are two kinds of intranet structures: a decentralized model and a centralized model, both of which are discussed in the next section.

The users can set out their needs and desires, and the providers can respond with their ability and willingness to satisfy the requests. Either group alone is liable to create an intranet that is not as effective as it might be.

Questions to Be Answered

With the committee constituted, it should look at all the documents the company produces that fit within the policy guidelines. For each document, the following questions should be answered:

- How wide an audience does it have?
- How often is it produced, and is that schedule supportable on the intranet?
- Do the layout and graphics lend themselves to the document being easily placed on the intranet?
- Does the addition of intranet features such as searching, forms, and hyperlinks make it a particularly attractive candidate?

- Are there any pressing needs to get the document up on the intranet?
- Is the document going to be revised soon?

Based on the answers to these questions, a prioritized list of documents to go on the intranet should be drawn up, and the documents created and placed on the intranet in their designated order. The review process should be repeated periodically to confirm that the documents on the intranet should stay there and to determine what new documents should be added.

Types of Intranets

There are both decentralized and centralized intranets, and they each have pros and cons that you should consider.

Decentralized Intranets

An intranet is *decentralized* when more than one group within an organization creates and services a web site. Very large corporations tend to have decentralized intranets, especially if the corporation does not have a department that is responsible for organizing and maintaining an intranet. There are many good reasons for having a decentralized intranet:

- It allows a "grass-roots" approach to intranet development, so departments and groups have control over what content they want to put up in their area.
- Since many groups are involved in the development of their area of the intranet, they have bought in to it and are more inclined to use the entire intranet.
- The content of the intranet tends to change more quickly because more groups are involved with its upkeep.

However, there are some cons in having a decentralized intranet—the most significant of which are the strengths of a centralized intranet: consistent design, consistent frequency of update, and consistent quality of information. There is also the possibility that there may be several dispersed intranet servers (one per department, for example), and these servers will eventually need maintenance. This could put an extra load on the Information Services (IS) department if they are expected to maintain these servers.

Centralized Intranets

A *centralized* intranet is an intranet that has one central group (or person) who is responsible for developing the structure (both technical and informational) and maintaining the intranet. The benefits of having a centralized intranet are:

- A consistent interface design, which helps usability and navigability

- A consistent quality of information and frequency of updating that information
- Easier maintenance from a technical perspective, because usually there is only one server or server farm

However, there are also some cons to having a centralized intranet:

- Usage levels can be low due to lack of involvement in the development process
- Site content can get out of date more easily if one group is trying to keep many different groups' content up to date
- Growth of the intranet can be slow

Whichever model you choose, it is important to consider the pros and cons of your decision and strategize ways to maximize the pros and minimize the cons. One very important task that can make or break the success of an intranet is getting buy-in from end users.

Getting Buy-In from Users

In both types of intranets, probably the most important thing you can do before you begin building or even planning your intranet is to get buy-in from your end users. *Buy-in* is the understanding from the people you want to use the intranet of how important the intranet will be for them. Depending on who your end users are, you may need to develop a campaign for the intranet, promoting its virtues as a method of communication that your organization will understand and appreciate. It is very important that your end users are aware of the project, that they are asked to participate in its development, and that they are adequately trained to use it.

Building Your Infrastructure

This section broadly discusses building an intranet—covering the technical aspects of setting up your network infrastructure and providing appropriate security.

Setting Up and Configuring Your Environment

The first requirement in setting up your intranet environment is that you have a local area network (LAN) that supports the TCP/IP protocol. One highly recommended source of information on setting up LANs and networking is Tom Sheldon's *McGraw-Hill's Encyclopedia of Networking & Telecommunications* (published by Osborne/McGraw-Hill, 2001).

Once your LAN is functioning, you can use FrontPage as the basis for creating an intranet as small as two computers in the same office, or one that links many computers in a number of remote locations. The limits on growth for your intranet will be determined by the number of users and the amount of traffic on the LAN. For several computers in an office, you do not need a dedicated server. In other words, a Windows 98 or Windows 2000 or XP Professional computer running PWS or IIS can also be used for other tasks. As the number of users and the network traffic grow, a computer will need to be dedicated to running IIS.

For larger intranets, you should consider using a dedicated server running Windows NT, 2000, or XP and IIS as your HTTP server software. IIS is more powerful than PWS and is an integral part of Windows NT, 2000, or XP Server. FrontPage and the IIS FrontPage Server Extensions are completely compatible with the Windows Server versions.

Installing TCP/IP on Your Network

The first step in building an intranet on your local area network is to install the TCP/IP protocol if it is not already used. If you have a connection to the Internet, through either a dial-up or network connection, TCP/IP will already be installed and configured on your computer. If you need to install TCP/IP, follow these steps:

Note   *If you are using a dial-up connection for the Internet, you may still need to install TCP/IP for your LAN, so you should go through the next set of steps just to check it out.*

1. Open the Start menu and choose Settings | Control Panel in Windows 98, Me, and 2000 or Start | Control Panel in Windows XP.

2. When the Control Panel opens, double-click Network in Windows 98 and Me, or double click Network and Dial-up Connections in Windows 2000 or just Network Connections in Windows XP. In Windows 2000 and XP, you then need to double-click Local Area Connection and click Properties.

3. In Windows 98 and ME the Network dialog box will open; select the Configuration tab if it's not already selected. In Windows 2000 and XP, the Local Area Connection Properties dialog box will open; select the General tab if it isn't already selected. Your Network or Local Area Connection Properties dialog box should appear, similar to Figure 24-1.

   Figure 24-1 shows the TCP/IP protocol being used by the network interface card (NIC) for my LAN connection. If some other protocol such as NetBEUI (NetBIOS Enhanced User Interface) or IPX/SPX (Internetwork Packet Exchange/Sequenced Packet Exchange) were bound to the NIC, then TCP/IP would have to be added. Multiple protocols can be bound to these cards, so TCP/IP can be added to the network interface card without removing any existing protocols.

4. Click Add in Windows 98 and Me, or click Install in Windows 2000 and XP. In the Select Network Component Type dialog box, select Protocol and click Add.

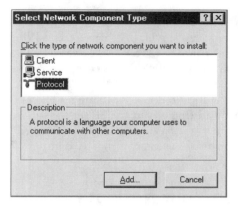

5. In the Select Network Protocol dialog box, in Windows 98 and Me select Microsoft from the Manufacturers list box, then select TCP/IP from the Network Protocols list box. In Windows 2000 and XP, select Internet Protocol (TCP/IP) from the Network Protocol list. In either case, click OK.

In a moment the Network or Local Area Connection Properties dialog box will be redisplayed, showing that the TCP/IP protocol has been installed.

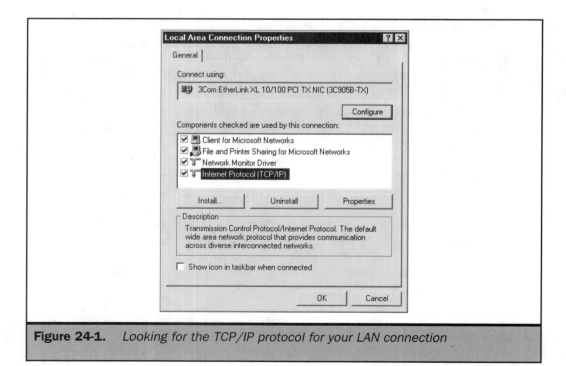

Figure 24-1. *Looking for the TCP/IP protocol for your LAN connection*

Configuring TCP/IP

If you are just installing TCP/IP you need to configure the protocol for the device it is being used with. For an intranet, the device is your network interface card. Configure your network card with these instructions:

1. In the Network or Local Area Connection Properties dialog box, select the TCP/IP component for your network card and click Properties. Your TCP/IP Properties dialog box will open, as shown in Figure 24-2 for Windows 2000 and XP.

2. In the TCP/IP Properties dialog box, select the IP Address or General tab if it's not already selected.

The IP (Internet Protocol) address is a group of four numbers that uniquely identify your computer on a TCP/IP network. For a dial-up connection to the Internet, your IP address will usually be assigned automatically by the server, as might be the case with large intranets using dedicated web servers. For small intranets using the PWS, you need to specify an IP address. You should consult your network administrator to learn what IP address you should use. However, on a small TCP/IP network, you can basically make up your own number—

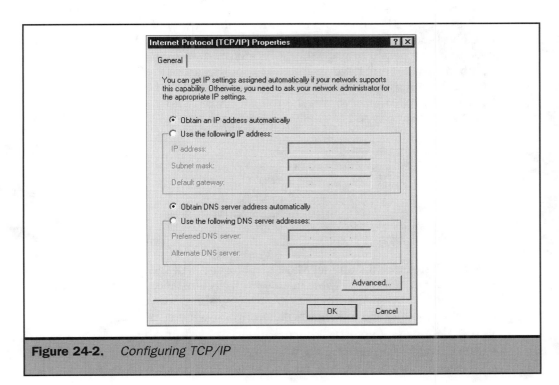

Figure 24-2.   *Configuring TCP/IP*

10.0.0.1, for example. You could then increment the number for each computer—10.0.0.2 for the next machine, and so on. As long as your computer does not try to use your IP addresses on the Internet (which it won't, if you use the dial-up adapter to connect to the Internet), you will not have a problem. The IP addresses you use for your network card will not affect your settings for your dial-up adapter.

An IP address is like a phone number. If you set up your own small phone system, you can use any phone numbers you want. But if you then connect your phone system to the outside world, you may have to use the phone numbers assigned by the outside authority. (Three series of numbers, though, 10.0.0.0 through 10.255.255.255, 172.16.0.0 through 172.31.255.255, and 192.168.0.1 through 192.168.255.255, have been set aside and are not currently assigned as Internet addresses. These are therefore available for you to use internally in your organization.)

Note   *Do not use an IP address beginning with 127 (for example, 127.0.0.1), as this is reserved as a localhost, or loopback, address.*

3. If your server does not automatically supply an IP address, click Specify An IP Address or Use The Following IP Address, click the left of the IP Address text box, and type your IP address. If any number is fewer than three digits, you'll need to type a period or press the RIGHT ARROW to move to the next block of numbers. If you don't have an assigned IP address, use the 10.0.0.*n* (*n* is a number between 1 and 255) set of numbers with 10.0.0.1 being the first. (Type **10**, press the RIGHT ARROW, type **0**, press the RIGHT ARROW, type **0**, press the RIGHT ARROW, and type **1** to get the address shown next.)

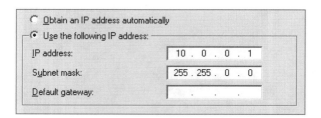

4. Click the left end of the Subnet Mask text box and type **2552550.0**. This is the default subnet mask, applicable in almost all circumstances; in most instances it is automatically entered for you. We're suggesting that you enter it here to cover the few instances where it will hang you up if it is missing.

5. In Windows 98 and Me, select the Bindings tab. Client For Microsoft Networks and File And Printer Sharing For Microsoft Networks should both be selected. Click them if they are not selected, and in any case click OK twice.

6. In Windows 2000 and XP, click OK to return to the Local Area Connection Properties dialog box. Client For Microsoft Networks and File And Printer Sharing For Microsoft Networks should both be selected. Click them if they are not selected.

7. Click OK or Close as necessary to close all open dialog boxes, then click Close to shut any open windows.

After changing your network settings, you may have to restart your computer for the changes to take effect. Make sure you save any open documents before restarting.

For TCP/IP on your dial-up adapter, you do not want to have File And Printer Sharing selected. This is for security. If you are connected to the Internet by use of your dial-up connection, it is possible (though unlikely) for others on the Internet to access your shared resources over the TCP/IP connection. You can still share resources with others on your network by using File And Printer Sharing on your LAN adapter.

Using Your FrontPage-Created Intranet

Once TCP/IP is configured properly on your network, accessing your FrontPage-created webs from any computer on the network is a simple process. First make sure IIS or PWS is running on the computer that will be the server. Then start your web browser on one of the other computers on the network. To access a web, use the URL http://*computername/webname* where *computername* is the computer's name running the server, and *webname* is the name of the web you want to open.

For example, I have two networked computers named "Marty" and "Server1." Marty runs Windows Me, Server1 runs Windows 2000 Server with IIS 5.0. The Exciting Travel web is on Server1. Here are the steps I went through to open the Exciting Travel web across my intranet on Marty:

1. Made sure to set up the TCP/IP protocol on both computers, as described earlier.

2. Restarted both computers.

3. Made sure IIS was running on the server. (This is done in different ways dependent on the operating system running on the server.)

If you do not see either PWS on Windows 98 or IIS on Windows NT, 2000, or XP, see Appendix A for instructions on installing one of them.

a) In Windows 98 open the Start menu, choose Programs | Internet Explorer | Personal Web Server | Personal Web Manager in Windows 98 original version or Programs | Accessories | Internet Tools | Personal Web Server | Personal Web Manager in Windows 98 SE, and then click Start if it is available. If it only says Stop, PWS is already running.

b) Windows Me does not have a web server associated with it, but if you have a copy of Windows 98 or Windows 98 SE, you can successfully install PWS from the Windows 98 disk (original or SE) on Windows Me by using the instructions in Appendix A for installing on Windows 98.

c) In Windows 2000 and XP Professional, open the Start menu, choose Settings | Control Panel, double-click Administrative Tools, double-click Computer Management, open Services And Applications, and click Internet Information Services. In the right pane of the second column, State, it should say "Running" for all services. If not, right-click Internet Information Services in the left pane and select Start.

d) In Windows 2000 and XP Server, open the Start menu, choose Programs | Administrative Tools | Computer Management, open Services And Applications, and click Internet Information Services. In the right pane of the second column, State, it should say "Running" for all services, as you can see in Figure 24-3. If not, right-click Internet Information Services in the left pane and select Start.

4. Start a browser on Marty, enter the address **http://server1/excitingtravel/**, and press ENTER. The Exciting Travel home page that was created earlier in this book appears as shown in Figure 24-4.

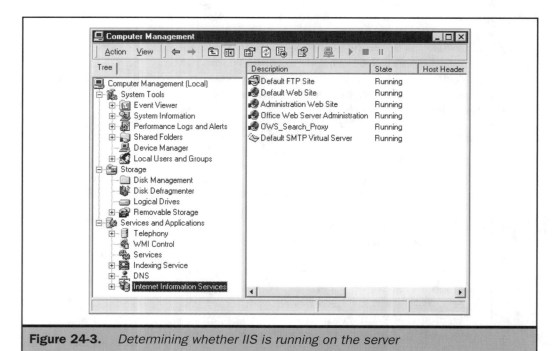

Figure 24-3. *Determining whether IIS is running on the server*

If your intranet doesn't immediately come up the first time you try, take heart; mine didn't either. Here is a list of troubleshooting questions:

■ Does your network otherwise function normally between the two computers you are trying to use with an intranet? If not, you must solve your networking problems before trying to use an intranet. See your network administrator or other technical network reference.

■ Has TCP/IP been successfully installed for your LAN adapter (not just to your dial-up adapter)? On *both* machines? Reopen your Network or Network And Dial-Up Connections control panel to check this.

■ Did you restart both computers after installing TCP/IP?

■ Is either PWS or IIS started and running on the computer where the webs are located? When you address this machine from the second machine, your hard disk light will blink.

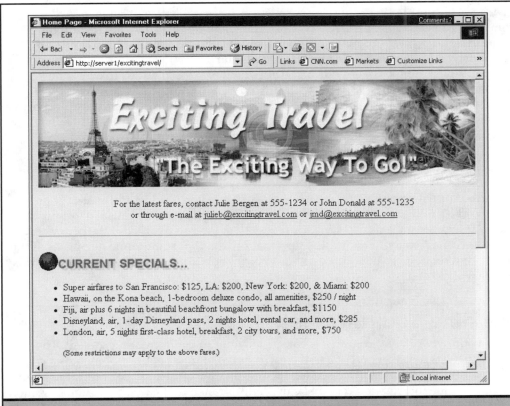

Figure 24-4. *Exciting Travel web received over an intranet*

- Have you entered the correct server name and web name in your browser? You can determine the server name and how well your TCP/IP network is operating by running the Network Test in the About Microsoft FrontPage dialog box; see Appendix A.

- Does the web you are trying to open have a Default.htm file? If not, you must specify the filename to open as well as the server and web name. For example, http://servername/webname/ will open if there is a Default.htm file. If not, you must enter http://servername/webname/filename.htm.

If you take a couple of minutes to make sure that each of the preceding questions is answered in the affirmative, your intranet will almost surely work. Errors I have made include forgetting to restart one of the computers and not spelling the web name correctly.

Security and Firewalls

Anytime you share resources over a network, the possibility exists that someone may access your files without your permission. The risk is greater when one or more computers on an intranet are also connected to the Internet. There are several things you can do to protect yourself and your files. One of the simplest, as mentioned previously, is to disable file and printer sharing for TCP/IP on your dial-up adapter. You can still share files over your LAN, but you have closed access to everyone on the Internet coming in through TCP/IP and your dial-up adapter.

Greater security can be achieved through the use of a firewall and possibly a proxy server, as was discussed in Chapter 22. A firewall is a computer that controls the flow of data between an intranet and the Internet by packet filtering.

Packet filtering passes or rejects IP packets based on the IP address that sent the packet. This allows you to configure your firewall to allow access from specific computers outside your intranet that you trust. This method isn't as secure as a proxy server because it's possible for someone to duplicate a trusted IP address.

Use of a proxy server means that every request and response must be examined by the proxy server. This can slow the response of your network, but the proxy server can also cache frequently requested information, thus speeding some responses. If the source of a request is a computer without permission to access your intranet, the proxy server will reject it.

Building Your Intranet

Once your network environment is complete, you can begin creating content. The needs analysis that you perform in the early stages of intranet development is a critical piece of information now. This section focuses on the "front end" of your intranet: the design and the information that make up your intranet. In the first topic in this section, you will get an overview of how to quickly put up documents on your intranet. Read this first if you are raring to go. Following this overview are more in-depth discussions of how FrontPage can help you create your intranet.

Overview

In Chapter 11, you read about importing existing, or legacy, files into FrontPage to create webs both on the Internet and on your intranet with examples of word processing, spreadsheet, and presentation files being used. In Chapter 19, you saw how to access database files in a FrontPage-created web. With the techniques in these chapters, just about all corporate information can be accessed through an intranet. Once you have imported the raw material from existing files, you can add any of the interactive features available with FrontPage. Among these are

- **Table of Contents Component** to quickly build an index of the material that is brought in
- **Web Search Component** to add the capability to search the material
- **Shared Borders** to place headers and footers on each page with link bars, time stamps, and mailto addresses
- **Forms** to solicit responses from the reader
- **Discussion web** associated with the legacy-derived web to promote a discussion about the contents of the legacy material
- **Interactive Spreadsheets and Charts** to allow users to interactively work with data that has been placed on the intranet

Most legacy material does not contain a lot of graphics or multimedia. Consider augmenting your legacy-derived webs with additional graphics and multimedia to make them more interesting to read and/or use.

One obvious question is: All the components, graphics, and multimedia are great, but I don't have time for all that. Can I quickly put my legacy documents on the company intranet and have them usable? The answer is yes—most definitely yes—if they have a consistently applied style in the documents. Look at the few steps it takes to put a single directory of titles on a web, and the neat results:

1. Load FrontPage, click New | Web. In the Web Site Template dialog box, click Import Web Wizard, name the folder **ImportTest**, and click OK. The Import Web Wizard dialog box will open.

2. Click From A Source Directory Of Files On A Local Computer Or Network. Browse your hard drive or network, and select the source directory containing the files you want to import. Click Include Subfolders if applicable, and click Next. (Make sure some Word files are in there!) Select the files in the directory that you *don't* want, and click Exclude (see next illustration). Click Next and then Finish. Your web is created!

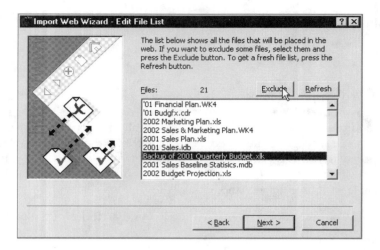

3. Without doing further work in FrontPage, close it, open your browser, type **//servername/ImportTest/**, and you should get a list of files associated with the web. Since we didn't specify a Default.htm file, a directory listing is displayed if "Directory Browsing Allowed" is turned on for the Default Web Site. (In Windows 2000 or XP Server, open Start, choose Programs | Administrative Tools | Internet Services Manager, open your local server, right-click Default Web Site, choose Properties, open the Home Directory tab, and click Directory Browsing in the middle left of the dialog box. Close both the dialog box and the Internet Information Services window. If one or more Inheritance Override dialog boxes appear, click OK to close them. In Windows 2000 or XP Professional, you need to open Start and choose Settings | Control Panel | Administrative Tools | Internet Services Manager. In the Windows 98 original version, open the Start menu, choose Programs | Internet Explorer | Personal Web Server | Personal Web Manager, or in Windows 98 SE, Programs | Accessories | Internet Tools | Personal Web Server | Personal Web Manager, click Advanced, and then Allow Directory Browsing.)

4. Click a Word document, the File Download dialog box opens, click Open From Source and OK, and voilà! your document appears as shown in Figure 24-5. (If your document has headings formatted as a headings style and you don't have the index on the side, open the View menu and choose Document Map if you are using Microsoft Word and Internet Explorer.)

If you have headings formatted as such, all of your headings are automatically made into a table of contents with hyperlinks to the actual headings in the document, so you have a built-in navigation system without doing anything. You can, of course, do much more to improve this document in FrontPage, but the point is that almost without doing anything, you have a web complete with navigation around a document.

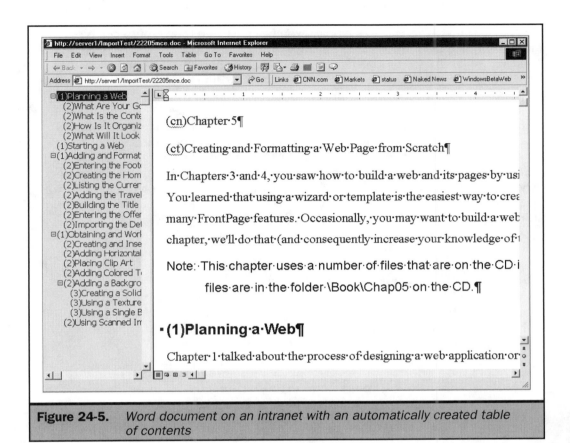

Figure 24-5.   *Word document on an intranet with an automatically created table of contents*

Creating an Intranet

With the needs analysis and other information collected in the planning stage of your intranet project, you can begin the process of creating an intranet. The first step of this is to organize the information you want to provide on your intranet. You can then bring the tools in FrontPage—including wizards, templates, and themes—to bear on your creation task.

Organizing Information

Earlier in the chapter, you read how planning and collecting information and conducting a needs analysis was critical to the success of your intranet. When you have completed assessing what the end users need to have on the intranet in order to meet its overall objective, and you have collected the necessary documents and other media, then you are ready to begin organizing this information.

Looking at what you have assembled, you will see that certain groups need certain information, and there is some information that all groups need—such as access to Human Resources information, the cafeteria menu, and how much vacation time they have left. Look for information people will want to have immediately at their fingertips. Take a large piece of poster board or butcher paper and write the word "Home" on it. This is your intranet home page, also known as the top-level page. What would people want to see at this level? Try to mimic the terms and structures that are in place and working within your organization—for example, if your Library, Office Supplies, and Imaging departments are known as Resource Services within your organization, then you will want to logically group these together under that same heading on your intranet. When you have arrived at a structure you think will work, go back to your committee and present your ideas. Be prepared to do this at least twice before you hit upon a structure that makes sense to the majority of your end users.

Once you have a structure that is approved by your committee of users, you are ready to begin physically building your intranet.

Using Wizards to Create an Intranet

As you saw in Chapter 3, FrontPage comes with wizards that walk you through the process of creating certain kinds of web sites, as well as wizards that help you import web sites from other locations. There are two wizards that are especially relevant to intranet development: the Import Web Wizard and the Discussion Web Wizard.

The Import Web Wizard   If any piece of your intranet already exists on any computer on your network, you can import this set of folders by using the Import Web Wizard. You can also import folders from your own hard drive, or from any computer on your LAN. You saw the process for doing this in the "Overview" section earlier in this chapter.

The Discussion Web Wizard   Another wizard that can be used in an intranet is the Discussion Web Wizard. The Discussion Web Wizard creates a FrontPage web that enables bulletin-board communication among users. Users submit topics by entering text in a form, they can search previous messages using a search form, and they access articles using a table of contents. See Chapter 3 for a thorough look at the Discussion web.

Using the Microsoft Intranet Template

Microsoft has provided a web site exclusively for intranet building. You can visit the Microsoft TechNet Intranet site at **http://www.microsoft.com/technet/intranet/** (see Figure 24-6).

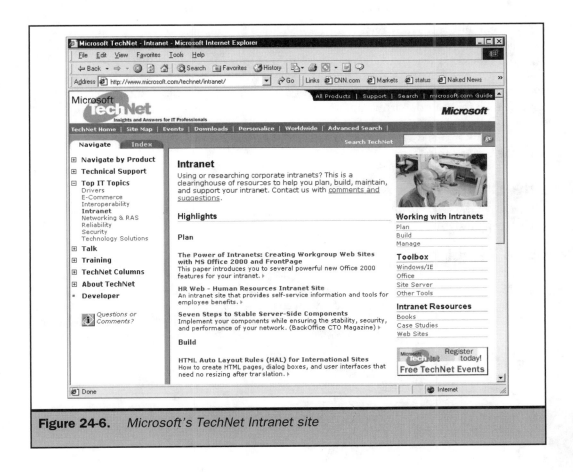

Figure 24-6.   *Microsoft's TechNet Intranet site*

Using Themes

Themes are a feature of FrontPage that can be particularly useful when you're creating an intranet—for a number of reasons:

■ Themes provide consistent graphical interfaces throughout the site.

■ Themes can be easily changed, so if you use one theme and later decide you don't like it, you can easily switch to another theme and change all of the parts of a web that use the theme.

■ The themes that come with FrontPage are well designed and provide a built-in hierarchy to aid in creating graphical user interfaces that work.

You can either initially create your web with a theme, or add it after you have created a new web by clicking Theme on the Format menu. Chapter 3 shows how to use themes and Chapter 10 shows how to customize them.

One obvious use of themes within an intranet would be to differentiate between departments. If each individual department did not have a graphic designer to create a unique look for their department, they could use themes as a quick way to get an interface up. Remember, though, to include a link back to the home page of the intranet—ideally a graphical link that is used throughout the site—so that users begin to associate that image with the home page.

Adding Content to Your Intranet

There are many ways to add content to a FrontPage web. This section discusses using page templates, dragging Office documents, and importing text into your FrontPage web.

Page Templates

Page templates are part of FrontPage's stock collection of content. The kinds of templates that are available to you are either content templates or formatting templates. Page templates are excellent starting points for creating intranet web pages. *Formatting* page templates enable you to easily create pages with complex layouts. *Content* templates (such as a bibliography or meeting agenda template) help you create common types of web pages often found on an intranet web site.

Examples of the content templates included with FrontPage are:

- Bibliography
- Confirmation Form
- Feedback Form
- Frequently Asked Questions
- Guest Book
- Photo Gallery
- Search Page

Some examples of formatting templates are:

- Narrow left-aligned body
- One centered column
- One column with contents sidebar
- One column with two sidebars
- Three-column body
- Two columns with contents

There are many other formatting templates for you to choose from. To access these page templates, open Page view, open the File menu, choose New | Page Or Web, and click Page Templates in the task bar. You will see a dialog box listing all the templates from which to choose, as shown in Figure 24-7.

To read more about page templates, see Chapter 4.

Dragging and Dropping Office Documents

Much of the content you will want to have on your intranet site will be in the form of Office documents. Most of the critical documents produced in an organization are created in either Word or Excel, and in some cases, it's ideal to keep these documents in their native form. For example, an Excel spreadsheet produced by the Finance department that includes interactive pivot tables might be of greater value in its native file format than if it was converted into HTML, because HTML is static. If you are using Internet Explorer as your intranet browser, you will want to take advantage of its ability to display Office documents over an intranet or Internet site in their native formats. Also with FrontPage, you can have the best of both a static HTML document and a fully interactive Excel spreadsheet and not run the risk of having your original spreadsheet changed by using the FrontPage Spreadsheet, PivotTable, or Chart components in an HTML page.

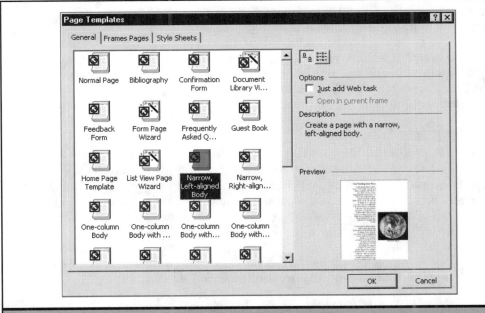

Figure 24-7.   *FrontPage's page templates*

When you are creating your intranet, you will have many documents you want to get into your FrontPage web quickly, and with FrontPage you can easily drag and drop files and folders from your hard drive or network directly into your FrontPage window. See Chapter 11 for more information on importing files.

The first time you import a particular file format, whether from Word, Excel, or some other program, you may be told that the file conversion program will need to be installed. If so, your Office or FrontPage CD must be inserted in its drive, then you click Yes to install the program.

You can select a formatting page template and drag text and graphic content to it by opening the page template in FrontPage and dragging the content files from the Windows Explorer.

Managing Content on Your Intranet

Managing an intranet is a challenging task. To manage a large site effectively, you need to have flexible tools that integrate with both your production process and your system infrastructure. This is where FrontPage really shines as a site management tool. FrontPage provides tools that check the quality of your site, allow you to perform sitewide managerial tasks, and provide flexibility in working with both large and small intranets. The tasks involved with managing an intranet site include link verification, task management, sitewide spelling, and when necessary, some level of overall site design and quality assurance.

If you have created subwebs for your departments or groups, then someone will need to become "webmaster" to each of these subwebs. These people will be responsible for managing the content of their respective webs. Web administrators can use FrontPage's management tools to perform management tasks on their web. The best place to start is in Reports view.

Using Reports View

FrontPage's Reports view, shown in Figure 24-8, provides the means to look at your web site and determine if you have problems, or if something needs attention. Reports view starts with a Site Summary, which gives you an overview of your site, including the number and size of your files, the pages that may be slow in loading, broken hyperlinks, and component errors among a number of other statistics and facts.

As a default, files in hidden folders, such as the _Private folder, are not included in the file counts. You can change that by opening the Tools menu, choosing Web Settings, Advanced tab, and clicking Show Hidden Files And Folders.

If you click many of the summary lines in the Site Summary, the lines will be expanded into full reports showing the individual web pages that have a certain

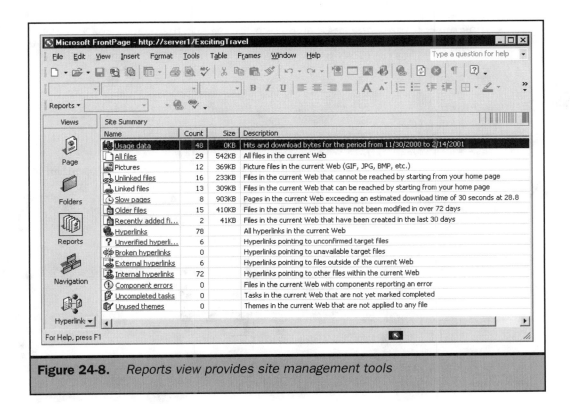

Figure 24-8.   *Reports view provides site management tools*

characteristic. In some cases, you can also set (in the Reporting toolbar) the criteria for determining if a page fits into a particular category. For example, for slow pages you can set the number of seconds that defines the threshold of "slow," like this:

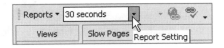

When you open a detail report, you can return to the Site Summary by selecting it in the Reports list on the left of the Reporting toolbar, or by opening the View menu and choosing Reports | Site Summary. Take time familiarizing yourself with the detail reports in Reports view. They can provide a lot of valuable information with which to manage a site.

Task Management

One of the most powerful tools in FrontPage for managing a site is the Task Manager. This allows you to establish tasks for creating and maintaining the site, attach those tasks to particular pages, assign the task to individuals, and then track the status of the tasks. Starting the task opens the associated page, and saving the page opens a dialog box asking if you want to change the task status. See how this is done with the following steps:

To have an associated task, you need to have a page opened when you create the task. If you create a task without a page open, you can still do it, but it won't be associated with a page.

1. To add a new task to the Tasks list, open the Edit menu, possibly extend the menu, and choose Tasks | Add Task. The New Task dialog box will open. Fill out the dialog box and click OK.

2. To begin working on a task, open Tasks view, right-click the task, and choose Start Task. The associated page will be opened in Page view for you to edit.

3. When you save the page, you will be asked if you want to mark the page as completed. If you choose No, the status will be changed from "Not Started" to "In Progress." If you choose Yes, the status will be marked "Completed." You can see the three possible statuses here:

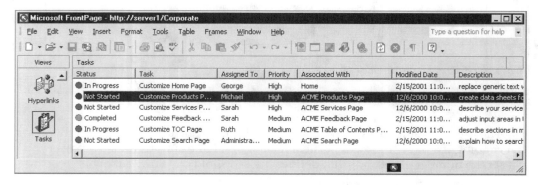

While it will take some effort to create and maintain the Tasks list, it will pay significant dividends in helping you manage a dynamic site.

Facilitating Site Design and Maintaining Quality

One of the more difficult tasks of managing an intranet's content is providing consistent global navigational tools that can be used throughout the various content areas and subwebs. One common strategy is to provide a single, global navigation bar or link bar with certain visual conventions, such as Home and Search buttons or other sitewide elements. This global link bar enables the different web authors working on the site to provide a way to get to the central areas of the site from within their subweb or content area. Providing this kind of tool ensures smooth navigation, because end users become accustomed to seeing this global link bar and will quickly learn how to navigate swiftly between content areas.

Providing a global link bar may sound like common sense; however, in very large intranets that are decentralized and maintained by many different web authors, it is common to see almost no consistent navigational convention. These intranets are true "web" experiences in that when you click around, you are definitely entering cyberspace. In an efficient intranet, though, it is critically important that users find the information they need quickly and easily, which demands a standardized set of navigational tools.

Creating Subwebs for Departmental Web Sites

It's a very good idea—in fact, it is highly recommended—that you break up your intranet into subwebs in order to manage the growing content areas. In the beginning, it might seem like overkill to assign each department its own subweb, but as the web grows, and more people take on the responsibility of creating content for it, having a separate subweb for areas that have a significant amount of content in them will end up being much more manageable.

When FrontPage webs get very large, the time it takes to open, edit, and save a page gets very irritating. This is because often when you open a page, the FrontPage Server Extensions processes every file and updates its private directories, especially if the pages are using web components such as image maps and included pages. If your web site gets to be more than about 50 pages, it's time to think about breaking sections of it into subwebs.

Using Permissions for Subwebs

When you partition your FrontPage intranet into subwebs that correspond to departments or groups within your organization, you can use your existing user/group permissions to grant access to the different subwebs. This means that any user in the Human Resources group can be granted author and browse access to the Human Resources subweb, but users outside of HR may only be able to browse, or they may be locked out all together. See Chapter 22 for more on and how to set permissions.

Verifying Hyperlinks Within an Intranet Site

One of the biggest maintenance problems in large, decentralized (or even centralized) intranet sites is ensuring that all of the links point to the correct files. In large web sites, this can be a full-time task without tools to help. FrontPage provides tools for verifying the hyperlinks in your web site. To verify that all your hyperlinks are valid in FrontPage, select Reports view and click Verifies Hyperlinks on the Reports toolbar. The Verify Hyperlinks dialog box appears, as you can see in Figure 24-9. Click Start. The Broken Hyperlinks report lists all broken hyperlinks, both internal and external.

The hyperlink verification process can be very slow. It is the kind of task that you want to start and then go to lunch. Hopefully, it will be done when you return. The status bar will tell you the progress.

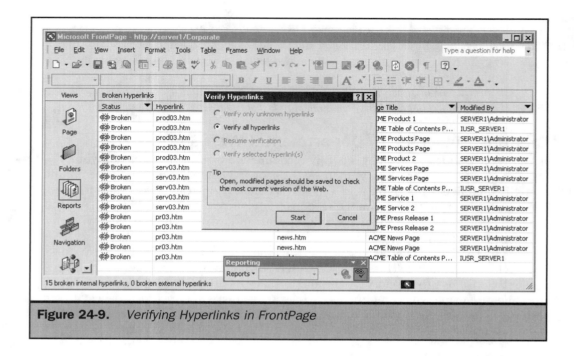

Figure 24-9.   *Verifying Hyperlinks in FrontPage*

To fix the broken hyperlinks, double-click the hyperlink entry in the Broken Hyperlink report. An Edit Hyperlink dialog box appears, as shown next, which allows you to replace the hyperlink with a new one for which you can browse, or you can edit the page containing the hyperlink and change it.

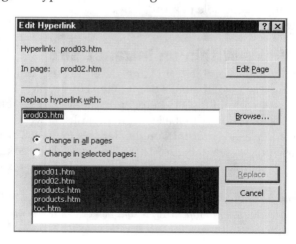

Sitewide Spelling

FrontPage has two tools to check spelling within web pages:

- In Page view, the Tools | Spelling command or the Spelling button on the toolbar checks the spelling within the active page.

- In all other views the same Spelling command or toolbar button opens the Spelling dialog box, where you can choose to check the spelling in just the selected pages or throughout the entire web, as shown next.

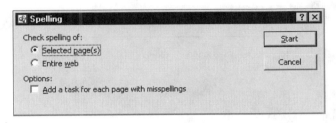

The cross-file spelling checker does not check pages open in Page view, so be sure to close all pages in Page view before using the spelling checker.

The Spelling dialog box also allows you to have pages with misspellings automatically added to the task list.

Using Web Components

Several web components are commonly used in successful intranet sites. Among these are the Web Search component and the Table of Contents Component to make finding information easy and intuitive, and the Include Page Component and Shared Borders to place consistent elements on every page.

The Search Component   The Search component provides a keyword search through all documents in a web. The Search component creates a form in which users type the text to locate, as you can see in Figure 24-10, and then displays a list of hyperlinks to pages containing the search text.

A Search component is added to either a new or an existing page in Page view by opening the Insert menu, choosing Web Component, and clicking Web Search | Current Web. The Search Form Properties dialog box will open, as shown next. After making the necessary changes, click OK and a search form will be added to the current page.

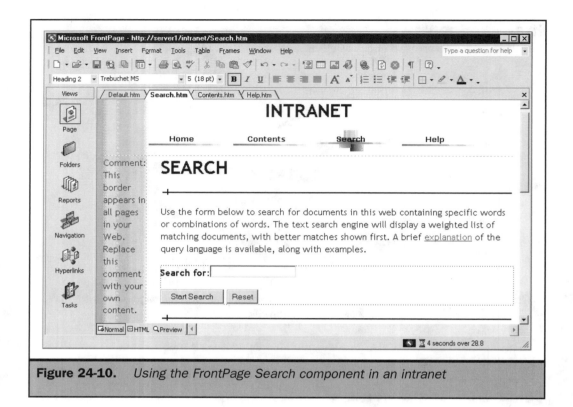

Figure 24-10. *Using the FrontPage Search component in an intranet*

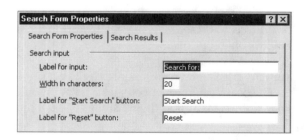

Tip

To protect pages from being found by users searching your web site with the Search form, move the pages into the _Private folder in the current FrontPage web. The Search form does not search in this folder.

Table of Contents Component   The Table of Contents Component creates a listing of all the pages on the site. You can add this component to either an existing or new page in Page view by opening the Insert menu and choosing Web Component | Table of Contents | For This Web Site. This will open the Table of Contents Properties dialog box, where you can specify the starting page in the web (normally the home page) and how the table of contents should be displayed, like this:

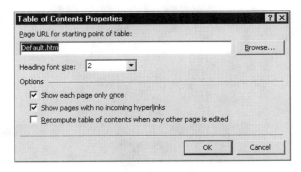

Note   *You will not be able to see the detail within a table of contents until you look at it in a browser. The table of contents is a dynamic feature that is rebuilt and displayed when someone accesses the page. When pages are added or deleted, they will automatically be added to or deleted from the table of contents when the table of contents is accessed.*

The options in the Table of Contents Properties dialog box are handled as follows:

- **Page URL For Starting Point Of Table**   Supply the relative URL of the page at which to start the table of contents. For a table of contents that encompasses the entire FrontPage web, type or browse to the URL of the web's home page.

- **Heading Font Size**   Select a heading style for the first entry in the table of contents. If you do not want a heading, select None.

- **Show Each Page Only Once**   Select this check box if you want each page in your FrontPage web to appear only once in the table of contents. A page can appear more than once if it is pointed to by multiple hyperlinks in your FrontPage web.

- **Show Pages With No Incoming Hyperlinks**   Select this check box to include orphan pages in your table of contents. Orphan pages are pages that cannot be reached by following hyperlinks from the home page.

- **Recompute Table Of Contents When Any Other Page Is Edited**   Select this check box to specify that the table of contents page should be re-created whenever any page in the current FrontPage web is edited. This can be a time-consuming process if the FrontPage web is large. If you do not select this check box, you can manually regenerate the table of contents by opening and saving the page containing the table of contents.

Include Page Component   The Include Page Component allows you to include the contents of one web page on another web page when you load the second web page in a browser. Include pages are good to use when you have content that can change and that appears on many pages in a web site. An *include page* references another file, so when the content of the include page changes, you do not have to modify the page in which it loads. Include pages can be used to add a consistent title or banner and link bar to every page in a web, or just as easily to add the contact, update, and copyright information at the bottom of every page.

For example, to add information at the bottom of every page, you would enter the information on a new blank page, shown next, and then save that page.

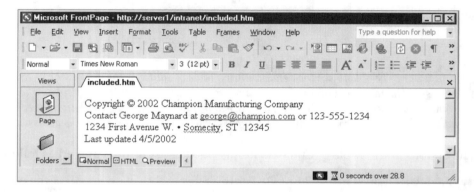

When you have the page you want included, open the page in Page view on which you want it included, open the Insert menu, and choose Web Component | Included Content | Page. The Include Page Component Properties dialog box will open and ask for the URL or name of the page to be included. You can either enter the URL or use Browse to locate it and then click OK. The contents of the included page will appear on the current page fully formatted with whatever theme is attached to the current page, as shown in Figure 24-11.

Shared Borders   FrontPage's Shared Borders allow you to add common sections, such as the top heading, navigation buttons, and bottom contact/copyright information to all pages in a web, much as you can with the Include Page Component. The difference is that with Shared Borders you can work on any of the pages that share the borders, and you don't have a separate page to maintain. You choose one or more of the four page borders to share, and anything you place in those border areas appears on every page. In the top and left borders you can include a set of navigation buttons. To add Shared Borders to a web, pick any page in the web, open the Format menu, and choose Shared Borders. The Shared Borders dialog box will open as you can see here:

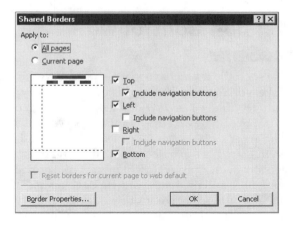

Make sure All Pages is set, choose which borders you want to share, and whether or not you want to include navigation buttons. When you click OK, all the pages in the web will have the shared borders. If you add a page to the web, it too will have the shared borders. Figure 24-11 has a shared top border with a navigation bar. If you want a particular page to not have one or more of the borders, open the page in Page view and then open the Shared Borders dialog box, click Current Page, and change the settings, which will only be reflected on the current page.

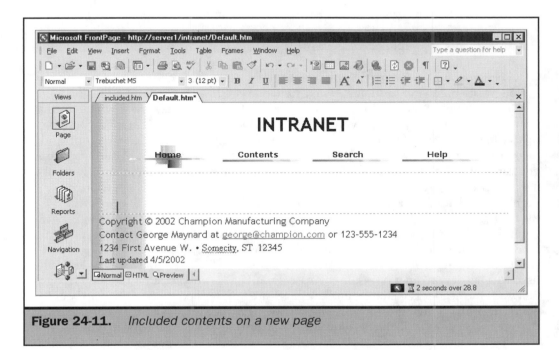

Figure 24-11.   *Included contents on a new page*

EXTENDING YOUR
WEB SITE

Web Page Version Control with Visual SourceSafe

If you have several—or especially if you have many—people working on creating material for your web site, you'll need a way to control the various versions of the many pages you'll end up with. FrontPage has provided help in this area by incorporating links between Microsoft Visual SourceSafe and the FrontPage Server Extensions running on a Windows NT/2000/XP Server.

Microsoft Visual SourceSafe is a separate product that you must purchase. It allows you to track various versions with a project orientation, while providing tools for storing, accessing, and organizing files, and mediating among developers. The project orientation allows the system, not the people, to keep track of the relationship between files.

Use of Visual SourceSafe with FrontPage requires that Visual SourceSafe be installed on the server where the FrontPage Server Extensions and the production webs in use are kept. If you have Visual SourceSafe installed this way, when you place a web on the server, you'll be asked if you want to make the web a Visual SourceSafe project. If so, when you recalculate the links, the files will be checked into Visual SourceSafe. You can then use Visual SourceSafe from a client workstation using FrontPage through three commands in the context menus (opened by right-clicking the file):

- **Check Out** to edit a file
- **Check In** to return a file that has been edited and have it update Visual SourceSafe accordingly
- **Undo Check Out** to return a file that has not been changed

When you are the first or only person to check out a file, a check mark will appear beside the filename in FrontPage. When someone else has checked out a file you are looking at, it will have a padlock beside the name. If you open Page view with a file that someone else has checked out, you'll see "(Read Only)" in the title bar, and you'll be unable to edit the file. If you open Page view with a file you have not checked out (and no one else has either), you'll see "(Not Checked Out)" in the title bar. In this latter case, you can still make changes to the file, but when you try to save the file, FrontPage will check to see if the file has changed since you opened it. If the file has not changed, FrontPage will automatically check it out and back in again in Visual SourceSafe. If the file has been modified, you will be asked if you want to overwrite the changes.

In some instances, changes you make to a page you have checked out affect pages that others have checked out. These changes fall into two categories: incidental changes and substantive changes. *Incidental* changes, for example, are like changing an included page used as a header on other pages. In this case, FrontPage is not concerned about the pages on which the header is included, and the pages are not checked to see if they are being edited. *Substantive* changes, like deleting or moving a page referenced by other pages that are checked out, will not be allowed, and an error message will tell you why.

Visual SourceSafe is a powerful tool to help maintain an intranet on which multiple people are working. It does assume, though, that you are using a separate Windows NT/2000/XP Server with the FrontPage Server Extensions and that you have published your webs to that server.

Using a SharePoint Team Web Site

The SharePoint Team Web Site is an intranet site set up to facilitate the communication and sharing of information among a team of people who work together. With a SharePoint Team Web Site, people can be invited to be team members, and once members, they need only a browser to add or access such group-common items as calendar events, phone numbers, names and addresses, to-do lists, and Office documents, as well as hold discussions and take polls. SharePoint does not require FrontPage, but FrontPage can be used to customize the site using themes, style sheets, and Web Components. SharePoint is a major resource and in many ways is a web-centric equivalent to Lotus Notes.

In Chapter 4, in the section entitled "Teaming Up with the SharePoint Team Web Site," there is a discussion of installing SharePoint on a local server and then using the SharePoint Team Web Site template to create a team collaboration web site. If you did not do that before, go back to Chapter 4 now and follow the instructions to build a site named "Team," and then come back here. Your site should be open in FrontPage as shown in Figure 24-12.

Using the Team Web Site, the next several sections will look at adding and managing team members and adding and managing content, as well as customizing. All work, except customization will be done in a browser.

Adding and Managing Members

Team members join the site through an invitation that includes the member's username and password. Once a member is on board, you can change the roles for which they have permission, delete them and make other modifications to their membership.

Inviting Members to the Team Site

Invite several members to your Team web with these steps:

1. With the Team Web Site displayed in FrontPage, click Preview In Browser. The Team site should appear in your browser.

2. Click Site Settings in the link bar at the top of the page. The Site Settings page will appear. Scroll down until you can see all of the Web Administration section, as shown in Figure 24-13. If you see Send An Invitation, skip to Step 5. Otherwise continue here.

3. Click Change Permissions. Select Use Unique Permissions For This Web Site and click Submit. The Permissions Administration page opens.

4. If you want to remove anonymous browsing, which is on as a default, click Change Anonymous Access Settings. Click Off and then click Submit.

5. Click Send An Invitation. Type the e-mail addresses, each on a separate line, of the people you want to invite to be team members and then click Next. Verify the e-mail address you have entered, enter the person's full name, and click Next.

Note
If you get a message that you can't send e-mail because the service is not set up on your server, open Start and choose Programs | Administrative Tools | Microsoft SharePoint Administrator. Click Set Installation Defaults. Scroll down until you see Mail Settings, enter the settings that are correct for you, and then click Submit. You must enter the actual mail server to which you go to send and receive mail.

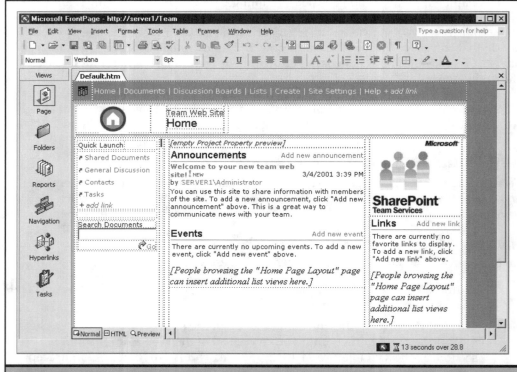

Figure 24-12.   *SharePoint Team Web Site in FrontPage*

6. Enter a personal message to the person you are inviting to the site, select the role (Administrator, Advanced Author, Author, Contributor, or Browser—see Chapter 22 for a description of these roles), and click Finish. A confirmation is displayed of the information you entered and your invitation is sent. Figure 24-14 shows what it looks like to the person receiving it.

7. Click Click Here to invite additional members or click Home to return to the Team Web Site.

If the person to whom you are sending an invitation is not already set up as a user on the server hosting the SharePoint Team Web Site, then a new password is generated for that person and sent to them in the invitation, as you can see in Figure 24-14. If the person is already set up on the server, the invitation is silent about the password with the assumption that the person will use their existing password.

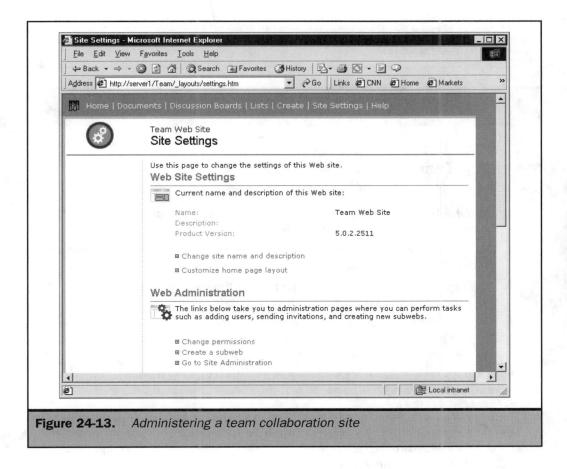

Figure 24-13. *Administering a team collaboration site*

```
Dear Carole Matthews,

SERVER1\Administrator has invited you to join the "Team Web Site" team web
site.

Here is a message from SERVER1\Administrator:
"Hi, Welcome to the team."

Your user name and password for accessing this site are:
         User name: SERVER1\cbm     Password: h!1DwNPd
Change your password as soon as possible to maintain security. You have been
added to the site with Contributor-level access. The description for
Contributor is "View pages and documents, view and contribute to
discussions.".

Click the following link to change your password: <http://server1/team/
vti bin/ vti adm/fpadmdll.dll?page=pwdmgr.htm&ReturnPage=http://server1/team>
Click the following link to view the Home page: <http://server1/team>

Welcome to Team Web Site!
```

Figure 24-14. *An invitation received by a new team member*

Managing Team Member Accounts

Change the role of a team member or make other changes to their account next.

1. From the Team site Home page, click Site Settings, scroll down beneath Web Administration and click Manage Users.

2. Click the user you want to manage. Click the new role you want assigned to the user and click Submit.

3. Add a user by clicking Add A User, entering the username and password, selecting a role, and clicking Add User.

4. Delete a user by clicking in the check box opposite the user and then clicking Remove Selected User(s) From All Roles. Click OK to confirm that you are sure you want to delete the user.

5. When you are done with managing users, click Home at the top of the page to return to the team site's home page.

There is not a clear distinction of when you use Send An Invitation and when Add A User is the appropriate way to go. Send An Invitation can generate a password and notify the new user. Add A User allows you to enter a password but doesn't do any notification. You choose which fits your needs the best.

You can manage your own membership record by opening Site Settings, scrolling down to User Information, and clicking Edit My Information. Your User Information page will open. Here you change your password, edit your user information, and manage personal subscriptions, like this:

```
Team Web Site
User Information: SERVER1\Administrator (SERVER1
\Administrator)

📝 Edit user information  |  Go back to user information list


Full Name:         SERVER1\Administrator
E-mail Address:
Notes:
     ⊠ Change password
     ⊠ Manage personal subscriptions
```

Adding and Managing Content

There are many ways to add a number of different types of content to a team site. From the Home page you can directly add a new announcement, a new event, or a new link. Then through Shared Documents you can add a new document or upload an existing one, through General Discussion you can start a new discussion group, and through Contacts and Tasks you can add and manage those types of items. All of these items use capabilities built into the default SharePoint Team Web Site. If these don't satisfy you, you can use the options at the top of the page to add additional document libraries, discussion boards, new lists, or create a new custom page. In the sections that follow, you'll look at a number of ways of adding content.

Adding and Managing Content Directly

The default Home page allows you to directly add announcements, events, and links. Follow these steps to see how:

1. On the Home page of the Team Web Site, click Add New Announcement. Enter a title, body and expiration date, shown in Figure 24-15. When you are done, click Save And Close. Your new announcement will appear on the Home page.

2. Click Add New Event. Enter a title, an event date, a date to remove the event, a description, and the location of the event. Click Save And Close. The event will appear on the Home page.

3. Click Add New Link. Enter the URL, a description, and comments, then click Save And Close.

4. Change or delete an announcement or event by clicking its title to open a page for that item where you can click Edit Item or Delete Item, as you can see next.

5. Clicking Edit Item opens the page where you originally entered the item. Click Go Back To List and you will be returned to the Home page.

You cannot change or delete a link in the same way you can announcements and events, because a link references the URL to which it points. To change a link, you must open the Lists option at the top of the page, click Links, and click the Edit icon next to the link you want to change. This opens the page where you originally enter the link.

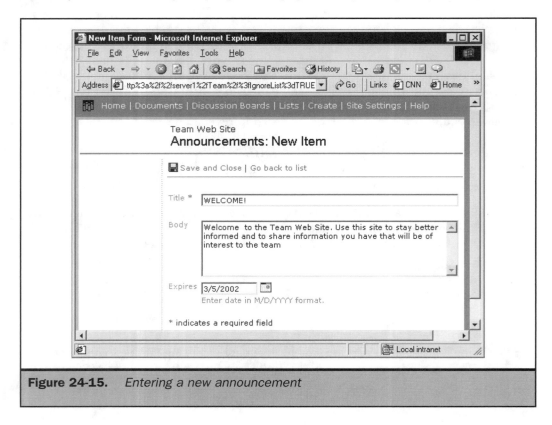

Figure 24-15.   *Entering a new announcement*

Here, you can then edit or delete it. Announcements and events, as well as tasks and contacts can be entered in the same way. When you have entered an announcement, event, and a link, your Home page should look like Figure 24-16.

Adding and Managing Content Indirectly

SharePoint classifies information in three ways; documents, discussions, and lists. The announcements, events, and links you directly entered are lists. In addition to these, there are contacts and tasks, which you access indirectly either through the Quick Launch area on the left of the Home page or through the Lists link or option at the top of the page where you can also create new lists. Documents and discussions are only accessed indirectly, either through the Quick Launch area or the links that are on the top of the page, where again you can create new document folders and discussion boards.

Working with Lists   You have seen how to directly enter items on the announcement, event, and link lists. See how this is done first through the Quick Launch area, and then through the option or link at the top of the page.

1. Click Contacts to open the Contacts page. Click New Item. Type in the information requested and click Save And Close. The new entry will appear in the list. You can click the last name to see a detailed listing of the item, as well as to edit, delete, or export it. You can also click the e-mail address to open a preaddressed e-mail message.

2. On the Contacts page, click Filter. Here in each field or column you can select an entry that has been made and display only items that contain that entry. The column you filter will have a funnel by its title and you can remove or change the filter by clicking Change Filter.

3. Click Import Contacts. You will be asked to choose a profile, of which Outlook is the only option, and click OK. If you have an Outlook contacts list, you will be asked to select the names to import. When you are done, click OK. You'll be told that a program is trying to access your Outlook e-mail addresses. Click Yes to allow this. The Outlook contacts will be brought in and added to the Team Web Site's list of contacts.

Note   *If you have not installed Outlook or set up a profile for it, you may be asked to insert your Office XP CD, go through the process of setting up an e-mail account, and adding a user before the importing can take place.*

4. Click Home to return there and click Tasks. You'll see a very comparable list structure with similar commands above the list. Click New Item. Enter a title, and select a status, priority, percentage complete, who it is assigned to, and finally start and due dates. When you are done, click Save And Close. The task will appear in the list.

5. Click Home and click Lists at the top of the page. The lists page will open showing all the lists currently in the Team Web Site. Click New List to do that.

Create Page will open. Click Custom List. In the New List page, enter the list name, description, and whether you want it on the Quick Launch bar, as shown in Figure 24-17.

6. Click Create. The new list will open with only a Title column. Click Modify Settings And Columns. Scroll down until you see Columns and click Add A New Column. Enter a column name, select the type of information you want the column to contain, a description, and other information. Click OK. When you have entered the columns you want, click Go Back To and the name of your new list.

7. Enter several items in your new list. After entering three or more items, click one of the column headings to sort the list by that field.

8. Return to the Home page. If you chose to include your new list in the Quick Launch area, you should see it there.

Working with Documents   Documents in SharePoint not only appear on a list of documents, as you saw in the various lists, but copies of the documents are stored there in the Document Library. Look at how this is handled with the following set of steps.

1. Click Shared Documents. Here you can create a new document in Word, upload an existing document from anywhere on the network, filter the list, and modify the settings and columns. The last two items are as you saw with lists. Click New Document. Microsoft Word opens.

Figure 24-16.   *An announcement, event, and link in the Team Web Site's Home page*

2. Type a short paragraph (it really doesn't need to say anything). Save the document in the default Shared Documents folder and close Word. The document will appear in the list on the Shared Documents page.

3. Click Upload Document, enter the document path and name or browse to the name and double-click it. Click Save And Close. Again the document will appear in the list on the Shared Documents page, as you can see in Figure 24-18.

4. Click a document filename in the list. You will be asked if you want to download it to your hard disk or open it. If you download it, you will be asked for the folder in which you want it saved, the file will be saved there and you can then open it in its associated program or return to the list. If you open it initially, the file will be opened in Internet Explorer. In either case, return to the Shared Document list.

5. Click Edit next to a document in the list. The filename and title will appear in a new page where you can delete the document, send it to someone for review

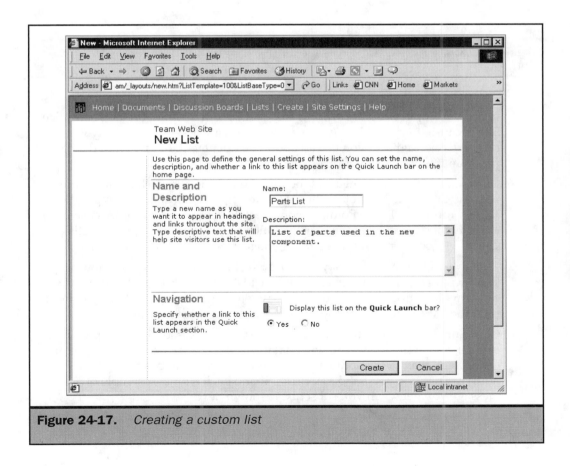

Figure 24-17.   *Creating a custom list*

EXTENDING YOUR
WEB SITE

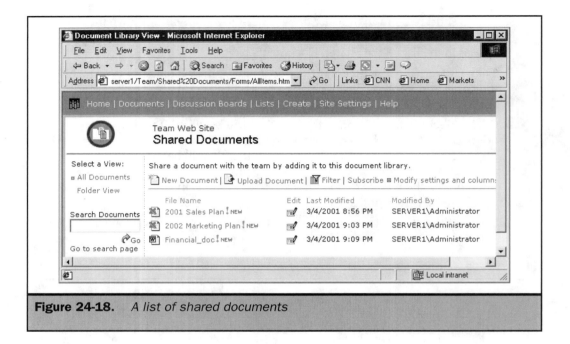

Figure 24-18. *A list of shared documents*

(since this implies you are sending it to someone who is not on the Team Web Site because they already have access to it, you are asked if you really want to do that), open a discussion thread about the document, or open it in the program it is associated with.

6. Click Home, click Documents at the top of the page, and click New Document Library. Enter the name of the library, a description, the template type (Word, Excel, FrontPage, PowerPoint, or none; pick Excel Document for this exercise) and whether it is to be in the Quick Launch area. When you are done, click Create. A document list will open, as you saw with Shared Documents.

7. Click New Document, and if you chose Excel Document in the previous step, Excel will open and you can create a spreadsheet. Like Shared Documents you can download documents and edit documents. As you saw with lists, you can filter the list of documents and modify the settings and columns.

8. Click Subscribe. Select the document library, list, or discussion group you want to subscribe to (meaning you will be notified if a change occurs), the type of change you want to be notified about, your e-mail address, and the time to notify you. When you are done, click OK and click Home. A sample of the message you get when you subscribe is shown next:

The following change(s) happened in the list <u>2002 Budget Documents</u>:

Event: Items were inserted into the list.
By: SERVER1\Administrator
Time: 2/19/2001 8:11:01 PM

Event: Items were modified in the list.
By: SERVER1\Administrator
Time: 2/19/2001 8:11:01 PM

<u>Click here to stop receiving this notification.</u>

Working with Discussion Boards   Discussion boards are threaded messages where anyone on the Team Web Site can enter a new message, someone else can reply or comment on the message, and a third person can reply or comment on the second message creating the thread. A fourth person can create a whole new thread by entering a new message unrelated to the first three. Discussion boards can be general in nature or on a specific topic. Here is how discussion boards are implemented in the Team Web Site:

1. From the Team Web Site Home page, click General Discussion in the Quick Launch area. The General Discussion page opens looking very much like the list and document library pages.

2. Click New Discussion. Enter a subject, the text of your message, and then click Save And Close.

3. Reply to an existing message by clicking it and then clicking Reply, entering the reply, clicking Save And Close, and then clicking Go Back To Discussion Board. Figure 24-19 shows what two discussion threads look like.

4. Click Home, click Discussion Boards, and click New Discussion Board. Enter the name of the discussion board, a description, whether it is to be in the Quick Launch area, and click Create. The new discussion board will open.

5. Click Home.

Customizing a Team Web Site

There are a number of ways to customize a SharePoint Team Web Site. You've seen how to add lists, document libraries, and discussion boards. You've also seen how you can add and change columns in a list. So here you'll look at other types of customizing, including modifying the Home page and adding a different type of document: surveys.

Customizing the Home Page

While there are a few items you can change in FrontPage, like the names "Quick Launch" and "Home" and the pictures, the majority of the page is generated and can only be changed by the mechanisms that have been built into the Team Web Site.

1. From the Home page, click Site Settings and under Web Site Settings click Change Site Name And Description. Make the changes you wish and click OK.

2. Back under Web Site Settings, click Customize Home Page Layout. As you can see in Figure 24-20, this allows you to choose the components displayed on the page. The Two columns on the right, shown in light blue, present the components currently displayed on the page, while the gray column on the left contains the components that are currently not displayed. To change what and where components are displayed, you drag them where they are to be placed.

3. Drag Shared Documents under Links in the right-most column. Drag Links back to the Available column on the left, and then drag the General Discussion under Shared Documents.

4. Click Save, returning you to the Home page, which now looks like Figure 24-21.

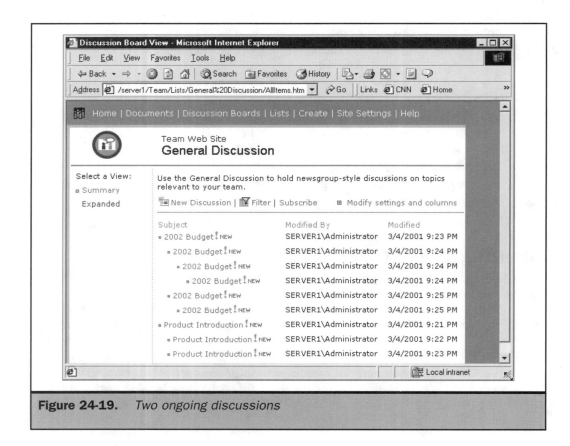

Figure 24-19. *Two ongoing discussions*

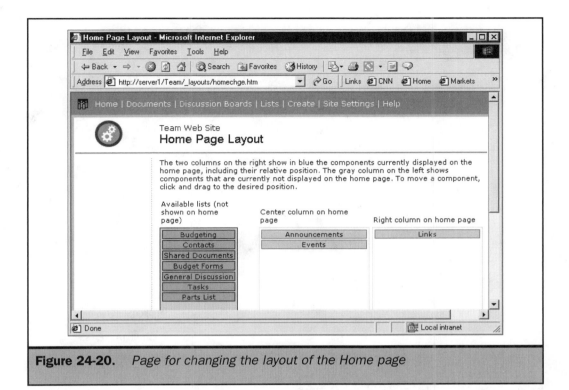

Figure 24-20.   *Page for changing the layout of the Home page*

Adding Surveys

There is one type of document that the Team Web Site can work with but is not in the default site. This is a survey of team members. See how to create a survey next.

1. From the Home page, click Create, then scroll down and click Survey. Afterward, enter the survey name, description, whether the survey is in the Quick Launch area, the survey options, and then click Next.

2. Enter the question you are asking, the type of answer, the choices for the answer, and the default value. When you are done, click OK. This opens a page where you can modify the survey that includes deleting it or putting an additional question on it.

3. Click Go Back To and the name of your survey. Click Respond To This Survey, answer the question and click Save And Close. Click Home to return there. You should see the survey in the Quick Launch area.

4. Click the Quick Launch entry and click Respond To This Survey. You will be told you are not allowed to respond to this survey because only one vote is allowed per person. You can look at a list of all responses, look at a graphical summary, or an overview, which for my survey looks like Figure 24-22.

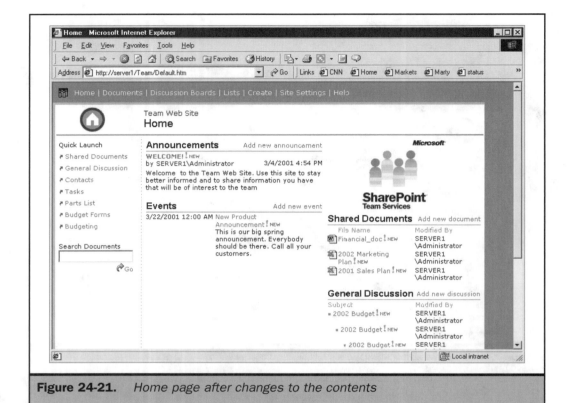

Figure 24-21.   *Home page after changes to the contents*

Conclusion

Throughout this chapter, you have seen how FrontPage can help you create an intranet site. It is a truly multifaceted tool that provides many options for creating, maintaining, and serving an intranet site. Its web-creation wizards enable you to produce fully functioning intranet sites quickly, and its page-creation templates give you a head start in creating web pages. FrontPage's ability to support Office document integration makes it possible to have access to existing documents in their native form, which is ideal for complex Word or Excel documents. With help from the many FrontPage tools, you have the ability to create complex intranet sites that take advantage of emerging technologies, such as channels, dynamic HTML, and Active Server Pages, in a fraction of the time it would take if you were to undertake the project from scratch. Also, FrontPage's site-management features and its ability to integrate with Visual SourceSafe provide the kind of control you need in an intranet environment where multiple authors are providing content simultaneously. Finally, SharePoint's Team Web Site provides a very powerful way for a team to collaborate using an intranet.

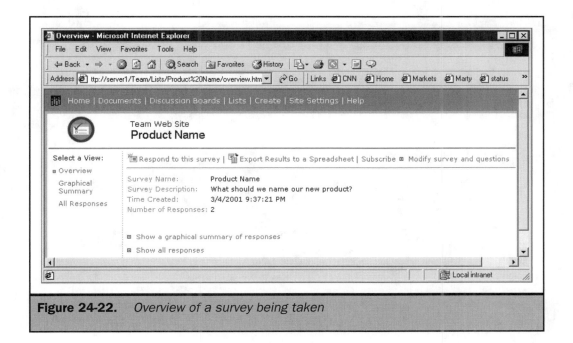

Figure 24-22.   *Overview of a survey being taken*

The Complete Reference

FrontPage 2002

Chapter 25

Publishing and Promoting Webs on the Internet

With the help of this book and FrontPage, by now you have created your own webs and possibly put them on your intranet or tested them on a local server. In this chapter, you will see how to make your efforts available to the millions of people worldwide who have access to the Internet. You'll do this by first publishing your web on a web server, a computer that is connected to the Internet. Then you'll promote your web site using web-based and traditional advertising.

Publishing Your Web Pages

Publishing a web means copying the files that contain the web's pages and graphics to a web server connected to the Internet. Unless you have your own such server, you will need to find a web presence provider (WPP) that will rent you space on their web server for your web. Also, to get the full functionality of your web, your WPP should support the FrontPage Server Extensions (FPSE).

Providing access to the Web has become a very competitive field, and you should be able to find several WPPs in your area to choose from. You can find a local WPP by asking others, by looking in your regional newspapers and other periodicals, and even by checking a current phone book. You can also use the Internet. Begin by using one of the many search engines available, such as AltaVista (**http://www.altavista.com**). Simply enter a search criterion such as **"Internet hosting [*your city*]"** (include the quotes). Another Internet site with a list of providers is Yahoo (**http://www.yahoo.com**). Microsoft also provides the ability to search for WPPs with FrontPage Server Extensions through the options at **http://www.microsoftwpp.com/wppsearch/**. With a little searching, you should be able to locate several WPPs in your area. It is not necessary that your WPP be located close to you. Most of your transactions will occur over the Internet, and there are a number of national providers, such as Earthlink (**http://www.earthlink.net/**) and AT&T's WorldNet Service (**http://www.att.com**), that offer the FrontPage Server Extensions as part of their service.

Generally, a WPP will provide dial-up access to the Internet, as well as hard disk storage for webs. Many offer space for a personal (noncommercial) web as part of their basic Internet access package. The amount of hard disk space allowed for a personal web site varies. In many areas, this basic service costs $10 to $30 a month with unlimited Internet access. (These rates are for 28.8 to 56.6 Kbps modems; rates for ISDN, DSL, and cable modems may be higher.)

Rates for commercial web sites can vary greatly—from under $20 to several thousand dollars a month—depending on the WPP, the amount of hard disk storage, and the bandwidth used. *Bandwidth* is the amount of data that is transferred from your web site over the WPP's Internet connection. For example, if your web is 1 megabyte (MB) in size and it was accessed 100 times in the course of a month, you used 100MB of bandwidth (or transfer bandwidth) that month.

Another point to consider is whether you want to have your own domain name. Without your own domain name, your web's URL would begin with the WPP's domain name, such as *http://www.WPPname.com/yourname*. With your own domain, your URL would be *http://www.yourname.com*. Your own domain is unnecessary for a personal web site, but it should be seriously considered for a commercial web. Your WPP can help you set up a domain name for your web site. Alternatively, you can contact InterNIC at **http://www.internic.net/** to get a list of accredited registrars. You then can go to one of those registrars and, with some information from your WPP and a fee (ranging from under $10 to over $50 per year; sometimes there is a minimum of two years), you can register your own domain name. Each registrar has complete instructions at their site. Also, at both the InterNIC and registrar's sites you can search for existing domain names using InterNIC's Whois facility to make sure the one you want is unique.

In deciding upon a WPP, you should be more concerned about the quality of the service than the price. The Internet is a little chaotic—new technologies (particularly in data transmission) are coming into play, and finding people who truly understand and can use these technologies is not always easy. Software doesn't always work as advertised, and keeping everything flowing smoothly sometimes requires a little "spit and baling wire." When evaluating a WPP, look at the design and features of their web site, and contact others who have their webs on the WPP's server. Choosing the cheapest WPP could be an expensive decision in the long run if they don't provide the services you need, such as the FrontPage Server Extensions.

FrontPage Server Extensions

HTML used to be written by hand using text editors such as Windows Notepad. When you wanted to include a form for the user to fill out, you had to make sure there was a script available on the server that would implement it. There were (and are) a number of scripts to do this, so you needed to know the syntax required by the particular script on your server. If your web page was transferred to another server with different scripts, your HTML probably had to be modified.

With FrontPage, those days are over. A great deal of the functionality and usefulness of FrontPage comes from the fact that it includes a standard set of server extensions that can run on virtually any HTTP server platform with any major server software. This means your FrontPage-created web can be placed on any web server running the FrontPage Server Extensions and will function correctly.

As a content creator, you need to know only that the latest FrontPage Server Extensions are installed on your WPP's web server. (On your local computer, the server extensions for Internet Information Services [IIS] or Personal Web Server [PWS] were installed as a part of the FrontPage or SharePoint installation; see Appendix A.) If they are, you are assured that any FrontPage Web Components, forms, or discussion groups you've included in your web will function on your WPP's server.

The FrontPage Server Extensions allow you to use Hypertext Transfer Protocol (HTTP) for uploading your webs in place of the older and more complex File Transfer Protocol (FTP). FrontPage Server Extensions will also help you maintain your web files by making sure the files on the web server are the same as those on your local hard disk and that all the hyperlinks are correct.

You might also want to check with your WPP to make sure their version of FrontPage Server Extensions is the same version or later as the FrontPage version you used to create your web application (although many of the FrontPage 2002 components are handled by the FrontPage 2000 Server Extensions).

Features that Require the Server Extensions

A number of FrontPage features and Web Components require the FrontPage Server Extensions. Since not all ISPs immediately install the latest extensions, the following lists are broken out by the oldest version of FrontPage Server Extensions that will support the feature (the newer versions will handle all the features of the earlier versions).

SharePoint is a superset of FrontPage 2002 Server Extensions.

Features Requiring SharePoint

- Lists and List view Web Component
- Document Libraries and Document Library view Web Component
- Surveys
- SharePoint-based Team Web Site

Features Requiring at Least FrontPage 2002 Server Extensions

- Custom link bars
- Multiple navigation structures
- Role-based security
- Shared border background properties
- Single page publishing
- Top 10 lists
- Usage analysis reports

Features Requiring at Least FrontPage 2000 Server Extensions

- Categories Web Component
- Database Results Wizard
- More than one level of subwebs
- Send To Database form
- Source Control, document check-in/check-out
- Style sheet links to multiple files

Features Requiring at Least FrontPage 98 Server Extensions

- Confirmation field
- Discussion form
- Image maps
- Hit counter
- Registration form
- Save results form
- Search form

Installing the FrontPage Server Extensions

If you are maintaining your own web server, you need to install the FrontPage Server Extensions on it (they are automatically installed when you install SharePoint on Windows 2000 Professional or Server and FPSE 2000 are installed with the Microsoft Personal Web Server [PWS]; see Appendix A). Alternatively, you may have to work with your WPP to install the FrontPage Server Extensions on their server. (For a variety of reasons, including security, WPPs can be reluctant to install every piece of software a client suggests.) Therefore, the next several paragraphs provide some of the reasoning behind the FrontPage Server Extensions, as well as an overview of the installation process.

For the most part, the FrontPage Server Extensions use the standard common gateway interface (CGI) found on all web servers. The CGI provides a standard protocol for the transfer and processing of data between a client (a web browser, for example) and a server. With Microsoft Internet Information Services (IIS), the server extensions are implemented as dynamic link libraries (DLLs). This allows the server extensions to take up less room and to execute faster. In any case, data is transferred to the FrontPage Server Extensions from the web server software. The server extensions then process the data and hand back the output to the server software. For example, in the case of a text search, the search criteria would be passed from the HTTP server to the appropriate FrontPage Server Extension. The specified information would then be searched using the specified criteria, and the results of the search would be handed back to the HTTP server. It would then be formatted with HTML and sent back to the client (web browser) that initiated the search.

Adding the FrontPage Server Extensions to an existing web server is a relatively simple process. The first step is to get a copy of the FrontPage Server Extensions for your web server. These are available at no charge from Microsoft's web site (**http:// www.microsoft.com/frontpage/wpp/default.htm**).

Microsoft currently provides FrontPage Server Extensions for the hardware, operating system, and web servers in the English language shown in Table 25-1. Many other languages are also available.

Note *No web server is included in Windows Me, but you can use PWS on the Windows 98 installation disk.*

Hardware Used	Operating System Used	Web Server Used
Digital Alpha	Windows NT 4.0 Server	Microsoft Internet Information Services 2.0 through 4.0
Digital Alpha	Windows NT 4.0 Workstation	Microsoft Peer Web Services
Digital Alpha	Digital UNIX 3.2c, 4.0.f, 5.0	Apache 1.1.3, 1.2.4, 12.5 CERN 3.0 NCSA 1.5.2 (not 1.5a or 1.5.1) Netscape Commerce Server 1.12 Netscape Communications Server 1.12 Netscape Enterprise 2.0 through 3.5.1 Netscape FastTrack 2.0, 3.01 Stronghold 2.3
Intel x86	UNIX-BSD/OS 2.1, 3.0–4.0 Linux 3.0.3–6.2 (Red Hat) SCO OpenServer Release 5 SCO UnixWare 7	See Digital Alpha running Digital UNIX
Intel x86	Windows 95/98 Windows NT Workstation Windows 2000 and XP Professional	Microsoft Personal Web Server (Windows 95 or 98) Microsoft Peer Web Services (Windows NT Workstation) Microsoft Internet Information Services 5.0 (Windows 2000 and XP Professional) FrontPage Personal Web Server Netscape FastTrack 2.0 O'Reilly & Associates WebSite

Table 25-1. *FrontPage Server Extensions Availability*

Hardware Used	Operating System Used	Web Server Used
Intel x86	Windows NT 4.0 Server Windows 2000 and XP Server, Advanced Server, and Datacenter Server	Microsoft Internet Information Services 2.0–4.0 and 5.0 (Windows 2000 and XP only) Netscape Commerce Server 1.12 Netscape Communications Server 1.12 Netscape Enterprise 2.0 through 3.51 Netscape FastTrack 2.0–3.01 O'Reilly & Associates WebSite and Website Pro 1.x and 2.0
HP (PA-RISC)	HP/UX 9.03, 10.01, 10.2, 11.0	See Digital Alpha running Digital UNIX
Silicon Graphics	IRIX 5.3, 6.2, 6.4, 6.5	See Digital Alpha running Digital UNIX
Sun (SPARC)	Solaris 2.4, 2.5, 2.7, 2.8 or SunOS 4.1.3, 4.1.4	See Digital Alpha running Digital UNIX

Table 25-1.   *FrontPage Server Extensions Availability* (continued)

As you can see, the FrontPage Server Extensions are available for most web server platforms and HTTP server software. Installation of the FrontPage Server Extensions varies depending on the platform, but complete instructions are available for each platform and are relatively simple. In addition, there is a FrontPage 2000 Server Extension Resource Kit v1.4 (SERK) that is available from the **http://msdn.microsoft.com/workshop/ languages/fp/** site.

The primary issue with a WPP about installing the FrontPage Server Extensions (besides being one more thing to learn and handle) will be security. When someone accesses a web page on a server, he or she is given certain permissions. Normally these are limited to reading data on the server. The user is usually not allowed to write to the server's hard disk or to change any of the files on the server outside of the user's personal folder. The reason is obvious: if a user is allowed to place a file on a server, that file, through malicious intent or simple ignorance, could wreak havoc on the server.

Network administrators protect their servers by restricting the type of access users are allowed (and some people make a hobby of beating the administrator's best efforts).

The FrontPage Server Extensions, like virtually every CGI application and script, need to allow the user to write to a file or folder on the server. The server's security is maintained by cordoning off these specific areas. Depending on the operating system and HTTP server software, the FrontPage Server Extensions generally require the same permissions as other CGI applications and do not represent an increased security risk.

The last word may simply be that FrontPage fills a tremendous gap in the quality of tools available for creating web content. If you remember the days of creating HTML in a text editor, you know how much more efficiently your time is used with FrontPage (if you don't remember, fire up Notepad and review Chapter 12).

Identifying Which Pages to Publish

When you create a new page, it is automatically identified as a page to be published. If you want, though, you can change this so that the page will not be copied to the web server. You might do this if you are not finished building a page but have other pages in the web you want published. When you are ready to publish a page, you simply have to identify the page as "Publish." It is also useful to mark certain files as "Don't Publish" if you don't want them recopied to the web server, such as pages with a hit counter or with a guest book, which would be zeroed out if they were republished. Use the following steps to identify the pages that you do and do not want published:

1. With FrontPage running and your local copy of the web that you want to publish open, click the View menu and choose Reports | Workflow | Publish Status. The Publish Status report will appear in the FrontPage window.

2. To change the status of a particular page, click the right side of the Publish field for that page to open the drop-down list of choices, as shown in Figure 25-1.

3. Click Publish or Don't Publish as desired. Your page will be so marked, and when you publish your web, your Publish setting will be followed.

Publishing to a Server with FrontPage Server Extensions

Once your FrontPage web is completed and tested on your local computer, it's ready for the big time: the World Wide Web. With any luck, your WPP has the FrontPage Server Extensions installed and has created a folder for your web on the web server. (Publishing your web to a server without the FrontPage Server Extensions is covered in the next section.)

To publish a FrontPage web to a server with FrontPage Server Extensions, you must first have permission to write files to the server. Your webmaster or server administrator will be able to assign the proper permission to your account. As an additional security measure, your webmaster or administrator may have you publish your web to a temporary folder. Once you have the proper permissions and location on the server for your web, use the following steps to publish your web.

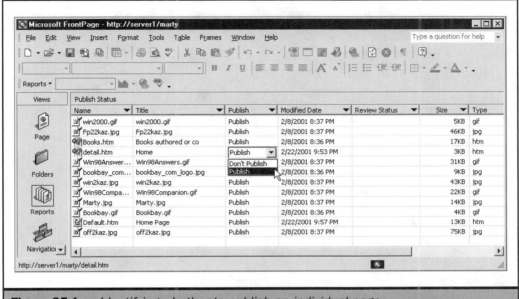

Figure 25-1. *Identifying whether to publish an individual page*

Note *If you do not have your own domain name and virtual or real server, your WPP may not let you create a new web or delete a web that is your primary folder, and FrontPage will not let you publish to a subsidiary folder. That means that you must create your web on your computer and publish it to your server. Then you can edit it, publish a new version of the web replacing the original version, add pages to it, and import other webs to it, but you can only delete individual folders and pages, you cannot delete the web itself.*

1. Start FrontPage if necessary. If you use a dial-up account to access the Internet, activate your Internet connection.

2. In FrontPage, open the web you will place on the web server.

3. Open the File menu and select Publish Web. The Publish Destination dialog box appears. Enter the URL or path to the server on which you want to publish and click OK. If asked, log on to your server by entering your username and password, and clicking OK. Click OK again to create a new web if one does not already exist. The Publish Web dialog box will be displayed as shown in Figure 25-2. (If your Publish Web dialog box only shows the left side, click Show.)

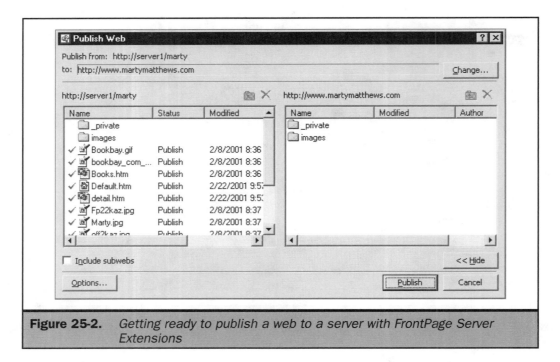

Figure 25-2. *Getting ready to publish a web to a server with FrontPage Server Extensions*

4. Click Publish. You'll see a message telling you how the publishing is going and a thermometer bar showing you how far along you are. When it is done, you'll see this message:

5. Test your web by clicking Click Here To View Your Published Web Site. Your web should appear in a browser, as mine does in Figure 25-3. When you are done looking at your web, close your browser and click Done.

In most cases, publishing your web to a server with the FrontPage Server Extensions will be this simple. The biggest hang-up is often that in your WPP communications, your URL, user ID, and password have been garbled and the correct ones were not used in the preceding steps. If you are having problems, this is the first thing you should check with your WPP.

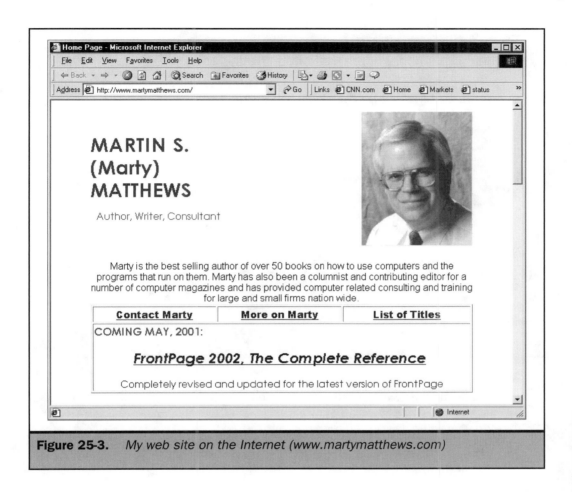

Figure 25-3. *My web site on the Internet (www.martymatthews.com)*

Editing a Web on a Server

One of the great beauties of putting your webs up on a server with the FrontPage Server Extensions is that you can directly edit your web on the server just as you would on your computer. To do this, follow these steps:

1. Make sure you can connect to the server by being connected to either the Internet or an intranet.

2. Open the File menu and choose Open Web to open the dialog box of the same name. If it is not already selected, click My Network Places or Web Folders, depending on your operating system. You should see both the original local version and the one on the WPP's server, as shown in Figure 25-4.

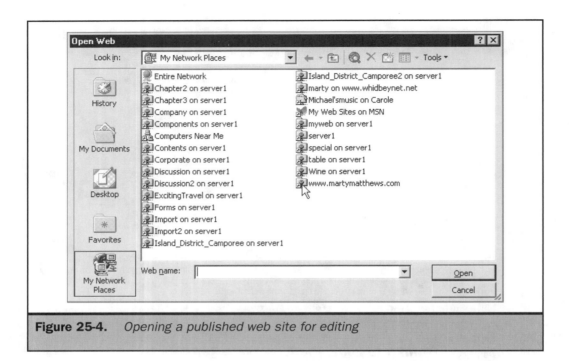

Figure 25-4.   *Opening a published web site for editing*

3. Double-click the web and click Open to open it in FrontPage. Except for the fact that you are doing it long distance, this is no different from editing on your own computer, as you can see in Figure 25-5.

4. When you are done, save and close the web as you would on your local server

 If you can't edit online because of policies your WPP has instituted or for any other reason, you can still edit the web on your computer and publish it again on the server (either the entire web or just the pages that have changed).

Deleting a Web on a Server

Another approach to correcting or changing a web on a server is to delete it from the server and copy it again.

 As explained earlier in this chapter, depending on how you are set up on your server, your WPP may not allow you to delete your entire web because it would be the same as deleting your primary folder on the server. You can instead delete all of the contents and republish the entire web to replace the contents.

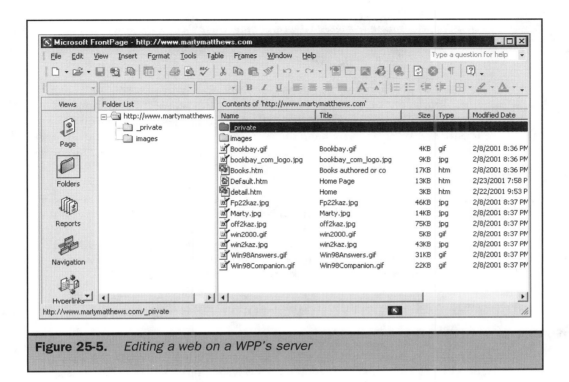

Figure 25-5. Editing a web on a WPP's server

To delete your web:

1. In FrontPage, with your Internet connection active, open the web as just described to edit it.

2. When the web has opened in FrontPage, select Delete Web from the File menu. You may be asked for your username and password. In the Confirm Delete dialog box, you are asked to choose Remove FrontPage Information From This Web Only, Preserve All Other Files And Folders, or Delete This Web Entirely. To fully remove a web, you need to choose Delete This Web Entirely. Make your choice and click OK.

Note   *If you don't have Delete Web on the File menu, you can add it by opening the Tools menu and choosing Customize to open the Customize dialog box. Select the Commands tab, click File in Categories, scroll through the commands until Delete Web is visible, and drag Delete Web to the File menu in your FrontPage window. The File menu will open and allow you to put the command where you want it in the menu (I put it just below Close Web).*

To delete single or multiple pages in a web, simply delete them on your local computer and then republish your web. FrontPage will compare your local web with the one you published and ask if you want a particular page deleted.

Once the web is deleted, repeat the steps given previously to again copy the web to the web server. If you continue to have problems doing this, contact the webmaster or server administrator. It may be possible to delete individual files from the web server outside of FrontPage (provided you have the correct permissions), but this can confuse FrontPage. FrontPage keeps track of all the components of your web; if you change any of them outside of FrontPage, it may end up looking for files that no longer exist or are in a different place.

If you successfully copy your web to the server but find that some elements don't function correctly, first make sure that the web works correctly on your local server. Then contact your webmaster or server administrator and explain the problem. If other webs using the same feature work correctly on the web server, the odds are that the problem is in your web. If the problem is common to other webs on the web server, then the FrontPage Server Extensions might not be installed correctly.

Publishing to a Server Without FrontPage Server Extensions

You can also publish a web created in FrontPage to a web server that isn't running FrontPage Server Extensions. While any features relying on the server extensions (forms, Web Components, and so on) will not function, all the standard HTML functions, such as hyperlinks, will be unaffected.

Using FrontPage's Publish Web option to publish to a web server without the FrontPage Server Extensions is very similar to publishing with the FrontPage Server Extensions. The Publish Web option publishes your web pages to an FTP (File Transfer protocol) server, rather than a web server. The FTP server usually provides access to the same directories as the WPP's web server, so a web browser can immediately open your web pages. In some cases, the webmaster or server administrator will have to activate your pages once they are uploaded to the FTP server. You will need permission to write to the destination FTP server. Your webmaster or server administrator will be able to assign the proper permission to your account.

The following instructions show you how to publish a FrontPage web to a server without the FrontPage Server Extensions using the Publish Web option. (The first several steps are exactly like those given earlier for publishing to a server with the FrontPage Server Extensions.)

1. Start FrontPage if necessary. If you use dial-up networking to access the Internet, activate your Internet connection.

2. In FrontPage, open the local copy of the web you want to place on the web server.

3. Open the File menu and select Publish Web. The Publish Destination dialog box will open.

4. Enter the URL to your web site as you would if you used the FrontPage Server Extensions, except precede it with **ftp://** similar to this:

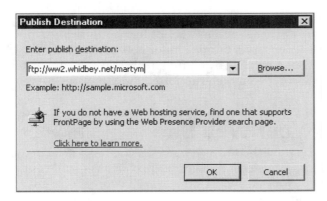

Your folder path for an FTP transfer is probably different from the URL used in a web browser. Be sure to clearly understand from your WPP the path to use for each.

5. Click OK. If and when asked, enter your username and password and click OK. If you are told that web does not exist, click OK to create a web at that location.

6. When the Publish Web dialog box opens and a connection has been established, click Publish. You'll see a message about how the publishing is going and how much of the process has completed. When the web is published, you'll see a completion message similar to the one you saw when publishing to a server with the FrontPage Server Extensions, except that you can't immediately go and view your web.

7. To test your web, start your favorite browser and enter the URL that you have been told to use (it may not be the same server name and path that you used in Step 4). Your web should appear.

Entering the correct information in these steps is crucial. If anything is wrong, it won't work. Be very clear with your WPP about the server name to which you will publish through FTP your web (Step 4); the path to your web site on that server (Step 4); the user ID and password to use (Step 5); and the URL, user ID, and password to access the Internet and view your site with a browser (Step 7). Carefully look for typos and spurious characters. Do not assume that any of the example information used in these steps is correct for you; it probably isn't. Keep trying. If you are using a correct server name, path and folder, and user ID and password, this will work.

The specific information that you should enter for the FTP server name and path is unique to a WPP or network installation. If after several attempts the copying is not working, you need to contact your WPP or network/server administrator.

Even if the web server that will host your web pages does not have the FrontPage Server Extensions, you may still be able to have the same functionality. For example, most servers will have an application or script for handling form input. You will need to ask your webmaster or server administrator how to access the application and then incorporate it into your web page by editing the HTML. Of course, it would be much easier if the server hosting your web supported the FrontPage Server Extensions.

Promoting Your Web Site

Once your web site is published to a web server, you need to let people know that it is there. If your web site is business related, the first step is to tell your existing customers about it. You might include an announcement with your regular invoicing, for example. You should also include your URL in all your conventional advertising, including your business cards, invoices, statements, purchase orders, drawings, reports, and any other document you produce. It's not uncommon to see URLs on everything from television commercials to billboards.

*A good reason to get your own domain name is that the address is usually easier to remember and easier to include on other literature than if your web were hosted on another domain. For example, consider **http://www.yourserver.com/yourweb/** compared to **http://www.yourdomain.com**.*

Being Found by a Search Engine

You also need to make sure you can be found on the Web by anyone looking for the products and services you offer. A number of search engines for the Web have been developed. Some, like Digital's AltaVista, actively search the Web for information. Others, like Yahoo, which also searches the Web, allow web sites to suggest their sites to them. Figure 25-6 shows Yahoo's How To Suggest Your Site page (**http://docs.yahoo.com/info/suggest**).

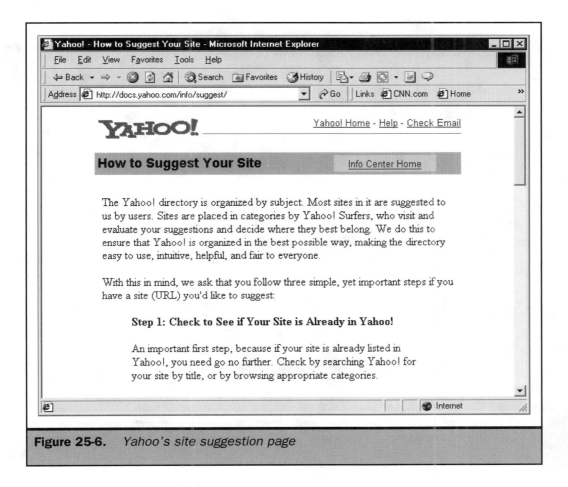

Figure 25-6.   *Yahoo's site suggestion page*

You can also suggest your web site to virtually all the search engines. A simple way to reach a number of search engines is to use the Submit It! web site (**http://www.submit-it.com/**), where for a fee (currently $59 for two URLs), your single entry is submitted to up to 400 search engines and directories that you select, as shown in Figure 25-7.

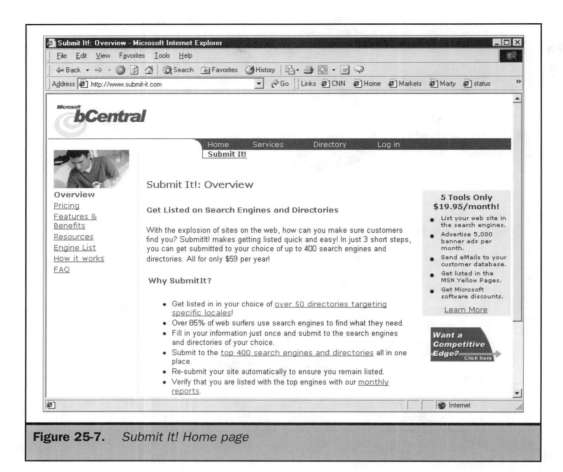

Figure 25-7.   *Submit It! Home page*

Table 25-2 gives names and addresses of a few of the search engines that you should make sure you are correctly listed on.

Search Engine	Web Address
800Go	http://www.800go.com/
AltaVista	http://www.altavista.com/
AOL Search	http://search.aol.com/
Ask Jeeves	http://www.ask.com/

Table 25-2.   *Search Engines*

Search Engine	Web Address
Excite	http://www.excite.com/
Google	http://www.google.com/
GoTo	http://www.goto.com/
Hot Bot	http://www.hotbot.com/
Infoseek	http://www.go.com/
Lycos	http://www.lycos.com/
MSN Web Search	http://search.msn.com/
NorthernLight	http://www.northernlight.com/
Switchboard	http://www.switchboard.com/
Web Crawler	http://www.webcrawler.com/
Yahoo!	http://www.yahoo.com/

Table 25-2. *Search Engines* (continued)

Making Your Web Search Engine–Friendly

Since many search engines are actively searching the Web for sites, it helps to have an introductory paragraph on your home page that gives a concise description of your site. The introductory paragraph should include the keywords that apply to your site. You can also enter a page title (as distinct from the title at the top of the page) and keywords or *meta tags* on your home page; some search engines will reference your page title and index your web based on the keywords. The page title and keywords can be entered in the Page Properties dialog box or directly in the HTML view of your page. Here are the steps to use the Page Properties dialog box:

1. With the web you want titled and indexed, open FrontPage, open the home page in Page view, open the File menu, and choose Properties (you may have to expand the menu). The Page Properties dialog box will open, as shown in Figure 25-8.

Note *The automatic page titles that get generated during page creation are often not useful for purposes of searching, such as the Home Page title shown in Figure 25-8. It is therefore important that you look at this and set the page title to something more appropriate.*

Page Properties

General | Background | Margins | Custom | Language | Workgroup

Location: http://server1/marty/Default.htm

Title: Home Page

Base location:

Default target frame:

Background sound

    Location: _____ Browse...

    Loop: 0 ☑ Forever

Design-time control scripting

    Platform: Client (IE 4.0 DHTML)

    Server: Inherit from Web

    Client: Inherit from Web

Style...

OK Cancel

Figure 25-8. *Changing the page title and keywords*

2. Replace the page title with one that is more descriptive of the web and open the Custom tab.

3. In the User Variables section, click Add to open the User Meta Variable dialog box. In the Name text box, type **keywords**. In the Value text box, type the words you want indexed separated by commas, as shown here:

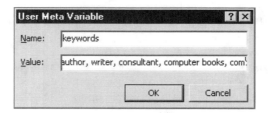

User Meta Variable

Name: keywords

Value: author, writer, consultant, computer books, com

OK Cancel

4. When you have entered all the keywords you can think of, click OK twice to close both the User Meta Variable dialog box and the Page Properties dialog box.

5. In FrontPage, click the HTML tab. In the Head section at the top of the listing, you should see the page title and keywords that you entered, similar to these for Marty's web:

```
<html>

<head>
<title>Martin S. Matthews, author, writer, consultant</title>
<meta http-equiv="Content-Type" content="text/html;
charset=windows-1252">
<meta http-equiv="Content-Language" content="en-us">
<meta name="GENERATOR" content="Microsoft FrontPage 5.0">
<meta name="ProgId" content="FrontPage.Editor.Document">
<meta name="keywords" content="Martin S. Matthews, Martin
     Matthews, Marty Matthews, author, writer, consultant,
     computer books, computer magazines, computers, software,
     Windows XP, Windows 2000, Windows 98, FrontPage 2002,
     FrontPage 2000, FrontPage 98, Office XP, Office 2000,
     Office 97, Osborne/McGraw-Hill, Microsoft Press">
<style>
```

You can see how you can also go into the HTML tab and directly enter or change a title and keywords.

Other Promotional Steps You Can Take

A useful tool for promoting your web site is *reciprocal links*. These are simply hyperlinks on your web page that point to someone who has a link to your site. Say you sell mountain climbing equipment. You could search the Web for climbing clubs and other groups with web sites relating to climbing. You then contact the owners of the sites, offering to put a link from your site to theirs if they will return the favor. This way, anyone who finds any of the sites you're linked to has a direct link to your site. If you gather enough links on your site, it may become a starting point for people who are surfing the Net.

You shouldn't overlook a press release, either. When your web site goes online or you make a major addition to your site, let the press and publications related to your business know about it. What you should *not* do is advertise your web site or business in newsgroups, unless the newsgroup is specifically run for that purpose. Say you decide to have a sale on climbing equipment. In your zeal to let the world know, you post a message on a recreational climbing newsgroup. The one result you can count on is that you will be flooded with "flames" (rather unpleasant, pointed e-mail messages), and frankly, you will deserve them.

A surefire way to get your web site widely known is to produce an outstanding web site. Today there are approaching 100 million web sites on the World Wide Web. Aim to be in the top 5 percent of your particular organization. In the era of conventional marketing, that goal would have been virtually impossible for a small business, but the web is a new paradigm. Creativity and content count more than advertising budgets. Give people a reason to visit your site by providing content that is unique and useful to them. Then package it in an effective, pleasing design. Review the section entitled "Rich Content" toward the end of Chapter 1. Take the time to explore the Web and gather ideas for your own site. (Gathering ideas is fine; however, gathering graphics or other actual content, no matter how easy it is, is a violation of copyright laws.)

The World Wide Web, whether you use it for business or pleasure, is having an effect on society as fundamental as the invention of the printing press. With FrontPage, you have the tools to participate in this new world.

Case Study: Promoting the BookBay

The BookBay is a small rural bookstore located on Whidbey Island in Puget Sound in Washington state. Its owner, Brad Bixby, is also the innovative creator of the web site, **http://www.bookbay.com/**, which you can see in Figure 25-9. Since the BookBay is a small independent bookstore, the problem of trying to promote its site loomed quite large. As a result, we asked him what his secrets were. Here are his answers.

"I advertise my web site address in everything my customers see, from yellow page ads to fliers, bag stuffers, bookmarks, and business cards.

"It is important to know how each of the search engines (or directories—since they work a bit differently) operate. Do they use page titles, meta tags (company name, description, and keywords), first paragraph text, keyword frequency, or submitted site descriptions, or all of them in their search? These are the things that put your page on top of everyone else's."

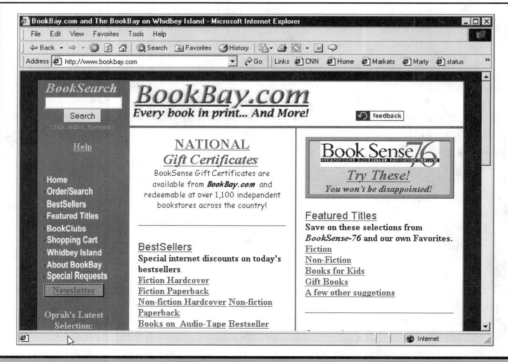

Figure 25-9. *BookBay's home page*

As another example of how meta tags are used, the BookBay's meta tags are shown next:

```
<html>
<head>
<meta name="description" content="BookBay.com - Serving whidbey Island and the world - Every
    Book In Print... And More!">
<meta name="keywords" content="BookBay, Book, Bay, whidbey, washington, Bookstore, Oprah,
    winfrey, Book Club, Northwest, Freeland, Fiction, Cooking, Computer, Gay, Lesbian,
    Bestsellers, Childrens, Gifts, Art, Jewelry, Brad, Bixby, Forward, Seattle,  Langley,
    Coupeville, Clinton, Oak Harbor, Puget, ">
<title>BookBay.com and The BookBay on whidbey Island</title>
</head>
```

"Also, think like someone surfing the web and tailor your keywords, titles, meta tags, etc., accordingly. What are they looking for? What keyword queries would they use in a search engine? The statistics I gather on my web site include information on referring links. Especially helpful are links from search engines, which often detail the keywords entered by the visitor.

"Develop a 'hook' to bring people to your page. It may not be a direct income source, but the first thing you need to do is get them to your site. Not one sale has ever been made on the Internet from someone who doesn't know you exist. One hook on my page is book clubs. Another is local authors. A hook not only gives people a reason to come to my page, it gives them a reason to come back. I also have Whidbey Island and Freeland (the town where I'm located) history pages to attract people interested in the area. If someone is just looking for a bookstore or books, they are probably not going to find me, but if they are looking for the Oprah Winfrey Book Club, Whidbey Island, or Freeland, they are very likely to see my site in the top of the list.

"After I have submitted my site to the major search engines, I check the top ones to see how I compare to other sites that have similar information, and in the book industry, that's a lot. If I am listed thirtieth, chances are people are not going to get to me. My objective is to be in the top ten listings when people go searching for any of my hooks. For example, using the search phrase 'bookstores Whidbey' on MSN Search at the time this is written [Spring 2001], I turned up first, as you can see in Figure 25-10; but unfortunately that is not always the case.

"You may hear about promoting your web site using reciprocal links. For a personal or informational site I think that is a good idea. The problem with using links to other sites from a commercial site is that if someone uses the link, there is a good chance you have lost them before they have seen everything you have to offer. It's kind of like having a store that has all the popular items right next to the front door. The customers never get to the back of the store to see what else is offered. You may get some people linking to your site from elsewhere, but is that more important than keeping the ones you have in your site? I have seen very few commercial sites that use reciprocal links.

EXTENDING YOUR
WEB SITE

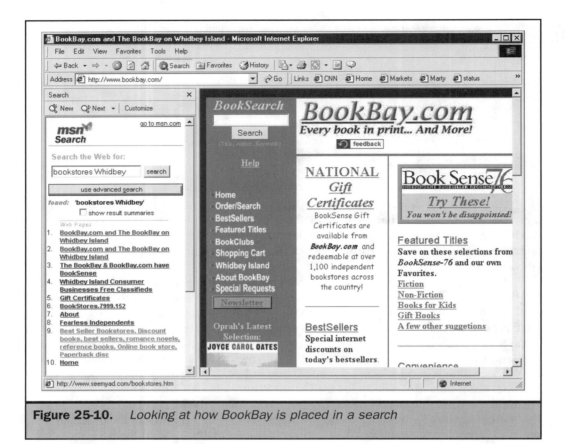

Figure 25-10. *Looking at how BookBay is placed in a search*

"If I find it necessary to link to another site, I do so in frames. Visitors are able to link to another site, but my logo and a link back to my site is always present."

Brad Bixby, the BookBay ***http://www.bookbay.com/***
(The name "BookBay" and the quotations from Brad Bixby are used with the permission of the BookBay.)

Probably the two most important tips that Brad mentioned were to use every means possible to promote your web and to repeatedly test to see how your web is coming out on searches. By testing your ranking and then changing your title, meta tags, and keywords, you can fine-tune how people will find you. Brad has certainly done this successfully and provides a good example.

The
Complete
Reference

FrontPage
2002

Part V

Appendixes

The
Complete
Reference

FrontPage
2002

Appendix A

FrontPage 2002
Installation

Installing FrontPage 2002 is an easy task, as you'll discover in this appendix. The onscreen instructions are clear, the steps are few, and with the information in this appendix, you will soon have FrontPage ready to use.

FrontPage 2002 is available in two ways: as a component of several Microsoft Office XP editions, and as a stand-alone product. In both cases, the software comes in a CD package with several other products. In addition to FrontPage, this appendix will discuss the installation of SharePoint, FrontPage 2002 Server Extensions, Internet Information Services 5.0, and Microsoft Personal Web Server 4.0.

What You Need to Install FrontPage 2002

To install FrontPage 2002, you'll need the following minimum software and hardware:

- Windows 98, Windows 98 SE, Windows Me, Windows NT 4.0 with Service Pack 6 or later, Windows 2000, or Windows XP (Windows 95 does not support Office XP)

- A PC with a Pentium 133 or higher

- 64MB of memory for Windows 98, Windows Me, or Windows NT 4.0; 96MB of memory for Windows 2000 or Windows XP

- 229MB of free disk space for the default installation of Office XP on Windows Me, Windows 2000, or Windows XP, or if installing over Office 2000 SR1, 279MB of free disk space otherwise. SharePoint, which includes the FrontPage Server Extensions will require another 14MB, while the FrontPage Server Extensions alone will require 10MB

- Super VGA (800×600) or higher with 256 or more colors from your video adapter and monitor

- Microsoft Mouse or compatible pointing device

- CD-ROM or DVD drive

- 28.8 baud or faster modem or connection through a LAN to the Internet

Note   *When installing on Windows 98 or Windows NT 4.0, Setup may detect that you have some out-of-date system components and go through a Microsoft Office System Files Update process before launching into the normal Office XP setup.*

To access the Internet or an intranet network in which FrontPage will be used, you also must have installed the TCP/IP network protocols (see Chapter 1 for a discussion of the protocols and Chapter 24 for the installation of TCP/IP) on a dial-up network using a modem and/or on a local area network (LAN) with its adapter card. If you are using an Internet browser with Windows 98/Me/NT/2000/XP, you have already installed and correctly configured TCP/IP. If you are just now coming up on the Internet or a network, you need to install TCP/IP. The easiest way to do so is to use the Internet Connection Wizard discussed in the "Connecting to the Internet" section later in this appendix.

If you are upgrading from an earlier version of FrontPage (98 or 2000), you need to have one of those versions installed on your computer, or have the floppy disk or CD available.

Installing FrontPage 2002

The only difference between the stand-alone version of FrontPage 2002 and one of the Office XP versions that includes FrontPage is the other components included in Office. FrontPage itself is exactly the same in both versions. In terms of installation, the only difference is that more components can be installed with the Office XP. For that reason, we will limit ourselves to discussing that edition.

You may use the defaults set up in the installer to determine which components of FrontPage to install, or use either the complete or custom installation procedure. In the custom installation, you determine what to install. If you use the defaults, recommended for most users, all FrontPage Components will be installed except the additional themes, which will automatically be installed the first time you try to use them (given you put the Office or FrontPage CD in its drive). The default installation is the choice assumed in this book and reflected in its examples and illustrations. If you choose Complete, all facets of Office XP are installed (including the additional themes in FrontPage), whereas if you choose Custom, you can choose which components to install.

 In Office XP or FrontPage 2002, the folder or directory path for installing Office and/or FrontPage software will be chosen for you. You no longer have a choice of where to install the applications. The Setup program creates the default directories in which Office and/or FrontPage will be installed.

Using the Default Installation

Follow these steps for the default installation of FrontPage:

1. Insert the first Office XP CD into your drive. You will see several messages to the effect that the installer is being set up. Then a dialog box will appear, requesting your name, initials, organization name, and CD key (located on the back of the CD case or sleeve). Enter these and press Next. The End User License Agreement (EULA) will appear.

2. Accept the license agreement and click Next. The dialog box shown in Figure A-1 appears—here you can choose between a default installation, a custom version, or a complete installation.

3. Click Install Now and then click Next. You are shown the list of applications that will be installed. This list will depend on the version of Office you are installing (but should always include FrontPage). If it doesn't, click Back, choose Custom, and go to the "Performing a Custom Installation" section to see if FrontPage is on the Office XP CD (it is not in every version of Office).

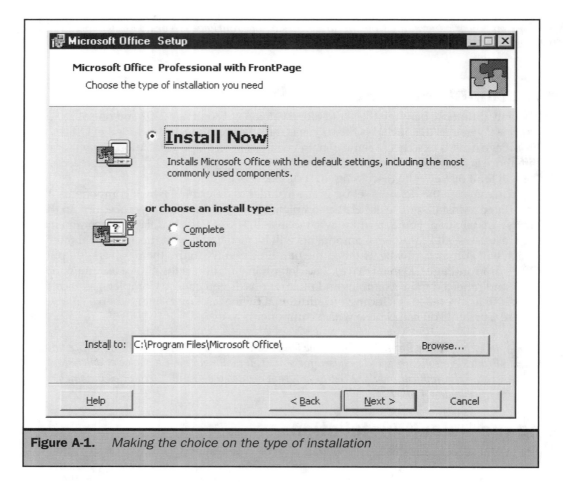

Figure A-1. *Making the choice on the type of installation*

4. Click Install. If you are upgrading from an earlier version of Office or FrontPage, Setup will tell you that it will examine your system to confirm the existence of the previous version. Click Continue. If Setup can't find a qualifying product, a dialog box will appear telling you so. If you have FrontPage on another drive, or if you have already removed it but have the original disk, you need to tell Setup which drive to search. Click Locate. A Locate Directory dialog box will appear. If you want a CD or floppy searched, insert it in its drive. Select the correct drive and directory and click OK.

5. You will see a dialog box that says Now Installing Office, with a display of the installation's progress. When the installer has finished, you will be told the installation was completed successfully. Click OK.

6. Start FrontPage by opening the Start menu and choosing Programs | Microsoft FrontPage. You are asked if you want to activate your copy of FrontPage or

Office. Click Yes or No and, if Yes, follow the instructions. To do so, you will either need to be connected to the Internet or call in the information on the telephone using an 800 number. When activation is completed, the FrontPage window will open with a new page in Page view, as shown in Figure A-2. You have proven that the installation was completed successfully. Close FrontPage.

If your installation did not complete successfully, look carefully at the error messages you have received. Correct any anomalies that are mentioned, like exiting from all programs that are running except Windows, or providing more disk space, and then rerun Setup.

Performing a Custom Installation

Use the Custom installation when you want to install only some of the Office or FrontPage component programs—for instance, if you are reinstalling FrontPage 2002. If you are installing FrontPage over a previous copy, you will want to use the same directory structure you used originally, in order to preserve access to your webs. If you want to use a different directory, you will have to uninstall the first copy, and then reinstall the program to the desired directory.

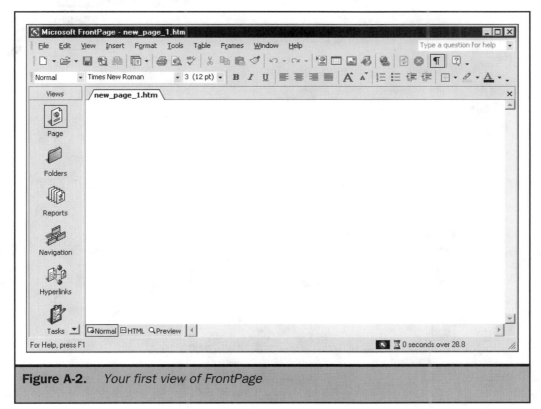

Figure A-2.   *Your first view of FrontPage*

To perform a Custom installation, follow these steps:

1. Complete the first two steps in the default installation until you arrive at the window where you choose the type of installation you want. Click Custom.

2. Select the Office applications you want to install, and whether you want the typical options or a detailed installation of each application. If you choose the typical options, you will be shown the list of applications to be installed (as in Step 3 of the default installation), which will then continue as described in the previous section. Note the detailed installation process.

3. Click Choose Detailed Installation Options For Each Application and click Next. Click the plus sign (+) next to Microsoft FrontPage For Windows. The FrontPage options will appear, as shown in Figure A-3. A gray container means only some of the options will be installed. A white container means all the options will be installed, and the numeral one in a container means the option will be installed on first use (at which time the CD will be needed).

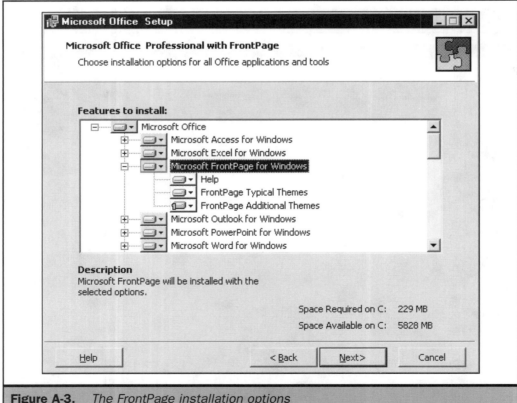

Figure A-3.   *The FrontPage installation options*

When you select a choice, its description is shown in the lower part of the dialog box.

4. Click FrontPage Additional Themes and choose Run From My Computer and you'll see the FrontPage parent container change from gray to white, meaning that all FrontPage options will be installed. Make any other selections appropriate for you. Click Next. You will be shown the list of applications to be installed.

5. Click Install. The Now Installing Office dialog box will appear as in Step 5 of the default installation and will continue as described in the previous section.

Connecting to the Internet

If you are not connected to the Internet and wish to be, this section will help you. It is not necessary to be connected to the Internet to use FrontPage, but if you wish to put your webs on an Internet server and your company does not have an Internet server to which you have a LAN connection, then you need to be connected to the Internet. Use these steps to do so:

1. Click the Internet Connection Wizard if it is on your desktop. (All versions of Windows from Windows 98 forward have the Internet Connection Wizard on the desktop by default; it will be labeled "Connect to the Internet" if the connection has not been made.)

2. If Internet Connection Wizard is not on the desktop, it is highly likely you are already connected to the Internet or have the ability to be (Windows XP in many circumstances automatically sets up the connection). To test this, double-click the Internet Explorer on the desktop or open the Start menu and select it. It should open with the current day's web page from MSN or the home page chosen for this computer. If you see an Internet page without a date, type **http://www.msn.com** in the Address field at the top and MSN should open.

3. If you are not connected to the Internet, open Windows Explorer and the C:\Program Files\Internet Explorer\Connection Wizard folder. Double-click the Icwconn1.exe file.

4. When the Internet Connection Wizard opens (as shown in Figure A-4), select how you want to connect to the Internet, via phone lines or your LAN. If you choose LAN and click Next, skip to Step 6.

 The figures here show the dialog boxes in Windows 2000. Those in Windows 98, and Windows XP are slightly different.

5. If you choose Connect Using My Phone Line and click Next, you are asked to enter the phone number, country, and area code (if needed). Click Next again.

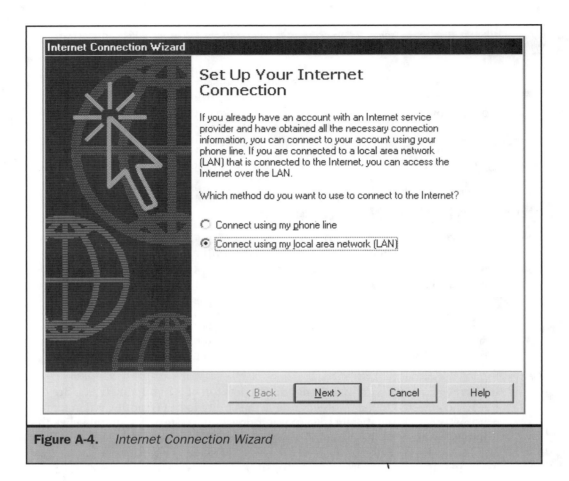

Figure A-4. *Internet Connection Wizard*

6. Enter the username and password given to you by your Internet Service Provider (ISP), then click Next. Enter the name of the connection and click Next again. When asked if you want to set up an Internet Mail Account, for now choose No, click Next, and then Finish. The new connection should appear in the Dial-up or Network and Dial-up Connection dialog box.

7. Double-click your new connection. If you are trying to connect and your modem is not set up, you are told that will be done next. Follow the instructions to do this, and finally click OK to restart your computer. If necessary, double-click your new connection again, and voila, you should be connected. An icon should appear in the system tray on the right of the taskbar. Again try opening your Internet Explorer as described previously. It should now work.

8. If you are told that file and printer sharing is turned on for your Internet connection, and that it should be turned off to protect you from someone on the Internet accessing your files, click OK.

9. Close Internet Explorer, double-click the connection icon in the system tray, and click Disconnect or Disconnect Now to shut down your Internet connection.

If you are having trouble with your Internet connection, the problem is probably related to one of several things: your modem; or the ID, password, or setting associated with your Internet account. To check your account, call your network administrator or Internet service provider (ISP) and go over what you are using. If that is not the problem, look into the modem by opening the Control Panel and double-clicking Modems or Phone and Modem Options. In the latter case, open the Modems tab, select your modem and click Properties. In the dialog box that opens, click the Diagnostics tab and then click either Query Modem or More Info. You should get a list of commands and responses, as shown next. If not, click Help in the Modems control panel or the Control Panel window itself and utilize the Modem Troubleshooter Troubleshooting Modems.

Installing a Local Web Server

A local web server allows you to publish your webs on your computer, and lets others on your network view your webs. It is not necessary to have a personal web server to create FrontPage webs; you can keep your files on your computer as disk-based webs as you are creating them and then publish them to a remote server when you are ready for others to see them. Neither version (Office XP or stand-alone) of FrontPage 2002 comes with a web server, but depending on your operating system you may have one available. If you are using Windows NT 4.0, Windows 2000 (either Server or Professional), or Windows XP (either Server or Professional) you have Internet Information Services (IIS) available to you. If you are using Windows 98 (either original or Second Edition), you have the Microsoft Personal Web Server (PWS) available on the Windows 98 disk. If you are using Windows Me and have the Windows 98 CD, you can install the Windows 98 PWS on Windows Me. This book recommends and assumes you have installed and are using either IIS or PWS. The installation of these two web servers will be described next.

If you are installing across a network—the installation files are located on a network server instead of a CD—use the Windows Explorer to open the appropriate folder on that server instead of using the CD in the following sections.

Installing Internet Information Services

Microsoft Internet Information Services included with Windows NT 4.0 Server or Windows 2000, XP Server and Professional, is a powerful, full featured commercial web server and is the web server you need to run either a full World Wide Web site or a major intranet. Most importantly, IIS allows you to create and support a large number of complex webs. The version of IIS in Windows 2000 Professional or Windows XP Professional does not allow subwebs (webs within webs). It also has some limitations on the number of simultaneous connections, and you cannot control the bandwidth used by any one user. Other than this, it has all the capabilities of the server version. To determine if you have IIS already installed, or to install IIS, you must have the operating system CD available, either directly or across the network, and then perform the following steps:

1. Open the Start menu, choose Settings | Control Panel (in XP you don't have to click Settings), and double-click Add/Remove Programs. The Add/Remove Programs dialog box will open.

2. Click Add/Remove Windows Components. The Windows Components dialog box will open. Scroll down until you see Internet Information Services (IIS). If it is checked, as shown in Figure A-5, then IIS is already installed and you can use it.

3. If IIS is not checked, insert the Windows CD in its drive or connect to the Windows CD files over the network, click the IIS check box, and click Next. Dialog boxes will appear telling you how the installation is progressing. When you are told you have successfully completed installation, click Finish.

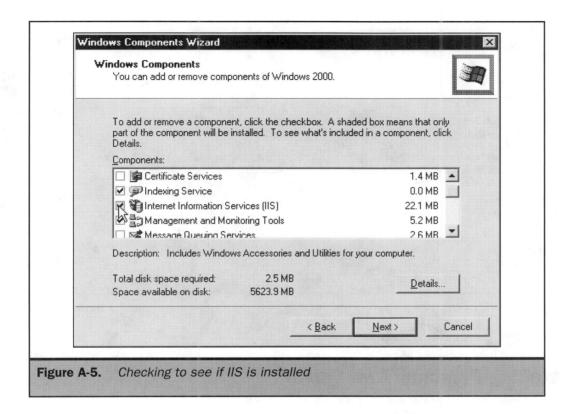

Figure A-5.   *Checking to see if IIS is installed*

4. To check to see if IIS is installed in either Windows 2000 or XP Professional, double-click Control Panel | Administrative Tools and then double-click Internet Services Manager. In either Windows 2000 or XP Server, open the Start Menu and choose Programs | Administrative Tools | Internet Services Manager.

5. Open your server and click Default Web Site. In the toolbar, four new buttons will appear. The three buttons on the right allow you to Start, Stop, and Pause IIS. The Start button should be dimmed, as shown in Figure A-6, meaning that IIS is running and ready to start delivering your webs over your network. You can see the same thing by right-clicking Default Web Site. In the context menu that opens, Start will be dimmed, while Stop and Pause will be black (active). The fourth new button, the red X, allows you to delete items.

6. Close the Computer Management dialog box and the Control Panel window.

There is much that you can do with IIS. To learn more after installing IIS, open your browser and in the Address text box, type **localhost/iishelp**, and press ENTER. A great deal of documentation will be presented to you. Unfortunately, this is beyond the scope of this book.

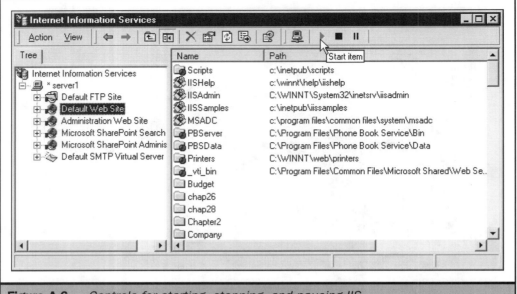

Figure A-6. *Controls for starting, stopping, and pausing IIS*

Installing Personal Web Server

The Microsoft Personal Web Server is based on Internet Information Services and is tightly integrated with Windows 98. PWS gives you several options to customize it to your needs and have it support several webs. If you want to make your webs available to a few others on your network, and want to make extensive use of FrontPage, PWS will do that. Here are the steps to install PWS from the Windows 98 CD.

1. With the Windows 98 CD in its drive, open the \Add-ons\Pws folder and double-click Setup.exe, as shown in Figure A-7.

2. Click Next in the introductory dialog box, then click Typical and Next in the second dialog box, accept the default folders, and click Next in the third dialog box. You will see an Overall Progress thermometer bar that tells you how the installation is going.

3. When you see the Thank You For Choosing Microsoft Software message, click Finish. At the prompt, click Yes to restart your computer.

You should see a new icon in the system tray on the right of your taskbar for the PWS, and a new Publish icon on your desktop for the Publishing Wizard. The latter opens the Personal Web Manager, where you control the PWS and maintain your web site. The icon in the tray tells you the PWS is running. Use the following steps to check it out:

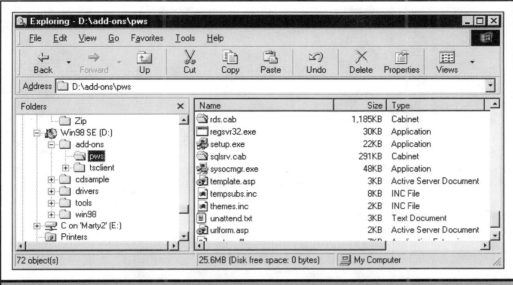

Figure A-7.   *Starting the installation of the Microsoft Personal Web Server*

1. Double-click the PWS icon in the taskbar to open the Personal Web Manager dialog box. Click Close in the Tip Of The Day dialog box, and the dialog box shown in Figure A-8 should appear.

2. In the Publishing section at the upper part of the dialog box, you can see the name of your server (**http://marty** in Figure A-8). To look at a web on your server, anyone on your network with the appropriate permission would just have to enter this server name, followed by a slash and the web name—for example, **http://marty/myweb**. Also, in the Publishing section, you see a Stop button to stop the PWS, hit it and the button changes to Start with the obvious effect. Below that, you can see the default home directory referred to often in this book. The lower part of the Main view shows you the usage of the PWS.

The HTTP address of the PWS is translated by the server to the physical disk address shown for your default home directory. Use this address as the Start Page in Internet Explorer to easily view your webs created in FrontPage.

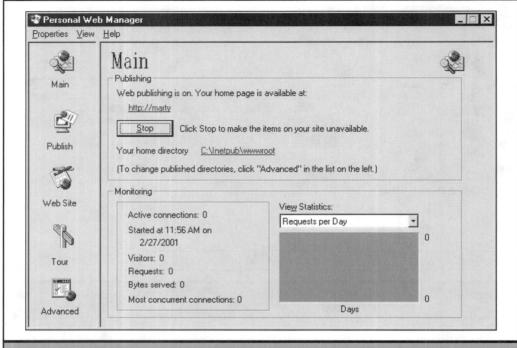

Figure A-8. *Personal Web Manager allows you to control the Personal Web Server*

3. Click Tour and run through a quick tour of the PWS. Here you will see how to use the PWS as an intranet host. The Publish and Web Site views allow you to add web pages to your web site and manage those pages. The Advanced view allows you to add HTTP aliases for the directories or folders on your hard disk (for example, the alias "Home" is automatically set for C:\Inetpub\wwroot), as well as the access permissions for those folders. The Advanced view also allows you to determine the name of your default home page—for example, Default.htm.

The name of your default home page is important because your server will automatically open it when a browser opens the web without specifying a page name. Microsoft's IIS and PWS both require Default.htm (or Default.asp) for this, while most UNIX-based servers require Index.htm (or Index.asp).

The PWS is a useful web server and will support small- to moderate-sized intranet sites very well.

Checking Your Network Setup

FrontPage includes the capability to test whether you are properly set up on a network with the TCP/IP protocol, and what your host name and IP address are. Run that test as follows:

1. From FrontPage, open the Help menu and click About Microsoft FrontPage. In the About Microsoft FrontPage dialog box, click Network Test. The FrontPage TCP/IP Test dialog box will open.

2. Click Start Test. You may be asked if you want to connect to your Internet service provider (ISP). If you want to use a local server for the creation of your webs, click Cancel in the Connect To dialog box. (The use of a local server is assumed and recommended in this book.)

3. Your test results will appear. If all is well, they will look similar to those shown here:

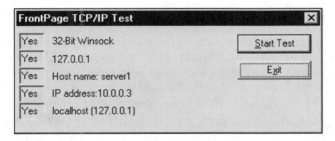

The following table explains each of the boxes in the FrontPage TCP/IP Test dialog box and what a negative answer might mean.

4. Click Exit to close the FrontPage TCP/IP Test dialog box, then click OK to close the About Microsoft FrontPage dialog box.

Element	Description
32-Bit Winsock	"Yes" verifies that the software connection between Windows and TCP/IP networking is present. "No" means that either TCP/IP is not installed, or you have a Windows problem and probably need to reinstall it. See the list of ideas and solutions for installing TCP/IP that follows.
127.0.0.1	"Yes" verifies that you have a local server available with this standard IP address. If the result is "No" and you want a local server, you need to install it.

APPENDIXES

Element	Description
Host name	"Yes" verifies the name of the server that will be used by FrontPage. If the result is "No" and Localhost is confirmed (see last item in table), you can use "localhost." "No" may mean that a server is not installed or not functioning.
IP address	"Yes" verifies the IP address of the server that will be used by FrontPage. If the result is "No" and Localhost is confirmed (see next item in table), you can use "localhost." "No" may mean that a server is not installed or not functioning.
Localhost	"Yes" verifies that the name "localhost" and its IP address can alternately be used in place of the host name. "No" means that a server is not installed or not functioning.

If any of the boxes in the TCP/IP dialog box says "No," you have a problem. Here are several ways to locate and solve these problems:

■ Is a web server, personal or otherwise, running or available on your computer? If you haven't already, you should install a web server. (This is not mandatory; you can use disk-based webs, but a web server allows you to stay on your computer while using your webs the way your clients will.) Otherwise you need to make a connection with your intranet or Internet web server.

■ Do you have two web servers assigned to port 80? If you have two servers available, only one can be assigned to port 80; the other needs to be assigned to port 8080, which can also be addressed by FrontPage.

■ Is FrontPage installed properly? Uninstall and reinstall it using nothing but defaults, and make absolutely sure nothing but Windows is running during installation.

■ If you are on a network, make sure the TCP/IP protocol has been set up. Do this by opening your Control Panel (Start menu, Settings, Control Panel or just Start | Control Panel in XP) and double-clicking Network, or Network and Dial-Up or Internet Connections in later versions of Windows. In Windows 2000 or XP, right-click Local Area Connection and choose Properties. In all cases, a dialog box should open and you should see the TCP/IP Internet protocol, as shown in Figure A-9. If you don't have TCP/IP as one of your protocols, click Add or Install in the Network or Local Area Connection dialog box, double-click Protocol, click Microsoft in the left list, then select TCP/IP on the right in earlier operating systems, or just double-click Internet Protocol (TCP/IP) in later operating systems. Click OK as needed and answer Yes to restarting your computer.

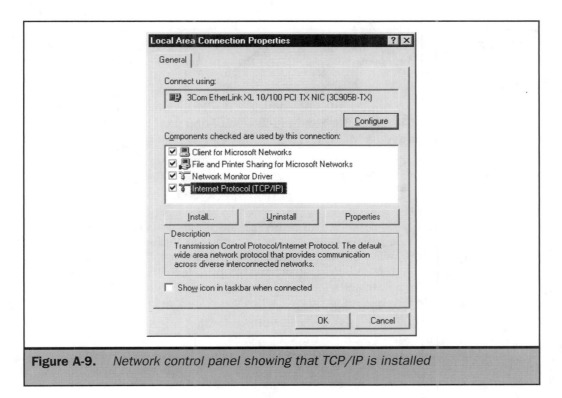

Figure A-9. *Network control panel showing that TCP/IP is installed*

- If you are accessing the Internet over a phone line, you need to have dial-up networking installed and the TCP/IP protocol assigned to it. Actually, the Internet Connection Wizard should already have installed this for you.

Installing SharePoint and FrontPage Server Extensions

SharePoint is a set of server tools for creating and running an extensive team collaboration web site on an intranet. SharePoint, which is a superset of the FrontPage 2002 Server Extensions, is described in detail in Chapter 24. SharePoint only runs under the Windows 2000 and Windows XP operating systems, either Professional or Server. Use these steps to install it.

> **Note** *If you are using Windows NT, Windows 2000, or Windows XP, and are still using FAT or FAT32, it is recommended you upgrade to NTFS (the NT File System). If you are using FAT or FAT32, you will get a message that you should upgrade, although you don't have to.*

1. With the Office XP or FrontPage first disk in its drive, open Windows Explorer, open the CD drive, open the Sharept folder, and double-click Setupse.exe, as shown in Figure A-10. Microsoft SharePoint Setup will start.

2. Enter your username, initials, organization, and product key as you did earlier in the chapter when installing Office or FrontPage. When you are ready, click Next.

3. Accept the End User License Agreement and click Next. You are shown you are about to install SharePoint, FrontPage Server Extensions, and other components. Click Install. If you are using FAT or FAT32 and Windows NT, 2000, or XP, you will get two messages recommending you upgrade to NTFS. If you don't want to, simply click OK twice, otherwise quit the SharePoint installation, insert your Windows CD, and follow the instructions to upgrade to NTFS. If you continue with the SharePoint installation, it will begin. You will then be told how the installation is progressing, including when it is completed.

4. Click OK. If directed to do so, restart your computer. Internet Explorer will open with the Server Administration page, as shown in Figure A-11. Here you can select the settings necessary to make SharePoint operate the way you want.

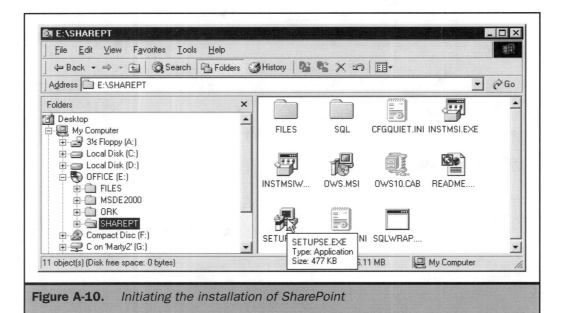

Figure A-10.   *Initiating the installation of SharePoint*

Figure A-11.   *Initial SharePoint Server Administration page*

5. Click Extend in the lower right of the Server Administration page. The Extend Virtual Server page will open. If the Administrator box is not filled in, do so. If you have a database server, fill in that information, select the site type you want, with the SharePoint-Based Web Site being the default, and click Submit. The virtual server will be created pointing to the default web site.

6. Click Administration. Here is where you do the primary administration of SharePoint. Click Go To Site Administration For Http://servername. This provides the administration of your particular server. Close the second instance of your browser and click Go To Http://servername. The SharePoint Home page should open, as seen in Figure A-12, showing you it is fully installed.

7. Familiarize yourself with the various administrative pages available. When you are ready, close both instances of your browser.

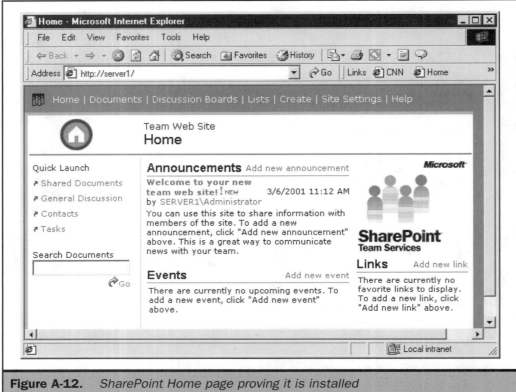

Figure A-12.   *SharePoint Home page proving it is installed*

> **Note**   *If you want to open the SharePoint Server Administration page later, open Start and choose Programs | Administrative Tools | Microsoft SharePoint Administrator in Windows 2000 or XP Server, or open Start, choose Settings | Control Panel, double-click Administrative Tools, and double-click Microsoft SharePoint Administrator in Windows 2000 or XP Professional.*

Installing FrontPage Server Extensions by Themselves

If you do not want to install SharePoint, but do want to install the FrontPage 2002 Server Extensions (FPSE) for all the reasons described in Chapter 25, you must first download the FPSE (they're free) and then install them. Here's how do to it:

1. Open your browser and the Microsoft web site **http://www.microsoftwpp.com/info**. Select the version of FPSE you want to download along with the supported platform you want to use.

2. Click OK to save the program to disk, then click OK to begin the download. The file is about 90MB, so it will take a fair amount of time depending on the speed of your Internet connection.

3. When the download is complete, double-click the file to unpack it. Select the folder where the FPSE will reside and click Unzip. When you are told the files were unzipped successfully, click OK and Close.

4. Double-click Setupse.exe, enter your username, initials, and organization, then click Next. Accept the End-User License Agreement and click Next. You are shown a list of what you will be installing—just the FrontPage Server Extensions.

5. Click Next. Installation will begin. You will be shown how far along you are and then told when the FPSE have been successfully installed. Click OK.

6. Restart your computer. To check the presence of the FPSE, open FrontPage. In the New Page or Web task pane on the right, click Web Site Templates, and double-click One Page Web.

7. Double-click the Default.htm file to open it in Page view, then open the Insert menu and choose Web Component.

If in Steps 6 and 7 you did not get any error messages about not having FrontPage Server Extensions installed, and if the only dimmed components in the Insert Web Component dialog box are List View and Document Library View (which are dependent on SharePoint), then you have successfully installed FPSE. If this is not the case, the first question to ask is did you restart your computer as requested in Step 6. If you did restart, then the installation did not go correctly. Did you get the successful completion message? Were there any error messages during installation? If so, these may point to a problem. The best solution is to try the installation again.

FrontPage, IIS or PWS, and SharePoint or FPSE should now all be installed. They represent a very powerful set of tools to develop and deliver web pages over either the Internet or an intranet. Turn to Chapter 1 to begin using them.

APPENDIXES

The Complete Reference

FrontPage 2002

Appendix B

FrontPage's Shortcut Keystrokes

When carrying out various FrontPage tasks, it is often easier to use a quick set of keystrokes instead of tedious mouse manipulations. In fact, many people prefer using the keyboard solely, rather than switching back and forth between mouse and keyboard. In light of this, a large number of shortcut keystrokes have been defined in FrontPage. This appendix lists these keystrokes according to the specific functions they perform, categorizing them so they loosely correspond to their related FrontPage menus (though not every keystroke listed is on the menu under which it is shown). They are as follows:

- File Menu Keystrokes
- Edit Menu Keystrokes
- View Menu Keystrokes
- Insert Menu Keystrokes
- Format Menu Keystrokes
- Tools Menu Keystrokes
- Table Menu Keystrokes
- Help Menu Keystrokes
- Other Keystrokes

 Many of FrontPage's shortcut keystrokes are common to other Office XP applications, especially Word.

File Menu Keystrokes

New Normal page	CTRL+N
Open page	CTRL+O
Close page	CTRL+F4
Save page	CTRL+S
Preview page in browser	CTRL+SHIFT+B
Print page	CTRL+P
Exit FrontPage	ALT+F4

Edit Menu Keystrokes

Undo action	CTRL+Z or ALT+BACKSPACE
Redo/repeat action	CTRL+Y or SHIFT+ALT+BACKSPACE

Cut selected text or graphics	CTRL+X or SHIFT+DELETE
Copy selected text or graphics	CTRL+C or CTRL+INSERT
Paste clipboard contents	CTRL+V or SHIFT+INSERT
Delete one character to the left	BACKSPACE
Delete one character to the right	DELETE
Delete one word to the left	CTRL+BACKSPACE
Delete one word to the right	CTRL+DELETE
Select all objects on a page	CTRL+A
Find text	CTRL+F
Replace text	CTRL+H
Check out a file from source control	CTRL+J
Check in a file to source control	CTRL+SHIFT+J

View Menu Keystrokes

Reveal HTML tags	CTRL+/
Refresh a page	F5
Switch between open pages	CTRL+TAB or CTRL+SHIFT+TAB

Insert Menu Keystrokes

Insert a line break	SHIFT+ENTER
Insert a non-breaking space	CTRL+SHIFT+SPACEBAR
Create a bookmark	CTRL+G
Create a hyperlink	CTRL+K

Format Menu Keystrokes

Display non-printing characters	CTRL+SHIFT+8
Change the font	CTRL+SHIFT+F
Change the font size	CTRL+SHIFT+P
Apply bold formatting	CTRL+B

Apply an underline	CTRL+U
Apply italic formatting	CTRL+I
Apply superscript formatting	CTRL+SHIFT+EQUAL SIGN
Apply subscript formatting	CTRL+MINUS SIGN
Copy formatting	CTRL+SHIFT+C
Paste formatting	CTRL+SHIFT+V
Remove manual formatting	CTRL+SHIFT+Z or CTRL+SPACEBAR
Center a paragraph	CTRL+E
Left align a paragraph	CTRL+L
Right align a paragraph	CTRL+R
Indent a paragraph from the left	CTRL+M
Indent a paragraph from the right	CTRL+SHIFT+M
Apply a style	CTRL+SHIFT+S
Apply the Normal style	CTRL+SHIFT+N
Apply the Heading 1 style	CTRL+ALT+1
Apply the Heading 2 style	CTRL+ALT+2
Apply the Heading 3 style	CTRL+ALT+3
Apply the Heading 4 style	CTRL+ALT+4
Apply the Heading 5 style	CTRL+ALT+5
Apply the Heading 6 style	CTRL+ALT+6
Apply the List style	CTRL+SHIFT+L

Tools Menu Keystrokes

Check spelling on a page	F7
Look up a word in the Thesaurus	SHIFT+F7
Display, edit, or run macros	ALT+F8
Display the Microsoft Script Editor	SHIFT+ALT+F11
Display the Microsoft Visual Basic Editor	ALT+F11
Create an Auto Thumbnail of a selected picture	CTRL+T

Table Menu Keystrokes

Insert a table	SHIFT+CTRL+ALT+T
Select the next cell's contents	TAB
Select the preceding cell's contents	SHIFT+TAB
Extend a selection to adjacent cells	Hold down shift and press an arrow key repeatedly
Select a column	Click in the column's top or bottom cell then hold down shift and press the up arrow or down arrow key repeatedly

Help Menu Keystrokes

Display the online Help	F1
Display context-sensitive Help	SHIFT+F1

Other Keystrokes

Select one character to the right	SHIFT+RIGHT ARROW
Select one character to the left	SHIFT+LEFT ARROW
Select to the end of a word	CTRL+SHIFT+RIGHT ARROW
Select to the end of a line	SHIFT+END
Select to the beginning of a line	SHIFT+HOME
Select one line down	SHIFT+DOWN ARROW
Select one line up	SHIFT+UP ARROW
Select to the end of a paragraph	CTRL+SHIFT+DOWN ARROW
Select to the beginning of a paragraph	CTRL+SHIFT+UP ARROW
Select one screen down	SHIFT+PAGE DOWN
Select one screen up	SHIFT+PAGE UP
Display the properties of a selection	ALT+ENTER
Cancel an action	ESC
Show the shortcut menu	SHIFT+F10

Activate menu bar	F10
Once active, select menu	RIGHT ARROW or LEFT ARROW
Once selected, open menu	DOWN ARROW
Select the next or previous command on the menu or submenu	UP ARROW or DOWN ARROW
Close the visible menu and submenu at the same time	ALT
Close the visible menu; or, with a submenu visible, close the submenu only	ESC
Open the program menu	ALT+SPACEBAR

Appendix C

Constructing
Web Templates

In Chapter 4, you saw how to create a page template. You even created a web template (although it was stored with the page templates). Here you will see how to create and properly store a full web template. A web template is just a web (simply a group of pages) stored in a special folder on your hard disk. The next exercise will show you how to create and save a web to use as a template.

1. Open FrontPage and create a new web using the Empty Web template. Name the web (and the folder in which it will be stored), **Budget**.

2. In Navigation view, click New Page on the toolbar to create a page automatically named Home Page.

3. Right-click the Home Page in Navigation view, and select Rename from the context menu. Type the new name, **Annual**, and press ENTER.

4. Click New Page again to add another page to your site. Click New Page three more times to create a total of five pages (the Home Page plus four more).

5. Click slowly twice (don't double-click) on each of the four pages in the Navigation pane and rename them **Q1**, **Q2**, **Q3**, and **Q4** respectively.

Tip *Press TAB to accept the first new page name change. This simultaneously moves you to the next new page.*

6. Slowly click twice on the page names in the left Folder List pane, one at a time. (If you do not see the files, press F5 to refresh; if your Folder List is not displayed, choose Folder List from the View menu.) Rename them so the page with the title "Q1" has a filename of **qtr1.htm**, "Q2" has a filename of **qtr2.htm**, and so on. The file with the title "Annual" should be renamed **Default.htm**. When you have renamed and retitled your pages, your Folder List and Navigation view should look like Figure C-1.

7. After you have completed the Budget web that will be used as a template, edit the content and structure of each page in the template, just as you would if building a normal web.

Note *Depending on the content you create, your files and folders may not match the examples precisely.*

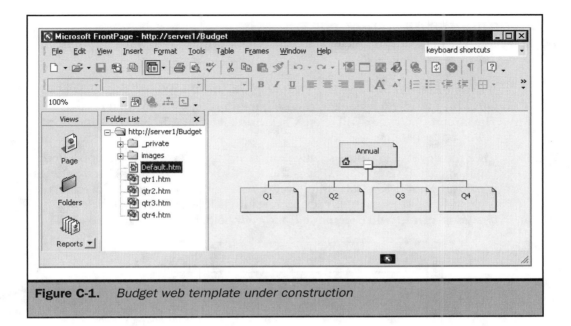

Figure C-1. *Budget web template under construction*

8. When you are happy with the web, save the Annual page (Default.htm) as a template (File | Save As, change the Save As Type to FrontPage Template, then click Save). In the Save As Template dialog box, change the Title to **Annual Budget**, change the Name to **Budget**, type **Create a quarterly budgeting model.** as the Description, click Save Template In Current Web, and click OK.

If you look at the FrontPage title bar, you will see that your template was saved in the C:\Windows\Application Data\Microsoft\FrontPage\Pages\Budget.tem folder in Windows 98 or Me. In Windows 2000 or XP, it is saved to the C:\Documents and Settings*username*\Application Data\Microsoft\FrontPage\Pages\Budget.tem folder. At this point, you have a normal web (not a template) of your full (five pages) Budget web that you want to be a template, and a single *page* template with the Annual page. To complete your web template, you need to import the special template pages into the original web, copy the web to the template Webs folder, and clean up several miscellaneous files.

Importing the Template Files

The easiest way to get the template files back into the original web is to import them. Do that now.

1. From the File menu, choose Close to close the newly created template page.

2. Open the File menu again and choose Import (expand the menu if necessary). The Import dialog box will open. Click Add File. The Add File To Import List dialog box will open.

3. Click the down arrow opposite Look In, select the C:\Windows\Application Data\Microsoft\FrontPage\Pages\Budget.tem or C:\Documents and Settings\ *username*\Application Data\Microsoft\FrontPage\Pages\Budget.tem folder, click Budget.dib, press CTRL, click Budget.inf, click Open, and then click OK. The two template files will be imported, and your Folders view will look like this:

Contents of 'http://server1/Budget'				
Name	Title	Size	Type	Modified Date
📁 _private				
📁 images				
📄 budget.dib	budget.dib	15KB	dib	3/12/2001 4:04 PM
📄 budget.inf	budget.inf	1KB	inf	3/12/2001 4:04 PM
📄 Default.htm	Annual	1KB	htm	3/12/2001 3:35 PM
📄 qtr1.htm	Q1	1KB	htm	3/1/2001 12:20 PM
📄 qtr2.htm	Q2	1KB	htm	3/1/2001 12:20 PM
📄 qtr3.htm	Q3	1KB	htm	3/1/2001 12:20 PM
📄 qtr4.htm	Q4	1KB	htm	3/1/2001 12:20 PM

Copying Files to Create a Web Template

Once you have created a web structure, you can transform it into a web template by copying all the files from the original folder to the web template folder, and modifying the special template files necessary for FrontPage to recognize the web as a template. You will copy and modify these files in Windows Explorer.

1. Locate the folder that holds all the files for the Budget web you just created. If you used the default installation for FrontPage, that folder will be C:\Inetpub\Wwwroot\Budget. When you locate and open the folder, you'll see the five HTML files you created, as well as other folders that contain additional files used in FrontPage webs, as you see in Figure C-2. The FrontPage folders (not all of which are in the current web or all webs) are described in Table C-1.

Figure C-2.   *The Budget web with the files and folders it contains*

Folder	Contents
_borders	Includes up to four .HTM files embedded in each page with the content of top, bottom, right, or left shared borders
_derived	Files that are currently checked out, as well as information for the Microsoft Indexing Service
_disc	Files for threaded discussions

Table C-1.   *FrontPage Web Folder Structure*

Folder	Contents
_fpclass	Files relating to a database results region, or relating to saving form results to a database
_private	Pages you don't want available to a browser or to searches; for example, Included pages
_sharedtemplates	Templates used in the web
_themes	Files used with themes including style sheets and images
_vti_bin	FrontPage-created common gateway interface (CGI) programs for controlling browse-time behavior, administrator, and author operations on the server
_vti_cnf	A configuration page for every page in the web, containing the name of the page, the created-by and modified-by names, and the creation and modification dates, among other variables
_vti_pvt	Several subfolders with both the current and historical To Do List files, meta-information for the web, and the dependency database
_vti_script	Visual Basic and Java scripts used in the web
_vti_txt	Text indexes used by Search boxes
*Connection*_interface	Files related to a database connection named *Connection*, created with the Database Interface Wizard
Editor	Web administration pages for managing a database created with the Database Interface Wizard
Fpdb	Files related to databases, including those created to hold form results, as well as those created by the Database Results Wizard and the Database Interface Wizard
Images	All images associated with a web
Table	Files containing the database tables or views named *Table*, created with the Database Interface Wizard

Table C-1.   *FrontPage Web Folder Structure* (continued)

2. Right-click the Budget web folder in the left pane of Windows Explorer, and select Copy from the context menu.

3. Click the folder where FrontPage web templates are stored to open it. If you used the default installation for FrontPage, this folder is C:\Windows\ Application Data\Microsoft\FrontPage\Webs in Windows 98 or Me, or C:\Documents and Settings*username*\Application Data\Microsoft\ FrontPage\Webs in Windows 2000 or XP.

4. With the Webs folder open in the right pane of Windows Explorer, right-click the right pane and select Paste from the context menu. You have now copied most of the files required for a template.

Working with the INF and MAP Files

In addition to the files you already copied, you will need to add one file and modify another in order for FrontPage to detect and use your template web. You need to add the MAP file, which stores the navigational links that the web may contain, and modify the INF file, which stores the information used to list your template in the Web Site Templates dialog box.

1. Open the folder for a web template that comes with FrontPage: the Personal template. The path to the Personal folder is C:\Program Files\Microsoft Office\Templates\1033\Webs\Personal.tem.

2. With the Personal.tem folder open, click Personal.map, as shown next. Press CTRL+C to copy the file.

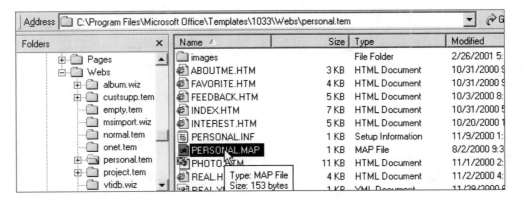

3. Open the new C:\Windows\Application Data\Microsoft\FrontPage\ Webs\Budget.tem or C:\Documents and Settings*username*\Application Data\Microsoft\FrontPage\Webs\Budget.tem folder you just created, right-click the right pane, and choose Paste to paste the MAP file into this folder.

4. Right-click the Personal.map file, and rename it **Budget.map**.

Note *While you will have to edit your own template files by hand (as described in the next several steps), to see how it works, you can use the Budget.inf and Budget.map files in the \Book\AppenC folder on the CD that came with this book.*

5. Double-click the Budget.inf file, and edit the contents using Notepad. The new contents of the file should look like this:

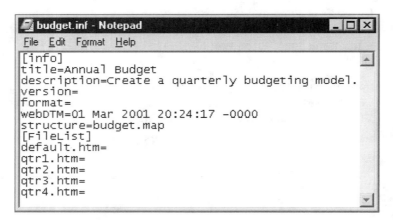

```
[info]
title=Annual Budget
description=Create a quarterly budgeting model.
version=
format=
webDTM=01 Mar 2001 20:24:17 -0000
structure=budget.map
[FileList]
default.htm=
qtr1.htm=
qtr2.htm=
qtr3.htm=
qtr4.htm=
```

Note *The webDTM line is your current date/time stamp and doesn't have to match what is shown here.*

6. Save and close the Budget.inf file.

7. Double-click the file Budget.map. If Windows does not recognize this file type, select Notepad as the application to open with MAP files.

8. Edit the file Budget.map so it looks like this (type the first line and then copy and change it for the other three lines):

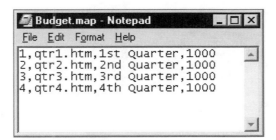

The MAP file changes the title of the page files from Q1, Q2, and so on, to 1st Quarter, 2nd Quarter, and so on.

9. Save and close the Budget.map file. Now that you have finished the INF and MAP files in your folder, your template will be recognized by FrontPage.

10. In FrontPage, open the File menu and choose Close Web to close the original Budget web. Then click the down arrow next to the New button in the toolbar and choose Web to open the Web Site Templates dialog box. Select Annual Budget and your description will appear, as shown here:

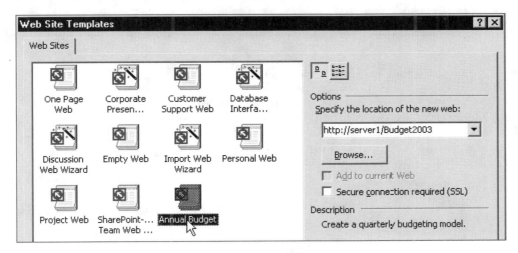

11. Enter a folder/web name of **Budget2003**, and then click OK to create a new web based on the template. The web opens with an already-designed structure and navigation links, all ready for you to customize the individual pages, as shown in Figure C-3 (your view might be different depending on the pages in your template).

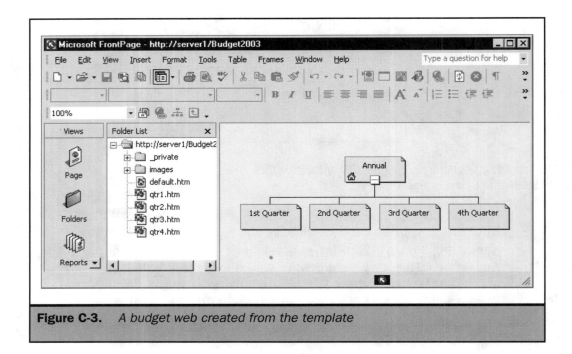

Figure C-3. *A budget web created from the template*

12. Delete the new web you just created and close FrontPage.

If your new web does not work as expected, look at the files in the template. Make sure all your files are placed where they should be and that the INF and MAP files look like those shown earlier. Since you have to edit the content of those files by hand (here, of course, you can use the CD files), it's easy to make a typing mistake.

FrontPage
2002

Appendix D

Using the Companion CD

947

The CD included with this book contains two items which are complementary to the paged text. The first, in the Book folder on the CD, holds files used within the book, organized by chapter. The second, in the Programs folder, contains many fine examples of freeware, shareware, and product demos that can enhance your FrontPage and web publishing experience.

Book Material

The materials from the book include files you are told to use in the instructions, as well as files and web pages for viewing if you choose. The best way to handle the web pages is to import them into an open web in FrontPage or create a new web using the Import Web Wizard. Click File | New | Page Or Web, select Web Site Templates, select the Import Web Wizard, provide a name for the web, and click OK. This places them in the root web on your system and properly creates all of the ancillary files.

Note *If you try to directly access the webs from the \Book\ folder on the CD, you may get a server error telling you they cannot be opened for writing. Importing the webs will fix this problem, but you can also correct it by copying the files to your hard disk, opening the Properties dialog box for \Book\Chap05\ExcitingTravel_vti_pvt\Service.lck, and removing the Read-only attribute that is automatically added to the file when it is written to the CD.*

Software Programs

The software programs on this CD have been gathered for your benefit and represent three types of software:

- **Freeware** costs nothing and can be used without further consideration. However, it has limited or no documentation and no upgrade policy. If it is copyrighted, it may not be distributed without permission from the creator.

- **Shareware** costs something. It is provided free of charge to evaluate whether you want to continue using it in your own environment. If you decide you do, you must pay a modest fee to the creator. You may then receive upgrades, printed manuals, technical support, and other benefits. If you do not pay for the product, you are expected to remove the software from your computer.

- **Demos** are provided by the vendor to let you see for yourself how the product works. There is no cost for the demo, but they are usually limited in some way—for instance, they may have fewer features, or time limits after which the product won't work.

In this appendix, we have included the vendor or creator's description of each program or script. The programs and scripts are housed in separate folders (inside the Programs folder) according to company name. In addition to the programs and scripts, helpful documentation may be found in the company folders, or perhaps listed as a help feature. In some cases, they may even be found online at a web site. If you have questions about any product, you must write or e-mail the source or vendor of the software whose name is included here and in the Readme or .TXT files on the CD. Do not contact the authors or publisher of this book, as we will not be able to help. The companies and the software they provide are as follows:

- Addsoft Corporation
  - StoreBot 2000 Standard Edition
  - StoreBot 2000 Professional Edition

- BulletProof Corporation
  - JDesignerPro 4.5

- ComCity Corporation
  - SalesCart, v.2.1 – 15-day Trial Demo
  - SalesCart PRO, v.1.5 – 15-day Trial Demo

- FerretSoft (A CNet Company)
  - WebFerret

- GoldWave, Inc.
  - GoldWave v4.21

- Stephen Le Hunte
  - HTMLib 4.0

- McWeb Software
  - J-Perk: Web Page Special Effects
  - Web Weaver 98 Gold

- Modelworks Software
  - SitePad Pro

- Quadralay Corporation
  - WebWorks Publisher Professional

- Spinwave
  - HVS ColorGIF 2.0 Demo
  - HVS JPEG 2.0 Demo

- WinZip Computing, Inc.
  - WinZip

> **Note** *The software and their descriptions are offered as is. Osborne/McGraw-Hill and the authors make no guarantee, either expressly or implied, as to the usability of the software or its fitness for a particular purpose. We do not recommend any of these packages, nor promise that they will work on your system. Subsequently, we assume no liability for damages, direct or consequential, that may result from using this software or its documentation.*

StoreBot 2000 Standard Edition

Addsoft Corporation

3094 Buckhaven Road
Chino Hills, CA 91709
Voice: (310) 338-3549
Fax: (909) 597-9962
E-mail: info@addsoft.net
Web: http://www.addsoft.net

StoreBot 2000 Standard Edition is a complete open source code shopping cart system with web-based store management. It runs on most Windows NT and 2000 Web servers, and is integrated with Microsoft FrontPage 98-2002. StoreBot 2000 uses a Microsoft Access database. Take five minutes to insert four WebBots—StoreFront, Payment, Invoice, and Manage—and your web site will be e-commerce ready. There are no monthly fees, and no programming is required. This program was designed to support SSL. Functions and features include:

- Microsoft Access database support
- Basic real-time online order tracking
- Allowance for item name, code, description, and image
- Support of single variant options (size, color, etc.)
- Built-in credit card number validation algorithm
- Online printable Invoice/Order Tracking System
- Customizable wording, font, and table layout regarding your web page

> **Note** *No documentation is included with this product. For complete online documentation and support, visit **http://www.addsoft.net/storebot**.*

StoreBot 2000 Professional Edition

Addsoft Corporation

3094 Buckhaven Road
Chino Hills, CA 91709
Voice: (310) 338-3549
Fax: (909) 597-9962
E-mail: info@addsoft.net
Web: http://www.addsoft.net

StoreBot 2000 Professional Edition contains everything in the Standard Edition, plus additional features such as:

- Basic remote browser-based administration
- Product searches
- An updateable regional tax table
- Support for up to two variant options (size, color, etc.)
- Product availability control
- International unit of measure support
- Custom defined payment method
- New order alerts

Note   *While fully functional and not time-limited, this software displays trial version notifications until registered. No documentation is included with this product. For complete online documentation, support, or to purchase and register this software, visit **http://www.addsoft.net/storebot**.*

JDesignerPro 4.5

BulletProof Corporation

20533 Biscayne Blvd. #451
Aventura, FL 33180
Voice: (305) 682-8187
Fax: (305) 933-1216
E-mail: support@bulletproof.com
Web: http://www.bulletproof.com

JDesignerPro 4.5 is a 100 percent Java, visual development and deployment solution for building data-driven intranet applications with both web-based and handheld-based clients. It easily meets design standards, and is used for cross-platform, interactive, professional, and scalable applications. JDesignerPro 4.5 includes a scalable application server deployment and supplies JDBC data access. JDesignerPro is compatible with any Java platform, JDBC, or ODBC database, any browser supporting Java, and both Palm and Pocket PC handheld devices.

SalesCart, v.2.1 – 15-day Trial Demo

ComCity Corporation

6690 Amador Plaza Rd., Suite 115
Dublin, CA 94568
Voice: (925) 556-6940
Fax: (925) 556-6945
E-mail: sales@comcity.com
Web: http://www.salescart.com

SalesCart is the original plug-in that allows anyone to add e-commerce capabilities to any new or existing Microsoft FrontPage web site. SalesCart adds itself to the FrontPage menu system and is an easy and economical way to add shopping cart capabilities to your FrontPage web sites. SalesCart requires no knowledge of HTML and allows you to design your shopping cart any way you like in FrontPage without having to learn new tools. A single license allows you to create an unlimited number of shopping carts.

SalesCart uses the open dynamic database capabilities of FrontPage, so it is compatible with any existing or new ODBC database used for your product cataloguing, including Sybase, Oracle, Informix, or Microsoft SQL. SalesCart is applicable to any size business, from small single-person operations up to large multi-national corporations. As your company grows, so does SalesCart. You can add additional functionality to SalesCart through a host of other SalesCart plug-ins, including:

- Real-time shipping modules
- Online product database management capabilities
- Online order retrievals
- Access to all major third-party transaction gateways, including: AuthorizeNet, SurePay, VeriSign, CyberCash, LinkPoint/CardService, Bank of America, and many others

*This is a 15-day fully functional time-out trial. After 15 days, the program will stop working. At that time, you are free to uninstall the product or contact ComCity at **http://www.salescart.com** to purchase a license and finish any work you have started on your e-commerce store.*

SalesCart PRO, v.1.5 – 15-day Trial Demo

ComCity Corporation

6690 Amador Plaza Rd., Suite 115
Dublin, CA 94568
Voice: (925) 556-6940
Fax: (925) 556-6945
E-mail: sales@comcity.com
Web: http://www.salescart.com

SalesCart PRO extends the features found in SalesCart and provides additional functionality, such as multi-level discounting, product optioning, and unlimited customization of the component.

*This is a 15-day fully functional time-out trial. After 15 days, the program will stop working. At that time, you are free to uninstall the product or contact ComCity at **http://www.salescart.com** to purchase a license and finish any work you have started on your e-commerce store.*

WebFerret

FerretSoft (A CNet Company)

1209 Hill Road North, Suite 109
Pickerington, OH 43147
Voice: (614) 755-3891
Fax: (614) 575-8355
E-mail: support@ferretsoft.com
Web: http://www.ferretsoft.com

WebFerret provides a handy and efficient way to use Web search engines to find information. It adds an entry to the Find option of your Windows Start button that lets you find web pages in addition to standard files and folders. Enter your search terms and WebFerret uses your Internet connection to check several popular search engines, including Lycos, AltaVista, Excite, Infoseek, Search.com, AOL Netfind, Euroseek,

LookSmart and others. You can also do more advanced searches, limiting the number of matches found or limiting the number of search engines used. Once the results are returned, tooltips give you a little more information about a site. Just double-click to bring up your browser and launch the page. WebFerret is fast, easy to use, and best of all—free!

System requirements: Windows 95, 98, ME, NT, or 2000

Key aspects of the WebFerret are as follows:

- **It's free**   WebFerret is free and may be shared in its original EXE form with friends, neighbors, even visitors to your web site or web pages. You may find it easier to simply provide a link to their site at **http://www.ferretsoft.com/** for download of the most current version.

- **It's stable and dependable**   WebFerret is over five years old, with more than 3,000,000 users worldwide.

- **It's easy to use**   Find web pages by simply entering a keyword and clicking "Find Now."

- **It's fast**   Finds results almost immediately, taking only a few seconds.

- **It provides quality results**   Searches can be narrowed by choosing to match any keyword, match all keywords, or by submitting the keywords as an exact phrase.

- **It uses a standard interface**   WebFerret uses the standard Windows interface and design of the Find utilities that come with the operating system.

- **It can be integrated with browsers**   Double-click a result or use the right mouse button to open the web page using your default browser.

- **It's always current**   WebFerret is designed to keep up with the changing nature of search engines by automatically updating how they operate. If the engines change, the WebFerret changes, too, so searches always work and are accurate.

GoldWave v4.21

GoldWave, Inc.

P.O. Box 51
St. John's, NF
Canada A1C 5H5
E-mail: chris3@cs.mun.ca
Web: http://www.goldwave.com/

GoldWave is a comprehensive digital audio editor for Windows. It is ideal for people who need to work with audio for CD editing, Java applications, web pages, games, radio and TV, or just for fun. You can use it to make everything from elaborate answering machine messages to professional CD audio content. It features real-time amplitude, spectrum and spectrogram oscilloscopes, large file editing, numerous effects, support for a wide variety of sound formats, and a CD audio extraction tool.

HTMLib 4.0

Stephen Le Hunte

155 Queens Drive, Flat 4
London,
United Kingdom N4 2AR
Voice: 44 181 450 8970
E-mail: htmlib@htmlib.com
Web: http://www.htmlib.com

HTMLib 4.0 is a complete HTML reference library that compares the three most popular web browsers for HTML functionality. The version on this CD contains no limitations. It covers Internet Explorer 4.01, Netscape 4.05, Mosaic 3.0 and later, with full cross-comparisons, examples, and screenshots. For up-to-date information on the status of the HTMLib, visit **http://www.htmlib.com**.

J-Perk: Web Page Special Effects

McWeb Software

31 Harris St., Ste 201
Brookline, MA 02446
Fax: (561) 423-4610
E-mail: info@mcwebsoftware.com
Web: http://www.mcwebsoftware.com

J-Perk adds Java animations, dynamic buttons, and special effects to web pages quickly and easily. It includes 35 special effects (that are easily customizable) to help make your web pages come alive. Simply input properties for each special effect, and J-Perk creates it with the click of a button. Put the J-Perk generated HTML code in your web page and it's ready to go! J-Perk special effects include animations, slideshows, rotating banners/billboards, Dynamic Buttons, Status Bar Text Ticker, Typewriter Text, Swirly Text, Image Fade effect, Image Cube effect, Fading Message, Dropdown menu, and Background Color Fade in/Fade out.

Includes 20 new special effects like: Scrolling Credits, Animated Buttons, Image Rollovers, Popup Alert Box, 8 new image effects and more!

APPENDIXES

This version of J-Perk can be evaluated for 30 days. After that time, you must order a registered copy from McWeb Software or remove Java Perk from your computer. Documentation for the evaluation copy is limited to online help.

Web Weaver 98 Gold

McWeb Software

31 Harris St., Ste 201
Brookline, MA 02446
Fax: (561) 423-4610
E-mail: info@mcwebsoftware.com
Web: http://www.mcwebsoftware.com

Web Weaver 98 Gold allows you to create great-looking web pages quickly and easily with a feature-rich HTML editor. Here are some of the features:

- Web Weaver 98 Gold has tutorials and wizards that help step you through web page creation.

- It features colored HTML code for easier editing; wizards for creating advanced HTML, such as imagemaps, frames, tables, and forms; easily accessible toolbars; context-sensitive help and an HTML glossary; spell-checking, web site/hyperlink checking tools, web page traffic analysis tools, and so on.

- Allows easy previewing of your web pages.

- Web Weaver Gold supports all HTML 2 and 3.2 tags, as well as Netscape and Internet Explorer HTML extensions.

- Includes free images, animated images, JavaScripts, and a form processing script.

- Ideal for beginners as well as advanced users.

 This version of Web Weaver can be evaluated for 30 days. After that, you must order a registered copy from McWeb Software or remove the program from your computer. Documentation is limited to online help for the shareware version.

SitePad Pro

Modelworks Software

Chet Murphy
14612 NE 169th St.
Woodinville, WA 98072

Voice: (425) 488-5686
Fax: (253) 830-7802
E-mail: cmurphy@modelworks.com
Web: http://www.modelworks.com

SitePad Pro is an integrated development environment (IDE) for Java, HTML, and VRML. It targets users who need to edit Java, HTML, VRML, and associated languages at the source-code level. Key features include the ability to write your own tools using JavaScript and a powerful editor supporting syntax coloring and code folding. Other features include an outline view of the content of open files, a project manager, a finder toolbar, support for both Sun and Microsoft Java tools, and much more.

Additional features include:

- Support for Sun's JDK Java tools
- Syntax coloring for HTML, Java, JSP, ASP, Perl, JavaScript, and many other file types
- A browser with class, package, and file views
- Dynamic help using script-generated indexes for Java (Javadocs) and other file types
- A project and package manager with build and rebuild commands
- Custom templates for creating new VRML, HTML, and Java files
- Custom menus, toolbars, hotkeys, and bookmarks
- Reformat command
- Block indent and un-indent
- Multilevel undo/redo
- Multiple file search and replace
- Split windows
- Line-number and column-number indicator
- Line numbers in the edit view
- Character ruler
- Input and output options for supporting Windows, UNIX, and Mac files
- Finder toolbar
- Abbreviated path name in window captions
- Support for adding new file types
- Custom scripting using JavaScript

SitePad Pro requires online registration for a 30-day trial. After the trial period expires, SitePad Pro will become a demo program restricted to opening files of 2,500 bytes or less. To continue using the product, you must order a license from Modelworks Software. Documentation is available in HTML pages and README files. All scripts include the source code.

WebWorks Publisher Professional

Quadralay Corporation

9101 Burnet Road, Suite 105
Austin, TX 78758
Voice: (512) 719-3399 x247
Fax: (512) 719-3606
E-mail: sales@webworks.com
Web: http://www.webworks.com

WebWorks Publisher Professional is the most powerful and cost-effective solution available for retargeting FrameMaker documentation when it comes to the rapidly growing and fast changing world of online formats. Using WebWorks Publisher Professional, you can easily transform FrameMaker documents and books into suitable online representations for use with the Web, online help systems, and CD-ROMs.

The following are a few key features that WebWorks Publisher Professional applies to FrameMaker:

- **Multiple online formats**   Produces documents formatted for HTML, HTML Help, WinHelp, JavaHelp, and Oracle Help for Java from a single source document or book. Even emerging online formats, like XML, are supported through WebWorks® Publisher's extensible templates and macro language.

- **Precise image control**   Controls all conversion aspects of individual graphics. Users can specify output parameters, including output file format, scaling, DPI, transparency, and rotation.

- **Enterprise integration**   Processes documents in batch mode for integration into your enterprise publication process. Ideal for large publication operations that require offline processing and automated delivery.

- **Multiple FrameMaker book support**   Preserves the full integrity of multiple cross-referenced FrameMaker books, all with a one-step conversion process.

- **Customizable character set support**   Character-by-character configurable support for nonstandard fonts. WebWorks Publisher is shipped with a library of GIF-sized characters to provide direct support for FrameMaker's Symbol font.

■ **Easily extensible user macros**   Easily modifies or creates macros for maintaining commonly used items such as running headers and footers. WebWorks Publisher includes many easy-to-customize prebuilt user macros that can be used as building blocks to suit a variety of needs.

■ **Easy and configurable online navigation**   Quickly creates easy-to-navigate online documents. WebWorks Publisher's built-in navigation macros are automatically applied to the document sequence in projects of any size. In addition, the end-user interface can be configured to take advantage of the latest HTML advances, such as frames or multiple windows.

To activate WebWorks Publisher Professional for evaluation, visit http://www.webworks.com/products/wwp_pro/default.asp and click "Try it", or e-mail them at sales@webworks.com to receive a 14-day key.

HVS ColorGIF 2.0 Demo

Spinwave

Dawn Ginn
1603 Orrington, Suite 990
Evanston, IL 60201
Voice: (870) 326-4455
Fax: (870) 326-4848
E-mail: info@spinwave.com
Web: http://www.spinwave.com

HVS ColorGIF Demo allows you to see your own images filtered by the HVS ColorGIF plug-in in a live preview window. It also shows you how big the resulting file would be and permits you to export the full product. It is full-featured for 15 days, after which you may purchase it online at **http://www.digfrontiers.com**.

Some of HVS ColorGIF 2.0's features are as follows:

■ The filter plug-in works with most major paint programs.

■ Command-F allows quick, no-intervention exports and batching.

■ File Export plug-in offers seamless action-based batch processing with Photoshop 4 and 5.

■ Produces small, high-quality GIFs.

■ Processes any combination of layers in Photoshop.

■ Filtering from a selection allows independent reduction and GIF export of a selected portion of an image.

- Image quality and GIF size preview gives immediate feedback on reduction settings.
- HVS Dithering controls intensity and masks to a selection.
- Reduces fixed palettes with Netscape, Mac, and Windows palettes built in. Fixed palettes can be modified and saved as presets.
- Includes Java-based stand-alone HVS Animator application.
- Saves and reloads custom-designed color tables.
- Multipalette feature factors multiple images into HVS algorithm to generate high-quality global palettes for animation, multimedia use.
- Allows an unprecedented level of control over image quality using pro-quality features like gamma and thresholding.
- Color Table Optimizer uses HVS algorithms to substantially reduce color table and image size in existing GIFs.
- Sophisticated transparency controls multiple colors, extended selection, and automatic ìmagic wandî-style similar-color selection.
- User presets and built-ins allow various reduction/export settings.
- Includes size and download time estimate with each change of settings.
- Includes an illustrated hyperlinked manual in HTML format.

HVS JPEG 2.0 Demo

Spinwave

Dawn Ginn
1603 Orrington, Suite 990
Evanston, IL 60201
Voice: (870) 326-4455
Fax: (870) 326-4848
E-mail: info@spinwave.com
Web: http://www.spinwave.com

HVS JPEG 2.0 Demo allows you to see your own images in the live preview window using the HVS JPEG plug-in. It also shows you how big the resulting file is and permits exporting. It is full-featured for 15 days, after which you may purchase it online at **http://www.digfrontiers.com**.

Some of HVS JPEG 2.0's features include:

- A filter plug-in, which works with most major paint programs
- Command-F, which allows quick, no-intervention exports and batching

- Batch processing with Photoshop 4 and 5
- A redesigned user interface to better support how artists work
- Small, high-quality JPEGs produced
- Automatic Q-Table Optimizer, which generates the best Q-table for the image
- User presets and built-ins for various quality settings
- Size and download time estimate with each change of settings
- Adobe Acrobat (PDF) format available

WinZip

WinZip Computing, Inc.

P.O. Box 540
Mansfield, CT 06268
E-mail: support@winzip.com
Web: http://www.winzip.com

WinZip 8.0 brings the convenience of Windows to the use of Zip files and other compression formats.

WinZip features include:

- **Windows 95/98/NT/2000 integration**   WinZip includes long filename support and tight integration with the Windows 95/98/NT/2000 shell. You can drag and drop to or from Explorer, or zip and unzip without leaving Explorer.

- **Internet support**   WinZip features built-in support for popular Internet file formats: TAR, gzip, UUEncode, XXencode, BinHex, and MIME. ARJ, LZH, and ARC files, which are supported via external programs. You can use WinZip to access almost all the files you download from the Internet. In addition, the freely downloadable WinZip Internet Browser Support Add-On lets you download and open archives with one click using Microsoft Internet Explorer or Netscape Navigator.

- **Automatic installation of most software distributed in Zip files**   If a Zip file contains a setup or install program, WinZip's Install feature will unzip the files, run the installation program, and clean up temporary files.

- **The WinZip wizard**   This optional feature uses the standard and familiar "wizard" interface to simplify the process of unzipping and installing software distributed in Zip files. The WinZip wizard is not targeted at experienced users, but is ideal for the rapidly growing number of PC users getting started with Zip files. When these users gain confidence or want to use more advanced zipping features, the full WinZip Classic interface is just a click away.

APPENDIXES

- **Favorite Zip folders**   WinZip lets you organize Zip files into one convenient list, sorted by date, that makes it easier to locate all Zip files regardless of where they came from or where they are stored. Unlike the standard File | Open Archive dialog box, the Favorite Zip Folders dialog box treats the contents of multiple folders as though they were one folder. A Search facility finds any Zip files lost on your hard disk.

- **Create files that unzip themselves**   WinZip Self-Extractor Personal Edition is now included with WinZip. Self-extracting files are ideal for sending compressed files to others who may not own or know how to use file compression software.

- **Virus scanner support**   WinZip can be configured to work with most virus scanners.

Note   *This version of WinZip is a shareware evaluation version, not the registered version of the current release of WinZip 8.0. After 21 days of evaluation, you can order the registered version from the web site at* **http://www.winzip.com.**

Index

I

X

INTERNATIONAL CONTACT INFORMATION

AUSTRALIA
McGraw-Hill Book Company Australia Pty. Ltd.
TEL +61-2-9417-9899
FAX +61-2-9417-5687
http://www.mcgraw-hill.com.au
books-it_sydney@mcgraw-hill.com

CANADA
McGraw-Hill Ryerson Ltd.
TEL +905-430-5000
FAX +905-430-5020
http://www.mcgrawhill.ca

**GREECE, MIDDLE EAST,
NORTHERN AFRICA**
McGraw-Hill Hellas
TEL +30-1-656-0990-3-4
FAX +30-1-654-5525

MEXICO (Also serving Latin America)
McGraw-Hill Interamericana Editores S.A. de C.V.
TEL +525-117-1583
FAX +525-117-1589
http://www.mcgraw-hill.com.mx
fernando_castellanos@mcgraw-hill.com

SINGAPORE (Serving Asia)
McGraw-Hill Book Company
TEL +65-863-1580
FAX +65-862-3354
http://www.mcgraw-hill.com.sg
mghasia@mcgraw-hill.com

SOUTH AFRICA
McGraw-Hill South Africa
TEL +27-11-622-7512
FAX +27-11-622-9045
robyn_swanepoel@mcgraw-hill.com

**UNITED KINGDOM & EUROPE
(Excluding Southern Europe)**
McGraw-Hill Education Europe
TEL +44-1-628-502500
FAX +44-1-628-770224
http://www.mcgraw-hill.co.uk
computing_neurope@mcgraw-hill.com

ALL OTHER INQUIRIES Contact:
Osborne/McGraw-Hill
TEL +1-510-549-6600
FAX +1-510-883-7600
http://www.osborne.com
omg_international@mcgraw-hill.com